THE OFFICIAL
TASP® Test Study Guide

NATIONAL EVALUATION SYSTEMS, INC.
AMHERST   AUSTIN

Printed in the United States of America
10 9 8 7 6 5 4

Library of Congress Catalog Card Number 88-63893
ISBN 0-89056-010-2

Dear Reader:

In 1987, an important bill was passed by the Texas Legislature. It called for testing the basic skills of all students entering public institutions of higher education in Texas. This bill is a far-reaching one, requiring colleges and universities to advise and assist students who are found to be underprepared in the basic skills. This legislation is a very important reform in Texas higher education. It was passed to help you achieve success in college.

Because of the resulting Texas Academic Skills Program (TASP), you will be tested, properly advised, and offered help if you need it in reading, writing, and mathematics. Your college or university will monitor your progress carefully to make sure that you get the best services available to help you be able to do college-level work. The purpose of this new program is to have fewer students drop out of college so that many more will finish their college careers.

So please prepare for this test knowing that it exists as a tool to help you get started right in college. Many resources are available to you in preparing for the TASP Test. Your college or university has information available to you, and we urge you to speak to faculty members or counselors on your campus. We believe The Official TASP® Test Study Guide can help you get ready to take the TASP Test. Its purpose is to provide the information necessary to understand the skills the test will measure. When you have these skills at your command, you will be on your way to reaching your college goals.

Our best wishes for your success in college.

Kenneth H. Ashworth
Commissioner
Texas Higher Education
  Coordinating Board

Lionel R. Meno
Commissioner
Texas Education Agency

Acknowledgments

Many people contributed to the development of *The Official TASP® Test Study Guide*. Especially, we want to recognize the following individuals.

For their valuable reviews of and comments on initial book outlines, book content design, and draft manuscript these current and former co-chairs of TASP committees.

Milton Bryant, *Prairie View A&M University*
  (TASP Bias Review Panel)
Jeffrey Campbell, *Midwestern State University*
  (TASP Content Advisory Committee, Writing)
Joseph Cude, *Tarleton State University*
  (TASP Content Advisory Committee, Mathematics)
Ann Faulkner, *Mountain View College*
  (Academic Skills Development Committee, Texas Academic Skills Council)
Jean Greenlaw, *University of North Texas*
  (TASP Content Advisory Committee, Reading)

Robert Jones, *Paris Junior College*
  (TASP Content Advisory Committee, Mathematics)
Hazelyn Lewis, *St. Philip's College*
  (TASP Content Advisory Committee, Writing)
Gail Platt, *South Plains College*
  (TASP Content Advisory Committee, Reading)
David Sanchez, *San Antonio College*
  (TASP Content Advisory Committee, Mathematics)
Faye Thames, *Lamar University*
  (TASP Content Advisory Committee, Mathematics)

For their help in conceptualizing the book and in reviewing initial book outlines and draft manuscript:

Richard Battaile, *Texas Education Agency*
Michael Kerker, *formerly of The Texas Higher Education Coordinating Board*
Joan Matthews, *Texas Higher Education Coordinating Board*

Leroy Psencik, *Texas Education Agency*
Ronald Swanson, *Texas Higher Education Coordinating Board*
Pamela Tackett, *Texas Education Agency*
Nolan Wood, *Texas Education Agency*

In addition, we are grateful to the many individuals at National Evaluation Systems who worked on editing the manuscript and in book design and production.

We thank you for your efforts and apologize to anyone whose name we may have omitted.

—National Evaluation Systems

CONTENTS

Foreword: How to Use *The Official TASP® Test Study Guide*

The Official TASP® Test Study Guide was prepared by National Evaluation Systems, Inc. (NES®), the organization contracted to develop and administer the test for the Texas Academic Skills Program (TASP®). The two agencies responsible for this program, the Texas Higher Education Coordinating Board (THECB) and the Texas Education Agency (TEA), reviewed this book. Staff members at both organizations and members of various TASP test development advisory committees reviewed the manuscript and provided comments and suggestions. *The Official TASP® Test Study Guide* is, therefore, your most authoritative resource for preparing to take the TASP Test.

The book consists of five sections. In Section I, Chapter 1 describes the goals and basic policies of the Texas Academic Skills Program. The second introductory chapter provides information on test preparation, including specific suggestions that you may find helpful in getting ready to take the test. Chapter 3 is devoted to the Quick Pre-Test. This short assessment can help you determine how well prepared you are for the type of content covered by this book.

Sections II, III, and IV deal with the skills eligible for inclusion on the TASP Test. The skills are grouped, as the test itself will be, into reading, mathematics, and writing. These skills chapters are instructional; they present a review of the fundamental content included within a skill. In addition, they contain numerous examples and practice exercises to permit you to check your understanding of the skills and to give you a sense of what the questions pertaining to these skills might be like.

In 1993, the THECB and TEA authorized changes in the mathematics skills. This revised version of *The Official TASP® Test Study Guide* incorporates those changes. Also, this edition of the *Study Guide* includes changes in the chapters that deal with the writing sample within the writing test.

Section V of the study guide contains a practice test, complete with an answer key and explanations of the correct responses. The Practice Test simulates the types of questions you will encounter on the actual TASP Test. Your results on the Practice Test can help you pinpoint skills with which you are having difficulty.

This book also contains a glossary of terms and study references—both features are designed to help you study and prepare for the TASP Test. Please note that there may be differences between the questions on the official TASP Test and those in the chapters in this book. For instance, the reading passages in Chapters 4–9 are generally shorter than those on the official TASP Test. The Practice Test at the end of the book is generally similar to the style of questions and passages that you will find on the official TASP Test.

Perhaps the most important point to make about the TASP Test is that it addresses skills that can be learned. Many tests that you encounter in your educational career are meant to measure your aptitude, or your capacity to learn. The TASP Test, in contrast, measures a series of skills you need if you are to perform effectively in college courses. You can master these skills, and indeed you should master them if you are to get the most out of your college experience. It is for these reasons that *The Official TASP® Test Study Guide* can be so helpful in preparing for the test.

The Texas Higher Education Coordinating Board, the Texas Education Agency, and National Evaluation Systems want you to succeed on this test. We believe that your success on the test is related to your preparation and study for the skills it addresses. This study guide is intended to be an effective tool for refreshing your memory about the skills to be tested and for providing instruction in areas where the material may be less familiar to you.

We call your attention to the feedback form at the end of the book. This short set of questions provides you with a way to help us improve subsequent editions of *The Official TASP® Test Study Guide*. We wish you every success on the TASP Test.

SECTION I

Preparing to Take the TASP Test

The *Official TASP® Test Study Guide* concentrates on providing instructional materials for the academic skills eligible for testing in the Texas Academic Skills Program (TASP®). It will be helpful for you to understand the background for the TASP. Section I of the study guide offers a brief overview of the goals and characteristics of the Texas Academic Skills Program.

In addition, Chapter 2 discusses some general test-preparation and test-taking skills and strategies that you may find helpful. It contains suggestions for how to get ready for the test both during the weeks and months before you take the TASP Test and in the few days immediately before your administration.

Chapter 3 is the Quick Pre-Test, a chance for you to assess your familiarity with the skills included in the TASP. The Quick Pre-Test is a set of questions, one per skill, that you can score instantly. The chapter also contains some suggestions for interpreting your score.

In short, Section I is meant to help you get started by providing background information about the Texas Academic Skills Program, suggestions for test preparation and test taking, and a Quick Pre-Test.

Chapter 1

INTRODUCTION TO THE TEXAS ACADEMIC SKILLS PROGRAM (TASP)

The Texas Academic Skills Program (TASP) is an instructional program designed to ensure that students attending public institutions of higher education in Texas have the academic skills necessary to perform effectively in college-level coursework. The TASP provides advisory programs and support for those students who demonstrate a need in those academic skills. While the TASP also includes a testing component to identify and provide diagnostic information about the academic skills of each student, it is important to emphasize that the focus of the TASP is advisement and educational support for Texas college students.

Program Background

A major impetus for the development of the TASP was *A Generation of Failure: The Case for Testing and Remediation in Texas Higher Education,* a report prepared by the Texas Higher Education Coordinating Board in July 1986. This report called attention to the problem of underpreparedness in academic skills of many Texas college students, a problem common to higher education across the country. The report contained specific recommendations for improving the academic skills of students in public institutions in Texas, including the commitment of resources to help those students identified as needing advisory and academic assistance. The report also advocated the development of a test to be used to identify students in need of this assistance.

Legislation. The legislative response to *A Generation of Failure* parallels the existing requirements for students entering teacher preparation programs. Since 1984, teacher education students have had to pass an academic skills test as a condition for admission into their programs. House Bill 2182, passed in spring 1987, extended this testing requirement to include all entering students at Texas public colleges and universities and mandated academic assistance for students who do not meet the state-wide standard. You should refer to the TASP Test Registration Bulletin for a comprehensive description of program policies, including who must take the test and when the test must be taken.

The Texas Higher Education Coordinating Board (THECB) and the Texas Education Agency (TEA) agreed to cooperate to develop a single test that would serve both as one of the criteria for admission to public and private teacher education programs and as the test mandated by House Bill 2182 for students entering public colleges and universities.

Test Development Process

The test development process for the Texas Academic Skills Program was a comprehensive one, involving thousands of faculty members from Texas colleges and universities. These individuals, working with the THECB, the TEA, and National Evaluation Systems, Inc. (NES) staff:

1. recommended the skills eligible to be measured on the test;

2. developed the specific test instrument to measure those skills; and

3. recommended performance standards for each section of the test.

What Are College-Level Skills? How Were They Selected?

In setting up the program, one of the issues was the definition of the specific academic skills to be assessed on the TASP Test. Committees of Texas educators developed a list of specific skills in reading, mathematics, and writing that students should have for effective performance at the college level. These skills were reviewed, revised, and validated through surveys sent to thousands of faculty members and students at colleges and universities in Texas. In the summer of 1988, the THECB and the State Board of Education officially adopted the skills eligible to be included on the test.

National Evaluation Systems drafted test questions matched to the approved skills. These questions were then reviewed by many groups of Texas educators who suggested revisions to the questions. In addition, a field test was conducted, and Texas educators reviewed the results.

The TASP Test, therefore, measures your level of proficiency with these skills. Your score on the test is determined solely on the basis of your performance on the skills. The test scores do not compare you to other students or compare students at one school with those at another school. The direct relationship between each test question and its TASP skill is the basis for score reporting and is an integral aspect of the goals of the program.

Thus, the resulting TASP Test measures skills that have been documented as necessary for effective performance by students in college-level courses, regardless of the type of institution they attend or the nature of their degree program. The test measures academic skills that are appropriate for all majors.

Changes in content. The test materials are continuously augmented and updated with the participation of advisory committees of Texas educators. Moreover, in 1993, the THECB and the State Board of Education authorized changes in the mathematics skills. New test materials, matched to the new and revised skills, were prepared using procedures parallel to those used during initial development.

Format. With the exception of the writing sample in the writing section, all questions are in multiple-choice format with four response alternatives per question. Each section of the test will have up to 55 multiple-choice questions.

Test fairness. The THECB, the TEA, and National Evaluation Systems designed a test development process that would ensure that the test materials are fair to all the diverse population groups involved in Texas. Since the test is a fundamental requirement for those students seeking to take upper-division courses toward a baccalaureate or an associate degree or certificate, or seeking admission to teacher education programs, it is essential that the test be equitable to all examinees. Consequently, all reviews of test materials by Texas educators dealt specifically with test fairness as a review criterion. In addition, the field test results were analyzed for potential problems, using sophisticated statistical techniques.

Test Preparation Support Materials

The content covered by the TASP Test is public information. The Coordinating Board, the Texas Education Agency, and NES have made an effort to distribute the list of skills eligible for assessment in each section of the test. *The Official TASP® Test Study Guide* provides valuable assistance both to students preparing for the test and to faculty members working with students. The study guide provides a wealth of general test-taking tips, information and practice questions about each of the skills, a review section of reading, mathematics, and writing skills, and a practice test.

Test Administration and Scoring Procedures

The *TASP Test Registration Bulletin* explains the procedures for administration of the TASP Test. It contains the TASP Test registration forms and the policies developed by the Coordinating Board and the Texas Education Agency for the administration of the test. These policies reflect several general goals.

Standardized administrations. The policies and procedures for administering the test will be the same at each test site. In this way, no student or group of students is either advantaged or disadvantaged by variations in administration procedures. It is important that your score on the test reflect only your preparedness in the academic skills and not factors related to the test site. The individuals administering the tests have been thoroughly trained and are provided with detailed manuals that cover procedures and circumstances in the test administration situation.

Convenience to examinees. The dates and sites for test administration were established for your maximum possible convenience. Because the testing component is a requirement that affects students at Texas public colleges and universities, and teacher education candidates at both public and private institutions, it is important that everyone has reasonable access to test administrations.

Test security. It is important that no student or group of students gain an advantage by having unauthorized access to the test or by being able to cheat in any way during the test administration. For this reason, the THECB, the TEA, and NES have created and implemented a series of procedures guaranteed to ensure the security of the test at all times. As an examinee, you should be relatively unaffected by these various procedures. More importantly, you can be confident that no examinees will have an unfair advantage through unethical or unauthorized means.

Individualized treatment. National Evaluation Systems regards each examinee as a client, deserving of courteous and professional service and attention. For this reason, the test is administered through an individualized registration process. In this way, you are assured that an individual record of your performance on the test is maintained and that the possibility of any loss of information is minimal. Overall, these procedures are designed to reduce any anxiety that you may feel about the program and to facilitate and simplify your involvement in the testing process.

Diagnostic reporting. The score results that you will receive provide diagnostic information as to your performance on each section of the test. This information will help you and your college or university faculty determine appropriate advisement and academic assistance.

Pre-TASP Test (PTT®). One feature of the program is the availability on some college and university campuses of the "campus" version of the test, the Pre-TASP Test. The PTT provides you with an opportunity to take and to receive diagnostic score reports on a shorter version of the official TASP Test. While campus version PTT scores do not count toward satisfying the requirements of state law, they do afford you an opportunity to gain familiarity with the TASP Test format and to discover areas of possible weakness in your academic preparation. Knowing in advance about potential problems will assist you in preparing for the official version of the TASP Test.

Policies and procedures. Policies and procedures governing the development, administration, and score reporting for the TASP Test are developed jointly by the Texas Higher Education Coordinating Board, the Texas Education Agency, and National Evaluation Systems. These policies and procedures reflect a commitment to provide services of the highest professional quality and maximum convenience to examinees and institutions of higher education. Moreover, policies and procedures are reviewed on a regular basis for continual improvements by staff of these three organizations.

Scoring the test. The reading, mathematics, and multiple-choice portions of the writing section are scored electronically. Your scores reflect only the number of questions you answer correctly.

The writing sample is scored using a technique called *focused holistic scoring*. This means that your writing sample will receive a single overall score. Each paper is read by two readers, each of whom scores it independently (i.e., the second person to read it does not know the score the first person assigned to it). If the two readers disagree substantially in their scores, there is a process for reviewing the paper and resolving the difference.

The writing sample is scored on a 4-point scale. Because each paper is read by two scorers, you will receive a score between 2 and 8 on the writing sample. If your score is 6, 7, or 8, you automatically pass the writing section of the TASP Test, regardless of your performance on the multiple-choice questions of the writing section. Conversely, if your score is 2, 3, or 4, you will not have passed the writing section regardless of your performance on the multiple-choice questions.

If your combined score is a "5," your performance on the multiple-choice questions of the writing section is used to determine your pass/not pass status.

In other words, you *must* complete the writing sample and you should do as well as you can on the multiple-choice questions of the writing section.

TASP Test Skills

Each section of the test (reading, mathematics, and writing) addresses a number of specific skills. These skills define the content included in that section.

The reading section includes a skill related to vocabulary and one related to study skills. Four other skills assess your ability to comprehend written materials. These skills include main idea, writer's intent, organization of ideas, and critical reasoning. All questions are in multiple-choice format.

The mathematics section includes two skills related to fundamental mathematics, five related to algebra, two related to geometry, and two related to problem solving. All questions are in multiple-choice format.

The writing section includes the writing sample, which will be evaluated on seven dimensions. The multiple-choice portion covers three skills in elements of composition and two in sentence structure, usage, and writing mechanics.

All the skills eligible for testing are described below.

Reading Skill Descriptions

Determine the meaning of words and phrases.
This skill includes using the context of a passage to determine the meaning of words with multiple meanings, unfamiliar and uncommon words and phrases, and figurative expressions.

Understand the main idea and supporting details in written material.
This skill includes identifying explicit and implicit main ideas and recognizing ideas that support, illustrate, or elaborate the main idea of a passage.

Identify a writer's purpose, point of view, and intended meaning.
This skill includes recognizing a writer's expressed or implied purpose for writing; evaluating the appropriateness of written material for various purposes or audiences; recognizing the likely effect on an audience of a writer's choice of words; and using the content, word choice, and phrasing of a passage to determine a writer's opinion or point of view.

Analyze the relationship among ideas in written material.
This skill includes identifying the sequence of events or steps, identifying cause-effect relationships, analyzing relationships between ideas in opposition, identifying solutions to problems, and drawing conclusions inductively and deductively from information stated or implied in a passage.

Use critical reasoning skills to evaluate written material.
This skill includes evaluating the stated or implied assumptions on which the validity of a writer's argument depends; judging the relevance or importance of facts, examples, or graphic data to a writer's argument; evaluating the logic of a writer's argument; evaluating the validity of analogies; distinguishing between fact and opinion; and assessing the credibility or objectivity of the writer or source of written material.

Apply study skills to reading assignments.
This skill includes organizing and summarizing information for study purposes; following written instructions or directions; and interpreting information presented in charts, graphs, or tables.

Mathematics Skill Descriptions

FUNDAMENTAL MATHEMATICS

Solve word problems involving integers, fractions, decimals, and units of measurement.
Includes solving word problems involving integers, fractions, decimals (including percents), ratios and proportions, and units of measurement and conversions (including scientific notation).

Solve problems involving data interpretation and analysis.
Includes interpreting information from line graphs, bar graphs, pictographs, and pie charts; interpreting data from tables; recognizing appropriate graphic representations of various data; analyzing and interpreting data using measures of central tendency (mean, median, and mode); and analyzing and interpreting data using the concept of variability.

ALGEBRA

Graph numbers or number relationships.
Includes identifying the graph of a given equation or a given inequality; finding the slope and/or intercepts of a given line; finding the equation of a line; and recognizing and interpreting information from the graph of a function (including direct and inverse variation).

Solve one- and two-variable equations.
Includes finding the value of the unknown in a given one-variable equation, expressing one variable in terms of a second variable in two-variable equations, and solving systems of two equations in two variables (including graphical solutions).

Solve word problems involving one and two variables.
Includes identifying the algebraic equivalent of a stated relationship and solving word problems involving one and two unknowns.

Understand operations with algebraic expressions and functional notation.
Includes factoring quadratics and polynomials; performing operations on and simplifying polynomial expressions, rational expressions, and radical expressions; and applying principles of functions and functional notation.

Solve problems involving quadratic equations.
Includes graphing quadratic functions and quadratic inequalities; solving quadratic equations using factoring, completing the square, or the quadratic formula; and solving problems involving quadratic models.

GEOMETRY

Solve problems involving geometric figures.
Includes solving problems involving two-dimensional geometric figures (e.g., perimeter and area problems) and three-dimensional geometric figures (e.g., volume and surface area problems), and solving problems using the Pythagorean theorem.

Solve problems involving geometric concepts.
Includes solving problems using principles of similarity, congruence, parallelism, and perpendicularity.

PROBLEM SOLVING

Apply reasoning skills.
Includes drawing conclusions using inductive and deductive reasoning.

Solve applied problems involving a combination of mathematical skills.
Includes applying combinations of mathematical skills to solve problems and to solve a series of related problems.

Writing Skill Descriptions

ELEMENTS OF COMPOSITION

Recognize purpose and audience.
This skill includes recognizing the appropriate purpose, audience, or occasion for a piece of writing; and recognizing writing that is appropriate for various purposes, audiences, or occasions.

Recognize unity, focus, and development in writing.
This skill includes recognizing unnecessary shifts in point of view or distracting details that impair the development of the main idea in a piece of writing and recognizing revisions that improve the unity and focus of a piece of writing.

Recognize effective organization in writing.
This skill includes recognizing methods of paragraph organization and the appropriate use of transitional words or phrases to convey text structure, and reorganizing sentences to improve cohesion and the effective sequence of ideas.

SENTENCE STRUCTURE, USAGE, AND MECHANICS

Recognize effective sentences.
This skill includes recognizing ineffective repetition and inefficiency in sentence construction; identifying sentence fragments and run-on sentences; identifying standard subject-verb agreement; identifying standard placement of modifiers, parallel structure, and use of negatives in sentence formation; and recognizing imprecise and inappropriate word choice.

Recognize edited American English usage.
This skill includes recognizing the standard use of verb forms and pronouns; recognizing the standard formation and use of adverbs, adjectives, comparatives, superlatives, and plural and possessive forms of nouns; and recognizing standard punctuation.

The Writing Sample

The following characteristics may be considered in scoring the writing samples.

Appropriateness—the extent to which the student addresses the topic and uses language and style appropriate to the given audience, purpose, and occasion.

Unity and Focus—the clarity with which the student states and maintains a main idea or point of view.

Development—the amount, depth, and specificity of supporting detail the student provides.

Organization—the clarity of the student's writing and the logical sequence of the student's ideas.

Sentence Structure—the effectiveness of the student's sentence structure and the extent to which the student's writing is free of errors in sentence structure.

Usage—the extent to which the student's writing is free of errors in usage and shows care and precision in word choice.

Mechanical Conventions—the student's ability to spell common words and use the conventions of capitalization and punctuation.

Chapter 2

PREPARING FOR AND TAKING THE TASP TEST

The best way to perform well on the Texas Academic Skills Program Test is to understand and be familiar with the skills measured by the test. No amount of "tips" or strategy suggestions will compensate for inadequate reading, mathematics, or writing skills. The Official TASP® Test Study Guide is designed to help you review and improve those academic skills.

Many suggestions, however, may make it easier for you to perform to the best of your ability. Students sometimes leave a test feeling that they have not really done as well as they could have. In general, your score cannot be higher than what you really know, but you can do things to help reach that highest level. This chapter contains a discussion of study methods and strategies for effective test performance.

Study Methods

There are many ways to study for this test. One approach is described below. We strongly suggest that students should, at least, review the list of specific reading, mathematics, and writing skills covered on the test. In this way, you can identify areas with which you are unfamiliar.

1. Review the skills and skill descriptions. You should begin by reviewing the skills and descriptions in the previous chapter. Read each one carefully, and think about whether you are familiar with the types of questions you are likely to be asked and with the content implied by each skill description. You might want to make a list of those skills with which you feel somewhat unfamiliar or unsure. Think about the types of questions that might be asked for each skill.

Each skill is defined by a number of subskills. Texas college and university faculty members believe this content is important for successful performance in college, so the test may cover any part of the materials listed with each skill.

For example, one skill in the writing section is "recognize edited American English usage." It includes the subskill of recognizing the standard use of verb forms and pronouns. It also includes the standard formation and use of adverbs, adjectives, comparatives and superlatives, and the plural and possessive forms of nouns. Last, it includes recognizing standard punctuation. If, for example, you are not sure what is meant by the terms *comparatives* and *superlatives*, you should plan to spend time reviewing material on this topic. Also, the word *standard* implies that the punctuation and the capitalization are of the format and conventions that are typically found in grammar textbooks or dictionaries published in the United States. If you are uncertain as to what is meant by *standard,* you should review the discussion of this skill later in this book.

2. Take the Quick Pre-Test. After you review all the skills in reading, writing, and mathematics, you should take the Quick Pre-Test found in Chapter 3.

3. Evaluate your areas of strength and weakness. To determine your areas of strength and weakness, use the Quick Pre-Test and your own sense of familiarity with the skills. Where do you think you need the most work? With which skills are you the most comfortable?

While the Quick Pre-Test will not provide detailed information, it can give you a sense of how much preparation work you may need. For instance, if you do not answer any questions correctly, you may need to review in detail all the content of this study guide. On the other hand, if you answer all questions correctly, you may find that a short review is sufficient preparation for the TASP Test.

4. Review the study materials. Even if you performed well on the Quick Pre-Test and feel confident about your knowledge of the TASP skills, you should still plan to read the study materials in this book. These chapters will help refresh your memory about reading, math, and writing skills. After all, the Quick Pre-Test does not cover every topic in each area. There are aspects of math, for instance, that are not on the Quick Pre-Test but which may be on the official TASP Test.

Working through this material means exactly that. Do not simply look at the section heading and say, "I know that," and move on. Take the time to read everything carefully, even if you feel well prepared.

5. Focus your study. Plan to focus your study on the skills that you have identified as needing attention. One of the major benefits of the structure of the TASP Test is that it allows you to identify specific areas of strength and weakness and to concentrate on the latter. Spend your time where you need the most work, and your gain is likely to be greatest. You will have to take all sections of the test, so skipping things that you are uncomfortable with, but do not want to study, is not a wise strategy.

As you study, you may wish to expand beyond this book in the following ways.

> **Resource materials.** The discussions of reading, mathematics, and writing skills contain lists of textbooks and other materials that address the content of these skills. These resources (or similar ones) will provide additional information.

> **Your advisor.** It may be helpful to consult with your advisor or another faculty member about getting assistance. You may find that as you review these materials, you still have questions. Whatever you do, do not isolate yourself from the support that your college or university is committed to providing you. If you believe you need help, ask for it.

6. Take the Practice Test. Once you have completed your focused study and general review, you should take the Practice Test at the end of this book. Set aside enough time to take the test without interruption. Find a quiet place where you can concentrate. A reading room in a library might be an ideal place since it is similar to the actual testing situation (quiet, yet with other people around).

Use the answer key to score the test. Identify skills on which you performed poorly. This is where you should concentrate your study time. The scoring chart will help you link test questions to specific skills; directions are provided with the Practice Test.

7. Take the Pre-TASP Test. The Pre-TASP Test, available on some college campuses, is a shorter version of the TASP Test and is sometimes called the "campus" version. Although it does not fulfill your requirement to pass the TASP Test, the campus version is similar to the TASP Test and gives you a chance to practice the reading, writing, and math skills necessary for college-level work. Your advisor can help you make arrangements to take the Pre-TASP Test.

On some campuses, you may be encouraged to take the Pre-TASP Test early in your college career. Some institutions are asking students to take the Pre-TASP Test as a way of determining which students need additional help.

8. Review problem areas. At this point, particularly if you have taken the Pre-TASP Test, you should have a clear sense of where you still have problems. Now you should focus your study primarily on those areas. Remember that the faculty members at your college or university want to help you master the content in each of these skill areas. If you have questions, please ask for assistance.

9. Last review. A day or so before you take the TASP Test, it would be helpful to review all the skills included in each area. This will refresh your memory and is sound last-minute preparation for taking the test.

Study Techniques

As mentioned above, the best approach to master the skills in the Texas Academic Skills Program is regular study over a period of time, including during high school. A number of additional specific techniques deserve mention at this time.

Cramming. Generally, intensive study ("cramming") for a test in the day or two before you are scheduled to take it is not a particularly effective study technique. It may be helpful to review certain facts or details immediately before the test so they are fresh in your mind. But begin your preparation *as early as possible*. The type of knowledge that the TASP Test requires is best gained over a period of time. Also, if you find you are having difficulty, you will have enough time to get help.

Study groups. Sometimes it is helpful to work with other individuals preparing for the test. Reviewing the skill areas with other students may raise issues you would not have considered and may provide a source of information on skills with which you are less familiar.

You may find it helpful to work in a study group once you have already identified your own areas of possible weakness. In that way, you will know the content on which you should concentrate.

The writing test. The writing test includes a sample of your writing. You will not know the topic for the writing sample until you are in the test room. You can, however, practice your writing in advance. The topics for the writing sample will not require knowledge of specific facts. In other words, you will not have to know some particular body of knowledge to respond. In addition, scores on the writing samples will not be based on your opinions or sentiments. Rather, the scoring criteria include the organization and effectiveness of the writing. The skills listed in the previous chapter give you a sense of characteristics of effective writing that the readers will be seeking.

The discussion of the sample writing topic includes a description of the criteria used for scoring as well as sample writing assignments. The writing assignment is the topic statement to which you will respond. You are strongly encouraged to practice writing a variety of compositions in response to those assignments. You may find it helpful to share your work with faculty members, other students preparing for the test, or other individuals whose writing skills are strong. Their review can identify problems you may have in this area.

The Study Guide and the TASP Test

The main purpose of *The Official TASP® Test Study Guide* is to provide instruction on the skills that are eligible for inclusion on the TASP Test. If you master these skills, performance on the test will follow naturally. Mastery of the skills will help you benefit from your college courses, which is, after all, the major reason behind the Texas Academic Skills Program.

Thus, the instructional chapters in this study guide do not focus exclusively on test content. They include topics that may not appear on a given form of the TASP Test. The sample problems and exercises may use formats and difficulty levels different from those on the test. The Practice Test at the end of this book is similar but not identical to the actual TASP Test.

A changing test. Part of the reason for not focusing solely on the TASP Test is that the test may change over time. Any given test form used at a specific administration may include a different selection of skills. Item formats may change. Since the TASP Test may vary somewhat from administration to administration, it is difficult to prepare for its specific characteristics. We believe it makes more sense to build toward mastery of the skills that are eligible for testing.

Strategies for Effective Test Performance

As stated earlier, there is no substitute for study and preparation. Test-taking strategies alone will not allow you to perform well on a test for which you are not prepared. There are, however, things you can do to ensure that you perform up to your ability. No one wants to do less well than he or she is capable of, particularly if the reason for poor performance is avoidable. This section of the study guide discusses the particular things you can do to ensure that on the day of the test you are ready to do your best.

Before the test. This discussion covers both physical and mental preparation for the test. Remember that the test will require your concentration over a period of several hours. Therefore, you do not want to be fatigued or physically uncomfortable during the test. Exercise regularly, eat sensibly, and get enough rest on the days before the test. Get a good night's sleep the night before the test. If you are tired or unnecessarily nervous the day of the test, your performance may suffer.

On the day of the test, avoid eating or drinking things that may cause you to take frequent trips to the restroom (e.g., diuretics such as coffee). Plan to eat a well-balanced breakfast so that you do not get hungry during the test, but do not eat so much that you are groggy. Remember, you cannot take food of any kind into the test room. Wear comfortable clothes. Several layers of clothes allow you to adjust to room temperature fluctuations.

Your mental preparation is as important as your physical preparation. Avoid last-minute sources of tension like having to look for your admission ticket. Concerns of this sort at the last minute may interfere with your performance on the test.

You should set an alarm clock the day of the test. Make sure you are up in plenty of time to dress and to eat at a leisurely pace.

Review your admission ticket and other materials. You need to have your admission ticket and two pieces of identification, one with a photograph. *You also need to take No. 2 pencils; pencils are not provided at the test site.*

Make certain you know the location of the test center and when you have to be there. Your test performance will not be helped if you have to search for your test site. Review these materials enough in advance so that if you are uncertain where your test room is, you have time to find out. Leave in plenty of time to get to the test site. Allow for traffic and other factors that may delay you. Again, your best interests are served by a leisurely trip with plenty of time to get to the site. *DO NOT BE LATE, AS YOU WILL NOT BE ALLOWED TO ENTER THE TESTING ROOM AFTER THE TEST HAS BEGUN.*

In general, you want to avoid anything that will make you feel rushed. The more relaxed you are when you arrive at the test site, the better you are likely to perform.

At the Test

Understand the test policy. The TASP Test has three sections: reading, mathematics, and writing. All three sections are contained in a single test booklet. When you take the test, you can decide whether to take all three sections or to attempt only one or two (e.g., math and reading). There is no rule that keeps you from taking whichever section or sections you wish. If necessary, you can reregister and complete the remaining section or sections at a later date.

Please note that if you do not attempt a test section, you may be required to take remediation in that subject before you have an opportunity to retake the TASP Test. You should discuss with your academic advisor the consequences of not attempting a section of the test. We advise you to contact someone on your campus to learn what the policy is at your institution.

One suggested approach is to take all three sections of the test on your initial attempt. If you pass all three, you are finished with the requirement. If you do not pass a section, you know that you need further study and extra assistance from your college or university. The earlier you know that you need some help, the earlier you can begin to get it.

Please note that when you register for the TASP Test, you do not have to indicate which section or sections of the test you plan to take. For instance, you may think you will take all three sections, but at the test administration, you may decide to concentrate on only one or two sections. Also, while you are taking the test, you may answer the sections in any order you prefer, and you may move back and forth within or between sections. You will have five hours to complete the test.

In general, the TASP Test policies allow you flexibility. It is a good idea, however, to enter the test administration knowing what you want to do and in what order. Some people suggest that you complete the writing sample first when you are the most fresh rather than leaving this task for the end. Remember that you do not have to retake sections of the test you passed during an earlier administration. For instance, once you pass the reading section of the test, you can skip that section on all future administrations.

When you arrive at the test, you will be checked in and assigned to a seat. As you begin the test, you can do a number of things to perform at your best.

Follow directions carefully. You should read and follow all test directions carefully. This means both the instructions provided before the test begins and all the directions that are written in the test booklet. The test booklet will include both general directions and directions for individual questions or groups of test questions. If there is something you do not understand, raise your hand and ask the test administrators. They are there to help you.

Read individual test questions. The questions on the test will be scored in terms of the best answer. This means that you should carefully read each choice in a question. Read the directions and the test questions carefully. You have five hours so there is no need to rush by reading questions too quickly. Take the time to read the questions carefully, and evaluate all the answer choices before deciding how to mark your answer sheet. There is only one best answer for each question. The questions are not tricky but rather are worded in a straightforward manner.

Guess wisely. Your score will depend on the total number of test questions you answer correctly. You will not lose points for guessing. For that reason, you should mark an answer for every question, even if you are not sure what the right answer is.

Even where you do not feel you know the correct answer, you may be able to eliminate one or two of the answer choices. If you can eliminate one answer and guess from among the other choices, your chances are one in three of getting that question right. At any rate, do not skip questions. Make a guess; there is no penalty for doing so.

Mark the answer sheet carefully. The multiple-choice portions of the test will be scored electronically. The electronic scanners that read your sheet are extremely sensitive, so you must be careful in marking your answer sheet. It is critical that you use the right type of pencil and fill in your answer oval, or "bubble," carefully, darkly, and completely. If you change your mind about an answer, be sure to erase the old mark completely. Also, do not make any stray marks on the answer sheet. The electronic scanners are sensitive to such marks and may interpret them as incorrect responses. If you need to make notes to yourself while answering a question, do so in the test booklet.

Remember that if you skip a question, you must also skip that position on the answer sheet.

Think about sequence. You may complete the test sections in any order you wish. Consider whether there are advantages for you in taking the three sections in some specific sequence. For example, some people suggest doing the writing sample first rather than leaving it for last when you may be tired. Whatever you decide, remember that you have the ability to make this decision in your own best interests.

Pace yourself. You should have plenty of time to complete the sections of the test. Five hours are provided. You are in charge of allocating your time on each test. It is important to try to move through a test at a fairly steady rate. If you are having difficulty with a particular question, skip that question, marking it to come back to later. (Make sure you skip the corresponding position on the answer sheet.) You may find that you do not need all the time allotted for the test, but you should plan to stay the entire time. Do not schedule other activities or commitments during or immediately after the test.

There are many suggestions about how to pace yourself during a test. Some suggest that you start by quickly skimming the entire test so you get a general sense of what is covered. Most experts agree that you should not spend too much time on any one question. Try to answer as many questions as you can. Then go back to the ones that seem more difficult for you.

Check your answers. If you have time at the end of the test, you should go back through to check the accuracy of your work. You may have skipped questions that seemed too difficult when you first read them. Also, you should make sure that you have marked your answers in the correct spaces on the answer sheet and that you have erased any answers you changed.

In general, try to use all the time available to increase your score.

Read the passages with care. On the reading test in particular, many test questions relate to passages similar to those in college-level reading material. There are several approaches to dealing with passages. You should consider them and choose the one that feels the most comfortable to you.

One strategy is to read the questions first so you will have a sense of what is expected of you. Then read the passage with the questions in mind, returning to each question to answer it.

A second approach is to read the passage first, slowly and carefully. Then turn to the questions.

Third, some people suggest that you scan the passage quickly to get a general sense of what it is about, then answer each question, referring to the passage for your answers.

No way is best; you should use the practice test in this book to find the strategy with which you are most comfortable.

Estimate in math. Many questions on the math test require making calculations. Once you have completed the calculations, make sure your answer is reasonable. If possible, estimate the approximate value of the correct answer, and check whether the answer you calculated is reasonably close to your estimated answer. If not, redo your calculations.

At the beginning of the mathematics section of the test you will be given a series of formulas, standard abbreviations, and other information relevant to that section. You may preview this material by looking at the mathematics section of the Practice Test in this *Study Guide*.

Beginning with the November 2000 test administration, you may use a four-function, nonprogrammable calculator (with square root and percent keys). Remember that you are not permitted to use any other tools such as a ruler, protractor, or compass.

Plan your writing sample. Spend some time thinking through what you want to say before generating your writing sample on the writing test. You may find it helpful to prepare a detailed outline. On the other hand, a few notes may be sufficient. These techniques will make the writing easier for you and should improve the quality of your essay. You can make notes or an outline in the test booklet. You must, however, write your sample in the answer document. Only the materials in the answer document will be scored, not the materials in the test booklet.

Test Anxiety

There is disagreement over the definition of the term test anxiety. Certainly, most people feel some nervousness before and during any assessment or test. This is perfectly natural, and some people feel that some level of tension is helpful when approaching a test. It makes you alert and focuses your attention on the task at hand. That little rush of adrenaline is not the worst thing and may actually help.

On the other hand, some people become so anxious before and during a test that anxiety interferes with their ability to perform. High levels of anxiety can affect how well you do, so you should keep your tension level under control. Here are some suggestions that may help.

Control the details. Before the test, gather the materials you are taking in a safe place. Know where you have to go for the test and when. Do not leave for the test site at the last minute. In other words, do not set yourself up for needless tension on the day of the test. Understand the details of the situation so that you are not surprised or rushed. Avoid running around trying to find the test site when you should be focusing your attention on the test.

Study, and gain self-confidence. Knowing that you know the content of the test is the best antidote to needless tension. If you are prepared, you are much less likely to be nervous. This book and a variety of other resources are available to you. Take advantage of them. Study for the test well in advance.

Get help. Sometimes tension before a test comes from a feeling of isolation. Remember, you are not alone; talk to your fellow students. Your nervousness can be reduced if you realize that everyone is a little apprehensive. Try to work together. Sometimes it makes sense to get help from your advisor or other faculty members. They can help you prepare and gain self-confidence. Keeping your concerns and worries to yourself is not helpful. There are many resources designed to help you succeed in this program. Your advisor or other faculty members may be able to refer you to these resources. Take advantage of their help.

Chapter 3

THE QUICK PRE-TEST

This chapter contains a quick pre-test of the skills in the Texas Academic Skills Program. These questions, one per skill, are based on the exercises at the end of each chapter in this book.

What You Will Learn by Taking the Quick Pre-Test

The Quick Pre-Test is included because you are probably curious about how you might do on the official TASP Test. Logically, how much preparation and study you need depends on how comfortable you are with the academic skills that constitute the program.

The Quick Pre-Test is divided into three sections—reading, mathematics, and writing—as is the official TASP Test. Note that the Quick Pre-Test does *not* include a writing sample, which is a required component of the official TASP Test.

> *If you get all the questions right in a section,* you may want to devote more attention to sections where you did not do as well. Because the Quick Pre-Test includes only one question per skill, it does not reflect the possible range of content in the TASP Test. You should, therefore, review this study guide for material with which you are less familiar. It is not appropriate to assume that because you got one question right, you can skip a skill completely in your preparation. On the other hand, if you got all or most of the reading questions correct, for example, you are probably reasonably well prepared in reading.

> *If you get all the questions wrong in a section,* you should plan to spend time improving your skills in that area. As a general indicator, missing all or most of the questions indicates a lack of preparedness. You may even want to seek help on your campus from your advisor or other faculty members. Remember that these are skills that you can learn, so do not give up.

> *If you get some right and some wrong,* you should review the content of the study guide carefully to assess in more detail your preparedness. Try to identify the particular skills on which you believe you need the most work. Again, these are academic skills that you can master.

Taking the Quick Pre-Test. Simply mark your answers right on the study guide page. Read each question carefully, including all the response options. When you have completed the Quick Pre-Test (all three sections), use the Answer Key that follows the test to score yourself, marking the number correct in each section. Remember that the Quick Pre-Test may not accurately reflect your performance on the official TASP Test.

The Quick Pre-Test
Reading Section

1   As we all know, before a human being can survive on its own, it needs many years of parental care and instruction. We think of animals as creatures of instinct, but in fact they too learn by observing. A baby chimpanzee must spend years watching its elders and then practicing the skills they demonstrate before it can take care of itself.

2   What would happen if a chimpanzee raised by humans were to be transferred to the wild? Could it adapt itself to such different surroundings? Could an adult acquire the new skills required to survive? Would it learn to socialize with other chimpanzees instead of with humans? Would it learn to gather its own food rather than opening the refrigerator for a ready-made snack? These were the questions faced in the case of a chimpanzee named Lucy. She was born in a roadside zoo and then raised almost like a human daughter by the Temerlins, a pair of American psychologists. Lucy lived in a house, "read" magazines for amusement, and even learned to communicate extensively with sign language.

3   When Lucy's "parents" heard about a program in Africa to return captive chimps to the wild, they wanted to see if the program could work for her. They had long been searching for a way to bring Lucy's captivity to an end, and this program, run by Stella and Eddie Brewer, seemed ideal. So the Temerlins and Janis Carter, a student who had been involved with their project, flew Lucy to Africa.

4   In Africa, however, it became clear to the Temerlins and Janis that Lucy would not benefit from the Brewers' program and would not survive on her own without a great deal of special help. Unlike the Brewers' chimps, Lucy had been raised for years as a human. It would, therefore, take much extra time and effort to help her develop the skills she would need for survival in the wild. Although the Temerlins left after a brief stay, Janis remained in Africa to help Lucy adapt to her new home.

5   Janis ended up staying with Lucy and other chimps in an African island refuge for the next ten years. Janis had to live almost as a chimp herself. She showed the animals how to build sleeping platforms and demonstrated how to eat green figs and ants. When one of the chimps frequently forgot to nurse her newborn infant, Janis tied a doll to her chest in the nursing position.

6   At first Lucy was especially dependent upon her teacher. As the chimp acquired skills and related with the other chimps, however, Janis gradually withdrew her support. This was an important step in transforming Lucy from a pet back into a wild animal, but it was painful for both Janis and Lucy.

7   Eventually the time came for Janis to leave the island. She moved to the mainland, from where she would continue to visit and observe the chimps. Six months after moving, Janis visited Lucy for the first time since their separation. Lucy greeted her tenderly but soon moved off to rejoin the other chimps. Her behavior was no longer noticeably different from those of her fellow chimps who had been born in the wild, and her future seemed assured. With raised hopes, Janis left the area for her first vacation in ten years.

8   When Janis returned a month later, Lucy had disappeared. Janis organized a search, and eventually Lucy's skeleton was found. The cause of death? Janis could never be certain, but the most likely answer was that the chimp had been killed by human beings.

9   Although Janis was saddened by this tragedy, she managed to find consolation in the knowledge that Lucy had made a substantial contribution to our understanding of learning and behavior in animals. During her years in captivity, Lucy had learned to communicate in a way that far exceeded anything previously known or expected of animals. Subsequently she proved that even a creature that had lived for years in captivity could adapt to living in the wild.

1.   Which of the following best defines the word raised as it is used in paragraph 7 of the selection?

    A. advanced

    B. refined

    C. elevated

    D. inspired

2.   Which of the following statements best expresses the main idea of the selection?

    A. Psychologists have found that, with adequate training, chimpanzees such as Lucy can learn to live among, and communicate extensively with, human beings.

    B. Despite her unfortunate end, Lucy's experiences living first in a human home and later in the wild taught researchers much about chimpanzee learning and behavior.

    C. Compared with other types of animals, chimpanzees have a unique ability to learn complex skills through observation and practice.

    D. Lucy's problems adjusting to the wild should serve as a warning that the costs associated with the removal of animals from their natural environment may well outweigh any possible benefits.

3.   The writer's main purpose in this selection is to:

    A. explore the ability of chimpanzees to learn and adapt.

    B. compare the intelligence of humans and chimpanzees.

    C. analyze psychological theories explaining chimpanzee behavior.

    D. expose the negative results of experimentation with animals.

4.   Janis and the Temerlins did not believe that Lucy would benefit from the Brewers' program to return captive chimps to the wild because Lucy:

    A. could communicate only with sign language.

    B. lacked the animal instincts of other chimps in the program.

    C. had been born in a roadside zoo.

    D. possessed fewer survival skills than other chimps in the program.

5. Which of the following information included in the selection most directly supports the writer's view that, like humans, chimps learn by observing?

A. Janis showed the animals how to build sleeping platforms and demonstrated how to eat green figs and ants.

B. Janis's gradual withdrawal of support was an important step in transforming Lucy from a pet back into a wild animal.

C. In Africa, it became clear that Lucy would not benefit from the Brewers' program and would not survive on her own without special help.

D. Janis moved to the mainland, from where she would continue to visit and observe the chimps.

6. Which of the following statements best summarizes the information presented in the selection for study purposes?

A. Like human infants, baby chimps must spend years watching and learning from their elders before they can take care of themselves. As a result, chimps that have been raised to behave like human beings are unlikely to have the skills needed to survive in the wild. The case of Lucy demonstrated, however, that such chimps do have the capacity to develop these skills.

B. Lucy, a chimpanzee, was born in a roadside zoo and raised by the Temerlins, a pair of American psychologists. After teaching Lucy to live and communicate much like a human being, the Temerlins turned her over to Janis Carter, whose job it was to prepare the chimp for life in the wild.

C. Animals learn how to take care of themselves in much the same way that humans do: by watching and practicing the skills demonstrated by their elders. This idea was first set forth by the Temerlins, a pair of psychologists, and was later conclusively proven by Janis Carter in her work with Lucy and other chimpanzees.

D. Janis Carter devoted more than ten years to developing a program to help captive chimps learn the skills needed to survive on their own. Through her work Janis demonstrated that it was possible to teach such chimps how to build sleeping platforms, find food, and nurse their young. One of her more successful "students" was a chimpanzee named Lucy, who had been raised by two American psychologists.

Mathematics Section

7. According to a recipe, it takes 4 cups of flour to make 12 servings of pancakes. How many cups of flour are needed to make 2 servings?

   A. 24

   B. 6

   C. $\frac{2}{3}$

   D. $1\frac{1}{2}$

8. Use the graph below to answer the question that follows.

   Ticket Sales

   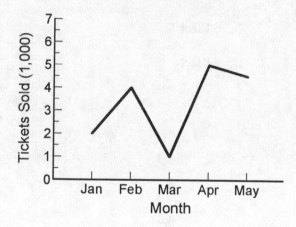

   By what percent did ticket sales increase from January to April?

   A. 50%

   B. 100%

   C. 150%

   D. 250%

9. Use the graph below to answer the question that follows.

   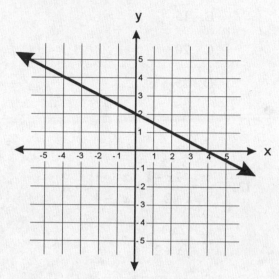

   Which equation is represented by this graph?

   A. $2y + x = 4$

   B. $y + 2x = 4$

   C. $2y - x = 4$

   D. $y - 2x = 4$

10. If $\frac{x+10}{2} = \frac{x+2}{10}$, what is the value of $x - 1$?

    A. -1

    B. -3

    C. -5

    D. -13

11. Five years ago, Zack was three times as old as Aaron. Five years from now, Zack will be twice as old as Aaron. How old is Aaron?

   A. 10

   B. 15

   C. 20

   D. 25

12. $\dfrac{x^2 - 2x + 1}{x + 2} \div \dfrac{x^2 - 1}{x^2 - 4} =$

   A. $\dfrac{2x + 1}{x + 2}$

   B. $\dfrac{x - 1}{x^2 + 3x + 3}$

   C. $\dfrac{x^2 - 3x + 2}{x + 1}$

   D. $\dfrac{2x^2 - 2x}{x^2 + x - 2}$

13. Which of the following quadratic equations has solutions given by

   $$x = \dfrac{3 \pm \sqrt{9 - 4(2)(-5)}}{4}?$$

   A. $2x^2 - 3x - 5 = 0$

   B. $3x^2 - 9x - 40 = 0$

   C. $4x^2 - 2x - 5 = 0$

   D. $12x^2 - 9x - 40 = 0$

14. A metal worker is building a wire frame for a cubic box that is to have a volume of 27 cubic feet. What is the minimum length of wire the metal worker will need?

   A. 27 feet

   B. 36 feet

   C. 54 feet

   D. 81 feet

15. Triangle ABC is similar to triangle EFG. If $\dfrac{AC}{EG} = 5$, and triangle ABC has a perimeter of 10, what is the perimeter of triangle EFG?

    A. $\dfrac{1}{2}$

    B. 2

    C. 10

    D. 50

16. Use the number sequence below to answer the question that follows.

    1, 9, 25, 49, ___

    What is the next number in the sequence?

    A. 64

    B. 73

    C. 81

    D. 97

17. Which of the following is the best **estimate** of the number square feet of material needed to make a spherical balloon with a volume of 256000 cubic feet?

    A. 1.2×10^3

    B. 1.9×10^4

    C. 2.8×10^4

    D. 8.5×10^5

Writing Section

Read the passage below, written in the style of a college history textbook. Then answer the questions that follow.

[1]More than any other factor, it was the steel rails and steam-powered locomotives of an expanding railroad system that shaped the course of United States economic development in the late nineteenth century. [2]During this era, the influence of railroads could be seen nearly everywhere. [3]They helped populate broad stretches of wilderness in the West. [4]They also opened up new markets for the producers of goods. [5]Enabling them to ship products long distances with unprecedented speed. [6]The decline of the passenger train was largely due to the growth of the commercial airline industry.

[7]In addition to facilitating the movement of goods and people, railroad expansion spurred growth in other industries. [8]The laying of track, construction of bridges, and manufacture of locomotives required vast quantities of steel. [9]And as steel output mounted, so did the demand for coal, which was the primary energy source in late nineteenth-century iron and steel mills. [10]In these and related ways, railroads set in motion a chain of economic activity that would make the United States a major industrial power.

18. Which of the following sentences, if added between Parts 8 and 9 of the second paragraph, would be most consistent with the author's purpose and intended audience?

   A. Between 1870 and 1890, annual steel production increased from 77,000 tons to 4.79 million tons.

   B. This must certainly have made a lot of steel manufacturers happy.

   C. I've always felt that the late nineteenth century must have been an exciting time to be alive.

   D. Can you imagine how many new mills were built to meet the demand?

19. Which of the numbered parts of paragraph 1 draws attention away from the main idea of the paragraph?

   A. Part 1

   B. Part 3

   C. Part 4

   D. Part 6

20. Which of the following parts of the passage is a nonstandard sentence?

   A. Part 1

   B. Part 5

   C. Part 8

   D. Part 9

Read the paragraph below, written in the style of an article in a natural history magazine. Then answer the questions that follow.

[1]With their strong, curved teeth, beavers are best know for their ability to cut down trees and build dams. [2]The main components of beaver dams are logs, branches, and rocks joined together with mud. [3]Beavers use the mud and stones to form the dam's base. [4] _____ .

[5]To strengthen the dam, beavers set the logs so that their tips point in the same direction as the water's current. [6]Then they cement together the sides of the logs with additional mud and stones. [7]When completed, some beaver dams are more than 300 yards long.

21. Which of the following sentences, used in place of the blank line labeled Part 4, would best fit the writer's pattern of development in the above paragraph?

A. They next add branches and log poles from trees they have cut down.

B. Unlike beaver dams, beaver lodges may be located on land or in the water.

C. Prior to the twentieth century, beavers were probably the most widely hunted animals in the United States and Canada.

D. Beavers that live in large lakes generally do not build dams.

22. Which one, if any, of the following changes is needed in the above paragraph?

A. Part 1: change "know" to "known."

B. Part 3: change "dam's" to "dams'."

C. Part 5: change "their" to "there."

D. None of these changes is needed.

Quick Pre-Test Answer Key

Here are the correct answers to the questions on the Quick Pre-Test.

Question	Answer	Skill
		Reading
1.	C	Meaning of words and phrases
2.	B	Main idea and details
3.	A	Writer's purpose and meaning
4.	D	Relationship among ideas
5.	A	Critical reasoning skills
6.	A	Study skills in reading
		Mathematics
7.	C	Word problems
8.	C	Data interpretation and analysis
9.	A	Graphs of number relationships
10.	D	One- and two-variable equations
11.	B	Word problems with variables
12.	C	Algebraic expressions and functional notation
13.	A	Quadratic equations
14.	B	Problems with geometric figures
15.	B	Problems with geometric concepts
16.	C	Apply reasoning skills
17.	B	Solve applied problems
		Writing
18.	A	Recognize purpose and audience
19.	D	Unity, focus, and development
20.	B	Effective sentences
21.	A	Effective organization
22.	A	Edited American English

Your Score

Reading   I answered _____ of 6 questions correctly.

Mathematics   I answered _____ of 11 questions correctly.

Writing   I answered _____ of 5 questions correctly.

SECTION II

Reading Skills Review

Introduction

The ability to read and comprehend college-level material is probably the most fundamental skill you will need during your college career. Almost every course requires some reading; many require substantial amounts.

The Texas Academic Skills Program addresses six reading skills. Each chapter in this section describes and provides instruction on one of the reading skills. Each of these skills may be covered on the TASP Test with multiple-choice questions that are associated with a passage. The passages are similar to the types of materials you will encounter in college-level textbooks and other instructional materials. The chapters in this section include many practice exercises modeled on this type of testing approach. In general, however, the passages on the TASP Test tend to be longer than the examples in these chapters.

Organization of This Section

Chapter 4 deals with vocabulary, the meaning of words and phrases. Comprehending what you read depends not only on your knowledge of words but also on your ability to determine the meaning of a word or a phrase from the context in which it is used. This chapter covers unfamiliar and uncommon words and phrases as well as figurative expressions.

Chapters 5 through 8 deal with four skills, each an aspect of reading comprehension. Chapter 5 covers identifying the main idea of a passage and ideas that support, illustrate, or elaborate on that main idea. Main ideas may be explicit or implicit; this chapter covers both types.

Chapter 6 provides instruction in recognizing a writer's purpose for writing and in evaluating the appropriateness of written material for various purposes or audiences. Written communication is generally planned with a specific intent and audience in mind. Writers match their vocabulary and style to their purpose and audience. Your ability to recognize the writer's purpose and intended audience is an important part of comprehension. Understanding purpose, audience, and point of view is also a key to determining a writer's opinion on a topic.

Chapter 7 involves the analysis of the relationship among ideas in written material. In many passages, events are described in sequence, cause-effect relationships are laid out, or ideas are contrasted with one another. Understanding the ways ideas are presented in writing improves comprehension. Your ability to draw conclusions from information that is stated or implied in a passage also depends on your understanding of the relationship among ideas in writing.

Chapter 8 offers instruction in the use of critical reasoning skills to evaluate stated or implied assumptions in a written passage. In working with a passage, we are often required to judge the relevance of the facts it provides, to consider the logic of a writer's argument, to evaluate the validity of an analogy, to distinguish between fact and opinion, and, in general, to assess the credibility or objectivity of the writing. Chapter 8 deals with these "higher-order" skills that go beyond understanding the passage.

Chapter 9, the last in this section, deals with the application of study skills to reading assignments. In many cases in college, you will be required to follow written instructions or to interpret information presented in charts, graphs, or tables. This chapter covers those skills and others related to organizing and summarizing information for study purposes.

Be aware that the purpose of this section of the book is to familiarize you with reading skills in general. In many instances, these chapters cover topics and ideas that may not appear on the official TASP Test. The goal of the study guide is to provide instruction on the skills upon which the TASP Test may be based, as opposed to preparing you solely to take the TASP Test. Indeed, the examples and practice exercises are not necessarily in the same format or at the same level of difficulty that you might experience on the official TASP Test.

Chapter 4

DETERMINE THE MEANING OF WORDS AND PHRASES

This skill includes using the context of a passage to determine the meaning of words with multiple meanings, unfamiliar and uncommon words and phrases, and figurative expressions.

Introduction

Throughout your undergraduate experience, you will encounter general and specialized words and phrases whose meanings at first may not be clear to you. Whenever you see such a word or phrase, careful examination of its context (i.e., the words and phrases surrounding it) may help you determine its intended meaning. By using context to discover the meaning of a previously unknown word or phrase, a word with multiple meanings, or a figurative expression, you will better understand the material you are reading. In addition, you will acquire new vocabulary to apply to future academic work. A good vocabulary is essential to effective reading in college and beyond. Words are, after all, the primary tools of thinking, speaking, reading, and writing.

You make use of context to some extent whenever you read. For a difficult reading assignment, context clues may indeed provide you with a great deal of valuable information and may often determine your ability to understand the assignment. This chapter will provide you with information and ideas about how to use context to determine the meaning of unknown words, words with multiple meanings, and figurative expressions.

Unfamiliar Words

How then do you unravel the mystery of an unknown word? Clues to the meaning of an unfamiliar word may be found in the words and phrases surrounding the unfamiliar word, or they may come in the form of definitions, restatements, examples, or explanations. In addition to using context clues, your knowledge of common roots and affixes may help in identifying the meaning of some unknown words. If you remain uncertain about the meaning of a word after examining its context and its structure, look it up in a glossary or dictionary.

1. Surrounding words and phrases. One of the easiest ways to figure out the meaning of an unfamiliar word is to read the words just before and just after that word, as described in the following example.

The vast *panorama* of sea and sky overwhelmed Balboa when he first saw the
Pacific Ocean in 1513.

Suppose you read the preceding sentence in a history text, but did not know the
meaning of the word *panorama*. First, examine the word that comes before it, *vast*.
You know *vast* means "very big" or "immense" and that it is being used to describe
the unfamiliar word, *panorama*. Next, read the words following *panorama*: "of sea
and sky." Now you know that the *panorama* consists of sea and sky. By reading
further, you find that Balboa was overwhelmed by the *panorama* when he saw the
Pacific Ocean for the first time. You can probably tell by now that *panorama* means
"view" or "vista." You have successfully used several context clues to arrive at the
meaning of an unfamiliar word. In this example, the context clues are
modifiers—adjectives, adverbs, and prepositional phrases—that help you
understand the unfamiliar word.

2. Definition. Writers often realize that you may not know a given word, so they
define it for you. Certain words and phrases (e.g., *is, consists of, means, refers to*)
may be used to signal the reader that a definition is coming.

> An *anarchist is* a person who does not believe in any form of established
> government.

> *Anaphylactic shock refers to* a severe reaction in an individual who has been
> exposed to a specific antigen, such as wasp venom, after previous sensitization.

Similarly, certain punctuation marks, particularly commas, dashes, and parentheses, often signal a definition. In these cases, the definition may consist of a brief
phrase immediately following the word and may be set off from the sentence by
comma(s), dash(es), or parentheses.

> The professor's *erudition (profound knowledge)* was respected in the academic
> community.

> The *geriatrician—one who treats diseases of old age*—is a relatively new type of
> specialist.

3. Restatement. A writer may also explain an uncommon word by restating its
meaning. Often key words or phrases, such as *that is, or,* and *in other words,* warn
you that a restatement is coming in the text.

> Cinderella's sisters were a *querulous* pair. *That is,* they found fault in everything
> Cinderella did.

> Ancient *cartographers, or* mapmakers, had to revise their charts and drawings of
> the world during the Age of Discovery.

> A new state program that encourages closer work with faculty has been developed
> to help stimulate and challenge *gifted* students. *In other words,* those who have a
> high IQ, an outstanding talent, strong leadership qualities, or exceptionally strong
> motivation will work with faculty on special projects.

In the first example of restatement, the meaning of *querulous*—"complaining"—is restated in the phrase *found fault.* In the second example, the unfamiliar word, *cartographer,* is defined by the term *mapmaker* and further explained by the phrase *charts and drawings.* In the third example, the term *gifted* is clarified by the set of defining characteristics that are listed following the phrase *in other words.*

4. Example. A writer often provides examples to clarify the meaning of a word. Key phrases—*for example* (or its Latin abbreviation, *e.g.*), *such as, for instance, including, like,* and *especially*—alert you to the use of examples.

> *Mammals, including for example* bears, squirrels, and humans, are warmblooded and usually have hair.

> The plot of a play usually revolves around a *protagonist, such as* Othello or Hamlet, and his or her struggles with an *antagonist, such as* Iago or King Claudius.

In these sentences, one or more specific examples may help you understand the meaning of the unfamiliar word.

5. Explanation. Sometimes a writer explains the meaning of an unfamiliar word in the same sentence or in the next sentence.

> Darlene's freckles were *ubiquitous.* They developed all over her hands, arms, legs, and face—wherever the sun had touched her skin.

> Julia Child evaluated the aspiring chef's new recipes. A graduate of a famous French cooking school and an expert on France's cuisine, Julia Child is a true *connoisseur* of French food.

In the first example, you can determine the meaning of *ubiquitous* from the second sentence. It states that Darlene developed freckles all over. You can now guess that *ubiquitous* means "everywhere."

In the second example, the fact that Julia Child graduated from a famous French cooking school and the fact that she is an expert in French cuisine are clues that come *before* the word in question. A *connoisseur* is a "person who has extensive knowledge in a particular field."

6. Roots and affixes. The way that an unfamiliar word is formed may offer clues to its meaning. Most of the words in the English language are formed from ancient Greek, Latin, or Anglo-Saxon *roots,* whose meanings may be modified by *affixes,* or additions to the beginning or end of a root. There are two kinds of affixes: *prefixes,* which are attached to the beginning of a word, and *suffixes,* which are attached to the end.

The Greek root *scope,* for example, which means "see," is used with the prefixes *micro-* ("small"), *tele-* ("far"), and *peri-* ("around") to form the words *microscope, telescope,* and *periscope.* By looking for common root words and affixes, you can often determine the meaning of a word that is new to you.

The prehistoric paintings were discovered in a *subterranean* cavern.

Aquaculture is a promising source of food for developing nations.

In the first example, the word *subterranean* is formed from the Latin word *terra,* meaning "earth" (as in *terrain* and *territory*), and the prefix *sub-,* meaning "under." These two clues should make it clear that *subterranean* means "underground." This is confirmed by the context of the sentence. In the second example, the word *aquaculture* is composed of two Latin words: *aqua,* meaning "water" (as in *aquarium* and *aquatic*), and *cultus,* meaning "grown" (as in *cultivate* and *agriculture*). The combination of these two roots means "water farming" and usually refers to the raising of fish.

Affixes can denote a variety of concepts, including time (e.g., *pre*war, *post*war), direction (e.g., *de*scend, *a*scend), and number (e.g., *uni*cycle, *bi*cycle, *tri*cycle). They are also used to form nouns (e.g., employ*ee*, teach*er*), verbs (e.g., popular*ize*, activ*ate*), adjectives (e.g., combat*ive*, lov*able*), and adverbs (e.g., steadi*ly*, quick*ly*). You should pay careful attention to affixes because they can change the meaning of a word or even reverse its meaning altogether, as in *un*happy, *ir*regular, *a*typical, and *dis*similar.

Many books include a list of common roots, prefixes, and suffixes. Keeping such a list handy and reviewing it from time to time may help you figure out unfamiliar words you find in your reading.

Words with Multiple Meanings

Many words have more than one meaning. The words *type, fall, low, interest,* and *main,* for instance, each have a number of very different meanings. They may also be used as different parts of speech (that is, used to serve different functions in the sentence). How, then, do you find the one meaning intended by the writer? As you read, you choose the one meaning that best fits the sentence and passage. When you do so, you will again make use of context.

At the press conference, the senator will *air* his views on toxic waste disposal.

Lena played an *air* that she had composed for the occasion.

In the first example, *air* means "to speak publicly." Context clues, such as "at the press conference" and "views," indicate that the senator will communicate his ideas in a public way. In the second example, the verbs *played* and *composed* are clues to the fact that *air* is intended by the writer to mean "a song or tune." In these examples, *air* has two very different meanings, which, in turn, differ from the word's most common meaning—"the mixture of invisible gases surrounding the earth."

After a *vain* attempt to start his car, Rob decided to take the bus to work.

Karen is quite *vain.* She spent hours fussing before her image in the mirror.

In the first example involving the word *vain*, Rob ends up taking a bus to work, so you can infer that his car would not start. Therefore, *vain* must mean "fruitless" or "without success." In the second example, the second sentence explains the intended meaning of *vain*—"excessively proud of one's appearance."

Figurative Language

You have probably heard the expressions, "It's as dry as a bone," or "He's as stubborn as a mule!" Most likely, you are familiar with these and other common figurative expressions. Often, however, writers make up new figurative expressions to convey a specific idea in a fresh way. As a student, you will need to interpret the meanings of such figurative expressions. They occur most commonly in literature, but may be found in all types of writing. Writers use figurative language to give emphasis and liveliness to their writing. Four of the most common types of figurative language are simile, metaphor, personification, and hyperbole.

1. Simile. Writers use similes to compare two dissimilar things. A simile shows that basically unlike things are alike in some way. You can spot a simile easily because words such as *like, as, than,* and *similar to* introduce the comparison.

> The smog hung over Los Angeles *like* a thick blanket of insulation.

> Dean's mood was *similar to* the day—gray and cloudy.

In the first example, you can get an idea of the intensity of the fog when the writer compares it to a heavy blanket of insulation. In the second example, Dean's mood is compared to a gray and cloudy day. Here, to understand the writer's meaning, you must also examine the implied meanings of *gray* and *cloudy. Gray* suggests darkness and dullness; *cloudy* suggests gloom. With the simile, therefore, the writer suggests that Dean is in a troubled mood.

2. Metaphor. Metaphors also draw a comparison between two dissimilar things and emphasize their common qualities. However, unlike the comparison in a simile, the comparison created by a metaphor is implied—that is, it is presented without the use of introductory words such as *like, as,* etc.

> The banyan tree was a massive octopus with giant tentacles radiating from its great head.

Here the writer compares a banyan tree to a massive octopus with its giant tentacles radiating from its head. Even if you have never seen a banyan tree (they are found in tropical swamps), you can picture what the tree is like through the writer's use of metaphor.

3. Personification. Personification is a type of figurative language in which nonhuman things, objects, or ideas are given human qualities.

> The daisies nodded their heads in the summer breeze.

> The sea gulls scolded us as we walked on the beach.

In the first example, the moving daisy blossoms are likened to people's nodding heads. In the second example, sea gulls are given the quality of human speech.

4. Hyperbole. Hyperbole, or overstatement, is simply exaggeration. Writers may use hyperbole to produce either a comic or a serious effect. When writers use hyperbole, you must not take their words literally. Instead, you should look for the ideas or impressions they are trying to communicate through their overstatements.

> A swim in Maine water will freeze your blood.

> The salmon rocketed out of the river.

> Building your own home is about as easy as walking to the North Pole!

In the first example, the writer knows that the Maine water will not really freeze your blood; it may, however, make you feel extremely cold. In the second example, the salmon clearly was not propelled by a rocket (although it may have looked that way); instead, it leaped swiftly under its own power. Similarly, in the third example, it is clear that, although building your own home is difficult, it is a manageable task and one that is not nearly as difficult as trudging to the North Pole. In each case, the writer is attempting to create a stronger effect than he or she would by writing the simpler, more literal version of these sentences: "A swim in Maine water will make you cold," "The salmon leaped out of the river," and "Building your own home is difficult."

Practice Exercises

The following exercises will help you review the skills covered in this chapter. Many of the types of questions presented here will be similar to those on the test; others will not. Remember that the purpose of the exercises is to give you practice on the skills rather than merely to prepare you for the test. Following these exercises are the Practice Exercise Explanations. They explain each question, the correct answer, and why the remaining choices are incorrect.

The fiery ball sank lower and lower in the sky. For a moment, it was a strange, round-cheeked maiden with brilliant curly locks blowing out behind her in the wind. She floated, suspended above the rippled carpet of clouds, then silently slipped from sight.

1. Which of the following is the best meaning of the word locks as it is used in this selection?

    A. tufts of wool

    B. hair

    C. firm holds

    D. fasteners

2. In this selection, the writer uses the phrase the round-cheeked maiden to refer to:

    A. a cloud.

    B. the wind.

    C. a young woman.

    D. the sun.

Retin-A is a drug whose long- and short-term effects are currently being investigated by medical researchers. Originally used to treat acne, the drug was recently used on 30 patients aged 35–70. In this study, Retin-A was found to reverse the effects of photoaging among individuals who have been exposed to excessive amounts of ultraviolet radiation. After applying a cream with Retin-A for four months, patients showed fewer wrinkles and sun spots and, overall, smoother, healthier-looking skin.

Preliminary results indicate that Retin-A, or tretinoin, helps to promote the growth and renewal of skin cells and of the tiny blood vessels in the skin. This, in turn, thickens and compresses the outer layer of skin.

However, there are limitations to the drug. First, it only works when the patient continues to use Retin-A. If the patient discontinues the drug application, the skin reverts to its former condition. In addition, some people show little improvement even after faithful use of the drug.

3. Which of the following best defines the term photoaging as it is used in the first paragraph of this selection?

A. a procedure used to make a photograph look older or antique

B. a chemical reaction induced by light

C. skin damage caused by repeated exposure to ultraviolet radiation

D. excessive sensitivity to light

4. Which of the following is the best meaning of the word promote as it is used in the second paragraph of this selection?

A. advance to a higher position

B. acquire by devious means

C. publicize or advertise

D. help bring about change

5. In paragraph 3 of this selection, the term reverts means:

A. leaps backward.

B. returns to the owner.

C. goes back.

D. returns to an ancestral type.

X-ray, CAT scan, and MRI are image systems available to modern medicine. Most of us are familiar with the X-ray, which is used so often to check for cavities and for broken bones. Likewise, the CAT scan (computerized axial tomography), used for the last 15 years to image internal bodily structures, has become a familiar term to us. But what is MRI?

MRI (magnetic resonance imaging) produces an image by putting the patient in a highly magnetized field, thus causing the protons in the patient's body to line up. The patient lies on a movable table that slides into a tube, similar to that used in a CAT scan. However, the MRI tube is constructed over a giant magnet. As the patient lies motionless in the tube, a radio wave is sent through the body, which temporarily knocks the protons out of axis. As the protons return to their axis, they give off a signal of their own, which is recorded, measured, and imaged by the computer.

6. Which of the following is the best meaning of the word image as it is used in the first paragraph of this selection?

    A. to describe vividly

    B. to imagine

    C. to symbolize or stand for

    D. to picture

7. In the second paragraph of this selection, the word field refers to an area:

    A. in which a given effect exists.

    B. that is visible through the lens of a microscope.

    C. in which sports events occur.

    D. that is used for cultivation or pasture.

Jason listened carefully. The horses neighed restively in their stalls. The henhouse practically shook with the birds' anxious squawking. Drummer, the beagle puppy, barked uneasily at Jason's heels. All the animals seemed to sense that something was about to happen. Then, suddenly, the ranch was as quiescent as a deserted battlefield.

Jason's eyes widened as he studied the dull sky. A strange yellow-green light overspread the horizon. Jason grabbed Drummer and ran for the old root cellar. They cowered together as far from the cellar door as possible. Outside they heard the whoosh of the whirling wind, then sounds like clattering cans and banging boards. Finally, there were loud booms that sounded like fireworks.

At last the silence returned. Jason and Drummer waited, then Jason inched to the door and opened it. The sky was blue again, the sun shone. The horses whinnied and the hens began to cluck.

With Drummer at his heels, Jason emerged from the cellar and surveyed the ranch. The house, the barn, the henhouse, and the corral were all standing, but his porch—the new porch that he and his neighbors had just built—was a storm-smashed raft tossed on a grassy sea.

8. Which of the following is the best meaning of the word restively as used in the first paragraph of the selection?

   A. anxiously

   B. sleepily

   C. quietly

   D. happily

9. In the first paragraph of this selection, the writer notes that the ranch was as quiescent as a deserted battlefield. The writer uses this simile to indicate that the ranch was:

   A. full of tension.

   B. very busy.

   C. extremely still.

   D. unpredictable.

10. As used in the last paragraph of this selection, the term surveyed means:

    A. questioned people.

    B. measured land.

    C. viewed completely.

    D. determined boundaries.

11. In the last paragraph, the writer uses the metaphor a storm-smashed raft tossed on a grassy sea to indicate that the porch:

    A. was the only structure left standing in a sea of destruction.

    B. was completely under water as a result of the storm.

    C. had been smashed by a wooden raft left on the grass before the storm.

    D. had been blown completely off the house and onto the grass.

Practice Exercise Explanations

1. **Correct Response: B.** Information in the selection indicates that the *locks* belong to a "maiden" and that they are "curly." Thus, given context clues, it is clear that *locks* must mean *hair. Tufts of wool, firm holds,* and *fasteners* are all alternative meanings of the word *locks,* but none of these meanings fits the context of the selection.

2. **Correct Response: D.** In this selection, *the round-cheeked maiden* is used as a metaphor for the sun. The reader knows this because context clues, such as "sank lower and lower in the sky" and "slipped from sight," indicate that the writer is describing a sunset. Although choices A and B, *a cloud* and *the wind,* are both mentioned in the paragraph, an examination of context clues indicates that the metaphor is intended to describe neither of these. Choice C is incorrect because it is a literal interpretation of a phrase intended as a metaphor.

3. **Correct Response: C.** In the first paragraph, we learn that *photoaging* refers to some negative effect and occurs "among individuals who have been exposed to excessive amounts of ultraviolet radiation." Therefore, choice C is the correct response. Choices B and D are incorrect because they relate only to the first part of the word, *photo-* (a prefix meaning "light"), and ignore the second part of the word, *-aging.* Choice A is incorrect because the passage does not have anything to do with photography.

4. **Correct Response: D.** Although all four answer choices represent actual meanings of the word *promote,* only choice D fits the context of the sentence in which the word appears. This sentence makes the point that Retin-A results in, or helps bring about change related to, the growth and renewal of skin cells and the blood vessels in the skin. Alternatively, information included in the sentence is unrelated to any person or thing that advances to a higher position (choice A), that is acquired by devious means (choice B), or that is publicized or advertised (choice C).

5. **Correct Response: C.** When you substitute *goes back* for *reverts* in the selection, the sense of the selection remains the same. Moreover, the same idea—that the skin returns to its former state—is restated in the previous sentence when the writer warns that the improvement remains only if Retin-A use is continued. This implies that once the drug is stopped, a relapse will occur. Choice A is incorrect because it suggests actual physical movement backward. Choice B refers to a different meaning of *revert,* one that would typically be used in a legal context. Choice D refers to still another meaning of *revert,* one that would likely be more appropriate in an anthropological or biological context.

6. **Correct Response: D.** As indicated in the selection, the CAT scan, like the X-ray and the MRI, is used to form a computerized picture of internal body structures. Therefore, of the response options given, the best meaning of the word *image,* used in this case as a verb, is *to picture.* This meaning is relatively new and may not be listed in some dictionaries. Choice A is incorrect because it refers to the literary use of the word *image,* in which a writer describes a subject using vivid language and figurative expressions. Choice B does not fit the context, since *to imagine* refers to the ability to make a picture in one's mind, an ability unrelated to anything discussed in the selection. Similarly, choice C is incorrect because MRI is used to make pictures, not *to symbolize or stand for* anything else.

7. **Correct Response: A.** As used in the first sentence of the second paragraph, the term *field* refers to a magnetized area in which a patient is placed; therefore, of the choices given, *field* is best defined as an area *in which a given effect exists*. Choice B, although related to medical technology, is not correct because the selection includes no mention of looking through an instrument such as a microscope. Choices C and D refer to quite different meanings of *field*. Neither of these choices is correct since the selection makes no reference to either sports or farming.

8. **Correct Response: A.** From the context, you know that the hens and the puppy, Drummer, are uneasy and anxious. In addition, the writer notes that all the animals "seemed to sense that something was about to happen." Using this information, you can infer that, like the hens and the puppy, the horses are also uneasy and anxious. The word *restive* therefore means "anxious" (choice A). Choices B, C, and D do not fit the context, since there is no evidence that any of the animals are sleepy, quiet, or happy. Sleepy and quiet may be suggested by the first part of the word *restive* (i.e., *rest-*), but here the syllable *rest-* does not mean the same as the word *rest*.

9. **Correct Response: C.** According to the selection, the animals were making anxious sounds, when suddenly the ranch became like a *deserted battlefield*. In this context, the writer's use of the word *suddenly* suggests change. Moreover, you can infer that a battlefield, which is noisy and active during battle, would seem *extremely still* when it is deserted. Choice A is incorrect because we know that the ranch, or at least the animals in it, changed suddenly from a state of tension to some other state. Choice B, which means the opposite of the correct response, does not fit the context of the story or the image of a deserted battlefield. Choice D also does not fit the image of a deserted battlefield.

10. **Correct Response: C.** You know from the context that when Jason emerged, he viewed his house, his barn, the henhouse, and the corral; in other words, he looked over his ranch completely. Therefore, choice C is the correct response. Choices A, B, and D refer to other meanings of the word *survey,* which do not fit the context of this passage. Choice A refers to the process of collecting data for a specific purpose by questioning people. Choices B and D refer to the work of a surveyor, an individual who measures land using special instruments and the principles of geometry and trigonometry.

11. **Correct Response: D.** Jason sees that all the structures on the ranch except his porch are intact after the storm. Using a metaphor, the writer compares the remains of the porch to a raft smashed by a storm on the sea; in other words, the porch as it sits broken apart on the grass looks like a raft that has been tossed helter-skelter on a stormy sea. Choice A is incorrect because the writer indicates earlier in the paragraph that other structures on the ranch were all standing after the storm. In choice B, the term *sea* is taken literally rather than figuratively, thus resulting in misinterpretation. In choice C, the term *raft* is taken literally rather than figuratively; this also leads to a misinterpretation of the writer's intended meaning. From information included in the selection, there is no indication either that the ranch is located near the sea or that a wooden raft was responsible for ruining the porch.

Study Ideas

Read the chapter and the practice exercises carefully. Be sure you understand the examples and practice exercises, including the explanations for the correct answers. Follow the steps listed below to develop your vocabulary further.

1. Read a variety of materials. Also be on the alert for new words used in conversation.

2. When reading, note new uses of familiar words, and unfamiliar words and figurative expressions.

3. Always try to figure out the meanings of unfamiliar words and phrases from the context. Use signal words and punctuation clues. Look particularly for definitions, restatements, examples, and explanations to help you.

4. If uncertain of a word's meaning after examining the context, look it up in the glossary of the text or in a dictionary. Note the part of speech, pronunciation, and particular meaning that matches the context of the material. Note other meanings as well.

5. Add each new word to your personal vocabulary list—write the word, the part of speech, the definition(s), and a sentence using the word.

6. On a piece of notebook paper, write the word, the definition, and the sentence in three separate columns. You can fold over one or two columns to test your retention of the word, its meaning, and its use.

7. Another way to build your vocabulary is to write each new word on one side of a 3 x 5 card with its definition on the reverse side. Study these cards often. Simple memorization tasks such as these are best accomplished in brief, frequent study periods. So take the cards with you and review them several times each day.

8. If you have access to a computer, use it to keep a running list of new vocabulary words.

9. Examine the structures of words. Learn common prefixes, suffixes, and word roots, and their meanings. Learn groups of new words that use the same prefix, suffix, or root.

10. Use new words in conversation, in class discussion, and in your writing. Watch for them as you read.

Chapter 5

UNDERSTAND THE MAIN IDEA AND SUPPORTING DETAILS IN WRITTEN MATERIAL

This skill includes identifying explicit and implicit main ideas and recognizing ideas that support, illustrate, or elaborate the main idea of a passage.

Introduction

Accurately identifying the main idea of a piece of writing is essential for making sense of what you read. You may be reading a Shakespearean tragedy, a history of the women's movement, a chapter on photosynthesis, or an auto repair manual. You may be reading because you have been assigned a paper on a particular subject, or you may be reading to entertain yourself. Whatever you are reading and for whatever purpose, your response to the material depends on your ability to understand the writer's point.

As you approach any reading passage, you should begin by skim reading the material to determine its general organization and structure. Typical organizational patterns include, for example, cause-and-effect organization, comparison-contrast organization, and argumentative organization. (See Chapter 7 for a detailed discussion of these patterns and techniques for identifying them.) Identifying the organizational structure of a reading passage before you actually begin to read is likely to help you see the larger point that the writer is trying to convey and the way each part of the work contributes to that larger point.

When you encounter a longer passage, it is helpful, in addition, to preview it by reading the first and last paragraphs in their entirety, as well as the first sentence of each remaining paragraph in the passage. The first paragraph will generally provide you with an introduction to the main idea, while the last paragraph will typically summarize for you the important points made by the writer throughout the work. Because it is common in the English language to place the most important idea of a paragraph first, reading the first sentence of each remaining paragraph will usually allow you to gain an excellent overview of the flow of the passage. Such an overview is important because it can help you focus and organize your thinking about the passage as you read.

Finally, you are more likely to recognize the point of what you read when you approach your reading actively rather than passively; that is, when you constantly ask yourself questions about what the writer is saying. Two important questions to ask are: "Who (or what) is the subject of the passage?" and "What is the writer saying about the subject?" As noted above, the answers to these questions are often found in the first sentence of a paragraph, or in the first paragraph of a longer selection. Moreover, writers frequently repeat their most important points at the end of a selection. After all, their goal is to communicate ideas clearly, not to mystify you. Signal words such as *in conclusion, in summary, therefore, finally, last,* and *most important* will help you find restatements of main ideas.

Besides a main idea, each piece of writing typically includes supporting details, or information used by the writer to develop the main idea or argument. Supporting details may take various forms, including reasons, examples, facts and statistics, description, and definition. These will be discussed in more detail later in the chapter, following the discussion below that focuses on how to identify a main idea.

Main Ideas in Narrative and Expository Writing

Narrative writing. Narrative works are those that tell a story or give an account of particular events. The main idea of a narrative passage may be either stated or implied, and it generally answers the question, "What is happening?" Following is an example of a narrative paragraph.

> Justina stared for a long time at the smashed window. Peering inside, she saw that the carpet was soaked. The rain had stopped shortly after midnight, so she concluded that an intruder had broken in sometime before that.

In this paragraph, the main idea is that Justina is interpreting evidence of a robbery. Note that this main idea is implied rather than stated in any one sentence you read. Although each sentence provides information, the main idea is something you must infer. In this example, you are using inductive reasoning to arrive at the main idea. That is, you infer the main idea from the combined evidence: Justina notices the broken window, she sees the wet carpet, she knows when it stopped raining, and evidently she is thinking ("she concluded") about all these things. (See Chapter 7 for a more complete discussion of inductive reasoning.)

Expository writing. As a college student, you will read a great deal of expository writing. Expository writing explains a process or a body of knowledge, or it makes an argument. To find the main idea of an expository passage, you should ask: "What is the writer trying to communicate?" The paragraph that follows is an example of expository writing that is written in the style of a college geology textbook and is designed to explain a process.

> Of the three basic types of rock, sedimentary rocks are most directly the product of erosion. A brittle piece of shale, for example, consists of thousands or millions of particles. Each of these particles was once a piece of silt, worn away by wind or water from some older rock, then transported by a stream, and deposited at the bottom of a lake or quiet stretch of river. Over a period of centuries, these particles were lithified.

The main point of the paragraph above is a fact stated in the first sentence: sedimentary rocks are the product of erosion. The rest of the paragraph illustrates that point by describing the process that generates one kind of sedimentary rock. (You might need to look up the word *lithified,* but you can probably figure out from the context that it means "turned into rock.")

Some expository writing presents an argument. Below is an example of such writing.

> Although traditional historians regard A.D. 476 as the year when the Roman Empire fell, its essential characteristics survived until the eighth century A.D. It is true that the city of Rome itself was overrun in 476 by invaders from the north, but Roman institutions continued in much of the Mediterranean world for hundreds of years after that date. Only in the year 711, when the Moors invaded Spain from North Africa, did the Roman Empire lose its position as the foremost political and cultural force in the Western world.

To find the main idea of this material, you must first ask yourself what the writer is trying to do. You note that the writer makes an assertion (i.e., the Roman Empire survived until the eighth century) that contradicts another, more widely held belief. It is the writer's assertion that constitutes the main idea. The writer must then defend this assertion with some sort of compelling argument. The reader, in turn, must be able to identify the points of the argument in order to accept or reject the writer's assertion. (Compare this paragraph with the one about sedimentary rocks. No one disagrees that sedimentary rocks are the result of erosion.)

Stated vs. Implied Main Idea

As seen in the preceding examples, the main idea of a passage may be either stated explicitly or implied. The following selections will give you additional practice in determining both stated and implied main ideas.

> Five members of the Mayor's Council on Aging resigned yesterday in protest over the administration's recent budget cuts. James Owens, Shirley Johns, Anita Moralez, Timothy Franklin, and Janice Ray submitted their resignations to Mayor Harrington yesterday morning, citing as their reason the administration's decision to cut as much as 20 percent from the budgets of a number of key programs affecting senior citizens. According to the administration's spokesperson, the cuts were necessary to compensate for predicted revenue shortfalls.

In a newspaper article such as the example above, the main idea is usually stated in the first sentence so the reader can get the most important information in the least amount of time. In the example, the first sentence tells you the point of the article. The rest of the article provides details that support and elaborate that point. In general, once you identify the main idea of a piece of writing, you should be able to see how the writer develops that idea, whether by means of examples, reasons, facts and statistics, description, or definition.

Joseph Conrad spoke Polish as his native language and learned French as a child. Determined to pursue a career at sea, and determined particularly to serve on a British ship, he set about in his twenties to learn English—partly by engaging in conversations with English speakers, but primarily by reading English books. As he began to write in English, he was able to use accurately some English words he did not even know how to pronounce. While serving as second officer on a British merchant ship, Conrad wrote his first novel, *Almayer's Folly*.

The main idea of this passage is not stated in any one sentence. To determine the main idea, look first at the topics included by the writer: Conrad's language learning, his sea career, and his writing. The main idea must somehow combine these subjects. Of course, the main idea can be worded in more than one way. Here are two possibilities:

Joseph Conrad's desire to serve on English ships played an important role in his future career as an English novelist.

Joseph Conrad learned English for one career and used it to make a name for himself in another.

The first of these two sentences mentions sailing and writing; the second sentence mentions learning English. Neither mentions all three topics explicitly, but each sentence is an accurate interpretation of the relationship among the three topics.

Supporting Details

Whether a main idea is stated or implied, it is normally supported by information in other sentences, or by whole paragraphs in a longer reading passage. That is, after all, what writing is: taking an idea and elaborating on it, sentence by sentence, thought by thought.

For most readers, supporting information is crucial to their reading experience. For example, the reader of a detective story wants details. It is no fun simply to be told that someone broke in and stole the secret documents; the fun is in piecing together the evidence and figuring out what happened. Similarly, if you are preparing for a career as a petroleum geologist, you need to know more than a quick definition of "sedimentary rock"; you need to know in detail how that rock was formed. Likewise, if you learned in high school that the Roman Empire fell in 476 A.D., but your college history text asserts that this date is inaccurate, you may be curious to know why the writer is saying this.

A main idea may be developed in several ways. One is by citing one or more *examples* that support the main idea, as illustrated in the following selections.

The popularity of karate has increased greatly in the United States. Athletes study karate to improve their confidence and concentration. Many others have taken up the discipline as a means of self-defense. Finally, because karate demands flexibility, stamina, strength, muscle control, and coordination, large numbers of people now study karate just to improve their overall fitness.

Community gardening is a great way to generate a sense of community spirit and support among the residents of a neighborhood or town. In Atkins Park last year, our neighborhood association put aside space for about 40 garden plots. By early summer, gardens were flourishing and so were ideas. All those using our plots met and agreed to limit their use of chemical pesticides. We also organized a system of refuse collection and designated an area as a compost heap. A number of people even took the time to plant a lovely flower garden at the entrance to our neighborhood's gardening area. Word of our productive and beautiful gardens has spread. Now other neighborhoods around the city plan to use our experience as a model.

In the first paragraph, the main idea—that karate has become increasingly popular in the United States—is supported by *examples* of those groups for whom interest in the discipline has increased (e.g., athletes, or others who wish to improve their fitness). In the second paragraph, the story of one neighborhood's experience with community gardening provides an example to support the writer's contention that such ventures are good for generating community spirit and support.

Supporting details may also be provided through *facts* and *statistics*. A *fact* is a statement that can be proved to be true, while a *statistic* is a fact in numerical form. The first example below uses facts to support its main point; the second uses statistics.

By modern standards, the ancient city of Pompeii was remarkably sophisticated in its design. Excavations of the city, which was buried beneath the ash of the Mount Vesuvius eruption, reveal cleverly designed buildings on a logical grid of streets. Pompeiian streets were lined with handsome paving stones and even had "speed bumps" to regulate chariot traffic.

In our society, the proportion of individuals who are over 65 years old has increased steadily during the past century. In 1900, only 4 percent of the U.S. population was in this age group. By 1972 the proportion had risen to approximately 10 percent, and experts estimate that this figure will double to reach 20 percent by the year 2050. What this trend means is that we must begin to plan now to ensure that adequate resources will be available to meet the needs of this ever-growing segment of our society.

In the first paragraph, *facts* about the ancient city of Pompeii are used to support the idea that that city exhibited sophisticated design features. Similarly, the second paragraph offers facts in the form of *statistics* to support the view that planning is required to ensure that adequate resources will be available for the growing number of elderly citizens in our society.

Writers may also use reasons to develop a main idea, as shown in the two selections below.

Television programs designed to allow consumers to shop at home are offering their viewers a valuable service. Shopping at home is much more convenient than the traditional method of going from store to store, particularly for those who have limited access to transportation or who have a medical condition that may limit their mobility. The person who shops at home is also able to avoid many of the typical problems of going out to shop, including traffic jams, inadequate parking facilities, crowded stores, unpleasant salespeople, and long lines at cash registers. Furthermore, shopping at home, like shopping in person, allows consumers to use their credit cards and to return most items if they are found to be unsuitable.

Some people are arguing that our state should institute a mandatory 11-month school year for all public school students. There are a number of reasons for opposing this idea. First, the institution of a longer school year does not guarantee that students will learn more; rather, they may simply end up spending more time learning the same amount of material. Second, an 11-month school year would rob many students of the valuable work, camp, or travel experiences they currently enjoy. Finally, many of our best teachers could well decide to quit their jobs in our state's public schools to work in other states that offer them a shorter work year.

In the first example, the writer cites a number of specific *reasons* for taking a positive view of television programs that allow people to shop at home. The writer is able to make a convincing argument by showing that shopping at home allows consumers to avoid many of the disadvantages of shopping in stores while retaining many of the advantages. In the second example, the writer provides three *reasons* for opposing an 11-month school year.

In the following paragraph, a main idea is developed through *definition*.

Demography is the study of populations. Demographers use statistics to describe trends in population size and structure over time, and to characterize patterns of population distribution through space. Demographers do more than simply describe the trends and patterns they observe, however. They also investigate the human and environmental causes underlying them.

In this paragraph, the writer describes demography by essentially *defining* for the reader what that area of study involves.

Finally, writers often use *description* to develop a main idea.

By noon, the enormous hall had become so full of people it was impossible for those inside to see more than a distance of five feet in any direction. The entire room seemed to be a swirling clutter of festive clothing, animated faces, and waving arms. The music and the thousand separate conversations combined to produce one continuous roar, while an incredible heat, generated by the crowd in the tightly packed space, enveloped the whole scene.

Here the writer uses *descriptive details* to develop the idea that the hall in question was crowded and to help the reader envision the situation.

You should also note that in a single passage, or even in a single paragraph, writers may use two or more of the types of support discussed in this section. For example, *reasons* provided by a writer are often strengthened through the use of *facts* or *statistics* that support them. As you work on the practice exercises that follow, try to notice the methods each writer has used to present supporting details.

Practice Exercises

The following exercises will help you review the skills covered in this chapter. Many of the types of questions presented here will be similar to those on the test; others will not. Remember that the purpose of the exercises is to give you practice on the skills rather than merely to prepare you for the test. Following these exercises are the Practice Exercise Explanations. They explain each question, the correct answer, and why the remaining choices are incorrect.

Many people assume that music composed by the great composers of the world is entirely original and unique. However, this has never been the case. Throughout the history of music, composers have often adapted folk tunes and turned them into more "serious" works. Mozart and Beethoven took simple German and Austrian tunes and arranged them in a variety of ways to form themes for great symphonies. Anton Dvorak based parts of his *New World Symphony* on folk dances from his native Czechoslovakia. The most memorable part of Aaron Copland's beloved ballet, *Appalachian Spring,* is the section incorporating the old Shaker hymn, "'Tis a Gift to Be Simple." In each of these cases, an artist has reaffirmed the connection between old tradition and new creation.

1. Which of the following sentences from the selection best expresses the main idea?

    A. Many people assume that music composed by the great composers of the world is entirely unique and original.

    B. Throughout the history of music, composers have often adapted folk tunes and turned them into more "serious" works.

    C. Mozart and Beethoven took simple German and Austrian tunes and arranged them in a variety of ways to form themes for great symphonies.

    D. The most memorable part of Aaron Copland's beloved ballet, *Appalachian Spring,* is the section incorporating the old Shaker hymn, "'Tis a Gift to Be Simple."

Typically, athletes and average exercisers think of sit-ups as the ideal abdominal exercise, and in general they are right. However, in any attempt to strengthen the abdominal muscles, care must be taken to avoid straining other muscles. If you do sit-ups by lying on the floor, clasping your hands behind your neck, and raising your torso until you can touch your knees with your elbows, all the while keeping your legs straight, you risk doing as much harm as good. Pulling yourself up and over like this can overutilize the muscles of the lower back and upper thigh, two sets of muscles that can be strengthened more safely with other exercises. A better way to do sit-ups is to lie with your knees bent, to cross your arms on your chest, and to raise your head and shoulders only as far as your stomach muscles alone can lift them.

2. Which of the following best expresses the main idea of the selection?

   A. People who think sit-ups are the best exercise for the abdominal muscles are right.

   B. Exercises that develop one set of muscles may often result in damage to another set.

   C. Sit-ups are safest when they are done so as to exercise only the abdominal muscles.

   D. One should not clasp one's hands behind one's neck when doing sit-ups.

In his long and illustrious career, Winston Churchill was successful not only because he was intelligent and inspiring to others, but also because he was lucky. Once, in school, this future prime minister of Great Britain was preparing to take an important geography test. He knew that the biggest question on the test would require a thorough description of the geography of one major country somewhere in the world. He also knew that his classmates would be spending hours studying every country in their atlases and geography books. He decided, however reckless the decision may have been, on a different study method.

Churchill wrote on small pieces of paper the names of all the major countries in his atlas, put the pieces into his hat, and then drew one out. The country name he drew was New Zealand. He proceeded to spend all of his study time learning everything he could about New Zealand. On the day of the test, Churchill discovered that the country the teacher had chosen was New Zealand.

3. What is the main idea of this selection?

   A. Churchill once took a geography test that changed his approach to learning.

   B. Churchill was basically a mediocre student who often got lucky.

   C. Churchill owed part of his considerable success to luck.

   D. Churchill's best subject in school was geography.

4. Which of the following details best supports the main idea of this selection?

   A. Churchill was intelligent and could inspire others.

   B. Churchill studied only one country for his big geography test.

   C. Churchill's classmates studied atlases and geography books.

   D. Churchill knew the test would include a question about New Zealand.

The country of Nepal has approximately the same geographical area as the state of Tennessee, but it has several times the population. Most people in Nepal live in poverty and depend largely on local resources. In this type of situation, conflicts sometimes arise between the short-term needs of the population and the long-term survival of the environment.

For example, Nepalese law restricts the cutting of wood as one means of preserving the environment. In the Himalayan foothills, however, practically everyone depends on firewood as the primary fuel for cooking and heating. Kerosene is available, but buying kerosene is more expensive than cutting down trees. Besides, residents of small, isolated villages in the hills can get kerosene only by walking for days to a large town. Thus, rural villagers commonly ignore the law in order to get fuel.

However, removing trees from the steep slopes of the Himalayan foothills makes the land susceptible to erosion by the melting snow from the mountains and the heavy rains of late summer. With fewer and fewer trees to hold it in place, more and more soil is washed away each year. This erosion causes dangerous floods and mudslides, and it robs the hills of the land that villagers need in order to grow food.

5. Which of the following statements best expresses the main idea of the third paragraph of this selection?

A. Melting snow is the underlying cause of the floods and mudslides that threaten the Himalayan foothills region.

B. Nepalese villagers have no idea of the harm they cause when they remove the trees from their land.

C. Nepal could largely eliminate its poverty problem through better management of its natural resources.

D. The continued use of trees for fuel has led to serious environmental problems for some Nepalese villagers.

6. Which of the following statements from the selection best supports the writer's assertion that conflicts sometimes arise in Nepal between the short-term needs of the population and the long-term survival of the environment?

A. The country of Nepal has approximately the same geographical area as the state of Tennessee, but it has several times the population.

B. Removing trees from the steep slopes of the Himalayan foothills makes the land susceptible to erosion.

C. Nepalese law restricts the cutting of wood as one means of preserving the environment.

D. Most people in Nepal live in poverty and depend largely on local resources.

Fats are classified according to their molecular structure. A molecule of fatty acid contains a long chain of carbon atoms, each of which is bonded to one or two hydrogen atoms. If every carbon atom in the chain is bonded to two hydrogen atoms, the fat is said to be "saturated." If, on the other hand, one or more carbon atoms is bonded to only one hydrogen atom, the fat is said to be "unsaturated." Unsaturated fats are either monounsaturated (one carbon atom is bonded to a single hydrogen atom) or polyunsaturated (at least two carbon atoms are bonded to one hydrogen atom). Saturated fats are the main fats in meat, butter, eggs, and other animal foods. Monounsaturated and polyunsaturated fats are found mostly in vegetable and fish oils.

In general, nutritionists regard any high-fat diet as unhealthy. High fat intake is commonly associated with higher levels of cholesterol and triglycerides, both of which are strongly correlated with increased risk of heart disease. For years, however, it has appeared that polyunsaturated fats pose less risk than saturated fats. A diet in which most of the fat is polyunsaturated—for example, fish broiled with a little sunflower oil—appears actually to lower the body's cholesterol levels, while a diet of bacon and eggs raises them.

Some recent research now indicates that a diet in which most of the fat is monounsaturated may also be very healthful. A study conducted in 1986 suggested that monounsaturated fats can lower the body's levels of low-density lipoprotein cholesterol—the so-called "bad" cholesterol—without lowering its levels of high-density lipoprotein cholesterol, which is thought to help prevent heart disease.

7. Which of the following is the main idea of the first paragraph of this selection?

    A. There are two major types of fat: monounsaturated and polyunsaturated.

    B. A fat is considered "saturated" if all its carbon atoms are bonded to two hydrogen atoms.

    C. Each type of fat is typically found in only certain types of food.

    D. Each category of fat displays a characteristic type of molecular structure.

8. Which of the following facts from the selection best supports the writer's contention that some kinds of fats are healthier than others?

    A. Researchers conducted a nutrition study in 1986.

    B. Polyunsaturated fats appear to lower cholesterol levels.

    C. The carbon chains of saturated and unsaturated fats differ.

    D. Nutritionists regard any diet that is high in fat as unhealthy.

Practice Exercise Explanations

1. **Correct Response: B.** In this example, all four answer choices are sentences taken verbatim from the selection. The writer's main idea, that famous composers have often made use of traditional folk tunes in composing their works, is stated in choice B, which is the third sentence in the selection. You should be able to figure out that choice B is the main idea because the examples provided throughout the selection support that statement. The alternative answer choices, although linked in some way to the main idea, do not themselves constitute the main idea of the selection. Choice A is an introductory sentence used by the writer to present a popular misconception about the development of great music. The writer then goes on to show by example that the idea presented in this sentence is false. Choices C and D are incorrect because the selection is about a larger subject than one or two particular composers; instead, it is about something that many composers do. Rather than providing a main idea, these two sentences offer examples that support the main idea.

2. **Correct Response: C.** In this selection, the main idea is implied rather than stated. Choice C condenses into a few words a point that is not made explicitly in any one sentence, but that is nevertheless the main idea of the selection. Although choice A, which restates the first sentence of this selection, is basically an accurate statement, it serves only to introduce the more specific point that forms the main idea of the selection. Choice B is also accurate, but it is a statement that is much broader in scope than information included in the selection. Although choice D identifies one detail that helps to explain the main idea, it is not the main idea.

3. **Correct Response: C.** In this selection, the main idea is presented in the opening sentence and is then developed through the use of a single anecdote, or brief story, which focuses on Churchill's extraordinary good luck in studying for a big exam. Of the choices given, only choice C, which is a brief restatement of the first sentence, focuses on the main idea of the piece. Choices A and D erroneously focus on elements of the anecdote rather than on the main idea.

   In addition, both of these choices include a misinterpretation of the information included in the anecdote. Choice B is a general statement about Churchill, but it is not clearly supported by the information in the passage. Given only the information provided by the writer, Churchill may have normally been a diligent student who took a risk in studying for this one test. (In fact, Churchill later described himself as an average student at best, but this information is not included in the passage.)

4. **Correct Response: B.** Of the choices provided, only choice B gives a detail that supports the main idea of the selection (i.e., that Churchill was often lucky in his life). After all, a student who studies only one country, when a test could ask about any one of a number of countries, is very lucky indeed if that one country turns out to be the one included on the test. Choice A repeats a point made in the first sentence of the selection. The fact that Churchill was intelligent and inspiring, however, does not support the idea that Churchill was lucky. Although choice C provides information that has relevance to the anecdote, this fact does not support the main idea. Choice D is false; Churchill did not know which country would be on the test. That is why the story is so interesting. If you thought choice D was the right answer, you probably should have read the passage more closely.

5. **Correct Response: D.** The third paragraph provides an example to illustrate the main idea of the entire selection, which is that poorer countries such as Nepal often face conflicts between short-term population needs and long-term environmental needs. Of the alternative answer choices provided, choice D best summarizes the example given in the third paragraph. Choice A represents a misinterpretation of the paragraph's main idea, since it places ultimate blame for environmental problems on melting snow rather than on tree removal. Choice B goes outside the scope of the selection; the reader is not told whether villagers are aware of the consequences of their actions. Choice C is another misinterpretation of the information presented; neither the third paragraph nor any other part of the selection discusses what it would take to eliminate poverty in Nepal.

6. **Correct Response: B.** Choice B provides a specific example of how the shorter-term fuel needs of the Nepalese population have had a negative long-term effect on the environment of Nepal. Thus, this statement clearly supports the writer's assertion noted in the question. Choice A is a detail that provides the reader with some general information about Nepal, but it does not support the given assertion. Choices C and D also provide specific information about Nepal. Although in both cases the information given relates to some aspect of the writer's assertion, neither choice actually deals with both the short-term and long-term issues that are part of the assertion.

7. **Correct Response: D.** The first paragraph focuses on an explanation of the chemical difference between saturated and unsaturated fats. Choice D, which is a rewording of the first sentence of the first paragraph, best expresses this idea. Choice A reflects a misinterpretation of information given in the first paragraph and in later paragraphs; the two major categories of fat are saturated and unsaturated, not monounsaturated and polyunsaturated. Although choices B and C are true statements, each represents only one of the elements discussed in the first paragraph and not the main idea of the paragraph.

8. **Correct Response: B.** Choice B is correct because it is the only response option that directly relates a particular kind of fat (i.e., polyunsaturated) to a health factor (i.e., reduced cholesterol levels). Although choices A, C, and D are all true statements and are all details that contribute to the meaning of the passage, none of these choices directly supports the specific idea noted in the question. Choice A is incorrect because it mentions nothing about the results of the study (which in fact do support the main idea). Choice C makes a general statement about how the chemical composition of fats differs, but says nothing about the comparative healthfulness of different types of fats. Choice D presents the view that any high-fat diet is bad and thus makes no distinction among kinds of fats in terms of their healthfulness.

Study Ideas

The following study hints will help you understand main ideas and identify supporting details in your reading.

1. Ask questions about what you read: *Whom* or *what* is the paragraph or selection about? What is the writer saying about that subject?

2. When you are about to start reading a book, begin by giving yourself a general sense of what is to come by reading its table of contents and introduction, as well as the beginnings of a couple of chapters. This preview of the book will help you recognize main ideas and read in a more directed and efficient manner.

3. Look first for the main idea in the first sentence of a paragraph or in the first paragraph of a longer selection. It may not be there, of course, but you will find it there more often than not.

4. Look for a restatement of the main idea of a paragraph in the final sentence. Or look for a restatement of the main idea of a longer selection—an essay, textbook chapter, or journal article—in the final paragraph or summary.

5. Remember that writers may imply rather than state the main idea. Use the two questions in Study Idea #1 to find the implied main idea.

6. Test what you believe to be the main idea by asking if all the details, facts, reasons, and examples given by the writer support this key idea in some way.

7. Preview a long reading assignment by reading just the first and last paragraphs and the first sentence of each remaining paragraph. Using this method, you can identify many main points and see how the writer arranges these points to build an argument or to explain a process or body of knowledge.

8. Read your assignments in their entirety, noting how the details support the main points.

Chapter 6

IDENTIFY A WRITER'S PURPOSE, POINT OF VIEW, AND INTENDED MEANING

This skill includes recognizing a writer's expressed or implied purpose for writing; evaluating the appropriateness of written material for various purposes or audiences; recognizing the likely effect on an audience of a writer's choice of words; and using the content, word choice, and phrasing of a passage to determine a writer's opinion or point of view.

Introduction

You pick up a book, article, or short story. You are reading an assignment for class, or reading just for pleasure. Within minutes, you are deeply engrossed, and soon you are convinced of a new point of view or excited by a new idea.

Your reading experience is directly related to the writer's ability to express a purpose, or intent, for writing. You may agree or disagree with the writer's perspective. You may be drawn to sympathize with the writer's point of view. With careful reading, you will notice how the writer of an effective reading passage has used appropriate language, a clear method of development, and a well-chosen tone to add to the effectiveness of his or her message. You will also notice that a successful work addresses a particular audience, be it a specific group or a general one. These factors—language, structure, audience, and tone—are all shaped according to the writer's intent.

Asking the following questions can help you discover a writer's intent:

- Why was this article (short story, analysis, theme) written?

- For whom is the writer writing?

- What does the writer accomplish with this piece of writing?

- How does the writer accomplish that goal?

A writer's intent shapes critical writing choices. First of all, the writer must have a specific audience in mind. Form and content must be relevant and readable for that audience. Furthermore, every writer hopes for a specific outcome: perhaps to interest, to inform, or to persuade the reader. Recognizing the writer's purpose, as well as the methods used to achieve that purpose, helps you to interpret, analyze, and enjoy a piece of writing. When you know the writer's purpose, you will have a solid basis for deciding whether the writing is effective and how the writing has meaning for you, the reader.

Imagine that you are reading an article from a literary magazine. To respond fully to the article, you need to note the five factors that communicate the writer's intent: language, structure, audience, tone, and point of view. By doing this, you are participating actively in completing the piece of writing. Without your participation, the writer's purpose is not fully realized.

Recognizing Writer's Intent

How do you recognize a writer's intent? Use the criteria below as guidelines when you are reading.

Language. First, consider the writer's use of language. Is it formal or informal, humorous or serious, direct or subtle? Do certain words or phrases stand out? What effect do those words or phrases have? Does the writer's choice of words provoke your sympathy, your empathy? Or, conversely, does it provoke your anger, your disbelief?

Structure—Method of Development. Consider the structure of the writing; that is, the way in which the writer organizes the information and ideas presented. Is each paragraph short and to the point? Or is each paragraph long, presenting a thesis statement, a careful analysis, and a final conclusion? Does the writer use a particular sequential order or a particular method for supporting his or her ideas (e.g., cause-effect analysis, comparison-contrast)? Are some elements emphasized and repeated often by the writer, while others are de-emphasized or ignored completely? Does the writer come back to the main idea many times? Or does the writer's conclusion surprise you?

Audience. Consider the writer's use of language and structure together. For example, are technical terms used in a detailed analysis? If the answer is "yes," then the writer is probably writing for a limited technical audience. If the language is descriptive and figurative, and the form is less rigid, then the writer is probably writing for a literary or more general audience.

Tone. Examine the writer's tone, or the way in which information and ideas are expressed. The tone may be formal or informal; it may also be humorous, serious, sarcastic, neutral, nostalgic, polite, and so on. You can determine the writer's tone by examining language, choice of detail, method of organization, sentence structure, even punctuation. Material found in textbooks and manuals, for example, is usually written in a neutral tone, while newspaper editorials, which generally seek to persuade, are often written using a more personal, emotional tone.

Point of View. The writer's point of view, or attitude toward the subject, may be explicit or it may be hidden, depending upon the writer's purpose. For example, a writer may argue a point to present a personal point of view. In this case, the writing will express opinions and present evidence that the writer hopes will be compelling. On the other hand, a writer might want you, the reader, to examine the evidence and draw your own conclusions. Then, the writing will be balanced, and the writer's point of view will be unstated.

Examples of Writer's Intent

As you read each of the following examples, use the criteria above to identify the writer's intent. Examples I and II are about the same general subject, but their purposes and points of view are very different. Each uses different content and a different style to achieve a different outcome. As you read each passage, notice the writer's language, structure, and intended audience. Why did the writer write this article? What audience does the writer hope to reach? What does the writer accomplish and how?

Example I

In 1977, a government construction crew attempted to erect a barbed wire fence near Big Mountain on the Navaho Reservation in Arizona. The fence was being erected as a result of the Navaho-Hopi Land Settlement Act, which was passed by Congress in 1974 and called for the division of the Hopi-Navaho territory. With the support of tribal councils created by the U.S. government, a number of corporations had successfully lobbied Congress to pass the act. The corporations were motivated by the desire to have access to the billions of dollars worth of coal and uranium located on the land owned in common by the Hopi and Navaho tribes.

The government agreed to build a fence along the partition line and to force local Navahos and Hopis to relocate. (The removal of the area's inhabitants had to occur before the energy companies could take the minerals.) As a result, over 10,000 self-sufficient rural sheepherders and farmers, mostly Navaho, are being uprooted and deprived of their only means of livelihood.

The philosophical views of the Navaho people make the government's relocation plan particularly distressing to them. They recognize the earth as a living being and the source of all that is needed for life. Without regard for their beliefs and traditions, the coal and uranium companies are damaging the sacred land, air, and water of these Native Americans.

Relocation has caused particular concern among Navaho women. The Navahos are a matrilineal people; that is, their homes, their livestock, and their land pass from generation to generation through the women of the tribe. Thus, Navaho women in some sense have the most to lose and are leading the resistance against forced removal from their land.

In Example I, you can determine the writer's intent by analyzing a number of elements in the selection. First, the writer describes the situation on the Navaho Reservation in Arizona and the developments leading up to that situation. The writer's point of view begins to become clear when, in the first paragraph, the corporations' desire for money is emphasized as the major motivating force behind the relocation plan. Then the writer goes on to try to persuade the reader that the relocation of the native populations is destroying their economic base and their traditional way of life. The writer supports this argument with facts that include some explanation of the philosophical beliefs of the Navahos and the role of women in Navaho society. The language and tone also contribute to the writer's ability to get the point across to the reader. The writer uses words such as *deprived* and *uprooted* to establish a tone that is sympathetic to the native population. The inclusion of the term *matrilineal* lends credibility to the writer's position because through the use of such terminology the writer appears knowledgeable about the Navaho culture. In this passage, the writer's intent is clearly not only to tell you about the plans for coal and uranium mining, but also to persuade you that these plans are unfair and will result in substantial damage to Navaho and Hopi life.

Example II

In 1977, a government construction crew attempted to erect a barbed wire fence near Big Mountain on the Navaho Reservation in Arizona. The fence was being erected as a result of the Navaho-Hopi Land Settlement Act of 1974, a law that allows corporations to take advantage of the coal and uranium resources on the Navaho and Hopi land.

When the construction crew approached the designated area to begin work, they were met by a group of rebellious Navaho women. The women made an illegal attempt to block the crew's access to the land, and so they were immediately arrested. Such resistance to land development is one example of a growing, nationwide movement designed to hinder our economic development and to keep our society immobilized. Coal and uranium mining are essential for technological progress, which, in turn, is necessary for a healthy, forward-looking society.

Our nation prides itself on being in the forefront of the modernization process. Let us not let a few misguided individuals slow our progress. We are now the technological leader of the world. Continued technological advancement is the key to our ability to maintain our powerful position.

Although both Example I and Example II are written to persuade their audience, the writers of these two passages use very different methods and hope for very different results. In contrast to Example I, Example II is designed to convince readers that they should side with the corporations and against the Navaho resistance effort. The writer of Example II uses a variety of techniques in an effort to accomplish this goal. First, unlike the writer of the previous passage, the writer of this passage provides no background information about the life and culture of the native populations. Thus, the reader of this passage is not drawn to sympathize with those who are being relocated. Second, the writer of Example II implies that the goals of the corporations are positive ones (e.g., economic development, technological progress, modernization), rather than selfish ones, as was implied in Example I. Similarly, the writer of the second passage tries to appeal to the patriotic sentiments of readers by implying that failure to mine the coal and uranium in question would damage the "powerful position" of the United States and hinder its ability to modernize and advance. In the second paragraph, it is even implied that the Navaho women who attempted to block the construction crew's access to their land were part of a larger movement whose aim is to ruin the U.S. economy. A careful reading of the selection shows, however, that no evidence is provided to support such claims. The writer also uses strong and opinionated language (i.e., "*rebellious* Navaho women," "keep our society *immobilized*," "a few *misguided* individuals") to arouse the emotions of readers and to convince them of a particular point of view. Overall, the writer offers many generalities and opinions, but very few facts that are truly relevant to the particular situation in question.

Example III

This season's drought reminds us of our relationship with our most needed and nurturing friend: mother nature. In our town, there is a lot of talk about the drought. Most people attribute the intense dry heat to a cycle of nature that is beyond our control. It is true that we cannot control the natural cycles that bring about feast or famine. But we can care for the delicate balances in nature that have kept our planet functioning for centuries.

For example, the earth is made to absorb and hold water. Therefore, even during long dry spells, vegetation should continue to grow. However, our repeated and prolonged use of heavy farm machinery has compacted the soil, thereby greatly diminishing the ability of the earth to retain water. The misuse of chemicals is another factor contributing to the reduced ability of the earth to absorb and hold water. Although some chemicals are helpful, others serve in the long run to deplete valuable nutrients and permanently destroy nature's chemical balance.

These are just two of the issues that have led the Town Council and the Farm Board to decide that the time has come to take action to preserve our rich natural environment. A first step in this direction is their decision to promote organic farming in our area. We support the efforts of these two groups. Through their work, we all can learn to produce a bountiful food supply, while at the same time preserve the balance of nature.

Example III illustrates another type of persuasive writing, the editorial. In this example, the writer appeals to a general audience by using simple, direct language. The goal is to encourage the reader to think about nature and the need to maintain natural balances. Without giving too much technical information, the writer tries to persuade the reader that steps taken to preserve the environment, such as the decision of the Town Council and the Farm Board to promote organic farming, are in the best interest of the town and the individual, as well as nature itself.

Example IV

Disabled individuals have long been denied many educational and professional opportunities in our society, but in 1973 the U.S. Congress took action to remedy this form of discrimination. In Section 504 of the Rehabilitation Act, Congress provided that handicapped citizens may not be excluded from any program receiving assistance from the federal government. The enactment of this law has meant many important changes at all levels of our education system.

What must we at the university do to comply with both the letter and the spirit of Section 504? A threefold approach is indicated. First, we must see that academic programs are accessible to individuals with different types of handicapping conditions. This requires, for example, the removal of architectural barriers, the hiring of sign-language interpreters, and the provision of those educational materials required by learners with special needs. Second, we must see that all nonacademic services, such as housing, transportation, financial aid, and health services, are fully available to persons who are disabled. Third, we must make it possible for handicapped individuals to participate in all aspects of student life outside the classroom, including campus cultural activities, athletics, and social organizations.

In Example IV, the writer's purpose becomes explicit in the second paragraph with the question: "What must we at the university do to comply with both the letter and the spirit of Section 504?" The entire selection is built around this question. It is clear that the writer's audience is the general university community and that the writer's purpose is to encourage members of the university community to address the problem of discrimination against individuals with handicapping conditions. The writer achieves this purpose through the use of formal language, a serious, neutral tone, and a balanced, rational approach. The writing is carefully structured, and the writer's points are presented as a logical sequence of ideas that most readers would be expected to understand and accept.

Practice Exercises

The following exercises will help you review the skills covered in this chapter. Many of the types of questions presented here will be similar to those on the test; others will not. Remember that the purpose of the exercises is to give you practice on the skills rather than merely to prepare you for the test. Following these exercises are the Practice Exercise Explanations. They explain each question, the correct answer, and why the remaining choices are incorrect.

Something woke Anne. With a shiver, she got up and padded down the hall to the bathroom. The wind rushed through every crack in the old house. Gusts shook the shutters and rattled the back door.

Looking out the window, Anne was suddenly transfixed by a strange sight: a hazy black shadow darting across the yard. She stood mesmerized, unable to move, following the eerie shape with her eyes. Then, behind the shadow, an intense white light, far too bright to be moonlight, began to shine.

Moments later, Anne found herself gliding through the icy air. Two hooded creatures seemed to be guiding her toward the light. The creatures flew without wings and appeared to communicate without sound. Just as Anne noticed that the light was emanating from a large, elliptical object hovering above the ground, she began to feel as if she were being pulled in two. She was terrified, yet somehow she knew she was in no danger.

1. In the first paragraph of this selection, the writer notes, "The wind rushed through every crack in the old house" and "Gusts shook the shutters and rattled the back door." The writer includes these details mainly to:

    A. let the reader know that the house in which the story takes place is haunted.

    B. help the reader visualize and sympathize with the character's situation.

    C. inform the reader that the weather will play an important role in the story.

    D. focus the reader's attention away from the main character and toward the house itself.

2. The writer of this selection includes the following phrases: "Anne was suddenly transfixed," "She stood mesmerized," "Anne found herself gliding," and "she began to feel as if she were being pulled in two." The combined effect of these phrases is to indicate to the reader that Anne:

    A. is still asleep as the action is occurring.

    B. has supernatural powers and abilities.

    C. has little control over her situation.

    D. is a person who enjoys adventure.

Educators today are more and more often heard to say that computer literacy is absolutely necessary for college students. Many even argue that each incoming freshman should have permanent access to his or her own microcomputer. What advantages do computers offer the college student?

Any student who has used a word processor will know one compelling reason to use a computer: to write papers. Although not all students feel comfortable composing on a word processor, most find revising and editing much easier on the computer. One can alter, insert, or delete just by pressing a few keys, thus eliminating the need to rewrite or retype. Furthermore, since the revision process is less burdensome, students are more likely to revise as often as is necessary to end up with the best paper possible. For these reasons, many freshman English courses require the use of a word processor.

Computers are also useful in the context of language courses, where they are used to drill students in basic skills. Software programs reinforce ESL (English as a Second Language) instruction, as well as instruction in French, German, Spanish, and other languages. By using these programs on a regular basis, students can improve their proficiency in a language while proceeding at their own pace.

Science students take advantage of computers in many ways. Using computer graphic capabilities, for example, botany students can represent and analyze different plant growth patterns. Medical students can learn to interpret computerized images of internal body structures. Physics students can complete complex calculations far more quickly than they could without the use of a computer.

Similarly, business and accounting students find that computer spreadsheet programs are all but indispensable to many aspects of their work, while students pursuing careers in graphic arts, marketing, and public relations find that knowledge of computer graphics is important. Education majors learn to develop grading systems using computers, while social science students use computers for analyzing and graphically displaying their research results.

It is no wonder, then, that educators support the purchase and use of microcomputers by students. A versatile tool, the computer can help students learn. And that is, after all, the reason for going to college.

3. In this selection, the writer's main purpose is to:

    A. analyze the advantages and disadvantages of computer use among college students.

    B. persuade educators to increase computer use in their own classrooms.

    C. describe how computers can be used to facilitate foreign language instruction.

    D. identify some of the ways that computers benefit college students.

4. In this selection, the writer refers to a number of specific academic fields, including foreign languages, graphic arts, marketing, education, and botany. The writer refers to these fields mainly to show that computers:

    A. have wide applicability in a college context.

    B. are very useful in some areas, but not at all useful in others.

    C. are so easy to master that all students can learn to use them.

    D. are more useful in a college environment than elsewhere.

5. In this selection, the writer's argument is developed primarily through the use of:

    A. cause-effect analysis.

    B. examples.

    C. anecdotes.

    D. comparison and contrast.

Studies of the accuracy of eyewitness testimony constitute an area of psychological research that is of great importance to the criminal justice system. Studies in this area indicate that evidence given by witnesses is often unreliable. This finding is significant because, next to physical or scientific evidence, eyewitness testimony is most likely to affect a jury's decision.

Researchers have discovered, for example, that the way in which witnesses are questioned affects the answers they give. In an experiment conducted by Elizabeth Loftus of the University of Washington, test subjects who viewed a film of an automobile accident were later asked one of two questions: "How fast were the cars going when they smashed into each other?" or "How fast were the cars going when they contacted each other?" Those who were asked the first question, which used the word smashed, gave much higher estimates of the speed of the cars than those who were asked the second question, which used the word contacted.

Other studies show that people add or subtract details from their recollections of events to make those recollections fit with what they think they have seen. In another experiment conducted by Loftus, two students left a bag in one section of a train station and then went off to check train schedules. Another student came along,

reached into the bag, pretended to place something under his coat, and then hurried off. When the first two students returned, one of them looked in the bag and cried out that her tape recorder had been stolen. Questioned later about the incident, about half of those who observed the incident were able to describe the tape recorder that was supposedly stolen, even though they could not possibly have seen one!

Psychological research further indicates that the recollections of witnesses often change over time to conform to contradictory recollections of other witnesses. That is, witnesses tend to alter their description of a situation until their recollections agree with what they have heard from others. These witnesses are not consciously lying, nor are they aware that their memory of events has changed. Rather, they continue to state confidently that they are reporting only what they have seen and heard.

Because the outcome of many trials hinges on the accounts of eyewitnesses, psychological research on eyewitness testimony has raised important issues for our legal system. This research demonstrates the importance of learning more about the way people view events and the way they recollect what they have seen. Only through such research can the court system ever hope to be able to evaluate eyewitness testimony adequately.

6. Which of the following statements from the selection best supports the writer's assertion that eyewitness evidence is often unreliable?

    A. Next to physical or scientific evidence, eyewitness testimony is most likely to affect a jury's decision.

    B. Those who were asked the first question, which used the word smashed, gave much higher estimates of the speed of the cars.

    C. When the first two students returned, one of them looked in the bag and cried out that her tape recorder had been stolen.

    D. Psychological research on eyewitness testimony has raised important issues for our legal system.

7. Which of the following best describes the writer's primary purpose for writing this selection?

    A. to argue for the importance of psychological studies designed to assess the accuracy of eyewitness testimony

    B. to criticize the criminal justice system for depending too heavily on eyewitness testimony

    C. to review all major psychological studies conducted to date on the issue of eyewitness reliability

    D. to recommend ways that the courts can overcome problems regarding poor eyewitness reliability

8. Given the information included in this selection, the writer would most likely agree that problems related to the accuracy of eyewitness testimony are primarily the result of:

    A. insensitivity on the part of judges and juries.

    B. the manipulation of eyewitnesses by those in authority.

    C. overall bias throughout the U.S. court system.

    D. unconscious processes within the minds of eyewitnesses.

Practice Exercise Explanations

1. **Correct Response: B.** After reading the selection in its entirety, it becomes clear that Anne, the main character, is the focus of the selection and that virtually all the details included in the selection are intended to help the reader picture Anne's situation. The writer thus provides information about the wind rushing through the cracks in the house and shaking the shutters and back door primarily in order to help the reader visualize and sympathize with the main character and her situation (choice B). Choice A is incorrect because there is no evidence that the house is haunted; to the contrary, information given later in the selection seems to imply that extraterrestrial visitors are probably responsible for the events described. Similarly, since neither the weather nor the house figures prominently in the narrative after the first paragraph, there is no reason to believe that the weather will play an important role in the story (choice C) or that the writer wishes to focus the reader's attention away from Anne and toward the house (choice D).

2. **Correct Response: C.** From the first words of the story, it is apparent that the main character is responding to a situation that is largely outside her control (i.e., "Something woke Anne"). This idea is continually reinforced by the writer through words and phrases indicating that outside forces are controlling Anne's thoughts (e.g., she was "transfixed" and "mesmerized") and actions (e.g., she "found herself gliding," she felt "as if she were being pulled in two"). Concerning the other answer choices, the reader knows from the first sentence in the selection that Anne cannot still be asleep (choice A), while there is no evidence to indicate either that she has supernatural powers (choice B) or that she particularly enjoys adventure in this or any other situation (choice D).

3. **Correct Response: D.** The purpose of the selection becomes clear when, in the first paragraph, the writer asks the question, "What advantages do computers offer the college student?" The rest of the selection goes on to answer this question, the idea of which is restated in choice D, the correct response. Choice A is incorrect because the writer does not address possible disadvantages of computer use. Concerning choice B, there is no evidence either that educators are the intended audience for this selection or that the writer's goal is to persuade the members of such an audience to modify their classroom instructional techniques. If this had been the writer's purpose, the selection would probably have been developed quite differently (e.g., with more detailed examples, with more explanation framed in the terms and concepts commonly employed by professional educators). Choice C is incorrect because, although the writer does note how computers can be used to facilitate foreign language instruction, this is used merely as one example to illustrate the writer's larger point and is not itself the main purpose of the selection.

4. **Correct Response: A.** In this selection, the writer refers to a number of specific academic fields in order to give the reader a sense of the wide variety of fields within which college students may benefit from the use of computers. Choice B is incorrect because the specific fields mentioned in the piece are not intended to provide an exhaustive list of those in which computers may be of help to students; rather, they are merely intended to serve as examples of the many fields in which this is the case. Choice C is incorrect because the writer's focus is on the idea that computers have many uses in a college context; there is no discussion at all, however, regarding the ease or difficulty with which students can learn to use computers. Similarly, the selection makes no mention of computer use outside the college environment, so choice D is also incorrect.

5. **Correct Response: B.** Except for the introductory and concluding paragraphs, the writer's focus is almost entirely on providing examples to support the view that computer literacy and access to computers are essential for contemporary college students. Therefore, choice B is the correct response. Although the second paragraph employs a small amount of *cause-effect analysis* (choice A) and *comparison and contrast* (choice D), these development techniques are not relied upon by the writer to nearly the same extent as is the use of *examples*. *Anecdotes* (choice C), which are brief stories intended to illustrate a point, are not used at all in the selection.

6. **Correct Response: B.** In the first paragraph, the writer notes that the evidence given by eyewitnesses is often unreliable. Throughout most of the rest of the selection, the writer discusses specific types of psychological research that have led to this conclusion. The statement given in choice B summarizes, at least in part, one of the key research studies cited to show that eyewitness testimony may be inadvertently influenced by many factors (in this case, the wording used by questioners). Therefore, choice B can be said to support the writer's main assertion. The statements given in the other answer choices do not directly support the writer's assertion that eyewitness evidence is unreliable. The statement in choice A is intended instead merely to indicate that eyewitness testimony is an important factor in court cases. It says nothing about the reliability or lack of reliability of such testimony. The statement in choice C is intended to explain how one of the studies discussed was set up, but does not in itself support the writer's assertion about eyewitness reliability. Meanwhile, the statement in choice D notes only that the issue of eyewitness testimony is an important one.

7. **Correct Response: A.** The purpose of this selection is indicated in the first and last sentences of the piece. Choice A essentially restates the point presented in these sentences: that continued psychological research is needed to clarify and evaluate issues related to the accuracy of eyewitness testimony. The writer's purpose is not to criticize the criminal justice system for depending on eyewitness testimony (choice B); rather, the writer is warning that the criminal justice system should be more aware of some of the pitfalls related to the use of such testimony. The writer's purpose is also not to review all major studies conducted to date on the issue of eyewitness reliability (choice C). Only two specific studies are described, and their function is to provide examples to illustrate a larger point. If the writer's main purpose had indeed been to provide a review of the major studies that have been conducted, many more studies and researchers would have been included. Finally, the writer includes no mention of specific steps courts can take to overcome problems regarding poor eyewitness reliability (choice D), and so this also cannot be considered the main purpose of the selection.

8. **Correct Response: D.** In reading this selection, it should become clear that the problems discussed by the writer occur as a result of unconscious processes that take place in the minds of eyewitnesses (choice D). This point is implied, for example, in the last paragraph when the writer notes, "the importance of learning more about the way people view events and the way they recollect what they have seen." Here, both of the areas cited by the writer as important areas for future study focus primarily on unconscious rather than conscious psychological processes. The same point is made in a more explicit way when, in the fourth paragraph, the writer notes that the "witnesses are not consciously lying, nor are they aware that their memory of events has changed." On the other hand, the selection includes no information to support the idea that problems of eyewitness reliability result from the insensitivity of judges and juries (choice A), manipulation by those in authority (choice B), or bias throughout the court system (choice C).

Study Ideas

The best way to learn to recognize and analyze a writer's intent is to ask yourself the following questions each time you read:

1. Who is the writer's intended audience? Is it an instructor? a college class? the academic community? a technical audience? the business community? the general public?

2. What is the intended goal of the writer? Is it to express his or her own thoughts and feelings? to create a work of art? to entertain an audience? to inform readers? to persuade them?

3. How does the writer achieve this goal?

    A. What kind of *language* does the writer use? Is it formal or is it informal? Is it descriptive or is it technical?

    B. What kind of *structure* does the writer use? Is information presented in a particular sequential order? as a cause-effect analysis? as a comparison-contrast? as an argument? Are the paragraphs long or are they short? Is the thesis presented first? Is it presented last? Or is it only implied and never stated explicitly?

    C. What is the writer's *tone?* Is it serious? humorous? sarcastic? ironic? formal? angry? nostalgic?

4. What is the writer's point of view? Is the writer neutral? Or does the writer show either a positive or a negative attitude toward the subject of the work?

Chapter 7

ANALYZE THE RELATIONSHIP AMONG IDEAS IN WRITTEN MATERIAL

This skill includes identifying a sequence of events or steps, identifying cause-effect relationships, analyzing relationships between ideas in opposition, identifying solutions to problems, and drawing conclusions inductively and deductively from information stated or implied in a passage.

Introduction

The materials you read in college typically include a large number of facts and ideas. To get the desired point across, writers must be sure not only to include all these facts and ideas in their works, but also to organize them in ways that make their relationships to one another clear. You, as a reader, must meanwhile be able to recognize both stated and implied relationships among the elements included in the materials you read. This is important to ensure your full understanding of those materials.

Most college materials are organized in one or more of the following ways: in sequential order (temporal or spatial), by cause and effect, or in terms of ideas in opposition (e.g., comparison-contrast, argumentative). In addition, some materials focus on the presentation of a problem and one or more of its possible solutions. As you read, being aware of how a writer has structured and organized the facts and ideas he or she is presenting can help you identify and retain important information more efficiently.

In addition to identifying the organizational relationships among the elements included in written materials, it is also important to be able to use the facts and ideas presented by a writer to draw your own conclusions. Drawing conclusions may, for example, involve recognizing relationships that are never stated, but only implied, in a writer's work. It may also require using information that is explicitly stated by the writer in order to form a generalization or to make a judgment that is not itself directly addressed in a work. In any case, the ability to draw conclusions requires that you be able not only to comprehend the facts and ideas presented by the writer, but also to think logically about possible further implications of those facts and ideas.

In the chapter that follows, you will learn more about how to identify relationships among the ideas included in written material and how to draw conclusions from the materials you read.

Organizational Patterns and Relationships in Written Materials

As noted above, most of the materials you read in college are organized using one or more of the following patterns: sequential order, cause and effect, ideas in opposition, or problem and solution(s). Each of these organizational patterns will be discussed and illustrated in the following sections.

Sequential Order. In a written work, sequential organization may reflect either a *chronological* (or *temporal*) sequence (i.e., ordering by time of occurrence) or a *spatial* sequence (i.e., ordering by location). Sequential ordering of one type or the other may be found in most kinds of writing, including *narrative, process*, and *descriptive* writing.

Narrative writing tells a story and includes both fictional and nonfictional accounts. Since the main purpose in narrative writing is to relate a story that involves a particular sequence of events, narrative writers generally organize their works according to a *chronological* sequence. The following is a brief example of narrative writing that is structured according to a chronological sequence of events.

> Sonya looked at her watch: 7:30 p.m. What was wrong? Why hadn't Doug come or called? He was always on time.
>
> Then the phone rang. "Sonya, I can't come. . . . Ahhh, I'll talk to you tomorrow."
>
> Sonya could tell by the sound of Doug's voice that something was terribly wrong. She grabbed her car keys and headed out the door.

This passage exhibits a clear sequence of events: Sonya looks at her watch, she hears the phone ring, she listens to Doug on the phone, she grabs her car keys, and she heads out the door. Most narrative works use this type of straightforward sequencing of events. Writers may also vary their chronological sequencing as, for example, with the use of *flashbacks*, which interrupt a straightforward chronological sequence to return to earlier events.

Process writing, like narrative writing, is organized using a chronological, or temporal, sequence. Instead of telling a story, however, process writing describes a series of steps or events that lead to the same outcome whenever they are duplicated. Process writing might describe, for example, how to conduct an experiment, how to assemble or operate a piece of machinery, or how an economic principle works in practice. In much process writing, it is particularly important that all information be stated in a clear and orderly fashion so the reader will be able to duplicate the process. When you read process writing, you should be able to answer the questions: "How does it happen?" and "In what order does it happen?" Consider the following passage, written in the style of a graphic arts manual.

The silk-screening process is not a difficult one. First, gather your materials: a silk screen, blockout, film, ink, a sponge, a squeegee, and paper towels.

Next, wash your screen to remove all dirt and oils. *Now,* adhere your handcut or photographed stencil. Do so by putting the film onto the screen, emulsion side down. Gently rub a wet sponge over the emulsion, blot with paper towels, *then* let the film dry.

Once the film is dry, use blockout to cover the areas of exposed screen and let dry.

Now, you are ready to start printing. Put the material to be printed—such as a T-shirt—in place and smooth out any wrinkles. Remove the backing sheet from the film so that the ink can pass through the film.

Put a generous amount of ink on one end of the screen, press the screen down hard on your material, *then* squeegee the ink over the film.

Finally, lift the screen gently. You should have a silk-screened T-shirt in the color and design of your choice.

This passage is written in a straightforward manner, using clear wording and concise sentences. It includes details that will be important to a reader trying to follow the directions. It also presents the required steps in the correct order and uses transitional words (e.g., *next, now, then, finally*) to help guide the reader from one step to the next. As a reader, you depend on a writer's clarity of style and organization, as well as the inclusion of important details and transitional words, as keys to understanding process writing.

Descriptive writing describes a place, a person, or an object. This type of writing often uses a sequential organization that is based on *spatial* relationships. That is, the writer describes first one part, then another, progressing in an orderly fashion until the description is complete. Following is an example of a descriptive paragraph that is developed using a spatial sequence.

The student lounge had a pleasant and relaxing atmosphere. A patterned blue and green carpet covered the central part of the well-maintained oak floor. A number of chairs and love seats, all upholstered in pale green and sky blue, were positioned in clusters throughout the room. Each cluster had as its focal point an oak coffee table. On the walls, which were painted a warm beige, there hung a variety of inexpensive, but tasteful, posters and prints. From the ceiling hung a large, antique chandelier that lent the entire lounge an air of elegance.

In this paragraph, the writer describes a room, using a spatial sequence that begins with the floor, goes on to the furniture and walls, and ends with the ceiling. As in all writing of this type, there is no reason why the description had to proceed in this particular way; the writer might just as easily and effectively have begun with a description of the ceiling and ended with a description of the floor. The most important issue for the reader of a descriptive passage that uses spatial sequencing is to be able to visualize mentally the writer's description.

Cause-and-Effect Organization. Writers often want to explain why something has happened or what results one should expect from a particular event or situation. Writing of this type includes three major organizational patterns: one that focuses on *cause(s)*, one that focuses on *effect(s)*, and one that focuses on a *causal chain* (i.e., a sequence of events in which each event in the sequence causes the next event to occur). Many texts that involve cause-effect relationships actually include all three patterns. The following selection is developed specifically with a focus on *causes* and allows you to answer the question: "Why does it happen?"

> There are many *causes* for the failure of marriages in our society. In some cases, people marry when they are too young and do not know what they really want and expect from a spouse or even from themselves. Other times, people who have much in common may marry, and then find some years later that they have developed new interests and priorities and have grown apart. Often, too, the stresses of daily life simply get in the way of effective communication between spouses, leading eventually to misunderstanding, resentment, and a decision to terminate the marriage.

In this paragraph, the writer addresses the question: "Why do marriages fail?" One clue to the kind of organization used here is the use of the signal word *causes* in the first sentence. Other transitional or signal words that alert you to causal analysis include, for example, the terms *because, since, reasons,* and *due to.*

A writer might also choose to concentrate on the *effects* of a particular event or situation. When a selection is developed with a focus on effects, you should be able to identify one or more results or outcomes, as in the paragraphs that follow.

> American farmers are suffering. This summer's scarce rain and high temperatures have *led to* a dramatic reduction in crop production. *As a result,* farmers' incomes will drop, and once again many of those with smaller farms will have to consider selling out.

> The severe drought is also having psychological *effects*. Many farmers and farm family members are anxious and depressed. *Consequently,* the demand for counseling and support groups now far exceeds the supply in many rural areas.

In this passage, the writer focuses on the *effects* of a drought. Included among those effects are reduced crop production, lower income for farmers, and depression and anxiety among farm families. Again, transitional and signal words, including *led to, as a result, consequently,* and *effects,* can help you recognize that this passage is developed with a focus on effects.

The next paragraph, which continues describing aspects of the drought mentioned in the previous passage, provides an illustration of a *causal chain* organizational pattern.

CHAPTER 7: RELATIONSHIP AMONG IDEAS

The continued dry heat will affect farm animals, too. A reduced crop yield means less feed, which in turn means that the price of feed will rise. With less feed available and feed prices rising, more and more farmers will begin selling their animals, often at prices far below those they might have received under better conditions.

In this paragraph, the writer explains how one event causes a second event, which in turn causes a third event, and so on. This type of causal analysis is called a *causal chain.* You may also find it referred to as the *domino effect.* When reading about a causal chain, you must first make sure you are able to identify in sequence each of the events presented by the writer. Then, you must also make sure you understand how each event, or link, in the chain follows logically from the preceding event.

Ideas in Opposition. Works that focus on *ideas in opposition* typically have one of two goals: to present opposing views on a topic or to compare and contrast two (or more) people, places, objects, or ideas. Works that emphasize the first of these goals are referred to as *argumentative,* while those that emphasize the second are referred to as *comparison-contrast* works.

Argumentative writing may present opposing views in a strictly objective or neutral manner, so that the writer seems to favor neither one side nor the other. In such cases, the writer will usually give approximately the same amount of space to the pros and the cons of both sides. On the other hand, a writer may argue strongly in favor of one side by providing as much support as possible for that side, while refuting or contradicting the views of the opposing side. In the passage that follows, the writer gives more or less the same amount of space to both sides of the issue, although by the end of the passage it seems fairly clear that the writer probably agrees more with one side than with the other.

In some states, smoking in public buildings is now restricted to designated areas. Some smokers are so upset they have sworn to overturn the new law. They argue that it is their right to be able to smoke wherever they want. Nonsmokers, however, argue that they have a more basic right: the right to breathe clean air.

Smokers further argue that smoke in the air will not harm nonsmokers to any appreciable degree. Yet, recent studies strongly refute this claim. People closely associated with smokers have a higher incidence of respiratory problems than those who have a smoke-free home and workplace.

Smokers also assert that it is inconvenient and inefficient for them to leave their work areas to go to designated smoking areas. Nevertheless, given current sentiment against smoking, they should feel fortunate to be able to smoke indoors at all. If antismoking activists have their way, new and stricter laws will soon be enacted to further limit smoking and clean up the environment.

In this example of *argumentative* writing, the pros and the cons of each side follow each other closely. Signal words such as *yet, however, further, nevertheless,* and *also* help you identify the shift from one side to the other, as well as the overall argumentative pattern. Whenever you see this type of writing, you will need to determine the issue, the major arguments pro and con, and the writer's position. Then you might also think about which side you believe is right.

Another type of writing that focuses on ideas in opposition is called *comparison-contrast* writing. The term *comparison* implies a focus on the similarities between two people, places, objects, or ideas; the term *contrast,* on the other hand, implies a focus on their differences. Writers often address similarities and differences together in the same selection.

Comparison-contrast writing has four main functions. First, it can be used to explain something that is unfamiliar by comparing and contrasting it to something that is more familiar to the audience. For example, a writer may help readers visualize the work of an unknown painter by comparing and contrasting it to the work of a painter with whom readers are likely to be very familiar. Second, a comparison-contrast approach is often used by writers who wish to evaluate the relative worth or appeal of two objects, ideas, etc. A writer for a consumer magazine might, for example, compare and contrast the specific characteristics and overall quality of two brands of stereo systems in order to help readers determine which is the better buy. A third function of comparison-contrast writing is to emphasize the differences between objects that are generally considered similar (e.g., South American vs. African monkeys). Finally, this type of writing can also be used to emphasize the similarities between objects that are generally considered different (e.g., Earth and Mars). Following are two examples of comparison-contrast writing.

> If you know all about baseball, then you will understand some aspects of the game of cricket. Cricket, *like* baseball, uses a bat and a hard leather ball. Also, the wicket keeper in cricket crouches behind the wicket, just as the catcher in baseball crouches behind home plate. Both players wear leg pads and padded gauntlets or gloves.
>
> *Both* games are played on a large field with one team on the field and the other at bat. *However,* the cricket field centers around two wickets, each defended by a batsman, *whereas* the baseball diamond has four bases. In cricket, there are 11 players on a team, *compared with* baseball's 9.
>
> The object in baseball is to score runs by hitting the ball and running the bases. *Likewise,* the object in cricket is to score runs by running between the two wickets and, at the same time, not allowing the other team to knock down the wicket with the ball.
>
> Play is started by the bowler, *like* the pitcher in baseball. In cricket, there are usually two innings per side with ten outs each, *while* in baseball there are usually nine innings with three outs per team.

In this passage, the writer helps an American audience understand and visualize the British game of cricket by comparing and contrasting cricket to the more familiar game of baseball. Note the italicized signal words that help you identify this as a comparison-contrast work. Note also how the writer's use of the comparison-contrast method allows you to grasp at least the essentials of cricket without having to read extensively on the topic.

> They rented the same farmhouse for the summer, but seemed worlds apart in their interests. Carla was an artist and Kim was a long distance runner. Carla was short and dark; Kim was lanky and fair. Carla's main exercise was a short walk into the fields or to a stream to set up her easel. Kim jogged ten miles across the fields and alongside the stream each day.
>
> However, Carla and Kim were *similar* in other respects. *Both* rose early every morning and spent long, solitary hours concentrating on their respective vocations. Later, at dinner, they talked of wildflowers, lizards, snakes, birds, sunsets, and of their plans for the future.
>
> These two *commonalities*—strong motivation and an appreciation of nature—were enough to bond these two otherwise very different housemates.

In this passage, the writer emphasizes meaningful similarities between two people, an artist and a long distance runner, who appear to be very different. Note that although the writer begins by identifying some of the key differences between the two, the focus of the piece soon turns to an analysis of their common features. The italicized words in the passage are terms often used to signal a work in which the similarities between two or more objects (or, in this case, people) are emphasized.

Problem and Solution(s). Writers often wish to focus their attention on a particular problem and one or more of its possible solutions. Both technical and nontechnical materials may use this *problem and solution* method of organization. In a nontechnical context, for example, a newspaper columnist might note that stress is becoming an increasing problem in our society and then go on to discuss various strategies that readers may find effective in combating this problem. In reading such materials, you should begin by asking yourself, "What is the problem?" Then, to identify the solution(s), ask yourself, "What can be done about the problem?" If a writer mentions several solutions, you should also try to determine whether the writer favors one or more particular solutions and, if so, why. The following passage illustrates the *problem and solution* method of organization as used in a technical context.

> When using your 35-mm camera to take a picture in intense sunlight, you must remember to follow one extra procedure. If you fail to do so, your light meter may be overinfluenced by the background sunlight; consequently, the subject in your foreground will come out too dark.
>
> To correct this problem, simply press the backlight control button and hold it down until after you press the shutter button. You will find the backlight control button on the front of your camera, just to the left of the aperture ring and just above the exposure preview switch. Assuming that your other settings are correct, use of the backlight control button should assure you a successful shot.

Now that you have read this passage, ask yourself, "What is the problem?" The answer is: trying to take a good picture in bright sunlight. Now ask yourself, "What can be done to solve the problem of excessive sunlight?" According to the passage, using the backlight control button will solve the problem.

Drawing Conclusions from Written Materials

As a student, you may often be asked to draw conclusions based on your reading. This task requires that you do more than simply comprehend the words that are written on the page. You must also use reasoning skills to infer meaning. The two types of reasoning skills you use are referred to as *inductive* and *deductive* reasoning.

When you reason *inductively,* you move from particular facts, examples, and observations to a general conclusion. Read and think about the following pieces of information. Then use those pieces of information to draw a conclusion that fits with what you have learned.

— John is speaking in angry, emotional tones.

— He has a bruised left arm and a fresh bandage on the left side of his face.

— The door on the driver's side of the car is so severely dented that it will not open.

What conclusion can you draw from this information? You probably concluded that John was in an accident very recently while he was driving his car. You were able to infer this because John was angry and upset, and his injuries were on his left side, as was the damage to his car.

When trying to arrive at a valid conclusion, be sure to examine all the evidence carefully. The more evidence you have, the more likely you are to arrive at a correct conclusion.

When you are asked to choose which one of several possible conclusions is most valid given particular evidence, you should weigh each alternative conclusion carefully against the facts and observations that are available to you. In the previous example, for instance, you might have concluded that John was injured in a bicycle accident and that his car had been dented on a previous occasion. Similarly, you could perhaps have concluded that John was injured in a fist fight with the driver who damaged his car. If you weigh these two conclusions against the previous one, however, and go back to examine the information that was initially given, you should find that the original conclusion is the best one. Of the three possible conclusions, the one given first fits the facts best and requires the fewest leaps of imagination.

When you choose the most probable or best conclusion, you make what is sometimes called an *inductive leap.* That is, you are "leaping" from the evidence to a conclusion. You do so by reviewing and thinking about the evidence. Often, considering the evidence in relation to your own life experience can help you gain further insight.

Be sure to watch out for the two common pitfalls of inductive reasoning. First, if you make an inductive leap too soon (i.e., without considering all the evidence), you will have "jumped to a conclusion," and possibly the wrong conclusion. Second, when drawing a conclusion, be sure to avoid assuming evidence that is not given. In the previous example, for instance, you should not assume that John is upset because he has no collision insurance. That assumption has no basis in any of the facts provided to you and may well be false. In other words, when you are asked to draw a conclusion that requires inductive reasoning, be sure to use all the information available to you, but avoid making assumptions concerning information that is not given.

Deductive reasoning involves using logic to move from general principles to specific conclusions. When a writer uses deductive reasoning, he or she must begin with a general premise that you, the reader, will accept. An example of such a premise might be, for example, that all students who receive A's in high school algebra and geometry have good math skills. Starting from a general premise, the writer must then build a logical argument before arriving at a specific conclusion.

The basic form of deductive reasoning is known as the *syllogism*. In a syllogism, the writer moves from a *major premise* (a general statement), to a *minor premise* (a related, but more specific, statement), to a *conclusion* that can be drawn from these two premises. Each premise must be true and the conclusion must follow logically from the major and minor premises.

> major premise: Students who receive A's in algebra and geometry have
>   good math skills.
> minor premise: Susan has received all A's in algebra and geometry.
> conclusion: Susan has good math skills.

Thus for you, as a reader, drawing a conclusion using deductive reasoning might involve reading a passage that includes both the major and the minor premise above, and then using those premises to conclude that the student in question has good math skills.

Practice Exercises

The following exercises will help you review the skills covered in this chapter. Many of the types of questions presented here will be similar to those on the test; others will not. Remember that the purpose of the exercises is to give you practice on the skills rather than merely to prepare you for the test. Following these exercises are the Practice Exercise Explanations. They explain each question, the correct answer, and why the remaining choices are incorrect.

The sea organisms referred to as lancelets and tunicates both belong to the phylum Chordata. They each have a stiff rod of cartilage called a notochord along their dorsal side. As sea dwellers, both also have gill pouches, a dorsal nerve cord, and a ventral heart.

However, the lancelet and the tunicate are very different in appearance, method of feeding, and locomotion. The lancelet has a streamlined body, pointed at each end, which rather resembles the body of a fish. Although it usually lives partly buried in the sand, it is able to swim. The lancelet gets food from water, which passes into its body through numerous gill slits.

A single tunicate, on the other hand, resembles a tubular bud; in groups, these organisms look like a large, open blossom. Tunicates attach one of their two openings to a rock and do not swim. A tunicate obtains its food from water funneled into its mouth.

Thus lancelets and tunicates, although both chordates, look, feed, and move very differently.

1. According to information in the selection, which of the following is a difference between lancelets and tunicates?

   A. Only lancelets have a dorsal nerve cord.

   B. Only tunicates attach themselves to rocks.

   C. Only lancelets are chordates.

   D. Only tunicates get food from sea water.

2. Which of the following conclusions may be drawn from information presented in the selection?

   A. Organisms that include quite dissimilar characteristics may be grouped in the same phylum.

   B. One area of similarity among chordates is their method of feeding.

   C. Lancelets have more gill slits than most other marine organisms.

   D. Chordates spend approximately equal amounts of time in and out of the water.

A lake is not an unchanging ecosystem. During its life, it undergoes a process of change called <u>succession</u>. Over the course of many years, sediment begins to accumulate at the bottom of the lake. The areas around the lake's shoreline fill in first. There, simple plants that include mosses and various shrubs begin to grow.

Meanwhile, sediment continues to collect on the lake bottom as more and more plants grow in the fertile soil along the shoreline of the ever-diminishing lake. As time goes on, shoreline shrubs are replaced by trees. Eventually, the lake disappears altogether and is replaced by forest.

3. According to this selection, which of the following occurs last to the shoreline of a lake that is undergoing succession?

   A. Sediment builds up.

   B. Soil fertility increases.

   C. Trees replace shrubs.

   D. Mosses become established.

4. Which of the following conclusions can be drawn from information presented in the selection?

   A. Lakes constitute a unique type of ecosystem in that they alone undergo succession.

   B. Succession from a lake to a forest occurs over a long period of time.

   C. Only a relatively small number of lakes eventually turn into forests.

   D. Once sediment begins to accumulate on a lake bottom, the process of succession proceeds very rapidly.

5. Information provided in the selection indicates that the fertile soil found along the shoreline of a lake undergoing succession is primarily due to:

   A. forest development.

   B. plant growth.

   C. reduced lake size.

   D. accumulated sediment.

The once widespread use of DDT to eliminate plant pests had a number of harmful effects. For instance, exposure to DDT resulted in increased resistance to pest-control chemicals among the members of some pest populations (e.g., mosquitoes, houseflies). Because of this, such pests became harder than ever to kill.

DDT also affected animal populations. DDT tends to build up in the fatty tissue of animals. In small doses, DDT is only harmful to insects, but in higher doses it can be harmful and even deadly to fish, birds, and mammals. DDT also hurt large birds in an indirect way. By causing large birds to produce thin, fragile eggshells in which embryos could not survive, DDT severely reduced some populations of eagles, ospreys, falcons, and pelicans.

Given these and other problems, it is not surprising that the regular use of DDT was banned in the United States in 1972. Since that time, the use of some other pesticides has been restricted as well. Despite their problems, however, it is also important to remember that pesticides such as DDT help ensure a high-crop yield for a growing world population and also help maintain pest-free food for consumers. For these reasons, pesticide research needs to continue until pesticides can be developed that are able to break down rapidly into harmless substances. Another direction for researchers might also be to find ways to apply pesticides directly to pests, rather than by aerial spraying.

6. According to the selection, which of the following is a result of DDT use?

   A. reduced eagle populations

   B. poor crop yields

   C. increased human illness

   D. poor food quality

7. According to the writer, one solution to the pesticide problem would be to:

   A. use machines rather than people to spray pesticides.

   B. keep fish, birds, and mammals affected by pesticides in wildlife preserves.

   C. discover a more direct way to apply pesticides.

   D. conduct genetic research on mosquitoes and houseflies.

If you follow these simple steps, you will be able to record one television program on your video cassette recorder (VCR) while you are viewing another program.

First, on your VCR, flip the power switch to the "on" position, the select switch to the "TV" position, and the speed switch to the "LP" or "SP" position. If the program you wish to record is longer than two hours, use LP (long playing); otherwise, use SP (standard playing).

Next, turn on the television set and select the channel that you wish to view now.

Then, insert a cassette in your VCR. After inserting the cassette, select the channel you wish to record by pressing the corresponding numbers on the channel selector key pad. Now, hold down the "record" button and press the "play" button. You are now ready to watch one program while the other one is being recorded.

8. This selection uses which of the following methods of organization?

    A. cause and effect

    B. argumentative

    C. comparison and contrast

    D. sequential

9. According to the selection, which of the following steps should you take immediately before pressing the "record" button on the VCR?

    A. Insert a cassette in the VCR.

    B. Set the speed switch to either the "LP" or the "SP" position.

    C. Press the "play" button.

    D. On the channel selector key pad, indicate the channel you wish to record.

Gambling casinos in Detroit? That would be a colossal mistake. It is true enough that Detroit, like many cities, is facing some serious economic problems, including unemployment, homelessness, pollution, and a one-industry economy. But rather than solving these problems, legalized gambling casinos would only add to them.

Advocates say that the establishment of gambling casinos would mean more jobs for Detroit's citizens. According to these advocates, moreover, the new jobs that would open up in casinos, hotels, restaurants, and other parts of the service sector would be high-paying ones. These claims are unfounded, however. From the experiences of other cities, we know that the vast majority of the new jobs that would become available would be low-level jobs that pay low-level wages. In addition, many jobs that open up would be temporary ones that would be at least partly filled by transient workers. Moreover, the best jobs would go to people imported from outside Detroit by national hotel chains.

Another reason to vote down the casinos is that gambling would surely attract organized crime. Although some insist that organized crime would stay away from legalized gambling because the winnings are taxed, we have already seen time and time again that wherever gambling appears, organized crime is soon to follow.

We don't want to be another Las Vegas or Atlantic City! We have built Detroit's positive image by developing green parks, cultural centers, and skyscrapers. Surely, there are more positive approaches we can use to solve our problems than by legalizing gambling.

Call or write the mayor or city council and tell them to keep gambling casinos out of Detroit.

Vote YES on August 2 to pass the city ordinance prohibiting casino gambling in Detroit. Remember, a YES vote says NO to gambling.

10. In which of the following statements from the selection does the writer respond most directly to those who claim that legalized gambling casinos would help solve Detroit's current economic problems?

   A. The best jobs would go to people imported from outside Detroit by national hotel chains.

   B. Gambling would surely attract organized crime.

   C. We have built Detroit's positive image by developing green parks, cultural centers, and skyscrapers.

   D. The new jobs that would open up would be high-paying ones.

11. The writer of this selection would most likely agree with which of the following statements?

   A. Detroit would be wise to follow Atlantic City's example.

   B. Poor voter turnout is one of our greatest problems.

   C. Legalized gambling works well in some cities.

   D. Detroit voters can make a difference in their city.

Practice Exercise Explanations

1. **Correct Response: B.** This selection focuses on comparing and contrasting two types of sea organisms: lancelets and tunicates. Information provided in the first paragraph of the selection indicates that *both* lancelets and tunicates have a dorsal nerve cord; therefore, choice A is incorrect. Similarly, the first and fourth paragraphs indicate that *both* types of organisms are chordates (referred to as "the phylum Chordata" in the first paragraph and "chordates" in the fourth paragraph); therefore, choice C is also incorrect. In the second and third paragraphs, which describe among other things how these two types of organisms obtain their food, we also learn that *both* obtain food from sea water (although through different mechanisms); choice D is thus also incorrect. Only choice B describes a way in which tunicates and lancelets actually differ. According to the information given, only tunicates attach themselves to rocks, while lancelets spend much of their time partly buried in the sand.

2. **Correct Response: A.** Of the four choices given, only choice A represents a conclusion that can be reasonably drawn from information provided in the selection. In the first sentence of the selection, the writer notes that lancelets and tunicates belong to a single phylum. The writer then goes on in the second paragraph to note that these two types of organisms differ substantially in a number of important ways. Thus, it is reasonable to conclude more generally that organisms with quite different characteristics may be grouped in a single phylum. Choice B is incorrect because we know from the selection that two types of chordates, lancelets and tunicates, *differ* in their method of feeding. Concerning choice C, the selection includes no reference to other types of marine organisms besides lancelets and tunicates; therefore, although we do know that lancelets have "numerous" gill slits, we have no way of knowing whether it is true that lancelets have more gill slits than most other marine organisms. Similarly, there is no evidence in the selection to indicate that either lancelets and tunicates, or chordates in general, spend approximately equal amounts of time in and out of the water (choice D). In fact, information presented indicates that lancelets spend most of their time buried in the sand, while tunicates appear to spend most of their time attached to rocks.

3. **Correct Response: C.** This selection uses sequential organization to describe the process of succession as it occurs to a lake. Of the four phenomena noted in the answer choices, the last to occur is the replacement of shrubs by trees (choice C). According to the selection, this takes place only *after* sediment builds up along the shoreline (choice A), which in turn increases the shoreline's soil fertility (choice B) and allows "simple plants that include mosses" to become established (choice D). Thus, trees take over after other plants, including mosses and shrubs, are established.

4. **Correct Response: B.** Words and phrases like *over the course of many years, as time goes on,* and *eventually* imply that the changes described are gradual and occur over a very long period of time. In addition, from your own experience, you can probably imagine that it takes quite a long time for an area containing small, simple plants to become a forest full of grown trees. Therefore, given information from the selection as well as your own experience, you should be able to conclude that choice B is correct. Although the writer does not mention any other type of ecosystem, there is no reason to conclude from the information given that lakes are unique in that they alone undergo succession (choice A). Choice C is incorrect because the writer implies that the process occurs to all, or at least most, lakes. Similarly, the writer implies throughout that the entire process of succession is a very gradual one; there is no indication that the process begins to speed up at any point. Therefore, choice D is also incorrect.

5. **Correct Response: D.** This question requires that you identify the cause of increased soil fertility along the shoreline of a lake undergoing succession. In the first paragraph, the writer notes that the shoreline area of a lake fills in first with sediment. In the second paragraph, the writer notes further that as sediment continues to collect, more and more plants begin to grow in the fertile soil along the shoreline. Thus, it seems most likely that the fertile soil found along the shoreline of a lake undergoing succession is primarily due to accumulated sediment (choice D). Meanwhile, it is clear from the selection that *forest development* (choice A) and *plant growth* (choice B) are both *results* of increased soil fertility rather than causes. Choice C, *reduced lake size,* similarly cannot be considered a cause of the fertile soil along a lake's shoreline. Instead, reduced lake size, like fertile soil, is itself a *result of* accumulated sediment.

6. **Correct Response: A.** The writer explains at the end of the second paragraph that DDT affected some large birds, including eagles, by causing them to produce eggs with thin, fragile eggshells. This meant that many of the embryo offspring of these birds failed to survive which, in turn, led to a reduction in the population size of the birds. Thus, it is true that DDT use led to *reduced eagle populations* (choice A). As noted in the last paragraph, however, DDT helps "ensure a high-crop yield" and "maintain pest-free food for consumers." Therefore, choices B and D are incorrect. Since the selection includes no information about the effects of DDT on human health, choice C is also incorrect.

7. **Correct Response: C.** In the last paragraph, the writer notes that one possible solution to the problem of pesticides would be to "find ways to apply pesticides directly to pests," presumably so that only pest populations would be affected by the pesticide chemicals. Therefore, choice C is the correct response. Choice A is incorrect because the writer notes in the last sentence that spraying is itself a problem. Choices B and D are incorrect because, although one or both of these strategies might possibly be of some help in solving the problem, the writer says nothing in the selection about either wildlife preserves or genetic research.

8. **Correct Response: D.** This selection describes how to record one television program on a VCR while watching another program. The writer describes the steps involved in this procedure in sequential order; therefore, choice D is the correct response. Words such as *first, next, then,* and *now* help you identify this method of organization. Choice A is incorrect because the selection discusses neither the causes nor the effects of anything. Choice B is incorrect because the writer neither discusses pros and cons nor argues for or against anything. The selection also does not examine similarities or differences between any two objects, so choice C is also incorrect.

9. **Correct Response: D.** According to information presented in the selection, the correct step to take immediately before pressing the "record" button is to "select the channel you wish to record by pressing the corresponding numbers on the channel selector key pad." Therefore, choice D is the correct response to the question. Although inserting a cassette in the VCR (choice A) and setting the speed switch to "LP" or "SP" (choice B) also occur before the "record" button is pressed, careful reading shows that neither of these is the step that occurs *immediately* before the "record" button is used. Concerning choice C, information provided in the third paragraph indicates that the "play" button should be pressed at the same time as or immediately after the "record" button is pressed. Therefore, choice C is also incorrect.

10. **Correct Response: A.** It is clear throughout the selection that the writer believes that any possible benefits of legalized gambling would be more than outweighed by its costs. Of the four answer choices given, only choice A is used by the writer to respond directly to the claim that legalized gambling would help Detroit economically. The writer uses the statement in choice A to argue specifically that legalized gambling would fail to improve substantially the job situation for Detroit citizens. Although the statement in choice B points to a problem that is likely to result from legalized gambling, the statement has little direct bearing on the particular issue of Detroit's economic problems as described in the first paragraph. Choice C, which merely states that the city of Detroit currently has a positive image, does not serve directly to counter the argument that gambling would help solve Detroit's economic problems. Choice D, meanwhile, reflects the view of proponents of legalized gambling casinos, rather than those of opponents such as the writer.

11. **Correct Response: D.** The purpose of this selection is to discourage legalized gambling in Detroit and to encourage people to get out and vote against it. Thus, the writer clearly believes that through their vote, Detroit citizens can have a significant effect on the future of their city (choice D). Choice A is incorrect because the writer specifically states in the fourth paragraph, "We don't want to be another Las Vegas or Atlantic City." Choice B is incorrect because although the writer is urging voters to get out and vote against legalized gambling, there is no indication that the writer believes that poor voter turnout is a problem in Detroit or elsewhere. Choice C is incorrect because the writer argues against legalized gambling throughout the selection and nowhere indicates that it may work well in some places.

Study Ideas

The following study hints will help you understand the relationships among the ideas included in the materials you read.

1. For each work you read, determine the type or types of organization the writer has used: sequential, cause and effect, argumentative, comparison and contrast, or problem and solution.

2. Look for signal words and phrases to help you determine how a selection is organized and how specific points included in the selection relate to one another. Because writers sometimes include one structure within another, be sure you have correctly identified the *overall* structure of the selection.

3. Ask yourself the following questions as you read: What is the writer's goal in the selection? How are the facts and ideas broadly organized to achieve the writer's intended goal? How does each idea presented relate to the writer's broad goal and to other specific ideas included in the selection (e.g., as a cause, an effect, a solution, a pro argument, a con argument)?

4. If, after reading a selection, you remain unsure about how some of the facts and ideas discussed relate to one another, try developing a rough diagram to help you visualize those relationships as you reread the part or parts you found confusing. Keep rereading the selection until you are sure you understand all the important ideas and relationships mentioned.

Chapter 8

USE CRITICAL REASONING SKILLS TO EVALUATE WRITTEN MATERIAL

This skill includes evaluating the stated or implied assumptions on which the validity of a writer's argument depends; judging the relevance or importance of facts, examples, or graphic data to a writer's argument; evaluating the logic of a writer's argument; evaluating the validity of analogies; distinguishing between fact and opinion; and assessing the credibility or objectivity of the writer or source of written material.

Introduction

Much expository writing is intended to convince you, the reader, to accept a writer's point of view about some issue or topic. If a writer is going to convince you of an opinion, an interpretation of events, or a scientific theory, that writer must construct an effective *argument*. It is not enough just to state an idea and insist on the truth of that idea.

On the other hand, if you intend to think for yourself, it is also not enough for you simply to accept a writer's argument and conclusions. You need to be a *critical reader;* that is, you need to understand how an argument is constructed, and you need to judge the strengths and weaknesses of the argument. As a critical reader, you will be able to decide what the information and opinions presented by a writer are worth.

In earlier chapters, you studied ways to identify the components (e.g., main idea, supporting details) and structure (e.g., cause and effect, argumentative, comparison and contrast) of written materials. To be a critical reader, you need to go one step further. You must also be able to evaluate the assumptions upon which a writer bases an argument, as well as the strength, objectivity, and logic of the argument itself. This requires that you be an *active reader;* that is, that you ask questions about what you read and take nothing for granted. Too often, readers erroneously assume that whatever they read must be true simply by virtue of its having been put into print in the first place.

In this chapter, you will have an opportunity to review the steps that are required to examine critically the materials you read. These steps include: identifying the writer's main idea or argument; identifying the assumptions underlying the writer's argument; identifying the types of support the writer uses to present or defend the argument; evaluating the completeness, relevance, validity, and objectivity of the support used; and assessing the overall logic and credibility of the argument.

Steps in Critically Evaluating Written Materials

1. Identifying the writer's main idea or argument. Before you can actually begin to evaluate a writer's argument, you must first be sure that you have a solid grasp of just what it is that the writer is trying to say. Only after you have identified the main idea or argument can you assess whether the writer has supported his or her point in an adequate and convincing way. If you are unsure about how to recognize a main idea, refer to Chapter 5. Consider also the passage below. Can you find its main idea?

> The California condor is both the largest and the rarest bird in North America. In the 1960s, the total population of California condors was less than 100. By the 1980s, this number had declined to less than 20. In 1987, the last known California condor still living in the wild was captured and put into a zoo. Scientists argue that in the zoo they can protect the condor and use it, along with a handful of other condors captured earlier, to participate in a breeding program. This breeding program should be applauded. Through it, enough condor chicks will eventually be produced to ensure that one day these great birds will again soar over the hills and valleys of California.

In this passage, the main idea is not presented immediately. Rather, the writer first builds an argument and does not directly address the main idea until near the end of the piece. At that point, it becomes clear that the writer's main purpose is to argue that the capture of California condors, and their subsequent placement in a breeding program, were the best way to ensure their survival as a species.

2. Identifying the assumptions underlying a writer's argument. In nearly any written material, the writer must make one or more assumptions upon which the material presented is based. Occasionally, writers state their assumptions explicitly at the outset. More often, however, it is up to the reader to determine both what a writer's assumptions are and whether these assumptions appear justified. In trying to determine a writer's assumptions, you must ask yourself, "What does the writer take for granted?" Often, whether you accept or reject an argument depends on your opinion about a writer's assumptions.

If you examine the passage about condors again, you may be able to see for yourself that the writer's argument depends on various assumptions. First of all, the writer makes an important assumption involving values; that is, it is assumed that saving endangered species is a worthwhile goal. Second, a number of assumptions are made involving factual issues: it is assumed, for example, that condors continue to live a reasonably healthy life when they are placed in captivity, that condor chicks born in captivity can be successfully released into the wild, and that captured condors will be able to breed in zoos. We will examine the last of these assumptions, which is perhaps the most crucial to the writer's argument, in somewhat more detail in the following paragraphs.

Your ability to recognize the assumption concerning the ability of captured condors to breed in captivity may depend partially on your previous knowledge of the subject. You may already know that not all animals have bred with success in captivity. In that case, it should occur to you to ask whether condors will be able to lay and hatch eggs in a zoo environment. However, even if you do not possess prior knowledge about this subject, careful reading and a little thought should help you see that the writer is making an assumption that he or she hopes you will share.

In fact, this particular assumption may or may not be valid. Before the last known condor was captured, some experts argued that putting the condors in zoos was *not* a good idea and that they were more likely to survive if they were left to find their own nesting sites. These experts argued that human beings should concentrate on protecting the birds in the wild, not capturing them and placing them in zoos. This argument was lost, however. No one could prove which side was right, but the more commonly accepted assumption was that if the condors continued to live in the wild, their numbers would continue to decline, presumably to zero.

3. Identifying types of support. A writer may use one or more types of support to convince readers of the validity of an argument. Such support may be provided in the form of facts, reasons, examples, expert opinion, or analogy.

The passage on condors illustrates some of these types of support. For instance, the writer uses *reasons* to support a position when implying that the California condor is important because it is the largest and rarest bird in North America. The inclusion of these observations suggests to the reader that the bird in question is in some respects unique and important, and thus worthy of being saved in the first place. The writer also uses *facts*, in the form of numerical data, to describe the decline of the California condor population from the 1960s until 1987. Here we learn that the number of wild condors fell from somewhat less than 100 in the 1960s, to less than 20 in the 1980s, and finally to one single condor in 1987. Finally, the writer uses *expert opinion* to support the argument when it is stated, "Scientists argue that in the zoo they can protect the condor and use it . . . to participate in a breeding program."

Besides reasons, facts, and expert opinion, writers often use *examples* to support an argument. Examples describe specific instances that illustrate a more general point. They often add a "human element" to an argument and thus serve to increase the reader's interest. Similarly, they tend to strengthen the impact of an argument by making it less abstract for readers and helping them see the practical implications of the issues involved.

> The lax enforcement of environmental protection legislation in our state under this administration has had negative effects that may now take decades to undo. Look at the Plains River, for example. The failure of the administration to ensure that industries along the river comply with regulations for dumping toxic waste has led to a dramatic reduction in the river's fish population and a startling increase in its concentrations of toxic elements.

In this passage, the writer uses a specific example to support the more general argument that lax enforcement of environmental protection legislation has had negative effects. In this case, the example provides evidence that appears to be both relevant and appropriate to the issue in question. Unfortunately, writers sometimes use examples to obscure rather than clarify an issue. For example, a writer who wishes to complain about a new town law might describe a family that has suffered as a result of the law, while failing to mention that this is the exceptional case and that the great majority of families in town have indeed benefited from enactment of the new law.

One further type of support is the *analogy*. An analogy is used to explain one relationship or idea in terms of another. In an analogy, the two ideas or relationships are basically different but exhibit one or more important similarities. Following is an example of an analogy.

> An administrator at Harvard University once opposed the idea of hiring the famous novelist Vladimir Nabokov to teach modern literature at Harvard. "After all," the administrator argued, "we wouldn't hire an elephant to teach zoology, would we?"

In this example, the administrator uses an analogy, in which he compares Nabokov to an elephant, to argue against hiring Nabokov to teach literature at Harvard. According to the analogy, because an elephant is an animal does not mean that it is competent to teach zoology (the study of animals); similarly, the fact that Nabokov writes great literature does not mean that he is competent to teach students about literature. Whether you think the administrator's argument is valid depends on whether you accept the analogy; that is, whether you agree that a novelist has the same relationship to the study of literature as an elephant has to the study of animals. Someone opposed to the administrator's view might indeed come back with another analogy: We *would* hire a former professional quarterback to coach a college's football team, wouldn't we?

4. Evaluating the types of support used. Being a critical reader implies more than simply checking to see if a writer has included facts, opinions, and ideas to support a point. You must also evaluate the significance and worth of the writer's supporting evidence in relation to the particular point the writer wishes to make. It is important to realize that any type of evidence can be *misused;* that is, presented in ways that are designed to mislead readers into supporting the writer's view. Moreover, even if a writer is not trying intentionally to mislead readers, he or she probably *is* selectively including or excluding evidence; that is, choosing to include evidence that will support the desired conclusion and to exclude evidence that might call the conclusion into question. Thus, it is up to you, the reader, to judge whether the evidence supplied by the writer is complete, relevant to the argument, valid (i.e., well supported by facts), and objective (i.e., based on fact rather than on opinion).

Concerning the issue of *completeness,* the passage on condors is instructive. In at least two instances, the writer chose facts selectively and thereby omitted evidence that would be important for a reader who is trying to decide whether the placement of wild condors in zoos is a good idea. First, the writer cited only those experts who were in favor of the action; the fact that there were other experts who opposed it was never even mentioned. Second, the writer provided facts about the dwindling condor population, but failed to provide similar evidence concerning potential problems related to the survival and breeding of condors in a zoo environment. Clearly, the information that the writer chose *not* to include might well have been sufficient to make readers seriously question the writer's conclusion.

You should also be careful to determine whether all the evidence a writer uses to support an argument is indeed *relevant* to the argument in the first place. Read the following passage, paying particular attention to the last two sentences:

> One recent development in the fitness boom is the use of hand weights. Carrying these weights, which range from a half pound to three pounds each, is supposed to increase a runner's arm strength and, at the same time, improve the runner's breathing and blood circulation. However, laboratory tests have shown that gripping even a small weight while exercising will raise one's blood pressure and lead to long-term negative effects. Besides, most runners find that hand weights are awkward to carry.

The last two sentences in this paragraph are intended to support the conclusion, which is not directly stated, but implied, that carrying hand weights may be detrimental to the health of people who are running for fitness. Are these two sentences relevant to the argument? The next-to-last sentence, which links the use of hand weights to heightened blood pressure and other "long-term negative effects," certainly is. The last sentence, however, is not so clearly relevant. If you like to run, but find that carrying hand weights while you run feels awkward, then you might indeed decide against using hand weights. On the other hand, the perception that carrying hand weights is awkward has nothing to do with whether the practice is a healthy one.

The *validity* of a writer's evidence is often more difficult to determine than either its relevance or its completeness. This is particularly true where the writer cites specific information related to a specialized area and you, as a reader, have little choice but to assume that what the writer is telling you is well-supported, generally accepted fact. This is rarely much of an issue with college textbooks, since presumably most such works are based on this type of fact. In some works, writers may also help you assess validity by citing the sources for the facts, data, and opinions they include. When the source seems to be a legitimate one, such as the U.S. Census Bureau or a respected scientist, you can be quite sure of the validity of the evidence. (Note that you still cannot be sure you are getting *all* the facts, but at least you can assume that what you *are* getting is well supported.) When a writer cites either a questionable source or no source at all, you must simply trust the writer or, if it seems important enough, track down additional information yourself.

In evaluating an argument's support, one final area of concern is *objectivity;* that is, whether the evidence and the conclusions are based on substantiated fact or merely someone's feelings and opinions. In this regard, it is important that you be able to distinguish fact from opinion. In the passage on condors, for example, the writer states a personal opinion rather than an objective fact when concluding that the breeding program "should be applauded." The following sentences further illustrate the difference between fact and opinion:

> FACT: The president appointed to the Supreme Court a judge who was an outspoken opponent of busing.

> OPINION: With the appointment of the new judge, the president made the Supreme Court too conservative for the good of the nation.

The first statement is not a matter of opinion. Either the judge spoke out against busing, in which case the statement is true, or the judge did not, in which case the statement is false. The second statement, however, is an opinion. You may or may not believe that the president was making the Supreme Court "too conservative," depending on how conservative you think the Court should be. If you support busing, you might agree with the opinion; if you oppose it, you might not share the writer's opinion that adding a busing opponent to the Court makes the Court too conservative. (Note also the use of the key word, *too*, which often indicates that an opinion is being expressed.)

5. Assessing the overall logic and credibility of the argument. After you have identified and evaluated the individual pieces of support used by a writer to construct an argument, you must then proceed to put your observations together to determine whether the work in its entirety seems to be both logical (i.e., uses correct reasoning) and credible (i.e., is believable). The overall logic and credibility of an argument depends primarily on three factors: first, the reasonableness and acceptability of the writer's assumptions; second, the types of evidence the writer has used; and third, the ways in which the writer has put the evidence together to form a coherent and convincing whole. An argument that is characterized by reasonable assumptions, adequate evidence, and a coherent structure is said to be an argument that "has no holes."

The logic of an argument may be either explicitly stated or implied. In the case of the passage on condors, the logic of the argument is implied and goes something like the following: We know that condors in the wild have been dying. We know also that there is only one condor left in the wild. Therefore, it is reasonable to conclude that if something is not done, the last condor in the wild will also die. It is further reasonable to conclude that capturing the last wild condor, placing it in a zoo, and hoping it reproduces is better than doing nothing at all. This argument seems basically to be a logical and credible one, although it is also important to remember, as noted in previous sections, that the evidence provided by the writer is rather limited and one-sided.

When assessing the logic of an argument, you may find that it contains one or more logical flaws in its construction. Such errors in reasoning are referred to as *logical fallacies*. If you are aware of the major types of logical fallacies, you will be more likely to be able to spot them in the works you read.

One common logical fallacy, referred to as "begging the question," or "arguing in a circle," occurs when a writer tries to prove a point simply by stating the point using different words. This is illustrated in the following statement:

> James cannot be trusted because he never keeps his word.

In this case, the writer presents no real evidence to support this point, but rather tries to convince the reader that James is untrustworthy merely by repeating the original assertion using other words; that is, "never keeps his word" means essentially the same thing as "cannot be trusted."

A second type of logical fallacy is *oversimplification,* which is often found in cause-and-effect reasoning. With oversimplification, the writer assumes that anything that occurs earlier than a given phenomenon can be considered the cause of that phenomenon, as in the example that follows:

> The unemployment rate has been rising ever since the president was elected last November. The president must therefore be responsible for our nation's increased unemployment.

Whenever you encounter reasoning such as this, you should ask yourself the following questions: 1. Is the presumed cause sufficient to produce the effect? 2. Could there be other causes that are responsible for producing the effect? 3. Could the fact that the later event followed the earlier one be the result of chance alone?

Either-or arguments are another kind of oversimplification. Here, the writer presents the reader with two extreme options, both of which are often in fact wrong, in order to convince the reader of a particular point of view.

> Either you can study hard and be a success in life or you can be lazy about your schoolwork and end up on skid row.

Clearly, there are numerous possibilities between the two extremes noted in this sentence. Since this is the case with most important issues, you should always view such either-or arguments with suspicion.

A fourth type of logical fallacy is the *hasty generalization,* in which a writer bases a conclusion on inappropriate or inadequate examples.

> Bud Hanks and Charlotte Winston, who are from the two richest families in the state, are both members of the state legislature. One can conclude, therefore, that only the wealthiest people in the state stand a chance of being elected to the legislature.

After reading this example, you should be able to see that the fact that two members of a legislative body happen to be rich provides inadequate evidence for concluding that only the rich can be elected.

Ignoring the question is yet another type of logical fallacy. In this case, the writer presents arguments that have little or no bearing on the issue in question.

> Mr. Sanchez should have been appointed coach of the football team. He has long been a favorite teacher at our school and has always shown a great deal of school spirit in his support of our sports programs.

In this example, the writer has lost sight of the main issue, Mr. Sanchez's qualifications to be coach of the football team. The argument presented only lets the reader know that Mr. Sanchez is well liked and supports school sports; it says nothing about why he would make a better football coach than the person who was selected.

One final type of logical fallacy is a *false comparison,* also referred to as a *false analogy*. As you recall from an earlier discussion, an analogy is used to explain one relationship or idea in terms of another one. In that discussion, the example used to explain the concept focused on the comparison between a novelist, Vladimir Nabokov, and an elephant. It is fairly safe to assume that that was in fact a *false* analogy. That is, the argument that Nabokov would be as bad at teaching literature as an elephant would be at teaching zoology is probably an oversimplification, which, in addition, offers no relevant evidence at all to support the point.

Practice Exercises

The following exercises will help you review the skills covered in this chapter. Many of the types of questions presented here will be similar to those on the test; others will not. Remember that the purpose of the exercises is to give you practice on the skills rather than merely to prepare you for the test. Following these exercises are the Practice Exercise Explanations. They explain each question, the correct answer, and why the remaining choices are incorrect.

The recent city council vote to build a new parking garage, at an estimated cost of $4.5 million, is a misguided effort to solve the city's parking problems. In the first place, the garage is sure to cost more than the estimated amount. When a similar garage was built in our neighboring town of Springfield in 1985, the final cost was more than double the original estimate that was approved by the Springfield mayor's office. We may be able to afford $4.5 million, but we cannot afford $9 million.

Second, the city council members have no respect for the advice of the parking consultants that they themselves hired. In a report published in this newspaper last month, those consultants noted that the parking problem would be solved if the city simply bought three new buses. These new buses would cost an estimated $1.2 million and would be able to bring shoppers and business people from the outskirts of the city to the downtown area. In voting to build the garage instead of buying buses, the council has acted like a patient who insists on having all his teeth pulled when his dentist has simply recommended a couple of fillings.

Third, the only available site for the garage is presently occupied by four run-down apartment buildings. Instead of demolishing these buildings and forcing the present occupants to seek housing elsewhere, the city should spend some of its money to improve those buildings. The city would thus provide better housing for some of its poorest inhabitants.

1. Which of the following statements from the selection expresses a fact rather than an opinion?

   A. The recent city council vote to build a new parking garage is a misguided effort to solve the city's parking problems.

   B. The city council members have no respect for the advice of the parking consultants.

   C. These new buses would cost an estimated $1.2 million.

   D. The city should spend some of its money to improve the run-down apartment buildings.

2. Which of the following is an assumption on which the writer's argument is based?

   A. The city council is trying to make downtown parking easier for people who live on the outskirts of town.

   B. People who have not been able to find parking places downtown would be willing to ride a bus downtown instead.

   C. The city can afford to build both the new garage and new housing for the occupants of the demolished apartments.

   D. Improving the downtown parking situation is a more important priority than saving four apartment buildings.

3. In the second paragraph of the selection,
    the writer makes a comparison between the
    city council's response to its consultants
    and a patient's response to his dentist.
    Which of the following best expresses the
    writer's reason for making the comparison?

    A. The council members have rejected
        their hired consultants'
        recommendation and decided to do
        something more expensive.

    B. The council has voted to do something
        that will cause great discomfort to the
        entire community.

    C. Most of the council members are in
        poor health and seem unable to exhibit
        good judgment.

    D. The council is prejudiced in favor of
        private automobiles and against public
        transportation such as buses.

4. Which of the following facts from the
    selection best supports the writer's
    contention that the new parking garage will
    cost $9 million?

    A. Buying more buses would be less
        costly than building a garage.

    B. The Springfield garage cost twice what
        was estimated.

    C. The city hired consultants to study the
        parking problem.

    D. The projected garage site is now
        occupied by four buildings.

About one person in ten occasionally suffers from the breathing problems associated with asthma: pain in the chest, shortness of breath, a general feeling of having difficulty breathing. In many cases, an attack of asthma can be brought on by running or other vigorous exercise. After a few minutes of exercise, the airways in the person's lungs become constricted, and the person finds it difficult to get enough air. This is called exercise-induced asthma.

Our recent experiment with 20 people who suffer from exercise-induced asthma suggests a way to deal with the problem. When the members of our test group jogged at an even pace on a track, we found that for the first six to eight minutes every one of them could exercise comfortably. During this time, their airways were expanding. When they exercised longer, however, they began to notice symptoms of asthma. These symptoms were worst after an average of 14.3 minutes of exercise.

Some of our subjects stopped to rest at this point. Others continued to exercise despite the discomfort. An interesting phenomenon we noticed was that, in both those who stopped exercising and those who continued, the symptoms gradually disappeared. After an average of 28.1 minutes from the beginning of exercise, all subjects could breathe normally and could resume exercise at the original rate with no further symptoms.

We have concluded that all those who suffer from exercise-induced asthma can deal with the problem by planning their exercise carefully. If the asthma is mild, they can jog slowly for 15-25 minutes, until the symptoms disappear, and then they can exercise freely for an hour or more. If it is severe, they can jog for 6-8 minutes, then rest for 20 minutes, and then resume exercise.

5. Which of the following statements from the selection is an opinion rather than a fact?

A. In many cases, an attack of asthma can be brought on by running or other vigorous exercise.

B. Our recent experiment included 20 people who suffer from exercise-induced asthma.

C. The symptoms were worst after an average of 14.3 minutes of exercise.

D. All those who suffer from exercise-induced asthma can deal with the problem by planning their exercise carefully.

6. Using the logic outlined by the writer in this selection, one would expect that those with severe asthma who exercise for 15 minutes without resting will:

A. show significantly reduced signs of asthma.

B. have open airways in their lungs.

C. begin feeling signs of an asthma attack.

D. experience great difficulty breathing.

7. Which of the following assumptions provides a basis for the writer's argument in this selection?

    A. Exercise-induced asthma is one of the most serious health problems in today's society.

    B. The average person is concerned about being able to breathe comfortably.

    C. The 20 people in this experiment are typical of most people who get exercise-induced asthma.

    D. The more often people exercise, the less likely they are to suffer from exercise-induced asthma.

8. Which of the following best assesses the writer's credibility?

    A. Although the writer may have overstated somewhat the implications of the research, careful observations and clearly stated conclusions make the findings highly credible.

    B. Because the writer does not provide information about his or her professional credentials or the names of those who participated in the experiment, the credibility of the findings is quite suspect.

    C. The writer's clear and concise description of the breathing problems associated with exercise-induced asthma provides strong evidence that the findings are highly credible.

    D. The writer's findings lack credibility for two main reasons: only 20 people participated in the experiment and those who did participate were not interviewed afterward.

Practice Exercise Explanations

1. **Correct Response: C.** Facts are verifiable statements. Choice C is the best response because the price of a bus is verifiable. By comparison, not everyone would agree that the city council's recent vote was *misguided* (choice A), that *council members have no respect for the advice of the parking consultants* (choice B), or that *the city should spend some of its money to improve the run-down apartment buildings* (choice D). Therefore, choices A, B, and D are all opinions rather than facts.

2. **Correct Response: B.** The writer's main point in the selection is that the city should buy more buses rather than build a new parking garage. In the second paragraph, the writer indicates that the buses would help solve the parking problem mainly by bringing people into the downtown area from the outskirts of the city. This implies further that *people who have not been able to find parking places downtown would be willing to ride a bus downtown instead* (choice B). Concerning the other response options, choice A may be true, but provides neither a basis of nor support for the writer's argument; choice C is unsupported by any information provided in the selection; and choice D is a statement that, if anything, is contrary to the view of the writer.

3. **Correct Response: A.** This question requires an understanding of how analogies are used in written materials. Choice A is the best response because the writer's main purpose in the second paragraph is to show that the city can save money by purchasing more buses rather than building a new parking garage. The analogy is thus used to illustrate how the decision of the council results in more expense than necessary and is therefore financially unsound. Concerning choice B, although the council's decision will cause problems for a small portion of the community, there is no indication that it will cause "great discomfort" to the "entire" community. Furthermore, this is an issue that is not discussed until the next paragraph and so is unlikely to be the basis for the analogy in question. Concerning choice C, there is no indication that the writer is questioning the health of council members. Concerning choice D, although council members may indeed have some bias against public transportation (as reflected in their vote), the analogy has no bearing on this issue.

4. **Correct Response: B.** This question assesses the ability to judge the relevance of particular facts to a writer's argument. Choice B is the best response because in the first paragraph the writer notes that the estimated cost of the city's garage is $4.5 million and then cites the Springfield garage as an example of a typical cost overrun. Choice A is incorrect because the writer's comparison of the cost of buses and the cost of the proposed garage has nothing to do with the comparison between the estimated cost of the garage and the cost overrun that the writer believes to be likely. Similarly, neither the hiring of consultants (choice C) nor the current state of the projected garage site (choice D) offers any direct evidence concerning the actual cost of the new garage.

5. **Correct Response: D.** Of the alternative answer choices given, only choice D is an opinion rather than a fact. You can tell this is so because the writer states explicitly that this is a *conclusion;* that is, it is an opinion based on what has been observed and does not necessarily represent an absolute certainty. Concerning the other responses, choices A, B, and C are facts because each is a statement that is absolutely verifiable.

6. **Correct Response: D.** This question requires an understanding of the logic of the writer's argument. In the selection, the writer states that those who suffer from exercise-induced asthma, including those with severe asthma, are likely to experience breathing problems beginning after six to eight minutes of exercise. The writer further states that such people show the worst symptoms after about 14 minutes and that severe asthmatics, in particular, should rest for 20 minutes after exercising for the initial six to eight minutes. Given this information, it is logical to conclude that a severe asthmatic who exercises for 15 minutes (i.e., less than a minute after peak discomfort occurs) without resting *would experience great difficulty breathing* (choice D). It can therefore also be concluded that individuals in this group would not *show significantly reduced signs of asthma* (choice A), nor would they *have open airways in their lungs* (choice B), which would be a sign of easy breathing. Concerning choice C, this group would have been experiencing breathing difficulties for some time after having exercised for 15 minutes, and would thus not be just beginning to feel signs of an asthma attack.

7. **Correct Response: C.** In this question, you are asked to recognize a major assumption upon which the validity of an argument depends. Choice C is the best response because in any experiment the group studied must be assumed to represent a much larger segment of the population. If this were not the case, then experimental results would have no meaning at all for anyone outside the experimental group itself. Of the other choices listed, the writer provides no indication that he or she believes *exercise-induced asthma is one of the most serious health problems in today's society* (choice A), or that *the more often people exercise, the less likely they are to suffer from exercise-induced asthma* (choice D). Concerning choice B, the writer makes the point that only about one person in ten suffers from breathing problems associated with asthma. Although the work may be based at least partially on the assumption that *these* people have a particular concern about being able to breathe comfortably, there is no reason to assume that the *average* person (i.e., one of the great majority who have no breathing problems) would have such a concern.

8. **Correct Response: A.** This question assesses your ability to evaluate a writer's credibility. Choice A is the best response because the precision, clarity, and logic with which both the observational data and the conclusions are reported do give the work credibility (i.e., believability), although the writer probably overstates the case somewhat when it is concluded in the last paragraph that the type of planning described can help "*all* those who suffer from exercise-induced asthma." Of the various objections raised in choices B and D (i.e., failure to list professional credentials, failure to provide the names of study participants, failure to interview participants afterward, participation of only 20 individuals in the study), the only one that might truly raise doubts about the validity or credibility of the work is the fact that only 20 people participated in the study. However, since the writer clearly states this from the beginning, it is far more likely to be viewed as a potential limitation of the study rather than a serious blow to the credibility of the writer. Concerning choice C, the writer's description of the breathing difficulties associated with exercise-induced asthma is background information that adds little or nothing to the credibility of the writer or the research.

Study Ideas

The best way to become a critical reader is to practice the critical reasoning skills discussed in this chapter whenever you read expository writing. This means following the steps listed below:

1. Identify the writer's main point or argument.

2. Identify the assumptions underlying the writer's main point or argument.

3. Identify the types of support the writer uses to present the point or argument.

4. Evaluate the completeness, relevance, validity, and objectivity of the support used.

5. Assess the writer's overall logic and credibility.

Chapter 9

APPLY STUDY SKILLS TO READING ASSIGNMENTS

This skill includes organizing and summarizing information for study purposes; following written instructions or directions; and interpreting information presented in charts, graphs, or tables.

Introduction

With recreational reading, you may choose to read whatever you wish, and read with no conscious goal beyond enjoying yourself. You need not make an effort to remember any details, characters, or concepts. In college courses, however, your instructors will assign you hundreds of pages of textbook material and expect you to understand, remember, and apply that material in tests and to further learning. Reading for learning, or study reading, thus differs greatly from recreational reading. Study reading requires analyzing and organizing written materials so you can comprehend, remember, and apply what you read.

How do you analyze and organize textbook material that is important for an exam, essay, or research paper? In earlier chapters, we discussed how to identify main ideas, supporting details, and writers' organizational patterns. Another vital aspect of the learning process is taking down, in your own words, the important points included in your reading. This involves the ability to organize and present the important information you read in the form of notes, an outline, or a "map" (a graphic form of notetaking). Besides providing you with a concise reference for later study, notetaking, outlining, and mapping also help make reading a process you engage in actively rather than passively.

Summarizing is another reading study skill that serves to engage you actively with the text. A summary, which is a concise statement of main ideas and their supporting details, allows you to check your understanding of material. Like notetaking or mapping, a summary also gives you the opportunity to state important information in your own words and thereby provides you with a tool for studying for tests or doing research.

Another study skill important to your understanding of complex data is the ability to read and interpret information in charts, graphs, and tables. Information discussed over several pages may be summarized concisely in graphic form. Charts, graphs, and tables can often serve to clarify, illustrate, or elaborate information presented in a text.

Finally, one last skill that is crucial to your success on assignments, exams, projects, or papers is your ability to follow written instructions. To master this skill, you must read carefully and pay special attention to detail and order. As is true for other reading skills, you can improve this skill with practice.

This chapter will provide you with guidelines for organizing written materials for study purposes (by taking notes, outlining, mapping, summarizing), interpreting information presented in graphic form, and following written instructions.

Notetaking, Outlining, and Mapping

In college, simply reading your assigned texts does not guarantee success. To do well on exams and papers, and to be able to understand and use what you read, you need to take notes in addition to reading. As you take notes, you are reinforcing the main ideas in your reading, and you are compressing the information you read into manageable form. Your notes then become a handy study tool. Notes may take one of several forms: list notes, formal outline notes, or "map" (or diagram) notes. By experimenting with alternative methods, you will find the one that works best for you. Whatever method you decide to use, the guidelines for notetaking that are provided below will remain the same.

1. Identify the main idea(s) and supporting details from a selection you have read. For purposes of organization, you may wish to divide the selection into manageable parts, such as chapter subsections.

2. Write down the main ideas in your own words. Be as concise as possible, but be sure to include *all* main ideas, since they are the skeleton of the material.

3. Emphasize the main ideas visually, leaving space for supporting details.

4. Write down important supporting details for each main idea, using your own words and being as concise as possible. Be sure to include details that may be used as examples, since examples frequently demonstrate major concepts and can aid you in understanding and remembering the material. You may also wish to include comments of your own that will help you remember or understand the material.

5. Be selective in recording supporting details. Do not include information that seems irrelevant or unimportant.

6. In general (although you may add comments and examples of your own), attempt to preserve the tone, logic, order, and emphasis of the original selection.

Read the following selection. Then examine the various forms of notes that can be used to organize the information in the selection for study purposes.

Economic Exchange Past and Present

Gold and silver form the basis of our economic system, but they are very rarely used as a medium of exchange in everyday life. Over the last eight centuries, the danger of theft or loss has increasingly discouraged the use of gold and silver coins. The development of banks has provided safer methods of making business transactions. Recent trends in banking have in fact led some observers to conclude that we will eventually live in a "cashless society."

The first substitutes for gold and silver coins were developed in Europe during the Middle Ages. Travelers in those days ran a high risk of highway robbery, so merchants began depositing gold and silver at one bank and receiving a "bill of exchange" that they could redeem at another bank when they arrived at their destination. Paper money, representing a fixed value in gold or silver, was first developed in China in the tenth century A.D. to encourage trade. This practice was later adopted by countries all over the world.

In today's modern banking system, even paper money is being phased out as an everyday medium of exchange. Individuals and businesses pay for most of their purchases, especially large ones, with checks that the seller can redeem for cash, or with credit cards that allow the purchaser to be billed later.

The advent of electronic banking has brought still more dramatic changes in commercial practices: "point of sale" computer terminals can now transfer funds automatically from the account of the buyer to the account of the seller, thus eliminating even the need for checks or credit cards.

List Notes. List notes, such as those below, emphasize main ideas by forming the left margin, while supporting details appear indented under the appropriate main idea. In developing list notes, the specific entries you include may consist of a word, a phrase, or even an entire sentence. You may also find that underlining or highlighting key words and phrases included in your list notes can help you study and remember those points and terms that seem most important. Overall, guidelines for developing list notes are very flexible. Since the purpose of such notes is to help you learn, use whatever works best for you.

Economic Exchange Past and Present

Long-Term Trends in Economic Exchange
    Risk of theft or loss using gold or silver for exchange
    Banks provide safer methods for making business transactions
        Trend toward a "cashless society"

Early Substitutes for Gold and Silver
    Merchants in the Middle Ages used "bills of exchange"
    Paper money developed in China in the 900s

Modern Substitutes for Paper Money
    Checks
        Seller redeems for cash
    Credit cards
        Buyer is billed later
    Automatic transfers
        Computerized
        No need for checks or credit cards

Formal Outline Notes. Formal outline notes differ from list notes in that they use a standard numbering and lettering system. Roman numerals are used to designate the broadest, most encompassing information and ideas, while capital letters, Arabic numerals, and lower-case letters are used to designate progressively less inclusive information and ideas. The numbers and letters in this type of outline can help you focus on both the ordering and the relative importance of ideas presented in written materials.

Economic Exchange Past and Present

I. Long-Term Trends in Economic Exchange
   A. Risks of using gold and silver
      1. theft
      2. loss
   B. Banks provide safer methods for making business transactions

II. Early Substitutes for Gold and Silver
   A. Medieval merchants used "bills of exchange"
      1. deposited money in one city
      2. picked up cash in another city
   B. The Chinese developed paper money (tenth century)
      1. represented a specific amount of gold or silver
      2. encouraged trade throughout China

III. Modern Banking—Substitutes for Paper Money
   A. Checks (seller can redeem for cash)
   B. Credit cards (buyer is billed later)
   C. Automatic transfers
      1. seller's account credited electronically
      2. computerized—no need for checks or credit cards

Map Notes. Map notes are another effective method of highlighting and organizing the information you encounter in written materials. Unlike list notes and outline notes, however, map notes do not take the form of a list. Instead, map notes provide you with a diagram that represents visually the important points in a work and the connections among those points. The major benefit of using map notes is that they can provide more types of information about the various ways the ideas in a selection may relate to one another than either list notes or outline notes can provide. In addition to providing information about the hierarchical structure of ideas (e.g., main ideas versus supporting details), map notes also allow you to represent other types of relationships (e.g., connections *between* two or more main ideas). Diagram notes may be as simple or complex as you wish and may illustrate schematically as many or as few relationships as you wish. As with list notes and outline notes, however, you should attempt to focus your attention on the most important ideas and relationships; otherwise, your map may become so complex and cluttered that its usefulness will be diminished.

Economic Exchange Past and Present

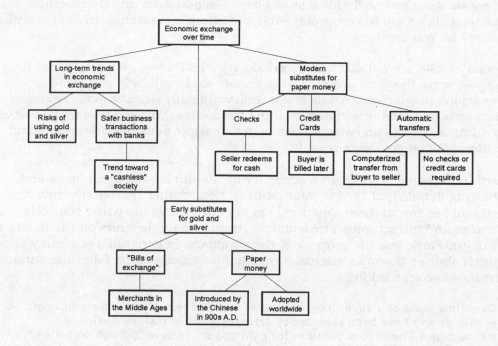

In each form of notetaking, main ideas stand out visually, with supporting details subordinate to them. Formal outline notes, with their standard system of numbering and lettering, are the most structured type of notetaking. This format tends to invite additional detail and to emphasize order. In addition, because you probably organize and plan your own essays by composing an outline, taking notes in a similar format may help provide you with a clearer view of a writer's plan and organization. On the other hand, you may be more comfortable with less formal list notes. This format lends itself to speedy notetaking and depends entirely on visual presentation for organization and subordination rather than on a number and letter sequence as with an outline. The most graphic form of notes, map notes, may suit you best if you have good visual memory and wish to be able to represent graphically a variety of relationships among ideas.

Whichever form works best for you, remember to strive for conciseness, completeness, and accuracy. Succinct notes will encourage more rapid and focused studying.

Summary

Like notes, a summary distills a large body of information into its essential elements. It is an aid in comprehending and retaining material. In short, writing a summary helps you think.

Summary skills are helpful when you take notes for a research paper and later when you write the final draft. Good summary skills will help you avoid unconscious plagiarism, in which you unintentionally use the exact or nearly exact words of a source without crediting the source. You will also make use of your summary skills on essay exams to demonstrate your understanding and retention of what you have read.

As with notetaking, you begin a summary by identifying the main ideas and supporting details included in your reading. Next, rather than presenting a shorthand version of them, rewrite them in your own words using complete sentences and paragraphs. The length of the summary depends on the length of the original work and the purpose of the summary. In general, a summary should be much shorter than the original. Consider, for example, the following summary of the passage on banking.

> Over time, gold and silver have been used less and less often as a medium of exchange and have been replaced by safer methods of making business transactions. The first substitutes for gold and silver were "bills of exchange," which were developed in Europe during the Middle Ages for use by traveling merchants. Then paper money was developed in China during the tenth century and was eventually adopted worldwide. More recently, even paper money has been largely replaced, first by checks and credit cards, then by automatic transfers involving the use of computers.

Interpretation of Information in Graphic Form

We live in an age of "information explosion." Television, newspapers, magazines, and textbooks bombard us with facts and statistics. Much of this information is presented concisely in graphic form so that we can more easily understand, absorb, and use it. Graphs, charts, and tables can confuse you, however, if you do not learn to read them accurately.

By following these steps, you should be able to interpret accurately data presented in charts, graphs, and tables.

1. Read the heading or title to determine the subject.

2. Read the notation that gives the source of information presented.

3. Read all labels, often given in bold print or italics, to decide what all bars, numbers, lines, or figures represent.

4. Pay special attention to numbers. Note particularly whether they indicate, for example, percents, dollars, thousands, or millions.

5. *Think* about the data. How does it relate to the text? Notice especially extremes, trends, and averages. Draw conclusions about the main point being made. Ask yourself what the information means, and ask yourself questions for further study.

Following is a brief passage accompanied by a pie graph. Read the passage, then study the graph.

During the early nineteenth century, most U.S. banks operated under widely varying state controls. They established separate lending rules, extended credit based on their individual decisions, and even issued their own paper currencies. After the Civil War, however, the federal government passed laws designed to bring banking under its control and to establish consistency among banking institutions. The national banks formed by this legislation were the forerunners of today's Federal Reserve System (FRS). Today, we have a mixed system of banking, with the total number of banks, both state and national, shrinking each year. In 1925, U.S. banks totaled 28,479, with 9,538 FRS members and 18,941 nonmembers. As you can see in the graph below, the proportion of member to nonmember institutions did not change a great deal through 1983, but the total number of banks did decrease significantly.

U.S. Banks, According to Membership in the Federal Reserve System (1983)

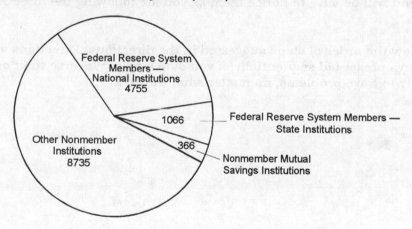

Be sure to follow the steps outlined above as you attempt to interpret this graph. Notice also the important information included in the graph. For example, as of 1983, somewhat over one-third and under one-half of all U.S. banks belonged to the Federal Reserve System. In addition, of the total number of FRS member institutions, national banks outnumbered state banks by a ratio of nearly 5 to 1. After you identify such information, try to connect the data presented in the graph to the information provided in the text. What trends are illustrated? What conclusions can you draw by comparing the text's 1925 data to the graph's 1983 data? Finally, ask some probing questions. For example, why don't more banks belong to the FRS? What changes might updated data reveal?

Following Written Instructions

To assemble a bicycle, run a computer, or make chocolate éclairs, you need to read and follow written directions carefully and accurately. You know that if you leave out the sugar in the éclairs, they will lack flavor, or if you attempt to attach the bicycle handlebars before the stem, you will fail to get the bike on the road. Similarly, if you try to complete a college chemistry lab experiment after a hasty and cursory reading of the directions, you will not get the desired results (and may, in fact, get disastrous results). Likewise, if you dive into an essay exam with only a quick glance at the instructions, you may answer unnecessary questions, spend too much time on certain topics, or write a response that does not address the question asked. To make sure you follow written directions accurately, consider the following.

1. Pay attention to the directions. No matter how familiar you think you are with a task or subject, you may have something to learn.

2. Read directions *completely* before beginning the task or project.

3. Read directions *carefully*. Do not skip over sections or read hastily, either because you assume you know the content or because you feel pressed for time. Accurate reading may well save you time.

4. Before you begin the task or project, underline or circle key instruction words so you will be sure to notice them as you are following the directions step by step.

5. Follow the order of steps suggested in the directions. Directions are nearly always presented sequentially; if you skip steps or reverse their order, you are likely to have problems, no matter what the task.

Practice Exercises

The following exercises will help you review the skills covered in this chapter. Many of the types of questions presented here will be similar to those on the test; others will not. Remember that the purpose of the exercises is to give you practice on the skills rather than merely to prepare you for the test. Following these exercises are the Practice Exercise Explanations. They explain each question, the correct answer, and why the remaining choices are incorrect.

A woman drifts pleasantly in her mind as she sits quietly reciting a phrase; a young child tosses in his crib, moaning and whimpering; an air traffic controller focuses complete attention on the screens before her; you lie motionless in bed and awaken, convinced you have had a dreamless night. All these states represent phases in the wide spectrum between total alertness and coma. Scientists have long focused attention on these states of consciousness, particularly the different levels of sleep. Though many questions about sleep remain unanswered, modern medical technology has provided numerous tools, such as the electroencephalogram (EEG) and magnetic resonance imaging (MRI), to aid scientists in analyzing states of sleep. Researchers have shown particular interest in learning what happens to our brains and bodies when we fall asleep and whether all sleep is the same.

What they have found is that there are two major states of sleep. During slow-wave sleep, also known as non-rapid eye movement sleep (non-REM sleep), we receive very little data from our sensory centers, and our brains rest at "idle." In this phase, which makes up approximately 80 percent of our sleep time, we rest quietly and show little movement. Scientists have concluded that dreams do not occur during this sleep phase.

The other major state of sleep is referred to as rapid eye movement sleep (REM sleep), which accounts for the remaining 20 percent of sleep. REM sleep differs from non-REM sleep in several ways. First, the sleeper's brain waves show activity much like that associated with a waking state. Second, the sleeper is much more active, twitching fingers, moving the eyes rapidly beneath the lids, and even exhibiting a higher rate of respiration. Finally, we dream during this phase. Even if you think you do not dream often, studies have demonstrated that we all experience dreaming about 20 percent of the time we are sleeping. We shift back and forth during the night between non-REM and REM sleep and will only recall dreams if we wake during the REM phase. Thus, if you think you never dream, you must rarely wake during the dream state.

1. Which of the following outlines best organizes the material from the selection?

    A. I.   People experiencing different states of consciousness
        II. Questions scientists have about sleep and conscious states
        III. Types of sleep

    B. I.   Different states of sleep
        II. Different types of dreams

    C. I.   Sleep research: questions and methods
        II. Characteristics of non-REM vs. REM sleep
        III. Dreaming and different states of sleep

    D. I.   EEG and MRI technology
        II. Brain-wave activity during REM and non-REM sleep

2. Which of the following would provide the most accurate and complete set of study notes to prepare for a quiz on the information presented in the second and third paragraphs of the selection?

    A. Non-REM sleep
        —slow-wave sleep
        —brain rests at "idle"
        —sleeper is active
        REM sleep
        —differs from non-REM sleep
        —accounts for 20% of sleep time
        —sleeper shows little movement

    B. Non-REM sleep
        —makes up about 80% of sleep time
        —sensory centers receive little data
        —absence of dreams
        REM sleep
        —brain waves show activity
        —eye movement and increased respiration
        —occurrence of dreams

    C. Non-REM sleep
        —sleeper rests quietly
        —makes up 20% of sleep time
        —little data received from sensory centers
        REM sleep
        —brain waves slow
        —similar to waking state
        —eye and finger movement

    D. Non-REM sleep
        —sensory centers are inactive
        —sleeper shows little movement
        —dreaming occurs
        REM sleep
        —high activity level
        —rapid eye movements
        —shifting back and forth

To print a document with the FLEXTECH Word Processing System, follow the charted directions below. Notice that you have two print paths to choose from as a time-saving feature. Pay special attention to repeat loops and help messages.

1. *Turn on printer.*
Locate the on/off switch in the left rear
and move it to the UP position. A red
light will appear in the lower
right-front corner of printer.

2. *Thread paper to printer.*
Run paper from the box to fit the spokes
on the feeder roll, being careful
to maintain evenness.

3. *Turn on video display screen.*
Press the green button in the lower
right corner of the screen.

4. *Turn on computer.*
Press the blue button in the lower
right corner of the machine.
Order is important. If you turn on
the machines in the improper order,
a WARNING signal will flash on the
screen. At the sign of a WARNING, hit
the *cancel/command* key, turn the machines
off, and return to step 3.

5. *Call up FLEXTECH program.*
A flashing cursor will appear in the
upper left of the screen, immediately
below the current date and time.
Type: FLEXTECH./ADA.

6. *Print with special format.* Next to FUNCTION, type: PRINT/FORMAT2.

7. *Select special format.* To print with double spacing, type: SSF next to the format type you want and press the *execute* key. If you make an error, hit the *cancel* and *home* keys simultaneously and return to step 5.

8. Go to step 7 of the "print standard" path.

6. *Print standard.* Next to FUNCTION, type: PRINT/STAND.

7. *Begin print run.* Next to PROCESS, type: RUN/FULL1. This will produce one copy of your document. If you want multiple copies, simply change the number at end of command line.*

8. *Print end.* When the print run is complete, wait for one minute before rolling the sheet to the break point.

*To stop the print process after step 7 in the "print standard" path, strike the PROLOCK key twice. Then, return to step 5.

3. According to information provided in the selection, which of the following steps should one take before choosing to print a document in either standard or special format?

    A. Strike the PROLOCK key twice.

    B. Turn off the red light on the printer.

    C. Type FLEXTECH./ADA.

    D. Type PRINT/FORMAT2 next to FUNCTION.

4. According to information provided in the selection, what should one do after making a mistake in the "special format" path?

    A. Disconnect the paper from the spokes on the feeder roll.

    B. Strike the cancel/command key and return to step 3.

    C. Wait for the WARNING signal to appear.

    D. Strike the cancel and home keys simultaneously and return to step 5.

Both marriage and divorce rates in the United States have increased in the twentieth century, though divorce rates have grown far more rapidly. In 1890, for example, the marriage rate stood at 9.0 per 1000 people and the divorce rate at only 0.5 per 1000. In 1983, the marriage rate was 10.5 per 1000 (only a slight increase over 1890), but the divorce rate had risen to 5.0 per 1000. Among the major reasons cited to explain the latter trend are changes in social attitudes, economic conditions, and divorce laws.

In the early twentieth century, family life represented the backbone of U.S. culture, and marriages tended to endure despite problems. People stayed together "for better or for worse," while the few who ended their marriages suffered considerable ostracism. During the course of the century, however, divorce has become more socially acceptable as people have begun to expect more of marriage and have become less willing to preserve marriages that failed to meet these expectations. At the same time, increased economic opportunities have made women less dependent financially on men, and relaxed divorce laws have made it easier to end a marriage.

Social disruptions, particularly wars, also precipitated great increases in divorce during the twentieth century. As the graph indicates, the number of divorces rose from 1915–1920, 1940–1945, and 1965–1975, the approximate time frames of World War I, World War II, and the Vietnam War. This is not especially surprising, given war's tendency to separate young married couples for long stretches of time and the general loosening of moral standards that has been known to occur during such periods.

In recent years, sociologists have noted a change in the above trends. Since the early 1980s, both the marriage and divorce rates have begun to level off somewhat, and there has even been a small decline in the number of divorces. It is much too early, however, to determine the significance of these changes: whether they represent a temporary departure from long-term trends or mark the beginning of a new phase in the history of marital relations.

Marriages and Divorces in the U.S.: 1890-1983
(numbers expressed in thousands)

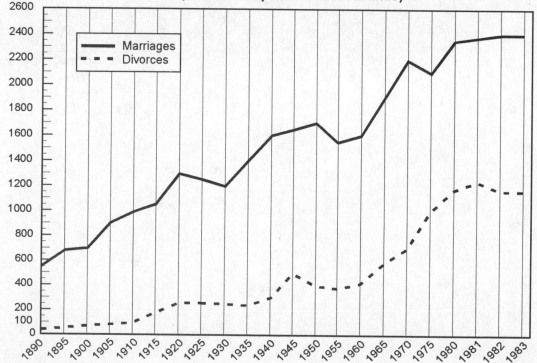

5. According to the graph, the number of divorces reached its peak in which of the following years?

   A. 1920

   B. 1945

   C. 1965

   D. 1981

6. According to the graph, during which of the following periods did the number of marriages per year undergo the greatest decline?

   A. 1920–1930

   B. 1940–1950

   C. 1960–1970

   D. 1970–1980

7. Which of the following maps best organizes the information in this selection?

A.

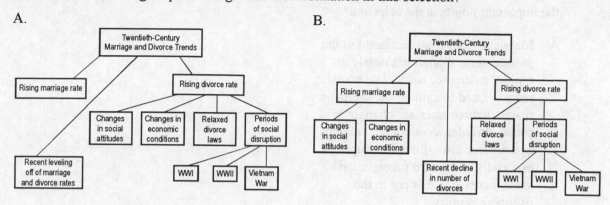

B.

C.

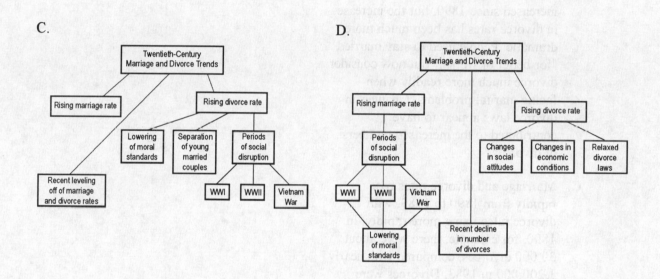

D.

8. Which of the following best summarizes
    the important points in the selection?

    A. Marriage rates have increased in the
        past century, though not nearly as
        rapidly as divorce rates. The main
        reasons cited to explain the dramatic
        rise in divorce rates are changes in
        social attitudes, economic conditions,
        and divorce laws. Social disruptions,
        especially wars, also precipitated a
        great increase in divorce in the
        twentieth century.

    B. Both marriage and divorce rates have
        increased since 1890, but the increase
        in divorce rates has been much more
        dramatic. People used to stay married
        "for better or worse," but now consider
        divorce much more readily when
        facing marital problems. Changes in
        divorce laws appear to have
        contributed to the increased numbers
        of divorces.

    C. Marriage and divorce rates rose
        rapidly from 1890 to 1983, with
        divorce rates rising more rapidly. In
        1890, for example, there were about
        30,000 divorces, compared with nearly
        1,200,000 in 1983. Divorces were
        especially common during the Vietnam
        War, when the numbers increased from
        approximately 400,000 per year to
        1,000,000 per year.

    D. Marriage and divorce rates have risen
        significantly in the past century.
        Sociologists speculate that people used
        to stay married even if they were not
        happy. Cultural tradition and societal
        pressure discouraged divorce in the
        nineteenth and early twentieth
        centuries.

Practice Exercise Explanations

1. **Correct Response: C.** Of the response options provided, only choice C represents a complete and accurate outline of the major themes presented in the selection. By comparison, choices A and D not only place too much emphasis on less relevant information, but also neglect to note the writer's main concern in the selection: the relationship between dreaming and different states of sleep. Although choice B correctly focuses on the selection's main topics (i.e., sleep and dreams), it does so in a misleading fashion, since at no point in the selection does the writer examine different types of dreams.

2. **Correct Response: B.** Choice B is the best response because it represents the most complete, accurate, and logical listing of pertinent details presented in the second and third paragraphs of the selection. By comparison, choices A, C, and D each contain at least two pieces of inaccurate information. In addition, choices A and C fail even to mention the writer's main point in the two paragraphs, that dreams occur only during REM sleep. Choice D does mention dreaming, but erroneously notes that dreaming occurs during non-REM sleep.

3. **Correct Response: C.** This question assesses the ability to understand and follow written directions. According to the instructions presented in the selection, it is necessary in step 5 to call up the FLEXTECH program by typing "FLEXTECH./ADA." (choice C) before moving on to step 6 and printing a document in either standard or special format. Of the other responses provided, the step listed in choice A is used to stop the print process in standard format, and the step described in choice D is needed only for printing in special format. Concerning choice B, the selection suggests that it is necessary to turn the printer off to extinguish the red light in its lower right corner, a step that would make it impossible to print in either format.

4. **Correct Response: D.** Step 7 in the special format column instructs users to hit the cancel and home keys simultaneously and to return to step 5 if they make an error. Therefore, choice D is the correct response. Of the other responses provided, at no point in the selection are users directed to disconnect paper from the feeder roll (choice A), while choices B and C relate to what happens and should be done when the machines are turned on in the improper order.

5. **Correct Response: D.** This question requires the interpretation of a line graph that provides information about the number of divorces occurring annually in the United States for the period between 1890 and 1983. Choice D is the correct response because the graph indicates that the number of divorces peaked in 1981 (with approximately 1,200,000 divorces occurring in that year), before declining slightly in more recent years. Although the number of divorces rose in the years immediately preceding 1920 (choice A) and 1945 (choice B), the total number of divorces in each of those years was considerably less than in 1981. Concerning choice C, the number of divorces in 1965 was only slightly greater than in 1945.

6. **Correct Response: A.** Of the response options provided, choice A represents the only time period during which the number of marriages per year actually decreased. The graph indicates that the number of marriages occurring annually declined between 1920 and 1930 from slightly more to slightly less than 1,250,000 per year. On the other hand, the graph indicates that from 1940 to 1950 (choice B) and from 1960 to 1970 (choice C), the number of marriages per year increased steadily. Concerning choice D, although the number of marriages per year declined between 1970 and 1975, this trend was more than compensated for by a substantial increase in the number of marriages occurring annually between 1975 and 1980.

7. **Correct Response: A.** Of the response options provided, only choice A represents an accurate, complete, and logical way to organize the main points presented in the selection. Of the other responses provided, choices B and D reflect a misinterpretation of the writer's argument, since no effort is made at any point in the selection to explain the rising number of marriages. Choice C, meanwhile, not only fails to list a number of the most important reasons for the increase in divorce, but also presents an illogical organization of information that appears in the selection.

8. **Correct Response: A.** Choice A is the most complete and accurate summary of the main points presented in this selection. Although choices B, C, and D all contain facts and conclusions that are accurate and support the writer's argument, they focus largely on less important details. At the same time, they all fail to list the most significant causes of the increase in divorce, which is the main theme of the selection.

Study Ideas

1. When taking notes on a reading selection, be sure to identify the main ideas and the most important supporting details. Visually distinguish main ideas from details by using an outline, map notes, or list notes.

2. A good summary, like notes, will contain information essential to the selection. Write a summary by rewriting a selection's main ideas concisely and in your own words.

3. To interpret information presented graphically, be sure to read and understand all headings, labels, and numbers.

4. When following written instructions, read the directions completely and carefully before beginning the task. The steps in a set of directions are usually presented sequentially, so pay particular attention to the suggested order.

Study References: Reading

These references for further study were suggested by members of the TASP Content Advisory Committee in Reading, the TASP Bias Review Panel, and the Remediation Subcommittee of the Texas Academic Skills Council.

Particular references are included because they relate to the TASP skills and are appropriate for college students. The titles listed here may also be available in learning centers and through developmental education programs on your campus.

Arnaudet, M. L., & Barret, M. E. *Approaches to Academic Reading and Writing.* Englewood Cliffs, NJ: Prentice Hall, 1984.

Avery, L. A., et al. *Read On!* Dubuque, IA: Kendall/Hunt Publishing Co., 1988.

Bromberg, M., & Gordon, M. *Words You Need to Know.* Hauppauge, NY: Barron's Educational Series, 1987.

Cortina, J., Elder, J., & Gonnet, K. *Comprehending College Textbooks.* New York: McGraw-Hill Inc., 1989.

DeVillez, R. *Step-by-Step: College Writing* (3rd ed.). Dubuque, IA: Kendall/Hunt Publishing Co., 1987.

Fry, E. *Reading Drills for Speed and Comprehension* (Advanced Level). Providence, RI: Jamestown Publishers, Inc., 1975.

Giroux, J. A. *Drawing a Conclusion* (Advanced Level). Providence, RI: Jamestown Publishers, Inc., 1974.

Giroux, J. A., & Williston, G. R. *Making an Inference* (Advanced Level). Providence, RI: Jamestown Publishers, Inc., 1978.

Giroux, J. A., & Williston, G. R. *Retaining Concepts and Organizing Facts* (Advanced Level). Providence, RI: Jamestown Publishers, Inc., 1974.

Giroux, J. A., & Williston, G. R. *Understanding the Main Idea* (Advanced Level). Providence, RI: Jamestown Publishers, Inc., 1974.

Griffith, K. J. *Writing Essays About Literature: A Guide and Style Sheet.* New York: Harcourt Brace Jovanovich, 1982.

Hawkins, M., et al. *The English Program.* Dubuque, IA: Kendall/Hunt Publishing Co., 1986.

Hawkins, M., et al. *Teacher's Manual: The English Program.* Dubuque, IA: Kendall/Hunt Publishing Co., 1986.

Maker, J., & Lenier, Minnette. *College Reading.* Belmont, CA: Wadsworth, 1986.

Morris, H. F. *Word Clues Level L.* Columbia, SC: EDL, 1979.

Porter, T., Kneupper, C., & Reeder, H. *The Literate Mind: Reading, Writing, Critical Thinking.* Dubuque, IA: Kendall/Hunt Publishing Co., 1987.

Sack, A., & Yourman, J. *One Hundred Passages to Develop Reading Comprehension.* Baltimore, MD: College Skills Center, 1983.

Seyler, D. *Read, Reason, Write.* New York: Random House, 1986.

Soteriou, P. E. *Integrating College Study Skills: Reasoning in Reading, Listening, and Writing.* Belmont, CA: Wadsworth, 1984.

Whimbey, A. *Analytical Reading and Reasoning*. Stamford, CT: Innovative Sciences, Inc., 1983.

Whimbey, A. *Mastering Reading Through Reasoning*. Stamford, CT: Innovative Sciences, Inc., 1985.

Wiener, H. S., & Bazerman, C. *Basic Reading Skills Handbook*. Dallas: Houghton Mifflin, 1988.

Wood, N. V. *College Reading and Study Skills*. New York: Holt, Rinehart & Winston, 1986.

Wood, N. V. *Improving Reading*. New York: Holt, Rinehart & Winston, 1984.

SECTION III

Mathematics Skills Review

Introduction

Familiarity with basic mathematical procedures and thinking is increasingly important for success in college. More and more areas of study include mathematics among their requirements, and college core curriculum requirements often include courses for which mathematics is needed.

Organization of This Section

This section of *The Official TASP® Test Study Guide* includes twelve chapters: one background chapter in which fundamentals of mathematics are reviewed and eleven chapters that discuss the eleven skills covered on the TASP Test. The TASP mathematics skills are grouped into four subsections: Fundamental Mathematics, Algebra, Geometry, and Problem Solving. As mentioned in the introductory chapters, there are several ways you can begin working with these materials. You may wish to start with the Quick Pre-Test to get a general sense of your strengths and weaknesses in the mathematical skills covered in this section.

Fundamental Mathematics. After an introductory chapter in which we review basic computational skills and concepts, the next chapter covers word problems involving integers, fractions, decimals and percents, and ratios and proportions. In addition, the use of units of measurement and conversions of such units in problem solving are also discussed, including the use of scientific notation for very large or very small numbers.

Another topic covered in this section is data interpretation and analysis. This topic includes the interpretation of information from line graphs, bar graphs, pictographs, pie charts, and tables. In addition, another important aspect of data analysis is covered: the use and interpretation of measures of central tendency (i.e., averages) and the concept of variability of data.

Much numerical information in college and beyond is summarized in terms of averages or presented in visual form through graphs or charts. Being able to understand, interpret, and evaluate such information accurately is important to your success in college.

Algebra. Algebra is the fundamental language of mathematics; it provides a way of expressing relationships among quantities. This subsection discusses five skills. One chapter deals with graphing numbers and number relationships, including equations, inequalities, and functions. The next two chapters involve solving one- and two-variable equations and systems of equations and solving word problems based on such equations. Many problems that you will encounter in college and beyond take the form of one- and two-variable equations.

Next is a chapter that discusses operations with algebraic expressions and functional notation. Techniques for factoring and simplifying polynomial, rational, and radical expressions are covered, as are procedures for performing mathematical operations involving such expressions. The final chapter in the Algebra section covers graphing and solving quadratic equations and inequalities.

In all these chapters, we have tried to present a step-by-step approach for understanding the content and we include many examples.

Geometry. The two chapters in the Geometry section cover problems involving two-dimensional and three-dimensional figures and the geometric concepts of similarity, congruence, parallelism, and perpendicularity. Many of the problems discussed in this section may seem familiar to you. Application problems involving geometric figures and concepts are among the most common in mathematics and, in fact, in everyday life.

Problem Solving. This section includes a chapter that reviews a number of reasoning skills that underlie much mathematical thinking, discussing the use of inductive and deductive reasoning to draw valid conclusions. Again, we present general principles and illustrate them by example. Finally, the last chapter deals with the realistic situation in which problems involving the use of more than one isolated mathematical skill are presented. This chapter provides some practice in putting together and using several of the skills that were covered in the rest of the Mathematics section of the Study Guide.

The purpose of this guide is to provide instruction in the skills necessary for success in college. Hence, we are providing broader coverage of topics than the test alone may include. Also, some of the practice exercises are in a format and at a level of difficulty different from what you may find on the TASP Test.

Mathematics Translations

Many mathematical expressions are presented in English. You have to be able to translate these English expressions into mathematical statements. This is particularly true in word problems, where you often encounter statements such as "John is three years older than Mary" or "If we cut two feet off a board. . . ." The table below presents several of the more common translations.

Mathematical Expression	English Statement
$=$	is, are, was, were, has, have, cost, costs
$x + y$ or $y + x$	the sum of x more than y, y more than x, x added to y, y added to x, x greater than y, y greater than x, x increased by y, y increased by x
$x - y$	y less than x, the difference between x and y, x decreased by y
$y - x$	x less than y, the difference between y and x, y decreased by x
xy or yx	the product of x and y, x multiplied by y, y multiplied by x, x times y, y times x
$\dfrac{x}{y}$ or x/y or $x \div y$	x divided by y, the quotient of x and y
$\dfrac{x}{100}$	x percent
x^2	x squared, x to the second power, x times itself

Sometimes expressions involve more than one of these statements. Here are some examples.

$\dfrac{x}{(y + z)}$ or $x \div (y + z)$	x divided by the sum of y and z
$x(y - z)$	x multiplied by the difference of y and z
$\dfrac{x}{100}(y - z)$	x percent of the difference between y and z

$x^2 - y$ y less than x times itself

$\frac{y}{x}(100)$ percent increase if x increases by y

$\frac{y}{x}(100)$ percent decrease if x decreases by y

$y + \frac{x}{100}(y)$ x percent greater than y

$y - \frac{x}{100}(y)$ x percent less than y

There are many other statements, but these are some of the most common.

Chapter 10

MATHEMATICS FUNDAMENTALS

This chapter describes fundamental principles, concepts, and operations of mathematics, including adding, subtracting, multiplying, and dividing fractions, decimals, and integers; using the order of operations to solve problems; solving problems involving percents; performing calculations involving exponents and scientific notation; estimating solutions to problems; and using the concepts of "less than" and "greater than."

Introduction

Most problems that we try to solve on a day-to-day basis involve some sort of operation with numbers. Depending on the problem, the operation required could include addition, subtraction, multiplication, or division; and the numbers involved could include fractions, decimals, integers, or percents. More sophisticated problems might require the use of scientific notation and exponents. Sometimes the most useful answer to a problem can be found by estimating or rounding numbers before performing operations. This chapter covers the fundamental concepts of numbers and the fundamental computation skills that are the basis of almost all mathematical problems. The concepts discussed in this chapter may not be tested directly on the TASP test, but they are required for understanding the skills that are tested on the TASP test and for solving the problems on the test that relate to those skills.

Basic Concepts

1. Numbers. We use numbers to describe the quantity of things around us. Numbers can be used to describe how many plates are on the table and how many spoons are next to each plate. When combined with units of measurement such as feet, pounds, and gallons, numbers can be used to describe something's size, weight, volume, or other such measurable characteristics. Numbers also have meaning on their own. When we say that 8 is greater than 3, we mean that the number 8 represents a larger quantity than the number 3, regardless of whether we are talking about cars, hats, or gallons of milk.

2. Signed numbers, absolute value, and the number line. The most familiar numbers are the numbers used in counting (1, 2, 3, 4, etc.). These numbers are called the natural numbers and can be represented in picture form on a number line.

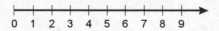

On this number line, numbers are represented by distances from the left end of the line. The left end represents zero, which is not one of the natural numbers, and is called the origin.

Notice that if you begin at the origin (zero point) and slowly move to the right, the numbers get larger. Notice also that the numbers are evenly spaced along the number line. This means that the difference in size or magnitude between the numbers 1 and 2 is the same as the difference between the numbers 2 and 3, which is the same as the difference between the numbers 3 and 4, and so on for as far as we care to extend the number line. The arrow at the end of the line indicates that we could extend this number line forever without running out of counting numbers.

If you move to the left, toward the origin, the numbers get smaller until you reach the origin. But what happens if you keep moving to the left of the origin?

Numbers less than zero are called negative numbers. Numbers greater than zero (including the familiar counting numbers) are called positive numbers. For every positive number there is a corresponding negative number. To understand what this means, the number line is extended to the left of the origin.

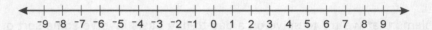

The numbers to the left of the origin are called negative numbers. Mathematicians indicate that a number is a negative number by placing a short horizontal line (–) to the left of it. Negative four is written ⁻4. A positive number is often indicated by a small + to the left of it, though this is not always necessary. For instance, the page numbers in this book are positive numbers, but nobody is confused by the fact that the + sign has been omitted. Numbers that have either a + or a – sign in front of them are called signed numbers.

What does a negative number mean? One way to think of a negative number (though not the only way) is as a number that has the same size or magnitude as its positive counterpart, but a different direction. A person who has 5 dollars might represent this amount by writing ⁺$5.00. A person who owes 5 dollars might represent this amount by writing ⁻$5.00. Both numbers represent the same size or magnitude (5), but in the first case the 5 represents an amount of money more than zero, and in the second case the 5 represents an amount of money less than zero.

Another example of negative numbers is the system used by astronauts and space scientists during a space launch. The time 2 seconds after launch is called ⁺2 seconds. The time 2 seconds before launch is called ⁻2 seconds. Each of these times is 2 seconds away from launch (that is, they have the same size or magnitude), but one represents 2 seconds before launch, and the other represents 2 seconds after launch.

The numerical part of a signed number, called its absolute value, represents magnitude or a distance from the origin of a number line. The absolute value of a number is indicated by two vertical lines around the number. Study the three examples below.

1. The absolute value of negative 4 is written |⁻4| and is 4, since ⁻4 is four units from zero.

2. The absolute value of positive 5 is written |⁺5| and is 5, since ⁺5 is five units from zero.

3. The absolute value of zero is written |0| and is 0, since there is no distance between 0 and itself.

The natural numbers along with their negatives and zero are called the integers (. . . , ⁻3, ⁻2, ⁻1, 0, 1, 2, 3, . . .). The dots before and after the integers indicate that this list can be extended in either direction. This is also indicated by the arrows at either end of the number line.

3. Fractions. A fraction is a way of representing a part of a whole or a part of a group. The number $\frac{1}{4}$ is an example of a fraction. The number above the line (1) is called the numerator, and the number below the line (4) is called the denominator. Another way to write this number is ¼. This fraction represents 1 of 4 equal pieces. When a pie is cut into 4 equal pieces, each piece is $\frac{1}{4}$ of the pie. The denominator indicates how many pieces make up the whole (in this case, 4), and the numerator indicates how many of these pieces are being represented by the fraction (in this case, 1). If the pie were cut into 5 pieces, each piece would be $\frac{1}{5}$ of the pie. Three pieces would be $\frac{3}{5}$ of the pie.

Mixed numbers are numbers that consist of both a whole number and a fraction (e.g., $3\frac{1}{2}$, $5\frac{3}{4}$, $10\frac{2}{3}$). Mixed numbers can be changed to fractions by multiplying the whole number by the fraction's denominator, adding that number to the fraction's numerator, and placing that number over the fraction's denominator.

   Convert $3\frac{1}{2}$ to a fraction.

   $3 \times 2 = 6$ *Multiply the whole number by the fraction's denominator.*

   $6 + 1 = 7$ *Add the result to the fraction's numerator.*

   $\frac{7}{2}$ *Place the result over the fraction's denominator.*

A fraction such as $\frac{7}{2}$, in which the numerator is larger than the denominator, is called an improper fraction.

Sometimes it is useful to be able to express fractions in more than one way. Multiplying or dividing both the numerator and the denominator of a fraction by the same number does not change the value of the fraction. For instance, both the numerator and the denominator of $\frac{1}{2}$ can be multiplied by 4 to produce the fraction $\frac{4}{8}$. Since both the numerator and the denominator of $\frac{1}{2}$ were multiplied by the same number (4), $\frac{1}{2}$ is equal to $\frac{4}{8}$. Similarly, the numerator and the denominator of $\frac{2}{4}$ can be divided by 2. When the numerator and the denominator of $\frac{2}{4}$ are divided by 2, the fraction $\frac{2}{4}$ becomes $\frac{1}{2}$. The fraction $\frac{2}{4}$ is equal to the fraction $\frac{1}{2}$. This means that taking one piece from a pie that is sliced into 2 equal pieces is the same as taking 2 pieces from a pie that is sliced into 4 equal pieces. A fraction that is in its simplest form (its numerator and its denominator cannot be divided by the same number; e.g., $\frac{1}{2}$, $\frac{3}{5}$, $\frac{8}{9}$) is said to be reduced to its lowest terms.

After converting a fraction to another form, a simple way to check your work is to cross-multiply. When two fractions are equal, the numerator of the first fraction multiplied by the denominator of the second fraction is equal to the numerator of the second fraction multiplied by the denominator of the first fraction.

Cross-multiply to verify that $\frac{1}{2}$ equals $\frac{4}{8}$.

$\frac{1}{2} = \frac{4}{8}$ $1 \times 8 = 8$ *Multiply numerator of first fraction by denominator of second fraction.*

$\frac{1}{2} = \frac{4}{8}$ $4 \times 2 = 8$ *Multiply numerator of second fraction by denominator of first fraction.*

Since the two products are equal (8 = 8), the two fractions are equal.

4. Decimals. A decimal is another way of representing a part of a whole. The number 3.576 is an example of a decimal. The value of this number can be determined by using the following illustration, which shows the place value of each position to the right of the decimal point.

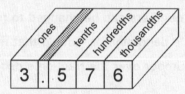

The position immediately to the right of the decimal point represents tenths, the next position to the right represents hundredths, the next position represents thousandths, and so on. As we continue to move to the right, each position represents one tenth of the position to its left. In the number 3.576, the number farthest to the right of the decimal point is in the thousandths position. Therefore, the number 3.576 equals $3\frac{576}{1000}$. Similarly, the number 1.28 equals $1\frac{28}{100}$, and the number 4.3 equals $4\frac{3}{10}$.

Fractions can be converted to decimals by dividing the numerator by the denominator. For instance, to convert $\frac{3}{4}$ to a decimal, divide 3 by 4. The result is 0.75. To convert the fraction $\frac{1}{3}$ to a decimal, divide 1 by 3. The result is 0.33333 . . . . The dots after the threes indicate that the threes will continue to repeat for as long as we are willing to keep dividing.

5. Percents. The symbol % represents percents. There are many situations in which percents are commonly used. You may receive a score of 85% on a math test, or you may hear that 45% of the people responding to a survey favor a particular candidate. A percent is a number that represents hundredths. The number 85% equals $\frac{85}{100}$, or 0.85. The number 45% equals $\frac{45}{100}$, or 0.45.

6. Exponents. An exponent describes the number of times some number (called the base) is to be used in multiplication. For example, $(2)^3 = (2)(2)(2) = 8$. The rules governing signed numbers raised to a power are the same as those for multiplication. When raising a positive base to any whole number power, just perform the successive multiplications to produce the result. When raising a negative base to a whole number power, the first step is to perform successive multiplications of absolute values to produce the numerical result. Then, if the power is odd, the sign of the result is negative; otherwise it is positive.

Calculate.
$(^-2)^4$

$(^-2)^4$	*The base is $(^-2)$. The exponent is 4.*
$(^-2)^4 = (^-2)(^-2)(^-2)(^-2)$	*Multiply the base 4 times.*
$(^-2)(^-2)(^-2)(^-2) = {}^+16$	*The exponent 4 is even; the result is positive.*

Calculate.
$(^-2)^3$

$(^-2)^3$	*The base is $(^-2)$. The exponent is 3.*
$(^-2)^3 = (^-2)(^-2)(^-2)$	*Multiply the base 3 times.*
$(^-2)(^-2)(^-2) = {}^-8$	*The exponent 3 is odd; the result is negative.*

7. Using variables to represent numbers. Mathematicians sometimes use letters to represent numbers. For instance, $x = 5 + 3$ means that some number (x) is equal to the sum of 5 and 3. The letter x in this case is called a variable since it stands for a number. The expression $1 + B = 3$ also contains a variable: the letter B. In this case, the variable B stands for the number 2, since only the number 2 can replace B and make the equation true. Later we will look at some ways of determining the value of variables in equations.

Operations with Signed Numbers

1. Operation signs and number signs. In order to evaluate an expression containing signed numbers, we must first learn to tell the difference between the operation signs and the number signs. You can recognize a number sign by the fact that it has no number immediately to its left. An operation sign will have a number to its left. The symbols + and – actually have two different meanings depending on whether they refer to operations (addition and subtraction) or to numbers (positive and negative).

In the expression $(^+3) + (^-4) - (^+2)$, there are five signs. The + sign before the 3 is a number sign, since there is no number to its left, and the number is read as positive three. The next + sign represents the operation of addition, since the number $^+3$ is to its left. The next sign refers to the 4 and is a number sign; therefore, it is read as negative four. The next – sign represents the operation of subtraction, since the number $^-4$ is to its left. The complete expression is read positive three, plus negative four, minus positive two. Remember that the words positive and negative refer to number signs while plus and minus refer to operations.

Identify each sign in the following expression.

$^-3 + 5 - 6$ *The first sign is a number sign, since there is no number to its left. The number is read "negative 3."*
The second sign is an operation sign, since the number $^-3$ is to its left; this sign indicates the operation of addition.
The last sign is an operation sign, since the number 5 is to its left; this sign indicates the operation of subtraction.

In the previous example there are no number signs associated with the 5 or the 6. When this occurs, the numbers are assumed to be positive. In fact, the expression could be written as $(^-3) + (^+5) - (^+6)$. This is a standard form for an expression containing signed numbers. Every number can have an associated sign and can be placed inside parentheses. All operations should be placed between the numbers. The first step in working with an expression is to rewrite it in standard form. Here is an example.

Expression	Standard Form
$6 - 3 + (^-4) + 2$	$(^+6) - (^+3) + (^-4) + (^+2)$
$^-5 - 6 + 2 + (^-2)$	$(^-5) - (^+6) + (^+2) + (^-2)$

2. Addition and subtraction of signed numbers. Performing operations with signed numbers involves remembering a few simple rules.

Rule 1: To add numbers that have the same sign, add their absolute values and place their common sign on the result.

Add.
$(^-3) + (^-4)$

$|-3| + |-4| = 3 + 4 = 7$ *Add absolute values.*
$^-7$ *Common sign is negative; answer is negative.*

Add.
$(^+4) + (^+5)$

$|^+4| + |^+5| = 4 + 5 = 9$ *Add absolute values.*
$^+9$ *Common sign is positive; answer is positive.*

Add.
$^-3 + (^-4) + (^-8)$

$|-3| + |-4| + |-8| = 3 + 4 + 8 = 15$ *Add absolute values.*
$^-15$ *Common sign is negative; answer is negative.*

Rule 2: To add two numbers that have unlike signs, first subtract the smaller absolute value from the larger absolute value. Place the sign associated with the larger absolute value on the result.

Add.
$(^-5) + (^+8)$

$|^+8| - |^-5| = 8 - 5 = 3$ *Subtract smaller absolute value from larger absolute value.*
$^+3$ *Sign associated with larger absolute value is positive.*

Add.
$6 + (^-10)$

$(^+6) + (^-10)$ *Convert to standard form.*
$|-10| - |^+6| = 10 - 6 = 4$ *Subtract smaller absolute value from larger absolute value.*
$^-4$ *Sign associated with larger absolute value is negative.*

Rule 3: To subtract signed numbers, change all operations of subtraction to addition, change the sign of the number immediately following the changed operation sign, and then proceed as in addition.

Subtract.
($^-$3) – ($^-$4)

($^-$3) + ($^+$4)   *Change from subtraction to addition. Change the sign of the number following the operation sign. Notice that this conversion always involves both a change in operation and a change in number sign.*

$|^+4| - |^-3| = 4 - 3 = 1$ *Subtract smaller absolute value from larger absolute value.*

$^+1$ *Sign associated with larger absolute value is positive.*

Subtract.
$^-$5 – 4

($^-$5) + ($^-$4)   *Change from subtraction to addition, and change the sign of the number following the operation sign.*

$|^-5| + |^-4| = 5 + 4 = 9$ *Add absolute values.*

$^-9$ *Common sign is negative; answer is negative.*

To simplify an expression involving more than two signed numbers, follow the procedure outlined below.

1. Place the expression in standard form.

2. Change all subtractions to additions, and change the signs of the numbers immediately following.

3. Add all numbers having like signs. That is, add all the positive numbers, and then add all the negative numbers.

4. Add the resulting unlike signed expressions.

Calculate.
$^-$3 + 5 – 6 + 9 + ($^-$8) + ($^-$1)

($^-$3) + ($^+$5) – ($^+$6) + ($^+$9) + ($^-$8) + ($^-$1)   *Convert to standard form.*

($^-$3) + ($^+$5) + ($^-$6) + ($^+$9) + ($^-$8) + ($^-$1)   *Convert subtractions to additions; change the signs of numbers immediately following changed signs.*

($^+$14) + ($^-$18)   *Add like signs.*

$^-$4   *Add unlike signs.*

Calculate.
5 – 6 – 8 + 4 + 2 – 7

($^+$5) – ($^+$6) – ($^+$8) + ($^+$4) + ($^+$2) – ($^+$7)   *Convert to standard form.*

($^+$5) + ($^-$6) + ($^-$8) + ($^+$4) + ($^+$2) + ($^-$7)   *Change subtractions to additions; change the signs of numbers immediately following changed signs.*

($^+$11) + ($^-$21)   *Add like signs.*

$^-$10   *Add unlike signs.*

3. Multiplication and division of signed numbers. When multiplying or dividing signed numbers, the solution is determined by multiplying or dividing the absolute values of the numbers and then assigning the proper sign to the result. The proper sign is determined by the number of negative signs in the problem. If there is an odd number of negative numbers, put a negative sign on the result; otherwise, put a positive sign on the result.

Before beginning the examples, recall that multiplication can be denoted by an $\times$, a dot, or parentheses with or without a dot. Division is denoted by a fraction bar or $\div$.

Multiply.
$(^-3)(^+4)$

$|^-3| \bullet |^+4| = 3 \bullet 4 = 12$ *Multiply absolute values.*
$^-12$ *Odd number of negative signs, so the result is negative.*

Multiply.
$^-2(^-4)(^+6)(^-1)$

$(^-2)(^-4)(^+6)(^-1)$ *Place in standard form (parentheses around number and its sign).*

$|^-2| \, |^-4| \, |^+6| \, |^-1| = 2 \bullet 4 \bullet 6 \bullet 1 = 48$ *Multiply absolute values.*
$^-48$ *Odd number of negative signs, so the result is negative.*

Divide.
$^-16 \div (^-2)$

$(^-16) \div (^-2)$ *Place in standard form.*
$|^-16| \div |^-2| = 16 \div 2 = 8$ *Divide absolute values.*
$^+8$ *Even number of negative signs, so the result is positive.*

Divide.
$18 \div (^-2)$

$(^+18) \div (^-2)$ *Place in standard form.*
$|^+18| \div |^-2| = 18 \div 2 = 9$ *Divide absolute values.*
$^-9$ *Odd number of negative signs, so the result is negative.*

Divide.
$\dfrac{15}{^-5} = 15 \div (^-5)$

$\dfrac{15}{(^-5)} = (^+15) \div (^-5)$ *Place in standard form.*

$|^+15| \div |^-5| = 15 \div 5 = 3$ *Divide absolute values.*
$^-3$ *Odd number of negative signs, so the result is negative.*

Operations with Fractions

The rules for operations of signed integers apply also to operations with fractions. There are, however, some additional rules that apply to fractions. Consider the rules that apply to each of the four operations involving fractions.

1. Addition of fractions. To add fractions, first you must change all the numbers to fractions having the same denominator, then add the numerators, and then simplify the final answer.

It is easier to add and subtract fractions that have a common denominator (the same denominator) than to add and subtract fractions that have different denominators. For example, it is easier to add $\frac{2}{3} + \frac{1}{3}$ than to add $\frac{2}{3} + \frac{2}{6}$. What, then, should be done to solve a problem that involves different denominators? You learned earlier that you can multiply or divide both the numerator and the denominator of a fraction by the same number without changing the fraction's value. This process provides a way to change denominators that are difficult to work with.

To add $\frac{2}{3} + \frac{2}{6}$, begin by multiplying both the numerator and the denominator of $\frac{2}{3}$ by 2 to produce the fraction $\frac{4}{6}$. This means that the two fractions, $\frac{2}{3}$ and $\frac{4}{6}$, are equivalent (equal). Now you have an easy way to add $\frac{2}{3}$ and $\frac{2}{6}$. First, change $\frac{2}{3}$ to $\frac{4}{6}$. Then add $\frac{4}{6}$ and $\frac{2}{6}$ to get $\frac{6}{6} = 1$.

To add fractions that have a common denominator, first add the numerators to find the numerator of the answer. The denominator of the answer is the common denominator.

> **Add.**
> $$\frac{3}{7} + \frac{1}{7}$$
>
> $3 + 1 = 4$ *Add the numerators. 4 will be the answer's numerator.*
>
> $\frac{3}{7} + \frac{1}{7} = \frac{4}{7}$ *The answer's denominator will be 7, since 7 is the common denominator.*

When you added $\frac{2}{3}$ and $\frac{2}{6}$, you changed $\frac{2}{3}$ to $\frac{4}{6}$ by multiplying the numerator and the denominator by 2. You could multiply by 4 instead. This would convert $\frac{2}{3}$ to $\frac{8}{12}$. Then you could multiply the numerator and the denominator of $\frac{2}{6}$ by 2 to convert $\frac{2}{6}$ to $\frac{4}{12}$. Our addition problem would then have been $\frac{8}{12} + \frac{4}{12} = \frac{12}{12} = 1$. You arrive at the same answer, but the first method is simpler. In the first example, the common denominator is 6. In the second example, the common denominator is 12. It is usually easiest to work with the smallest common denominator. This smallest common denominator is called the least common denominator (LCD).

To find the LCD, first factor the denominators into products of prime numbers. To do this, find all the numbers that must be multiplied to produce each denominator.

Find the LCD of the fractions $\frac{1}{4}$, $\frac{3}{8}$, and $\frac{7}{10}$.

Begin by noting that $4 = 2 \times 2$, $8 = 2 \times 4$, and $10 = 2 \times 5$.

$$4 = (2)(2) = 2^2$$
$$8 = (2)(4)$$
$$10 = (2)(5)$$

The numbers to the right of the equal signs (2, 2, 2, 4, 2, and 5) are called factors. The next step is to look at the list of factors and determine if any of them can be factored further. Eight was expressed as (2)(4), but the 4 can be expressed as (2)(2). Therefore, express 8 as (2)(2)(2) instead of as (2)(4). The new list of factors looks like the following.

$$4 = 2^2$$
$$8 = (2)(2)(2) = 2^3$$
$$10 = (2)(5)$$

Since none of the factors (2 and 5) can be factored further, the list is complete.

How do you determine the LCD from this list? The LCD is the product of the highest power of every factor that appears in the list. The only two factors in the list are 2 and 5. The highest power of 2 is 2^3. The highest power of 5 is 5^1, or 5. The LCD is, therefore, $(2^3)(5) = (8)(5) = 40$.

Find the sum.
$$\frac{1}{2} + \frac{1}{6} + \frac{1}{12}$$

1. Find the LCD.

$$2 = 2$$
$$6 = (2)(3)$$
$$12 = (2^2)(3)$$
The LCD is $2^2(3)$, or 12.

2. Convert each fraction to an equivalent fraction that has 12 (the LCD) as the denominator.

$$\frac{1}{2} + \frac{1}{6} + \frac{1}{12} = \frac{6}{12} + \frac{2}{12} + \frac{1}{12}$$

3. Add the numerators.

$$\frac{6}{12} + \frac{2}{12} + \frac{1}{12} = \frac{9}{12}$$

4. Reduce to lowest terms.

$$\frac{9}{12} = \frac{3}{4}$$

2. Subtraction of fractions. In many calculations, subtraction of fractions can be dealt with more easily if you change the problem to addition by changing the signs of the numbers, as you did earlier with integers. When changing the sign of a number, it is usually easier to change the sign of the numerator. Here is an example.

$$\frac{3}{4} - \frac{7}{8} = \frac{^+3}{4} - \frac{^+7}{8} = \frac{(^+3)}{4} + \frac{(^-7)}{8}$$

Note that the number signs are in the numerators.

Subtract.

$$\frac{2}{3} - \frac{1}{8} - \frac{4}{5}$$

$$\frac{2}{3} - \frac{1}{8} - \frac{4}{5} = \frac{(^+2)}{3} - \frac{(^+1)}{8} - \frac{(^+4)}{5} \qquad \textit{Convert to standard form.}$$

$$\frac{(^+2)}{3} + \frac{(^-1)}{8} + \frac{(^-4)}{5} \qquad \textit{Convert to addition, change signs in numerators.}$$

$$LCD = (2^3)(3)(5) = 120$$

$$\frac{80}{120} + \frac{(^-15)}{120} + \frac{(^-96)}{120} = \frac{(^-31)}{120} \qquad \textit{Convert to equivalent fractions that have 120 as the denominator; add the numerators.}$$

Final answer: $\dfrac{^-31}{120}$ or $-\dfrac{31}{120}$

The fraction is already in lowest terms.

3. Multiplication of fractions. There are two methods for multiplying fractions. The first involves multiplying the numerators to form the numerator of the result and multiplying the denominators to form the denominator of the result. You then reduce the result to lowest terms for the final answer. The problem with this approach is that it tends to generate large numbers.

The second method involves reducing all common factors first and then multiplying as described in the previous method.

Multiply.

$$\frac{5}{8} \cdot \frac{4}{15} \cdot \frac{2}{3}$$

$$\frac{5 \cdot 4 \cdot 2}{8 \cdot 15 \cdot 3} = \frac{40}{360} = \frac{1}{9} \qquad \textit{Method 1}$$

$$\frac{5 \cdot 2 \cdot 2 \cdot 2}{2 \cdot 2 \cdot 2 \cdot 5 \cdot 3 \cdot 3} = \frac{1}{9} \qquad \textit{Method 2}$$

4. Division of fractions. To divide fractions, first invert any fractions following a division sign. Inverting means switching the numerators and the denominators. Next, change the division sign to a multiplication sign, and then multiply the fractions and reduce the result to lowest terms.

Divide.

$$\frac{3}{11} \div \frac{9}{22}$$

$$\frac{3}{11} \times \frac{22}{9} \qquad\qquad \textit{Invert; switch to multiplication.}$$

$$\frac{3}{11} \times \frac{22}{9} = \frac{66}{99} = \frac{2}{3} \qquad \textit{Method 1}$$

$$\frac{(3 \times 11 \times 2)}{(11 \times 3 \times 3)} = \frac{2}{3} \qquad \textit{Method 2}$$

Divide.

$$\left(\frac{3}{11}\right) \div \left(\frac{4}{8}\right) \div \left(\frac{1}{2}\right)$$

$$\left(\frac{3}{11}\right) \times \left(\frac{8}{4}\right) \times \left(\frac{2}{1}\right) \qquad\qquad \textit{Invert; switch to multiplication.}$$

$$\frac{3 \times 8 \times 2}{11 \times 4 \times 1} = \frac{48}{44} = \frac{12}{11} = 1\frac{1}{11} \qquad \textit{Method 1}$$

$$\frac{3 \times 2 \times 2 \times 2 \times 2}{11 \times 2 \times 2 \times 1} = \frac{12}{11} = 1\frac{1}{11} \qquad \textit{Method 2}$$

Calculate.

$$\left(\frac{4}{7}\right) \div \left(\frac{8}{9}\right) \times \left(\frac{3}{5}\right)$$

$$\frac{4}{7} \times \frac{9}{8} \times \frac{3}{5} \qquad\qquad \textit{Invert; switch to multiplication.}$$

$$\frac{4}{7} \times \frac{9}{8} \times \frac{3}{5} = \frac{108}{280} = \frac{27}{70} \qquad \textit{Method 1}$$

$$\frac{2 \times 2 \times 3 \times 3 \times 3}{7 \times 2 \times 2 \times 2 \times 5} = \frac{27}{70} \qquad \textit{Method 2}$$

Operations with Decimals

Decimals and fractions are alternative ways of expressing a given quantity. Many problems involving operations with decimals involve decimals that are intermixed with fractions or integers. A few rules are used to carry out these operations.

1. Addition and subtraction of decimals. The rules applying to addition and subtraction of signed integers and fractions apply also to addition and subtraction of decimals. When adding or subtracting decimals, the numbers should be lined up vertically with the decimal points under one another. Then perform the operation (add or subtract), and position the decimal point in the result directly below its column.

Add.

13.2 + 0.25 + 1.261 + 8.04

13.2	*Align vertically.*
0.25	
1.261	
+ 8.04	
22.751	*Add, and place decimal point in the proper column.*

When fractions, decimals, and whole numbers are mixed in an expression, add the decimals, and add the fractions; then convert decimals to fractions, add, and reduce.

Calculate.

$$0.54 + 0.3 + 1 - \frac{1}{3}$$

$(1.84) + \left(\frac{-1}{3}\right)$	*Add decimals and whole numbers; change operation and number sign.*
$\frac{184}{100} + \left(\frac{-1}{3}\right)$	*Convert decimals to fractions.*
$\frac{552}{300} + \left(\frac{-100}{300}\right) = \frac{452}{300}$	*Find LCD and convert to equivalent fractions.*
$\frac{452}{300} = \frac{113}{75} = 1\frac{38}{75}$	*Reduce to lowest terms.*

Note that changing $\frac{1}{3}$ to a decimal in this problem and proceeding with the operations of decimals would have affected the accuracy of the answer because rounding 0.333 . . . to 0.33 or 0.333 would give us only an approximation.

Calculate.

$$0.37 + 1.2 + \frac{1}{2}$$

$1.57 + \frac{1}{2}$	*Add decimals and whole numbers.*
$1.57 + 0.5$	*Convert fraction to a decimal by dividing.*
2.07	*Add decimals.*

Note that in this case the fraction could be converted to a decimal without losing accuracy since $\frac{1}{2}$ is exactly equal to 0.5.

Calculate.

0.326 + 1.62 – 0.43 – 0.181

0.326	0.43	*Add absolute values of numbers that have like signs.*
+ 1.62	+ 0.181	
1.946	0.611	

1.946	*Subtract smaller absolute value from larger absolute value.*
– 0.611	
1.335	

⁺1.335	*Assign sign of larger absolute value.*

2. Multiplication of decimals. If finding a product involves multiplying fractions and decimals, it may help to change the fractions to equivalent decimals and perform the operations using the rules of decimals. However, if this is done, the final answer will be exact only if the decimals are exactly equal to the fractions. Otherwise, the problem should be completed using the operation of fractions in order to maintain accuracy. When multiplying decimals, multiply them as though they were integers. Count the *total* number of decimal places to the right of the decimal point in *all* numbers. Place the decimal point in the answer by counting the same number of places, beginning at the right of the last digit.

Multiply.
1.26 × 0.043

$$
\begin{array}{r}
1.26 \\
\times\ 0.043 \\
\hline
378 \\
504 \\
\hline
5418
\end{array}
$$

Multiply numbers as if they were integers.

There are a total of five digits to the right of the decimal point; two in 1.26 and three in 0.043.

.05418   *Beginning at the right of the number, count five places to the left; if there are not enough digits, as is the case here, add zeros to the left of the answer.*

0.05418   *If the result is between ⁻1 and ⁺1, put a zero to the left of the decimal point.*

Find the product.
$$\frac{4}{5}(0.3)(0.54)$$

$(0.8)(0.3)(0.54)$ *Convert $\frac{4}{5}$ to a decimal (0.8), since it has an exact value.*

0.1296   *Multiply, and place decimal point (4 places). Put a zero to the left of the decimal point.*

3. Division of decimals. The simplest method for dividing decimals is to make the divisor an integer. If it is necessary to move the decimal point in the divisor in order to create an integer, then move the decimal point in the dividend by the same amount. Each time you move the decimal point you multiply the dividend or divisor by 10. After moving the decimal points, perform division as with integers. Note that the decimal point in the answer should be directly above the decimal point in the dividend.

Solve and round answer to two decimal places.
0.23 ÷ 0.45

$$\frac{0.23}{0.45} = \frac{23}{45}$$

Multiply the numerator (dividend) and the denominator (divisor) by 100 to create an integer in the denominator.

```
        0.511
  45 |23.000
     22 5
        50
        45
        50
        45
```

Carry out the division to three places in order to round to two places.

0.51   *Round to two decimal places.*

Solve and round answer to two decimal places.
1.43 ÷ 0.781

$$\frac{1.43}{0.781} = \frac{1430}{781}$$

Multiply the numerator and the denominator by 1000 to create an integer in the denominator.

```
          1.830
  781 |1430.000
       781
       649 0
       624 8
        24 20
        23 43
           770
```

Carry out the division to three decimal places in order to round to two decimal places.

1.83   *Round to two decimal places.*

Remember that some fractions and decimals are exactly equivalent.

$$\frac{1}{2} = 0.5$$

$$\frac{4}{5} = 0.8$$

Other fractions result in repeating patterns. For example, $\frac{1}{3} = 0.3333 \ldots$. This is why you should work with fractions instead of decimals unless the fractions have exact decimal equivalents.

Operations with Exponents

To perform operations involving exponents, you must be familiar with the following rules of exponents.

Rule 1: To multiply numbers that have the same base, add the exponents.

$$(a^r)(a^s) = a^{r+s}$$

$$(2^3)(2^4)(2^8) = 2^{3+4+8} = 2^{15}$$

Rule 2: To divide numbers that have the same base, subtract the exponents.

$$a^r \div a^s = a^{r-s}$$

$$2^5 \div 2^2 = 2^{5-2} = 2^3$$

Rule 3: To raise an exponential expression to a power, multiply the exponents.

$$(a^r)^s = a^{rs}$$

$$(2^2)^3 = 2^{(2)(3)} = 2^6$$

Rule 4: To raise a base consisting of two or more factors to a power, each factor individually must be raised to that power.

$$(ab)^r = (a^r)(b^r)$$

$$(2x)^3 = (2^3)(x^3) = 8x^3$$

This problem illustrates the fact that only the number nearest the exponent is raised to the power unless parentheses are used to indicate otherwise. In the term $2x^3$, only x is raised to the third power.

Rule 5: To raise a fraction to a power, raise both the numerator and the denominator to that power.

$$\left(\frac{2}{3}\right)^3 = \frac{2^3}{3^3} = \frac{8}{27}$$

Rule 6: If an exponent is negative, the expression is equivalent to a fraction that has a 1 in the numerator and the same base and positive exponent in the denominator.

$$a^{-r} = \frac{1}{a^r}$$

$$2^{-3} = \frac{1}{2^3} = \frac{1}{8}$$

Rule 7: Any number, except 0, raised to an exponent of 0 is 1, and any number raised to an exponent of 1 is the number itself.

$$a^0 = 1, a \neq 0$$

$$a^1 = a$$

$$3x^0 = 3 \cdot 1 = 3 \qquad \textit{Note that the exponent applies only to x.}$$

Most problems involving exponents will require the use of more than one of these seven rules. You should take care to apply these rules properly and accurately.

Simplify.

$$\frac{(2x^2)^3}{x^5}$$

$$\frac{(2x^2)^3}{x^5} = \frac{(2^3)(x^2)^3}{x^5} \qquad \textit{Rule 4}$$

$$\frac{(2^3)(x^2)^3}{x^5} = \frac{(2^3)(x^6)}{x^5} \qquad \textit{Rule 3}$$

$$\frac{(2^3)(x^6)}{x^5} = (2^3)(x^1) = (2^3)(x) \qquad \textit{Rules 2 and 7}$$

$$(2^3)(x) = 8x$$

Calculations Using Scientific Notation

A number is said to be in scientific notation if it is in the form $N \times 10^p$ where N is a number between 1 and 10.

To place a number in scientific notation, move the decimal point to produce a number between 1 and 10. The absolute value of the exponent is equal to the number of places the decimal point is moved. If moving the decimal point creates a number less than the original, the exponent is positive. If the move creates a number larger than the original, then the exponent is negative. If no move is required, the exponent is zero.

Number	Scientific Notation
0.0035	3.5×10^{-3}
350	3.5×10^2
2.6	2.6×10^0

You can see that when you move the decimal to the right, the exponent is negative. Moving the decimal to the left generates a positive exponent. Scientific notation is typically used to designate either very large or very small numbers.

$$3,500,000,000,000,000,000 = 3.5 \times 10^{18}$$
$$0.000000000000035 \qquad\quad = 3.5 \times 10^{-14}$$

Addition and subtraction. To add or subtract two or more numbers that are in scientific notation and that have the same power of 10, use the following rule.

$$(a \times 10^x) + (b \times 10^x) + (c \times 10^x) = (a + b + c) \times 10^x$$

Simplify.
$(3 \times 10^8) + (6 \times 10^8) + (4 \times 10^8)$

$(3 \times 10^8) + (6 \times 10^8) + (4 \times 10^8) = 13 \times 10^8$
$13 \times 10^8 = 1.3 \times 10^9$

Notice the last step of this example. To change 13×10^8 to an equivalent number in scientific notation, 13 is divided by 10 (the decimal point is moved one place to the left) in order to obtain a number with one non-zero digit to the left of the decimal point. To offset this change, the power of 10 is multiplied by 10 (the exponent is increased by 1).

If the numbers in the original problem do not have the same powers of 10, they can be changed to equivalent numbers with the same power of 10 by using the method that follows.

Add.
$(6 \times 10^4) + (5 \times 10^5)$

$(6 \times 10^4) + (5 \times 10^5) = (0.6 \times 10^5) + (5 \times 10^5) = 5.6 \times 10^5$ or
$(6 \times 10^4) + (5 \times 10^5) = (6 \times 10^4) + (50 \times 10^4) = 56 \times 10^4 = 5.6 \times 10^5$

Multiplication and division. Problems involving multiplication and division of numbers in scientific notation can best be completed by using the rules of exponents discussed earlier in the chapter.

Perform the indicated operations.
$$\frac{(2 \times 10^3) \cdot (2.4 \times 10^4)}{10^8}$$

$\dfrac{4.8 \times 10^7}{10^8}$ *Multiply (2)(2.4).*

4.8×10^{-1} *Exponent rule 2*

You can see this work out if all the 10's are put in the numerator and in the denominator.

$$\frac{2(10)(10)(10) \cdot 2.4(10)(10)(10)(10)}{(10)(10)(10)(10)(10)(10)(10)(10)} = \frac{4.8(10)(10)(10)(10)(10)(10)(10)}{(10)(10)(10)(10)(10)(10)(10)(10)}$$

$$\frac{4.8}{10} = 0.48 = 4.8 \times 10^{-1}$$

Order of Operations

1. General rules. Many complex expressions involve addition, subtraction, multiplication, and division. The order in which you do the operations is important and follows a set of standard rules. As a rule, you should perform multiplication and division first from left to right and then perform addition and subtraction from left to right. Parentheses are often used to indicate the order of operations.

1. Simplify expressions in parentheses (or brackets and braces, respectively), working from the innermost expressions outward.

2. Raise all terms to the proper power if there are exponents in the expression.

3. Perform multiplication and division operations from left to right.

4. Perform addition and subtraction operations from left to right.

Until you practice and gain confidence, you should perform one operation per line in an evaluation process.

Perform the indicated operations.

$3 - 4(^-2)$

$(^+3) - (^+4)(^-2)$	*Place in standard form. Note that there are no exponents.*
$(^+3) - (^+4)(^-2) = (^+3) - (^-8)$	*Multiply first. There are no terms to divide.*
$(^+3) - (^-8) = (^+3) + (^+8) = {}^+11$	*Subtract.*

Perform the indicated operations.

$^-3 + (^-1)^3(^-2)^2$

$(^-3) + (^-1)^3(^-2)^2$	*Place in standard form.*
$(^-3) + (^-1)(^-2)^2$	*Raise first power.* $(^-1)^3 = (^-1)(^-1)(^-1) = {}^-1$
$(^-3) + (^-1)(^+4)$	*Raise second power.* $(^-2)^2 = (^-2)(^-2) = {}^+4$
$(^-3) + (^-4)$	*Multiply.*
$^-7$	*Add.*

Perform the indicated operations.

$2 \cdot (^-5)^3 \div 25 \cdot (^-2) - 3$

$(^+2)(^-5)^3 \div (^+25)(^-2) - (^+3)$	*Place in standard form.*
$(^+2)(^-125) \div (^+25)(^-2) - (^+3)$	*Calculate* $(^-5)^3$.
$(^-250) \div (^+25)(^-2) - (^+3)$	*Multiply* $(^+2)(^-125)$.
$(^-10)(^-2) - (^+3)$	*Divide* $(^-250) \div (^+25)$. *Remember to perform multiplication and division from left to right. If you multiply* $(^+25)(^-2)$ *before dividing* $(^-250) \div (^+25)$, *you will not get the correct result.*
$(^+20) - (^+3)$	*Multiply* $(^-10)(^-2)$.
$^+17$	*Subtract* $(^+20) - (^+3)$.

2. Grouping symbols. Grouping symbols such as parentheses, brackets, and braces are used to alter the order of operations. When grouping symbols appear in an expression, the quantity within the group must be evaluated first. Remember, expressions within sets of grouping symbols are evaluated from the inside out.

Perform the indicated operations.

$(^-3 + 4 \bullet (^-2)) \bullet (^-2)$

$((^-3) + (^+4)(^-2))(^-2)$	*Place in standard form.*
$((^-3) + (^-8))(^-2)$	*Do work inside parentheses according to the order of operations. Multiply $(^+4)(^-2)$.*
$(^-11)(^-2)$	*Add $^-3$ and $^-8$.*
$^+22$	*Multiply.*

Perform the indicated operations.

$6 - 2 \bullet \{(^+3) \bullet [(^-2) - (^-3)(^-4)]\}$

$(^+6) - (^+2) \bullet \{(^+3) \bullet [(^-2) - (^-3)(^-4)]\}$	*Place in standard form.*
$(^+6) - (^+2) \bullet \{(^+3) [(^-2) - (^+12)]\}$	*Evaluate innermost group according to order of operations. $(^-3) \bullet (^-4) = {}^+12$*
$(^+6) - (^+2) \{(^+3)(^-14)\}$	*Evaluate brackets.*
$(^+6) - (^+2)(^-42)$	*Evaluate braces. $(^+3) \bullet {}^-14 = {}^-42$*
$(^+6) - (^-84)$	*Multiply.*
$^+90$	*Add.*

Calculations Using Percents

Calculations involving percents usually take one of the following three forms.

1. What is *a*% of *b*?
2. *a* is *b*% of what number?
3. *a* is what percent of *b*?

Let us analyze each case, keeping in mind that the word *of* implies multiplication and the word *is* implies equality.

Case 1: What is *a*% of *b*? This statement can be interpreted as some unknown number = *a*% • *b*. In other words, change *a*% to a decimal by removing the percent sign and moving the decimal two places to the left; then multiply by *b*.

What is 3% of 50?

$(0.03)(50) = 1.5$ *Convert the percent to a decimal, and then multiply. Likewise, 18% of 46 = (0.18) • (46) = 8.28*

Case 2: *a* is *b*% of what number? The mathematical interpretation is *a* = *b*% • some unknown number, or $\frac{a}{b\%}$ = unknown number. This is the opposite of the question posed in Case 1. In other words, change *b*% to a decimal, and divide into *a*.

3 is 50% of what number?

$$\frac{3}{50\%} = \frac{3}{0.5} = \frac{(10)}{(10)}\frac{(3)}{(0.5)} = \frac{30}{5} = 6 \quad \textit{Convert the percent to a decimal (50\% = 0.5),}$$
$$\textit{and divide into 3.}$$

17 is 20% of what number?

$$\frac{17}{20\%} = \frac{17}{0.2} = \frac{170}{2} = 85$$

Case 3: a is what percent of *b*? This statement can be interpreted as $\frac{a}{b}$ = unknown number. To solve the problem, divide *a* by *b,* and then change the answer to a percent.

3 is what percent of 50?

$$\frac{3}{50} = 0.06 \qquad\qquad \textit{Divide.}$$

$$0.06 = 6\% \qquad\qquad \textit{Convert to a percent.}$$

7 is what percent of 28?

$$\frac{7}{28} = 0.25 = 25\%$$

Estimation

It is helpful at times to be able to estimate the answer to a problem. If the example consists of integers, round off each number to the place value of the digit farthest to the left unless the directions indicate otherwise. When rounding, use the digit immediately to the right of the place value you wish to round. If it is 5 or more, add 1. If it is less than 5, the number remains the same. For example, 384 should be rounded to the hundreds place, since the leftmost digit (3) is in the hundreds place. Round 384 to 400, since the digit to the right of 3 (8) is greater than 5. Round 5021 to 5000, since the 0 is less than 5. If the problem consists of decimals, apply the same rule. 23.82 is nearer 20 than to 30 if you are rounding to the nearest ten units. If you find that you prefer more accuracy, you may round to a different place value. If the problem consists of fractions, change them to decimals, and proceed in the same manner.

Estimate the answer of the following problem to the nearest 10 units.

$$\frac{32(466)}{6} \qquad\qquad \textit{Before starting to solve the problem, round each number}$$
$$\textit{to the nearest tens place.}$$

$$\frac{30(470)}{10} = 3(470) = 1410 \quad \textit{Notice that this problem is made easier by dividing the}$$
$$\textit{numerator and the denominator by 10 before multiplying}$$
$$\textit{to obtain the final answer.}$$

Comparison of Numbers

You will find it helpful in many types of problems to compare the values of numbers, whether those numbers are in the form of fractions, decimals, or mathematical expressions. By expressing the numbers in the same form, you can easily compare them. If the numbers are in the form of fractions, change them to equivalent fractions that have the same denominator (LCD), and compare the numerators.

Which of the following fractions is largest?

$$\frac{1}{3}, \frac{2}{5}, \frac{8}{15}, \frac{13}{30}$$

$$\frac{1}{3} = \frac{10}{30}$$ *Change all fractions to equivalent fractions that have a denominator of 30 (the LCD).*

$$\frac{2}{5} = \frac{12}{30}$$

$$\frac{8}{15} = \frac{16}{30}$$

$$\frac{13}{30} = \frac{13}{30}$$

Find the largest fraction by comparing numerators. The largest fraction is $\frac{16}{30}$, which represents $\frac{8}{15}$; therefore, the largest fraction in the original problem is $\frac{8}{15}$.

The numbers could also be presented in the form of mathematical expressions, which should be calculated in order to compare them.

Which is larger?
15% of 6480 or 18% of 7100

$0.15 \cdot 6480 = 972; \ 0.18 \cdot 7100 = 1278$
18% of 7100 is larger.

The symbols listed below are used frequently in describing a comparison of quantities.

>   greater than
≥   greater than or equal to
<   less than
≤   less than or equal to

Consider the arrangement of numbers on a number line, where number values increase from left to right. If one number is positioned to the left of another, the first number is less than (<) the second number. If a number lies to the right of another number, the first number is greater than (>) the second number.

Insert the symbols <, ≤, >, ≥ to make the following comparisons true.

5 _____ 26	*5 < 26*	
0 _____ ⁻4	*0 > ⁻4*	
3 _____ 3	*3 ≤ 3 or 3 ≥ 3*	

Practice Exercises

The following exercises will help you review the concepts covered in this chapter. Although the types of questions presented here may not appear on the test, the concepts they cover are essential for solving many of the problems on the test. The purpose of these exercises is to give you practice on fundamental math concepts and skills rather than merely to prepare you for the test. Following these exercises are the Practice Exercise Explanations. They explain each question, the correct answer, and why the remaining choices are incorrect.

1. Find the sum.

    $(^+4) + (^-8) + (^+2) + (^-3)$

    A. $^-5$

    B.   5

    C.   17

    D.   192

2. Perform the indicated operations.

    $(^-4) - (^-2) - (^+1)$

    A. $^-5$

    B. $^-3$

    C. $^-1$

    D.   5

3. Perform the indicated operations.

    $4(^-2) \div (^-4)2$

    A. $^-64$

    B.   1

    C.   4

    D.   64

4. Find the sum.

    $\dfrac{3}{8} + \dfrac{2}{9} + \dfrac{1}{2}$

    A. $\dfrac{5}{17}$

    B. $\dfrac{6}{19}$

    C. $\dfrac{43}{72}$

    D. $\dfrac{79}{72}$

5. Perform the indicated operations.

    $\dfrac{1}{2} - 2\dfrac{2}{3} - 1\dfrac{1}{5}$

    A. $\dfrac{^-101}{30}$

    B. $\dfrac{^-13}{6}$

    C. $\dfrac{13}{6}$

    D. $\dfrac{131}{30}$

6.   Perform the indicated operations.

$\frac{1}{2} \div \frac{4}{3} \bullet \frac{6}{7}$

A. $\frac{9}{28}$

B. $\frac{4}{7}$

C. $\frac{7}{16}$

D. $\frac{16}{7}$

7.   Perform the indicated operations.

$0.32 - 1.4 + \frac{1}{4} - \frac{1}{2}$

A.   ⁻1.33

B.   ⁻0.38

C.   1.33

D.   2.47

8.   Perform the indicated operations.

$0.75 \div 3(0.4)$

A.   0.1

B.   0.625

C.   0.9

D.   1

9.   What percent of 100 is 62?

A.   0.38

B.   0.62

C.   38

D.   62

10. Simplify.

$\frac{(2x)^{-3}}{3x^{-2}}$

A. $\frac{1}{6x}$

B. $\frac{1}{24x}$

C. $\frac{8x^5}{3}$

D. $\frac{2x^5}{3}$

11. Simplify and express the answer in scientific notation.

$$\frac{2 \times 10^3 + 8 \times 10^3}{(3 \times 10^3) \bullet (2 \times 10^3)}$$

A. 1.66×10^{-3}

B. 1.66×10^0

C. 1.66×10^3

D. 1.66×10^9

12. Which of the following is the best estimate of $3288(5263 + 8928)$?

A.   42,000

B.   420,000

C.   4,200,000

D.   42,000,000

13. Which of the following is *largest*?

$$\frac{1}{3}; \frac{5}{9}; \frac{1}{2}; \frac{7}{15}$$

   A. $\frac{1}{3}$

   B. $\frac{5}{9}$

   C. $\frac{1}{2}$

   D. $\frac{7}{15}$

14. $3(^-4) - 12 \div (^-2)^2 =$

   A.   9

   B.   0

   C. $^-9$

   D. -15

15. Convert 0.034 to scientific notation.

   A. 3.4×10^2

   B. 3.4×10^{-2}

   C. 0.34×10^{-1}

   D. 34×10^{-3}

16. Which of the following is true?

   A. $\frac{1}{2} < \frac{1}{3}$

   B. $\frac{2}{5} \geq 0.40$

   C. $1\frac{1}{2} > 1\frac{4}{6}$

   D. 10% of 50 < 5% of 70

17. Which of the following is the *smallest*?

   A. 5% of 950

   B. 20% of 500

   C. 40% of 110

   D. 75% of 150

18. Perform the indicated operations.

$$\frac{9-5}{^-3+5}$$

   A. $^-4$

   B. $^-2$

   C. 0.5

   D. 2

19. What is 20% of 90?

   A. 0.18

   B. 4.5

   C. 18

   D. 70

20. Which of the following is the best estimate of $\frac{0.62 \times 68}{0.49}$?

   A.   8

   B.   20

   C.   80

   D.   200

Practice Exercise Explanations

1. **Correct Response: A.** $(^+4) + (^-8) + (^+2) + (^-3) = (^+6) + (^-11) = {}^-5$
    Choice C is the result of confusing the multiplication rules of signed numbers with the addition rules and concluding that $(^-8) + (^-3)$ is 11. Choice B results from assigning the incorrect sign to the final answer. Choice D is the result of finding the product instead of the sum of the numbers.

2. **Correct Response: B.** $(^-4) - (^-2) - (^+1) = (^-4) + (^+2) + (^-1) = {}^-3$
    Choices A and C result from improperly changing signs when converting from subtraction to addition. Choice D results from changing the sign of $(^-4)$.

3. **Correct Response: C.** $(^+4)(^-2) \div (^-4)(^+2)$
    $(^-8) \div (^-4)(^+2)$
    $(^+2)(^+2)$
    4

    You may have been tempted to do the multiplication first and the division last (choice B), rather than performing the operations from left to right. Choice A results from using the opposite of $^-4$ rather than the reciprocal when changing to multiplication. Choice D results from multiplying the four numbers.

4. **Correct Response: D.** The LCD is $2^3 \times 3^2$, or 72.

    $$\frac{3}{8} + \frac{2}{9} + \frac{1}{2} = \frac{27}{72} + \frac{16}{72} + \frac{36}{72} = \frac{79}{72}$$

    Often students are tempted to add the numerators and the denominators (choice B). Choice A results from adding the numerators and the denominators of the first two fractions only. Choice C is the sum of the first two fractions only.

5. **Correct Response: A.** $\left(\frac{^+1}{2}\right) + \left(\frac{^-8}{3}\right) + \left(\frac{^-6}{5}\right)$ LCD = 30

    $$\frac{(^+15)}{30} + \frac{(^-80)}{30} + \frac{(^-36)}{30} = \frac{(^-101)}{30}$$

    Choice B is the result of subtracting $2\frac{2}{3}$ from $\frac{1}{2}$ and disregarding the third term $\left(\frac{6}{5}\right)$. Choice C is the result of subtracting the numerators and the denominators. Choice D is the result of adding the three fractions.

6. **Correct Response: A.** $\frac{1}{2} \times \frac{3}{4} \times \frac{6}{7} = \frac{3}{8} \times \frac{6}{7} = \frac{18}{56} = \frac{9}{28}$ or

$\frac{1}{2} \times \frac{3}{2 \times 2} \times \frac{3 \times 2}{7} = \frac{9}{28}$

Notice that both the numerator and the denominator can be divided by 2 to reduce $\frac{18}{56}$ to $\frac{9}{28}$. Choice B is the result of changing the operation of division to multiplication without taking the reciprocal of the second number. Choice C is the result of multiplying the second and third fractions first, which violates the principle of performing operations from left to right. Choice D results from taking the reciprocal of the first fraction rather than the second. In solving this problem, it is important to perform the operations from left to right.

7. **Correct Response: A.** $(^+0.32) - (^+1.4) + \frac{(^+1)}{4} - \frac{(^+1)}{2}$

$(^+0.32) + (^-1.4) + \frac{(^+1)}{4} + \frac{(^-1)}{2}$

$(^-1.08) + \frac{(^+1)}{4} + \frac{(^-1)}{2}$

$\frac{(^-108)}{100} + \frac{(^+1)}{4} + \frac{(^-1)}{2}$

$\frac{(^-108)}{100} + \frac{(^+25)}{100} + \frac{(^-50)}{100} =$

$\frac{(^-133)}{100} = {}^-1.33$

Choice C results from assigning the wrong sign to the answer rather than remembering that the sign of a product or quotient is determined by the number of minus signs in the problem. Since there is an odd number of minus signs in this problem (1), the final answer is negative. Choice D results from adding two negative numbers to obtain a positive result. Choice B results from errors in handling place values when performing the operations.

8. **Correct Response: A.** $\left(\frac{^+0.75}{^+3}\right)(^+0.4)$

$(^+0.25)(^+0.4) = {}^+0.1$

Choice B is the result of performing the multiplication operation first, and choice C is the result of multiplying all three numbers. Choice D results from a misplaced decimal point.

9. **Correct Response: D.** $\dfrac{62}{100} = 0.62 = 62\%$

    Choice B results from confusing 0.62% and 62%. This is a common mistake. Choice C results from subtracting 62 from 100. Choice A is similar to choice C but confuses 0.38% and 38%.

10. **Correct Response: B.**

    $$\frac{(2x)^{-3}}{3x^{-2}} = \frac{1}{(2x)^3 3x^{-2}} = \frac{1}{8x^3 3x^{-2}} = \frac{1}{24x}$$

    If you did not bring $(2x)^{-3}$ to the denominator to make it $(2x)^3$ but instead treated it as $(2x)^3$ in the numerator, you probably picked choice C. If you did not simplify $(2x)^3$ by raising both 2 and x to the third power, then choice A would have been your answer. If you combined both of these errors, choice D would have been your answer.

11. **Correct Response: A.**

    $$\frac{2 \times 10^3 + 8 \times 10^3}{(3 \times 10^3) \bullet (2 \times 10^3)} = \frac{10 \times 10^3}{6 \times 10^6} = \frac{5}{3} \times 10^{-3} = 1.66 \times 10^{-3}$$

    Choice B results from adding exponents in the numerator. This is correct in multiplication problems but not in addition problems. Choice D is the result of adding rather than subtracting exponents in the last step. Choice C results from assigning the wrong sign to the exponent in the final step.

12. **Correct Response: D.** To estimate the answer to this problem, round each number to the nearest 1000. This results in the simplified form below.

    3000(5000 + 9000) = 3000(14,000) = 42,000,000

    The three incorrect responses result from errors in the placement of the decimal point. The actual answer to the original problem is 46,660,008. Only choice D is a good approximation of this answer.

13. **Correct Response: B.** The least common denominator (LCD) for the four fractions is 90.

    $$\frac{1}{3} = \frac{30}{90}; \frac{5}{9} = \frac{50}{90}; \frac{1}{2} = \frac{45}{90}; \frac{7}{15} = \frac{42}{90}$$

    The largest of the four fractions is $\dfrac{5}{9}$, since it has the largest numerator when all four fractions are converted to the same denominator.

14.   **Correct Response: D.** $(^+3)(^-4) - (^+12) \div (^-2)^2$

$(^+3)(^-4) - (^+12) \div (^+4)$

$(^-12) - (^+12) \div (^+4)$

$(^-12) - (^+3)$

$(^-12) + (^-3) = ^-15$

Choice B is incorrect, since subtraction was performed before division. Choice C results from a sign error in evaluating $(^-2)^2$. Choice A results from a sign error in multiplying $(^+3)(^-4)$.

15.   **Correct Response: B.** In 0.034, the decimal point must be moved two places to the right to produce a number between 1 and 10 (3.4). Therefore, the correct exponent is $^-2$. Choice A is incorrect, since the original number was increased and should have a negative exponent. Choices C and D are incorrect, since 0.34 and 34 are not numbers between 1 and 10.

16.   **Correct Response: B.** $\frac{2}{5} = 0.40$; therefore $\frac{2}{5}$ is greater than or equal to 0.40.

Choice A is incorrect because $\frac{1}{2} = \frac{3}{6}$, and $\frac{1}{3} = \frac{2}{6}$, so $\frac{1}{2} < \frac{1}{3}$. Choice C is

incorrect, since $1\frac{1}{2} = \frac{3}{2} = \frac{9}{6}$, and $1\frac{4}{6} = \frac{10}{6}$. Choice D is incorrect, since 10% of

50 is 5, and 5% of 70 = 3.5.

17.   **Correct Response: C.** To answer this question, the percents should first be converted to decimals and then multiplied by the numbers given.

5% = 0.05	0.05 × 950 = 47.5
20% = 0.20	0.20 × 500 = 100
40% = 0.40	0.40 × 110 = 44
75% = 0.75	0.75 × 150 = 112.5

The smallest of the four numbers is 40% of 110, since it results in the smallest number when all four expressions are evaluated.

18.   **Correct Response: D.** The numbers in the numerator and the denominator should be subtracted and added before dividing.

$$\frac{9 - 5}{^-3 + 5} = \frac{4}{2} = 2$$

Choice A results from treating the two sides as individual fractions $\left(\frac{9}{^-3} \text{ and } \frac{^-5}{^+5}\right)$ and then adding them. Choice B assigns an incorrect sign to the result. Choice C adds $^+3$ to 5 in the denominator.

19. **Correct Response: C.** The percent is calculated by multiplying the decimal form of 20% (0.2) by 90. Choice A results from misplacing the decimal when multiplying. Choice B results from dividing 90 by 20. Choice D results from subtracting 20 from 90.

20. **Correct Response: C.** To estimate, the decimals should be rounded off to the nearest tenth and 68 should be rounded off to the nearest ten.

$$\frac{0.6 \times 70}{0.5}$$

$$\frac{42}{0.5}$$

$$\frac{40}{0.5} = 80$$

Choice A results from dividing by 5 instead of 0.5 in the last step. Choice B results from multiplying by 0.5 in the last step. Choice D results from multiplying by 5.

Study Ideas

A careful study of the above exercises and the explanations of the answers will help you review important number concepts and computations. In these exercises, you were asked to work with fractions, decimals, integers, and percents; to use the order of operations to solve problems; to perform calculations with exponents and scientific notation; to estimate; and to use the concepts of "less than" and "greater than." The exercises are designed to give you practice in using these concepts. You may wish to reread parts of the chapter that address specific concepts with which you have difficulty.

You should be aware of these fundamental mathematics concepts and skills and apply them to your work in college, at home, and on the job.

Chapter 11

SOLVE WORD PROBLEMS INVOLVING INTEGERS, FRACTIONS, DECIMALS, AND UNITS OF MEASUREMENT

This skill includes solving word problems involving integers, fractions, decimals, percents, ratios, proportions, units of measurement, and conversions (including scientific notation).

Introduction

The fundamental math skills discussed in the previous chapter may now be used to solve various kinds of problems. In these problems, which are often called word problems, you must do more than simply perform calculations. You must apply math skills to real-life situations. You must translate words into numbers and mathematical symbols, creating equations that allow you to find an answer to the question stated in the problem.

The word problems in this chapter will involve integers, fractions, ratios and proportions, decimals, percents, units of measurement, and conversions. The chapter will help you develop problem-solving skills and strategies that will prepare you to deal with word problems.

Word problem strategy. There are many different kinds of word problems. Of course, it is not possible to come up with a single, foolproof method for solving *all* word problems. Each problem has unique features that make it different from every other problem. There are, however, four steps that you can use in solving any word problem.

1. Read and understand the problem.
2. Develop a mathematical plan for solving the problem.
3. Carry out the plan accurately.
4. Check your answer to make sure it is reasonable.

We will now look at each of these steps in more detail.

1. Read and understand the problem. The first step in solving any math problem is to make sure you understand the question being asked. In order to do this, you should read all the information provided in the problem. Some information may be presented in words, while some will be given in numbers. Be sure you have a clear idea of what the words and the numbers mean, and what the question is asking you to find. As you read the problem, be certain to *identify the question* that is being asked.

Look at all the numbers given in the problem. In most cases, assume that you should use all the numbers in the problem to answer the question.

Use the words in the problem to help you determine what the problem is asking you to find. For example, words such as *cost, savings,* and *discount* may indicate that you must calculate an amount of money, while words such as *further, mileage,* and *length* may show that you need to find a distance. Words such as *increase* and *more* may mean that you need to use addition to find an answer. The words *times* and *double* often indicate that you must multiply to solve the problem. When the words *less, remainder,* or *decrease* appear in a problem, you may need to subtract or divide.

The last sentence in a word problem often states the actual question being asked. Be sure that you read this sentence carefully and understand the information in it. If this is not the case, locate the sentence that does contain the unknown value.

2. Develop a mathematical plan for solving the problem. After you have read the problem carefully and understood it, develop a plan for finding your answer. Use key words or phrases in the problem to form a mathematical plan for solving the problem. Here are a few examples of key words and phrases that will help you in your planning.

What is the total of . . . ? (Add)
What is the sum of . . . ? (Add)
What is the difference between . . . ? (Subtract)
What is the product of . . . ? (Multiply)
What is the ratio of . . . ? (Divide)
What is the quotient of . . . ? (Divide)
What is the average of . . . ? (Add and then divide)
Approximately (or about) how many . . . ? (Estimate)

Use the key words and phrases from the problem to write an equation, a statement that tells how you are going to solve the problem. You can use words or numbers to write your equation, but be sure that you write a clear statement telling what you are going to do. As you prepare your plan, remember that some problems have more than one step. For example, if you need to find the average daily temperature for a particular week, you need to add the daily temperatures and then divide by the number of days in the week. Be sure to include in your plan all the important numbers from the problem. In most cases, all the numbers that appear in the problem will be used.

Once you have written down your plan, review it to make certain that you are answering the question presented in the problem. For example, if a problem asks you to calculate how much time is remaining in a basketball game, be sure your plan will allow you to calculate the time left in the game, not the time that has already been played.

3. Carry out the plan accurately. After you have developed a plan, you will need to follow it. This will often mean performing more than one mathematical operation. It is important that you perform the operations in the correct order. You must also be certain that you use the correct mathematical signs (positive or negative) and that you accurately copy all numbers in the problem. Do all calculations slowly and carefully, and be sure to check your work as you go along.

4. Check your answer to make sure it is reasonable. After you have finished the first three steps of the problem-solving process, check your answer and decide if it is reasonable. Look at the problem again, and see if your answer makes sense. For example, if a problem tells you the regular price of a pair of shoes and then asks how much the shoes would cost if they were on sale for 30% below the regular price, your answer should be less than the regular price of the shoes. Use common sense to decide if your answer is reasonable. If your solution does not make sense, ask yourself why. Recheck your plan and your calculations. Try to find an answer that is reasonable.

Using these four steps will make it easier to solve mathematical problems. You may find that you use these steps a little differently for each problem. For example, for one problem you may spend a great deal of time developing a plan, but then you may carry out your plan very quickly. For other problems, you may develop a plan very easily but spend a longer time carrying out the plan. As you work on the problems, you should ask yourself questions such as: "Am I answering the question that was asked?," "Does my plan solve the problem?," and "Did I use all the available information?" Asking yourself these questions will help remind you to use the steps in the problem-solving process.

The following problems show how the four steps can be used to solve math problems. First, try to solve the problem yourself. Then read the explanation that follows each problem. Each explanation will present one way in which the four problem-solving steps can be used to find an answer to the problem. Keep in mind that you may find another way to use these steps in answering the question. You do not have to use exactly the method shown in the explanation to find the correct answer. There is no single right way to solve each problem.

Using the Problem-Solving Method to Answer Problems

The problems in this section cover many different topics. They will require you to use a wide variety of mathematical skills. These problems are typical of word problems you may encounter.

> Joan purchased a box of diskettes for her computer for $10.50, a printer ribbon for $4.75, a package of computer paper for $9.00, and a box of envelopes for $6.25. What was the total price of the supplies Joan bought?

The first step in answering this question should be to read the problem carefully. The problem contains a number of prices that are important in finding the correct answer. The last sentence also contains the word *total*. In this problem, that word indicates that the numbers should be added.

An appropriate plan for this problem should list all the prices given in the problem and should indicate that these prices must be added.

$10.50 + $4.75 + $9.00 + $6.25 = ?

This plan could also be written as follows.

```
     $10.50   (diskettes)
       4.75   (ribbon)
       9.00   (paper)
   +   6.25   (box of envelopes)
     $  ?
```

To carry out the plan for this problem, all the numbers listed must be added together.

$10.50   (diskettes)
 4.75   (ribbon)
 9.00   (paper)
+ 6.25   (box of envelopes)
$30.50

Once an answer has been calculated, it should be checked to determine whether or not it is a reasonable solution to the problem. In this situation, the most appropriate way to check the answer is to round off the price of each item purchased and to estimate the total cost. The diskettes and paper cost approximately $10.00 each. The combined price of the ribbon and the box of envelopes is also close to $10.00. This means that the combined price of the items should be around $30.00. The answer that was calculated for the problem, $30.50, is therefore a reasonable solution.

If the numbers of items purchased had been larger, it might have been easier to use a slightly different method to solve this problem. For example, suppose the problem had been as follows.

Joan purchased 10 boxes of diskettes for her computer at $10.50 each, 6 printer ribbons for $4.75 each, and 8 packages of computer paper at $9.00 each. What was Joan's total bill?

In this situation, it would be much easier first to multiply the cost of each item by the number of items purchased and then to add all the costs together.

$10 \times \$10.50 = \$105.00$ (cost of 10 boxes of diskettes)
$6 \times \$ 4.75 =   28.50$ (cost of 6 ribbons)
$8 \times \$ 9.00 =   72.00$ (cost of 8 packages of paper)
                    205.50 (total cost of all items)

The next problem also requires two separate operations to find the correct answer.

The librarian at a high school needs to order enough labels to mark all the books in the school library. Each shelf holds approximately 50 books, and there are 200 shelves in the library. If the labels are sold in packages of 300, what is the smallest number of packages of labels the librarian needs to order to relabel all the books in the library?

The first step in solving this problem must be to calculate the total number of labels needed to mark all of the books. The number of labels must equal the number of books in the library. You can determine how many labels are needed by using the information from the problem to calculate how many books there are.

Step 1:   50 books per shelf × 200 shelves = 10,000 books

          10,000 books = 10,000 labels needed

You must now determine how many packages of labels the librarian must order to obtain 10,000 labels. The problem says that the labels come in packages of 300. To find out how many packages are needed, you must divide 10,000 by 300.

$$10,000 \div 300 = 33\frac{1}{3}$$

Obviously, the librarian cannot order $33\frac{1}{3}$ packages of labels. You must use your common sense to realize that the librarian needs to order a whole number of packages. The number must be rounded to 34, which is the smallest number of packages the librarian must order.

Another two-step problem involves finding averages. The following problem shows how to apply the problem-solving method to such problems.

A student receives two scores of 85, one score of 86, and two scores of 87 on tests in a history class. What is the average of the student's scores?

When you carefully read the problem, you discover that it asks for an average. Knowing that you are looking for an average helps you develop a plan for the problem. To find an average, you must add several numbers together and then divide by the number of items added. In this case, you must add the five scores. Next, you need to divide the sum of the scores by 5. An appropriate plan for solving this problem must include both steps.

Step 1: $85 + 85 + 86 + 87 + 87 = ?$

Step 2:   Answer to Step 1 ÷ 5

Remember that the problem says that the student received *two* scores of 85 and *two* scores of 87. As a result, the numbers 85 and 87 must be added twice to find the correct average.

The plan for this problem must be carried out in two separate steps. It is important to check your calculations after each step.

Step 1:   85
           85
           86
           87
         + 87
          430   Step 2: $\frac{430}{5} = 86$

An average should be a value that is approximately in the middle of all the numbers being added. Look at the numbers given in the problem. The numbers range from 85 to 87. As a result, the calculated answer, 86, is reasonable.

Many word problems ask you to find an average. You may be asked to find average scores (as in this problem), the average amount of time it takes to do something, or the average of several measurements (e.g., Elliott weighed 7 bags of peaches and found that their weights were as follows. . . . What is the average weight of the bags of peaches?). The key to solving problems that involve averages is to include all the numbers given in the problem and to divide by the number of values added.

In addition to integers, word problems may involve fractions, ratios and proportions, decimals, and percents. They may also involve calculation of units of measurement and conversions between equivalent but different units of measurement. The problems in the next five sections discuss strategies for solving problems involving values that are not whole numbers and problems involving units of measurement.

Problems Involving Fractions

Remember that a fraction is a value that represents part of a whole. For example, if you cut a pie into 6 equal-sized pieces, each piece is $\frac{1}{6}$ of the whole pie.

In general, word problems that contain fractions are very similar to word problems that use only whole numbers. You can still apply the four-step problem-solving process presented earlier in this chapter to find the answer to a word problem involving fractions. Solving problems that contain fractions does require some special math skills, however. Reread the section on fractions in the previous chapter to review the math skills you will need to solve word problems involving fractions.

Remember that the top number in a fraction is called the numerator and the bottom number is called the denominator. You must keep in mind that you have to find a common denominator for all the fractions in a problem before the fractions can be added or subtracted. It is important to include the process of finding a common denominator in your plan for solving a word problem.

The following example shows a problem that involves finding a common denominator.

> A car's gasoline tank is $\frac{7}{8}$ full at the beginning of a trip and $\frac{1}{4}$ full at the end of the trip. If the tank holds 20 gallons when full, how many gallons of gasoline were used on the trip?

Carefully reading the problem shows that you must find the number of gallons of gasoline used. You must calculate how much gasoline was used from the time the tank was $\frac{7}{8}$ full to the time it was $\frac{1}{4}$ full. You know that the tank, when it is full, holds 20 gallons of gasoline. The plan for solving this problem should involve three steps. First, you must find a common denominator for the fractions $\frac{7}{8}$ and $\frac{1}{4}$. Second, you must find the difference between $\frac{7}{8}$ and $\frac{1}{4}$ (that is, you must find out how much less $\frac{1}{4}$ is than $\frac{7}{8}$). Finally, you must find out what fractional part of 20 gallons was used during the trip. One plan for solving this problem would be written as follows.

Step 1:   Find common denominator

Step 2: $\frac{7}{8} - \frac{1}{4} = ?$

Step 3:   Answer from Step 2 times 20 gallons

To find the common denominator of $\frac{7}{8}$ and $\frac{1}{4}$, you must get the two denominators to be the same. To do this, you must multiply the fraction $\frac{1}{4}$ times $\frac{2}{2}$, as follows.

Step 1: $\frac{1}{4} \times \frac{2}{2} = \frac{2}{8}$

Now you are ready to do Step 2 of the plan.

$$\frac{7}{8} - \frac{2}{8} = \frac{5}{8}$$

Step 2 tells you that the car used $\frac{5}{8}$ of a tank of gasoline during the trip. You know from the problem that one whole tank of gasoline contains 20 gallons. You now need to calculate how many gallons there are in $\frac{5}{8}$ of a tank.

Step 3: $\frac{5}{8} \times 20 = \frac{100}{8} = 12\frac{1}{2}$ gallons

The calculations indicate that the car used $12\frac{1}{2}$ gallons of gas during the trip. The next step in the problem-solving process is to check that answer to see if it is reasonable. In problems involving fractions, you can often determine by estimation whether or not your answer is reasonable. In this problem, for example, $\frac{5}{8}$ of a tank is just slightly more than $\frac{1}{2}$ of a tank ($\frac{4}{8} = \frac{1}{2}$). If the full tank holds 20 gallons of gasoline, $\frac{1}{2}$ of the tank would contain 10 gallons of gasoline. Since $\frac{5}{8}$ is a little bit more than $\frac{1}{2}$, the number of gallons in the answer should be just a little more than 10 gallons. Therefore, $12\frac{1}{2}$ gallons is a reasonable answer.

You could also solve this problem by finding the number of gallons in the tank at the beginning of the trip and the number of gallons in the tank at the end of the trip. You would then subtract the ending amount from the beginning amount to find the number of gallons used during the trip.

Step 1:   (gallons in the tank at the beginning of the trip)

$$\frac{7}{8} \times 20 = \frac{140}{8} = 17\frac{1}{2} \text{ gallons}$$

Step 2:   (gallons in the tank at the end of the trip)

$$\frac{1}{4} \times 20 = \frac{20}{4} = 5 \text{ gallons}$$

Step 3:   (gallons used on the trip)

$$17\frac{1}{2} - 5 = 12\frac{1}{2} \text{ gallons}$$

Often, problems about cars and gasoline involve finding the distance a car has traveled or finding the number of miles a car can go on a gallon of gasoline. For example, suppose the problem given above had said the following.

A car's gasoline tank holds 20 gallons and the car gets 22 miles per gallon. If the car uses $12\frac{1}{2}$ gallons of gasoline on a trip, how many miles did the car travel on the trip?

To solve this problem, you must find the number of miles driven on the trip. Since the car gets 22 miles per gallon, the most appropriate plan would be to multiply the number of gallons used by 22. Therefore, the number of miles driven on the entire trip is as follows.

$$12\frac{1}{2} \times 22 = 275 \text{ miles}$$

The next example involves other math skills that are commonly used in solving problems that contain fractions.

A construction worker has a cable that is $22\frac{1}{2}$ feet long. The builder needs to use $\frac{2}{3}$ of the cable in a construction project. The rest of the cable will not be used. How long is the piece of cable that will not be used?

The information in the problem makes it clear that you must find the length of the piece of cable that will not be used. A two-step plan will be needed to find out how much of the cable will not be used.

Step 1:   Find out what fractional part of the cable will not be used.

Step 2:   Find the length (in feet) of the piece of cable that will not be used.

You know that $\frac{2}{3}$ of the cable will be used. To find out how much of the cable will not be used, you must subtract the amount of cable that will be used from the entire cable. The entire cable counts as 1 whole cable (remember that the number 1 can be converted to a fraction by using the same number in the numerator and in the denominator; in this case, $1 = \frac{3}{3}$). Carry out Step 1 of the plan by subtracting $\frac{2}{3}$ from the length of 1 whole cable.

$$1 - \frac{2}{3} = \frac{3}{3} - \frac{2}{3} = \frac{1}{3}$$

You now know that $\frac{1}{3}$ of the cable will not be used. You need to find out how many feet equal $\frac{1}{3}$ of $22\frac{1}{2}$ feet, the length of the whole cable. To do this, you must multiply $\frac{1}{3}$ times $22\frac{1}{2}$.

Step 2: $\frac{1}{3} \times 22\frac{1}{2} = \frac{1}{3} \times \frac{45}{2} = \frac{15}{2} = 7\frac{1}{2}$ feet

This is a reasonable answer since we can easily estimate that $\frac{1}{3}$ of $22\frac{1}{2}$ is something close to 7. The key is to focus on the amount that will not be used. You could also solve this problem by determining the amount being used ($\frac{2}{3} \times 22\frac{1}{2} = 15$) and subtracting that from $22\frac{1}{2}$.

The following problem uses many of the same skills as the preceding problem, but this problem requires one additional step.

A developer has 15 acres of land available and is going to divide the land into $\frac{1}{4}$-acre and $\frac{1}{2}$-acre lots, using all the available land. If there are to be 26 $\frac{1}{4}$-acre lots, how many $\frac{1}{2}$-acre lots will there be?

The problem asks for the number of $\frac{1}{2}$-acre lots of land that can be made. The answer clearly depends on how much land is available after the $\frac{1}{4}$-acre lots have been made. The first step in solving this problem is to calculate the amount of land that will be used to make 26 $\frac{1}{4}$-acre lots.

$$26 \times \frac{1}{4} = \frac{26}{4} = \frac{13}{2} = 6\frac{1}{2} \text{ acres}$$

The second step in solving this problem is to find out how many acres are available for the $\frac{1}{2}$-acre lots.

$$15 - 6\frac{1}{2} = 8\frac{1}{2} \text{ acres}$$

Finally, you must calculate the number of $\frac{1}{2}$-acre lots in $8\frac{1}{2}$ acres.

$$8\frac{1}{2} \div \frac{1}{2} = \frac{17}{2} \times \frac{2}{1} = 17$$

A common mistake here would be to multiply $8\frac{1}{2}$ by $\frac{1}{2}$ to get $4\frac{1}{4}$ lots. However, this does not make sense. If you use your common sense, it is clear that there must be more than $4\frac{1}{4}$ lots of $\frac{1}{2}$ acre each in $8\frac{1}{2}$ acres.

Sometimes, it is difficult to tell that a problem involves fractions until you read it carefully and develop a plan to solve it. The following problem shows one such case.

On a trip, a car travels 10 miles at 40 miles per hour. How many *minutes* does the entire trip take?

To solve this problem, it helps to know about a special mathematical relationship between distance and time. This relationship is described by the equation Distance = Rate × Time. This equation means that you can find the distance traveled on a trip by multiplying the speed of the car times the length of time the car was moving. When someone says that a car is traveling at 50 miles per hour, he or she is using this principle to describe the distance the car goes in terms of how fast it is moving and how long it takes to move. Many textbooks and tests include lists of equations like this one. Be sure to check for such a list of equations before you begin to work on this type of problem.

The first step in solving this problem is to determine what you must find. You are looking for the number of *minutes* the trip took. The equation Distance = Rate × Time is intended to find the distance traveled. To use this equation, you must first convert it to a form that can be used to find *time.* You can do this by dividing both sides of the equation by *rate.*

$$\frac{\text{Distance (D)}}{\text{Rate (R)}} = \frac{\text{Rate (R)}}{\text{Rate (R)}} \times \text{Time (T)}$$

This gives you the new equation.

$$\frac{D}{R} = T$$

This new equation tells you that you can find the time required for the trip by dividing the distance traveled by the speed of the car. You can substitute 10 miles for D and 40 mph for R.

$$\frac{10 \text{ miles}}{40 \text{ mph}} = \frac{1}{4} \text{ of an hour}$$

This tells you that the car traveled for $\frac{1}{4}$ hour. Notice, however, that the problem requires you to state your answer in minutes. This means that you must now convert time from hours to minutes. You can do this by multiplying $\frac{1}{4}$ (the portion of an hour required for the trip) times 60 (the number of minutes in an hour).

$$\frac{1}{4} \text{ hour} \times 60 \text{ minutes/hour} = 15 \text{ minutes}$$

Problems Involving Ratios and Proportions

A ratio is a special value that is used to compare two numbers by division. Ratios can be thought of as fractions. For example, a recipe may call for 1 cup of water and 2 cups of flour. In the recipe, the ratio of water to flour would be 1 (water) to 2 (flour). This ratio would be written $\frac{1}{2}$.

A proportion is a mathematical statement that says that two ratios are equal. For example, a car that travels 100 kilometers in 4 hours is traveling at the same speed as a car that goes 50 kilometers in 2 hours (both cars are traveling at 25 kilometers/hour). A proportion describing this relationship would be written $\frac{100}{4} = \frac{50}{2}$.

Word problems involving ratios and proportions often ask you to find a relationship between two things (such as the relationship between time and work done or the relationship between time and distance traveled).

To solve word problems involving ratios and proportions, you should generally treat these quantities as if they were fractions.

The following problems involve the use of ratios and proportions.

> If it takes 6 hours to put together a swing set, what part of the job would be completed after 2 hours and 40 minutes of work?

The question asks you to find the part of the job that can be done in a certain amount of time. To find an answer, you must find out about the relationship between time and work done. This suggests that you will need to use ratios to solve the problem. The first step in planning how to solve this problem should involve finding the ratio of time actually worked and the time needed to do the whole job.

Step 1:   (Finding the ratio)

$$\frac{2 \text{ hours and } 40 \text{ minutes}}{6 \text{ hours}} \quad \text{(time actually worked)} \atop \text{(time needed to do whole job)}$$

As you can see, however, the numerator and the denominator contain different units. The second step in solving this problem must be to change either the numerator or the denominator so that both have the same unit. If you use hours as the units, you need to convert 40 minutes to a portion of an hour. Since 1 hour contains 60 minutes, 40 minutes $= \frac{40}{60}$ of an hour $= \frac{2}{3}$ of an hour. Now that you have the same unit in both parts of the fraction, you can calculate what part of the job can be completed in $2\frac{2}{3}$ hours.

Step 3: $\dfrac{2\frac{2}{3} \text{ hours}}{6 \text{ hours}} = \dfrac{8}{3} \div 6 = \dfrac{8}{3} \times \dfrac{1}{6} = \dfrac{8}{18} = \dfrac{4}{9}$ of the job can be completed.

You could also solve this problem by converting both the numerator and the denominator to minutes. Then the calculations would be as follows.

$$\frac{2 \text{ hours and } 40 \text{ minutes}}{6 \text{ hours}} = \frac{160 \text{ minutes}}{360 \text{ minutes}} = \frac{4}{9}$$

You can use estimation to decide if this is a reasonable answer. The entire job of putting the swing set together should take 6 hours. This means that it would take 3 hours to finish $\frac{1}{2}$ of the job. Since 2 hours and 40 minutes is close to 3 hours, the correct answer should be close to (but less than) $\frac{1}{2}$. The calculated answer, $\frac{4}{9}$, is close to but slightly less than $\frac{1}{2}$. Therefore, $\frac{4}{9}$ is a reasonable answer.

In the next problem, you must use both ratios and estimation to find a solution.

> There are 347,583 houses in Sutton City. Approximately 3 of every 5 houses have at least one television. Which of the following is the best estimate of the number of houses in Sutton City that do not have a television?

It is very important for you to read problems like this one carefully. First, you should notice that the question asks you to find the number of houses in Sutton City that do *not* have televisions, rather than the number of houses that do have them. Second, the problem contains several key words that will help you solve it. The words *approximately* and *estimate* are key words in this problem. They indicate that you will not be able to find an exact answer. This means that you can use rounding to help you solve the problem, rather than struggling with numbers that are difficult to use in calculations. The first step in solving this problem, therefore, is to round 347,583 to 350,000.

The second step in solving this problem is to find the ratios you need to estimate how many houses do *not* have televisions.

You know that approximately 3 of every 5 houses have a television. From this information you can create the ratio.

$\frac{3}{5}$ (televisions)
 (houses)

If every house had a television, the ratio of televisions to houses would be:

$\frac{5}{5}$ (televisions)
 (houses)

You can find out how many houses do *not* have televisions by subtracting the number of houses that do have televisions from the number of houses that *could* have televisions.

$$\frac{5}{5} - \frac{3}{5} = \frac{2}{5}$$

This tells you that approximately $\frac{2}{5}$ of the houses do *not* have televisions. The final step in solving this problem is to use the ratio you have just found to estimate how many houses (out of 350,000) do not have televisions.

$$\frac{2}{5} \times 350,000 = 140,000 \text{ (houses)}$$

Approximately 140,000 houses in Sutton City do not have televisions.

The next problem shows you how proportions may be used to solve some word problems.

You can obtain 5 tablespoons of lemon juice by squeezing 2 lemons. How many tablespoons of juice can be squeezed from 11 lemons?

The question asks how much juice you can get from 11 lemons. To solve the problem, you must find out about the relationship between lemons and lemon juice. The first sentence states that you can get 5 tablespoons from 2 lemons. First, you need to find out how much juice you could get from 1 lemon.

Step 1:   2 lemons give 5 tablespoons of juice
          1 lemon = $\frac{1}{2}$ of 2 lemons

Therefore, the amount of juice you can get from 1 lemon should be $\frac{1}{2}$ the amount of juice you would get from 2 lemons:

$$\frac{1}{2} \text{ of } 5 = 2\frac{1}{2} \text{ tablespoons of juice from 1 lemon}$$

Step 2:   You can now calculate the total amount of juice that could be squeezed from 11 lemons by multiplying as follows.

$$11 \times 2\frac{1}{2} = 27\frac{1}{2} \text{ tablespoons of juice}$$

You could also solve this problem by setting up a proportion. The proportion would be made up of two fractions that describe the relationship between lemons and the amount of juice. A proportion for this problem would look like this.

$$\frac{5 \text{ tablespoons}}{2 \text{ lemons}} = \frac{? \text{ tablespoons}}{11 \text{ lemons}}$$

To find an answer, you must cross-multiply. This means that you should multiply the numerator of one ratio by the denominator of the other.

$$5 \times 11 = ? \times 2$$

$$\frac{55}{2} = ?$$

$$\frac{55}{2} = 27\frac{1}{2}$$

Problems Involving Decimals

Like fractions, decimals represent a part of a whole. To solve word problems involving decimals, you must use many of the same skills you use to solve other kinds of problems. You must also use a variety of special skills. You can review the math skills for working with decimals by rereading the appropriate sections in the previous chapter.

One common problem that occurs in working with decimals has to do with the placement of the decimal point. In some problems, the decimal point must shift positions when you perform certain math operations. Be sure to check that the decimal point is in the correct place as you solve problems involving decimals.

The following problem involves performing regular math operations on decimals.

A family monitors their gas-meter readings for several months. The meter readings tell how much gas was used each month. The meter reading was 100.4 on June 1, 108.7 on July 1, 118.0 on August 1, 126.2 on September 1, and 135.2 on October 1. Between which two dates was the *greatest* amount of gas used?

This problem asks you to calculate the amount of gas used by the family. To do this, you must subtract the meter reading for the beginning of one month from the meter reading for the beginning of the following month. You must subtract several times to find the answer to the problem. An appropriate plan for this problem would be as follows.

Meter reading in July – reading in June = 108.7 – 100.4 = 8.3
Reading in August – reading in July = 118.0 – 108.7 = 9.3
Reading in September – reading in August = 126.2 – 118.0 = 8.2
Reading in October – reading in September = 135.2 – 126.2 = 9.0

After carrying out the plan, it can be determined that the greatest amount of gas was used between July 1 and August 1.

Problems Involving Percents

Percents are also used to represent the parts of a whole. They are often used in problems involving sales and discounts, taxes, measurements, and test scores. Percents show how many 100ths of a whole are present. Percents can often be written as fractions by using the number in the percent as the numerator and using 100 as the denominator. For example, 75% can be written as $\frac{75}{100}$.

Although percents can be thought of as fractions, problems involving percents have some special characteristics. In problems involving percents, it is almost always necessary to change the percents to fractions or to decimals before you can do any mathematical operations. For that reason you should be very familiar with the method for converting percents to fraction or decimal form. Here is an example.

$$26\% = \frac{26}{100} = 0.26$$

Another fact that may help you deal with problems involving percents concerns key words. In a percent problem, the word *of* means that you should multiply. For example, to answer the question, *What is 25% of 50?* you should multiply 0.25 times 50.

The following problem shows some of the special math skills needed to solve problems involving percents.

Robin purchased a baseball glove for 30% off the original price of $52.00 and a bat for 25% off the original price of $15.00. What was the total cost of the two sale items?

When you read this problem, you will find that several steps will be required to solve it. You must calculate the sale price of each item, and then you must find the total cost of the items at their sale prices. It is very important for you to develop a thorough plan for solving problems like this one.

Step 1:   (Calculating the percent price of each item)

The original price of the glove is discounted by 30%. This means that the actual cost of the glove is 100% (the original price) minus 30% (the discount), which means that the glove costs 70% of the original price.

The original price of the bat is discounted by 25%. The actual cost of the bat will be 100% minus 25%, which means that the bat costs 75% of the original price.

Step 2:   (Calculating the cash price of each item)

To determine the cash price of the bat and the glove, you must find the discounted price of the glove by taking 70% of $52.00 and the discounted price of the bat by taking 75% of $15.00.

70% of $52.00 = $52.00   75% of $15.00 = $15.00
                 ×   0.70   ×   0.75
             $36.40 (glove) $11.25 (bat)

Step 3:   (Finding the total cost of the two items)

The problem asks you to find the total cost of buying the bat and the glove when they are on sale. To do this, you must add the discounted price of the glove to the discounted price of the bat.

    $36.40 (glove)
+ 11.25 (bat)
    $47.65

The following problem also shows some of the special math skills needed to solve problems involving percents.

A car dealer buys a used car for $3000. He decides to give the car a selling price that is 40% above his cost, but the car does not sell at that price. The dealer then marks down the selling price by 20%. If the car is sold at the reduced price, what is the dealer's profit in dollars?

The question asks you to find the dealer's profit (profit is the difference between the selling price and what the seller paid for the item in the first place). You must go through several steps to find the answer to this problem. First, you must find the price of the car when it is marked up by 40%. Next, you must determine the cost of the car when the original selling price is marked down by 20%. Finally, you must calculate the difference between the price at which the car is sold and the original cost of $3000.

Step 1:   (Finding the original selling price)

The original selling price is 40% more than $3000. There are two ways to find the original selling price: 1) compute 40% of $3000 and add that amount to $3000, or 2) compute 140% (100% + 40%) of $3000.

Method 1: $3000 $3000   Method 2: $3000
          × 0.40   + 1200   × 1.40
          $1200 $4200 $4200

The original selling price is $4200.

Step 2:   (Finding the discounted selling price)

The next step in solving this problem is to find the discounted selling price, which is 20% less than the original selling price of $4200. Again, there are two ways to calculate the discounted selling price: 1) compute 20% of $4200 and subtract the result from $4200, or 2) compute 80% (100% − 20%) of $4200.

Method 1: $4200 $4200   Method 2: $4200
            × 0.20   – 840   × 0.80
            $ 840 $3360 $3360

Step 3:   (Finding the car dealer's profit)

To find the dealer's profit, you must subtract the amount the dealer originally paid for the car (the dealer's cost) from the discounted selling price of the car.

$3360 – $3000 = $360

In this problem, it is very important to perform each of these steps in the correct order. This is because the two percents in the problem are percents of different quantities (40% of the dealer's cost and 20% of the original selling price). If you do not find the percents of the correct quantities, you will get the wrong answer.

Problems Involving Units of Measurement and Conversions

Numbers that define the size of something are called measurements. You can measure many different qualities of an object, such as length, area, volume, weight, capacity, or time. For each type of measurement, there are appropriate units of measurement that will fit the attribute being measured. For example, you can measure distance in miles, but not in quarts. You need to be familiar with the units that can be used to measure each quality.

The following table lists some of the units used for different types of measurements. Also in the table are the conversions that you will need to know in order to solve many problems involving measurement.

Conversions for Units of Measurement

U.S. Standard		**Metric**	
Length	12 inches = 1 foot 3 feet = 1 yard 5280 feet = 1 mile	**Length**	10 millimeters = 1 centimeter 100 centimeters = 1 meter 1000 meters = 1 kilometer
Volume (liquid)	2 pints = 1 quart 4 quarts = 1 gallon	**Volume**	1000 milliliters = 1 liter 1000 liters = 1 kiloliter
Weight	16 ounces = 1 pound 2000 pounds = 1 ton	**Weight**	1000 milligrams = 1 gram 1000 grams = 1 kilogram
Time	60 seconds = 1 minute 60 minutes = 1 hour 24 hours = 1 day		

For problems involving measurement, it is especially important to be consistent in the use of units of measurement. For example, multiplying hours by minutes or feet by inches will produce erroneous results. Remember to read the problem carefully and to note which unit of measurement is being used. Your answer must be in units consistent with the ones used in the question that is being asked. In many cases, keeping units of measurement consistent will require that you perform a conversion from one unit (e.g., millimeters) to another unit (e.g., meters).

Following are some examples of problems involving units of measurement and conversions.

On average, a woman's heart beats approximately 60 times per minute. About how many times a day will a woman's heart beat?

You need to convert 1 day to minutes to answer this question.

1 day = 24 hours
1 hour = 60 minutes

1 day = (24)(60) minutes
1 day = 1440 minutes

heartbeat rate = 60 times per minute
beats per day = (60)(1440)
               = 86400 beats per day

A woman's heart beats approximately 86,400 times per day.

A recipe for fruit punch calls for mixing 2 pints of fruit juice with enough water to make 3 gallons of the punch. How much water will be needed to make the 3 gallons of punch?

To answer this question you need to subtract 2 pints from 3 gallons. To do this you need to convert the gallons to pints.

1 gallon = 4 quarts
1 quart = 2 pints

      so

1 gallon = (4)(2) pints
1 gallon = 8 pints
3 gallons = 24 pints
3 gallons – 2 pints = 24 pints – 2 pints = 22 pints

It will require 22 pints of water to make the 3 gallons of punch.

An Olympic athlete can run 1 mile in 4 minutes. How fast is that in miles per hour?

This problem can be solved using ratios.

1 mile : 4 minutes
x miles : 1 hour

You must convert the hour to minutes.

$$\frac{1 \text{ mile}}{x \text{ miles}} = \frac{4 \text{ minutes}}{60 \text{ minutes}} \quad \text{or} \quad \frac{1 \text{ mile}}{4 \text{ minutes}} = \frac{x \text{ miles}}{60 \text{ minutes}} \qquad \textit{Write a proportion.}$$

$60 = 4x$ $60 = 4x$ *Cross multiply.*
$x = 15$ $x = 15$ *Solve for* x.

The athlete can run 15 miles per hour.

The next problem requires the use of *scientific notation,* which is a convenient way to rewrite very large or very small numbers. Remember that scientific notation involves expressing a number as the product of a number between 1 and 10 and an exponent of 10. Thus the number 93,000,000 (93 million) becomes 9.3×10^7 in scientific notation. The exponent of 7 results from moving the decimal point seven places to the left.

Scientific notation often involves rounding (usually to what will be two decimal places) and then setting up the proper exponent. Thus, the number 128,653,531,126 would be rounded to 129,000,000,000 and then rewritten as 1.29×10^{11}.

In working with numbers written in scientific notation it is important to remember how to multiply and divide numbers with exponents. Note that:

$10^x \cdot 10^y = 10^{x+y}$ (i.e., in multiplication, exponents are added)

and $\dfrac{10^x}{10^y} = 10^{x-y}$ (i.e., in division, exponents are subtracted)

Consider the following problem.

For a science project, a student is making a scale drawing of Mercury and Jupiter. Jupiter's diameter, which is 1.44×10^5 km, he drew 30 inches long. How long should he draw Mercury's diameter if it is 4.88×10^6 m long?

This problem involves ratios and scientific notation. Since you are comparing the diameter of Jupiter, which is in kilometers, to the diameter of Mercury, which is in meters, you should first convert both to the same unit of measure.

4.88×10^6 m = Mercury's diameter

1000 m $= 1$ km or m $= \dfrac{\text{km}}{1000}$ *See table of conversions.*

$\dfrac{4.88 \times 10^6 \text{ m}}{1000}$ = Mercury's diameter in km   *Divide m by 1000 to get km.*

$\dfrac{4.88 \times 10^6}{10^3} = 4.88 \times 10^3$ km   *Use scientific notation and the property $\dfrac{10^x}{10^y} = 10^{(x-y)}$.*

Now set up a proportion to solve the problem.

$$\dfrac{\text{Jupiter's diameter}}{\text{Mercury's diameter}} = \dfrac{\text{Jupiter's scale diameter}}{\text{Mercury's scale diameter}}$$

$$\dfrac{1.44 \times 10^5 \text{ km}}{4.88 \times 10^3 \text{ km}} = \dfrac{30 \text{ in.}}{x \text{ in.}}$$

$$1.44 \times 10^5 x = 4.88 \times 10^3 (30)$$
$$= 146.40 \times 10^3$$
$$= 1.46 \times 10^2 \times 10^3$$
$$= 1.46 \times 10^5$$
$$x = \dfrac{1.46 \times 10^5}{1.44 \times 10^5}$$
$$= \text{approximately 1 inch}$$

Mercury's diameter should be drawn approximately 1 inch long.

Summary

As we pointed out earlier in this chapter, there is no single correct way to solve all word problems. That does not mean, however, that you should guess at an answer or skip a problem completely just because you have never seen that kind of problem before. Instead, you should keep in mind the general principles discussed in this chapter and use them as you work through each word problem. Most of the word problems you will encounter can be solved if you use the four basic steps that follow.

1. Read and understand the problem.

2. Develop a mathematical plan for solving the problem.

3. Carry out the plan accurately.

4. Check your answer to make sure it is reasonable.

Practice Exercises

The following exercises will help you review the skills covered in this chapter. Many of the types of questions presented here will be similar to those on the test; others will not. Remember that the purpose of the exercises is to give you practice on the skills rather than merely to prepare you for the test. Following these exercises are the Practice Exercise Explanations. They explain each question, the correct answer, and why the remaining choices are incorrect.

1. Jane estimates that she spends $\frac{1}{3}$ of each paycheck on rent and $\frac{1}{4}$ of each paycheck on food. If her paycheck is $300.00, how much does she have left over after paying for rent and food?

    A. $125.00

    B. $175.00

    C. $214.29

    D. $275.00

2. If Betty drives the 425 miles to Tulsa at a rate of 50 miles per hour, how many minutes away from Tulsa is she after 8 hours?

    A. $12\frac{1}{2}$

    B. 25

    C. 30

    D. 50

3. If 4 packages of spaghetti cost $2.10, how much will 6 packages cost at the same rate?

    A. $ 0.55

    B. $ 3.15

    C. $ 4.20

    D. $11.43

4. By working at a store, Bob gets a 15% employee discount. A bicycle that he wants usually sells for $80.00, but it is on sale at 35% off. How much will Bob have to pay for the bicycle after both the 35% reduction and the 15% discount?

    A. $ 4.20

    B. $ 7.80

    C. $40.00

    D. $44.20

5. Jan purchases 2 tapes at $3.95 each and 1 tape for $6.00. To the nearest cent, what is Jan's average cost per tape?

    A. $13.90

    B. $ 4.98

    C. $ 4.63

    D. $ 3.32

6. In Smith County, about $\frac{1}{3}$ of the 61,029 households have a dog. About how many households in Smith County do not have a dog?

    A. 43,000

    B. 40,000

    C. 20,000

    D.   2,000

7. After deductions totaling 25% of her pay, Ann received a paycheck of $270.00 (her net). What was her pay before deductions (her gross)?

    A. $ 67.50

    B. $ 202.50

    C. $ 360.00

    D. $1080.00

8. At the beginning of March, the Johnsons' water tank was $\frac{3}{4}$ full. At the end of the month it was $\frac{1}{8}$ full. If the tank's capacity is 200 gallons, how much water did the Johnsons use in March?

    A. 175 gal

    B. 150 gal

    C. 125 gal

    D.   25 gal

9. Mr. Diaz bought 10 boxes of alarm clocks for each of his 3 stores. If there are 12 alarm clocks in each box, how many alarm clocks did Mr. Diaz buy?

    A.   40

    B.   42

    C. 120

    D. 360

10. A 12.5-liter punch bowl is filled with 3.5 liters of orange juice, 1.5 liters of pineapple juice, and 7.5 liters of ginger ale. Approximately what percent of the punch is made of orange and pineapple juices?

    A. 10

    B. 30

    C. 40

    D. 60

11. On a map, 2 centimeters represents 50 kilometers. If 2 cities are 10 centimeters apart on the map, what is the actual distance between the 2 cities?

   A.   10 kilometers

   B.   50 kilometers

   C.   100 kilometers

   D.   250 kilometers

12. A supermarket has 36 crates of apples, 7 crates of bananas, 18 crates of oranges, and 11 crates of grapefruit. What is the ratio of crates of apples to crates of oranges in the supermarket?

   A. $\frac{3}{4}$

   B. $\frac{2}{3}$

   C. $\frac{1}{2}$

   D. $\frac{2}{1}$

13. Julia's lawn is rectangular and measures 500 feet by 300 feet. One bag of fertilizer will cover approximately 600 square yards. How many bags of fertilizer must she buy to fertilize her lawn?

   A.   15 bags

   B.   28 bags

   C.   84 bags

   D.   250 bags

14. Ice weighs approximately 0.92 grams per cubic centimeter. A sculptor is using a block of ice measuring 4 meters by 0.5 meters by 2 meters. Approximately how many grams does the block weigh?

   A. 3.68×10^6 grams

   B. 4.35×10^6 grams

   C. 3.68×10^7 grams

   D. 4.35×10^7 grams

15. The speed of light is approximately 3×10^8 meters per second. How long would it take light from a star 1.5×10^8 kilometers away to reach Earth?

   A.   0.5 seconds

   B.   2 seconds

   C.   2.5 minutes

   D.   8.3 minutes

Practice Exercise Explanations

1. **Correct Response: A.** You can solve this problem in two ways. First, you might find $\frac{1}{3}$ of $300.00 and $\frac{1}{4}$ of $300.00, add those two figures, and then subtract their sum from $300.00.

    $\frac{1}{3}$ of $300.00 = $\frac{1}{3}$ × $300.00 = $100.00   Amount left: $300.00

    $\frac{1}{4}$ of $300.00 = $\frac{1}{4}$ × $300.00 = $ 75.00   − $175.00

     Total: $175.00 $125.00

    Or, you could first add the fractions $\frac{1}{3}$ and $\frac{1}{4}$ to get $\frac{7}{12}$. Then find $\frac{7}{12}$ of $300.00 and subtract that number from $300.00.

    $$\frac{1}{3} + \frac{1}{4} = \frac{4}{12} + \frac{3}{12} = \frac{7}{12}$$

    $$\frac{7}{12} \times \$300.00 = \$175.00$$

    $300.00 − $175.00 = $125.00

    Response B is incorrect because it calculates the amount spent, not the amount left over. Response C is the result of incorrectly adding $\frac{1}{3}$ and $\frac{1}{4}$. Response D results from multiplying rather than adding $\frac{1}{3}$ and $\frac{1}{4}$.

2. **Correct Response: C.** To solve this problem, use the equation Distance = Rate × Time to find how far Betty has traveled.

    50 mph (rate) × 8 hours (time) = 400 miles (distance)

    Thus after 8 hours, the distance left is 425 − 400 = 25 miles. Again, use a form of the distance equation, Time $= \dfrac{\text{Distance}}{\text{Rate}}$, to find out the time left in the trip.

    $\dfrac{25 \text{ miles (distance)}}{50 \text{ mph (rate)}} = \dfrac{1}{2}$ hour (time), or 30 minutes

    Response A is the result of incorrect division. Response B incorrectly refers to the number of miles left, not to the time. Response D refers to the speed of travel, 50 mph.

3. **Correct Response: B.** You can solve this problem in two ways. First you can determine the cost per package, then multiply that number by 6.

    If 4 packages cost $2.10, 1 package costs $\dfrac{\$2.10}{4}$ = $0.525

    6 packages cost 6($0.525) = $3.15.

    You may also use a proportion to solve the problem.

    $$\frac{4 \text{ packages}}{\$2.10} = \frac{6 \text{ packages}}{\$x}$$

    $4x = 6(\$2.10) = \$12.60$

    $x = \$3.15$

Response A refers to the cost of only 1 package. Response C finds the cost of each package to be $0.70. Response D is the result of incorrectly setting up the proportion as $\frac{4}{2.10} = \frac{x}{6}$.

4. **Correct Response: D.** To solve this problem, you must first recall that 100% represents the entire quantity, so a 35% reduction leaves 65% remaining.

$100\% - 35\% = 65\%$

65% of $\$80.00 = (0.65)(80) = \$52.00$

Then, $100\% - 15\% = 85\%$

85% of $\$52.00 = (0.85)(52) = \$44.20$

Response A incorrectly finds 35% of $80.00 and then 15% of that number. Response B uses the 15% discounted amount of $52.00. Response C adds the two discounts of 35% and 15% to get 50%. This is incorrect because the discounts are on two different prices. Remember to check answers for common sense. In this example, you could probably eliminate responses A and B for that reason.

5. **Correct Response: C.** To solve this problem, you must add the 3 tape prices and divide by the number of tapes.

$\$3.95 + \$3.95 + \$6.00 = \$13.90$

Average $= \$13.90 \div 3 = \$4.63$

Response A adds the 3 prices but neglects to divide. Response B adds 2 prices and divides by 2. Response D adds 2 prices and divides by 3. You can check the answer choices for common sense if you recall that an average has to lie between the highest and the lowest values that were used to determine it. In this problem, the average has to be between $3.95 and $6.00, so you can eliminate $13.90 right away.

6. **Correct Response: B.** In this problem, the word *about* indicates that the fraction $\frac{1}{3}$ is approximate. Therefore, you should use 60,000 as an estimate.

$\frac{1}{3}$ of $60,000 = \left(\frac{1}{3}\right)(60,000) = 20,000$ have dogs

$60,000 - 20,000 = 40,000$ do not have dogs

Response A incorrectly rounds off 61,029 to 65,000 instead of to 60,000.

Response C incorrectly finds how many do have dogs. Response D incorrectly finds $\frac{1}{3}$ of 60,000 to be 2000, a computation error.

7.   **Correct Response: C.** To solve this problem, you must use a proportion.

100% of Ann's pay − 25% deductions = 75% of the pay

Thus, 75% of her pay is $270.00.

The proportion is $\frac{75}{100} = \frac{270}{n}$, $75n = 27{,}000$, $n = \frac{27{,}000}{75}$, $n = \$360.00$.

Response A incorrectly finds 25% of Ann's net pay. Response B incorrectly finds 75% of her net pay. Response D incorrectly solves the problem using 25% of gross pay, not 75%.

8.   **Correct Response: C.** To solve this problem, you can first determine the amount of water in the tank at the beginning of March and then the amount in the tank at the end of the month.

$\frac{3}{4}$ of 200 gal $= \left(\frac{3}{4}\right)(200) = 150$ gal (start)

$-\frac{1}{8}$ of 200 gal $= \left(\frac{1}{8}\right)(200) = \underline{-25 \text{ gal (end)}}$

125 gal used

Response A adds rather than subtracts the quantities. Response B finds only $\frac{3}{4}$ of 200 gallons. Response D finds only $\frac{1}{8}$ of 200 gallons.

9.   **Correct Response: D.** To solve this problem, first multiply the number of boxes by the number of stores, and then multiply by the number of alarm clocks in each box.

10 boxes × 3 stores = 30 boxes

30 boxes × 12 clocks = 360 clocks

Response A multiplies the number of boxes by the number of alarm clocks in a box and then divides by the number of stores. Response B incorrectly adds the number of alarm clocks in one box to the total number of boxes. Response C incorrectly multiplies 10 boxes by 12 alarm clocks.

10. **Correct Response: C.** To solve this problem, add the amount of orange juice and pineapple juice, and divide this total by 12.5 to calculate the percent.

3.5 + 1.5 = 5.0 $\frac{5.0}{12.5} = 0.4$ 0.4 × 100 = 40%

Response A incorrectly divides the number of liters of pineapple juice by the total. Response B incorrectly divides the number of liters of orange juice by the total. Response D multiplies, instead of divides, to get the percentage.

11. **Correct Response: D.** To solve this distance problem, you must use a proportion:

$\frac{2 \text{ centimeters}}{50 \text{ kilometers}} = \frac{10 \text{ centimeters}}{x \text{ kilometers}}$

$2x = 500$

$x = 250$ kilometers

Response A incorrectly equates centimeters and kilometers. Response B uses the scale of 50 kilometers without using the proportion. Response C incorrectly multiplies the scale units given.

12. **Correct Response: D.** The ratio of crates of apples to crates of oranges equals the total number of crates of apples divided by the total number of crates of oranges.

$$\frac{36 \text{ crates of apples}}{18 \text{ crates of oranges}}$$

This simplifies to $\frac{2}{1}$.

Response A incorrectly adds the numbers for apples and oranges and divides by the total number of crates. Response B incorrectly divides the number for apples by the number for apples plus oranges. Response C gives the inverse of the correct ratio.

13. **Correct Response: B.** The area of the lawn in square feet ($500 \times 300 = 150{,}000$) must be converted to square yards by dividing by 9. This number must be divided by 600 to get the number of bags. Thus:

$$\frac{150{,}000}{9} \cdot \frac{1}{600} = \frac{50{,}000}{(3)600} = \frac{500}{18} = \frac{250}{9} = 27.78$$

Since the number of bags must be a whole number, 28 bags is the answer. Response A is the result of incorrectly finding the area of the lawn. Response C is the result of dividing the square feet of the area by 3 instead of 9 to convert to square yards. Response D results from failing to convert feet to yards.

14. **Correct Response: A.** To calculate the volume of the ice in cubic centimeters, each dimension must be converted to centimeters. Since 1 meter = 100 centimeters, the dimensions are 400 cm by 50 cm by 200 cm. The volume is thus $(400)(50)(200) = 4{,}000{,}000$ cubic centimeters. In scientific notation this becomes 4×10^6 cubic centimeters. To find the weight, we multiply this number by 0.92, or $\frac{92}{100}$.

$$4 \times 10^6 \cdot \frac{92}{100} = \frac{(4.92) \times 10^6}{10^2}$$

$$= \frac{368 \times 10^6}{10^2}$$

$$= \frac{3.68 \times 10^2 \times 10^6}{10^2}$$

$$= 3.68 \times 10^6 \text{ grams}$$

Response B results from choosing the wrong operation when changing the volume to weight. Responses C and D are the result of incorrectly converting the meters to centimeters. Also in response D, an error was made in choosing the operation when changing volume to weight.

15. **Correct Response: D.** Two conversions are needed for this problem. First we convert to meters the distance of the star from the Earth. The distance becomes $1.5 \times 10^8 \times 10^3$. Dividing this by 3×10^8 gives us

$$\frac{1.5 \times 10^8 \times 10^3}{3 \times 10^8} = \frac{1.5 \times 10^3}{3} = 0.5 \times 10^3 = 500 \text{ seconds.}$$

Response B results from dividing backwards and disregarding the conversion of km to m. Responses A and C are the result of incorrect conversions from km to m.

Study Ideas

A careful study of the above exercises and the explanations of the answers will help you review important skills relating to word problems. In these exercises you were asked to solve problems involving integers, fractions, decimals, percents, ratios and proportions, units of measurement, and conversions. The exercises are designed to give you practice in these skills. You may wish to reread parts of the chapter that address specific kinds of word problems with which you have difficulty.

You should be aware of the techniques for solving word problems. You are likely to come across similar problems in college, at home, and on the job.

When solving word problems, be sure to remember the following:

1. Many word problems reflect real-life situations.

2. Use your basic computation skills to complete the word problem (see the previous chapter for a review of these skills).

3. Read each problem carefully, noticing key words and values.

4. Identify the actual question you are being asked to solve.

5. Be sure to develop a plan for solving the problem and carry out that plan accurately.

6. No matter how simple the problem may appear, remember to check your answer to verify that the result is reasonable.

Chapter 12

SOLVE PROBLEMS INVOLVING DATA INTERPRETATION AND ANALYSIS

This skill includes interpreting information from line graphs, bar graphs, pie charts, pictographs, and tables; recognizing graphic representations of data; and analyzing and interpreting data using measures of central tendency and the concept of variability.

Introduction

Graphs and tables are used to present information in an organized way. It is often much easier to see trends and relationships among numbers if they are presented in picture form. This chapter explains how graphs and tables are constructed and how data are displayed using graphs and tables. You will learn to read and create bar graphs, pie charts, line graphs, and pictographs, and to draw conclusions from data presented in tabular form.

Just as pictures and tables help us understand the meaning of numbers, so do various kinds of summaries of numbers. Two important concepts related to summarizing numerical information are *central tendency* and *variability*. Measures of central tendency tell us something about the middle or center of a group of numbers; the several kinds of *averages* that can be drawn from lists of numbers are all measures of central tendency. Measures of variability tell us something about how similar or how different from the average the entire group of numbers is; numbers that are tightly clustered around a center have little variability, while numbers that are scattered widely around a central number have greater variability. If you understand measures of central tendency and variability, you will be better able to evaluate data presented as a list of numbers or a graph and to compare two or more sets of data. These topics are discussed in this chapter.

Bar Graphs

The graph below is a bar graph. It is one of the simplest means of presenting data (information) in pictorial form.

State University Enrollment

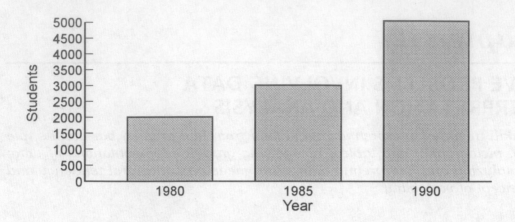

The title of this graph is *State University Enrollment,* and it presents enrollment data for the years 1980, 1985, and 1990. Notice that the lines that form the bottom and the left side of the graph are labeled and have numbers printed at regular intervals along their lengths. Each of these labeled lines is called an *axis* (plural is *axes*). The vertical axis, sometimes called the *y-axis,* is labeled *Students* and represents student enrollment. The axis is marked at intervals by very short lines called *ticks.* Each tick is labeled (0, 500, 1000, 1500, etc.). The distance between two ticks represents 500 students. The horizontal axis, sometimes called the *x-axis,* is labeled *Year* and represents the years 1980, 1985, and 1990.

The labels along the horizontal axis (the base of the graph) indicate that the three shaded bars represent student enrollment for the years 1980, 1985, and 1990. The leftmost bar represents enrollment for the year 1980, the middle bar represents enrollment for the year 1985, and the rightmost bar represents enrollment for the year 1990. The height of each bar corresponds to the student enrollment for that year. The numbers along the vertical axis (left side of graph) allow us to assign a value (number of students) to the height of each bar.

To determine the number of students enrolled in 1985, first find the bar that represents 1985 by reading the labels along the bottom of the graph. The middle bar represents 1985. Next, draw a horizontal line from the top of the middle bar to the vertical axis. Look at the point at which this horizontal line meets the vertical axis. This point is labeled *3000.* This indicates that the student enrollment for the year 1985 was *3000.* A taller bar represents a larger student enrollment.

A few observations about student enrollment can be made by just looking at the graph. First, the largest increase in enrollment occurred between 1985 and 1990, since the change in height between these two bars is the greatest. Second, enrollment increased between 1980 and 1985, and between 1985 and 1990, since the bars are taller for each successive year. Third, the largest enrollment was in 1990, and the smallest was in 1980.

It is not always easy to read values directly from an axis; sometimes you must estimate to obtain values. That is because it is difficult in drawing the columns to be precise enough to distinguish between small differences. For instance, in 1985 there were about 3000 students. It would be difficult to distinguish on this graph between bars representing 2995 and 3005 students.

The graph below represents spending by the Defense Department for the years 1970, 1975, 1980, 1985, and 1990.

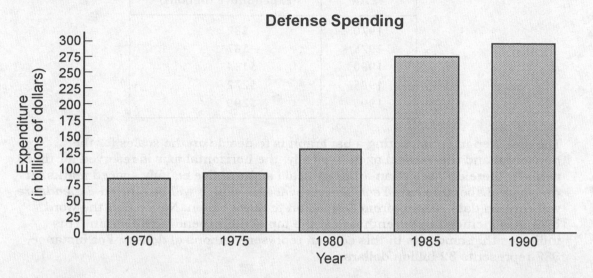

To determine the expenditure for the year 1980, draw a horizontal line from the top of the bar representing 1980 to the vertical axis. This line meets the vertical axis at a point that is between the points labeled *125* and *150*. To determine the expenditure for 1980, you must *interpolate,* or read between the lines. Each labeled point on the vertical axis represents $25 billion. Note that the line intersects the scale *about* one fifth (0.20) of the way between the marks; therefore, the interpolation is 125 + (0.20)(25) = 130. The one-fifth is a visual estimate, not a precise measurement. An interpolated value for 1970 might be 75 + (0.33)(25) = 83.25. You can see that an interpolation is computed by multiplying the value of each subdivision by a fractional estimate of the distance between the marks on the axis and adding that number to the lower subdivision. It must be emphasized that an interpolation is simply an estimate, or an educated guess.

Additional observations that could be made about these data are as follows.

1. Defense spending has increased during each five-year period.

2. The largest increase in spending occurred between 1980 and 1985.

3. The smallest increase occurred between 1970 and 1975.

4. If the trend continues, a projection can be made that defense spending will be greater than $300 billion in 1995. (Predicting values beyond the limits of a graph in this way is called *extrapolation.*)

As an aid to understanding bar graphs, return to the previous example, pretend that the graph has not yet been constructed, and use the actual data to construct the graph. A government publication indicates that defense expenditures for 1970, 1975, 1980, 1985, and 1990 were $82 billion, $87 billion, $134 billion, $272 billion, and $299 billion, respectively. There are many ways to organize these data; one method is described below.

YEAR	Expenditure (billions)
1970	$82
1975	$87
1980	$134
1985	$272
1990	$299

The first step in constructing a bar graph is to decide on the scales for the horizontal and the vertical axes. Typically, the horizontal axis is reserved for time periods; therefore, select an arbitrary scale and use five equally spaced marks for the years. Label this axis *Year*. The vertical axis, which will be labeled *Expenditure,* will contain data ranging from $82 billion to $299 billion. Notice that the word *billions* is included in parentheses at the top of the expenditure column. This indicates that amounts in this column represent billions of dollars. For instance, $82 represents 82 billion dollars.

The selection of a scale for the vertical axis is also arbitrary; however, as a general rule, subtract the starting value from the largest value, divide by 10, and round to a convenient number. In this example, use 0 as the smallest value and $299 as the largest. The computation is $\frac{(299 - 0)}{10}$, which we will round down to 25 since 25 is a convenient number to use. The scale will contain equally spaced tick marks representing $25 billion each. Once the graph has been sketched, the scales may be altered to emphasize differences in data. The first step in reading a graph is to check the scale of the axes, as variation in scale may lead to a different view.

For instance, suppose you wish to show the same data but make the data appear to increase at a slower rate. By altering the vertical scale such that each mark represents $50 billion, you can produce the following graph.

Defense Spending

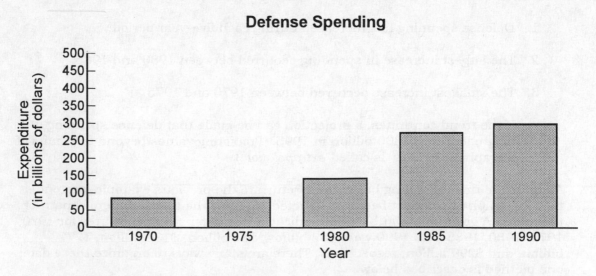

This presents the same data in a different light. Because of the change in the interval chosen for the vertical axis, it looks like there is less difference from year to year. Another alteration commonly used to change the appearance of data is to begin numbering the axes at values other than zero. When viewing a graph, be very careful to examine the numbering along the axes. A small change can make a very large difference. You should always check the scales and pay attention to the actual numbers.

Bar graphs may also be presented on their sides. The vertical axis may be the year and the horizontal axis the data. The way you construct your graph is a matter of personal preference.

Consider the information below.

Personal Expenses (dollars)

	1980	1985	1990
Utilities	1000	1200	1500
Food	2000	3000	2500
Insurance	500	800	1000

This table presents the amount of money spent on utilities, food, and insurance during three specified years. Notice that for each of the three years, there are three values to consider: one for utilities, one for food, and one for insurance. This requires a type of bar graph slightly different from the two used in the previous examples.

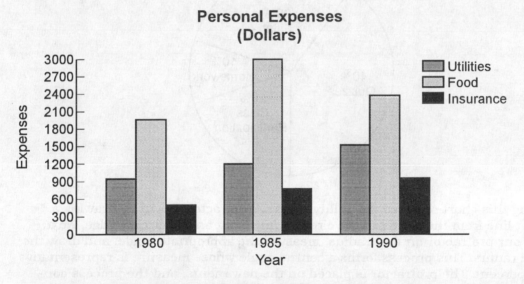

In the graph above, different types of shading are used to separate visually the three categories of expenses. The graph illustrates that utilities and insurance have increased steadily over the years, while food expense declined from 1985 to 1990. The data could have been grouped by category of expense rather than by year. Then different shadings would have been used for the years 1980, 1985, and 1990. Determining which approach makes more sense depends on the purpose of the chart: to compare expenditures as a whole over time or to focus on a particular category of expense such as food.

Pie Charts

A pie chart or pie graph is a graph in the form of a circle (a pie) that is sliced into a number of wedges (slices). The relative size of each wedge represents the relative value of the data. For example, if the income of a certain company is $300 million and one department accounts for $100 million, then the size of the pie wedge representing that department would be $\frac{100}{300}$, or $\frac{1}{3}$, of the circular area. This is converted to degrees by multiplying that fraction by 360 (the number of degrees in a circle). In this case, the central angle that forms the wedge would be $\frac{1}{3} \times 360$, or 120 degrees.

The pie chart below shows the composition of a final grade in a college course. The grade is based on the following percents: 10% for homework; 20% for class participation; 30% for the final examination; and 40% for hour examinations and quizzes. Each of the four percents is multiplied by 360 degrees to compute the central angle for the corresponding wedge. Each angle is plotted with a *protractor* (a tool used to measure and construct angles) until all quantities have been sketched. See the following figure.

Course Grade

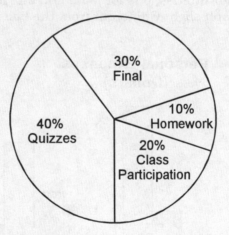

Drawing this chart requires the ability to use a protractor. Begin by drawing a straight line from the center of the circle to any point on the circle's edge. Next, place your protractor on that radius, measure the appropriate angle, and draw the second radius. This process forms a central angle whose measure is representative of the percent. The protractor is placed on the new radius, and the process continues until all central angles have been sketched. Sometimes, each wedge is shaded in a different fashion, and a key is provided next to the graph to show what the different shadings represent.

Working with values. A different procedure is used to construct a pie chart when values rather than percents are known. In this case, you must first calculate the percents by dividing each value by the total. The angle is computed by multiplying this result (the percent) by 360 degrees. Consider the following hypothetical data.

Military Spending (billions)

Branch	Expenditure	Percent	Angle (degrees)
Army	50	25%	90
Navy	60	30%	108
Marine Corps	30	15%	54
Air Force	60	30%	108
Total	200		

In this type of example, only the branch and expenditure columns are usually provided. The percent column is computed by dividing each entry in the expenditure column by the total expenditure, $200 billion, and converting the result to a percent. That percent is multiplied by 360 degrees to produce the corresponding central angle.

Military Spending

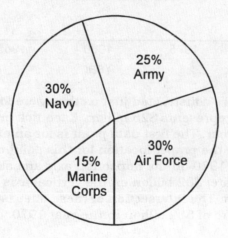

Line Graphs

Another type of graph that is used to present data is the line graph. Like a bar graph, a line graph has both a horizontal axis and a vertical axis. On a line graph, data are represented by points rather than by bars, and all the points on the graph are connected by a line. We will use the data below to illustrate how a line graph is constructed.

Year	Expenditure (billions)
1970	$82
1975	$87
1980	$134
1985	$272
1990	$299

As with the bar chart example, we will let the horizontal scale represent the year and the vertical scale, the expenditure.

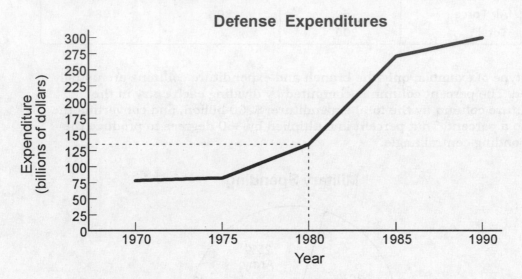

The scales for the axes are constructed just as they were for the bar graph. Each tick on the vertical axis represents $25 billion. Each tick on the horizontal axis represents a particular year. The first data point is for an expenditure of $82 billion in the year 1970. To find the proper location for this point on the graph (called *plotting the point*), locate 1970 on the horizontal axis and sketch a light vertical line through it; locate (estimate) $82 billion on the vertical axis and sketch a light horizontal line through it. The intersection of these lines is the point that represents an expenditure of $82 billion in the year 1970.

The procedure for reading a line graph is similar to the procedure for plotting points on a line graph. For instance, to determine the defense expenditure for the year 1980, first find 1980 on the horizontal axis. Next, draw a vertical line through this point and extend it until it meets the graphed line. Draw a horizontal line through the point where these two lines meet, and extend it until it meets the vertical axis. Read the value (or estimate the value) for defense expenditures for 1980 from the vertical axis ($134 billion). The vertical and horizontal lines that need to be drawn are included on the graph above.

Sometimes two sets of data are plotted on the same graph. This is most often done when comparisons are to be made. The graph below presents sales data for two stores. The solid line represents sales for store A. The dotted line represents sales for store B. By looking at the line, we can see that store B's sales were higher than store A's sales for the years 1984, 1985, and 1986. For the years 1987 and 1988, store A's sales were higher.

Total Sales; Stores A and B

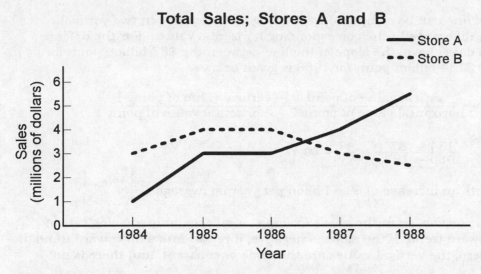

Store A
Store B

Slope. It is easy to detect a trend or rate of change by using a line graph. The rate of change between two points on a line graph is called *slope*. The slope of a line is the vertical change in the line (called the *rise*) over a horizontal distance of 1 unit (called the *run*). Look at the following three graphs. Line A has a rise of 2 units for each run of 1 unit. It has a slope of 2. Graph B has a rise of 1 unit for each run of 1 unit. It has a slope of 1. Graph C has a rise of 0 (it does not have a vertical change) for each run of 1 unit. It has a slope of 0.

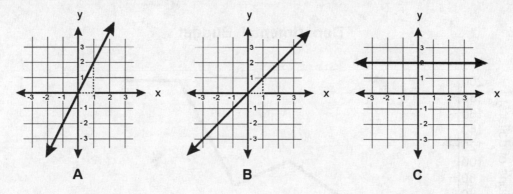

A   B   C

The slope of a line can be computed by dividing the difference in two vertical values by the difference in the corresponding horizontal values. For the defense expenditures data above, the slope of the line between the $87 billion point for 1975 and the $134 billion point for 1980 is given below.

$$\text{slope} = \frac{\text{vertical value of point } 2 - \text{vertical value of point } 1}{\text{horizontal value of point } 2 - \text{horizontal value of point } 1}$$

$$= \frac{134 - 87}{1980 - 1975} = \frac{47}{5} = {}^{+}9.4$$

This represents an increase of $9.4 billion per year on average.

If the slope is positive, as in the above example, it reflects an increasing rate of change or upward trend. If the slope is negative, it represents a downward trend. If the slope is zero, the vertical values are the same or constant, and there is no change.

Consider the following budget data and related line graph.

Departmental Budget (millions of dollars)

Year	1985	1986	1987	1988	1989	1990
Budget	20	50	100	70	200	200

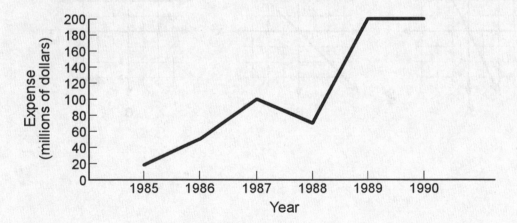

Departmental Budget

For convenience, data points will be enclosed in parentheses, with the horizontal value and vertical value separated by a comma. The first data point above would be written (1985,20).

According to the graph, the spending level for 1986 was $50 million. This represents an increase from the previous year, 1985, when the budget figure was $20 million. The rate of increase for data points (1985,20) and (1986,50) is computed below.

$$\text{slope} = \text{rate of change} = \frac{50 - 20}{1986 - 1985} = {}^{+}30$$

Note that a positive slope describes a line that rises as it goes from left to right. If this same rate were to continue, you could predict that the next budget would be $80 million; however, as you can see from the data, the 1987 budget was $100 million. This illustrates one problem with trying to make predictions: trends do not always continue. The rate of change that occurred between 1986 and 1987 (an increase of 50) is more than the rate of change that occurred between 1985 and 1986 (a change of 30).

Notice that between 1987 and 1988 the budget decreased. The data points were (1987,100) and (1988,70). The slope is computed below.

$$\text{slope} = \text{rate of change} = \frac{70 - 100}{1988 - 1987} = {}^-30$$

The negative sign in the above result indicates a downward trend. Notice that the line slants downward between 1987 and 1988, indicating a decreasing rate or negative slope.

You may compare data points over a longer period to examine a trend rather than to determine the slope. A slope can only be determined by using points that lie along the same straight line. Suppose you wish to determine the trend from 1985 to 1990. The computation is given below.

$$\text{rate of change} = \frac{200 - 20}{1990 - 1985} = \frac{180}{5} = {}^+36$$

The positive value indicates an increase in spending over this period.

Another interesting observation may be made about the line between (1989,200) and (1990,200). Note the calculation below.

$$\text{slope} = \frac{200 - 200}{1990 - 1989} = \frac{0}{1}$$

This indicates that there was no change in the budget over this period. Notice that the line between 1989 and 1990 is horizontal.

The table below summarizes the budget data.

Departmental Budget

Year	Budget	Rate of Change from Previous Year
1985	20	No data on 1984
1986	50	⁺30
1987	100	⁺50
1988	70	⁻30
1989	200	⁺130
1990	200	0

The smallest budget was $20 million in 1985; the largest budget was $200 million in both 1989 and 1990. The greatest annual increase occurred between 1988 and 1989; the largest decrease occurred between 1987 and 1988; the budget remained unchanged between 1989 and 1990.

Pictographs

Another type of graph is the pictograph. A pictograph uses symbols or simple drawings to represent data. The following table provides voter registration figures for three towns.

Registered Voters

Town	Number of Voters
Carlisle	8500
Darlington	6500
Gates	4000

Town	Number of Registered Voters 🚶 = 1000 Voters ⌐ = 500 Voters
Carlisle	🚶🚶🚶🚶🚶🚶🚶🚶⌐
Darlington	🚶🚶🚶🚶🚶🚶⌐
Gates	🚶🚶🚶🚶

The graph above is a pictograph of these data. In this pictograph, each figure represents 1000 voters, and half of a figure represents 500 voters. Since Carlisle has 8500 voters, there are $8\frac{1}{2}$ figures representing Carlisle. To find the number of voters in Darlington, count the number of whole figures (6), multiply this number by 1000 (the number represented by each figure), and add 500 to it since there is also half of a figure.

$$6 \times 1000 = \begin{array}{r} 6000 \\ + 500 \\ \hline 6500 \end{array}$$

Interpretation of Tables

Data are often presented in the form of a table. Reading a table usually involves finding the appropriate row and column for a given problem and then reading a number at the point where the row and column intersect. Sometimes it is necessary to be able to scale the values upward or downward in the table. For example, suppose that a chart indicates that there are 250 calories in 2 ounces of cheese, and you would like to know how many calories there are in 6 ounces of cheese. Since 6 ounces of cheese represents 3 2-ounce servings, you could multiply 250 calories by 3 to get 750 calories. An easier method for scaling data is to set up a proportion. The calculation for this same example is described using a proportion as follows.

$$\frac{2 \text{ ounces}}{6 \text{ ounces}} = \frac{250 \text{ calories}}{x}$$ *One side for ounces, the other for calories.*

$$2x = (6)(250)$$ *Cross-multiply and solve for x.*

$$x = \frac{1500}{2}$$

$$x = 750$$

You could also set the problem up as:

$$\frac{250 \text{ calories}}{2 \text{ ounces}} = \frac{x \text{ calories}}{6 \text{ ounces}}$$

$$2x = (6)(250)$$ *Cross-multiply and solve for x.*

$$x = 750$$

The following data represent the nutritive value of 1 ounce of various dairy products.

Food	Calories	Protein (grams)	Fat (grams)	Calcium (grams)
Whole milk	19	1	1	36
Cheddar cheese	115	7	9	204
Cream cheese	100	2	10	23
Swiss cheese	105	8	8	272

How many calories are there in 3 ounces of milk and 6 ounces of cream cheese?

Calories in 3 ounces of milk: Calories in 6 ounces of cream cheese:

$$\frac{1 \text{ oz.}}{3 \text{ oz.}} = \frac{19 \text{ cal.}}{x} \quad \text{or} \quad \frac{19 \text{ cal.}}{1 \text{ oz.}} = \frac{x \text{ cal.}}{3 \text{ oz.}}$$ $$\frac{1 \text{ oz.}}{6 \text{ oz.}} = \frac{100 \text{ cal.}}{x} \quad \text{or} \quad \frac{100 \text{ cal.}}{1 \text{ oz.}} = \frac{x \text{ cal.}}{6 \text{ oz.}}$$

$$x = 57 \text{ cal.} \qquad\qquad x = 57 \text{ cal.}$$ $$x = 600 \text{ cal.} \qquad\qquad x = 600 \text{ cal.}$$

$$57 \text{ cal.} + 600 \text{ cal.} = 657 \text{ calories}$$

Which has more fat: 5 ounces of cheddar cheese or 5.5 ounces of Swiss cheese?

5 oz. of cheddar cheese: 5.5 oz. of Swiss cheese:

$$\frac{1\text{ oz.}}{5\text{ oz.}} = \frac{9\text{ g}}{x} \quad \text{or} \quad \frac{9\text{ g}}{1\text{ oz.}} = \frac{x\text{ g}}{5\text{ oz.}} \qquad \frac{1\text{ oz.}}{5.5\text{ oz.}} = \frac{8\text{ g}}{x} \quad \text{or} \quad \frac{8\text{ g}}{1\text{ oz.}} = \frac{x\text{ g}}{5.5\text{ oz.}}$$

x = 45 grams   x = 45 grams   x = 44 grams   x = 44 grams

Therefore, 5 ounces of cheddar cheese contains more fat than 5.5 ounces of Swiss cheese.

Summary of Graphs and Tables

Bar graphs. To read a bar graph, follow these steps.

1. Check the vertical and horizontal scales.
2. Extend a line from the top of the bar to the vertical axis.
3. Interpolate, if necessary. Interpolation involves adding a fractional estimate of the distance between two marks on the scale.

To construct a bar graph, follow these steps.

1. Determine the scales. The vertical scale is computed by dividing the difference between a starting value and the largest value by 10.
2. Plot the height of each bar on the vertical axis.

Pie charts. To construct a pie graph, follow these steps.

1. Convert the data to fractions or percents by dividing the value for each category by the total.
2. The measure of the central angle for each category is the product of the fractional value and 360 degrees.
3. Begin with an arbitrary radius and use a protractor to plot successive angles.
4. Label each wedge.

Line graphs. To construct a line graph, follow these steps.

1. Set scales as in a bar chart.
2. Plot points by locating the horizontal position and then the vertical position using the scales.
3. Connect each data point with a line.

By studying the slope of the line between data points, you may determine if quantities increase, decrease, or remain the same. A line that rises as you move from left to right represents an increase; a line that falls represents a decrease. If the line is horizontal, it represents a quantity that remains the same.

Pictographs. To construct a pictograph, follow these steps.

1. Determine what number each symbol will represent (scale).
2. Determine how many symbols are needed to represent each value by dividing each value by the scale.
3. Arrange proper number of symbols in each row.
4. Label the pictograph.

To read a pictograph, follow these steps.

1. Count the number of symbols in a row.
2. Multiply this number by the scale of the pictograph to obtain a value for that row.

Tables. To read a table, remember that values in a table are read just as you would read a point on a graph. Row and column headings replace the vertical and horizontal scales. A value is determined by locating its corresponding horizontal and vertical position (its row and column), and its meaning is determined by its associated description. To scale values from a table, use proportions.

Measures of Central Tendency and Variability

Measures of central tendency. To analyze data meaningfully, it is often important to know the *central tendency* of the data—the number that represents the middle or central value of the data. Data tend to be grouped around a value; this central value can often give you a sense of the meaning of the numbers. Because the numbers you will analyze usually are measures of some quality possessed by persons or things (e.g., temperature, batting ability, cost, academic achievement, weight, speed), an understanding of the central tendency of the numbers that measure the quality can provide insight into the past, present, or future status of that quality. By analyzing the central tendencies of numbers, you may be able to perceive that air temperatures are generally high during a certain time period, but growing cooler; that a baseball player's hitting is only fair, but getting better; that costs are rising more slowly this year than last year; and so on.

Three measures of central tendency are widely used to analyze sets of numbers: *mean, median,* and *mode.* Although the terms may be unfamiliar, the concepts that underlie them are used every day. When you look at the change in your pocket and observe that you have more dimes than anything else, you are using the concept of mode. When you say, "My average grade on math quizzes this semester was 82," you are using the concept of mean. And when you check with your classmates and find that, compared to their grades, your grade on the most recent math test was "right in the middle," you are using the concept of median.

Mean. The *mean* of a set of numbers is the arithmetic average of that set of numbers. The mean is the most frequently used measure of central tendency, and you are probably familiar with the procedure for calculating it. First you add all the values in the set and then you divide that sum by the number of values in the set. Consider the following example.

A student in an algebra class received grades of 86, 75, 88, 90, 50, and 80 on six tests this year. What was the student's mean test grade?

The mean is the sum of the grades divided by the number of grades.

$$\text{Mean} = \frac{86 + 75 + 88 + 90 + 50 + 80}{6}$$

$$= \frac{469}{6}$$

$$= 78.17$$

The student's mean test grade is 78.17.

Median. The *median* of a set of numbers is the middle value in the set when the numbers are arranged in order of size. If the number of values in the set is odd, there will be one middle value and that value will be the median. If the number of values in the set is even, there will be two middle values and the median will be the mean of those two values (i.e., the sum of the two numbers divided by two, or the number exactly halfway between the two numbers).

For example, the list of algebra scores above contains 6 values, which (arranged in ascending order) are: 50, 75, 80, 86, 88, and 90. Since 6 is an even number, the median will be the mean of the two middle numbers, 80 and 86. Half of (80 + 86) is 83, which is the median score. Here is another example.

The number of lawnmowers sold by Grisham's Hardware Store between April and October is listed in the following table.

Number of Lawnmowers Sold

Apr.	May	June	July	Aug.	Sept.	Oct.
5	8	7	8	6	4	2

What is the median number of lawnmowers sold per month during this period?

To find the median, first arrange the numbers in order of size (either smallest to largest or largest to smallest):

2 4 5 6 7 8 8

Notice that the value 8 is listed twice because it appears twice in the table. Since there are 7 numbers in the set, the median value will be the middle one, the one with the same number of values below and above it. In this case there are three values above the median and three below:

2 4 5 6̲ 7 8 8

The median number of lawnmowers sold per month during this period was 6.

Mode. The third measure of central tendency is the *mode*. The mode is usually the easiest measure of central tendency to find. The mode of a set of numbers is simply the value that occurs most frequently. Here is an example.

First County Bank keeps track of the number of deposits over $5000 it receives from its customers. Over a recent ten-day period, the daily totals of such deposits were 50, 28, 61, 32, 28, 46, 34, 21, 41, and 30. What is the mode of these numbers?

If you inspect the list of numbers, you will find that on two days there were 28 deposits of more than $5000. Since this number occurs more frequently than any other number of deposits, the mode of this list of numbers is 28.

A set of data may have one mode, more than one mode, or no mode. The above set of data had one mode. An example of a set of data with more than one mode is:

6, 8, 24, 26, 27, 29, 30, 30, 32, 32

In this set of data, the numbers 30 and 32 occur twice each; as a result there are two modes: 30 and 32. Note that if this set of data had contained three values of 30 and two of 32, there would be only one mode: 30.

An example of a set of data with no mode is 2, 4, 5, 7, 8, 10, and 12. Each number appears only once, and so the set has no mode.

Choosing a measure of central tendency. The different measures of central tendency have different uses and advantages. If you have a large number of basically similar values (e.g., a set of test scores for a class), the mean will probably be the most accurate way to summarize your data. But if your set of data contains one or two highly unusual values and there are not enough other values in the set to counterbalance these values, the mean may be misleading.

For example, if the test scores of six students in a calculus class are 57, 58, 59, 60, 61, and 100, reporting the mean score (65.8) gives a less accurate sense of the central tendency of the scores than reporting the median score (59.5). Similarly, government figures on average family incomes in a particular country are usually given as medians rather than means. The very high salaries of a few workers may give a mean figure that is too high; the median (i.e., middle) figure is probably more typical of the set of data.

The mode is most appropriately used when the set of data is likely to contain values that occur frequently and when the question that it makes sense to ask is "Which value occurs most often?" Thus, the average noontime temperature of a vacation spot during the month of August would probably best be given as a mode rather than as a median or a mean. Similarly, if you wanted to report on the average or typical population of the municipalities in various countries, you would probably produce the most accurate answer by first grouping the municipalities into a few categories by size (e.g., "towns with populations under 5000," "towns with populations between 5001 and 50,000," and so on) and then reporting the mode (i.e., the category with the largest number of entries) for each country.

Interpretation of the different measures. Because the three measures of central tendency can produce different results for the same set of data, the choice of measure to use may depend on the intent of the presenter. As an interpreter of data presented by others, you would be wise to consider the question of probable intent and to look very carefully at the numbers to see which measure of central tendency has been presented. Sometimes, the presenter may use the measure of central tendency that is most favorable to his or her purposes rather than the one that most accurately represents the data.

For example, a company that wishes to be known for its high salaries might calculate both its mean and its median salaries and report as its average salary the one (usually the mean) that is higher. Or a company that doesn't want to appear careless might use the measure with the lowest value to report the average number of industrial accidents that it experiences per month. To interpret data on averages accurately, it is important to understand which "average" is being reported and, if possible, to analyze the data from which the average was calculated.

Consider this example.

What are the mean and the median of the numbers 65, 75, 79, 84, 120, and 150?

The mean is the sum of the numbers (573) divided by 6 = 95.5.

Since there is an even number of values in the set, the median is the mean of the middle two numbers = (79 + 84)/2 = 81.5.

These two results are very different; they can mean different things and be put to different uses. If the set of numbers represented the rental costs of the rooms in a hotel, the hotel might use the median to report that the average cost of a room was $81.50. On the other hand, if the numbers represented the total points scored by a college basketball team in its first six games of the season, a coach might use the mean to report that the team averaged 95.5 points per game. Be careful and look closely when you are analyzing and interpreting figures reported as "averages."

Variability. The question of central tendency inevitably brings up the concept of variability. We have already mentioned the degree of similarity in a set of numbers as one consideration in determining which measure of central tendency to use. The concept of similarity of numbers in a set is related to the variability of the data in the set.

The *variability* of a set of data is the spread of the data around the mean. Two sets of data will often be discussed in terms of their means; however, without considering the variability displayed by the data, such a discussion may be misleading.

Suppose two cities are reported as having a mean temperature of 50 degrees during a six-day period in April. At first glance it would seem that the two cities must have similar climates and would be equally comfortable during the six-day period. However, a closer look at the data underlying these temperatures gives a different impression.

Temperatures in Two Cities
Six Days in April

	Day 1	Day 2	Day 3	Day 4	Day 5	Day 6
City A	40	50	50	50	50	60
City B	10	30	50	50	70	90

One interesting observation about these data is that the means, medians, and modes of both cities are exactly the same: all six figures are 50 degrees. Thus, identical measures of central tendency can sometimes result from data that are not at all similar. In this case, knowing the details of the measure of central tendency that was used to report the figures would not help us see the difference between the two cities. The difference is one of variability.

The difference in temperature patterns for the two cities can be seen clearly in a graph of both sets of data.

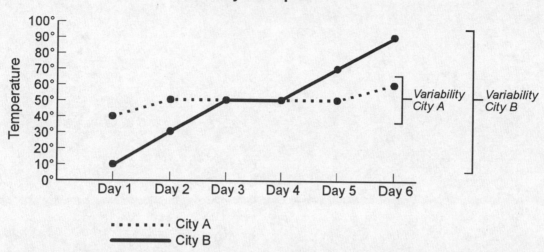

**Temperatures in Two Cities
Six Days in April**

The graph reveals that even though the measures of central tendency for both sets of data are exactly the same, the spread, or variability, of the data in each set is very different. In City A all of the temperatures were clustered around 50 degrees. In City B the temperatures were spread over a wider range from 10 to 90 degrees. The temperatures in City A during this period were consistent; those in City B varied from extremely cold to extremely hot. For most people, City A would have been more comfortable during this period than City B.

One quick way to evaluate the variability of a set of data is to look at the *range* of values from lowest to highest. The range is simply the highest value minus the lowest value; it is usually the case that the greater the range in a set of values, the greater the variability. In the case of the two cities above, the temperature range for City A over the six-day period was 20 degrees (60 – 40 = 20); for City B it was 80 degrees (90 – 10 = 80). Therefore, the range of temperatures over this time period was greater for City B than for City A; City B's temperature variability was greater.

To analyze and interpret summary data accurately, remember that it is important to consider the details of both the central tendency and the variability of the data before you draw or accept any conclusions.

Practice Exercises

The following exercises will help you review the skills covered in this chapter. Many of the types of questions presented here will be similar to those on the test; others will not. Remember that the purpose of the exercises is to give you practice on the skills rather than merely to prepare you for the test. Following these exercises are the Practice Exercise Explanations. They explain each question, the correct answer, and why the remaining choices are incorrect.

Use the graph below to answer the questions that follow.

Ticket Sales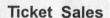

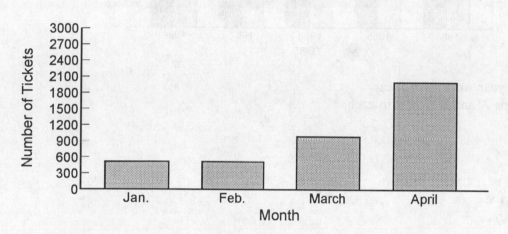

1. Approximately how many tickets were sold in February?

    A.   about 300

    B.   about 500

    C.   about 600

    D.   about 900

2. In which two months were the same number of tickets sold?

    A.   January and February

    B.   February and March

    C.   March and April

    D.   January and April

3. Which of the following statements is accurate?

    A.   The trend is toward increasing ticket sales.

    B.   The trend is toward decreasing ticket sales.

    C.   Ticket sales increased each month.

    D.   Ticket sales decreased each month.

Use the bar graph below to answer the questions that follow.

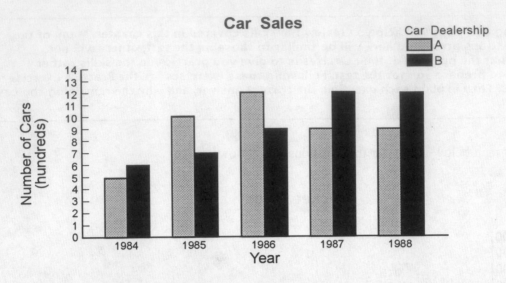

4. In which year were sales at car
   dealerships A and B closest to each
   other?

   A. 1984

   B. 1985

   C. 1987

   D. 1988

5. Between which two years did sales at
   dealership A show the greatest increase?

   A. 1984 and 1985

   B. 1985 and 1986

   C. 1986 and 1987

   D. 1987 and 1988

Use the pie chart below to answer the questions that follow.

Flavor Preference Survey

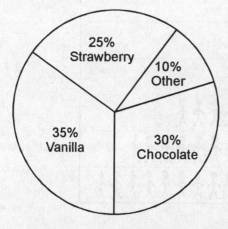

6.   What percent of the people in the survey chose either chocolate or vanilla?

A.   5%

B.   30%

C.   35%

D.   65%

7.   The greatest number of people in the survey preferred:

A.   chocolate.

B.   vanilla.

C.   strawberry.

D.   a flavor other than chocolate, vanilla, or strawberry.

8.   Use the pictograph below to answer the question that follows.

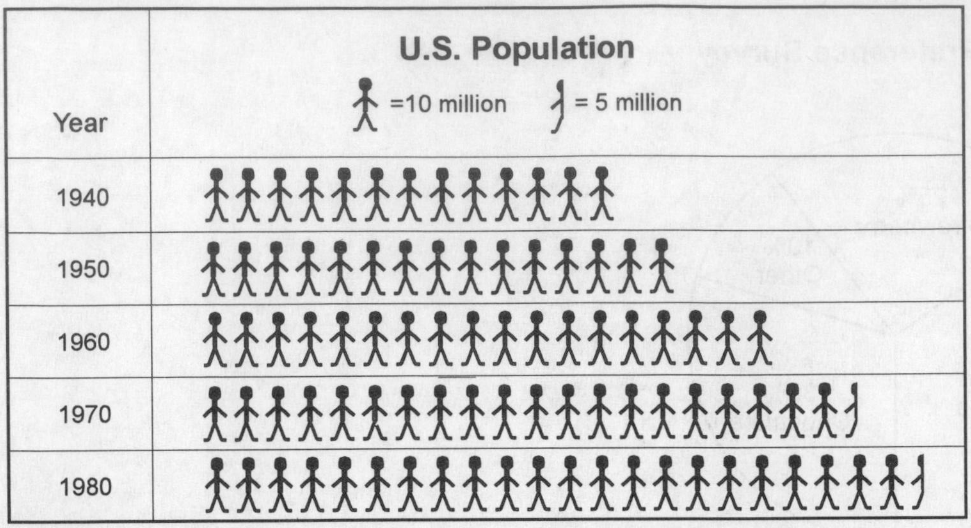

Year	U.S. Population 👤 =10 million ⌡ = 5 million
1940	👤👤👤👤👤👤👤👤👤👤👤👤👤
1950	👤👤👤👤👤👤👤👤👤👤👤👤👤👤👤
1960	👤👤👤👤👤👤👤👤👤👤👤👤👤👤👤👤👤👤
1970	👤👤👤👤👤👤👤👤👤👤👤👤👤👤👤👤👤👤👤👤⌡
1980	👤👤👤👤👤👤👤👤👤👤👤👤👤👤👤👤👤👤👤👤👤👤👤⌡

How much greater was the U.S.
population in 1970 than in 1950?

A.   5.5 million

B.   11 million

C.   25 million

D.   55 million

Use the tables below to answer the questions that follow.

POSTAL RATES

First-Class

Weight, not exceeding pound(s)	Zone/Rate					
	1, 2, & 3	4	5	6	7	8
1	$2.40	$ 2.40	$ 2.40	$ 2.40	$ 2.40	$ 2.40
2	2.40	2.40	2.40	2.40	2.40	2.40
3	2.74	3.16	3.45	3.74	3.96	4.32
4	3.18	3.75	4.13	4.53	4.92	5.33
5	3.61	4.32	4.86	5.27	5.81	6.37
6	4.15	5.08	5.71	6.31	6.91	7.66
7	4.58	5.66	6.39	7.09	7.80	8.67
8	5.00	6.23	7.07	7.87	8.68	9.68
9	5.43	6.81	7.76	8.66	9.57	10.69
10	5.85	7.39	8.44	9.44	10.45	11.70
11	6.27	7.97	9.12	10.22	11.33	12.71
12	6.70	8.55	9.81	11.01	12.22	13.72
13	7.12	9.12	10.49	11.79	13.10	14.73
14	7.55	9.70	11.17	12.57	13.99	15.74
15	7.97	10.28	11.86	13.36	14.87	16.75

Fourth-Class

Weight, not exceeding pound(s)	Zone/Rate						
	1 & 2	3	4	5	6	7	8
2	$1.69	$1.81	$1.97	$2.24	$2.35	$ 2.35	$ 2.35
3	1.78	1.95	2.20	2.59	2.98	3.42	4.25
4	1.86	2.10	2.42	2.94	3.46	4.05	5.25
5	1.95	2.24	2.65	3.29	3.94	4.67	6.25
6	2.04	2.39	2.87	3.64	4.43	5.30	7.34
7	2.12	2.53	3.10	4.00	4.91	5.92	8.30
8	2.21	2.68	3.32	4.35	5.39	6.55	9.26
9	2.30	2.82	3.55	4.70	5.87	7.17	10.22
10	2.38	2.97	3.78	5.05	6.35	7.79	11.18
11	2.47	3.11	4.00	5.40	6.83	8.42	12.14
12	2.56	3.25	4.22	5.75	7.30	9.03	13.09
13	2.64	3.40	4.44	6.10	7.78	9.65	14.03
14	2.69	3.48	4.56	6.27	8.02	9.96	14.50
15	2.75	3.55	4.67	6.44	8.24	10.24	14.94

9. How much would it cost to send a 12-pound package to a person in zone 3 by first-class mail?

A. $2.56

B. $3.25

C. $6.70

D. $8.55

10. How much would be saved by sending a 5-pound package to zone 7 by fourth-class instead of first-class mail?

A. $1.14

B. $2.39

C. $4.67

D. $5.81

Use the line graph below to answer the questions that follow.

Union Benefits

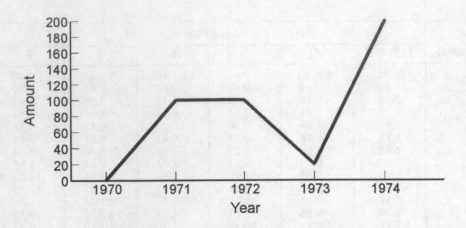

11.   Between which two years was the
      increase in benefits the greatest?

      A.   1970 and 1971

      B.   1971 and 1972

      C.   1972 and 1973

      D.   1973 and 1974

12.   Between which two years was there
      no change in benefits?

      A.   1970 and 1971

      B.   1971 and 1972

      C.   1972 and 1973

      D.   1973 and 1974

13.   Use the table below to answer the question that follows.

Basketball Team Players Height Chart

Player	1	2	3	4	5
Height in inches	82	79	84	81	77

The heights in inches of five members of
the high school basketball team are given
in the table. What is the median height of
these five players?

A.   84 inches

B.   81 inches

C.   80.6 inches

D.   81.5 inches

14.   Use the table below to answer the question that follows.

Daily Low Temperatures in Johnsville

Day	Monday	Tuesday	Wednesday	Thursday	Friday
Wind chill Temperature	–10° C	–34° C	2° C	3° C	–1° C

Daily low temperatures were recorded
over a five-day period in Johnsville.
These temperatures are given in the
table. What is the mean of the daily low
temperatures for the five-day period?

A.   –1° C

B.   2° C

C.   –8° C

D.   10° C

15. A student received the following grades
     on quizzes in a history course: 80, 88,
     75, 93, 79, 95, 75, and 96. Which of the
     following statements about these grades
     is true?

     A.   The mode is the most typical grade
          and should be used as the average.

     B.   The median and the mode of this
          set of data are equal.

     C.   This set of data has two medians.

     D.   The mean of this set of data is
          higher than the median.

16.   Use the graph below to answer the
       question that follows.

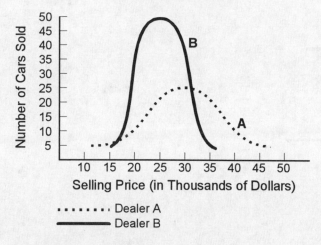

**Number of Cars Sold and Selling Prices
by Two Dealers
(January–June)**

Which of the following is an accurate
interpretation of the information
presented in the graph?

A.   Dealer A had a greater variability
      in selling price than Dealer B.

B.   Dealer B's median selling price
      was higher than Dealer A's.

C.   The mode of the selling prices at
      Dealer A was equal to that at
      Dealer B.

D.   Dealer A's mean selling price was
      lower than Dealer B's.

17. As the experience of a typist increases, typing speed increases until it reaches a maximum. Which graph below correctly depicts this situation?

A.

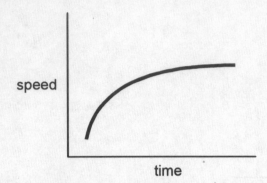

B.

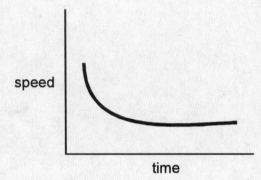

C.

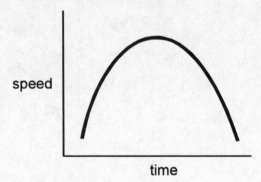

D.

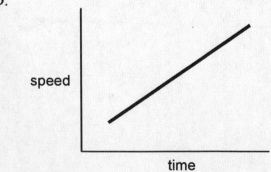

Practice Exercise Explanations

1. **Correct Response: B.** Because the bar on the graph for February lines up with a point in between 300 and 600 on the y-axis, you need to interpolate to estimate the value. The February bar is higher than 300 and approximately $\frac{3}{4}$, or 0.75, of the way to 600.

   (0.75)(300) = 225
   225 + 300 = 525

   Rounding 525 to the nearest 100 gives 500 as the answer. Choice A does not add the additional amount over 300. Choice C reads the value from the nearest tick instead of interpolating. Choice D uses the bar for March and rounds down to 900.

2. **Correct Response: A.** If the same number of tickets are sold in two months, the bars for these months will be the same height. Only January and February have bars of the same height. Choices B, C, and D compare months with bars that are not similar in height.

3. **Correct Response: A.** The graph shows an overall increase in ticket sales from January, with sales of approximately 500 tickets, to April, with sales of approximately 2000 tickets. Choice B is an incorrect summary, as ticket sales did not decrease overall. Choice C is incorrect because, although the trend is toward an increase, ticket sales did not change between January and February. Sales did not, therefore, increase each month. Choice D is incorrect because sales never decreased.

4. **Correct Response: A.** To compare the sales of the dealerships each year, you must compare the heights of the differently shaded bars for each year. The heights are most similar in 1984. They correspond to a difference of approximately 1000 cars. Choices B, C, and D are incorrect because there is a difference of approximately 3000 cars in each case.

5. **Correct Response: A.** For this question, you must compare the heights of only the bars shaded for car dealership A. The bars increased in height by the largest amount between 1984 and 1985. This change in height corresponds to approximately 5000 cars more in 1985 than in 1984. Choice B represents an increase of 2000 cars. Choice C indicates years in which there was a decrease of 3000. Choice D indicates years in which there was no change in sales.

6. **Correct Response: D.** To determine the percent of people who chose either chocolate or vanilla, you need to add the percents for those choices together. 30% + 35% = 65%. Choice A represents the difference between the popularity of vanilla and the popularity of chocolate. Choice B gives the percent for chocolate only, and choice C for vanilla only.

7. **Correct Response: B.** This question is asking for the category that has the highest percentage. The highest is 35%, which is for vanilla. Choice A corresponds to 30%, choice C to 25%, and choice D to 10%—all are less than 35%.

8. **Correct Response: D.** The number of figures for 1970 is 20 plus a half-figure. Each whole figure is equal to 10 million, and each half-figure to 5 million. Therefore, the total for 1970 is 20(10 million) + 1(5 million) = 205 million. The number of figures for 1950 is 15. 15(10 million) = 150 million. Therefore, the difference between 1950 and 1970 is 205 – 150 = 55 million. Choice A incorrectly counts figures as equal to 1 million each, choice B counts them as 2 million each, and choice C counts them as 5 million each.

9. **Correct Response: C.** To determine the mailing cost, you must refer to the table labeled *first-class.* In the left-hand column, you can find the weight of 12 pounds. Because the package is going to zone 3, you must use the column labeled *1, 2, & 3* to find the correct rate. Look across the row for 12 pounds; the rate in the column for zones 1, 2, & 3 is $6.70. Choice A uses the wrong table and the column for zones 1 and 2. Choice B uses the wrong table, but the column for zone 3. Choice D uses the correct table, but the column for zone 4 instead of the column for zone 3.

10. **Correct Response: A.** This question requires you to compare values between the two tables. The first-class rate for a 5-pound package is $5.81. The fourth-class rate for a 5-pound package is $4.67. The difference is $5.81 – 4.67 = $1.14. Choice B compares the cost for sending a 7-pound package to zone 5. Choice C gives the cost for fourth-class and choice D the cost for first-class.

11. **Correct Response: D.** This question requires you to compare sets of two adjacent points on a line graph. The values for each set of two years is found by finding the value for each on the y-axis and taking the difference. The value for the year 1973 is 20, and the value for the year 1974 is 200. The difference between the values for the years 1974 and 1973 is $^{+}$180. This is the largest increase shown on the graph. The difference between the values for the years 1970 and 1971 (choice A) is 100 – 0 = $^{+}$100. The difference between the values for the years 1971 and 1972 (choice B) is 100 – 100 = 0. The difference between the values for the years 1972 and 1973 (choice C) is 20 – 100 = $^{-}$80.

12. **Correct Response: B.** Using the same comparisons as you did for question 11, you can find the set of two years in which there was no change (i.e., the difference is 0). The two years that had a difference of 0 are 1971 and 1972. Choices A, C, and D as calculated above have differences of $^{+}$100, $^{-}$80, and $^{+}$180, respectively.

13. **Correct Response: B.** To find the median height, first arrange the heights of the five players in order of size: 77, 79, 81, 82, and 84 inches. The median height is the height in the middle—the one with same number of heights above it as below it. Since there are five height measurements, the median height is the third height in the list (two above it, two below it), 81 inches. Response A is the middle height in the table, but since the heights in the table are not arranged in order of size, 84 inches is not the median height. Response C is the mean of the five heights (77 + 79 + 81 + 82 + 84 = 403/5 = 80.6), not the median. Response D is the result of taking the mean of the third and fourth values in the ordered list, a procedure that would be appropriate if there was an even number of heights in the list.

14.   **Correct Response: C.** To find the mean temperature, add all the temperatures and divide by the number of temperatures in the list:

$$\text{Mean temperature} = \frac{(-10)+(-34)+(2)+(3)+(-1)}{5} = \frac{-40}{5}$$

Mean temperature = –8°C

Response A is the median temperature, not the mean. Response B is the middle temperature in the table. Response D results from failing to consider negative signs when calculating the mean.

15.   **Correct Response: D.** Reordering the numbers in the set of data gives the following:

75, 75, 79, 80, 88, 93, 95, 96

From this arrangement it is clear that the mode (the most frequently occurring grade) is 75 and the median (the middle grade) is (88–80)/2, or 84. The mean is

$$\frac{75+75+79+80+88+93+95+96}{8} = \frac{681}{8} = 85.1$$

Therefore, the mean (85.1) is higher than the median (84) and Response D is correct. Response A is incorrect because in this data set the mode (75) represents the lowest score rather than a typical or central score. Response B is incorrect because the mode (75) is not the same as the median (84). Response C is incorrect because the two middle values in the data set must be averaged (i.e., their mean must be calculated) to produce the median.

16.   **Correct Response: A.** The variability in selling prices was greater at Dealer A because the range of prices of cars sold was greater, running from about $12,000 to about $48,000. This is a range of about $36,000, compared with a range of about $22,000 at Dealer B. From the graph, the mean, median, and mode of selling prices at Dealer A appear to be about the same: approximately $30,000. The mean, median, and mode at Dealer B appear to be approximately $25,000. Therefore, Responses B, C, and D are incorrect.

17.   **Correct Response: A.** Since the speed initially increases and then eventually levels off (becomes flat) over time, Response A is correct. Response B is incorrect because it shows an initial decrease in speed and then a leveling off of speed over time. Response C is incorrect because it shows an increase in speed followed by a corresponding decrease in speed over time. Response D in incorrect because it shows a consistent increase in speed, with no leveling off over time.

Study Ideas

A careful study of the above exercises and the explanations of the answers will help you review important skills relating to graphs, tables, and charts, and to measures of central tendency and variability. In these exercises, you were asked to interpret information in line graphs, bar graphs, pie charts, and pictographs, and to solve problems involving means, medians, modes, and variability. The exercises are designed to give you practice in these skills. You may wish to reread parts of the chapter that address specific skills with which you have difficulty.

You should be aware of the principles for understanding material presented in graphic form. It is likely that you will be called upon to interpret such information in college, at home, and on the job.

When working with graphs, tables, and charts, be sure to note the vertical and horizontal scales, and the specific units used. Misinterpreting data in this way is a common error.

You should also be aware of the different ways to calculate and interpret measures of central tendency. You should understand the differences in the various measures and the importance of the concept of variability. Information about data in textbooks, newspapers, magazines, and in the broadcast media is often presented in summary form as an "average." The skills discussed in this chapter should help you to understand this information accurately.

Chapter 13

GRAPH NUMBERS OR NUMBER RELATIONSHIPS

This skill includes identifying the graphs of equations or inequalities; finding the slopes and the intercepts of lines; finding the equations of lines; and recognizing and interpreting information from the graph of a function, including direct and inverse variation.

Introduction

In math, graphing is used to show a picture of the answers to an equation or an inequality. When you graph an equation/inequality, you are actually drawing a picture of the solution set of that equation/inequality. The solution set contains all the possible correct answers for an equation or an inequality. The values in the solution set all make the equation or the inequality into a true statement.

Some equations and inequalities have no solutions at all. Others have many solutions. When an equation or an inequality has many possible answers, it may not be practical to list the solutions. In those situations, it may be more practical to show the solutions in picture form. In those cases, you must draw a graph.

For this section on graphing equations and inequalities, it is assumed that you are familiar with the number line. Remember that each point on the number line has a coordinate. Each coordinate is actually the distance of that point from the origin, which is the point on the number line with the coordinate "zero." By using the number line, you should be able to answer questions like the following.

1. What is the coordinate of point P?

2. What point has coordinate $^-5$?

3. What point is halfway between coordinate O and point R?

4. What point is four units to the right of point S?

5. What is the coordinate of the point $\frac{1}{2}$ unit to the left of point P?

6. What is the coordinate of the point $2\frac{3}{4}$ units to the right of Q?

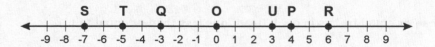

Answers: 1) 4; 2) T; 3) U; 4) Q; 5) $3\frac{1}{2}$; 6) $-\frac{1}{4}$

Graphing on the Number Line

1. Graphing sets of numbers on the number line. To graph a number on the number line, place a filled-in circle on the coordinate of the number. For example, to graph the number ⁻5, you would place a filled-in circle on the number line at the coordinate ⁻5, as indicated below.

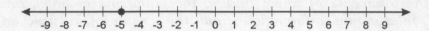

Graph the points 2, 0, ⁻3, and 5.

Solution:

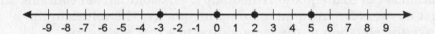

List the set of numbers that is graphed on the number line below.

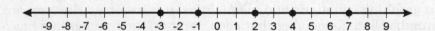

Solution: {⁻3, ⁻1, 2, 4, 7}

2. Inequalities. When drawing graphs, you often have to work with inequalities. In working with inequalities, it is important to know how to read the inequality symbols. The list below shows the four inequality symbols and explains what each one means.

> "is greater than," as in a > b (read "a is greater than b")

< "is less than," as in c < d (read "c is less than d")

≥ "is greater than or equal to," as in e ≥ f (read "e is greater than or equal to f")

≤ "is less than or equal to," as in g ≤ h (read "g is less than or equal to h")

You should also keep in mind that inequality symbols can help you find the position of the values that solve an inequality on a number line.

The graph of an inequality on a number line shows the solution set of the inequality statement (that is, it shows all the numbers that will make the original statement true). The graph of an inequality consists of a number line, a ray (or arrow pointing to the left or to the right and covering all the points that are possible solutions to the inequality), and the endpoint of the ray.

It is easiest to graph inequalities that have the following characteristics.

1. The inequality has only one variable.

2. The variable is by itself on the left of the inequality symbol, and the variable is positive.

3. The numerical value is on the right side of the inequality symbol.

The following examples show inequalities in this form.

$$x \geq 3 \qquad\qquad a < {}^-5 \qquad\qquad x > 0$$

$$C \leq 6 \qquad\qquad p > {}^-5$$

When the inequalities are in this form, the endpoint of the graph will be the numerical value (shown on the right side of the inequality symbol). The ray in the graph will point in the same direction as the inequality symbol in the statement. The endpoint of the ray should be an open circle if the inequality symbol is ">" or "<," but the endpoint should be a filled-in circle when the inequality symbol is "≥" or "≤." A filled-in circle indicates that the point at the circle is included in the graph. An open circle indicates that the graph ends at, but does not include, that point.

Graph x ≥ 3.

This inequality is read "x is greater than or equal to 3." The graph of this inequality should be drawn as follows.

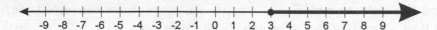

In this example, the inequality symbol is ≥. This means that the endpoint of the ray is a filled-in circle. Also, the variable is on the left side of the statement. This means that the inequality symbol points in the direction that the ray in the graph must point, which is to the right.

Graph a < ⁻5.

This inequality is read "a is less than negative five" and is graphed as follows.

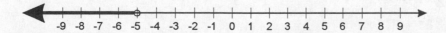

Whenever you must graph a simple inequality statement on a number line, you should use the following steps.

1. Make sure that the inequality is written with the variable on the left side of the statement and the number on the right side of the statement.

2. Make sure that the variable is by itself on the left side of the statement, and make sure that it is positive.

3. Look at the inequality symbol to determine whether to use a filled-in circle or an open circle as an endpoint (filled in if the inequality symbol has a line under it, open if the symbol does not have a line under it).

4. Draw the appropriate endpoint on the number line (filled in or open) at the point indicated by the number in the inequality.

5. Draw a ray pointing in the same direction as the inequality symbol.

6. Check the graph. To do this, pick any number that is covered by the ray. Put the number you have chosen into the inequality statement in place of the variable. If the graph is correct, this procedure will produce a true statement. If putting the number into the inequality creates a false statement, there is an error in your graph. You should check your work again to identify the mistake.

3. Complex inequality statements. Sometimes inequalities are more complex than those discussed in the previous section. When you have to graph these more complex inequalities, you must perform some additional steps in order to get the inequality in a form that can be easily drawn. For example, you might be given an inequality to graph such as $2x \geq {}^-10$ or one such as $4 - 3x < 7$. Before you can graph these inequalities, you must use the same basic arithmetic operations you would use to solve simple equations: adding, subtracting, multiplying, or dividing. Your goal in performing these operations is to rearrange the inequality so that the variable is by itself. You are trying to get the inequality into the form discussed in the previous section (with the variable on the left side of the statement and the numerical value on the right side of the statement). Once you have converted the inequality to that form, it will be easy to graph its solution set.

In most cases, performing math operations on an inequality is the same as performing math operations on a simple equation. There is one exception to this rule, however. When you multiply or divide an inequality by a negative number (for example, $^-2$), you must reverse the direction of the inequality symbol. The following examples show why you must change the direction of the inequality symbol in these special cases.

For example, the inequality $5 > 4$ is a true statement. Five is greater than four. If you multiply both sides of this inequality by $^-1$, however, you get the statement $^-5 > {}^-4$. This statement says that $^-5$ is greater than $^-4$, which is false. To correct the error, you must reverse the direction of the inequality symbol, creating the true statement $^-5 < {}^-4$.

You must reverse the direction of the inequality symbol whenever you multiply or divide both sides of an inequality by a negative number. Here is another example that shows that this is necessary. The inequality ⁻3 < 6 is a true statement. Negative three is less than six. But if you divide both sides of the statement ⁻3 < 6 by ⁻3 (without changing the direction of the inequality symbol), the result is 1 < ⁻2. Since 1 is greater than ⁻2, this new inequality is false. To make the inequality true, you must change the inequality symbol from < to >, creating the true statement 1 > ⁻2.

To solve the inequality ⁻2x < 4, you must divide both sides of the inequality by ⁻2. This gives you the simplified inequality x > ⁻2. To solve the inequality $-\frac{1}{3}x > ⁻2$, you must multiply both sides by ⁻3, which gives you the statement x < 6.

Remember that you do not have to reverse the direction of the inequality symbol when you multiply or divide an inequality by a positive number. The example below shows an inequality that is simplified by performing basic arithmetic operations with a positive number.

Graph 2x ≥ ⁻10.

$\frac{2x}{2} \geq -\frac{10}{2}$ *Convert the inequality to a simpler form by dividing both sides of the statement by 2.*

x ≥ ⁻5   *Notice that you do not need to reverse the direction of the inequality symbol since you are dividing by a positive number.*

The next step in solving this problem is to graph the inequality x ≥ ⁻5 on the number line. This number line shows the graph of the inequality x ≥ ⁻5.

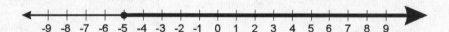

Remember that you can check the graph by replacing x with any number that is covered by the ray.

(2)(0) ≥ ⁻10   *Replace x with the value 0 in the original inequality.*

0 ≥ ⁻10   *This is a true statement. This indicates that the graph is accurate.*

You can also check your graph by choosing a number that is not covered by the ray and using that value to replace x in the original inequality. Doing this should create a false statement. For example, ⁻8 is not covered by the ray in the graph. If ⁻8 is substituted for x in the original statement, the result is ⁻16 ≥ ⁻10, which is a false statement.

The Cartesian Plane

Placing points and rays on the real number line is the most basic type of graphing. The next type of graphing is slightly more complicated, but it involves many of the same procedures you use to graph points on a number line. The previous section discussed ways to graph numbers or sets of numbers on a number line. In that section, all the statements you graphed contained only one variable. This section will discuss how to graph equations or inequalities that involve two variables.

A number line is not sufficient to graph equations and inequalities in two variables. To graph this type of statement, you must use a new system called the Cartesian coordinate system. The Cartesian coordinate system, which is also called the Cartesian plane, is made up of two real number lines, one that is horizontal (i.e., left to right) and one that is vertical (i.e., up and down). The two lines are perpendicular to one another. These two number lines are called the axes (plural of axis) of the Cartesian plane. The horizontal axis is usually called the x-axis, and the vertical axis is usually called the y-axis. The point at which the x- and y-axes intersect is called the origin of the Cartesian plane. The origin represents the point at which the coordinates on both number lines are equal to 0.

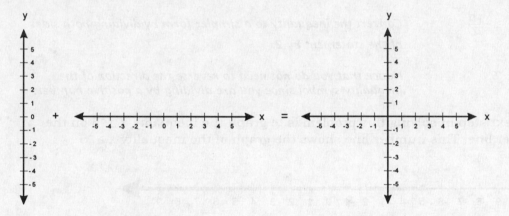

The Cartesian plane is divided into four separate regions called quadrants. Each of the four quadrants is labeled by a Roman numeral. The numbering process begins in the upper right quadrant and proceeds counterclockwise as follows.

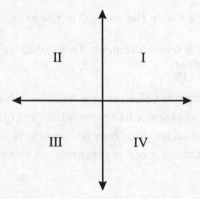

As with a single number line, each point on the Cartesian plane has a coordinate associated with it. On the Cartesian plane, however, two numbers are needed to describe the location of a point. The first number indicates the location of the point in relation to the x-axis, and the second number indicates the location of the point in relation to the y-axis. The two numbers used to describe the position of a point on the Cartesian plane are called an ordered pair. For example, (⁻3,5) is an ordered pair that tells you that a point is located at ⁻3 on the x-axis and at 5 on the y-axis. Notice that this point is not actually on either axis. Instead, it is in quadrant II. The numbers in an ordered pair, which describe the location of a particular point, are called the coordinates of the point.

To find the coordinates of a point on a graph, you must first identify the location of the point as measured on the x-axis and then find its location as measured on the y-axis. The first number in an ordered pair (which identifies a point's location on the x-axis) is called the x-coordinate of the point. The second number in the ordered pair (which identifies a point's location on the y-axis) is called the y-coordinate.

The following examples show how to find the coordinates of a point on the Cartesian plane.

What are the coordinates of points A, B, C, and D?

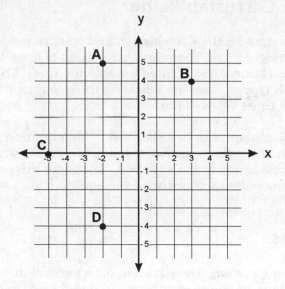

Solution: A = (⁻2,5); B = (3,4); C = (⁻5,0); D = (⁻2,⁻4)

Graph each of the following points: E = (4,⁻5); F = (5,0); G = (⁻3,5);
H = (0,⁻3); I = (⁻2,⁻3).

Solution:

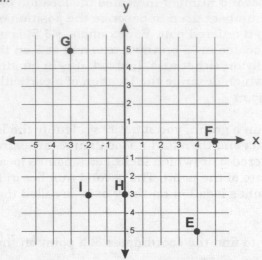

Graphing Lines on the Cartesian Plane

Once you can graph individual points on the Cartesian plane, you are ready to
begin the process of graphing straight lines. There are three types of lines that you
can graph: vertical lines, horizontal lines, and slanted (or oblique) lines. There is a
unique method for graphing each type of line. The following three sections discuss
ways to prepare graphs for these three types of lines.

Every straight line in the Cartesian plane can be described by an equation in the
two variables, x and y. The graph of the line represents the set of points whose
coordinates, when substituted for x and y in the equation, will make the equation
a true statement. For example, the point (3, 2) satisfies the equation x − y = 1.

Graphing Vertical Lines

Every line can be described by an equation. The equation for a vertical line can be
put into a particular form. That form contains an x-term, an equal sign, and a
number (e.g., x = 2). There is no y-term in the equation of a vertical line. It is
easiest to graph a vertical line when the equation for the line is written with a
positive x-term by itself on the left side of the equal sign and the number on the
right side of the equal sign. Equations in this form are said to be in the x = k form.
Notice that all the points on the vertical line have the same x coordinate. That is, x
is constant even though the y coordinates vary. In the x = k form, if k is positive,
the line lies to the right or positive side of the origin; if k is negative, the line lies to
the left or negative side of the origin.

Sometimes, equations for vertical lines are written in a more complicated form.
When this occurs, you should convert the equation to the x = k form before you try
to graph the line. The table below lists several equations for vertical lines and
shows how to change them into the x = k form. The equations on the left of the
table are more complex; the equations on the right are simplified versions of the
same equations.

x = 3 becomes x = 3	No change.
x - 5 = 0 becomes x = 5	Add 5 to both sides.
2x = $^-$6 becomes x = $^-$3	Divide both sides by 2.
$^-$2x = 5 becomes x = $-\frac{5}{2}$	Divide both sides by $^-$2.
$\frac{1}{3}$x = $^-$4 becomes x = $^-$12	Multiply both sides by 3.

Once you have decided that an equation represents a vertical line (i.e., you have found that it can be put in the x = k form), you should use the following steps to graph the equation.

1.   Put the equation in the x = k form. If the equation is not in that form, convert it to the appropriate form.

2.   The value k always serves as the x-coordinate of the vertical line. Find the value of k on the x-axis, and draw a small circle on it.

3.   Draw a vertical line that passes through the circle and that is parallel to the y-axis.

The following examples show how to use these steps to graph vertical lines on the Cartesian plane.

Graph 2x = 6.

$\frac{2x}{2} = \frac{6}{2}$ *Convert the equation to the x = k form*
                      by dividing both sides by 2, then solve for x.

x = 3

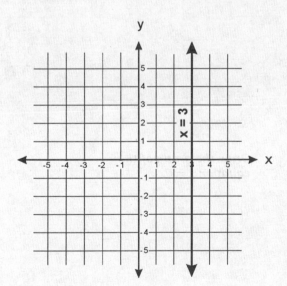

Draw the graph of the equation
x = 3.

Graph 3x = ⁻5.

$$\frac{3x}{3} = -\frac{5}{3}$$

$$x = -\frac{5}{3}$$

Convert the equation to the $x = k$ form by dividing both sides by 3, then solve for x.

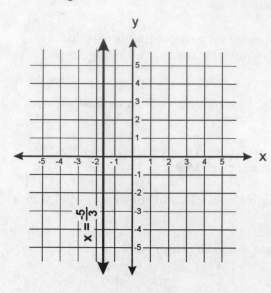

Draw the graph of the equation $x = -\frac{5}{3}$.

Graph 3x = 0.

$$\frac{3x}{3} = \frac{0}{3}$$

$$x = 0$$

Convert the equation to the $x = k$ form by dividing both sides by 3, then solve for x.

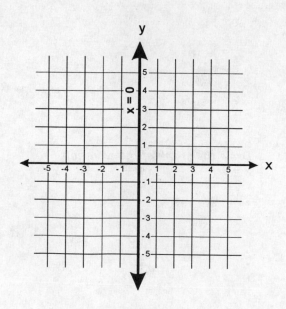

Draw the graph of the equation $x = 0$.

Graphing Horizontal Lines

Horizontal lines can also be described by equations that have a particular form. That form contains a y-term, an equal sign, and a number (e.g., y = 7). There is no x-term in the equation of a horizontal line. It is easiest to graph a horizontal line when the equation for the line is written with a positive y-term by itself on the left side of the equal sign and with the number on the right side of the equal sign. Equations in this form are said to be in the y = c form. All the points on a horizontal line have the same y coordinate. In the y = c form, if c is positive, the line lies above or on the positive side of the origin. If c is negative, the line lies below or on the negative side of the origin.

When equations for horizontal lines are written in a more complicated form, they should be converted to the y = c form before you graph the line. The table below lists several equations for horizontal lines and shows how to change them into the y = c form. The equations on the left of the table are more complex; the equations on the right are simplified versions of the same equations.

y = ⁻5 becomes y = ⁻5   No change.

⁻4y = 8 becomes y = ⁻2   Divide both sides by ⁻4.

$2y = {}^-3$ becomes $y = -\frac{3}{2}$ Divide both sides by 2.

After you have identified the equation as representing a horizontal line, use the following steps to graph the equation.

1. If the equation is not in the y = c form, convert it to that form.

2. The value c always serves as the y-coordinate of the horizontal line. Find the value of c on the y-axis, and draw a small circle on it.

3. Draw a horizontal line that passes through the circle and is parallel to the x-axis.

Graph 3y = 9.

$$\frac{3y}{3} = \frac{9}{3}$$ *Convert the equation to the y = c form by*
                                        dividing both sides by 3, then solve for y.
$$y = 3$$

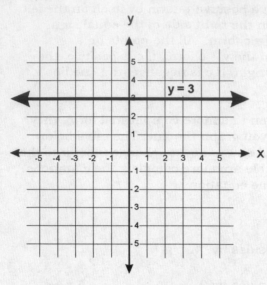

Draw the graph of the
equation y = 3.

Graph 2y = ⁻5.

$$\frac{2y}{2} = -\frac{5}{2}$$ *Convert the equation to the y = c form by*
                                         dividing both sides by 2, then solve for y.
$$y = -\frac{5}{2}$$

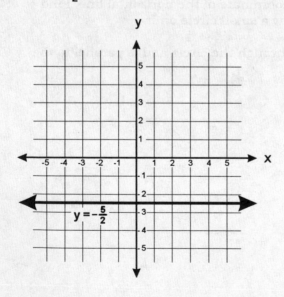

Draw the graph of the
equation $y = -\frac{5}{2}$.

Graph $\frac{y}{^-5} = 0$.

$(^-5)\left(\dfrac{y}{^-5}\right) = (^-5)(0)$ *Convert the equation to the y = c form by*

                                                       multiplying both sides by $^-5$, then solve for y.

$y = 0$

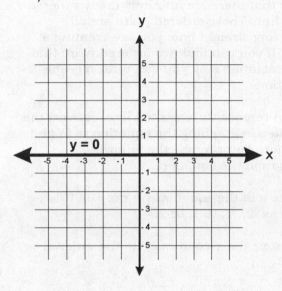

Draw the graph of the equation y = 0.

From the examples above, you should notice that the equation of the x-axis is y = 0, and the equation of the y-axis is x = 0. This is an important fact to remember.

Graphing Slanted Lines

The equations of all slanted (or oblique) lines (lines that are not horizontal or vertical) contain an x-term, a y-term, and sometimes a number (a constant). The graph of a slanted line in the Cartesian plane is the set of points the coordinates of which, when substituted for x and y in the equation, will make the equation true. This is the same principle that applied to vertical and horizontal lines as discussed above. The following represent equations of slanted lines.

2x + 3y = 6

4x − y = 8

$^-x = ^-3y$

Notice that all these equations can be put in the y = mx + b form. The equation of any slanted line can be written in this form. This is the easiest form to use when you are graphing the equation of a slanted line. When you graph a slanted line, remember that y should be positive and should be by itself on the left side of the equal sign. The table below lists several equations of slanted lines and shows how to change them into the y = mx + b form. The equations on the left of the table are more complex; the equations on the right are simplified versions of the same equations.

$2x + 3y = 6$ becomes $y = -\frac{2}{3}x + 2$

$x - y = 1$ becomes $y = x - 1$

$^-x = 3y$ becomes $y = -\frac{1}{3}x$

Using ordered pairs to graph slanted lines. One method for graphing slanted lines uses sets of ordered pairs. Remember that there are infinitely many ordered pairs that satisfy the equation of a straight line. These ordered pairs are all solutions to the equation. When you graph any straight line, you are creating a picture of the solution set for the equation. If you can find two ordered pairs that satisfy the equation (i.e., that belong to the solution set), you can draw a graph that will show all the solutions to the equation.

Once you have determined that an equation represents a slanted line, convert the equation to the $y = mx + b$ form. The next step in graphing the equation is to find several ordered pairs that satisfy the equation. You can use the following procedure to find the ordered pairs and to graph the equation.

1. Pick a number, then use it to replace x in the equation $y = mx + b$. It is usually best to pick a number such as $^-2$, $^-1$, 0, 1, or 2.

2. The number you chose will now become the x-coordinate of the ordered pair.

3. Solve the equation for y. The number you get when you solve for y will become the y-coordinate of the ordered pair.

4. Write the x-coordinate (the number you chose) and the y-coordinate (the number you got when you solved the equation for y) as an ordered pair. Be sure to write them in a place where you can refer back to them easily.

5. Repeat Steps 1–4 (using a different number for x each time) until you have 3 to 5 different ordered pairs.

6. On a Cartesian plane, graph the ordered pairs you have found.

7. Draw the line connecting the points you have graphed, and then label the line by writing the original equation next to it.

The following examples show how to use these steps to graph the equations of slanted lines.

Graph $2x + 3y = 6$.

$2x + 3y = 6$	*Convert to the $y = mx + b$ form by subtracting 2x from both sides and then dividing both sides by 3.*
$y = -\frac{2}{3}x + 2$	
Let $x = 3$.	*Pick a value to replace x in the equation, and then solve for y.*
$y = -\frac{2}{3}(3) + 2$	*Solve for y (if $x = 3$).*
$y = ^-2 + 2$	
$y = 0$	
$(3,0)$	*Write the ordered pair.*

Repeat the steps above until 3 to 5 ordered pairs are obtained. Only two ordered pairs are necessary; the additional pairs serve as a check.

Let x = 0.

$y = -\frac{2}{3}(0) + 2$

y = 2

(0,2)   *Write the ordered pair.*

Let x = ⁻3, x = ⁻6, x = 6 and find the corresponding ordered pairs.

They are (⁻3,4), (⁻6,6), and (6,⁻2).

Locate these points on the Cartesian plane. Draw a line that passes through all the points you marked, and then label the line by writing the equation 2x + 3y = 6 next to it.

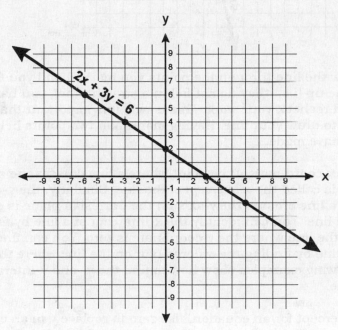

Graph 4x – y = 1 by finding ordered pairs that satisfy the equation.

4x – y = 1   *Convert the equation to the y = mx + b form by subtracting 4x from both sides and then dividing both sides by ⁻1.*

y = 4x – 1

x = ⁻2 → y = ⁻9 (⁻2,⁻9)   *Pick values to replace x in the equation, then solve for y.*
x = ⁻1 → y = ⁻5 (⁻1,⁻5)
x = 0 → y = ⁻1 (0,⁻1)
x = 1 → y = 3 (1,3)
x = 2 → y = 7 (2,7)

Draw the graph using the ordered pairs you found.

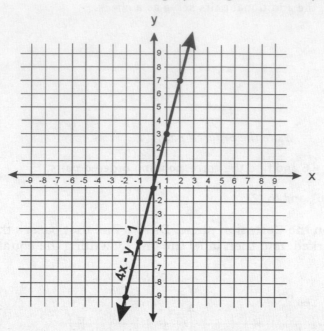

If you try to draw the line through the points you marked and you find that the points do not line up (i.e., they do not fall in a straight line), you have made an error and should recheck your work. This is why it is important that you use more than two points to draw your line. Having more than two points helps you see any errors you may have made.

Intercepts. The x-coordinate of the point where a line crosses the x-axis on the Cartesian plane is called the *x-intercept* of the line. Similarly, the y-coordinate of the point where a line crosses the y-axis on the Cartesian plane is called the *y-intercept* of the line. You can identify the x-intercept of a line by finding the ordered pair on the line where the y-coordinate is zero. You can find the y-intercept of a line by finding the ordered pair on the line where the x-coordinate is zero. The following examples show how to find the x- and y-intercepts for the equation of a line.

To find the x-intercept for an equation, use zero to replace y in an equation of the $y = mx + b$ form. Then solve for x. The value you obtain for x is called the x-intercept of the equation.

The examples below show how to find the x-intercept of an equation.

Find the x-intercept of 2x + 3y = 6.

Let $y = 0$.   *Use zero to replace y in the equation.*

$2x + 3(0) = 6$ *Solve for x.*

$2x = 6$
$x = 3$

Therefore, the x-intercept for this equation is 3. The ordered pair that represents the point where the line crosses the x-axis is (3,0).

Find the x-intercept for 4x – y = 18.

Let y = 0.   *Use 0 to replace y in the original equation.*

4x – 0 = 18   *Solve for x.*

4x = 18

$x = \dfrac{18}{4}$

$x = \dfrac{9}{2} = 4\dfrac{1}{2}$

Therefore, the x-intercept is $4\dfrac{1}{2}$. The coordinates of the point where the graph of the line crosses the x-axis are $(4\dfrac{1}{2},0)$.

You can find the y-intercept (the y-coordinate of the point where a line crosses the y-axis) by using a similar procedure as follows.

Find the y-intercept for 2x + 3y = ⁻6.

Let x = 0.   *Use 0 to replace x in the equation.*

(2)(0) + 3y = ⁻6   *Solve for y.*

3y = ⁻6

y = ⁻2

Therefore, the y-intercept is ⁻2, and the coordinates of the point where the line crosses the y-axis are (0,⁻2).

All slanted lines have both an x-intercept and a y-intercept. Vertical and horizontal lines, however, each have only one intercept. Since the graph of a vertical line is parallel to the y-axis, it will never cross the y-axis. As a result, a vertical line has no y-intercept. Every vertical line has only an x-intercept. Likewise, since the graph of a horizontal line is parallel to the x-axis, it will never cross the x-axis. As a result, a horizontal line has no x-intercept. Every horizontal line has only a y-intercept.

There are two special cases for which this is not true: when the vertical line runs along the y axis or a horizontal line runs along the x axis. The equations for these lines would be x = 0 and y = 0. But since these lines do not cross the axes at a single, unique point, we do not consider them to have intercepts.

Remember that the equation for a vertical line can be written in the x = k form. When the equation for a vertical line is written in this form, the x-intercept of the line is the value k.

Find the x-intercept for 3x = 12.

$\dfrac{3x}{3} = \dfrac{12}{3}$ *Convert the equation to the x = k form.*

x = 4   *Solve for x.*

Therefore, the x-intercept is 4, and the coordinates of the point where the line crosses the x-axis are (4,0).

Remember that the equation for a horizontal line can be written in the y = c form. When the equation for a horizontal line is written in this form, the y-intercept of the line is the value c.

Find the y-intercept for 2y = ⁻7.

$$\frac{2y}{2} = -\frac{7}{2}$$ *Convert the equation to the y = c form by*

$$y = -\frac{7}{2}$$ *dividing both sides by 2.*

Therefore, the y-intercept is $-\frac{7}{2}$, and the coordinates of the point where the graph of the line crosses the y-axis are $(0, -\frac{7}{2})$.

Slope

The slope refers to the amount of slant that the graph of a line has. Mathematically, the slope is the ratio of the amount of vertical change to the amount of horizontal change between any two points on the line. You can find the slope of a line from its graph, from the coordinates of any two points on the line, or from its equation.

Using the Graph of a Line to Find the Slope

The following list explains how to find the slope of a slanted line by using its graph.

1. Find a point on the graph of the line, and draw a vertical line through it.

2. Choose a second point on the line, and draw a horizontal line through it so that the line you draw intersects the vertical line that you drew from the first point. The horizontal and the vertical lines that you have drawn should form two sides of a triangle. The original line should be the third side of the triangle (see the example following Step 5).

3. Starting at either point on the line, count up (or down) along or parallel to the y-axis until you reach the horizontal line drawn in Step 2. If you counted up, write a positive number telling how many places you counted to get to the intersection (e.g., if you counted up 6 places along the y-axis, write 6). If you counted down, write a negative number telling how many places you counted to get to the intersection (e.g., if you counted down 6 places along the y-axis, write ⁻6). Next, start at the place where the lines you drew intersect, and count to the right (or left) along the x-axis to the second point you chose on the original line. If you counted to the right, write down a positive number telling how many places you counted (e.g., if you counted 4 places to the right, write 4). If you counted to the left, write a negative number telling how many places you counted (e.g., if you counted 4 places to the left, write ⁻4). When you do this counting procedure, you should start at one point on the original line and end at the second point that you chose on the original line.

4. The distance you counted up (or down) is called Δy (delta y). This distance tells how much y has changed between the first point and the second point on the original line. The distance you counted right (or left) is called Δx (delta x). This distance tells how much x has changed between the first and the second points on the original line.

5. In equations, the slope of the line is represented by the letter "m." The slope is usually written as a ratio of Δy to Δx or $m = \frac{\Delta y}{\Delta x}$.

The following examples show you how to use these steps to find the slope of a line.

Find the slope of the line below.

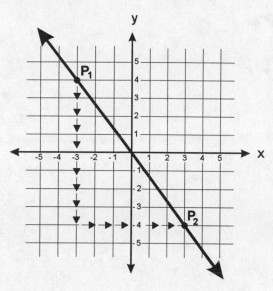

Start at P_1.

Count down 8 → $\Delta y = {}^-8$.

Count right 6 → $\Delta x = 6$.

$$m = \frac{\Delta y}{\Delta x}$$

$$m = -\frac{8}{6}$$

$$m = -\frac{4}{3}$$

Find the slope of the line below.

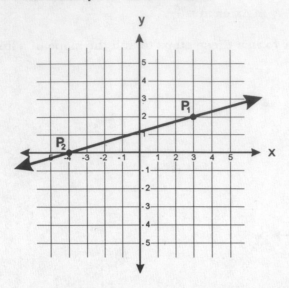

Start at P_1.

Count down 2 → $\Delta y = {}^-2$.

Count left 7 → $\Delta x = {}^-7$.

$$m = \frac{\Delta y}{\Delta x}$$

$$m = \frac{{}^-2}{{}^-7}$$

$$m = \frac{2}{7}$$

It is somewhat difficult to use this method to find the slope of horizontal or vertical lines. When you try to do the counting procedure on a vertical line, you find that the distance in a right/left direction between any two points on the line is zero. Therefore, when you substitute in the slope formula, you obtain $\frac{\Delta y}{0}$.

Remember that a ratio can be thought of as a fraction and that a fraction cannot have zero in the denominator. Because you cannot write a real ratio in this situation, a vertical line is said to have no slope, or, technically, an undefined slope.

When you apply the counting procedure to a horizontal line, you find the up/down distance between points is zero. As a result, the slope formula is $\frac{0}{\Delta x}$. Since the numerator of the ratio is zero, the value of the fraction is zero. As a result, the slope of a horizontal line is zero. The examples below show what happens when the counting procedure is used with horizontal and vertical lines.

Find the slope of the vertical line below.

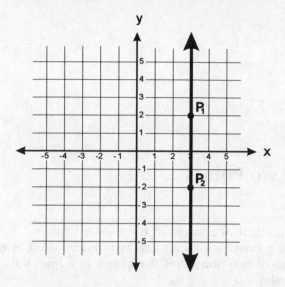

Start at P₁.

Count down 4 → Δy = ⁻4.

Count right/left 0 → Δx = 0.

$m = \dfrac{\Delta y}{\Delta x}$

$m = -\dfrac{4}{0}$

m = no slope (undefined slope)

Find the slope of the horizontal line below.

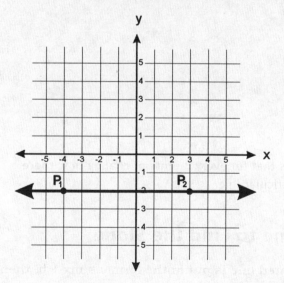

Start at P_1.

Count up or down $0 \rightarrow \Delta y = 0$.

Count right $7 \rightarrow \Delta x = 7$.

$$m = \frac{\Delta y}{\Delta x}$$

$$m = \frac{0}{7}$$

$$m = 0$$

Using the Coordinates of Two Points on a Line to Find the Slope

The slope of a line (m) represents the amount of change in the y-coordinates divided by the amount of change in the x-coordinates for any two points on a line. If (x_1, y_1) and (x_2, y_2) are the coordinates of two points on the graph of a line, you may use the formula below to find the slope.

$$m = \frac{y_2 - y_1}{x_2 - x_1}$$

Remember that $\Delta y = y_2 - y_1$ and $\Delta x = x_2 - x_1$.

The following example shows how to use this formula to find the slope of a line.

Find the slope of a line containing the points (⁻7,2) and (3,5).

$(x_1, y_1) = (^-7,2)$ and $(x_2, y_2) = (3,5)$

$x_1 = ^-7$, $y_1 = 2$, $x_2 = 3$, and $y_2 = 5$

$$m = \frac{y_2 - y_1}{x_2 - x_1}$$

$$m = \frac{5 - 2}{3 - (^-7)}$$

$$m = \frac{3}{10}$$

The slope of the line is $\frac{3}{10}$. This means that for every 3 units of change in y, there are 10 units of change in x on this particular line.

Using the Equation of a Line to Find the Slope

Slanted lines. If the equation of a slanted line is put in the form y = mx + b, then m (the coefficient of x) is the slope of the line, and b is the y-intercept.

Find the slope of ⁻2x + 3y = 6.

3y = 2x + 6   *Convert the equation to the y = mx + b form by dividing both*
                     sides by 3.

$\frac{3y}{3} = \frac{2x}{3} + \frac{6}{3}$

$y = \frac{2}{3}x + 2$

The slope of the line is $\frac{2}{3}$, and the y-intercept is 2.

Find the slope of 6x – 4y = 5.

6x – 4y = 5   *Convert the equation to the y = mx + b form by subtracting*
                     6x from both sides and then dividing by ⁻4.

$y = \frac{^-6}{^-4}x + \frac{5}{^-4}$

$y = \frac{3}{2}x - \frac{5}{4}$ *Reduce the fractions.*

The slope of the line is $\frac{3}{2}$, and the y-intercept is $-\frac{5}{4}$.

Vertical and horizontal lines. To find the slope of a vertical or a horizontal line given its equation, remember the following facts.

1. All vertical lines have the equation x = k.

2. All vertical lines have no slope (undefined slopes).

3. All horizontal lines have the equation y = c.

4. All horizontal lines have zero slope.

With this information, you can easily identify the slope of vertical and horizontal lines.

Find the slope of 2y = 6.

$\frac{2y}{2} = \frac{6}{2}$ *Convert to the y = c form by*

                     dividing both sides by 2.

y = 3

Remember that a horizontal line has a slope of zero, therefore m = 0.

Find the slope of 3x = 7.

$\frac{3x}{3} = \frac{7}{3}$ *Convert to the x = k form by*

                     dividing both sides by 3.

$x = \frac{7}{3}$

Remember that a vertical line has no slope, therefore m = no slope.

Graphing a Line Using the Slope-Intercept Method

Another method that can be used to graph a line involves the use of the slope and the y-intercept of the line. This method is called the slope-intercept method of graphing. It is most useful when you have to graph slanted lines. You should use the following steps to graph lines according to the slope-intercept method.

1. Convert the equation to the y = mx + b form.

2. Identify the slope and the y-intercept of the equation (remember that m = slope and b = y-intercept).

3. Draw a small circle on the y-intercept on a Cartesian plane.

4. A slope is usually written in the form of a fraction. The numerator of the fraction tells the change in y, and the denominator tells the change in x. (NOTE: If m is a whole number, use that whole number as the numerator of the fraction and the number 1 as the denominator of the fraction.) Using the y-intercept as a starting point, count up or down along the y-axis the number of places indicated by the numerator of the slope. Next, count right or left along the x-axis the number of places indicated by the denominator of the slope. For example, if the equation tells you that the slope of the line is $\frac{2}{5}$, you should count two places up and five places to the right from your starting point. (Remember that positive numbers require counting up or to the right and that negative numbers require counting down or to the left.) After you have finished counting, draw a point at the new point you have found.

5. Find the coordinates of the point that you found in Step 4. Use the coordinates of that point to replace x and y in the original equation. The result should be a true numerical statement. If it is not, you have made an error and should check your work before proceeding to Step 6.

6. If you have not made any errors, draw a line connecting the y-intercept and the point that you found in Step 4.

7. Label the line by writing the original equation next to it.

Graph 2x + 3y = 6, using the slope-intercept method.

2x + 3y = 6   *Convert to the y = mx + b form by subtracting 2x from both sides and then dividing both sides by 3.*

$y = -\frac{2}{3}x + 2$

This indicates that $m = -\frac{2}{3}$ and $b = 2$. The coordinates of the y-intercept are (0,2). Counting two places down from this point (because the numeration of the slope is ⁻2) and three places to the right (because the denominator of the slope is 3) gives the point (3,0). Let us use this point as a test point to replace x and y in the original equation.

Test point: (3,0)

$2x + 3y = 6$

$2(3) + 3(0) \overset{?}{=} 6$

$6 + 0 \overset{?}{=} 6$

$6 = 6$

This is a true statement, and the line can now be labeled.

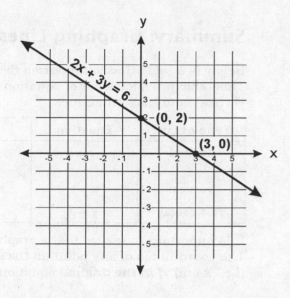

Graph 4x − 5y = 10 by using the slope-intercept method.

$y = \dfrac{4}{5}x - 2$

Convert to the y = mx + b form by subtracting 4x from both sides and then dividing both sides by ⁻5.

Therefore, $m = \dfrac{4}{5} = \dfrac{\Delta y}{\Delta x}$ and b = ⁻2, which indicates that (0,⁻2) are the coordinates of the y-intercept. Counting 4 places up and 5 places to the right from this point gives the point (5,2).

Test point: (5,2)

$4x - 5y = 10$

$4(5) - 5(2) \overset{?}{=} 10$

$20 - 10 \overset{?}{=} 10$

$10 = 10$

This is a true statement. The line in the graph is accurate.

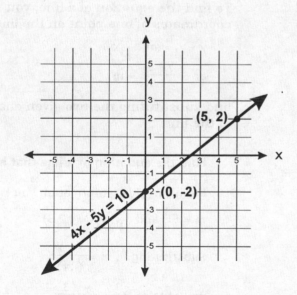

Summary: Graphing Lines

Below is a table that summarizes the information covered in the previous sections. This table provides a list of equations, slopes, and x- and y-intercepts for slanted, vertical, and horizontal lines.

Type of Line	Equation	Slope	x-intercept	y-intercept
Slanted	$y = mx + b$	m	Let y = 0. Solve for x.	b
Vertical	$x = k$	no slope	k	none
Horizontal	$y = c$	0	none	c

It is important to realize that a graph represents all the solutions of an equation. The coordinates of any point on the graph can be substituted for the variables (i.e., x and y) in the original equation, and a true statement will result.

Finding the Equation of a Line

In the preceding sections of this chapter you have been given the equation of a line, and by extracting information from the equation, you have been able to graph the line on the Cartesian plane. In this section you will learn to reverse this process. You will be given some of the characteristics of a line and you will be asked to find the equation of the line with those characteristics.

To find the equation of a line, you need to know only the slope of the line and the coordinates of one point on the line. Using the point-slope form:

$$y - y_1 = m(x - x_1)$$

or $\quad \dfrac{y - y_1}{x - x_1} = m \qquad\qquad$ *Divide both sides by $(x - x_1)$.*

and substituting the two given characteristics, you will be able to find the equation of the line.

Find the equation of a line that has a slope of $-\dfrac{1}{3}$ and contains the point (-2,3).

From the given information you know:

$m = -\dfrac{1}{3}$ and $(x_1, y_1) = (-2,3)$

Substituting in $m = \dfrac{y - y_1}{x - x_1}$

you obtain: $-\dfrac{1}{3} = \dfrac{y - 3}{x - (-2)}$

Solving and simplifying gives: $-\dfrac{1}{3} = \dfrac{y - 3}{x + 2}$

$$
\begin{aligned}
-1(x + 2) &= 3(y - 3) & &\textit{Multiply both sides by (x + 2) and by 3.}\\
-x - 2 &= 3y - 9 & &\textit{Remove parentheses.}\\
-x - 3y &= -7 & &\textit{Move variables and numbers.}\\
x + 3y &= 7 & &\textit{Solve for y.}\\
3y &= -x + 7 \\
y &= -\dfrac{1}{3}x + \dfrac{7}{3}
\end{aligned}
$$

It is easy to verify that the equation you obtained is correct. You can check the slope by rewriting the equation in slope-intercept form, $y = mx + b$. For this equation, rewriting gives $y = -\frac{1}{3}x + \frac{7}{3}$, which produces a slope of $-\frac{1}{3}$, as required. To check that the point ($^-$2,3) is on the line, simply substitute the values from this ordered pair into the equation $x + 3y = 7$. This gives you:

$$(^-2) + 3(3) \stackrel{?}{=} 7$$
$$^-2 + 9 \stackrel{?}{=} 7$$
$$7 = 7$$

Since both characteristics satisfy the equation you found, you can conclude that the equation of the line with a slope of $-\frac{1}{3}$ and containing the point ($^-$2,3) is $x + 3y = 7$.

In some situations, the slope of the line and the coordinates of a point on the line are not both given. In such situations you must first use the information that *is* given to find the slope of the line and the coordinates of one point on the line, and then proceed as before.

Find the equation of the line that contains the points ($^-$3,5) and (2,7).

First use the coordinates of the two points to find the slope.

Using ($^-$3,5) = (x_2, y_2) and (2,7) = (x_1, y_1) substitute into $m = \frac{y_2 - y_1}{x_2 - x_1}$ to find the slope of the line.

$$m = \frac{5 - 7}{^-3 - 2}$$

$$m = \frac{^-2}{^-5}$$

$$m = \frac{2}{5}$$

Now using the slope of $\frac{2}{5}$ and the point (2,7) = (x_1, y_1), substitute as before:

$$m = \frac{y - y_1}{x - x_1}$$

substituting:

$$\frac{2}{5} = \frac{y - 7}{x - 2}$$

$2(x - 2) = 5(y - 7)$	*Multiply both sides by 5 and by (x – 2).*
$2x - 4 = 5y - 35$	*Remove parentheses.*
$2x - 5y = {}^-31$	*Move variables and numbers.*

Check by substituting the original ordered pairs into the equation you obtained to determine if the two points satisfy the equation $2x - 5y = {}^-31$.

Check: ($^-$3,5)   Check: (2,7)

$$2x - 5y = {}^-31$$

$$2(^-3) - 5(5) \stackrel{?}{=} {}^-31$$

$$^-6 - 25 \stackrel{?}{=} {}^-31$$

$$^-31 = {}^-31$$

$$2x - 5y = {}^-31$$

$$2(2) - 5(7) \stackrel{?}{=} {}^-31$$

$$4 - 35 \stackrel{?}{=} {}^-31$$

$$^-31 = {}^-31$$

Since both ordered pairs satisfy the equation, you can conclude that $2x - 5y = {}^-31$ is the equation of the line passing through ($^-$3,5) and (2,7).

Use the chart to determine the linear equation that models the data given.

y	x
5	$\frac{1}{2}$
7	1

Using (x,y) ordered pairs, the table gives the coordinates of two points on a line whose equation you are asked to find. The coordinates of these points are $\left(\frac{1}{2},5\right)$ and (1,7). Proceeding as before, and letting $(x_2,y_2) = \left(\frac{1}{2},5\right)$ and $(x_1, y_1) = (1,7)$, you can substitute these pairs into the point-slope formula to determine the linear equation that models the information in the table.

Substituting in $m = \dfrac{y_2 - y_1}{x_2 - x_1}$

you obtain $\quad m = \dfrac{5 - 7}{\frac{1}{2} - 1}$

$$m = \dfrac{-2}{-\frac{1}{2}}$$

$$m = 4$$

Thus the required linear equation has a slope of 4. Now you can use the point-slope form as before to find the linear equation. Simply use the slope found above (m = 4) and either of the two known ordered pairs. We will use $(x_1, y_1) = (1,7)$.

$m = \dfrac{y - y_1}{x - x_1}$	*Use the point-slope form.*
$\dfrac{4}{1} = \dfrac{y - 7}{x - 1}$	*Substitute m = 4 and $(x_1, y_1) = (1,7)$.*
$4(x - 1) = y - 7$	*Multiply both sides by (x – 1).*
$4x - 4 = y - 7$	*Remove parentheses.*
$4x - y = {}^{-}3$	*Move variables and numbers.*

Check the accuracy of this equation by substituting the original ordered pairs.

Check: $\left(\frac{1}{2},5\right)$ Check: (1,7)

$$4x - y = {}^{-}3 \qquad\qquad\qquad 4x - y = {}^{-}3$$

$$4\left(\frac{1}{2}\right) - 5 \overset{?}{=} {}^{-}3 \qquad\qquad 4(1) - 7 \overset{?}{=} {}^{-}3$$

$$2 - 5 \overset{?}{=} {}^{-}3 \qquad\qquad\qquad 4 - 7 \overset{?}{=} {}^{-}3$$

$${}^{-}3 = {}^{-}3 \qquad\qquad\qquad\qquad {}^{-}3 = {}^{-}3$$

The two ordered pairs satisfy the equation. You can conclude that the linear equation $4x - y = {}^{-}3$ models the data given.

Given the graph below, determine the equation of the line that passes through points A and B.

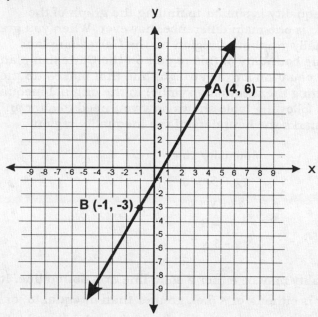

Use the coordinates of the two points to determine the slope of the line, as follows:

Let $(x_2, y_2) = (4, 6)$ and $(x_1, y_1) = (^-1, ^-3)$. Substitute into $m = \dfrac{y_2 - y_1}{x_2 - x_1}$.

$$m = \frac{6 - (^-3)}{4 - (^-1)}$$

$$m = \frac{6 + 3}{4 + 1}$$

$$m = \frac{9}{5}$$

Now use $m = \dfrac{9}{5}$ and $(x_1, y_1) = (^-1, ^-3)$ and substitute once more.

$$m = \frac{y - y_1}{x - x_1}$$

$$\frac{9}{5} = \frac{y - (^-3)}{x - (^-1)}$$

$$\frac{9}{5} = \frac{y + 3}{x + 1}$$

$$9(x + 1) = 5(y + 3)$$

$$9x + 9 = 5y + 15$$

$$9x - 5y = 6$$

Therefore, the equation of the line that passes through points A and B on the graph is $9x - 5y = 6$.

Check the accuracy of this equation by substituting the coordinates on the graph.

Check: (4,6)

$$9x - 5y = 6$$
$$9(4) - 5(6) \stackrel{?}{=} 6$$
$$36 - 30 \stackrel{?}{=} 6$$
$$6 = 6$$

Check: $(^-1, ^-3)$

$$9x - 5y = 6$$
$$9(^-1) - 5(^-3) \stackrel{?}{=} 6$$
$$^-9 + 15 \stackrel{?}{=} 6$$
$$6 = 6$$

The coordinates of both points satisfy the equation. The equation $9x - 5y = 6$ fits the line on the graph.

Graphing Linear Inequalities

Finding the graph of a linear inequality is similar to finding the graph of the equation of a straight line. There is one main difference, however. When you graph a linear inequality, you are actually graphing a region on the Cartesian plane rather than just a single line. The boundary of this region on the Cartesian plane is a straight line. You can find the equation for the straight line that makes up the boundary of the region by changing the inequality symbol in the original inequality statement to an equal sign. The following table shows how you need to alter an inequality to find the line that marks the boundary of the inequality region.

Inequality	Boundary Line
$2x + 3y \geq 6$	$2x + 3y = 6$
$5x - y < 8$	$5x - y = 8$
$x \geq 3$	$x = 3$
$y - 5 \leq 7$	$y - 5 = 7$

The boundary line for an inequality may be either a solid line or a dotted line. It is a solid line when the inequality is either $\geq$ or $\leq$ (i.e., greater than or equal to, or less than or equal to). Here, the solution includes the line itself since the "equal to" part of the expression reflects the line. It is a dotted line when the original inequality is > or < (i.e., greater than or less than). The line itself is not a part of the solution set.

The steps in graphing the solution set for a linear inequality are as follows.

1. Rewrite the inequality statement as an equation.

2. Graph the equation on a Cartesian plane by using a solid or a dotted line as indicated by the inequality sign in the original equation.

3. The boundary line you have graphed separates the plane into two regions (see the example following Step 7). Pick an ordered pair that represents a point in one of those regions.

4. Use the ordered pair to replace the variables (i.e., x and y) in the original inequality statement. Then solve the inequality, and determine if the resulting numerical statement is true or false.

5. Now choose a point in the second region of the Cartesian plane. Use the coordinates of that point to repeat Step 4.

6. One of the ordered pairs you chose should make the inequality statement true. The other ordered pair should make the statement false. If this does not occur, check your work. The ordered pair that makes the statement true is in the region that represents the solution set of the inequality.

7. Shade the region that contains the ordered pair that makes the inequality true. The coordinates of any point in the shaded region should make the original inequality true. You can check your work by choosing another point in that region and using its coordinates to solve the inequality. If you get a true statement, you have shaded the correct region.

Graph the solution set of 2x + 3y ≥ 6 by using the slope-intercept method.

Since the original inequality contains ≥, we know that the boundary line will be solid.

$y = -\frac{2}{3}x + 2$ *Convert to the y = mx + b form by subtracting 2x from both sides and then dividing both sides by 3.*

The equation indicates that m = $-\frac{2}{3}$ and b = 2. The coordinates of the y-intercept are (0,2). We can find the coordinates of the x-intercept by letting y = 0 and solving for x.

$$2x + 3y = 6$$
$$2x + 3(0) = 6$$
$$2x = 6$$
$$x = 3$$

Therefore, the point (3,0) is on the line and, since we know two points on the line, we can graph it.

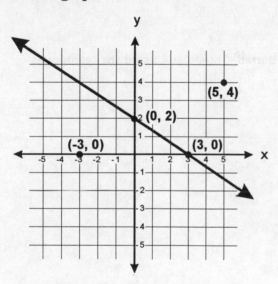

Now choose two test points, one on each side of the line. We will use (⁻3,0) and (5,4). By substituting each ordered pair into the original inequality, we should obtain one true statement and one false statement, as follows.

Test point: (⁻3,0)   Test point: (5,4)

$2x + 3y ≥ 6$ $2x + 3y ≥ 6$

$2(⁻3) + 3(0) ≥ 6$ $2(5) + 3(4) ≥ 6$

$⁻6 + 0 ≥ 6$ $10 + 12 ≥ 6$

$⁻6 ≥ 6$ $22 ≥ 6$
False   True

Since the point (5,4) produced a true statement, we should shade the region containing (5,4).

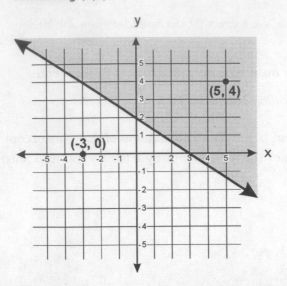

The coordinates of any point in the shaded region will make the original inequality true.

Graph the solution for y < 4.

The inequality is < so the boundary line is dotted. Graph y = 4 using the techniques previously discussed.

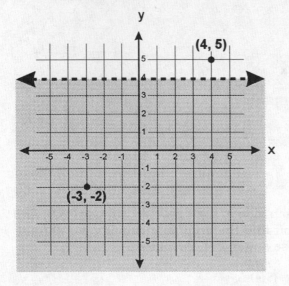

Test point: (⁻3,⁻2)   Test point: (4,5)

Results in ⁻2 < 4   Results in 5 < 4
True   False

Shade the region containing (⁻3,⁻2).

Variation

Variation is a mathematical way of telling how a change in one thing can cause a change in another thing. For example, a student may sell newspapers to make extra money. If the student sells more newspapers, he or she will earn more money. The fewer papers sold, the less money earned. A change in one value (i.e., the number of newspapers sold) causes a change in another value (i.e., money earned).

1. Direct variation. In *direct variation,* two values change in the same way. The example of a student selling newspapers is a type of direct variation. When one value (the number of papers sold) goes up, the other value (the money earned) also goes up. In the same way, when one value goes down, the other value also goes down. The relationship between these two values can be written as a ratio. For example, if the student sells 20 papers and gets $0.50 for every newspaper sold, the ratio would be written as $\frac{20}{\$10.00}$. In this relationship, the amount of change in the two values is constant (i.e., the amount of money earned will increase or decrease by $0.50 times the number of papers sold). In this situation, therefore, $0.50 is the constant of variation. If you consider the number of papers sold to be the value x and the total amount of money earned to be the value y, you can write the following equation to describe the relationship between the two values.

> y = kx (NOTE: In this equation, k is the constant of variation. The value of k *cannot* be zero.)
> y = total amount earned and x = total number of papers sold
> k = $0.50

In the previous example, the constant is known. In many cases, you need to find the constant. To find the constant, you must solve the equation for k, which gives you the equation $\frac{y}{x} = k$.

Solve the following problem.

> The weight of an object on the moon varies directly with its weight on Earth. An astronaut weighs 150 pounds on Earth and weighs 25 pounds on the moon. A student weighs 102 pounds on Earth. How much would the student weigh on the moon?
>
> Let x = weight on the moon.
> Let y = weight on Earth.

$\frac{y}{x} = k$ *Use the equation* $\frac{y}{x} = k$.

$\frac{150}{25} = k$ *Substitute the weights of the*

$k = 6$ *astronaut for x and y, then solve for k.*

To find the student's weight, use the value of k that you calculated.

y = 102
x = ?
k = 6
$\frac{102}{x}$ = 6
x = 17 pounds

This shows that for each unit of change in x, there are 6 units of change in y. A table of ordered pairs shows this relationship.

x   y

1   6   Note that when x increases by
2   12   one unit, y increases by
3   18   6 units.
4   24

2. Inverse variation. In *inverse variation,* two values change in opposite ways. For example, if a person travels 500 miles in a car, the length of time needed to make the trip will depend on the speed that the car travels. If the speed of the car increases, the amount of time needed to finish the trip decreases. If the speed of the car decreases, the amount of time needed to finish the trip increases. The speed of the car and the time needed to make the trip are said to vary inversely.

Inverse variation can also be described by an equation. The equation for inverse variation also uses the variables x and y, and a constant of variation, k. The equation for inverse variation can be written as follows.

xy = k, when k is not zero   *This equation may also be written*
                                    in the form of y = $\frac{k}{x}$.

The following example shows how to use this equation to solve inverse variation problems.

If y varies inversely with x, and y = 7 when x = 28, find x when y = 4.

xy = k   *First find the value of k by using*
28(7) = k   *the equation xy = k.*
k = 196

Next, find x when y = 4 by using the value of k that you just calculated.

xy = k
x(4) = 196
x = 49

You can solve problems involving either direct or inverse variation by using the following steps.

1. Decide if the problem involves direct or inverse variation.

2. Write down the appropriate formula, either y = kx (for direct variation) or xy = k (for inverse variation).

3. Use the values given in the problem to solve for k (the constant of variation).

4. Use the variation equations and the value that you calculated for k in order to find any remaining unknown values.

If y varies directly with x, and x = 10 when y = 3, find y when x = 5.

$y = kx$	*The problem says that you are finding direct variation, so use the formula y = kx.*
$3 = k(10)$	*Substitute known values into the equation.*
$k = \frac{3}{10}$	*Solve for k (the constant of variation).*
$y = \left(\frac{3}{10}\right)(5)$	*Use $k = \frac{3}{10}$ and x = 5 to solve for y.*
$y = \frac{3}{2}$	

When x = 5, y will equal $\frac{3}{2}$.

If x varies inversely with y, and x = 3 when y = 2, find the value of x when y = 18.

$x = \frac{k}{y}$	*The problem asks you to calculate inverse variation, so use the formula xy = k (converted to $x = \frac{k}{y}$).*
$3 = \frac{k}{2}$	*Substitute known values into the equation.*
$k = 6$	*Solve for k.*
$x = \frac{6}{18}$	*Use k = 6 and y = 18 to solve for x.*
$x = \frac{1}{3}$	

You may need to find the graphs of equations that describe direct or inverse variation. It is usually easiest to graph this type of equation by finding ordered pairs that can be used to substitute for x and y in the appropriate equation (i.e., ordered pairs that make the equation a true statement). Graph the ordered pairs on a Cartesian plane, and connect the points you have marked. This gives you the graph of the equation.

There are a few facts that may help you graph equations describing direct or inverse variation. First, you should remember that the equation for direct variation, y = kx, is the equation of a straight line. If you convert this equation to the y = mx + b form, you can see that the direct variation formula is a straight line in which b = 0 (b is the y-intercept of the line on the Cartesian plane) and m = k (m is the slope of the line when it is drawn on the Cartesian plane). Notice that when b = 0, the coordinates of the y-intercept are (0,0), which is the origin of the Cartesian plane. (You can calculate this by using 0 to replace y and b in the y = mx + b form of the equation.) This means that the graph of every direct variation equation is a straight line that passes through the origin.

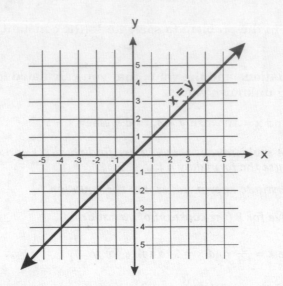

Drawing the graph of an equation that describes inverse variation is slightly more difficult. The graph of an inverse variation is not a straight line. Instead, its graph is a special figure called a hyperbola. A hyperbola is a curved line, the ends of which come close to, but never quite touch, the axes of the Cartesian plane. The diagram below shows an example of a hyperbola.

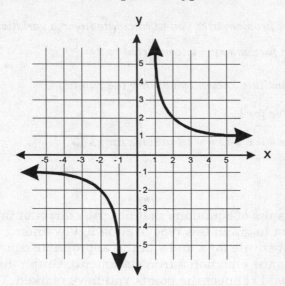

The best way to graph an inverse variation equation is to first find k, then pick a number to replace x in the equation and solve for y. Use the value of x that you chose and the value of y that you calculated to create an ordered pair. Draw a small circle at the appropriate point on the Cartesian plane. Repeat this procedure until you have several points on the plane. Then draw a curve to connect the points, forming the graph. Remember, the graph should look like a hyperbola. If it does not, go back and recheck your work.

Practice Exercises

The following exercises will help you review the skills covered in this chapter. Many of the types of questions presented here will be similar to those on the test; others will not. Remember that the purpose of the exercises is to give you practice on the skills rather than merely to prepare you for the test. Following these exercises are the Practice Exercise Explanations. They explain each question, the correct answer, and why the remaining choices are incorrect.

1. Which equation represents the line graphed below?

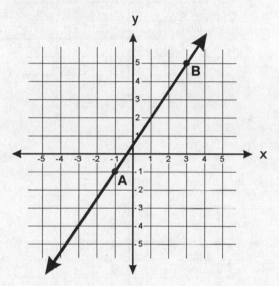

A. $2x - 3y = {}^{-}9$

B. $3x - 2y = {}^{-}1$

C. $3x - 2y = {}^{-}9$

D. $2x - 3y = {}^{-}1$

2. What is the x-intercept of a line whose equation is $2x - 6y = {}^{-}12$?

A. $^{+}6$

B. $^{-}2$

C. $^{+}2$

D. $^{-}6$

3.   Which of the following is the graph of the inequality $y < 3$?

A.

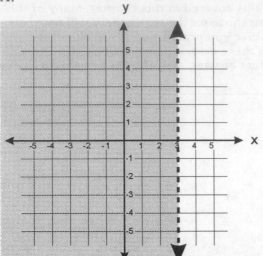

B.

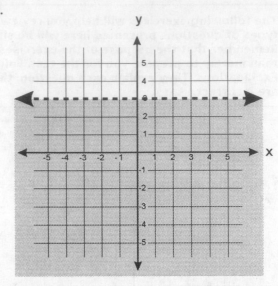

C.

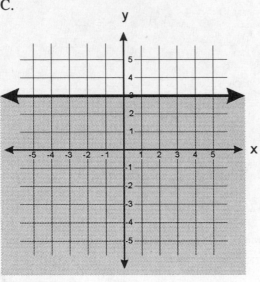

D.

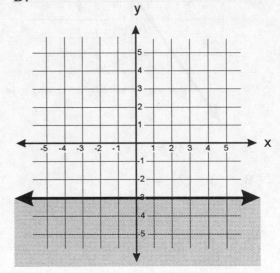

4.   Which of the following points is part of
     the solution set of $3x - y = 6$?

     A.   (3,0)

     B.   (0,2)

     C.   (⁻2,0)

     D.   (0,⁻6)

5. Which of the following equations has
    (2,⁻3) as one of its solutions?

    A. $2x + 3y = ^-13$

    B. $2x - 3y = 13$

    C. $^-2x + 3y = 5$

    D. $^-2x - 3y = ^-5$

    Use the graph below to answer the two
    questions that follow.

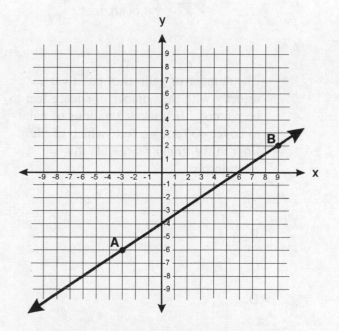

6. What are the coordinates of the
    y-intercept of line AB on this graph?

    A.   (0,4)

    B.   (⁻4,0)

    C.   (0,⁻4)

    D.   (4,0)

7. What is the slope of line AB on the graph
    above?

    A. $\frac{3}{2}$

    B. $-\frac{2}{3}$

    C. $-\frac{3}{2}$

    D. $\frac{2}{3}$

8. Use the graph below to answer the
    question that follows.

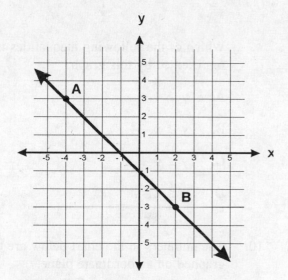

    Which of the following equations
    represents line AB?

    A. $y = ^-x - 1$

    B. $^-2y = x + 1$

    C. $y = x - 1$

    D. $2y = ^-x + 1$

9. Use the graph below to answer the question that follows.

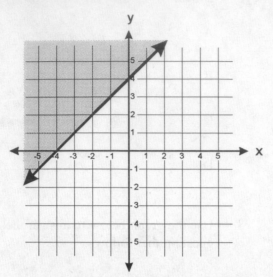

—   Which of the following inequalities is represented by this graph?

A. $y \geq 4 + x$

B. $y \geq x - 4$

C. $y \leq 4 + x$

D. $y \leq x - 4$

10. The numbers in the chart below are to be graphed on a coordinate plane.

x	3	5	7	9	11
y	9	15	21	27	33

Which of the following statements best describes the graph that will result?

A.   It represents a function in which x and y are unrelated.

B.   It represents a function in which y varies inversely with x.

C.   It represents a function in which y varies directly with x.

D.   It is not a linear function.

11. Use the graph below to answer the question that follows.

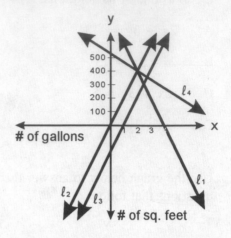

The number of gallons of paint varies directly with the number of square feet to be painted. If it takes 2 gallons of paint to cover 400 square feet, which of the lines in the graph represents this relationship?

A. ℓ_1

B. ℓ_2

C. ℓ_3

D. ℓ_4

12. On a particular job, the number of workers varies inversely with the amount of time it takes to complete the job. If 5 workers can complete the job in 12 hours, how long would it take 15 workers to complete the job?

A.   4 hours

B.   5 hours

C.   36 hours

D.   60 hours

Practice Exercise Explanations

1. **Correct Response: B.** The coordinates of A and B are A $(^-1,^-1)$ and B $(3,5)$. Let $(x_2,y_2) = (^-1,^-1)$ and $(x_1, y_1) = (3,5)$ and substitute in $m = \frac{y_2 - y_1}{x_2 - x_1}$. When simplified, this produces $m = \frac{3}{2}$. Using the slope of $\frac{3}{2}$ and the point $(x_1, y_1) = (3,5)$ in the point-slope formula gives the equation $3x - 2y = ^-1$. Substituting the coordinates of point A $(^-1,^-1)$ into response A gives $1 = ^-9$, a false statement. Likewise, substituting A $(^-1,^-1)$ in response C yields $^-1 = ^-9$ (a false statement), and substituting the same coordinates into response D produces $1 = ^-1$, which is also false. Only selection B satisfies the conditions shown in the graph.

2. **Correct Response: D.** Since the x-intercept is a point whose y-coordinate is 0, the x-intercept of a line can be found by substituting 0 for y in the original equation. This results in the equation $2x - (6)(0) = ^-12$, or $x = ^-6$. Response A results from incorrectly changing the sign. Response B solves for the y-intercept and also changes the sign. Response C solves for the y-intercept.

3. **Correct Response: B.** To graph the inequality $y < 3$, first graph the equality $y = 3$. The graph of $y = 3$ is a horizontal line, 3 units above the x-axis. Since the inequality indicates *less than* rather than *less than or equal to,* the line $y = 3$ should be a dotted line rather than a solid line. Since the original inequality indicates *less than* rather than *greater than,* you should shade the area under the line rather than above the line. Answer A is the graph of $x < 3$. Answer C is the graph of $y \le 3$. Answer D is the graph of $y \le ^-3$.

4. **Correct Response: D.** Since every solution must satisfy the original equation, you merely have to substitute each ordered pair into the original equation. The substitution that gives a true numerical statement is a solution. Substitute $(0,^-6)$ and obtain $3(0) - (^-6) = 6$, or $6 = 6$ which is a true statement. For response A, you would substitute $(3,0)$ and obtain $3(3) - 0 = 6$, or $9 = 6$ which is false. For response B, you would substitute $(0,2)$ and obtain $3(0) - 2 = 6$, or $^-2 = 6$ which is false. For response C, you would substitute $(^-2,0)$ and obtain $3(^-2) - 0 = 6$, or $^-6 = 6$ which is false.

5. **Correct Response: B.** Using the substitution process of problem 4, you obtain $2(2) + ^-3(^-3) = 13$, or $13 = 13$, a true statement. For response A, $2(2) + 3(^-3) = ^-13$, or $^-5 = ^-13$, a false statement. For response C, $^-2(2) + 3(^-3) = 5$, or $^-13 = 5$, a false statement. For response D, $^-2(2) + ^-3(^-3) = ^-5$, or $5 = ^-5$, a false statement.

6. **Correct Response: C.** The coordinates of the y-intercept are the coordinates of the point where the graph of the line crosses the y-axis. To find these coordinates, start at the origin and count down to the point indicated. Since you moved down 4 units the y-coordinate is $^-4$. Therefore the coordinates of the y-intercept are $(0,^-4)$. Since the y-intercept is on the y-axis, you may exclude responses B and D, which are on the x-axis. It is clear from the graph that the line crosses the y-axis below zero; this eliminates response A, since $(0,4)$ is above the x-axis.

7. **Correct Response: D.** Noting that two points on the line in the graph are $(0, ^-4)$ and $(3, ^-2)$, use the slope formula $m = \frac{y_2 - y_1}{x_2 - x_1}$ to determine that the slope of this line is $\frac{2}{3}$. Responses A and C result from inverting the formula by using the change in x $(x_2 - x_1)$ as the numerator and the change in y $(y_2 - y_1)$ as the denominator. Response B applies the formula correctly but inaccurately produces the wrong sign (i.e., a negative number instead of a positive one).

8. **Correct Response: A.** You can find the correct equation based on the y-intercept $(^-1)$ and the slope of the line $(^-1)$. Only response A contains these values. By substituting a point from the line (e.g., $(^-1,0)$), you find that response A gives a solution that is true.

    $(0) = ^-(^-1) - 1 = 1 - 1 = 0$ True

    Response B is incorrect because, when converted to $y = mx + b$ form, it shows a slope of $-\frac{1}{2}$ and a y-intercept of $-\frac{1}{2}$. Response C is incorrect because it has a positive slope $(^+1)$. Response D is incorrect because it has a slope of $-\frac{1}{2}$ and a y-intercept of $+\frac{1}{2}$, which can be seen when it is converted to $y = mx + b$ form.

9. **Correct Response: A.** One convenient way to solve this problem is by determining the equation of the boundary line of the inequality. The slope of this line is $^+1$ and its y-intercept is $^+4$. Therefore, the equation of this line is $y = x + 4$. Responses B and D are incorrect, since their boundary line equations are $y = x - 4$. To choose between responses A and C, a test point (e.g., $(^-5,2)$) from the shaded region can be used. These coordinates can then be substituted into equations A and C.

    Response A: $2 \geq 4 + (^-5)$ or $2 \geq ^-1$ A true statement
    Response C: $2 \leq 4 + (^-5)$ or $2 \leq ^-1$ A false statement

    Therefore, response A is correct.

10. **Correct Response: C.** The ratio of $\frac{y}{x}$ for all ordered pairs in the chart is $\frac{3}{1}$. This represents a direct variation in which $y = 3x$. Since graphing the ordered pairs would produce a straight line, response D is incorrect. Response B is incorrect because y does not grow smaller as x grows larger, which would be the case with inverse variation. Since x and y are related by the function $y = 3x$, response A is incorrect.

11. **Correct Response: B.** The question describes a direct variation: as the number of gallons of paint increases, the number of square feet that can be painted also increases. We know that the point representing (2 gallons, 400 square feet) must be on the line and that the line will satisfy the direct variation formula $y = kx$. By substitution (400 sq. ft. = k (2 gal.)), we know that k, the constant of variation or the slope, is positive (i.e., it is 200). Only ℓ_2 has a positive slope and passes through the point representing (2 gal., 400 sq. ft.). Line ℓ_3 does not pass through this point and ℓ_1 and ℓ_4 have negative slopes.

12. **Correct Response: A.** Since the question describes an inverse variation, the formula $xy = k$ can be used. By substitution we know that $k = 60$, since $(12)(5) = k$. If x is the number of hours and y is the number of workers, we can now calculate the number of hours it would take 15 workers to do the job: $15x = 60$, or $x = 4$ hours. Response B results from calculating the wrong value of k by multiplying $(5)(15)$, and then dividing the result by 15 workers. Response C results from treating the variation as direct instead of inverse. Response D is the result of multiplying 5 workers by 12 hours and going no further.

Study Ideas

A careful study of the preceding exercises and the explanations of the answers will help you review important skills relating to graphing numbers and number relationships. In these exercises, you were asked to identify graphs of equations and inequalities, find the equations of lines, find the slopes and intercepts of lines, and recognize and interpret direct and inverse variation. The exercises are designed to give you practice in these skills. You may wish to reread parts of the chapter that address specific skills with which you have difficulty.

Chapter 14

SOLVE ONE- AND TWO-VARIABLE EQUATIONS

This skill includes finding the value of the unknown in one-variable equations, expressing one variable in terms of a second variable in two-variable equations, and solving a system of two equations in two variables.

Introduction

Definitions. Let us begin by reviewing several definitions. A *term* is a number, a variable, or a product of numbers and variables. The expression $2x^2 + 3x + 5$ consists of three terms: $2x^2$, $3x$, and 5. The numerical part of a term is called a numerical coefficient or, simply, coefficient. The number 2 in the first term above is a numerical coefficient. A *polynomial* is an expression whose terms may be placed in the form ax^n, where n, the exponent, may be zero or a positive integer. The expression $2x^3 + 3x - 5$ is a polynomial consisting of three terms; however, the expression $\frac{2}{x} + 4$ is not a polynomial, since $\frac{2}{x} = 2x^{-1}$, which violates the definition.

An *equation* is a statement of balance or equality and consists of a left side, an equal sign, and a right side. For example, $2x + 3 = 11 - 2x$ represents an equation with a left side of $2x + 3$ and a right side of $11 - 2x$. A *solution* to an equation is a value which, when substituted for the variable in the original equation, yields a true statement. In the above example, the solution is $x = 2$.

The *absolute value* of a number can be described as the distance of that number from zero on the number line. The symbol for absolute value is two vertical bars. For example, $|^-5|$ is read, "the absolute value of negative five" and is equal to 5 since $^-5$ is five units away from zero. More specifically, for any real number x,

$|x| = x$ if $x \geq 0$ (x is zero or positive)
$|x| = {}^-x$ (the opposite of x) if $x < 0$ (x is negative).

Sometimes you will be asked to solve two equations in two variables simultaneously. Each equation would have a solution set consisting of ordered pairs. When you solve a *system* of equations such as

$3x = 2y = 6$ and $x - 3y = 4$

you are looking for the ordered pairs that will make both equations true.

The *degree* of a polynomial is the largest exponent present in the expression. The expression $3x^3 + 2x - 5$ is a third-degree polynomial. A first- degree polynomial is called *linear,* and an equation whose terms consist of numbers or first-degree polynomials is said to be a *linear equation.* A second-degree polynomial is called a *quadratic.* The equation $4x^2 - 3x = 0$ is an example of a *quadratic equation,* since two is the highest power of the variable x that it contains.

To check the solution to $2x + 3 = 11 - 2x$, substitute 2 for x in the original equation. Since you are checking the solution and are not yet certain that it is correct, leave out the equal sign.

$2x + 3$	$11 - 2x$
$(2)(2) + 3$	$11 - (2)(2)$
$4 + 3$	$11 - 4$
7	7

$$7 = 7$$
$$x = 2$$

An equation may also contain an absolute value expression. The equation $|x - 2| = 5$ is an example of this type of equation. Absolute value equations will have one, two, or no solutions. For this example, there are two values of x that make the statement true: 7 and ⁻3. This is illustrated below when these values are substituted for x.

$|x - 2|$	5		$|x - 2|$	5
$|7 - 2|$	5		$|{-3} - 2|$	5
$|5|$	5		$|{-5}|$	5
5	5		5	5

$$x = 7 \text{ or } {}^-3$$

When you check a solution to any equation, the value is substituted for the variable in the original problem, and each side is evaluated independently. If both sides evaluate to the same quantity, the solution is correct. It is helpful to sketch the lines shown above in the check as a reminder to evaluate each side separately.

A summary follows.

$2x + 1 = 5$ is a linear equation.

$x^2 + 2 = 4$ is a quadratic equation, since x^2 is a second-degree term.

$\frac{2}{3}y + 5 = 10$ is a linear equation. The numerical coefficient may be a fraction.

$\frac{3}{y} + 10 = 3$ is not a linear equation. The term $\frac{3}{y}$ is not a polynomial. Variables cannot be in the denominator.

$|x + 3| = y$ is an equation involving absolute value.

$$\left.\begin{array}{rcl} x^2 +2 & = & y \\ \frac{1}{2}x+y & = & 5 \end{array}\right\}$$ is called a system of simultaneous equations.

Linear Equations

Linear equations can be written as one-variable equations, such as $2x + 4 = 5$. For one-variable equations the solution set will contain either one value, an infinite number of values, or no value. Linear equations can also appear as two-variable equations, such as $4x - 3y = 10$. For two-variable equations the solution set will contain an infinite number of ordered pairs. Each ordered pair will define a value for each of the variables in the equation. The solution set of a linear equation in two variables can always be graphed as a line on the Cartesian coordinate plane.

Solving Linear Equations of the Form ax = b

The simplest linear equation contains a single variable term on one side and a number on the other. For example, $3x = 15$ is a simple linear equation. You may guess the solution to this equation by translating it into words: 3 times a number is 15. Obviously, the missing number is 5. A trial-and-error technique works for a simple equation. We must, however, develop an approach that will solve all linear equations. The method we will use makes use of the fact that in an equation, the left and the right side are equal. Therefore, any operation performed on one side must also be performed on the other side if the two sides are to remain equal. Solving an equation involves converting the equation to a form in which the variable is by itself on one side of the equal sign. To solve the equation $3x = 15$, you must first remove the 3 from the x. To do this, perform the following opposite, or inverse, operation of multiplication (which is division).

Solve 3x = 15 for x.

$3x = 15$

$\frac{3x}{3} = \frac{15}{3}$ *Divide both sides by 3.*

$x = 5$ $\frac{3x}{3} = x$ and $\frac{15}{3} = 5.$

Check:

3x	15
3(5)	
15	15

There is no difference between the equations $5x = 10$ and $10 = 5x$. You can always switch the left and the right sides of an equation. To solve either form, you must divide both sides by 5 to get $2 = x$ or $x = 2$. A check proves this correct. Again, the operation between the 5 and x is multiplication; therefore, to solve the equation, apply the inverse operation of division to both sides. Many times you will have an equation of the form $^-x = 3$. Recall that ^-x is really ^-1x. To solve, you can either multiply or divide both sides by $^-1$ to get $x = ^-3$.

When solving applied problems, you may encounter decimal coefficients, such as
$0.03y = 9$. The solution is as follows.

Solve $0.03y = 9$ for y.

$0.03y = 9$

$\dfrac{0.03y}{0.03} = \dfrac{9}{0.03}$ *Divide both sides by the coefficient 0.03.*

$y = 300$

Solve $2t = 5$ for t.

$2t = 5$

$\dfrac{2t}{2} = \dfrac{5}{2}$ *Divide both sides by the coefficient 2.*

$t = \dfrac{5}{2}$

Check:

$2t$	5
$2\left(\dfrac{5}{2}\right)$	
5	5

Solving Linear Equations of the Form ax + b = c

Another type of equation results from adding a constant on the same side of the
equation as the variable term. Consider the equation $x + 3 = 10$. Again, it may be
possible to guess the solution. What number added to 3 produces 10? The answer
is 7. To find the answer algebraically, remove the 3 by subtracting 3 from both
sides of the equation. The complete solution is as follows.

Solve $x + 3 = 10$ for x.

$x + 3 = 10$

$x + 3 - 3 = 10 - 3$ *Subtract 3 from each side.*

$x = 7$

Check:

$x + 3$	10
$7 + 3$	
10	10

Solve $2x + 1 = 9$ for x.

The first operation is to isolate the term involving the unknown, $2x$. To do this,
remove the 1 by subtracting it from both sides. The final step is to remove the 2 by
using division.

$2x + 1 - 1 = 9 - 1$ *Subtract 1 from each side.*

$2x = 8$

$\dfrac{2x}{2} = \dfrac{8}{2}$ *Divide each side by 2.*

$x = 4$

Check:

2x + 1	9
2(4) + 1	
8 + 1	
9	9

Note the sequence of operations. Isolate the variable term on one side and the number on the other, then divide. This is the approach used for all linear equations.

Solve 3x – 5 = 31 for x.

$3x - 5 = 31$

$3x - 5 + 5 = 31 + 5$ *Add 5 to both sides.*

$3x = 36$

$\dfrac{3x}{3} = \dfrac{36}{3}$ *Divide both sides by 3.*

$x = 12$

Check:

3x – 5	31
3(12) – 5	
36 – 5	
31	31

Solve 14 = 10 – 4x for x.

$14 - 10 = 10 - 4x - 10$ *Subtract 10 from both sides to isolate the variable term.*

$4 = {}^{-}4x$

$\dfrac{4}{{}^{-}4} = \dfrac{{}^{-}4x}{{}^{-}4}$ *Divide each side by ⁻4.*

${}^{-}1 = x$

Check:

14	10 – 4x
	10 – 4(⁻1)
	10 – (⁻4)
14	14

Solving Linear Equations of the Form ax + b = cx + d

A more advanced problem occurs when both numbers and variable terms appear on both sides of the equal sign. The first step is still to isolate the variable terms. Even though it makes no difference where the variable term is isolated, it is easier to choose the side with the larger coefficient. Note the following example.

Solve 3x + 5 = 2x − 2 for x.

3x + 5 = 2x − 2

3x + 5 − 2x = 2x − 2 − 2x   *Subtract 2x from both sides since the larger coefficient is 3.*

x + 5 = ⁻2

x + 5 − 5 = ⁻2 − 5   *Subtract 5 from each side.*

x = ⁻7

Check:

3x + 5	2x − 2
3(⁻7) + 5	2(⁻7) − 2
⁻21 + 5	⁻14 − 2
⁻16	⁻16

In the example above, the decision to isolate the unknown on the left side was determined by the fact that the larger coefficient 3 was on that side.

Solve ⁻3x − 4 = 8x + 9 for x.

⁻3x − 4 + 3x = 8x + 9 + 3x   *Add 3x to each side to isolate the variable terms.*

⁻4 = 11x + 9

⁻4 − 9 = 11x + 9 − 9   *Subtract 9 from each side.*

⁻13 = 11x

$\dfrac{-13}{11} = \dfrac{11x}{11}$ *Divide by the coefficient.*

$\dfrac{-13}{11} = x$

In this example, the unknown term is isolated on the right side since the coefficient 8 is larger than ⁻3. This approach requires that all numbers be isolated on the left side. Finally, division produces the results.

Solving Linear Equations by Transposition

A more efficient way to isolate terms is called transposition, which replaces the addition/subtraction step. You must remember that when a term crosses the equal sign its sign changes, since this is the same as adding or subtracting the same quantity from both sides. In the problem above, there were four terms: ⁻3x, 4, 8x, and 9. The variable terms were isolated on the right side. This requires moving or transposing ⁻3x to the right side. The result is ⁻4 = 8x + 9 + 3x. The numbers must be shifted to the left side. This requires transposing +9 to the left side. The result is ⁻4 − 9 = 8x + 3x = 11x. The final step is division. Note that you cannot transpose the 11 as it is part of a term. You can only transpose complete terms. The previous example is worked by using transposition as follows.

Solve ⁻3x – 4 = 8x + 9 for x.

$^-3x - 4 = 8x + 9$

$^-4 = 8x + 9 + 3x$ *Transpose 3x to isolate the variable term on the right side.*

$^-4 - 9 = 11x$ *Transpose the 9.*

$^-13 = 11x$

$-\dfrac{13}{11} = \dfrac{11x}{11}$

$-\dfrac{13}{11} = x$

Transposition eliminates the addition/subtraction step. Remember that you can transpose only complete terms.

Solve 3x + 9 = ⁻x – 5 for x.

$3x + x = {}^-5 - 9$ *Transpose variable terms to left side, numbers to right side.*

$4x = {}^-14$

$\dfrac{4x}{4} = -\dfrac{14}{4}$ *Divide both sides by the coefficient.*

$x = -\dfrac{14}{4}$

$x = -\dfrac{7}{2}$

Check:

$3\left(-\dfrac{7}{2}\right) + 9$	$^-\left(-\dfrac{7}{2}\right) - 5$
$-\dfrac{21}{2} + 9$	$+\dfrac{7}{2} + (^-5)$
$-\dfrac{21}{2} + \dfrac{18}{2}$	$\dfrac{7}{2} + \left(-\dfrac{10}{2}\right)$
$-\dfrac{3}{2}$	$-\dfrac{3}{2}$

Solve 5y = 8y for y.

$5y = 8y$

$0 = 8y - 5y$ *Transpose 5y. Note 0 is placed on left side, since you really subtracted 5y from both sides.*

$0 = 3y$

$\dfrac{0}{3} = \dfrac{3y}{3}$ *Divide both sides by the coefficient.*

$0 = y$

Linear Equations Containing Fractions

Recall that $\frac{1}{2}x = \frac{x}{2}$ and $\frac{3}{2}x = \frac{3x}{2}$. The first operation to perform in solving a linear equation involving fractions is to multiply every term on both sides by the least common denominator (LCD) of the fractions. This operation will remove, or clear, the fractions after reduction. Then proceed to the solution as before.

Solve $\frac{2x}{3} = 10$ for x.

$3\left(\frac{2x}{3}\right) = 3(10)$ *Multiply both sides by the LCD 3.*

$2x = 30$

$\frac{2x}{2} = \frac{30}{2}$ *Divide each side by the coefficient.*

$x = 15$

Check:

$\frac{2x}{3}$	10
$\frac{2(15)}{3}$	
10	10

Solve $\frac{2x}{3} + 5 = \frac{1}{6}x + \frac{13}{2}$ for x.

$6\left(\frac{2x}{3}\right) + 6(5) = 6\left(\frac{1}{6}x\right) + 6\left(\frac{13}{2}\right)$ *Multiply by 6, the LCD.*

$2(2x) + 30 = 1(x) + 3(13)$ *Reduce.*

$4x + 30 = x + 39$

$4x - x = 39 - 30$

$3x = 9$

$x = 3$

Check:

$\frac{2x}{3} + 5$	$\frac{1}{6}x + \frac{13}{2}$
$\frac{2(3)}{3} + 5$	$\frac{1}{6}(3) + \frac{13}{2}$
$2 + 5$	$\frac{1}{2} + \frac{13}{2}$
7	7

Decimals. In applied problems, decimal equations often occur. To solve such equations, first multiply all terms by a factor that will eliminate the decimals.

Solve $0.04x + 3 = 0.06x$ for x.

$100(0.04x) + 100(3) = 100(0.06x)$ *Multiply each term by 100.*

$4x + 300 = 6x$

$300 = 6x - 4x$

$300 = 2x$

$150 = x$

Check:

$0.04x + 3$	$0.06x$
$0.04(150) + 3$	$0.06(150)$
$6 + 3$	9
9	9

Linear Equations Containing Parentheses

Equations often contain parentheses. Remember that operations in parentheses should be performed first when possible. Parentheses can sometimes be removed by using the distributive law. This law states that $a(x + y) = ax + ay$, or $a(x - y) = ax - ay$.

Solve $2(x - 1) + 3 = 4x$ for x.

$2x - 2 + 3 = 4x$ *Clear the parentheses by using the distributive law.*

$2x + 1 = 4x$

$1 = 4x - 2x$

$1 = 2x$

$\frac{1}{2} = x$

Solve $\frac{y - 1}{3} + 4 = 2y$ for y.

It is a good idea to enclose in parentheses any numerator or denominator having more than one term. The above equation should be rewritten as follows.

$\frac{(y - 1)}{3} + 4 = 2y$ *Enclose the numerator in parentheses.*

Now clear the fractions by multiplying each term by 3, and proceed to the solution.

$\frac{3(y - 1)}{3} + 3(4) = 3(2y)$ *Multiply each term by 3 to clear the fractions.*

$1(y - 1) + 12 = 6y$

$y - 1 + 12 = 6y$ *Clear the parentheses by using the distributive law.*

$11 = 5y$

$\frac{11}{5} = y$

Linear Equations in Two Variables

Any equation that can be put into the form $ax + by = c$ is called a linear equation in two variables, x and y. To solve a linear equation in two variables, you must use the same approach developed for the one-variable equation.

1. Clear fractions by using the LCD.

2. Clear parentheses by using the distributive law.

3. Use transposition to isolate the term or terms involving the unknown.

4. Divide by the coefficient of the unknown.

Solve 3x + 4y = 7 for y.

4y = 7 – 3x

Since there are no fractions or parentheses, skip to the third step and use transposition to isolate 4y, the term involving the unknown.

$y = \dfrac{7 - 3x}{4}$ or $\dfrac{7}{4} - \dfrac{3x}{4}$

Divide both sides by the coefficient of the unknown term, 4.

Solve $\dfrac{5}{2}x - \dfrac{3}{5}y - 4 = 0$ for x.

$10\left(\dfrac{5}{2}x\right) - 10\left(\dfrac{3y}{5}\right) - 10(4) = 10(0)$

Clear fractions by multiplying each term by 10, the LCD.

5(5x) – 2(3y) – 40 = 10(0)

25x – 6y – 40 = 0

25x = 6y + 40

Since there are no parentheses, isolate the unknown terms by using transposition.

$x = \dfrac{6y + 40}{25}$

Divide both sides by 25, the coefficient of the unknown term.

Solve 3a – 5b = c for b.

$^-5b = c - 3a$

Since there are no fractions or parentheses, isolate ^-5b, the term involving the unknown.

$\dfrac{^-5b}{^-5} = \dfrac{c - 3a}{^-5}$

Divide both sides by the coefficient of b, $^-5$.

$b = \dfrac{c - 3a}{^-5}$

Two Linear Equations in Two Unknowns

An example of two linear equations in two unknowns is given below.

2x + 3y = 5

3x – y = 2

This set of linear equations is also referred to as a system of linear equations.

There are many methods used to solve a system of linear equations. We will discuss two approaches, addition and substitution. First, we must clarify what is meant by a solution to a system of equations. There are three possibilities.

1. A single solution exists when there is exactly one pair of x and y values that satisfy both equations simultaneously. This occurs when the lines intersect.

2. No solution exists when, in the process of solving the system, the unknowns cancel and a false statement results. In this case, there are no x and y values that satisfy both equations. This occurs when the lines are parallel.

3. An infinite number of solutions exist when, in the course of solving the system, the unknowns cancel and a true statement results. In this case, there is an infinite number of pairs of x and y that satisfy both equations. This occurs when both equations represent the same line.

The addition method. The addition method is based on two concepts. First, the solution set of an equation is not changed when both sides are multiplied by the same quantity. Second, if equations are added to equations, the result is an equation. Before solving a system of equations by addition, you must place the system in proper form by using transposition. Corresponding unknown terms must be aligned on the same side of the equal sign, with the number terms on the other side. The following represents a system placed in proper form.

$3x = 2 - y$ becomes $3x + y = 2$.

$y = 7 - 3x$ becomes $3x + y = 7$.

Note that the x and the y terms are aligned on the same side of the equal sign with the numbers on the other side. This alignment is accomplished by using transposition.

Our task is to reduce the system to one equation with one unknown and then to solve it using previous methods. To accomplish this, multiply each equation by appropriate values to create equal but opposite signs on the coefficient of one variable; then add. This process eliminates one equation and variable, and it allows us to solve for the remaining variable.

Solve the following system.

$2x + 3y = 5$

$3x - y = 2$

Begin by multiplying the first equation by the opposite of the coefficient of x in the second equation. This is $^-3$. Next, multiply the second equation by the coefficient of x in the first equation, which is 2. Finally, add the two equations. The process is described as follows.

$2x + 3y = 5$
$3x - y = 2$

$(^-3)(2x + 3y) = (^-3)(5)$ *Multiply both sides of the first equation by $^-3$.*
$(2)(3x - y) = (2)(2)$ *Multiply both sides of the second equation by 2.*

$^-6x - 9y = ^-15$ *Simplify by multiplying and using the distributive law.*
$6x - 2y = 4$

$\begin{aligned}^-6x - 9y &= ^-15\\ \underline{6x - 2y} &= \underline{4}\\ ^-11y &= ^-11\end{aligned}$ *Add the second equation to the first equation:*
    $^-6x + 6x = 0$; $(^-9y) + (^-2y) = ^-11y$; $^-15 + 4 = ^-11$.

$y = 1$ *Divide both sides by $^-11$.*

You can use the same process to eliminate y and solve for x. Begin by multiplying the first equation by the opposite of the y-coefficient in the second equation. Next, multiply the second equation by the y-coefficient in the first equation. Then add the equations.

$2x + 3y = 5$
$3x - y = 2$

$2x + 3y = 5$ *Multiply both sides of the first equation by +1. Multiply*
$(3)(3x - y) = (3)(2)$ *both sides of the second equation by 3.*

$2x + 3y = 5$ *Simplify by multiplying and using the distributive law.*
$9x - 3y = 6$

$2x + 3y = 5$ *Add the second equation to the first equation:*
$\underline{9x - 3y = 6}$ $2x + 9x = 11x; (3y) + (^-3y) = 0; 5 + 6 = 11.$
$11x \quad = 11$

$x = 1$ *Divide both sides by 11.*

Note the multiplication of each equation by the coefficient of one variable from the other equation, with one of the coefficients changing signs in the multiplication. This procedure guarantees that at least one of the variables in the two equations will have opposite and equal coefficients so they can cancel when the equations are added.

To check the solution, substitute the x and y values in both equations. If true statements result, then the solution is correct.

Check:

$2x + 3y = 5 \quad 2(1) + 3(1) = 5$ *Both are true statements.*
$5 = 5$
$3x - y = 2 \quad 3(1) - (1) = 2$
$2 = 2$

Solve the following system.

$2x = 5 - y$
$^-4x - 2y = 3$

Place the system in proper form by using transposition.

$2x + y = 5$
$^-4x - 2y = 3$

Eliminate the variable x. Begin by multiplying the first equation by the opposite of the coefficient of x in the second equation. Multiply the second equation by the coefficient of x in the first equation.

$(4)(2x + y) = (4)(5)$ *Multiply both sides of the first equation by 4. Multiply*
$(2)(^-4x - 2y) = (2)(3)$ *both sides of the second equation by 2.*

$8x + 4y = 20$ *Simplify by multiplying and using the distributive law.*
$^-8x - 4y = 6$

$8x + 4y = 20$ *Add the second equation to the first equation:*
$\underline{^-8x - 4y = \ 6}$ $(8x) + (^-8x) = 0; (4y) + (^-4y) = 0; 20 + 6 = 26.$
$0 = 26$

When you attempted to eliminate x, you also eliminated y. Since a false statement resulted, the system has no solution and is called an *inconsistent system*.

Solve the following system.

$2x + y = 10$

$^-4x - 2y = ^-20$

Since the system is in proper form, proceed to eliminate the variable x.

$(2)(2x + y) = (2)(10)$	*Multiply both sides of the first equation by 2.*
$(^-4x - 2y) = (^-20)$	*Multiply both sides of the second equation by 1.*
$4x + 2y = 20$	*Simplify by multiplying and using the distributive law.*
$^-4x - 2y = ^-20$	

$$\begin{array}{l} 4x + 2y = 20 \\ \underline{^-4x - 2y = ^-20} \\ \qquad\quad 0 = 0 \end{array}$$

Add the second equation to the first equation:
$(4x) + (^-4x) = 0$; $(2y) + (^-2y) = 0$; $(20) + (^-20) = 0$.

When you attempted to eliminate x, you also eliminated y, and a true statement resulted. The system has an infinite number of solutions and is called a *dependent system.*

Solve the following system.

$2x - 5y = 1$

$y = \dfrac{1}{3}x$

When one or more equations contain a fraction, it is best to clear the fractions before attempting to eliminate a variable. In this example, clear the fraction and then place the system in proper form.

$2x - 5y = 1$

$y = \dfrac{1}{3}x$

$2x - 5y = 1$	*Multiply the second equation by 3.*
$3y = x$	
$2x - 5y = 1$	*Place the second equation in proper form by using transposition.*
$x - 3y = 0$	

Eliminate x.

$(^-1)(2x - 5y) = (^-1)(1)$	*Multiply both sides of the first equation by $^-1$. Multiply*
$(2)(x - 3y) = (2)(0)$	*both sides of the second equation by 2.*
$^-2x + 5y = ^-1$	*Simplify by multiplying and using the distributive law.*
$2x - 6y = 0$	

$$\begin{array}{l} ^-2x + 5y = ^-1 \\ \underline{2x - 6y = \;\;0} \\ \qquad\quad ^-y = ^-1 \end{array}$$

Add the second equation to the first equation.

$y = 1$ *Multiply both sides by $^-1$.*

Eliminate y.

$(3)(2x - 5y) = (3)(1)$	*Multiply both sides of the first equation by 3. Multiply*
$(^-5)(x - 3y) = (^-5)(0)$	*both sides of the second equation by $^-5$.*
$6x - 15y = 3$	*Simplify by multiplying and using the distributive law.*
$^-5x + 15y = 0$	

$$\begin{array}{l} 6x - 15y = 3 \\ \underline{^-5x + 15y = 0} \\ \quad x \qquad\qquad = 3 \end{array}$$

Add the second equation to the first equation.

Check:

$2(3) - 5(1) = 1$ *The solution satisfies both equations.*

$1 = \frac{1}{3}(3)$

The substitution method. The substitution method requires solving either equation for a variable and substituting that expression into the other equation. Since there is a choice of variable and equation, select the easiest variable to solve for: the one with a 1 or $^-1$ coefficient. If none exists, you might be better off using the addition method. When substituting, always use parentheses.

Solve the following system using substitution.

$2x + y = 3$

$x - y = 0$

Since the y-coefficient in the second equation is $^-1$, solve that equation for y.

$x - y = 0$
$y = x$

Substitute this expression for y in the first equation.

$2x + (x) = 3$

Solve the resulting equation for x.

$3x = 3$
$x = 1$

Substitute this x value into the equation you derived in the first step, and solve for y.

$y = x$
$y = (1)$
$y = 1$

Check:

$2(1) + (1) = 3$
$1 - 1 = 0$

Solve the following system.

$3x + y = 4$
$6x + 2y = 5$

Solve the first equation for y.

$y = 4 - 3x$

Substitute this expression for y in the second equation.

$6x + 2(4 - 3x) = 5$

Solve the resulting equation.

$6x + 8 - 6x = 5$
$8 = 5$

The unknown cancels, and the resulting equation is false. The original system has no solution and is classified as inconsistent.

Nonlinear Equations

Absolute Value Equations

There are many types of equations other than linear. The following sections will deal with these. One type is the equation involving absolute value. The simplest type of absolute value equation will have a linear expression appearing inside the absolute value symbol on one side of the equal sign and a number on the other, such as $|x| = 3$. There are two possible values that will satisfy this equation, $x = 3$ or $x = {}^-3$. The solution set for this equation is $\{3, {}^-3\}$.

A more complicated linear expression may appear inside the absolute value symbol. You can solve this type by writing two separate linear equations and solving those as illustrated in a previous section.

Find the solution set of $|x| = 10$.

$|x| = 10$
$x = 10$ or $x = {}^-10$ *Both $/10/$ and $/{}^-10/$ equal 10.*

The solution set contains two elements, $\{10, {}^-10\}$.

This method works because the equation asks you to find x such that x lies 10 units from the origin. (Remember that the absolute value of a number is its distance from zero.) There are two such numbers: ${}^-10$ and ${}^+10$. In other words $x = 10$ and $x = {}^-10$.

Find the solution set of $|x + 8| = 7$

$|x + 8| = 7$
$x + 8 = 7$ or $x + 8 = {}^-7$ *The expression in the absolute value symbol must equal 7 or ${}^-7$.*

Solve both equations separately.

$x = 7 - 8$ $x = {}^-7 - 8$ *Subtract 8 from both sides of the equations.*

$x = {}^-1$ $x = {}^-15$

The solution set contains two elements, $\{{}^-1, {}^-15\}$.

Check both solutions.

$|{}^-1 + 8|$	7		$|{}^-15 + 8|$	7
$|7|$	7		$|{}^-7|$	7
7	7		7	7

Here we are asked to find x such that $(x + 8)$ lies 7 units from the origin. There are two such numbers: $(x + 8)$ and ${}^-(x + 8)$. In other words, $(x + 8) = 7$ and ${}^-(x + 8) = 7$ satisfy the equation. ${}^-(x + 8) = 7$ can be written $x + 8 = {}^-7$.

Find the solution set of $|2x + 1| = 9$.

$|2x + 1| = 9$
$2x + 1 = 9$ or $2x + 1 = {}^-9$ *The expressions in the absolute value symbol must equal 9 or ${}^-9$.*

Solve both equations separately.

$2x = 9 - 1$	$2x = {}^-9 - 1$	*Subtract 1 from both sides.*
$2x = 8$	$2x = {}^-10$	
$x = 4$	$x = {}^-5$	*Divide both sides by 2.*

The solution set contains two elements, $\{4, {}^-5\}$.

Check both solutions.

$\lvert 2(4) + 1 \rvert$	9
$\lvert 8 + 1 \rvert$	9
$\lvert 9 \rvert$	9
9	9

$\lvert 2({}^-5) + 1 \rvert$	9
$\lvert {}^-10 + 1 \rvert$	9
$\lvert {}^-9 \rvert$	9
9	9

Absolute value expressions can also appear in two-variable equations. The solution set for an equation of this type will be an infinite set of ordered pairs. Since it is impossible to give a list of all solutions, the solution set is generally shown by a graph on the Cartesian plane. One simple method of drawing the graph is to plot points that satisfy the equation. The procedure for finding these ordered pairs was discussed in a previous section on graphing linear equations. Because the graph is a V-shape, you must use enough ordered pairs so that you can find the lowest point of the V. The graph will be symmetrical about the vertical line that passes through that point. Each half of the V-shape will be a line.

The following examples show how to graph equations in two variables involving absolute value.

Graph $y = \lvert x + 1 \rvert$

Let $x = {}^-3, {}^-2, {}^-1, 0, 1, 2$ *Choose enough values to replace x so that you can find the lowest point of the graph.*

$x = {}^-3 \qquad y = \lvert {}^-3 + 1 \rvert$
$\qquad\qquad y = \lvert {}^-2 \rvert$
$\qquad\qquad y = 2$
$\qquad ({}^-3, 2)$

$x = {}^-2 \qquad y = \lvert {}^-2 + 1 \rvert$
$\qquad\qquad y = \lvert {}^-1 \rvert$
$\qquad\qquad y = 1$
$\qquad ({}^-2, 1)$

$x = {}^-1 \qquad y = \lvert {}^-1 + 1 \rvert$
$\qquad\qquad y = \lvert 0 \rvert$
$\qquad\qquad y = 0$
$\qquad ({}^-1, 0)$

$x = 0 \qquad y = \lvert 0 + 1 \rvert$
$\qquad\qquad y = \lvert 1 \rvert$
$\qquad\qquad y = 1$
$\qquad (0, 1)$

$x = 1 \qquad y = \lvert 1 + 1 \rvert$
$\qquad\qquad y = \lvert 2 \rvert$
$\qquad\qquad y = 2$
$\qquad (1, 2)$

$$x = 2 \qquad y = |2 + 1|$$
$$y = |3|$$
$$y = 3$$
$$(2, 3)$$

Now plot those points.

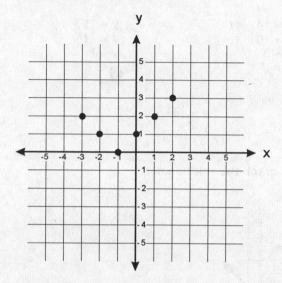

The axis of symmetry occurs at $x = ^-1$. Each half of the V-shape will be linear.

The solution set is illustrated as follows:

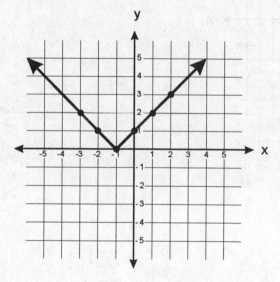

Graph $y = |x - 4|$

Let x = 0, 1, 2, 3, 4, 5, 6, 7

| x = 0 | y = \|0 − 4\| | x = 1 | y = \|1 − 4\| | x = 2 | y = \|2 − 4\| |

x = 0   y = $\lvert 0 - 4 \rvert$ x = 1   y = $\lvert 1 - 4 \rvert$ x = 2   y = $\lvert 2 - 4 \rvert$
          y = $\lvert ^{-}4 \rvert$ y = $\lvert ^{-}3 \rvert$ y = $\lvert ^{-}2 \rvert$
          y = 4   y = 3   y = 2
      (0, 4)   (1, 3)   (2, 2)

x = 3   y = $\lvert 3 - 4 \rvert$ x = 4   y = $\lvert 4 - 4 \rvert$ x = 5   y = $\lvert 5 - 4 \rvert$
          y = $\lvert ^{-}1 \rvert$ y = $\lvert 0 \rvert$ y = $\lvert 1 \rvert$
          y = 1   y = 0   y = 1
      (3, 1)   (4, 0)   (5, 1)

x = 6   y = $\lvert 6 - 4 \rvert$ x = 7   y = $\lvert 7 - 4 \rvert$
          y = $\lvert 2 \rvert$ y = $\lvert 3 \rvert$
          y = 2   y = 3
      (6, 2)   (7, 3)

Plot the ordered pairs found above and graph the solution set.

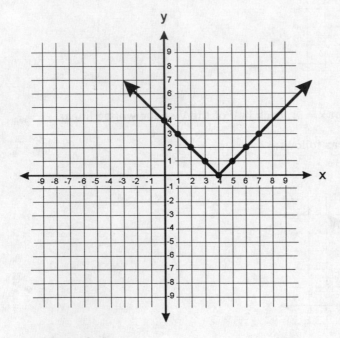

Graph y = $\lvert x \rvert - 2$

Let x = $^{-}3$, $^{-}2$, $^{-}1$, 0, 1, 2, 3

x = $^{-}3$ y = $\lvert ^{-}3 \rvert - 2$ x = $^{-}2$ y = $\lvert ^{-}2 \rvert - 2$ x = $^{-}1$ y = $\lvert ^{-}1 \rvert - 2$
          y = 3 − 2   y = 2 − 2   y = 1 − 2
          y = 1   y = 0   y = $^{-}1$
     ($^{-}3$, 1)   ($^{-}2$, 0)   ($^{-}1$, $^{-}1$)

x = 0   y = $\lvert 0 \rvert - 2$ x = 1   y = $\lvert 1 \rvert - 2$ x = 2   y = $\lvert 2 \rvert - 2$
          y = 0 − 2   y = 1 − 2   y = 2 − 2
          y = $^{-}2$ y = $^{-}1$ y = 0
     (0, $^{-}2$)   (1, $^{-}1$)   (2, 0)

x = 3   y = $\lvert 3 \rvert - 2$
          y = 3 − 2
          y = 1
     (3, 1)

Graph the solution set.

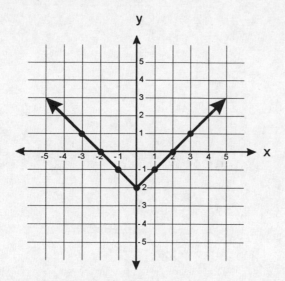

Graph y = |x| + 3

Let x = ⁻3, ⁻2, ⁻1, 0, 1, 2, 3

x = ⁻3 y = |⁻3| + 3 y = 3 + 3 y = 6 (⁻3, 6)	x = ⁻2 y = |⁻2| + 3 y = 2 + 3 y = 5 (⁻2, 5)	x = ⁻1 y = |⁻1| + 3 y = 1 + 3 y = 4 (⁻1, 4)
x = 0 y = |0| + 3 y = 0 + 3 y = 3 (0, 3)	x = 1 y = |1| + 3 y = 1 + 3 y = 4 (1, 4)	x = 2 y = |2| + 3 y = 2 + 3 y = 5 (2, 5)

x = 3   y = |3| + 3
y = 3 + 3
y = 6
(3, 6)

Graph the solution set.

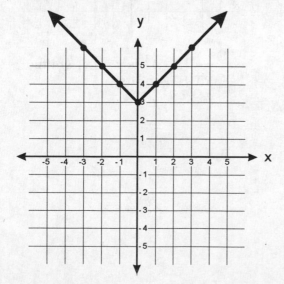

Compare the four sample problems with the graph of y = |x|.

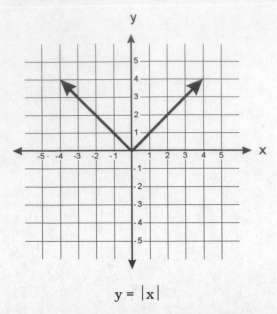

y = |x|

Notice that the graphs are all *congruent;* that is, they have exactly the same size and shape, differing only in where the V-shape is positioned.

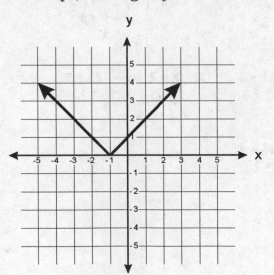

y = |x + 1| is y = |x| shifted LEFT 1 unit.

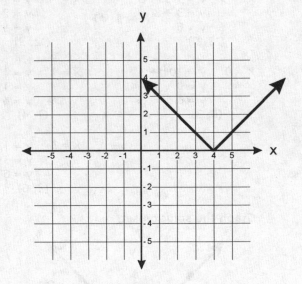

y = |x – 4| is y = |x| shifted RIGHT 4 units.

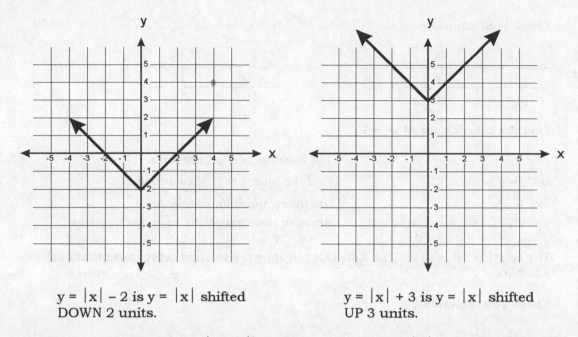

y = |x| – 2 is y = |x| shifted DOWN 2 units.

y = |x| + 3 is y = |x| shifted UP 3 units.

In general, the graph of y = |x + k| will be the graph of y = |x| shifted k units *left* if k is positive and k units *right* if k is negative. The graph of y = |x| + h will be the graph of y = |x| shifted h units *up* if h is positive and h units *down* if h is negative.

Quadratic Equations

A second type of nonlinear equation is the *quadratic equation*. The equation $x^2 = 25$ is called a quadratic equation because it consists of numbers and a second-degree polynomial. Since quadratic equations are dealt with in detail in another chapter, this section will discuss only the simplest of quadratic equations.

As you recall, solving an equation means finding values that will satisfy it. There will be two values that will satisfy $x^2 = 25$: x = 5 or x = ⁻5. All equations involving second-degree polynomials will have either one, two, or no solutions in the real number system. To solve simple quadratic equations, first put the equation in the form of $x^2 = a$ and then find the square root of each side. Remember that $\sqrt{x^2} = |x|$. Then follow the same steps as for the equations involving absolute value.

Find the solution set of $x^2 = 16$.

$x^2 = 16$	*The equation is in proper form.*
$\sqrt{x^2} = \sqrt{16}$	*Find the square root of each side.*
$|x| = 4$	*Use the relationship $\sqrt{x^2} = /x/$.*
x = 4 or x = ⁻4	*Absolute value equations have two solutions.*

The solution set is {4, ⁻4}.

Check your solutions.

x^2	16
4^2	16
16	16

x^2	16
$(^-4)^2$	16
16	16

Find the solution set of $x^2 = 5$.

$x^2 = 5$ *The equation is in proper form.*

$\sqrt{x^2} = \sqrt{5}$ *Find the square root of each side.*

$|x| = \sqrt{5}$ *Use the relationship $\sqrt{x^2} = |x|$.*

$x = \sqrt{5}$ or $x = ^-\sqrt{5}$ *Absolute value equations have two solutions.*

The solution set is $\{\sqrt{5}, ^-\sqrt{5}\}$. Note that this time the solution set involves irrational numbers.

Check your solutions.

x^2	5
$(\sqrt{5})^2$	5
5	5

x^2	5
$(^-\sqrt{5})^2$	5
5	5

Find the solution set of $x^2 - 4 = ^-3$.

$x^2 - 4 = ^-3$

$x^2 = ^-3 + 4$ *Put the equation in the form $x^2 = a$.*

$\sqrt{x^2} = \sqrt{1}$ *Find the square root of each side.*

$|x| = 1$ *Use the relationship $\sqrt{x^2} = |x|$.*

$x = 1$ or $x = ^-1$ *Absolute value equations have two solutions.*

The solution set is $\{1, ^-1\}$.

Check your solutions.

$x^2 - 4$	$^-3$
$1^2 - 4$	$^-3$
$1 - 4$	$^-3$
$^-3$	$^-3$

$x^2 - 4$	$^-3$
$(^-1)^2 - 4$	$^-3$
$1 - 4$	$^-3$
$^-3$	$^-3$

Find the solution set of $x^2 + 4 = 2$.

$x^2 + 4 = 2$

$x^2 = 2 - 4$ *Put the equation in the form $x^2 = a$.*

$x^2 = ^-2$

$\sqrt{x^2} = \sqrt{^-2}$ *Find the square root of both sides.*

There is no real number solution to this equation. That is, it is not possible to find a value for $\sqrt{^-2}$ in the real number system.

Quadratic Equations in Two-Variable Form

Quadratic equations can also appear in two-variable form. The equation $y = x^2 + 8$ is a simple example. The solution set for this type of equation is an infinite number of ordered pairs that can be illustrated in a graph. The graph of the solution set of a second-degree equation in two variables will form a U-shaped curve called a *parabola*.

The simplest way to graph equations like $y = x^2 + 8$ is to find ordered pairs that will satisfy the equation and join them to form a smooth curve. These graphs are symmetrical about a vertical line.

You should note the similarities between the solutions of two-variable quadratic equations, discussed here, and those of two-variable absolute value equations discussed earlier.

Graph $y = x^2 + 8$.

Let $x = {}^-2, {}^-1, 0, 1, 2$

$x = {}^-2 \quad y = ({}^-2)^2 + 8$
$\qquad\quad y = 4 + 8$
$\qquad\quad y = 12 \qquad\qquad\qquad ({}^-2, 12)$

$x = {}^-1 \quad y = ({}^-1)^2 + 8$
$\qquad\quad y = 1 + 8$
$\qquad\quad y = 9 \qquad\qquad\qquad ({}^-1, 9)$

$x = 0 \quad y = 0^2 + 8$
$\qquad\quad y = 0 + 8$
$\qquad\quad y = 8 \qquad\qquad\qquad (0, 8)$

$x = 1 \quad y = 1^2 + 8$
$\qquad\quad y = 1 + 8$
$\qquad\quad y = 9 \qquad\qquad\qquad (1, 9)$

$x = 2 \quad y = 2^2 + 8$
$\qquad\quad y = 4 + 8$
$\qquad\quad y = 12 \qquad\qquad\qquad (2, 12)$

Plot these points and join them in a smooth curve.

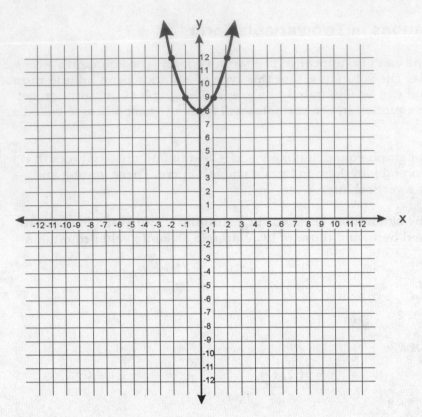

Graph $y = x^2 - 2$.

Let $x = ^-3, ^-2, ^-1, 0, 1, 2, 3$

$x = ^-3$	$y = (^-3)^2 - 2$	
	$y = 9 - 2$	
	$y = 7$	$(^-3, 7)$

$x = ^-2$	$y = (^-2)^2 - 2$	
	$y = 4 - 2$	
	$y = 2$	$(^-2, 2)$

$x = ^-1$	$y = (^-1)^2 - 2$	
	$y = 1 - 2$	
	$y = ^-1$	$(^-1, ^-1)$

$x = 0$	$y = 0^2 - 2$	
	$y = 0 - 2$	
	$y = ^-2$	$(0, ^-2)$

$x = 1$	$y = 1^2 - 2$	
	$y = 1 - 2$	
	$y = ^-1$	$(1, ^-1)$

$x = 2$	$y = 2^2 - 2$	
	$y = 4 - 2$	
	$y = 2$	$(2, 2)$

$x = 3$	$y = 3^2 - 2$	
	$y = 9 - 2$	
	$y = 7$	$(3, 7)$

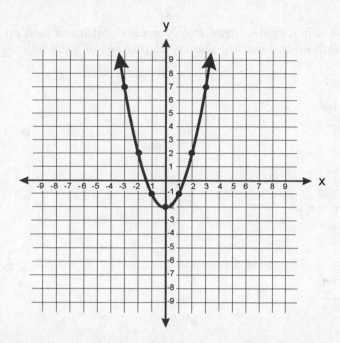

If you compare these samples with the graph of $y = x^2$, you will notice that the graphs are congruent, but differ in position.

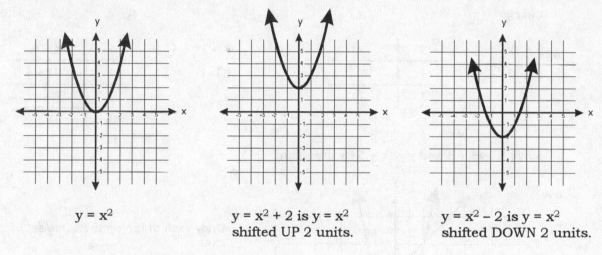

| $y = x^2$ | $y = x^2 + 2$ is $y = x^2$ shifted UP 2 units. | $y = x^2 - 2$ is $y = x^2$ shifted DOWN 2 units. |

In general, $y = x^2 + k$ will be congruent to $y = x^2$ but shifted k units *up* if k is positive and k units *down* if k is negative.

Solving Systems of Nonlinear Equations by Graphing

Systems of nonlinear equations can be solved by methods similar to those used for solving linear systems; however, graphing is often a simpler approach to finding ordered pairs that will satisfy both equations. Since the solution set for each equation in a system of nonlinear equations can be represented by a graph, the points of intersection of the graphs have coordinates that will satisfy the system of equations. For this method to result in precise solutions, it is important to draw very accurate graphs.

For example, $y = |x|$ and $y = 3x + 4$ is a system that involves one nonlinear and one linear equation. The graphs of both equations are shown on one set of axes below.

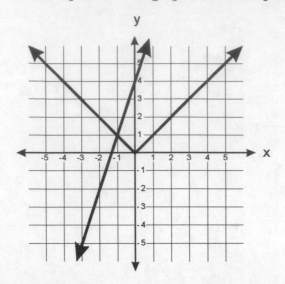

As you can see, the two equations have one point of intersection, (⁻1, 1). This is the ordered pair that will make both equations true.

Check.

$y = \|x\|$	y	$\|x\|$
(⁻1, 1)	1	$\|{}^-1\|$
	1	1

$y = 3x + 4$	y	$3x + 4$
(⁻1, 1)	1	$3({}^-1) + 4$
	1	⁻3 + 4
	1	1

Solve $y = x^2 + 3$ and $y = {}^-x + 5$ by graphing.

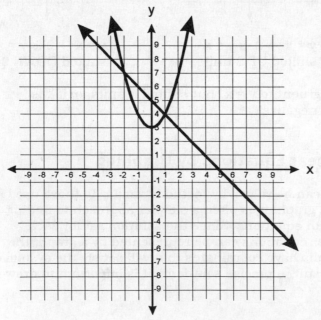

Draw each graph on the same set of axes.

Locate the points of intersection: (⁻2, 7), (1, 4)

Check each ordered pair in both equations.

$y = x^2 + 3$
$(^-2, 7)$

y	$x^2 + 3$
7	$(^-2)^2 + 3$
7	$4 + 3$
7	7

$y = ^-x + 5$
$(^-2, 7)$

y	$^-x + 5$
7	$^-(^-2) + 5$
7	$2 + 5$
7	7

$y = x^2 + 3$
$(1, 4)$

y	$x^2 + 3$
4	$1^2 + 3$
4	$1 + 3$
4	4

$y = ^-x + 5$
$(1, 4)$

y	$^-x + 5$
4	$^-(1) + 5$
4	$^-1 + 5$
4	4

Find the solution set of $y = |x - 4|$ and $y = 2x - 2$.

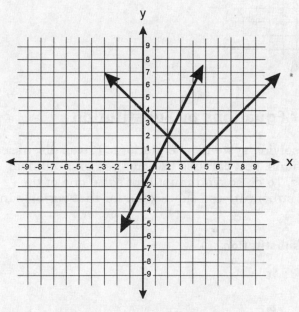

Graph both equations.

Find the point of intersection of the two graphs:
(2, 2)

Check the solution in both equations.

$y = |x - 4|$
$(2, 2)$

y	$|x - 4|$
2	$|2 - 4|$
2	$|^-2|$
2	2

$y = 2x - 2$
$(2, 2)$

y	$2x - 2$
2	$2(2) - 2$
2	$4 - 2$
2	2

Find the solution set of $y = x^2 - 1$ and $y = -\frac{3}{2}x - 3$.

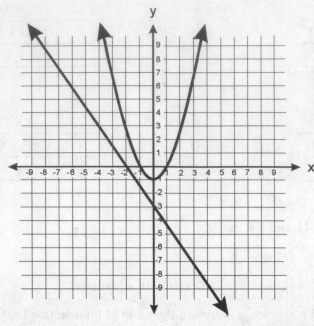

Graph both equations.

Notice that in this situation there is no point of intersection.

There is no solution for this system.

Solving Systems of Nonlinear Equations by Substitution

Substitution is another method for solving systems of equations. It was discussed above in the section on linear equations. You can use this method on nonlinear systems as well as on linear systems. To do so, you must first solve one of the equations for one variable and then substitute the expression for that variable into the other equation.

Solve the following system using substitution.

$x^2 + 3x - 10 = y$
$3x - y = 6$

Since the first equation is already solved for y, substitute that expression for y in the second equation.

$3x - (x^2 + 3x - 10) = 6$

Solve the resulting equation for x.

$3x - x^2 - 3x + 10 = 6$
${}^{-}x^2 + 10 = 6$
${}^{-}x^2 = 6 - 10$
${}^{-}x^2 = {}^{-}4$
$x^2 = 4$
$\sqrt{x^2} = \sqrt{4}$
$|x| = 2$
$x = 2 \text{ or } {}^{-}2$

Now find the value of y for each value of x.

$x = 2$
$y = x^2 + 3x - 10$
$y = 2^2 + 3(2) - 10$
$y = 4 + 6 - 10$
$y = 0$
$(2, 0)$

$x = {}^-2$
$y = x^2 + 3x - 10$
$y = ({}^-2)^2 + 3({}^-2) - 10$
$y = 4 - 6 - 10$
$y = {}^-12$
$({}^-2, {}^-12)$

Check both ordered pairs in the second equation.

$(2, 0)$

$3x - y$	6
$3(2) - 0$	6
6	6

$({}^-2, {}^-12)$

$3x - y$	6
$3({}^-2) - ({}^-12)$	6
${}^-6 + 12$	6
6	6

Find the solution set of $6x^2 - x + 3 = y$ and $6x^2 + 4x = y + 9 - x$ by substitution.

$6x^2 - x + 3 = y$
$6x^2 + 4x = y + 9 - x$

The first equation is already solved for y. Substitute the expression for y in the second equation.

$6x^2 + 4x = (6x^2 - x + 3) + 9 - x$
$6x^2 + 4x = 6x^2 - x + 3 + 9 - x$
$6x^2 + 4x = 6x^2 - 2x + 12$
$6x^2 - 6x^2 + 4x = {}^-2x + 12$
$4x = {}^-2x + 12$
$4x + 2x = 12$
$6x = 12$
$x = 2$

Find the value of y for $x = 2$.

$x = 2$
$y = 6x^2 - x + 3$
$y = 6(2^2) - 2 + 3$
$y = 6(4) - 2 + 3$
$y = 24 - 2 + 3$
$y = 25$

$(2, 25)$ is the solution for the system.

Check the ordered pair (2, 25) in the second equation.

$6x^2 + 4x$	$y + 9 - x$
$6(2^2) + 4(2)$	$25 + 9 - 2$
$6(4) + 4(2)$	32
$24 + 8$	32
32	32

Solve the following system.

$y + 4 = x^2$
$3y + x = x - 21$

Solve the first equation for y.

$y = x^2 - 4$

Substitute the expression for y in the second equation.

$3(x^2 - 4) + x = x - 21$
$3x^2 - 12 + x = x - 21$
$3x^2 - 12 + x - x = {}^-21$
$3x^2 - 12 = {}^-21$
$3x^2 = {}^-21 + 12$
$3x^2 = {}^-9$
$x^2 = {}^-3$

There is no real number solution for this system since a real number squared can never equal a negative value.

Practice Exercises

The following exercises will help you review the skills covered in this chapter. Many of the types of questions presented here will be similar to those on the test; others will not. Remember that the purpose of the exercises is to give you practice on the skills rather than merely to prepare you for the test. Following these exercises are the Practice Exercise Explanations. They explain each question, the correct answer, and why the remaining choices are incorrect.

1. If $\frac{5}{8}b + 2 = \frac{9}{2}$, what is the value of $6b - 3$?

   A. 4

   B. $6\frac{3}{8}$

   C. 21

   D. $30\frac{3}{5}$

2. If $h + 6.8 = 30.2$, what is the value of $h + 2$?

   A. 23.4

   B. 25.4

   C. 37.0

   D. 39.0

3. If $^-10x + 2y = 3x - \frac{16}{5}y$, what is the value of x in terms of y?

   A. $67\frac{3}{5}y$

   B. $\frac{2}{5}y$

   C. $\frac{18}{65}y$

   D. $\frac{^-6}{65}y$

4. Solve $3t + 5 = 5t + 7$ for t.

   A. 1

   B. $-\frac{1}{4}$

   C. $^-1$

   D. $1\frac{1}{2}$

5. If $\frac{2y}{3} + 5 = \frac{y}{2} - 5$, what is the value of y?

   A. -60

   B. 0

   C. -10

   D. 60

6. If $2x + 3y = 15$, what is the value of y in terms of x?

   A. $y = \frac{15-2x}{3}$

   B. $y = 15 - 2x$

   C. $y = 5 - 2x$

   D. $y = \frac{15 + 2x}{3}$

7. Solve $\frac{3a}{2} - 4b = 5$ for a.

   A. $a = \frac{8b + 5}{3}$

   B. $a = \frac{10-8b}{3}$

   C. $a = \frac{8b + 10}{3}$

   D. $a = \frac{4b + 10}{3}$

8. Solve this system for x.

   $2x - y = 3$
   $3x + 4y = 10$

   A. $\frac{13}{11}$

   B. $-\frac{22}{5}$

   C.   2

   D. $-\frac{7}{5}$

9. Solve this system for y.

   $2x - y = 3$
   $3x + 4y = 10$

   A. $\frac{29}{5}$

   B. $\frac{13}{11}$

   C.   0

   D.   1

10. Solve this system for y.

   $3x - y = 5$
   $^-6x + 2y = 15$

   A.   5

   B. $\frac{25}{4}$

   C.   There are an infinite number of solutions.

   D.   There is no solution.

11. Find the solution set of $|4x + 3| = 6$

   A. $\left\{\frac{3}{4}, -\frac{3}{4}\right\}$

   B. $\left\{\frac{3}{4}, -\frac{9}{4}\right\}$

   C. $\left\{\frac{3}{4}, \frac{9}{4}\right\}$

   D. $\left\{-\frac{3}{4}, -\frac{9}{4}\right\}$

12.   Which graph below represents the solution set for $y = |x - 5|$?

A.

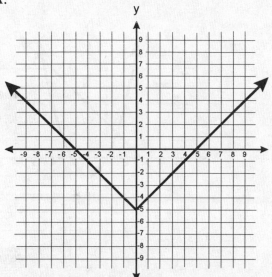

B.

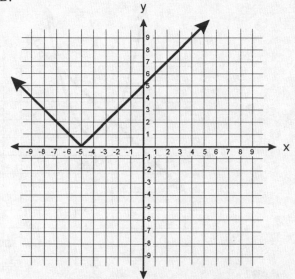

C.

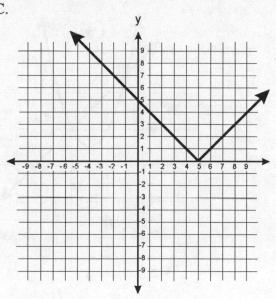

D.

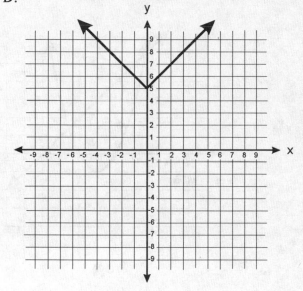

13.   Solve $y = x^2 - 2x - 12$ and
       $3y + 6x = ^-9$ for x.

       A.   {3, ⁻3}

       B.   {1, ⁻1}

       C.   {9, ⁻9}

       D.   There is no real solution.

14.   Which graph below shows the solution of $y = x^2 + 1$ and $y = {}^-x + 3$?

A.

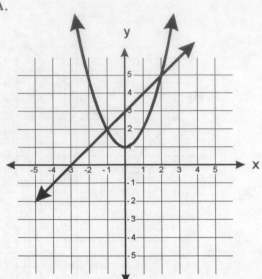

B.

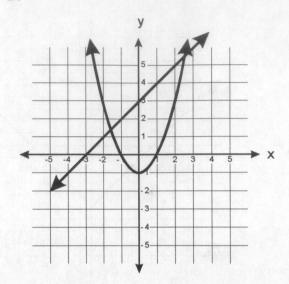

C.

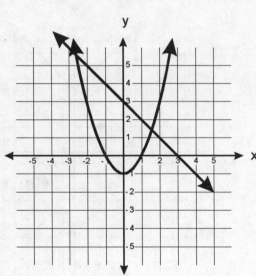

D.

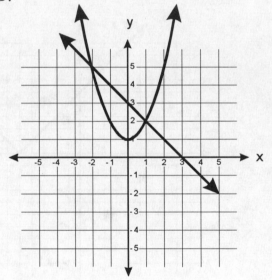

15.   Find the solution set of $3x^2 - 3y - 2 = 4$
      and $y = x^2 - 2$.

   A. $(0, {}^-2)$

   B. $(2, 2), ({}^-2, 2)$

   C.   There are an infinite number of
        solutions.

   D.   There is no real solution.

Practice Exercise Explanations

1. **Correct Response: C.** To solve the problem, you must first solve for b using the equation given.

   $$\frac{5}{8}b + 2 = \frac{9}{2}$$
   $$\frac{5}{8}b = \frac{9}{2} - 2 = \frac{9}{2} - \frac{4}{2} = \frac{5}{2}$$
   $$b = \frac{5}{2} \times \frac{8}{5} = 4$$

   You can then substitute the solution for b into the expression 6b – 3.

   6b – 3 = 6(4) – 3 = 21.

   Response A gives the value of b. Response B results from failing to invert $\frac{5}{8}$ to $\frac{8}{5}$ in the first equation. Response D results from incorrectly subtracting $\frac{9}{2} - 2 = \frac{7}{2}$.

2. **Correct Response: B.** To solve the problem, solve the first equation for h, and then add that value to 2.

   h + 6.8 = 30.2
   h = 30.2 – 6.8 = 23.4
   23.4 + 2 = 25.4

   Response A gives the value of h. Response C results from incorrectly transposing 6.8 by adding it to 30.2 and then giving the value of h. Response D results from the same transposition error as response C and then adding 2 to the result.

3. **Correct Response: B.** This problem is solved by transposing the x and y variables to isolate each variable on opposite sides of the equal sign.

   $$^-10x + 2y = 3x - \frac{16}{5}y$$
   $$2y + \frac{16}{5}y = 13x$$
   $$\frac{26}{5}y = 13x$$
   $$\left(\frac{1}{13}\right)\left(\frac{26}{5}y\right) = x$$
   $$\frac{2}{5}y = x$$

   Response A results from not inverting 13 to $\frac{1}{13}$. Response C results from incorrectly adding $\frac{16}{5} + 2 = \frac{18}{5}$. Response D results from incorrectly transposing $-\frac{16}{5}y$ as $-\frac{16}{5}y$ instead of $\frac{16}{5}y$.

4. **Correct Response: C.** To solve this equation for t, begin by isolating t on the left side of the equation.

   3t + 5 = 5t + 7
   3t – 5t = 7 – 5
   $^-$2t = 2
   t = $^-$1

   Responses A and B result from sign errors during transposition. Response D results from transposing through addition rather than through subtraction.

5. **Correct Response: A.** Solve this equation as follows.

$$\frac{2y}{3} + 5 = \frac{y}{2} - 5$$

$$\frac{4y}{6} + 5 = \frac{3y}{6} - 5 \qquad\qquad \textit{Convert fractions to LCD.}$$

$$\frac{4y}{6} - \frac{3y}{6} = {}^-5 - 5 \qquad\qquad \textit{Transpose.}$$

$$\frac{y}{6} = {}^-10 \qquad\qquad \textit{Subtract.}$$

$$y = {}^-60 \qquad\qquad \textit{Cross-multiply.}$$

Response B results from a sign error during transposition. Responses C and D result from improperly clearing fractions.

6. **Correct Response: A.** To find the value of y in terms of x, isolate y on the left side of the equal sign.

$$2x + 3y = 15$$

$$3y = {}^-2x + 15$$

$$y = \frac{{}^-2x + 15}{3} = \frac{15 - 2x}{3}$$

Response B results from failing to divide by the coefficient. Response C results from not dividing 2x by 3. Response D results from a sign error in transposition.

7. **Correct Response: C.** Solve this equation as follows.

$$\frac{3a}{2} - 4b = 5$$

$$\frac{3a}{2} = 5 + 4b \qquad\qquad \textit{Transpose.}$$

$$3a = 10 + 8b \qquad\qquad \textit{Multiply both sides by 2.}$$

$$a = \frac{10 + 8b}{3} = \frac{8b + 10}{3} \qquad\qquad \textit{Divide both sides by 3.}$$

Response A results from not multiplying (5)(2). Response B results from a sign error during transposition. Response D results from not multiplying (4b)(2).

8. **Correct Response: C.** Solve this system as follows.

$$2x - y = 3$$
$$3x + 4y = 10$$

$$(4)(2x - y) = (4)(3)$$
$$3x + 4y = 10$$

$$8x - 4y = 12$$
$$\underline{3x + 4y = 10}$$
$$11x \quad\;\; = 22$$

Response A results from improper application of the distributive law. Response B results from a sign error in the first equation. Response D results from an error in clearing the parentheses.

9.   **Correct Response: D.** Solve this system as follows.

$$2x - y = 3$$
$$3x + 4y = 10$$

$$(^-3)(2x - y) = (^-3)(3)$$
$$(2)(3x + 4y) = (2)(10)$$

$$^-6x + 3y = ^-9$$
$$\underline{6x + 8y = 20}$$
$$11y = 11$$
$$y = 1$$

Response A results from subtracting rather than adding the two equations. Response B results from failing to multiply the right sides of the equations. Response C results from incorrectly solving the equation at the final step.

10.   **Correct Response: D.** In this problem, the unknowns cancel; the system is called inconsistent when there is no solution. Response A results from a sign error caused by incorrectly multiplying the top equation. Response B also results from a sign error in multiplication. Response C results from an incorrect conclusion drawn when the unknowns cancel.

11.   **Correct Response: B.** Solve this absolute value equation as follows.

$$|4x + 3| = 6$$

$$4x + 3 = 6 \qquad \text{or} \qquad 4x + 3 = ^-6$$

$$4x = 6 - 3 \qquad\qquad\qquad 4x = ^-6 - 3$$

$$4x = 3 \qquad\qquad\qquad\quad 4x = ^-9$$

$$x = \frac{3}{4} \qquad\qquad\qquad\quad x = -\frac{9}{4}$$

Response A results from writing only one of the two equations and incorrectly assuming the second value should be the opposite of the first. Responses C and D result from a sign error in transposition.

12.   **Correct Response: C.** Response C is the graph of $y = |x|$ shifted 5 units right. Responses A, B, and D are all shifted in the wrong direction. To verify that C is correct, substitute the values 1, 2, 3, 4, 5, 6, 7, 8, and 9 for x in the equation. The ordered pairs that result from these substitutions are: (1, 4), (2, 3), (3, 2), (4, 1), (5, 0), (6, 1), (7, 2), (8, 3), and (9, 4), all of which are shown in response C.

13.   **Correct Response: A.** Solve the system by substitution.

$$y = x^2 - 2x - 12$$
$$3y + 6x = ^-9$$

$$3(x^2 - 2x - 12) + 6x = ^-9$$
$$3x^2 - 6x - 36 + 6x = ^-9$$
$$3x^2 - 36 = ^-9$$
$$3x^2 = ^-9 + 36$$
$$3x^2 = 27$$
$$x^2 = 9$$
$$\sqrt{x^2} = \sqrt{9}$$
$$|x| = 3$$
$$x = 3 \text{ or } x = ^-3$$

Response B results from incorrectly removing the parentheses. Response C results from incorrectly finding the value of $\sqrt{9}$. Response D results from a sign error when adding $^-9 + 36$.

14.   **Correct Response: D.** Response D shows the graph of $y = x^2$ shifted up 1 unit and a line passing through (0, 3) with slope of $^-1$. Responses A and B show the line drawn with an incorrect (positive) slope. Response C shows the curve shifted in the wrong direction (i.e., down 1 unit instead of up).

15.   **Correct Response: C.** Use substitution to solve this system.

$$3x^2 - 3y - 2 = 4$$
$$y = x^2 - 2$$
$$3x^2 - 3(x^2 - 2) - 2 = 4$$
$$3x^2 - 3x^2 + 6 - 2 = 4$$
$$4 = 4$$

The unknowns cancel, leaving a true statement. The system, therefore, has an infinite number of solutions (i.e., it is dependent). Response A results from a sign error when removing parentheses. Response B results from incorrectly simplifying the left side of the equation. Response D results from drawing an incorrect conclusion when unknowns cancel and leave a true statement.

Study Ideas

A careful study of the above exercises and the explanations of the answers will help you review important skills relating to one- and two-variable linear and nonlinear equations. In these exercises you were asked to find the value of the unknown in one-variable equations, express one variable in terms of a second variable in two-variable equations, and solve a system of two equations in two variables. The exercises are designed to give you practice in these skills. You may wish to reread parts of the chapter that address specific skills with which you have difficulty.

Chapter 15

SOLVE WORD PROBLEMS INVOLVING ONE AND TWO VARIABLES

This skill includes solving word problems that can be translated into one-variable equations or systems of two-variable equations and identifying the equation or equations that correctly represent the mathematical relationship(s) in word problems. Also included are problems with an infinite number of solutions and with no solutions.

Introduction

Solving word problems in one or two variables is much easier if you are able to set up the problems mathematically. In this chapter, you will be given the means to accomplish this.

Word problems may be classified by how many unknowns (variables) are required to set up the problem. In this chapter, we will deal with problems that involve either one or two unknowns (variables). Often, the same problem can be solved using either one or two variables. As an illustration, the problem below will be solved three different ways, two involving one variable and one involving two variables. The difference between these two types of problems is illustrated by the following example.

The sum of two numbers is 44. If the larger number is three times the smaller number, find the smaller number.

Word Problems Involving One Variable

Method A

The sum of two numbers is 44. If the larger number is three times the smaller number, find the smaller number.

Let x = the smaller number.

Then the larger number must be equal to $3x$, since the problem states that it is 3 times the smaller number.

Since, according to the problem, the sum of the smaller number (x) and the larger number ($3x$) is 44, set up the following equation.

$x + 3x = 44$

Now solve for x.

$4x = 44$
$x = 11$ and $3x = 33$

Since $11 + 33 = 44$, the solution is reasonable.

Method B

The sum of two numbers is 44. If the larger number is three times the smaller number, find the smaller number.

Let x = the smaller number.

Then the larger number must be equal to $44 - x$, since the problem states that the sum of the two numbers is 44.

NOTE: The preceding step is based on the fact that if $x + y = z$, then $x = z - y$ and $y = z - x$. In other words, if a number is divided into two parts, and one part is called x, then the other part is equal to the total minus x. In the preceding example, this meant that the larger number was equal to the sum $(44) - x$.

The problem states that the larger number, which we are calling $(44 - x)$, is three times the smaller number, which we are calling x. The problem can therefore be stated as follows.

$3x = 44 - x$

Solve.
$3x = 44 - x$

$3x + x = 44$
$4x = 44$
$x = 11$ and $(44 - x) = 33$

Solutions Involving Two Variables

The sum of two numbers is 44. If the larger number is three times the smaller number, find the smaller number.

Let x = the smaller number.
Let y = the larger number.

The equations are as follows.

$x + y = 44$ *The sum of the numbers is 44.*
$y = 3x$ *One number is three times the other.*

Using the substitution method for solving systems of equations described in the previous chapter, substitute $3x$ for y in the first equation.

$x + 3x = 44$
$4x = 44$
$x = 11$ and $y = (3)(11) = 33$

Again, $x + y = 11 + 33 = 44$.

The basic difference between the two approaches is the number of variables used to set up the problem. If *one variable* is used, only *one equation* is necessary to solve the problem. If *two variables* are used, then a system of *two equations* is needed to solve the problem. Which method you choose depends on the problem and on your personal preference. The key to successful solving of word problems is to set up correctly the one or two equations that describe the situation.

The following problem can be conveniently solved using one variable.

> Maria has $360.00. She spends 20% of it on her car and 25% of it on food. How much money does Maria have left?

> Let x = amount of money left.

> Maria spent 20% of her check on the car and 25% of it on food. Thus she spent 20% + 25% = 45% of the check. Since 100% is the whole check, she has (100% − 45%) = 55% left. Remember that 100% of a quantity is the entire quantity, and 50% is one half the quantity.

> (Since 55% is greater than half her check, the answer should be greater than half of $360.00, or close to $200.00.)

> x = 55% of 360.00
> x = (0.55)(360.00) = $198.00

Translating Words into Algebraic Terms

To solve word problems, you must first be able to translate the words they use into mathematical symbols and algebraic expressions. Some commonly used words, their mathematical meanings, and their equivalent algebraic expressions are summarized in the table below. Note that the letters used for variables are arbitrary; other letters could just as accurately be used.

Words	Example	Meaning	Expression
the sum of a and b; the total of a and b; or words like *in all* or *all together*	The sum of two numbers is 45.	Add a to b to equal 45.	a + b = 45 or b + a = 45
a more than b; a increased by b; a in addition to b. (But be careful: *more than* in the question part of the problem can mean subtract—see next entry.)	The sum of two numbers is equal to 45, and the larger number is 13 more than the smaller.	Add a to b to equal 45; then substitute for b the expression a + 13.	a + b = 45, expanded to a + (a + 13) = 45

Words	Example	Meaning	Expression
How much more than a is b? or How much less than b is a?	Ben and Kara read a total of 128 pages this weekend. If Ben read 45 pages, how many more pages than Ben did Kara read?	Subtract Ben's total, b, from the overall total to calculate Kara's total, k. Then subtract Ben's total from Kara's.	k = 128 − 45 k = 83 k − b = 83 − 45 k − b = 38
the difference between a and b	The difference between two numbers is 6.	Subtract b from a to equal 6.	a − b = 6
a decreased by b, or words indicating a decrease, such as *spend, lose, give away, take away, deduct,* etc.	The sum of two numbers decreased by 16 is 34.	Subtract 16 from the sum of a and b to equal 34.	(a + b) − 16 = 34
the product of x and y; x times y	The product of two numbers is 144. The larger number is 4 times the smaller.	Multiply x and y to equal 144; then substitute 4 times the smaller number for the larger number.	xy = 144 x(4x) = 144
the word *of* with percents and fractions	Lonnie spends N hours on each drawing. She estimates that she spends a third of that time planning and another 15 percent of the time revising her work. How much time does she spend on these two activities?	Multiply $\frac{1}{3}$ times N and 0.15 times N. Then add the two results to get the time, T.	$\frac{1}{3}$N + 0.15N = T
the quotient of p and r, or words like *per* and *each*	In r hours James read p pages. How many pages did he read per hour?	Divide p by r.	p/r or $\frac{p}{r}$

Note that words referring to algebraic expressions can be combined in word problems. Consider the following further examples.

1. **six more than the product of x and 5**
   6 + 5x or 5x + 6   6 added to the result of multiplying x and 5

2. **four less than twice the number y**
   2y – 4   4 subtracted from the product of 2 and y

3. **one third of 5 more than p**
   $\frac{p+5}{3}$ or $\frac{5+p}{3}$ add 5 and p, then multiply by $\frac{1}{3}$ or divide by 3

4. **three times the difference of 6 and w**
   (6 – w)3 or 3(6 – w)   multiply 3 by the result of subtracting w from 6

Solving Typical Word Problems

There are a few types of word problems that occur with regularity. These problems require certain formulas that should be memorized. The most common types are distance-rate-time problems, interest problems, mixture-solution problems, and perimeter-area problems.

Distance-Rate-Time Problems. To solve problems involving distance, rate of travel, and time, it is helpful to understand the equation D = RT, where D is the distance, R is the rate (in miles per hour, feet per second, etc.), and T is the time. This equation says that the distance that an object travels is equal to its rate of travel (speed) multiplied by the time the object has been traveling. For instance, a car that travels 50 miles per hour for 3 hours travels 50 miles x 3 hours, or 150 miles. Other forms of the equation include $R = \frac{D}{T}$ and $T = \frac{D}{R}$.

When using the formula D = RT, the units must agree. That is, if the distance is in feet, and the time is in seconds, the rate must be in feet per second. This means that in some distance-rate-time problems, you will have to convert units.

Example 1.

Rick runs at the rate of 4 miles/hour, while Paul runs at the rate of 6 miles/hour. If they start running at the same time and place and run in opposite directions, how far apart will they be after 30 minutes?

Let D = the distance that Rick and Paul are apart after 30 minutes of running. Since the rates are in miles per hour rather than in miles per minute, change 30 minutes to 0.5 hours.

Then D = the distance that Rick ran in 0.5 hours plus the distance that Paul ran in 0.5 hours.

Rick's distance = RT = (4 mph)(0.5 hrs.) = 2 miles
Paul's distance = RT = (6 mph)(0.5 hrs.) = 3 miles

D = 2 mi. + 3 mi. = 5 miles.
Rick and Paul will be 5 miles apart after 0.5 hours.

Example 2.

Dan is driving to visit a friend who lives 40 miles away. After driving for 1 hour at an average rate of 35 mph, Dan gets a flat tire. He walks at 4 mph the rest of the way to his friend's house. How long did the 40-mile trip take Dan?

The total time for the trip is the sum of the time in the car (1 hour) plus the time spent walking. Since Dan drove for 1 hour at 35 mph, he traveled 35 miles.

$D = RT = 35$ mph $\times$ 1 hr. $= 35$ miles

He traveled 35 miles before getting a flat tire, so Dan has 5 miles to walk. (Common sense should tell you that it should take Dan a little over an hour to walk this distance. Thus the answer to the problem should be a little greater than 2 hours.)

Since we are looking for the amount of time it takes Dan to walk the remaining 5 miles, we should transpose the formula $D = RT$ to $T = \frac{D}{R}$.

Thus $T = \frac{5 \text{ miles}}{4 \text{ mph}} = 1.25$ hours.

His time is 1 hr. + 1.25 hrs. = 2.25 hours.

An equation that includes both parts of the trip would be $T = \frac{D}{R} + \frac{D}{R}$, where the first term on the right side is the time spent driving, and the second term is the time spent walking.

Interest problems. To solve interest problems, you must know that $I = PRT$, where I is the amount of interest in dollars, P is the principal or the number of dollars you start with, R is the interest rate usually expressed as a percent, and T is the time. Thus, the amount of interest you earn on money in a bank account depends on the interest rate the bank pays, the amount of money in your account, and the length of time you leave the money in the account. If R is a percent per year, then T must be expressed in years. If the interest rate is expressed as a percent, it should be changed to a decimal when used in an equation. This is true for virtually every word problem involving percents. A problem that involves percents is easier to solve if you change the percent to a decimal.

Example 1.

Mary has a bank account that earns 6% interest per year. How much money must Mary have in the bank in order to make $60.00 in interest per year?

Let P = the principal or amount of money in the bank; I = the amount of interest, or $60.00; R = the rate of interest, or 6%; and T = the length of time the money is earning interest, or 1 year. Before beginning, convert 6% to 0.06.

I = PRT
60 = (P)(0.06)(1)
60 = 0.06P
6000 = 6P   *Multiply both sides by 100.*
1000 = P, or P = $1000

Example 2.

Susan decides to invest $5000 in two different savings certificates. One yields 4% interest per year; the other yields 6% interest per year. If the total yield from both certificates in one year is $244.00, how much did she invest at 4%?

Let x = amount at 4%.
Let y = amount at 6%.

The interest earned per year can be found using the equation I = PRT, where P is the principal, R is the interest rate, and T is the time. The interest earned on the 4% certificate is (x)(0.04)(1), or 0.04x, and the interest earned on the 6% certificate is 0.06y. The two equations are as follows.

x + y = 5000   *The sum of the amounts in the two*
                               accounts is $5000.
0.04x + 0.06y = $244.00   *The total interest, $244.00, is the sum*
                               of the interest in each account.

Recall that when an equation involves fractions, the fractions ought to be cleared by multiplying both sides by the least common denominator. Equations that contain decimals should be cleared by multiplying both sides by the power of 10 necessary to convert the decimals to integers. In the above equations, multiply both sides of the second equation by 100 to obtain the following system.

x + y = 5000
4x + 6y = 24,400

Eliminate y, since x (the principal at 4%) is the variable you want to solve for. Do this by multiplying the top equation by ⁻6 and adding the result to the second equation.

⁻6x − 6y = ⁻30,000
4x + 6y = 24,400

⁻2x = ⁻5600
x = $2800

This number represents the amount of money that Susan invested in the 4% certificate. Therefore, she must have invested $5000 − $2800 = $2200 in the account at 6%.

Example 3.

Suppose that Susan had her money in the 4% account for a year and a half and the money in the 6% account for nine months. Again, assume that she started with $5000 but that her total interest is $270.00. How much did she invest in each?

Let x be the amount (principal) at 4% and y the amount at 6% since the rates are 4% and 6%. Here the time is not 1 year as in the problem above but 1.5 years for the 4% account and 0.75 years for the 6% account. Nine months is three quarters of a year, or 0.75 year.

$x + y = 5000$
$(0.04)(1.5)x + (0.06)(0.75)y = 270$

$0.06x + 0.045y = 270$	*Multiply the decimals in the second equation.*
$60x + 45y = 270,000$	*Multiply by 1000 to clear the decimals in the second equation.*

$x + y = 5000$	*The system of equations is now written this way.*
$60x + 45y = 270,000$	

$^-60x - 60y = ^-300,000$	*Multiply the first equation by $^-60$.*
$^-15y = ^-30,000$	*Add the equations to eliminate x.*
$y = \$2000$ invested at 6%	

Hence, $5000 - $2000 = $3000 invested at 4%.

Mixture-solution problems. The first step in solving a mixture-solution problem is to rewrite the information in a more easily understood format. It is often easiest to set up a simple table to keep track of the information. The information in the table is then used to formulate an equation.

Example 1.

How many pints of 40% salt solution must be added to 10 pints of 80% salt solution to dilute the solution to 50%?

Salt Solutions

	Solution 1	Solution 2	Final Solution
Volume	10 pts.	x pts.	(10 + x) pts.
Concentration	80% salt	40% salt	50% salt

Formulate an equation by noting that the product of the final volume and the final concentration is equal to the product of the volume and concentration for solution 1 plus the product of the volume and concentration for solution 2.

80% of 10 pts. + 40% of x pts. = 50% of (10 + x) pts.	
$(0.80)(10) + (0.40)x = (0.50)(x + 10)$	
$(8)(10) + 4x = (5)(x + 10)$	*Clear the decimals by multiplying both sides by 10.*

$80 + 4x = 5x + 50$
$30 = x$
$x = 30$ pints

Example 2.

Chris must prepare a 40% salt solution. All she has available, however, is 100 cubic centimeters (cc) of a 50% salt solution. How many cubic centimeters of pure water (0% salt) must she add to the 50% solution to make a 40% salt solution?

Let x = amount of pure water.

(Because 100 cc of a 50% solution plus 100 cc of a 0% solution would result in a 25% solution, the answer should be less than 100 cc.)

100 cc	+	x cc	=	(100 + x) cc
50% salt		0% salt		40% salt

The total amount of salt on the left side of the equation is equal to the amount of salt on the right side. 50% of 100 cc + 0% of x cc = 40% of (100 + x) cc
$(0.50)(100) + 0x = 0.40(100 + x)$
$50 + 0x = 40 + 0.4x$

Clear the decimals by multiplying by 10, and collect like terms.

$500 = 400 + 4x$
$100 = 4x$
$x = 25$ cc

Perimeter-area problems. There are basically two kinds of geometric figures used for these problems: the rectangle and the circle. The formulas that are important for working with rectangles are as follows.

$P = 2l + 2w$ or $P = 2(l + w)$, where P is perimeter (the distance around the rectangle), l is the length, and w is the width.

$A = lw$, where A is the area, l is the length, and w is the width.

The formulas that are important for working with circles are as follows.

$C = 2\pi r$ or $C = \pi d$, where C is the circumference (the distance around the circle), π is the constant pi (which is approximately equal to 3.14 or $\frac{22}{7}$), r is the radius, and d is the diameter.

$A = \pi r^2$, where A is the area, π is the constant, and r is the radius.

For most problems in geometry, the first step should be to draw a diagram that summarizes the problem. Diagrams are often very helpful when doing any kind of geometric problem.

Example 1.

A rectangle has a perimeter of 220 ft. Its length is 20 ft. longer than its width. Find its width.

Let w = width.
Then length = w + 20.

Since the problem involves perimeter, use the formula P = 2l + 2w.

P = 2l + 2w
220 = 2(w + 20) + 2w
220 = 2w + 40 + 2w
220 = 4w + 40
180 = 4w
45 = w or w = 45 ft.

Example 2.

Clare plans to paint the walls of her apartment. The front and the back walls are each 20 feet long and 8 feet high. The side walls are 30 feet long and 8 feet high. If a gallon of paint covers 200 square feet, how many gallons will Clare have to buy?

The problem is best solved by dividing it into two parts. The first part is to find the area to be covered, while the second is to find the gallons of paint needed.

First, to find the area of the front wall, use the formula A = lw.

A = 20 ft. × 8 ft. = 160 sq. ft.

Since the back wall has the same dimensions as the front wall, it must also have an area of 160 sq. ft.

To find the area of each side wall, use the formula A = lw.

A = 30 ft. × 8 ft. = 240 sq. ft.

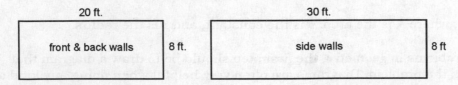

The total area is A = (2)(160) + (2)(240) = 800 sq. ft. (ft.^{2})

Next, since the total area is 800 ft.^{2}, and a gallon of paint covers 200 ft.^{2}, Clare needs the following.

$$\frac{800 \text{ ft.}^2}{200 \text{ ft.}^2/\text{gal.}} = 4 \text{ gal. of paint}$$

Problems with an Infinite Number of Solutions and with No Solutions

Occasionally you will correctly set up an equation to solve a word problem only to find that your solution seems to make no sense. This may be due to the fact that equations in one or two variables can have a solution set with an infinite number of members or one with no members.

An example of an open sentence with infinite solutions is $2 + x = x + 2$. This type of equation is called an *identity*. Any number replacement for x will result in a true statement. The solution set contains an infinite number of members.

In contrast, $x - 1 = x - 3$ will have no solution. Sentences of this type are called *inconsistent equations*. No matter what number you replace x with, you will never have a true statement. The solution set for this equation is the *null set*, a set containing no elements.

Example 1.

> The length of a rectangle is five feet more than its width. If the length is increased by 6 feet and the width is decreased by two feet, the new perimeter will be 8 feet longer than the old perimeter. Find the width of the old rectangle.

First draw a diagram and label the old length and width.
Let x = the old width.
Then x + 5 = the old length.

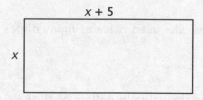

Now draw the new rectangle, labeling the new length and width.
New width = x – 2.
New length = x + 5 + 6.

Write an equation expressing the relationship between the old perimeter and the new perimeter. Use the formula $P = 2l + 2w$. The old perimeter plus 8 feet equals the new perimeter.

$$2x + 2(x + 5) + 8 = 2(x - 2) + 2(x + 5 + 6)$$

Now solve this equation for x.

$$2x + 2x + 10 + 8 = 2x - 4 + 2x + 10 + 12$$
$$4x + 18 = 4x + 18$$
$$18 = 18$$

The end result is a statement that is always true; therefore, this problem has an infinite number of solutions. (The dimensions are limited, however, to positive values only.)

Example 2.

The smaller of two numbers is eight less than the larger. Three times the larger is the same as the sum of twice the smaller and the larger increased by 16. Find the larger of the numbers.

Let x = the larger of the two numbers.
Then $x - 8$ = the smaller number.

Write an equation expressing the relationship stated in the problem.

$3x = 2(x - 8) + x + 16$

Solve the equation for x.

$3x = 2x - 16 + x + 16$ *Use the distributive property to simplify.*

$3x = 3x$ *Add like terms on the right side of the equation.*

The end result is a statement that is true for all values of x. Any number will solve this equation; there are infinitely many solutions for the word problem.

Example 3.

Maria paid a bill of \$2.00 with quarters and dimes. She used twice as many dimes as quarters. How many dimes did she use?

Let x = the number of quarters.
Then $2x$ = the number of dimes.
The value in dollars of all the quarters is $.25x$ and the value in dollars of all the dimes is $.10(2x)$.

Write an equation.

$.25x + .10(2x) = 2.00$

$25x + 10(2x) = 200$ *Clear all decimals by multiplying both sides by 100.*

$25x + 20x = 200$
$45x = 200$
$x = \dfrac{200}{45} = \dfrac{40}{9} = 4\dfrac{4}{9}$

In this case, the equation has a mathematical solution, $4\dfrac{4}{9}$, but the solution makes no sense in the context of the word problem. Since the number of quarters and the number of dimes must both be whole numbers, not fractions or mixed numbers, the problem has no solution.

Example 4.

Find the smallest of four consecutive integers such that three times the third added to the second is the same as twice the sum of the first and the fourth.

Let n = the first integer.
Then n + 1 = the second, n + 2 = the third, and n + 3 = the fourth.

Translate the word problem into an algebraic equation.

3(n + 2) + n + 1 = 2(n + n + 3)
3n + 6 + n + 1 = 2n + 2n + 6   *Simplify using the distributive property.*

4n + 7 = 4n + 6   *Combine like terms.*
7 = 6

The last statement will never be true, so there is no value of n that can be found to satisfy the original equation. This problem has no solution.

Systems of Equations with Infinite or No Solutions. Systems of equations in two variables can also result in infinite or no solutions. This can occur when the equations are dependent (i.e., they have infinitely many solutions), inconsistent (i.e., they have no solution), or impossible in the given situation.

If a *linear* system has no solution, then the graphs of the ordered pairs that make up each line will be parallel. If the equations are dependent, one equation will be equivalent to the other, and when graphed will produce the same line. Any solution of one equation will also be a solution of the other.

Example 1.

The sum of two numbers is $1\frac{2}{3}$ and twice the first number subtracted from 3 is the same as $\frac{1}{3}$ less than twice the second. Find the first number.

Let x = the first number and y = the second number.
First translate the problem into two algebraic equations.

$x + y = 1\frac{2}{3}$

$3 - 2x = 2y - \frac{1}{3}$

Next clear all fractions by multiplying both sides of each equation by 3.

3x + 3y = 5
9 - 6x = 6y - 1

Solve the system.

3x + 3y = 5   *Transpose the second equation to put*
⁻6x - 6y = ⁻10   *the terms in the proper order.*

6x + 6y = 10   *Multiply both sides of the first equation*
⁻6x - 6y = ⁻10   *by 2.*

0 = 0

The result is a statement that is always true. Any ordered pair (x,y) that will satisfy the first equation will satisfy the system. There are an infinite number of solutions to this problem.

Example 2.

The sum of three times the first of two numbers and the second number is the same as the first number subtracted from twice the second number. The second of the two numbers is one less than four times the first. Find the first number.

Let x = the first number and y = the second.

Translate the word problem as follows.

3x + y = 2y − x
y = 4x − 1

Solve this system using substitution.

3x + 4x − 1 = 2(4x − 1) − x

Now solve the above equation for x.

7x − 1 = 8x − 2 − x	*Use the distributive property to simplify.*
7x − 1 = 7x − 2	*Add like terms on the right side.*
⁻1 = ⁻2	*Subtract 7x from both sides.*

The result is a statement that is never true. There is no ordered pair (x,y) that will solve this problem and we say that the system has no solution.

Example 3.

John is eight years more than five times Bob's age. Three times John's age decreased by five is the same as twice Bob's age. Find Bob's age.

Let Bob's age = B and John's age = J.

Write two equations.

J = 5B + 8
3J − 5 = 2B

Solve this system by addition.

J − 5B = 8	*Transpose the equations.*
3J − 2B = 5	

⁻3J + 15B = ⁻24	*Multiply both sides of the first equation*
3J − 2B = 5	*by ⁻3.*

13B = ⁻19

$$B = -\frac{19}{13}$$

This time the result is a number, but because B represents Bob's age and an age cannot be negative, there is no solution to the word problem.

Suggestions for Problem Solving

When solving word problems, you should keep the following in mind.

1. Read the problem carefully, making sure that you *understand* exactly what is being asked of you.

2. In more complicated word problems, it is a good idea to *simplify* the problem by breaking it into smaller, more manageable parts.

3. A neat and large *diagram* with the essential parts labeled is helpful in finding a solution.

4. *Specify* what each variable that you use represents.

5. Carefully *translate* the word problem into algebra.

6. *Solve* for the variable that represents the quantity asked for in the problem.

7. After solving the problem, *use common sense* to determine whether your answer is a reasonable one based on the information given in the problem. After you read and understand the problem, you should form an opinion of what a reasonable answer will be. If, after completing your work, your answer is not close to your original opinion, then check your work. Your original opinion may have been incorrect, or you may have solved the problem incorrectly.

8. *Be confident* that you are capable of solving word problems.

Practice Exercises

The following exercises will help you review the skills covered in this chapter. Many of the types of questions presented here will be similar to those on the test; others will not. Remember that the purpose of the exercises is to give you practice on the skills rather than merely to prepare you for the test. Following these exercises are the Practice Exercise Explanations. They explain each question, the correct answer, and why the remaining choices are incorrect.

1. Barbara, a salesperson, gets $200.00 per week salary plus 5% commission on her total sales for the week. If she earned $230.00 in one week, what were her total sales?

   A. $ 6.00

   B. $ 40.00

   C. $400.00

   D. $600.00

2. Todd must take a taxi to work. The fare is $2.00 for the first mile and $.50 per mile for each additional mile. If Todd has $10.00, how many miles can he travel?

   A. 5 miles

   B. 8 miles

   C. 17 miles

   D. 20 miles

3. In her chemistry class, Betty must mix 5 liters of a 20% sugar solution with some quantity of a 50% sugar solution to produce a solution that is 40% sugar. How many liters of the 50% solution should she add?

   A. 0.1 liter

   B. 10 liters

   C. 30 liters

   D. 40 liters

4. Ten bags of Brand X fertilizer plus 6 bags of Brand Y fertilizer will cover 2600 square feet, while 3 bags of Brand X plus 1 bag of Brand Y covers 700 square feet. How many square feet can be covered with 4 bags of Brand X plus 4 bags of Brand Y?

   A. 400 square feet

   B. 800 square feet

   C. 1200 square feet

   D. 1400 square feet

5. Jeff borrowed $2000 in two one-year loans. He pays 8% interest per year on the first loan and 10% per year on the second. If the total interest charges for a year are $176.00, how much did he borrow at 8%?

    A. $ 800.00

    B. $1000.00

    C. $1200.00

    D. $2176.00

6. In Jorge's math class, his quiz average counts for 40% of his final grade, and his test average counts for the rest. His quiz average is 75. What must his test average be in order to earn a final grade of 81?

    A. 78

    B. 85

    C. 87

    D. 90

7. Jim must rent a truck in order to move. Company A quotes him a price of $20.00 plus $.35 per mile, while Company B quotes $30.00 plus $.25 per mile. At what distance will the cost for each company be the same?

    A.   50 miles

    B.   100 miles

    C.   200 miles

    D. 1000 miles

8. Alex and John each contribute money to an investment pool. Alex puts in $2000 and John puts in $3000. If the profit for the first year is $1500, and they are to split the profit in the same ratio as their respective contributions, how much should Alex receive?

    A. $ 500.00

    B. $ 600.00

    C. $ 900.00

    D. $1000.00

9. Airplane A takes 8 hours to travel from one airport to another airport. Airplane B, which travels 100 miles per hour more slowly than Airplane A, requires 10 hours to complete the same trip. How fast does Airplane A travel?

    A.   100 mph

    B.   500 mph

    C.   800 mph

    D. 1250 mph

10. Four less than 10 times Bob's age is the same as 20 added to 8 times his age. If B represents Bob's age, which equation correctly expresses the relationship described above?

    A. $4 - 10B = 20 + 8B$

    B. $(4 - 10)B = (20 + 8)B$

    C. $10B - 4 = 8B + 20$

    D. $10(B - 4) = 8(B + 20)$

11. The quotient of the number x increased by two and four is the same as the number x decreased by three. Which equation correctly expresses this relationship?

   A. $\frac{x}{4} + 2 = x - 3$

   B. $\frac{x+2}{4} = 3 - x$

   C. $\frac{x+2}{4} = x - 3$

   D. $\frac{x}{2} + 4 = 3 - x$

12. Six more than twice the width of a rectangle is the same as eight less than five times the width. If W represents the width of the rectangle, which equation correctly expresses this relationship?

   A. $6 + 2W = 5(W - 8)$

   B. $2W + 6 = 8 - 5W$

   C. $2(W + 6) = (5 - 8)W$

   D. $6 + 2W = 5W - 8$

13. The length of a rectangle is 9 cm more than four times the width. The product of three and three cm more than the width is the same as the difference of the length and the width. Find the width.

   A. 1.5 cm

   B. 6 cm

   C. There are an infinite number of solutions.

   D. There is no solution.

14. A bottle contains $2.10 in dimes and quarters. There are nine less than twice as many dimes as quarters. How many quarters are there in the bottle?

   A. 4

   B. 73

   C. There are an infinite number of solutions.

   D. There is no solution.

Practice Exercise Explanations

1. **Correct Response: D.** To solve this problem, first determine her commission, then divide by 5% to determine total sales.

   Let S = total sales
   $230 = 200 + (0.05)S$
   $30 = 0.05S$
   $S = \$600.00$

   Choice A results from a decimal point error: dividing by 5 instead of 0.05. Choices B and C result from using Barbara's salary instead of her commission and from making decimal errors.

2. **Correct Response: C.** The first step is to set up an equation to solve the problem. Let m equal the number of miles he can travel.

   $\$2.00(1) + \$.50(m - 1) = \$10.00$

   This represents $2.00 (times the first mile) plus $.50 for each subsequent mile (m minus the first mile). Now solve.

   $\$.50(m - 1) = \$8.00$
   $\$.50m = \$8.50$
   $m = 17$

   Choice A represents the distance he could travel at $2.00 per mile. Choice B results from subtracting rather than dividing. Choice D represents the distance he could travel at $.50 per mile.

3. **Correct Response: B.** Let L = liters of 50% sugar solution to be added.

   20% of 5 + 50% of L = 40% of (L + 5)   *(L + 5) = total number of liters*
                                                 at the end.

   $(0.2)(5) + 0.5L = 0.4(L + 5)$
   $1 + 0.5L = 0.4L + 2$ *Distributive law on the right side of the*
                                                 equation.

   $0.1L = 1$
   $L = 10$ liters

   Choice A represents an error in working with decimals. Choice C results from incorrectly adding the 20% and the 50% and subtracting the 40%.

   $20 + 50 - 40 = 30$

   Choice D results from an incorrect use of the distributive property in solving the equation.

   $1 + 0.5L = 0.4L + 5$
   $0.01L = 4$
   $L = 40$

4. **Correct Response: C.** The first step is to write equations to solve for Brand X and Brand Y coverage.

Let x = Brand X coverage.
Let y = Brand Y coverage.

$10x + 6y = 2600$
$3x + y = 700$
$(^-3)(10x) + (^-3)(6y) = (^-3)(2600)$ *Use multiplication method.*
$(10)(3x) + (10)(1y) = (10)(700)$

$^-30x - 18y = ^-7800$
$30x + 10y = 7000$ *Add equations.*

$^-8y = ^-800$
$y = 100$

$3x + y = 700$ *Substitute.*
$3x + 100 = 700$
$3x = 600$
$x = 200$

Then use the x and y values to calculate the coverage asked for in the equation.

$4(200) + 4(100) = $ total
$800 + 400 = 1200$ sq. ft.

Choice A results from solving for y, multiplying by 4, and omitting the x term. Choice B results from solving for x, multiplying by 4, and omitting the y term. Choice D incorrectly finds x and y to be 175 sq. ft. each.

$\frac{700}{4} = 175$ from the second equation

$4(175) + 4(175) = 1400$

5. **Correct Response: C.** First set up two equations using two variables. Let x = amount of loan at 8%, and let y = amount of loan at 10%.

$x + y = 2000$
$0.08x + 0.10y = 176$

Multiplying the second equation by 100 gives the following.

$x + y = 2000$
$8x + 10y = 17,600$

Multiply the first equation by $^-10$ to eliminate the y term.

$^-10x - 10y = ^-20,000$
$8x + 10y = 17,600$
$^-2x = ^-2400$
$x = \$1200$, the amount of the 8% loan

Choice A results from solving for the wrong variable, the 10% loan.

$^-8x + ^-8y = ^-16,000$
$8x + 10y = 17,600$
$2y = 1600$
$y = 800$

Choice B assumes that the two parts of the $2000 are equal, $1000 each. Choice D results from simply adding the principal and the interest, $2000 + $176.00 = $2176.

6. **Correct Response: B.** First, set up an equation to solve the problem. Let x = Jorge's test average.

    40% of 75 + 60% of x = 81
    (0.4)(75) + (0.6)(x) = 81
    30 + 0.6x = 81
    300 + 6x = 810
    6x = 510
    x = 85

    Choice A is the average of 75 and 81, a misunderstanding of the problem. Choice C results from computing the averages with equal weight for the two parts.

    $$\frac{(75 + x)}{2} = 81$$

    Choice D reverses the weights assigned to the quizzes and exams and assigns 40% to the test portion.

    (0.6)(75) + (0.4)(x) = 81
    x = 90

7. **Correct Response: B.** To solve the problem, set up an equation where D = the distance in miles.

    Since each equation is for cost, the two costs are the same as follows.

    20 + 0.35D = 30 + 0.25D
    2000 + 35D = 3000 + 25D
    10D = 1000
    D = 100 miles

    You can check this easily. $20.00 + $.35(100) = $55.00; $30.00 + $.25(100) = $55.00.

    Choice A results from simply adding $20.00 and $30.00 together, which would give a value in dollars, not miles. Choice C results from a computation error. Choice D results from multiplying the $20.00 and $30.00 by 1000 instead of 100 when clearing the decimals.

8. **Correct Response: B.** Since Alex contributed $2000 and John contributed $3000, the total contribution is $5000. Alex put in $2000 of the $5000, making his share $\frac{2}{5}$ of the total. Thus he should receive $\frac{2}{5}$ of the total profit of $1500, or $600.00.

    $$\frac{2}{5}(1500) = \$600.00$$

    Choice A uses the same calculation and ratio as choice D, and then subtracts the result ($1000) from the total profit. Choice C represents John's share of the profits. Choice D results from using the ratio of Alex's contribution to John's $\left(\frac{2}{3}\right)$ rather than the ratio of Alex's contribution to the total.

9. **Correct Response: B.** This problem can be solved using the distance formula (D = RT). Since the two planes travel between the same two airports, the distances traveled by the two planes are equal. If A is the speed of Airplane A, the following equation can be used to solve this problem.

    $$8A = 10(A - 100)$$
    $$8A = 10A - 1000$$
    $$10A - 8A = 1000$$
    $$2A = 1000$$
    $$A = 500$$

    Choice A results from using the difference in speed between Airplanes A and B as the speed of A. Choice C results from multiplying 8 by 100 mph. Choice D results from dividing both sides of the first equation by 10A to solve the equation rather than correctly distributing the factors by adding or subtracting.

10. **Correct Response: C.** The mathematical expression that represents the statement "less than 10 times Bob's age" (B) is $(10 \times B) - 4$ or $10B - 4$. The next part of the problem, "is the same as," indicates an equal sign. The last part, "20 added to 8 times" B, is represented as $20 + (8 \times B)$ or $8B + 20$. Choice C is the only one that shows all parts of the equation correctly. Choice A subtracts 10B from 4. Choice B includes a misuse of parentheses as well as the error contained in choice A. Choice D also misuses parentheses.

11. **Correct Response: C.** The first part of the sentence, "the quotient of a number x increased by two and four," is correctly translated $\frac{x+2}{4}$. Recall that a quotient is the result of division. The next part, "is the same as," indicates the equal sign. The last part, "the number x decreased by three," is written $x - 3$. Notice the order of the terms in the subtraction. Choice A divides x by 4, rather than $x + 2$ by 4. Choice B reverses the terms in the subtraction. Choice D divides the x by 2 and adds 4.

12. **Correct Response: D.** The first part of the sentence, "six more than twice the width," states that you must double the width and add 6 to it. The next four words, "is the same as," indicate an equal sign. The last part of the sentence, "eight less than five times the width," tells you to subtract eight from the result of multiplying 5 by the width. Notice the order of the terms in the subtraction. Choice A includes a misuse of parentheses. Choice B reverses the order of the subtraction. Choice C incorrectly uses parentheses in both parts of the equation.

13. **Correct Response: C.** First write an expression for the length of the rectangle in terms of the width. Then write an equation to solve the problem.

    Let x = the width of the rectangle.
    Then $4x + 9$ = the length of the rectangle.

    The problem becomes: $3(x + 3) = 4x + 9 - x$ (the product of 3 and $x + 3$ = the length – the width).

    Solve the equation for x.

    $$3x + 9 = 4x + 9 - x$$
    $$3x + 9 = 3x + 9$$

The result is an equivalence. This sentence is true for all values of x. There are infinitely many solutions to this problem. Any number greater than zero can be the width.

Choice A results from incorrectly translating the word problem to $3x + 3 = 4x + 9 + x$ and then disregarding a negative sign. Choice B is the result of an incorrect translation of the length of the rectangle to $4(x + 9)$. Choice D results from not using the distributive property correctly when multiplying 3 and $(x + 3)$.

14. **Correct Response: D.** First set up an equation to solve this problem.

Let x = the number of quarters.
Then $2x - 9$ = the number of dimes.

The value in dollars of all the dimes is $.10(2x - 9)$ and the value in dollars of all the quarters is $.25x$.

So the equation is

$$.10(2x - 9) + .25x = 2.10$$

You can clear all the fractions by multiplying the entire equation by 100.

$$10(2x - 9) + 25x = 210$$
$$20x - 90 + 25x = 210$$
$$45x - 90 = 210$$
$$45x = 300$$
$$x = \frac{300}{45} = 6\frac{2}{3}$$

Since the number of coins must be a whole number, this answer is not possible. Therefore, there is no solution to this problem.

Choice A results from a subtraction error in calculating $210 - (^-90)$. Choice B results from failing to use the value of the coins in the equation. Choice C is an incorrect interpretation of the result.

Study Ideas

A careful study of the above exercises and the explanations of the answers will help you review important skills relating to solving word problems in one and two variables. In these exercises you were asked to solve word problems that can be translated into one-variable linear equations or systems of two-variable linear equations and to identify the equation or equations that correctly represent the mathematical relationships expressed in word problems. You were also presented with problems for which there are infinitely many solutions and problems for which there are no solutions. The most common word problems are problems that deal with distance-rate-time, interest, mixture-solution, and perimeter-area. You are likely to come upon similar problems in college, at home, and at work. This chapter's exercises are designed to give you practice in these skills. You may wish to reread parts of the chapter that address specific skills with which you have difficulty.

Chapter 16

UNDERSTAND OPERATIONS WITH ALGEBRAIC EXPRESSIONS AND FUNCTIONAL NOTATION

This skill includes factoring quadratics and polynomials; adding, subtracting, multiplying, and dividing polynomial expressions; performing basic operations on and simplifying rational and radical expressions; and applying basic principles of functions and functional notation.

Introduction

Algebra is an important part of mathematics. It is the branch of mathematics that deals with the manipulation of expressions and equations that contain variables. The ability to recognize and work with algebraic expressions and equations is a necessary part of the solution to many problems.

An important aspect of algebra is the study of functions and functional notation. The ability to recognize and evaluate functions and polynomial expressions is essential to the study of college-level mathematics. This chapter will focus on many fundamental operations with polynomial expressions.

Simplifying Polynomial Expressions

One of the most basic skills in algebra is the ability to simplify polynomial expressions. Simplifying a polynomial expression may seem like a difficult task, but if it is approached in a logical and orderly manner, it can become a simple and routine procedure. To simplify a polynomial expression, first remove any parentheses, next combine like terms, then rewrite the polynomial in descending order of exponents.

Removing parentheses. When removing parentheses, observe the following rules.

1. If no sign precedes a set of parentheses, remove the parentheses and maintain the signs of the terms enclosed.

   $(2x - 3) = {}^+2x - 3$

2. If a plus sign precedes a set of parentheses, remove the parentheses and maintain the signs of the terms enclosed.

   ${}^+(3 - 4x) = {}^+3 - 4x$

3. If a minus sign precedes a set of parentheses, remove the sign and the parentheses, then change the sign of each term enclosed.

   ${}^-(3 - 4x) = {}^-3 + 4x$

4. If a quantity precedes a set of parentheses, apply the distributive law. Multiply each term in the parentheses by the quantity that precedes the parentheses.

$^-3(5x - 3) = ^-15x + 9$

Make sure that when you multiply an expression by a negative term, you change the sign of every term in the expression.

Combining like terms. After removing parentheses, the next step in simplifying a polynomial expression is to combine *like terms*. Like terms are terms in which the variables have the same exponent. For instance, in the polynomial expression $4 + 5x^3 + 5x^2 - 3x^7 + 4x^3 + 2x^7 + 3$, the like terms are $5x^3$ and $4x^3$ since each contains an x^3, $^-3x^7$ and $2x^7$ since each contains an x^7, and 4 and 3 since each contains no x. Notice that $5x^3$ and $5x^2$ are not like terms. Though they have the same coefficients, they do not have the same exponent.

Simplify.
$(2 - 5x) + (x^2) - 4x + 11$

$2 - 5x + x^2 - 4x + 11$	*Remove the parentheses.*
$x^2 - 9x + 13$	*Combine like terms 2 and 11, ^-5x and ^-4x, and carry x^2 along.*

Simplify.
$(2 - 3x) - 4(x - 2)$

$^+2 - 3x - 4x + 8$	*Remove parentheses.*
$^-7x + 10$	*Combine like terms.*

Simplify.
$x^2 + 3(2 - x^2) - (3 - 2x)$

$x^2 + 6 - 3x^2 - 3 + 2x$	*Remove parentheses.*
$^-2x^2 + 2x + 3$	*Combine like terms. Notice that the final expression is written in descending order of exponents: x^2, x, no x.*

Multiplying Polynomial Expressions

To multiply polynomial expressions means to write a product as an equivalent sum in simplified form. After multiplying, all parentheses should be removed and like terms combined.

A Monomial Times a Polynomial

To multiply a monomial by a polynomial, use the distributive law:
$a(b + c) = (ab + ac)$. Multiply each term of the polynomial, in this case $(b + c)$, by the monomial a.

Multiply.
3(2x + 5y)

3(2x + 5y) = 6x + 15y   *Use the distributive law.*

Each term has been multiplied by the monomial 3.

(3)(2x) = 6x; (3)(5y) = 15y

Multiply.
2a(3b – 4c + d)

2a(3b – 4c + d) = 6ab – 8ac + 2ad   *Use the distributive law.*

Each term has been multiplied by the monomial 2a.

(2a)(3b) = 6ab; (2a)($^-$4c) = $^-$8ac; and (2a)(d) = 2ad

The Product of Two Binomials

Multiplying two binomials is one of the most common operations in algebra. There are several methods for performing this task. As these methods are discussed, remember that they all produce the same result.

Method 1. The Distributive Law: a(b + c) = ab + ac

Multiply.
(2x + 3y)(5x + 4y)

$$(2x + 3y)(5x + 4y) = (2x + 3y)5x + (2x + 3y)4y$$

$a = (2x + 3y)$
$b = 5x$
$c = 4y$

$$= 10x^2 + 15xy + (2x + 3y)4y$$

$a = 5x$
$b = 2x$
$c = 3y$

$$= 10x^2 + 15xy + 8xy + 12y^2$$

$a = 4y$
$b = 2x$
$c = 3y$

$$= 10x^2 + 23xy + 12y^2$$ *Combine like terms.*

In the first step, the distributive law was used with a = (2x + 3y), b = 5x, and c = 4y. In other words, treat the binomial (2x + 3y) as a single term. Then the law was used twice more: (2x + 3y)5x and (2x + 3y)4y. Finally, like terms were combined to produce the simplified form of the product.

Method 2. FOIL

A method commonly used to multiply two binomials is called FOIL. The F represents the product of the first terms; the O represents the product of the outside terms; the I represents the product of the inside terms; and the L represents the product of the last terms.

Multiply.
$(2x + 3y)(5x + 4y)$

FOIL	Which Terms	Result
(F) (F)	First terms	$(2x + \quad)$ $(5x + \quad)$ $= 10x^2$
(O) (O)	Outside terms	$(2x + \quad)$ $(\quad + 4y)$ $= 8xy$
(I) (I)	Inside terms	$(\quad + 3y)$ $(5x + \quad)$ $= 15xy$
(L) (L)	Last terms	$(\quad + 3y)$ $(\quad + 4y)$ $= 12y^2$
		$= 10x^2 + 23xy + 12y^2$

Again, you have to combine like terms ($8xy + 15xy$) for the final solution. This method is limited to binomials.

Method 3. The Vertical Arrangement

This technique for multiplying two binomials arranges the binomials in a vertical order. Then each term of the bottom factor is multiplied by each term of the top factor until all products are found. This method is especially helpful when multiplying polynomials larger than binomials together.

Multiply.
$(2x + 3y)(5x + 4y)$

$$\begin{array}{r} 2x + 3y \\ 5x + 4y \\ \hline 8xy + 12y^2 \\ 10x^2 + 15xy \\ \hline 10x^2 + 23xy + 12y^2 \end{array}$$

First, the factors are arranged vertically.
Then each term of (2x + 3y) is multiplied by 4y.

Each term of (2x + 3y) is multiplied by 5x.

The like terms are combined, leading to the final form of the product.

In studying these examples, note that the different methods produce the same result, $10x^2 + 23xy + 12y^2$.

The Sum of Two Terms
Times the Difference of the Same Two Terms

To multiply the sum of two terms by the difference of the same two terms, use the rule $(a + b)(a - b) = a^2 - b^2$. The product is called the difference of two squares.

Multiply.
$(2x + 3y)(2x - 3y)$

$(2x + 3y)(2x - 3y) = 4x^2 - 9y^2$

Applying the rule, $a = 2x$ and $b = 3y$;
therefore, $a^2 = (2x)^2 = 4x^2$, and $b^2 = (3y)^2 = 9y^2$.

Multiply.
$(5a + 7b)(5a - 7b)$

$(5a + 7b)(5a - 7b) = 25a^2 - 49b^2$

Applying the rule, $a = 5a$ and $b = 7b$; therefore, $a^2 = 25a^2$, and $b^2 = 49b^2$.

You can see why this rule works by using the FOIL method on the original multiplication:

$(a + b)(a - b) = a^2 - ab + ab - b^2 = a^2 - b^2$.

The Square of a Binomial

To square a binomial (an expression that has two terms), use the rule

$(a + b)^2 = a^2 + 2ab + b^2$

$(a - b)^2 = a^2 - 2ab + b^2$.

This is one of the most frequently misperformed operations in algebra. Remember that when you square a binomial (two terms) you will always get a trinomial (three terms).

Again, you can see why this rule works by using the FOIL method on the two original multiplications:

$(a + b)^2 = (a + b)(a + b) = a^2 + ab + ab + b^2 = a^2 + 2ab + b^2$

$(a - b)^2 = (a - b)(a - b) = a^2 - ab - ab + b^2 = a^2 - 2ab + b^2$

Multiply.
$(2x + 3)^2$

$(2x + 3)^2 = 4x^2 + 12x + 9$

Applying the rule, $a = 2x$ and $b = 3$; therefore, $a^2 = (2x)^2 = 4x^2$, $2ab = (2)(2x)(3) = 12x$, and $b^2 = (3)^2 = 9$.

Multiply.
$(x - 4y)^2$

$(x - 4y)^2 = x^2 - 8xy + 16y^2$

Applying the rule, $a = x$ and $b = {}^-4y$;
therefore, $a^2 = x^2$, $2ab = 2(x)({}^-4y) = {}^-8xy$, and $b^2 = 16y^2$.

Factoring

To factor an expression means to rewrite the expression as an equivalent product. It is the inverse operation of multiplication, which you have just completed. Usually when an expression is factored, each of the factors is in prime or the lowest form, meaning they cannot be reduced further. Your ability to factor depends on recognizing different forms of expressions and the products that lead to these forms.

The Common Factor

A common factor is a factor that can be found in each term of the expression. It may be a number, a variable, a binomial, or even a polynomial. The first step in factoring is to determine if there is a common factor.

The common factor in $3x + 6y$ is 3, since 3 is a factor of both $3x$ and $6y$.
　　Factoring $3x + 6y$, you get $3(x + 2y)$.

The common factor in $ax^2 - 3xy$ is x.
　　Factoring $ax^2 - 3xy$, you get $x(ax - 3y)$.

The common factor in $2x^2y + 8xy^2$ is $2xy$.
　　Factoring $2x^2y + 8xy^2$, you get $2xy(x + 4y)$.

The common factor in $3x(a + b) - 4y^2(a + b)$ is $a + b$.
Factoring $3x(a + b) - 4y^2(a + b)$, you get $(a + b)(3x - 4y^2)$.

Factor the polynomial 6ax + 10bx - 9ay - 15by.

$6ax + 10bx - 9ay - 15by$ does not have an obvious common factor. However, if you group the first two terms and the second two terms, you have the following.

$(6ax + 10bx) - (9ay + 15by)$

Factor each of these parentheses separately and you will have the following.

$2x(3a + 5b) - 3y(3a + 5b)$

Now there is an obvious common factor: $(3a + 5b)$.
$(3a + 5b)(2x - 3y)$ is the complete factorization of the polynomial
$6ax + 10bx - 9ay - 15by$.

The Difference of Two Squares

An expression of the form $a^2 - b^2$ is called the difference of two squares and is factored into the two factors $(a + b)$ and $(a - b)$.

The factors of $4x^2 - 9y^2$ are $(2x + 3y)(2x - 3y)$.

The factors of $16a^2 b^2 - 25c^2d^2$ are $(4ab + 5cd)(4ab - 5cd)$.

The factors of $x^2 - 81$ are $(x + 9)(x - 9)$.

The factors of $a^4 - 9$ are $(a^2 + 3)(a^2 - 3)$.

The factors of $(x + y)^2 - 36$ are $[(x + y) + 6][(x + y) - 6]$
or $(x + y + 6)(x + y - 6)$.

The Perfect Trinomial Square

An expression of the form $ax^2 \pm 2ab + b^2$ is called a perfect trinomial square and is factored into $(a \pm b)^2$. Note that the signs of the first and third terms, which must be perfect squares, are the same, yet the second term may be positive or negative. It is the sign of the second term that gives the factored binomial its sign.

The factors of $x^2 + 6x + 9$ are $(x + 3)^2$.

The factors of $4x^2 - 12xy + 9y^2$ are $(2x - 3y)^2$.

The factors of $2x^2 - 20x + 50$ are $2(x - 5)^2$.
NOTE: The common factor 2 was factored to make the expression
$2(x^2 - 10x + 25)$; then, $x^2 - 10x + 25$ factors into $(x - 5)^2$.

The factors of $x^2 - 6xy + 9y^2 - 16$ are $(x - 3y + 4)(x - 3y - 4)$.
This example is a combination of the perfect trinomial square and
the difference of two squares. To factor, you must first recognize that
$x^2 - 6xy + 9y^2$ is a perfect square. It can be factored into $(x - 3y)^2$; thus the
expression can be written $(x - 3y)^2 - 16$, which is the difference of two
squares.

The General Quadratic

An expression of the form $ax^2 + bx + c$ is called a quadratic expression and is factored, when possible, by one of two methods. The first method is trial and error, while the second method follows a set procedure.

Method 1. Trial and Error

Case 1: $ax^2 + bx + c$, where $a = 1$.

Factor $x^2 + bx + c$.

1. Since the two binomial factors must produce, when multiplied, a first term of x^2, each must begin with the term x.
   (x   )(x   )

2. The sign of each binomial depends on the sign of the constant term c. If c is positive, each binomial has the same sign. If c is negative, the binomials have different signs.
   When factored, $x^2 + bx + c$ takes the form (x +   ) (x +   ).
   When factored, $x^2 - bx + c$ takes the form (x -   ) (x -   ).
   When factored, $x^2 + bx - c$ takes the form (x +   ) (x -   ).
   When factored, $x^2 - bx - c$ takes the form (x +   ) (x -   ).

3. Now you must find two factors (f_1 and f_2) of c whose sum/difference is b ($f_1 \times f_2 = c$).
   When factored, $x^2 + bx + c$ takes the form $(x + f_1)(x + f_2)$, where $f_1 + f_2 = b$.
   When factored, $x^2 - bx + c$ takes the form $(x - f_1)(x - f_2)$, where $f_1 + f_2 = b$.
   When factored, $x^2 + bx - c$ takes the form $(x + f_1)(x - f_2)$, where $f_1 - f_2 = b$.
   When factored, $x^2 - bx - c$ takes the form $(x + f_1)(x - f_2)$, where $f_2 - f_1 = b$.

4. Check by multiplying your binomials and getting back your original expression, $x^2 + bx + c$.

Factor $x^2 - 6x + 8$.

1. Since $a = 1$, the binomials each have x as the first term.
   (x   )(x   )

2. Since $c = 8$, each binomial has the same sign, the sign of the middle term.
   (x -   )(x -   )

3. You now must find two factors of 8 whose sum is 6. These are 2 and 4; hence, the factorization is as follows.
   (x - 2)(x - 4)

4. Check: $(x - 2)(x - 4) = x^2 - 4x - 2x + 8 = x^2 - 6x + 8$

Factor $x^2 - 2x - 15$.

1. Since $a = 1$, the binomials each have x as the first term.
   (x   )(x   )

2. Since $c = {}^-15$, the binomials have different signs.
   (x +   )(x -   )

3. Now you need to find two factors of 15 whose difference is 2. These are 3 and 5. Since the sign of the middle term is minus, the larger factor, 5, is associated with the minus sign.

$$(x + 3)(x - 5)$$

4. Check: $(x + 3)(x - 5) = x^2 - 5x + 3x - 15 = x^2 - 2x - 15$

Case 2: $ax^2 + bx + c$, where $a \neq 1$.

Factor $ax^2 + bx + c$.

The sign rules for Case 1 still apply; however, you must also find factors of a and c such that the factors are in the form $(px \pm r)(qx \pm s)$, where $pq = a$, $rs = c$, and $ps + qr = b$.

1. $(px\quad)(qx\quad)$; $pq = a$

2. $(\quad r)(\quad s)$; $rs = c$

3. $(px\quad)(\quad s)$
4. $(\quad r)(qx\quad)$ $\Big\}$ $ps + qr = b$

To factor $6x^2 - 11x - 10$, you should start by using your sign rules. Since $c = {}^-10$, your binomials will have the form $(px + r)(qx - s)$.

You need to find factors of 6 and 10.

1. $(px\quad)(qx\quad)$; $pq = 6$

2. $(\quad + r)(\quad {}^-s)$; $rs = {}^-10$

3. $(px\quad)(\quad {}^-s)$
4. $(\quad + r)(qx\quad)$ $\Big\}$ $ps + qr = {}^-11$

The possibilities for $pq = 6$ are $p = 1$, $q = 6$; $p = 6$, $q = 1$; $p = 2$, $q = 3$; and $p = 3$, $q = 2$.

The possibilities for $rs = {}^-10$ are $r = 1$, $s = {}^-10$; $r = {}^-10$, $s = 1$; $r = 10$, $s = {}^-1$; $r = {}^-1$, $s = 10$; $r = 2$, $s = {}^-5$; $r = {}^-5$, $s = 2$; $r = 5$, $s = {}^-2$; and $r = {}^-2$, $s = 5$.

The factorization becomes $(3x + 2)(2x - 5)$.

Although this technique appears to be complicated, with practice it is generally the method of choice for most people. You have to substitute possible values until you find the right combination.

Method 2. A Factor Algorithm

To factor $ax^2 + bx + c$, follow these steps.

1. Multiply a and c.

2. Find two factors of ac whose sum is b. If you can do this, the expression can be factored; otherwise, it cannot be factored.

3. Replace b by this sum.

4. Remove the parentheses; there will now be four terms.

5. Group into two groups of two terms each.

6. Factor each group separately by taking out the common monomial factor. This must leave a common binomial factor.

7. Factor the common binomial factor.

8. Check the result.

Now factor $6x^2 - 11x - 10$, using the factor algorithm. Remember, a = 6, b = ‾11, and c = ‾10.

1. ac = (6)(‾10) = ‾60

2. Now you must find two factors of ‾60 whose sum is ‾11. A table may be helpful.

Factor	Factor	Sum
1	‾60	‾59
‾1	60	59
2	‾30	‾28
‾2	30	28
3	‾20	‾17
‾3	20	17
4	‾15	‾11
‾4	15	11

3. Replace ‾11 by the sum (4 − 15) or (‾15 + 4).
The expression now becomes $6x^2 + (4 - 15)x - 10$.

4. Remove the parentheses.
$6x^2 + (4 - 15)x - 10 = 6x^2 + 4x - 15x - 10$

5. Group into two groups of two terms each.
$6x^2 + 4x - 15x - 10 = (6x^2 + 4x) - (15x + 10)$
(NOTE: Be careful when grouping. When the first term is negative, you must change all the signs.)

6. Factor each group.
$(6x^2 + 4x) - (15x + 10) = 2x(3x + 2) - 5(3x + 2)$

7. Factor the common binomial factor.
$2x(3x + 2) - 5(3x + 2) = (3x + 2)(2x - 5)$

8. Check.
$(3x + 2)(2x - 5) = 6x^2 - 15x + 4x - 10 = 6x^2 - 11x - 10$

Remember, both methods, trial and error and algorithm, are correct; you need to find the one that works best for you.

The Sum and Difference of Two Cubes

An expression of the form $a^3 + b^3$ is called the sum of two cubes and is factored into $(a + b)(a^2 - ab + b^2)$. The expression $a^3 - b^3$ is called the difference of two cubes and is factored into $(a - b)(a^2 + ab + b^2)$. Note that both a^3 and b^3 must be perfect cubes.

The factors of $x^3 - 8$ are $(x - 2)(x^2 + 2x + 4)$.

The factors of $y^3 + 125$ are $(y + 5)(y^2 - 5y + 25)$.

Polynomial Long Division

You probably remember the long division process from arithmetic. Four steps were repeated over and over in that process, as illustrated in the following example.

1. Estimate how many times the divisor can be divided into an appropriate portion of the dividend. ($32 \div 26 = 1$)
2. Enter the estimate (1) on top and multiply.
3. Subtract. ($32 - 26 = 6$)
4. Bring down the next digit in the dividend.
5. Repeat until the remainder is less than the divisor.

$$\begin{array}{r} 12 \\ 26\overline{)327} \\ 26 \\ \hline 67 \\ 52 \\ \hline 15 \end{array}$$

Since the remainder, 15, is less than the divisor, 26, the division is finished. The answer (i.e., the quotient) can be expressed as 12 R15 or $12 + \frac{15}{26}$.

You can check the answer by multiplying the divisor by the quotient. The result should be the dividend:

$$26 \left(12 + \tfrac{15}{26}\right) = ?$$
$$(26)(12) + (26)\left(\tfrac{15}{26}\right) = ? \qquad \textit{Apply the distributive law.}$$
$$312 + 15 = 327 \qquad \textit{The result is correct.}$$

The long division process in algebra uses the same four steps, but first you must:

1. put the terms in the dividend and divisor in descending power order (e.g., x^4 before x^3 before x^2 before x);

2. put a placeholding term with a coefficient of zero into the dividend for any missing powers (e.g., if there is an x^3 term but no x^2 term, insert $0x^2$ in the dividend).

Consider the following example.

Divide: $(15x^2 + 13x - 7) \div (5x + 1)$

1. Set up as a long division problem.
    (There is no need to reorder terms or insert
    placeholding terms, since all terms in the dividend
    are present in correct order.)
2. Estimate. $(15x^2 \div 5x = 3x)$
3. Put the estimate on top and multiply $3x (5x + 1)$.
4. Subtract. (Remember to change the signs mentally.)
5. Bring down the next term and repeat: $(2)(5x + 1)$.

$$
\begin{array}{r}
3x + 2 \\
5x+1 \overline{)15x^2 + 13x - 7} \\
\underline{15x^2 + 3x} \\
10x - 7 \\
\underline{10x + 2} \\
-9
\end{array}
$$

Since the remainder (-9) is of lesser degree than the divisor, the division is
finished. The answer can be expressed as $3x + 2 + \frac{-9}{5x+1}$.

To check the division multiply the quotient and the divisor:

$(5x + 1)(3x + 2 + \frac{-9}{5x+1}) =$

$(5x + 1)(3x) + (5x + 1)(2) + (5x + 1)(\frac{-9}{5x+1}) =$ *Apply the distributive law.*

$15x^2 + 3x + 10x + 2 + (-9) =$ *Remove parentheses.*

$15x^2 + 13x - 7$ *Gather like terms.*

Since this result is the same as the dividend, the long division is accurate.

Divide: $(6x^3 - 15x + 18) \div (3x + 6)$

In this example the dividend is missing an x^2 term, and so a placeholding x^2 term
with a coefficient of zero must be added. Because the coefficient is zero, the
expression is essentially unchanged; the x^2 term simply makes the long division
easier.

$$
\begin{array}{r}
2x^2 - 4x + 3 \\
3x+6 \overline{)6x^3 + 0x^2 - 15x + 18} \\
\underline{6x^3 + 12x^2} \\
-12x^2 - 15x \\
\underline{-12x^2 - 24x} \\
9x + 18 \\
\underline{9x + 18} \\
0
\end{array}
$$

Estimate and multiply.
Subtract and bring down.
Estimate and multiply.
Subtract and bring down.
Estimate and multiply.
Subtract: no remainder.

To check this answer, we multiply the quotient and the divisor.

$(3x + 6)(2x^2 - 4x + 3) =$
$(3x + 6)(2x^2) + (3x + 6)(-4x) + (3x + 6)(3) =$ *Apply the distributive law.*
$6x^3 + 12x^2 - 12x^2 - 24x + 9x + 18 =$ *Remove parentheses.*
$6x^3 - 15x + 18$ *Gather like terms.*

The answer is correct: the result, $6x^3 - 15x + 18$, is the original dividend.

Simplifying Rational Expressions

Rational expressions are just fractions. Since arithmetic follows the structure of algebra, the rules for working with algebraic expressions are the same as those in arithmetic. You may want to refer to number concepts and computation skills to review operations with numerical fractions.

To add, use $\frac{a}{b} + \frac{c}{b} = \frac{a + c}{b}$, where $b \neq 0$.

To subtract, use $\frac{a}{b} - \frac{c}{b} = \frac{a - c}{b}$, where $b \neq 0$.

To multiply, use $\frac{a}{b} \times \frac{c}{d} = \frac{ac}{bd}$, where $b \neq 0$ and $d \neq 0$.

To divide, use $\frac{a}{b} \div \frac{c}{d} = \frac{a}{b} \times \frac{d}{c} = \frac{ad}{bc}$, where $b \neq 0$, $c \neq 0$, and $d \neq 0$.

When working with rational expressions, there are three things to keep in mind.

1. To add or subtract, you must have the same denominators. This is usually thought of as a least common denominator (LCD). Think of it as making the terms like terms.

2. Your answers are expected to be in simplest form—all like terms are to be combined, and the numerator and the denominator do not share any common factors other than one (1).

3. The denominator of a rational expression must not be zero.

Now look at some examples of rational expressions.

Perform the indicated operation.
$\frac{2}{a} + \frac{3}{a}$, where $a \neq 0$

$\frac{2}{a} + \frac{3}{a} = \frac{2 + 3}{a} = \frac{5}{a}$

Since each term has denominator a, and $a \neq 0$, this is a straightforward application of the rule for the addition of two fractions.

Perform the indicated operation.
$\frac{2}{a} + \frac{3}{b}$, where $a \neq 0$ and $b \neq 0$

$\frac{2}{a} + \frac{3}{b} = \frac{2b}{ab} + \frac{3a}{ab} = \frac{3a + 2b}{ab}$

Since the denominators are not the same, you must find the least common denominator. The LCD for a and b is ab. Each fraction is then written as an equivalent fraction with this denominator. Finally, the rule for addition is applied.

Perform the indicated operation.

$\dfrac{2}{x - 1} + \dfrac{3}{x + 1}$, where $x \neq 1$ and $x \neq {}^-1$

$\dfrac{2}{x - 1} + \dfrac{3}{x + 1} = \dfrac{2(x + 1)}{(x - 1)(x + 1)} + \dfrac{3(x - 1)}{(x - 1)(x + 1)}$ *LCD is $(x - 1)(x + 1)$.*

$= \dfrac{2(x + 1) + 3(x - 1)}{(x - 1)(x + 1)}$ *Addition.*

$= \dfrac{2x + 2 + 3x - 3}{(x - 1)(x + 1)}$ *Use distributive law.*

$= \dfrac{5x - 1}{(x - 1)(x + 1)} = \dfrac{5x - 1}{x^2 - 1}$ *Combine like terms and multiply.*

Since the denominators, $(x - 1)$ and $(x + 1)$, are not the same, you must find the LCD. The LCD for $(x - 1)$ and $(x + 1)$ is $(x - 1)(x + 1)$ or $x^2 - 1$. Each fraction is then written as an equivalent fraction with this denominator. The rule for addition is applied, and the expression is simplified.

Perform the indicated operation.

$\dfrac{2}{x - 1} \cdot \dfrac{3}{x + 2}$, where $x \neq 1$ and $x \neq {}^-2$

$\dfrac{2}{x - 1} \cdot \dfrac{3}{x + 2} = \dfrac{6}{x^2 + x - 2}$ $\dfrac{a}{b} \times \dfrac{c}{d} = \dfrac{ac}{bd}$

This is a direct application of the rule for multiplication of fractions. Six is the product of 2 and 3, and $x^2 + x - 2$ is the product of the denominators, $(x - 1)$ and $(x + 2)$.

Perform the indicated operation.

$\dfrac{2}{a^2} \div \dfrac{4}{a}$, where $a \neq 0$

$\dfrac{2}{a^2} \div \dfrac{4}{a} = \dfrac{2}{a^2} \times \dfrac{a}{4} = \dfrac{2a}{4a^2} = \dfrac{1}{2a}$

Since the operation is division ($\div$), you must multiply by the multiplicative inverse (reciprocal) of $\frac{4}{a}$, which is $\frac{a}{4}$. Then use the rules for multiplication, and simplify the result.

Reducing Rational Expressions

All fractions, including complex rational expressions, are usually easier to work with if they are in reduced form. To obtain the reduced form of a fraction:

1. factor the numerator and denominator completely;

2. divide out (i.e., cancel) like factors in the numerator and denominator. A factor in the numerator divides out with a like factor in the denominator.

Let's look at some examples.

Reduce:

$$\frac{4a^2b^3}{8a^5b}$$

$\dfrac{2 \cdot 2 \cdot a \cdot a \cdot b \cdot b \cdot b}{2 \cdot 2 \cdot 2 \cdot a \cdot a \cdot a \cdot a \cdot a \cdot b}$ *Factor.*

$\dfrac{\cancel{2} \cdot \cancel{2} \cdot \cancel{a} \cdot \cancel{a} \cdot b \cdot b \cdot \cancel{b}}{\cancel{2} \cdot \cancel{2} \cdot 2 \cdot \cancel{a} \cdot \cancel{a} \cdot a \cdot a \cdot a \cdot \cancel{b}}$ *Divide out like factors in the numerator and denominator.*

$\dfrac{b^2}{2a^3}$ *Recombine.*

Reduce:

$$\frac{2x^2-8}{4}$$

$\dfrac{2(x^2-4)}{2 \cdot 2}$ *Factor.*

$\dfrac{2(x+2)(x-2)}{2 \cdot 2}$ *Factor further.*

$\dfrac{\cancel{2}(x+2)(x-2)}{\cancel{2} \cdot 2}$ *Divide out.*

$\dfrac{(x+2)(x-2)}{2}$ *Reduced form.*

Reduce:

$$\frac{5x^2-10x+5}{x^2-1}$$

$\dfrac{5(x^2-2x+1)}{(x+1)(x-1)}$ *Factor.*

$\dfrac{5(x-1)(x-1)}{(x+1)(x-1)}$ *Factor further.*

$\dfrac{5(x-1)}{(x+1)}$ *Reduced form.*

Perform the indicated operation.

$$\frac{4x^3y^2}{7a^2b} \cdot \frac{21a^3}{12x^5a}$$

$\dfrac{84a^3x^3y^2}{84a^3x^5b}$ *Apply the rule $\dfrac{a}{b} \times \dfrac{c}{d} = \dfrac{ac}{bd}$*

$\dfrac{y^2}{x^2b}$ *Reduce.*

Perform the indicated operation.

$$\frac{4a^3b^2}{5} \cdot \frac{25a^4}{9a^6b^5}$$

$\dfrac{(4)(25)a^7b^2}{(5)(9)a^6b^5}$ *Apply the rule $\dfrac{a}{b} \times \dfrac{c}{d} = \dfrac{ac}{bd}$*

$\dfrac{20a}{9b^3}$ *Reduce.*

Radical Expressions

An exponent attached to a base indicates the number of times that the base is to be used as a factor. For example, x^2 indicates that x is to be used as a factor 2 times; that is, x^2 is the same as (x)(x). When the exponent is 2 the resulting expression is called a *perfect square*. There are two things that you should remember about perfect squares:

1. A perfect square is always a positive number or zero.

2. A perfect square is obtained by multiplying two identical factors.

Perfect Square Number

Whenever you take a number and square it you obtain a perfect square number. For example:

$$0^2 = 0 \qquad 1^2 = 1 \qquad 2^2 = 4 \qquad 3^2 = 9 \qquad (-6)^2 = 36 \qquad (\tfrac{1}{2})^2 = \tfrac{1}{4}$$

Therefore, the numbers 0, 1, 4, 9, 36, and $\tfrac{1}{4}$ above are perfect square numbers.

Examples:

Find: **1.** 2^2 **2.** 5^2 **3.** the square of 7 **4.** the square of $\tfrac{2}{5}$ **5.** $(0.5)^2$

Answers: 1. 4 **2.** 25 **3.** 49 **4.** $\tfrac{4}{25}$ **5.** 0.25

Perfect Square Literal Expressions

Any literal factor (i.e., a factor that is a letter rather than a number) that has an even exponent is a perfect square. For example, x^2 is a perfect square since its exponent is even and it has two identical factors: $(x)(x) = x^2$. Likewise, x^{26} is a perfect square since it has an even exponent and therefore two identical factors: $(x^{13})(x^{13}) = x^{26}$.

Determine which of the following are perfect squares.

1. x^6 **2.** A^5 **3.** y^7 **4.** x^{256}

Answers: Examples 1 and 4 are perfect squares since they are literal terms with even exponents.

Finding Square Roots of Perfect Square Expressions

The mathematical symbol $\sqrt{}$ is a *radical sign*. The number inside the radical sign is called a *radicand*. Often there is a small number sitting on top of the hook on the left side of the radical sign. This is called the *index*. In the radical expression $\sqrt[3]{x}$, x is the radicand and 3 is the index.

The index indicates the root to be extracted. When no index is present, it is assumed that the square root of the radicand is to be found.

To find square roots of expressions, use the following statement:

$$\sqrt{X} = Y \text{ if and only if } (Y)^2 = X$$

For example, to determine $\sqrt{4}$ you would think:

$$\sqrt{4} = (?) \text{ if and only if } (?)^2 = 4$$

and you would try to determine a value to use in place of the ? to make the statement true. In thinking about this, you would discover that:

$$\sqrt{4} = +2 \text{ since } (+2)^2 = 4 \quad \textbf{and} \quad \sqrt{4} = -2 \text{ since } (-2)^2 = 4.$$

This means that there are actually two square roots of 4: +2 and –2. The positive root, +2, is called the *major root,* while the negative root, –2, is called the *minor root.* Every time you consider a square root problem, remember that there could be two square roots of the expression.

To eliminate confusion about major and minor roots, it is accepted practice to use a sign in front of the radical sign to indicate which root is wanted. For example, $+\sqrt{4}$ means +2 while $-\sqrt{4}$ means –2. If no sign appears in front of the radical, it is usually assumed that the positive root is wanted.

It should be remembered that if the radicand is a negative value, there is no real number square root. Think about –36. You are trying to replace the ? with a number which makes the following true:

$$\sqrt{-36} = (?) \text{ if and only if } (?)^2 = -36$$

If you think about this, you will find that there is no number than can replace the ? and produce a true statement. As a result, we cannot take square roots of expressions with negative values in the real number system.

Examples:

Find the square root indicated.

     1. $\sqrt{25}$ 2. $-\sqrt{36}$ 3. $\sqrt{16x^2}$ 4. $\sqrt{81x^6y^2}$ 5. $-\sqrt{9x^4}$

Answers:

    1. $\sqrt{25}$ is 5 since $(5)^2 = 25$

    2. $-\sqrt{36}$ is –6 since $(-6)^2 = 36$

    3. $\sqrt{16x^2}$ is 4x since $(4x)^2 = 16x^2$

    4. $\sqrt{81x^6y^2}$ is $9x^3y$ since $(9x^3y)^2 = 81x^6y^2$

    5. $-\sqrt{9x^4}$ is $-3x^2$ since $(-3x^2)^2 = 9x^4$

Simplifying Radical Expressions Containing Non-Perfect Square Radicands

Often the square root radical expressions you are trying to simplify contain radicands that are not perfect squares. To simplify this type of radical expression:

1. find the largest perfect square factor of the radicand;

2. rewrite the radicand as a product of the perfect square factor and another factor;

3. take the square root of the perfect square factor, move it outside the radical sign, and express its product with the non-perfect square factor inside the radical sign.

A square root radical expression is in its simplest form only if there are no perfect square factors in the radicand.

Consider these examples.

Simplify:

$\sqrt{45}$

$\sqrt{(9)(5)}$ *Factor the radicand into a perfect square and a non-perfect square.*

$3\sqrt{5}$ *Take the square root of 9 and move it outside the radical sign.*

Thus $\sqrt{45}$ is the same as $3\sqrt{5}$.

Simplify:

$5\sqrt{18}$

$5\sqrt{(9)(2)}$ *Factor the radicand.*

$(5)(3)\sqrt{2}$ *Take the square root of 9 and move it outside.*

$15\sqrt{2}$ *Finish the simplification.*

Thus $5\sqrt{18} = 15\sqrt{2}$.

Simplify:

$A^2B\sqrt{A^4B^3}$

$A^2B\sqrt{A^4B^2B}$ *Rewrite to reveal perfect square in radicand.*

$(A^2B)(A^2B)\sqrt{B}$ *Take the square root of A^4B^2 and move it outside.*

$A^4B^2\sqrt{B}$ *Multiply.*

Thus $A^2B\sqrt{A^4B^3} = A^4B^2\sqrt{B}$.

Simplify:

$-7\sqrt{75}$

$-7\sqrt{(25)(3)}$ *Factor.*

$(-7)(5)\sqrt{3}$ *Take square root and move.*

$-35\sqrt{3}$

Thus $-7\sqrt{75} = -35\sqrt{3}$.

Simplify:

$-3x\sqrt{20x^6y^3}$

$-3x\sqrt{(4x^6y^2)(5y)}$ *Rewrite.*

$(-3x)(2x^3y)\sqrt{5y}$ *Take square root and move.*

$-6x^4y\sqrt{5y}$ *Multiply.*

Thus $-3x\sqrt{20x^6y^3} = -6x^4y\sqrt{5y}$.

Multiplication of Radical Expressions

This is the rule for multiplying radical expressions:

$$(a\sqrt{b})\,(c\sqrt{d}) = ac\sqrt{bd} \text{ when } b \geq 0 \text{ and } d \geq 0$$

In other words, the product is found by multiplying coefficients by coefficients and radicands by radicands, and then simplifying the result. Here are some examples.

Multiply: $(2\sqrt{3})\,(4\sqrt{7})$

Applying the rule above gives:

$(2)(4)\sqrt{(3)(7)} = 8\sqrt{21}$

Multiply: $(-3\sqrt{5})\,(2\sqrt{6})$

$(-3)(2)\sqrt{(5)(6)} = -6\sqrt{30}$

Multiply: $(-4x\sqrt{x})(3\sqrt{y})$

$(-4x)(3)\sqrt{xy} = -12x\sqrt{xy}$

Sometimes once you have completed the multiplication, it will be necessary to simplify the radicand by removing any perfect square factors in it.

Multiply: $(2\sqrt{6})(3\sqrt{15})$

This produces $6\sqrt{90}$.

Now the radicand must be simplified:

$6\sqrt{(9)(10)}$ *Factor the radicand.*

$(6)(3)\sqrt{10}$ *Take square root and move.*

$18\sqrt{10}$ is the result.

Multiply: $(4\sqrt{5x})(-3\sqrt{15x^3y})$

$-12\sqrt{75x^4y}$ *Apply the multiplication rule.*

$(-12)\sqrt{(25x^4)(3y)}$ *Factor the radicand.*

$(-12)(5x^2)\sqrt{3y}$ *Take square root and move.*

$-60x^2\sqrt{3y}$ is the result.

To simplify radical expressions whose radicands are fractions, you apply the property:

$$\sqrt{\frac{a}{b}} = \frac{\sqrt{a}}{\sqrt{b}} \quad \begin{array}{l} a \geq 0 \\ b > 0 \end{array}$$

In other words, take the square root of the numerator and the square root of the denominator separately.

Simplify: $\sqrt{\dfrac{9}{16}}$

This becomes $\dfrac{\sqrt{9}}{\sqrt{16}}$ or $\dfrac{3}{4}$.

Simplify: $-\sqrt{\dfrac{25x^2}{36y^4}}$

This becomes $-\dfrac{\sqrt{25x^2}}{\sqrt{36y^4}}$ or $-\dfrac{5x}{6y^2}$.

Addition and Subtraction of Radical Expressions

Like Radicals

To add or subtract radical expressions you must first determine if the radical expressions are considered "like" or "unlike." Square root radical expressions are considered "like" expressions if their radicands are the same. If they are the same, then addition and subtraction are easy.

In the radical expressions $5\sqrt{2}$ and $-6\sqrt{2}$, the radicands are the same; they are therefore like radicals. On the other hand, the expressions $-3\sqrt{3}$ and $4\sqrt{2}$ are unlike radicals because their radicands are different.

Before determining if radical expressions are like or unlike, be sure to simplify each expression to simplest form. For example, in first looking at $2\sqrt{3}$ and $-5\sqrt{27}$, you might think that they are not like radicals since $3 \neq 27$, but if you simplify the second radical, you will come to a different conclusion.

$$-5\sqrt{27} \;\; = -5\sqrt{(9)(3)}$$

$$= (-5)(3)\sqrt{3}$$

$$= -15\sqrt{3}$$

The simplified versions of both radical expressions have the same radicand; they are therefore like radicals.

Determine if the following radical expressions are like or unlike:

1. $\sqrt{15}$ and $\sqrt{30}$ They are unlike since the radicands are simplified and unequal.

2. $\sqrt{4x^3}$ and $\sqrt{8x^5}$ Simplify to obtain $2x\sqrt{x}$ and $2x^2\sqrt{2x}$. Since the radicands are not equal, the radicals are unlike and cannot be combined.

3. $\sqrt{45xy^2}$ and $\sqrt{20x^3}$ Simplify and obtain $3y\sqrt{5x}$ and $2x\sqrt{5x}$. Since the radicands are the same, these are like radicals.

Adding and Subtracting Radical Expressions

Use the following property to add and subtract radical expressions:

$(a\sqrt{b}) + (c\sqrt{b}) = (a+c)\sqrt{b}$ and $(a\sqrt{b}) - (c\sqrt{b}) = (a-c)\sqrt{b}$ where $b \geq 0$.

Adding and subtracting radical expressions is sometimes referred to as combining radical expressions. Only like radicals can be combined. To combine like radicals, you merely combine (add or subtract) their coefficients.

Combine: $2\sqrt{3} + 5\sqrt{3}$

Since the radicands are equal, we merely add their coefficients.

$(2+5)\sqrt{3}$

$7\sqrt{3}$

Combine: $5\sqrt{2x} - 7\sqrt{2x}$

Since the radicands are equal, we combine their coefficients.

$(5-7)\sqrt{2x}$

$-2\sqrt{2x}$

Combine: $2\sqrt{8} - 5\sqrt{18}$

In this case, the radicands are unequal, so we must first simplify each radical expression.

$$2\sqrt{(4)(2)} - 5\sqrt{(9)(2)}$$
$$(2)(2)\sqrt{2} - (5)(3)\sqrt{2}$$
$$4\sqrt{2} - 15\sqrt{2}$$

Because the radicands are now the same, these are like radicals that can be combined.

$$(4 - 15)\sqrt{2}$$
$$-11\sqrt{2}$$

Exponential Notation for Square Roots

In addition to the radical sign, an alternative notation for indicating a square root radical is a fractional exponent. The use of an exponent of $\frac{1}{2}$ is the same as the use of the radical symbol.

$$\sqrt{x} = x^{\frac{1}{2}} \text{ when } x \geq 0.$$

When you must evaluate an expression with an exponent of $\frac{1}{2}$, it is easiest to rewrite the expression in radical form and then, using the properties for radicals, to simplify the expression.

Simplify: $(25)^{\frac{1}{2}}$

In radical form, this is $\sqrt{25}$, or 5.

Simplify: $-(72x^3)^{\frac{1}{2}}$

In radical form, this is $-\sqrt{72x^3}$. It can be simplified to $-\sqrt{36x^2 2x}$, or in the simplest terms $-6x\sqrt{2x}$.

Simplify: $(-36)^{\frac{1}{2}}$

In radical form, this is $\sqrt{-36}$. This expression cannot be simplified since the radicand is a negative number. As you recall, the radicand for square root radical expressions cannot be a negative number.

Functional Notation

Polynomials are sometimes expressed in the form $P(x) = x^2 + 7x - 2$. This form is sometimes referred to as *functional notation*. In this form, $P(x)$ identifies the name of the polynomial, P, and the name of the variable under consideration, x.

In the expression $G(y) = 2y - 5$, the name of the polynomial is G, the variable is y, and the polynomial expression is (2y–5).

This form of notation is useful for evaluating expressions for specific numerical values of the variable. For example, to find the value of P above when x assumes the value 2, you merely replace the x with the number 2 on both sides of the equal sign and then simplify the right side.

Evaluate: $P(x) = x^2 + 7x - 2$ for $P(2)$

$P(2) = 2^2 + 7(2) - 2$ *Replace each x term with the number 2.*

$P(2) = 4 + 14 - 2$ *Simplify.*

$P(2) = 16$

Evaluate: $G(a) = \sqrt{a^2 + 25}$ for $G(0)$

$G(0) = \sqrt{0^2 + 25}$ *Replace each a term with the value 0.*

$G(0) = \sqrt{25}$ *Simplify.*

$G(0) = 5$

Functional notation can also be used to indicate operations to perform on the values of polynomial expressions.

Find $P(-2) - P(1)$ if $P(x) = \dfrac{|x|}{5}$

First find $P(-2) = \dfrac{|-2|}{5}$ and $P(1) = \dfrac{|1|}{5}$.

Thus $P(-2) = \dfrac{2}{5}$ and $P(1) = \dfrac{1}{5}$

Therefore, $P(-2) - P(1) = \dfrac{2}{5} - \dfrac{1}{5}$ or $P(-2) - P(1) = \dfrac{1}{5}$

Practice Exercises

The following exercises will help you review the skills covered in this chapter. Many of the types of questions presented here will be similar to those on the test; others will not. Remember that the purpose of the exercises is to give you practice on the skills rather than merely to prepare you for the test. Following these exercises are the Practice Exercise Explanations. They explain each question, the correct answer, and why the remaining choices are incorrect.

1. Which of the following is a factor of $x^2 + x - 6$?

    A. $(x - 3)$

    B. $(x - 2)$

    C. $(x + 2)$

    D. $(x - 6)$

2. Which of the following is a factor of $x^2 - 16$?

    A. $(x + 16)$

    B. $(x - 1)$

    C. $(x + 4)$

    D. $(x - 16)$

3. Which of the following is a factor of $6x^2 + 7x - 20$?

    A. $(6x - 20)$

    B. $(3x + 4)$

    C. $(2x - 5)$

    D. $(3x - 4)$

4. Which of the following is a factor of $x^2 - 10x + 16$?

    A. $(x - 2)$

    B. $(x + 4)$

    C. $(x - 4)$

    D. $(x + 8)$

5. Which of the following is a factor of $9 - x^2 + 4xy - 4y^2$?

    A. $(3 - x - 2y)$

    B. $(3 - x + 2y)$

    C. $(3 + x + 2y)$

    D. $(3 - x + 4y)$

6. Subtract: $(5 - 2x) - (x^2 - 6x - 4) =$

    A. $^-x^2 - 8x + 1$

    B. $3x^3 + 9$

    C. $^-x^2 + 4x + 9$

    D. $x^2 + 4x + 9$

7. Which polynomial added to $x - 2(x + 3)$ yields the sum $x^2 - 5x - 5$?

    A. $^-6x + 1$

    B. $x^2 - 4x - 8$

    C. $x^2 - 8x - 2$

    D. $x^2 - 4x + 1$

8. $(3a + 2)(5a - 4) =$

    A. $15a^2 - 2a - 8$

    B. $15a^2 - 8$

    C. $15a^2 + 2a - 8$

    D. $15a^2 - 22a - 8$

9. $(x^2 - 6x + 5)(x^2 - 3x - 1) =$

    A. $x^4 + 18x^2 - 5$

    B. $x^4 - 9x^3 + 23x^2 - 21x + 5$

    C. $x^4 - 9x^3 + 22x^2 - 9x - 5$

    D. $x^4 - 3x^3 + 22x^2 - 21x - 5$

10. $\dfrac{2}{x - 7} + \dfrac{5}{x - 7} =$

    A. $\dfrac{7}{2x - 14}$

    B. $\dfrac{7}{x - 7}$

    C. $\dfrac{1}{x - 1}$

    D. $\dfrac{1}{x}$

11. $\dfrac{2}{x + 1} + \dfrac{x}{x - 2} =$

    A. $\dfrac{2 + x}{(x + 1) + (x - 2)}$

    B. $\dfrac{2 + x}{x^2 - x - 2}$

    C. $\dfrac{2x}{x^2 - x - 1}$

    D. $\dfrac{(x + 4)(x - 1)}{x^2 - x - 2}$

12. Multiply: $\dfrac{x - 1}{3} \cdot \dfrac{6}{x^2 - 1}$

    A. $\dfrac{(x - 1)^2 (x + 1)}{18}$

    B. $\dfrac{2}{x + 1}$

    C. $\dfrac{2}{x - 1}$

    D. $\dfrac{2}{x}$

13. $\dfrac{x^2 - x - 2}{x^2 + x - 6} \div \dfrac{x + 1}{x + 3} =$

   A.   1

   B. $\dfrac{x + 3}{x - 3}$

   C. $\dfrac{x + 2}{x - 2}$

   D. $\dfrac{(x + 1)^2}{(x + 3)^2}$

14.   Square: $(2y - 6)$

   A. $4y^2 + 36$

   B. $2y^2 - 12y - 36$

   C. $2y^2 - 36$

   D. $4y^2 - 24y + 36$

15.   Perform the indicated operation.

   $\dfrac{6a^3b^2}{3b^3} \bullet \dfrac{8a^3b^2}{14a^8}$

   A. $\dfrac{8ab}{7}$

   B. $\dfrac{b}{3a^2}$

   C. $\dfrac{8b}{7a^2}$

   D. $\dfrac{8}{7a^5b}$

16.   Reduce: $\dfrac{8x^2 - 24x - 32}{2x^2 - 4x - 6}$

   A. $\dfrac{4(x - 4)}{x - 3}$

   B. $\dfrac{8(x + 4)}{2x + 6}$

   C. $\dfrac{4(x - 4)}{x - 6}$

   D. $\dfrac{8(x - 2)}{2x - 3}$

17.   Determine the quotient.

   $(16x^2 + 12x - 7) \div (4x + 1)$

   A. $4x + 4 + \dfrac{-3}{4x+1}$

   B. $4x + 2 + \dfrac{-9}{4x+1}$

   C. $4x + 2 + \dfrac{-5}{4x+1}$

   D. $4x + 3 + \dfrac{-10}{4x+1}$

18.   Simplify: $\sqrt{216}$

   A. $6\sqrt{5}$

   B. $6\sqrt{6}$

   C. $12\sqrt{18}$

   D. $36\sqrt{6}$

19. Perform the indicated operation.

$\sqrt{15} \cdot \sqrt{6}$

A. $6\sqrt{5}$

B. $9\sqrt{10}$

C. $10\sqrt{3}$

D. $3\sqrt{10}$

20. Perform the indicated operation.

$-2\sqrt{27x^2} + 3\sqrt{12x^2}$

A. 0

B. $-6x\sqrt{3}$

C. $12x\sqrt{3}$

D. $x\sqrt{39}$

21. Evaluate $f(x) = 3x^2 - 5x + 6$
     for $f(2) - f(5)$.

A. -48

B. 48

C. 64

D. 174

22. Rewrite in simplest radical form.

$(x^2y^4)^{\frac{1}{2}}$

A. x^2y^2

B. $\sqrt{\dfrac{xy^2}{2}}$

C. xy^2

D. x^4y^8

Practice Exercise Explanations

1. **Correct Response: B.** Since this expression has the form $ax^2 + bx + c$, and $a = 1$, the trial-and-error method can be used.

   1. Each binomial must start with x as its first term.
      $(x\ \ )(x\ \ )$

   2. Since $c = ^-6$, the signs in the binomials must be opposite.
      $(x -\ )(x +\ )$

   3. Now you must find two factors of 6 whose difference is 1. The possible integer factors of 6 are 1 and 6, and 2 and 3. The pair that satisfies the condition of a difference of 1 is 2 and 3; hence, the factorization is as follows.
      $(x - 2)(x + 3)$

   Choices A and C are incorrect because of the wrong placement of the signs. Choice D would have to use the factors 1 and 6. Another correct response, not given, would be $(x + 3)$.

2. **Correct Response: C.** Since this expression has the form $a^2 - b^2$ (the difference of two squares), the rule to use is $a^2 - b^2 = (a + b)(a - b)$, where $a = x$ and $b = 4$. Therefore, the factorization is $x^2 - 16 = (x + 4)(x - 4)$.

   The incorrect choices A, B, and D are all the result of not taking the square root of 16. Another correct response would be $(x - 4)$. Note that when you have the difference or the sum of two squares, the factors must involve the square roots of the a and the b terms (here, 4 is a square root of 16).

3. **Correct Response: D.** Since this expression has the form $ax^2 + bx + c$, where $a \neq 1$, the factor algorithm method should be used.

   1. $(a \times c) = (6)(^-20) = ^-120$

   2. You need to find two factors of $^-120$ whose sum is 7. They are 15 and $^-8$. Draw a table if you have trouble finding these factors.

   3. Replace b with these factors as a sum.
      $6x^2 + 7x - 20 = 6x^2 + (15 - 8)x - 20$

   4. Remove parentheses.
      $6x^2 + (15 - 8)x - 20 = 6x^2 + 15x - 8x - 20$

   5. Group into two groups of two terms each.
      $6x^2 + 15x - 8x - 20 = (6x^2 + 15x) - (8x + 20)$

   6. Factor each group.
      $(6x^2 + 15x) - (8x + 20) = 3x(2x + 5) - 4(2x + 5)$

   7. Factor the common binomial factor.
      $3x(2x + 5) - 4(2x + 5) = (2x + 5)(3x - 4)$

   8. Check.
      $(2x + 5)(3x - 4) = 6x^2 - 8x + 15x - 20 = 6x^2 + 7x - 20$

   Choice A results from using the coefficient of x^2 and the constant term, $^-20$, as a set of factors. Note that the original expression does not have a common monomial factor, yet $6x - 20$ has the common factor 2. Therefore, choice A could not be the correct answer. Choices B and C are the result of using the wrong signs with the factorization. Another correct answer would be $(2x + 5)$.

4. **Correct Response: A.** Since this expression has the form $ax^2 + bx + c$, where $a = 1$, the trial-and-error method can be used.

    1. Each binomial must start with x as its first term.
        $$(x \quad)(x \quad)$$

    2. Since $c = {}^+16$, the signs in the two binomials must be the same as the sign of b. Since $b = {}^-10$, the signs must be negative.
        $$(x - \quad)(x - \quad)$$

    3. Now you must find two factors of 16 that have a sum of 10. The possible integer factors of 16 are 1 and 16, 2 and 8, and 4 and 4. The pair that satisfies the condition of a sum of 10 is 2 and 8; therefore, the factorization is as follows.
        $$x^2 - 10x + 16 = (x - 2)(x - 8)$$

    Incorrect choices B and C are included since many students recognize that 16 is a perfect square and factor it as a perfect square. However, $(x + 4)^2 = x^2 + 8x + 16$ and $(x - 4)^2 = x^2 - 8x + 16$, which are both incorrect factorizations. Choice D results from using the wrong sign with the factorization. Another correct answer would be $(x - 8)$.

5. **Correct Response: B.** To solve this problem, you must recognize that when grouped together the last three terms represent a perfect trinomial square and can be factored by the rule $a^2 - 2ab - b^2 = (a - b)^2$. The resulting expression takes on the form of the difference of two squares and can be factored by the rule $a^2 - b^2 = (a + b)(a - b)$. The solution when written out is as follows.

    $$9 - x^2 + 4xy - 4y^2$$
    $$= 9 - (x^2 - 4xy + 4y^2)$$
    $$= 9 - (x - 2y)^2$$
    $$= [3 + (x - 2y)][3 - (x - 2y)]$$
    $$= (3 + x - 2y)(3 - x + 2y)$$

    Choice A is the result of not distributing the minus sign correctly in the last step. Choice C may be the result of either not factoring the perfect square correctly or not distributing the minus sign properly in the last step. Choice D is the result of incorrectly factoring the perfect square. Another correct answer would be $(3 + x - 2y)$.

6. **Correct Response: C.** To subtract, or simplify, first remove parentheses and then combine like terms.

    $$(5 - 2x) - (x^2 - 6x - 4)$$
    $$= 5 - 2x - x^2 + 6x + 4 \qquad \textit{Remember to change signs.}$$
    $$= {}^-x^2 + 4x + 9$$

    Incorrect choices A and D result from incorrect distributions of the minus sign over the last polynomial $x^2 - 6x - 4$. Choice B results from combining the unlike terms ${}^-2x$, ${}^-x^2$, and $6x$ and adding exponents to get an x^3 term.

7. **Correct Response: D.** To find the answer, you need to subtract $x - 2(x + 3)$ from the sum $x^2 - 5x - 5$. First, simplify $x - 2(x + 3)$.

$x - 2(x + 3)$
$= x - 2x - 6$
$= {}^-x - 6$
$(x^2 - 5x - 5) - ({}^-x - 6) = x^2 - 5x - 5 + x + 6 = x^2 - 4x + 1$

Incorrect choice A is the result of distributing $(x - 2)$ over $(x + 3)$. Choices B and C result from different incorrect distributions of the negative sign over the second term $^-2(x + 3)$.

8. **Correct Response: A.** This problem involves the multiplication of two binomials. One method of finding this product is as follows.

$(3a + 2)(5a - 4) = (3a + 2)5a - (3a + 2)4$
$= 15a^2 + 10a - 12a - 8$
$= 15a^2 - 2a - 8$

You could also use FOIL—multiplying first, outside, inside, and last terms.

Choice B results from multiplying the first terms together and the last terms together and then combining them as the product. This is the most common error when multiplying two binomials. Choice C is the result of combining 10a and ^-12a and getting 2a instead of ^-2a, while choice D results from combining 10a and ^-12a and getting ^-22a.

9. **Correct Response: C.** This exercise involves the multiplication of two trinomials. The vertical arrangement method should be used.

$$\begin{array}{r} x^2 - 6x + 5 \\ x^2 - 3x - 1 \\ \hline {}^-x^2 + 6x - 5 \\ {}^-3x^3 + 18x^2 - 15x \\ x^4 - 6x^3 + 5x^2 \\ \hline x^4 - 9x^3 + 22x^2 - 9x - 5 \end{array}$$

Choice A results from multiplying the first terms, the second terms, and the third terms together and then combining them as the product. Choice B is the result of *not* combining $^-x^2$ with $5x^2$ and $18x^2$. This is a very common error. In the expressions x^2 and $^-x^2$, the coefficients are $^+1$ and $^-1$, respectively. Choice D is the result of incorrectly subtracting $^-3x^3$ from $^-6x^3$ to get $^-3x^3$ and incorrectly multiplying ^-6x by $^-1$ to get ^-6x.

10. **Correct Response: B.** This problem involves the addition of two rational expressions (fractions) having the same denominators. To solve, add the numerators and carry over the common denominator.

$$\frac{2}{x - 7} + \frac{5}{x - 7} = \frac{2 + 5}{x - 7} = \frac{7}{x - 7}$$

Choice A adds the numerators and adds the denominators. Choices C and D are both incorrect simplifications.

11. **Correct Response: D.** This problem involves the addition of two rational expressions that have different denominators. First, find the least common denominator. Change each term into an equivalent term with this denominator. Add the numerators while carrying over the denominators, and simplify.

The LCD for $(x + 1)$ and $(x - 2)$ is $(x + 1)(x - 2)$.

$$\frac{2}{x + 1} + \frac{x}{x - 2}$$

$$= \frac{2}{x + 1} \cdot \frac{x - 2}{x - 2} + \frac{x}{x - 2} \cdot \frac{x + 1}{x + 1}$$

$$= \frac{2(x - 2)}{(x + 1)(x - 2)} + \frac{x(x + 1)}{(x - 2)(x + 1)}$$

$$= \frac{2(x - 2) + x(x + 1)}{(x + 1)(x - 2)}$$

$$= \frac{2x - 4 + x^2 + x}{(x + 1)(x - 2)}$$

$$= \frac{x^2 + 3x - 4}{(x + 1)(x - 2)} = \frac{(x + 4)(x - 1)}{x^2 - x - 2}$$

$$= \frac{x^2 + 3x - 4}{x^2 - x - 2} = \frac{(x + 4)(x - 1)}{(x + 1)(x - 2)}$$

all equivalent forms

Choice A results from adding the numerators and the denominators. Choice B results from adding the numerators and multiplying the denominators. Choice C results from multiplying the two fractions.

12. **Correct Response: B.** This problem involves the multiplication of two rational expressions. To solve, multiply the numerators and the denominators, and then simplify.

$$\frac{x - 1}{3} \cdot \frac{6}{x^2 - 1} = \frac{6(x - 1)}{3(x - 1)(x + 1)} = \frac{2}{x + 1}$$

You have to remember to factor $(x^2 - 1)$.

Choice A results from dividing rather than multiplying. Choice C results from incorrectly factoring $x^2 - 1$ as $(x - 1)^2$. Choice D results from incorrectly simplifying $\frac{x - 1}{x^2 - 1}$ into $\frac{1}{x}$.

13. **Correct Response: A.** This problem involves the division of two rational expressions. The first step is to find the reciprocal (multiplicative inverse) of $\frac{x + 1}{x + 3}$, which is $\frac{x + 3}{x + 1}$. Now use the rules of multiplication to solve.

$$\frac{x^2 - x - 2}{x^2 + x - 6} \div \frac{x + 1}{x + 3}$$

$$= \frac{x^2 - x - 2}{x^2 + x - 6} \cdot \frac{x + 3}{x + 1}$$

$$= \frac{(x + 1)(x - 2)(x + 3)}{(x - 2)(x + 3)(x + 1)} = 1$$

Factor the two expressions $(x^2 - x - 2)$ and $(x^2 + x - 6)$.

Choices B and C both result from incorrect factorization. Choice D results from multiplying rather than dividing the two expressions.

14. **Correct Response: D.** This problem involves squaring a binomial.

$(2y - 6)^2$
$= (2y - 6)(2y - 6)$
$= 4y^2 - 12y - 12y + 36$
$= 4y^2 - 24y + 36$

Choice A results from taking the square of each term in the parentheses. Choices B and C result from errors in multiplication, and use the wrong sign for the last term.

15. **Correct Response: C.** Applying the rule $\frac{a}{b} \cdot \frac{c}{d} = \frac{ac}{bd}$ produces the result $\frac{48a^6b^4}{42a^8b^3}$, which reduces to $\frac{8b}{7a^2}$. Response A is the result of multiplying the exponents in the numerator instead of adding them to find the product. Response B is the result of adding the coefficients in the numerator instead of dividing them. In Response D, the coefficients are correctly multiplied, but the other terms in the numerator are not multiplied, a common error when such terms are identical.

16. **Correct Response: A.** This question involves factoring and reducing. The correct process is as follows.

$$\frac{8x^2 - 24x - 32}{2x^2 - 4x - 6} = \frac{8(x^2 - 3x - 4)}{2(x^2 - 2x - 3)}$$

$$= \frac{4(x-4)(x+1)}{(x-3)(x+1)}$$

$$= \frac{4(x-4)}{x-3}$$

Response C results from incorrectly factoring the denominator, and Responses B and D result from incorrectly factoring both the numerator and the denominator.

17. **Correct Response: B.** This question involves polynomial long division. The correct process is as follows.

$$\begin{array}{r}
4x + 2 + \frac{-9}{4x+1} \\
4x+1\overline{)16x^2 + 12x - 7} \\
\underline{16x^2 + 4x} \\
8x - 7 \\
\underline{8x + 2} \\
-9
\end{array}$$

Response A results from incorrectly subtracting in both steps. Response C results from incorrectly subtracting in the second step. Response D is the result of incorrectly multiplying the divisor in the first step and using 12x instead of 8x in the second step.

18. **Correct Response: B.** If $\sqrt{216}$ is factored correctly into $\sqrt{2 \cdot 2 \cdot 2 \cdot 3 \cdot 3 \cdot 3}$ and then regrouped into $\sqrt{(2 \cdot 2)(3 \cdot 3)(3 \cdot 2)}$, the result of $2 \cdot 3\sqrt{3 \cdot 2}$ is apparent, which simplifies to $6\sqrt{6}$. Response A results from adding the two factors left within the radical sign. Responses C and D are the results of grouping incorrectly and inappropriately moving a factor outside the radical sign without taking the square root.

19. **Correct Response: D.** The first step in solving this problem is to multiply the two radicals to produce $\sqrt{90}$. Then this result is factored into $\sqrt{9 \cdot 10}$ and the perfect square factor is moved outside the radical sign after its square root is calculated. Thus $\sqrt{9 \cdot 10}$ becomes $3\sqrt{10}$. Response A results from incorrectly factoring $\sqrt{90}$. Response B moves the perfect square factor outside the radical sign without taking its square root, and Response C moves the wrong factor outside while finding the square root of the factor left inside the radical sign.

20. **Correct Response: A.** To add two radical expressions it is first necessary to find out if they are like radicals. The radical expressions must be factored.

$$-2\sqrt{27x^2} + 3\sqrt{12x^2} = -2\sqrt{9 \cdot 3x^2} + 3\sqrt{3 \cdot 4x^2}$$

$$= (-2)(3)x\sqrt{3} + (3)(2)x\sqrt{3}$$

$$= -6x\sqrt{3} + 6x\sqrt{3}$$

Since these two expressions are like radicals (i.e., they have identical radicands), they can be added by adding their coefficients. This produces $0\sqrt{3}$, which is 0. Response B results from moving 9 and 4 outside the radical without taking their square roots. Response C results from a sign error. Response D attempts to add coefficients and radicands without achieving like radicals.

21. **Correct Response: A.** To evaluate this expression, first substitute 2 for x in the expression, then 5 for x, and then subtract the two resulting values, as follows.

f(2) $= 3(2)^2 - 5(2) + 6$
$= 12 - 10 + 6$
$= 8$

f(5) $= 3(5)^2 - 5(5) + 6$
$= 75 - 25 + 6$
$= 56$

Finally $8 - 56 = {}^-48$

Response B results from subtracting 56 – 8 (i.e., f(5) – f(2)). Response C results from adding 56 + 8. Response D is the result of using $(3 \cdot 2)^2$ and $(3 \cdot 5)^2$ instead of $3 \cdot 2^2$ and $3 \cdot 5^2$ in the evaluation of the expressions.

22.   **Correct Response: C.** The exponent "$\frac{1}{2}$" is a fractional exponent indicating square root. $x^{\frac{1}{2}} = \sqrt{x}$; therefore $(x^2y^4)^{\frac{1}{2}} = \sqrt{x^2y^4} = xy^2$. Response A results from applying the exponent to y^4 but not to x^2. Response B is a misinterpretation of the meaning of the exponent. Response D inappropriately doubles each exponent.

Study Ideas

A careful study of the above exercises and the explanations of the answers will help you review important skills relating to operations with algebraic expressions. In these exercises, you were asked to factor quadratics and polynomials; to add, subtract, multiply, and divide polynomial expressions; and to perform basic operations on and simplify rational and radical expressions. The exercises are designed to give you practice in these skills. You may wish to reread parts of the chapter that address specific skills with which you have difficulty.

You should be aware of these algebraic concepts for your work in college. You may choose to consult an algebra textbook for more detailed explanations of these topics.

Chapter 17

SOLVE PROBLEMS INVOLVING QUADRATIC EQUATIONS

This skill includes graphing quadratic equations and inequalities, solving word problems involving quadratics, identifying the algebraic equivalent of stated relationships, and solving quadratic equations and inequalities.

Introduction

Mathematics uses a number of special types of equations to solve problems. One important type of equation that is commonly used in math problems is the quadratic equation. Any equation that can be written in the form $ax^2 + bx + c = 0$ is called a quadratic equation. When a quadratic equation is written in the form $ax^2 + bx + c = 0$, it is said to be in standard form. (NOTE: For a quadratic equation to be in *standard form,* one side of the equation must be zero.) In this equation format, the letters a, b, and c represent numbers, and the letter x represents a variable (i.e., an unknown). Notice that this type of equation always contains a term that is squared (e.g., x^2).

This chapter discusses techniques you can use to solve quadratic equations and inequalities. It also describes how to graph these equations and inequalities and how to solve word problems involving quadratics. You should be aware that this chapter provides only an overview of the numerous math skills that may be applied to quadratic equation problems. You may wish to consult an algebra textbook for more information about solving quadratic equations and inequalities.

Solving Quadratic Equations

Before you attempt to solve quadratic equation problems, you should remember that all equations have a solution set. A solution set is a group of answers that satisfy an equation (i.e., that make the equation a true statement). A complete solution set contains all the values that make the equation true. A quadratic equation may have one, two, or no solutions. The solutions of a quadratic equation are also called the roots of the equation.

To solve quadratic equations, you generally use one of three methods: factoring, completing the square, or applying the quadratic formula. You can solve any quadratic equation by completing the square or applying the quadratic formula; you can use the factoring method only with certain equations.

Factoring a Quadratic Equation

Factoring is the process of finding two or more numbers that can be multiplied together to give a specific value. For example, to get the number 50, you could multiply 5 times 10 *or* you could multiply 25 times 2.

$$50 = (5)(10) \text{ or } 50 = (2)(25)$$

In this situation, 5 and 10, and 25 and 2, are said to be *factors* of 50.

When you use the factoring method to solve quadratic equations, you must find two values that can be multiplied together to produce a polynomial. You will not simply be multiplying two numbers together; instead, you will be multiplying monomials or binomials. The following table shows some examples of monomials and binomials.

MONOMIALS	BINOMIALS
3	$3 + x$
y	$5z - 9$
^-4xy	$7x - 2a$
$\frac{1}{5}b$	$^-3a^2 + 18$

Both in monomials and in binomials, the numerical part of a term is called the *numerical coefficient,* or simply the *coefficient.* For example, in the binomial $7x - 2a$, the numbers 7 and $^-2$ are the coefficients. The letters written in the statement are called *variables*.

Before you begin factoring quadratic equations, you may wish to review the sections on performing operations on polynomials in the previous chapter of this book.

To solve a quadratic equation by factoring, you must find two or more binomials that can be multiplied together to produce the quadratic. This task will be easier if you follow the procedure described below.

1. Convert the equation to standard form.

2. Factor the side of the equation that contains the polynomial.

3. Set each binomial factor equal to zero and solve for the variable.

4. Check your answer by substituting the values you found for the variables in the original equation.

The examples below show you how to use these steps to solve a quadratic equation.

Solve $x^2 - x - 6 = 0$ by factoring.

$x^2 - x - 6 = 0$	*Write the equation in standard form. In this case, the equation is given in the standard form, so it is unnecessary to convert it.*
$(x + 2)(x - 3) = 0$	*Factor the side of the equation that contains the polynomial.*
$(x + 2) = 0$ or $(x - 3) = 0$ $x = ^-2$ or $x = 3$	*Set each binomial factor equal to zero and solve for the variable.*

Both $^-2$ and 3 are solutions to (i.e., *roots of*) the equation $x^2 - x - 6 = 0$. You should check your answer by using these numbers to replace x in the original equation and solving. If these numbers make the original equation a true statement, your answers are correct.

$(^-2)^2 - (^-2) - 6 = 0$	*These are true statements.*
$4 + 2 - 6 = 0$	*The solutions are correct.*

and

$(3)^2 - (3) - 6 = 0$
$9 - 3 - 6 = 0$

When you solve a quadratic equation by factoring, you are using the *zero product property* of numbers. This property states that if a product is equal to zero, then at least one of the factors must equal zero (i.e., if two numbers multiplied together equal zero, then at least one of the two numbers must be zero). Because you are using this property, it is very important for you to remember to convert your equation to standard form so that one side is zero.

Sum of roots. In the example shown above, $^-2$ and 3 are roots of the equation. Usually, you will be asked to find the roots of an equation to solve a problem. Sometimes, however, you may be asked to find the sum of the roots of an equation. This means that you must add the roots together to find the correct answer. If you had been asked to find the sum of the roots for the example above, you would have added $^-2 + 3$, giving 1 as your answer. You should remember that if you find the sum of the roots, that value will not necessarily be a solution to the original equation. This means that you cannot substitute the sum of the roots into the original equation to check your work.

Solve $x^2 - 4x + 5 = 10$ by factoring.

$x^2 - 4x + 5 = 10$ $x^2 - 4x - 5 = 0$	*Convert the equation to standard form.*
$(x + 1)(x - 5) = 0$	*Factor the equation.*
$x + 1 = 0$ or $x - 5 = 0$ $x = ^-1$ or $x = 5$	*Set each factor equal to zero and solve.*

Both $^-1$ and 5 are solutions to the equation.

$(^-1)^2 - 4(^-1) + 5 = 10$ *Check your answer by using the solutions to replace*
$1 + 4 + 5 = 10$ *x in the original equation.*

   and

$(5)^2 - 4(5) + 5 = 10$
$25 - 20 + 5 = 10$

The sum of roots of this equation is $^-1 + 5 = 4$.

Solving Quadratic Equations by Completing the Square

When you solve a quadratic equation by completing the square, you are actually using a rather complicated method of factoring.

Sometimes when you factor a number, you find that it has two identical factors. For example, you could factor 36 by multiplying 6 times 6 ($6 \times 6 = 36$). The factors of 36 can be written as a square, $6^2 = 36$. This may also happen when you factor a quadratic equation. The example below shows a quadratic equation that has two identical factors.

$$x^2 + 10x + 25 = (x + 5)^2$$

When you solve a quadratic equation by completing the square, you are rearranging the equation so that its factors are the same (i.e., the factors can be written as a perfect square). It will be easiest for you to use this method if you follow the steps listed below. These steps assume that you are starting with an equation in standard form ($ax^2 + bx + c = 0$).

1. Convert the equation so that c is on the right side of the equal sign. (Leave a space where c used to be.)

2. Be sure the coefficient of x^2 is 1. If the equation is written in a form such that the coefficient of x^2 is a number other than 1, divide all the values in the equation by that coefficient so that x^2 has a coefficient of 1.

3. Find $\frac{1}{2}$ the coefficient of x (i.e., find $\frac{1}{2}$ of b).

4. Square the number you found in step 3.

5. Add the number you found in step 4 to both sides of the equation.

6. Factor the equation (i.e., rewrite the equation as a product of perfect squares).

7. Solve for x.

It may be easier for you to understand this process if you see how it works with an actual equation. The examples below show you how to use the process of completing the square to solve a quadratic equation.

Solve $x^2 + 10x - 18 = 0$ by completing the square.

$x^2 + 10x + \underline{\ ?\ } = 18$ *Convert the equation so that c is on the right side of the equal sign. (Leave a space where c used to be.) Notice that the coefficient of x^2 is already 1, so you do not have to do any other conversions.*

$\dfrac{10}{2} = 5$ *Find $\frac{1}{2}$ the coefficient of x (i.e., find $\frac{1}{2}$ of b).*

$(5)^2 = 25$ *Square the number you found in the previous step.*

$x^2 + 10x + 25 = 18 + 25$
$x^2 + 10x + 25 = 43$ *Add the number you found in the previous step to both sides of the equation.*

$(x + 5)^2 = 43$ *Factor the equation.*

$x + 5 = \pm\sqrt{43}$ *Solve for x.*

$x = \pm\sqrt{43} - 5$

The solutions to the equation $x^2 + 10x - 18 = 0$ are $+\sqrt{43} - 5$ and $-\sqrt{43} - 5$.

Solve $2x^2 + 12x - 4 = 0$ by completing the square.

$2x^2 + 12x + \underline{\ ?\ } = 4$ *Convert the equation so that c is on the right side of the equal sign. Leave a space where c used to be.*

$\dfrac{2x^2}{2} + \dfrac{12x}{2} + \underline{\ ?\ } = \dfrac{4}{2}$ *Divide all the numbers in the equation by the coefficient of x^2.*

$x^2 + 6x + \underline{\ ?\ } = 2$

$\dfrac{6}{2} = 3$ *Find $\frac{1}{2}$ the coefficient of x (i.e., find $\frac{1}{2}$ of b).*

$(3)^2 = 9$ *Square the number you found in the previous step.*

$x^2 + 6x + 9 = 2 + 9$
$x^2 + 6x + 9 = 11$ *Add the number you found in the previous step to both sides of the equation.*

$(x + 3)^2 = 11$ *Factor the equation.*

$x + 3 = \pm\sqrt{11}$ *Solve for x.*

$x = \pm\sqrt{11} - 3$

The solutions to the equation $2x^2 + 12x - 4 = 0$ are $+\sqrt{11} - 3$ and $-\sqrt{11} - 3$.

As a technique for solving quadratic equations, completing the square is best used when the equation can be put into the form $x^2 + $ (even number)$x = $ any number. When an equation is in this form, you can find $\frac{1}{2}$ of b easily, and you will not have to work with fractions. Even when equations appear in this form, however, completing the square is a complicated process, and you will most likely have to practice it several times before you feel comfortable with it.

Solving Quadratic Equations Using the Quadratic Formula

When the completing-the-square method is used to solve the equation $ax^2 + bx + c = 0$ for x ($a \neq 0$), the result is known as the *quadratic formula*. Solving for x results in the following equation.

$x = \frac{^-b \pm \sqrt{b^2 - 4ac}}{2a}$. This equation is called the quadratic formula and can be used to solve any quadratic equation. Notice that before using this formula to solve an equation, the equation must be converted to standard form, with zero on one side and the polynomial on the other.

> **The Quadratic Formula**
>
> $$x = \frac{^-b \pm \sqrt{b^2 - 4ac}}{2a}$$

The expression $b^2 - 4ac$ is called the discriminant. When it is equal to 0, the equation has one real root. When it is greater than 0, the equation has two unequal real roots. When it is less than 0, the equation has no real roots.

Solve $6x^2 = 5 - 13x$ using the quadratic formula.

$6x^2 + 13x - 5 = 0$ *Transpose terms so that the equation is in the form $ax^2 + bx + c = 0$. Next, identify a, b, and c.*

$a = 6$ *The coefficient of x^2 is 6.*
$b = 13$ *The coefficient of x is 13.*
$c = {}^-5$ *The constant term is $^-5$.*

Now, substitute these values for a, b, and c in the quadratic formula, and solve.

$$x = \frac{^-b \pm \sqrt{b^2 - 4ac}}{2a}$$

$$x = \frac{^-13 \pm \sqrt{(13)^2 - 4(6)(^-5)}}{2(6)}$$

$$x = \frac{^-13 \pm \sqrt{169 + 120}}{12}$$

$$x = \frac{^-13 \pm \sqrt{289}}{12} = \frac{^-13 \pm 17}{12}$$

$$x = \frac{^-13 + 17}{12} \text{ or } x = \frac{^-13 - 17}{12}$$

$$x = \frac{4}{12} = \frac{1}{3} \text{ or } x = \frac{^-30}{12} = {}^-\frac{5}{2}$$

Therefore, the solutions are $\frac{1}{3}$ and $^-\frac{5}{2}$, which may be easily checked.

The sum of the roots is $\frac{1}{3} + {}^-\frac{5}{2} = {}^-\frac{13}{6}$ or $^-2\frac{1}{6}$.

In this example, the term inside the radical sign (289) is a square, so we were able to take the square root (17) easily. In some cases, the number within the radical sign will not be the perfect square of an integer. In those situations, it is usual to leave the term in the radical sign rather than evaluating the square root. Therefore, you will often see answers like $\frac{\sqrt{17}}{4}$ or $\frac{\sqrt{23}}{6}$ in solutions to problems.

The quadratic formula can be used to solve any quadratic equation.

Graphing Quadratic Equations

Any equation that can be written in the form $y = ax^2 + bx + c$ (where $a \neq 0$) is called a quadratic equation. The graph of a quadratic equation is a curve that is closed on one end and open on the other end; this curve is called a *parabola*. When a parabola opens upward, it may look like a capital letter U, or a horseshoe. The open end of a parabola may also face down, to the right, or to the left.

All parabolas have a point on the closed end upon which the entire curve turns. The two open ends seem to curve away from this point. This point is called the *turning point,* or *vertex,* of the parabola.

An imaginary line, called the *axis of symmetry,* can be drawn through the turning point of a parabola. The axis of symmetry divides the parabola in half.

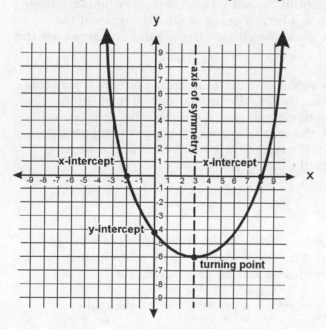

In many ways, graphing a quadratic equation is similar to graphing other kinds of equations. You must still graph the coordinates of points that satisfy the equation (i.e., ordered pairs) on the Cartesian plane. You may have to determine the x-intercept (i.e., the place where the parabola crosses the x-axis) or the y-intercept (i.e., the place where the parabola crosses the y-axis) as you graph the equation. You may find it useful to review the graphing techniques discussed in the previous chapter before you begin graphing quadratic equations.

You should also know some special characteristics of quadratic equations that may help you graph them. The list below contains some properties of quadratic equations that may make it easier for you to tell how the graph of a particular equation should look. Remember, quadratic equations can be written in the form $y = ax^2 + bx + c$ (where $a \neq 0$). This is called the standard form of the equation. When a quadratic equation is written in standard form, the following statements about its graph are true.

1. If $a > 0$, the parabola opens upward.

2. If $a < 0$, the parabola opens downward.

3. The value of c tells where the parabola crosses the y-axis. That is, c identifies the y-intercept.

You will often find that it is useful to determine the zeros of a parabola. The zeros of the parabola are the points where $y = 0$. You can calculate them simply by setting $y = 0$ and solving for x. You should be aware that there may be more than one zero for a parabola, or there may not be any zeros at all. The zeros of the equation tell you where, if at all, the parabola crosses the x-axis. The zeros are the x-intercepts of the graph.

You may also need to calculate the coordinates of the turning point of a parabola in order to graph a quadratic equation. Calculating the coordinates of the turning point also allows you to find the axis of symmetry of a parabola because for an equation in the form $y = ax^2 + bx + c$ the axis of symmetry passes through the x-coordinate of the turning point. To determine the coordinates of the turning point, you can use the following formula.

$$x = -\frac{b}{2a}$$

This formula allows you to find the x-coordinate of the turning point. After you have found the x-coordinate, you can find the y-coordinate by substituting the x-coordinate you calculated into the original equation and solving for y.

It will be easiest to graph quadratic equations if you use the following steps.

1. Be sure the equation is written in standard form (i.e., $y = ax^2 + bx + c$). If it is not, convert it to standard form.

2. Determine whether the value of a is greater than zero or less than zero. Use this information to decide whether the parabola will open upward or downward.

3. Use the value of c to find the y-intercept of the graph.

4. Find the coordinates of the turning point of the graph.

5. If necessary, find the zeros (i.e., the x-intercepts) of the graph.

The examples below show how to use these steps to graph quadratic equations.

Graph $y = x^2 - 2x - 8$.

$y = x^2 - 2x - 8$	*Be sure the equation is written in standard form (i.e., $y = ax^2 + bx + c$). This equation is in the correct form, so there is no need to do additional conversions.*
$a = 1$; therefore $a > 0$	*Determine whether the value of a is greater than zero or less than zero. Remember that a is the coefficient of x^2. In this case, $a > 0$, so the parabola will open upward.*
$c = {}^-8$	*Use the value of c to find the y-intercept of the graph. Since $c = {}^-8$, the graph will cross the y-axis at the point $(0, {}^-8)$.*
$x = -\dfrac{b}{2a}$	*Use the formula $x = -\dfrac{b}{2a}$ to find the turning point of the graph.*
$x = \dfrac{{}^-({}^-2)}{(2)(1)}$	*Remember that a is the coefficient of x^2 in the original equation and b is the coefficient of x.*
$x = 1$	*This calculation indicates that the axis of symmetry of the graph passes through $x = 1$.*
$y = 1^2 - (2)(1) - 8$	*Use the x-coordinate calculated in the previous step to replace x in the original equation, and solve for y.*
$y = 1 - 2 - 8$	
$y = {}^-9$	

The coordinates of the turning point of the parabola are $(1, {}^-9)$.

You could draw a rough sketch of the parabola with the information you have calculated in the steps shown above.

However, you can be more precise by taking the additional step of finding the zeros (i.e., the x-intercepts) of the graph, as indicated below.

$0 = x^2 - 2x - 8$	*Set $y = 0$ and solve for x.*
$0 = (x - 4)(x + 2)$	*By the factoring method.*
Therefore $x = 4$ or $x = {}^-2$	

This parabola will cross the x-axis when x = 4 and when x = ⁻2.

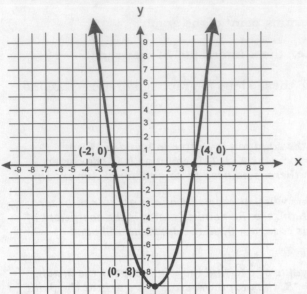

Solving for x.

The standard form of the quadratic equation is arranged so that you are solving for y ($y = ax^2 + bx + c$). Occasionally, however, you will find quadratic equations arranged so that you must solve for x. Such an equation is written in the form $x = ay^2 + by + c$.

Graphing a quadratic equation in which you must solve for x is very similar to graphing an equation in which you are solving for y. You can still use the properties of the quadratic equation to identify key points such as x- and y-intercepts, the vertex, and the axis of symmetry. The main difference between graphing quadratic equations in which you must solve for x is that the parabola described by the equation will open either to the right or to the left, rather than up or down.

The list below states several important facts that you can use to graph a quadratic equation in the form $x = ay^2 + by + c$.

1. If a > 0, the parabola opens to the right.

2. If a < 0, the parabola opens to the left.

3. For an equation in the form $x = ay^2 + by + c$, the value of c tells where the parabola crosses the x-axis. That is, the value of c identifies the x-intercept.

4. For an equation in the form $x = ay^2 + by + c$, the zeros of the equation identify the points where the parabola crosses the y-axis. You can find the zeros of the equation by setting x equal to zero and solving for y.

5. For an equation in the form $x = ay^2 + by + c$, you can find the turning point by using the equation $y = -\frac{b}{2a}$. This formula allows you to determine the y-coordinate of the turning point. You can then find the x-coordinate by substituting the value of y that you calculated into the original equation and solving for x.

The example below shows how to use these properties to graph a quadratic equation in the form $x = ay^2 + by + c$.

Graph the equation $x = -y^2 - 4y + 5$.

$x = -y^2 - 4y + 5$	*Be sure the equation is written so that the x is by itself on the left side of the equal sign. This equation is in the correct form, so there is no need to do additional conversions.*
$a = {}^-1$; therefore $a < 0$	*Determine whether the value of a is greater than zero or less than zero. Remember that a is the coefficient of y^2. In this case, $a < 0$, so the parabola will open to the left.*
$c = 5$	*Use the value of c to find the x-intercept of the graph. Since $c = 5$, the graph will cross the x-axis at the point (5,0).*
$y = -\dfrac{b}{2a}$	*Use the formula $y = -\dfrac{b}{2a}$ to find the turning point of the graph. Remember that a is the coefficient of*
$y = \dfrac{{}^-({}^-4)}{(2)({}^-1)}$	*y^2 in the original equation and b is the coefficient of y.*
$y = {}^-2$	*This calculation indicates that the axis of symmetry of the graph passes through $y = {}^-2$.*
$x = {}^-({}^-2)^2 - (4)({}^-2) + 5$ $x = {}^-4 + 8 + 5$ $x = 9$	*Use the y-coordinate calculated in the previous step to replace y in the original equation, and solve for x.*

The coordinates of the turning point of the parabola are $(9, {}^-2)$. This is enough information to draw a sketch of the parabola.

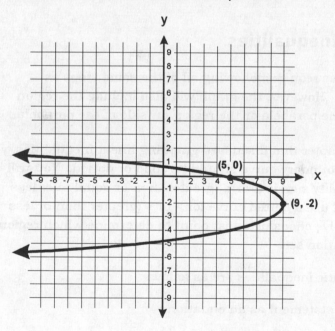

You may also find that you need to create a more precise graph. In that case, you would have to determine the zeros of the parabola using the following method.

$0 = -y^2 - 4y + 5$ *Set x = 0 and solve for y.*
$0 = {}^-1(y + 5)(y - 1)$ *By the factoring method.*
Therefore $y = {}^-5$ or $y = 1$

This parabola will cross the y-axis when $y = {}^-5$ and when $y = 1$, giving a more precise drawing of the graph.

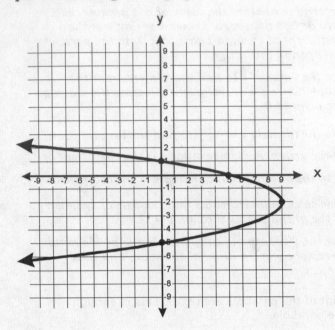

Graphing Quadratic Inequalities

Graphing quadratic inequalities requires following all of the same steps as graphing quadratic equations. However, the graph will also include the region of ordered pairs enclosed by the parabola or the region outside of the parabola.

As you may recall from the chapter that discussed graphing linear inequalities, you will need to determine if the boundary curve should be solid or dotted. You will use a solid curve if the inequality sign is $\geq$ or $\leq$ (greater than or equal to *or* less than or equal to), and you will use a dotted curve for $>$ or $<$ (greater than *or* less than). Your last step will involve choosing a test point to determine which region to include as part of your solution set.

The steps for graphing quadratic inequalities are as follows:

1. Rewrite the inequality statement as an equation.

2. Graph the equation on the Cartesian plane using the steps given in the preceding section on graphing quadratic equations. Use a solid or dotted curve as indicated by the inequality sign in the original equation (i.e., solid for $\geq$ or $\leq$; dotted for $>$ or $<$).

3. The curve separates the plane into two regions, one that is on the interior of the parabola and one that is on the exterior. Choose an ordered pair that represents a point in either one of those regions.

4. Use the ordered pair to replace the variables in the original inequality statement. Determine whether the resulting numerical statement is true or false.

5. Choose a point in the second region. Use that ordered pair to repeat step 4.

6. One of the ordered pairs should make the inequality statement true. The other should make it false. The ordered pair that makes the statement true is in the region that represents the solution set of the inequality.

7. Shade the region that contains the ordered pair that satisfies the inequality. You can check your work by choosing another point in the shaded region and using the coordinates in the inequality. If you get a true statement, you have shaded the correct region.

The examples below show how to use these steps to graph quadratic inequalities.

Graph $y \geq x^2 - 4x + 3$.

$y = x^2 - 4x + 3$	*Rewrite the inequality as an equation. Be sure the equation is written in standard form (i.e., $y = ax^2 + bx + c$).*
$a = 1$; therefore $a > 0$	*Determine whether the value of a is greater than or less than zero. In this case $a > 0$, so the parabola will open upward.*
$c = 3$	*Use the value of c to find the y-intercept of the graph. Since $c = 3$, the graph will cross the y-axis at the point $(0,3)$.*
$x = -\dfrac{b}{2a}$	*Use the formula $x = -\dfrac{b}{2a}$ to find the turning point of the graph.*
$x = \dfrac{^-(^-4)}{(2)(1)}$	*Remember that a is the coefficient of x^2 and b is the coefficient of x.*
$x = 2$	*This calculation indicates that the axis of symmetry of the graph passes through $x = 2$.*
$y = 2^2 - (4)(2) + 3$ $y = 4 - 8 + 3$ $y = ^-1$	*Use the x-coordinate calculated in the previous step to replace x in the equation $y = x^2 - 4x + 3$, and solve for y.*

The coordinates of the turning point are $(2,^-1)$. The y-intercept is $(0,3)$.

Take the additional steps to find the x-intercepts.

$0 = x^2 - 4x + 3$ *Set y = 0 and solve for x.*
$0 = (x - 3)(x - 1)$ *By the factoring method.*
Therefore $x = 3$ or 1

The x-intercepts are (1,0) and (3,0).

Sketch the graph. Use a solid curve since the original inequality sign was $\geq$.

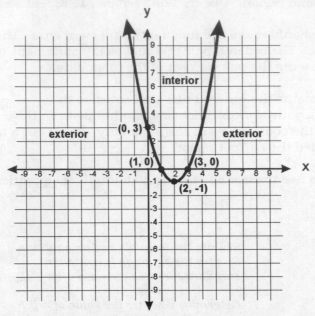

Notice the two regions labeled "interior" and "exterior." You must now determine which of these regions to shade.

Choose (2,2)   *Choose a point in one of the regions.*
                                      This point is in the interior of the curve.

$2 \geq 2^2 - 4(2) + 3$ *Substitute the values of x and y into the*

$2 \geq 4 - 8 + 3$ *original inequality. Determine whether*

$2 \geq {}^-1$ *the resulting statement is true or false.*

True

Choose ($^-$5,0)   *Choose a point from the other region.*
                                      This point is in the exterior of the curve.

$0 \geq (^-5)^2 - 4(^-5) + 3$ *Substitute the values of x and y into the*

$0 \geq 25 + 20 + 3$ *original inequality and determine*

$0 \geq 48$ *whether the resulting statement is true*
                                      or false.

False.

The point whose coordinates are (2,2) is to be included in the solution set. Shade the region that includes this point.

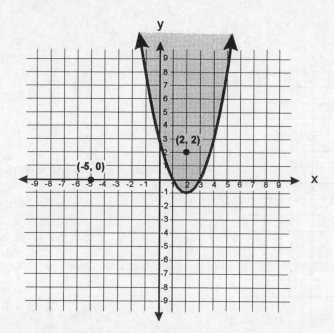

Graph y > ⁻5x² + 2x.

$y = {}^-5x^2 + 2x + 0$	*Rewrite the inequality as an equation. Be sure the equation is written in standard form.*
$a = {}^-5$; therefore $a < 0$	*The parabola will open downward.*
$c = 0$	*The y-intercept is at (0,0).*
$x = -\dfrac{b}{2a}$	*Determine the turning point.*
$x = -\dfrac{2}{2({}^-5)}$	
$x = \dfrac{1}{5}$	*The axis of symmetry passes through* $x = \dfrac{1}{5}$.
$y = {}^-5\left(\dfrac{1}{5}\right)^2 + 2\left(\dfrac{1}{5}\right)$	*Find the y-coordinate of the turning point.*
$y = {}^-5\left(\dfrac{1}{25}\right) + \dfrac{2}{5}$	
$y = -\dfrac{5}{25} + \dfrac{2}{5}$	
$y = -\dfrac{1}{5} + \dfrac{2}{5}$	
$y = \dfrac{1}{5}$	*The turning point is at* $\left(\dfrac{1}{5},\dfrac{1}{5}\right)$.
$0 = {}^-5x^2 + 2x$	*Determine the x-intercepts.*
$0 = x({}^-5x + 2)$	*Factor.*
Therefore $x = 0$ or $\dfrac{2}{5}$	*The x-intercepts are at (0,0) and $(\dfrac{2}{5},0)$.*

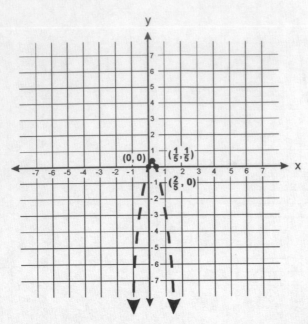

Sketch the graph using a dotted curve.

Choose (0,⁻4)   *Choose a test point. This one is in the*
                                       interior of the curve.

⁻4 > ⁻5(0)² + 2(0)   *Determine whether it results in a true*
                                       or false statement.

⁻4 > 0

False

Choose (5,0)   *Choose a second test point. This one is*
                                       in the exterior of the curve.

0 > ⁻5(5²) + 2(5)   *Determine whether it results in a true*
                                       or false statement.

0 > ⁻125 + 10

0 > ⁻115

True

Shade the appropriate region.

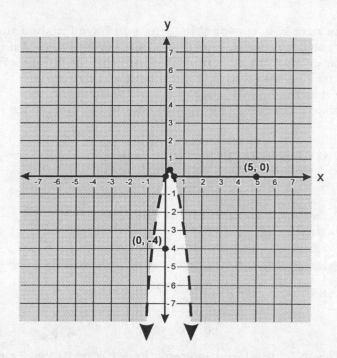

Solving Word Problems Involving Quadratic Models

To become proficient in solving word problems, you need to develop some basic problem-solving strategies and some confidence in their use. Consider the following plan for solving word problems.

1. **Read and understand the problem.** The first step in solving any math problem is to read all the information provided. Some information will be given in numbers, but some may be presented in words. In most cases you will need to use all the information in the problem to answer the question. Be sure you have a clear idea of what the words and the numbers mean.

The last sentence in a word problem often states the actual question being asked. Be sure that you read this sentence carefully and understand what is being asked.

2. **Develop a mathematical plan for solving the problem.** After you have read the problem carefully and understood it, develop a plan for finding your answer. Use key words or phrases in the problem to form a mathematical plan for solving the problem. Solving word problems with quadratics often involves translating the problem into algebraic terms. Choose variables to represent the values that you are given and those that you are asked to find. It is helpful if the variables have some relevance to the value they represent. For instance, d is a good choice for distance, r for radius, n for number, and t for time. All relevant information should be put into algebraic terms. A diagram, a picture, or a table is often helpful in the planning process.

Your objective at this stage is to write an equation or a system of equations that represent the conditions of the problem or the situation described in the problem.

3. **Solve the problem.** After you have developed a plan, you will need to follow it. This will often mean using algebra to solve the equations developed in step 2. Replace as many variables as possible with numbers given in the problem. Do all calculations slowly and carefully.

4. **Check your answer to make sure it is reasonable.** After you have finished the first three steps of the problem-solving process, check your answer and decide if it is reasonable. The solutions may or may not be compatible with the conditions of the problem. For instance, you may be asked to find the length of a figure. The algebraic solution may indicate that the length is either 12 or ⁻3. However, ⁻3 could never represent the length of a geometric figure and should be rejected as a solution to the problem.

A canvas tarp has the shape of a rectangle, and its area is 15 square meters. The width of the tarp is 2 meters less than its length. Find the length of the tarp.

This problem gives the area of a rectangle and asks for the length. A diagram may be helpful. Let l = length.

area = 15

width = l – 2
(width is 2 less than length)

length = l

Since the area of a rectangle is given by the formula area = length × width, you can form the equation $15 = l(l - 2)$.

Solve the equation $15 = l(l - 2)$

$$15 = l(l - 2)$$
$$15 = l^2 - 2l$$
$$0 = l^2 - 2l - 15$$
$$0 = (l - 5)(l + 3)$$

$l - 5 = 0$ or $l + 3 = 0$

$l = 5$ $l = {}^-3$

The solutions to the equation $15 = l(l - 2)$ are 5 and ⁻3. These must now be checked. If the length is 5 meters, the width is l – 2, or 3 meters, and the area of the rectangle is 5 × 3, or 15 square meters. This agrees with the conditions of the problem. If the length of the rectangle is ⁻3, the problem has no meaning in the real world since a negative length has no meaning. Therefore, the mathematical solution ⁻3 is rejected as an answer to the problem.

Practice Exercises

The following exercises will help you review the skills covered in this chapter. Many of the types of questions presented here will be similar to those on the test; others will not. Remember that the purpose of the exercises is to give you practice on the skills rather than merely to prepare you for the test. Following these exercises are the Practice Exercise Explanations. They explain each question, the correct answer, and why the remaining choices are incorrect.

1.   Which of the following is a solution of the equation $x^2 - 5x - 14 = 0$?

   A.   2

   B.   ⁻7

   C.   -2

   D.   14

2.   Find the sum of the roots of the equation $8x^2 + 2x - 3 = 0$.

   A. $-\dfrac{1}{4}$

   B. $\dfrac{1}{2}$

   C. $\dfrac{1}{4}$

   D. $-\dfrac{3}{4}$

3.   Solve for x.

   $2x^2 - 3x - 1 = 0$

   A. $\dfrac{1}{2}, {}^{-}1$

   B. $\dfrac{3 \pm \sqrt{17}}{2}$

   C. $\dfrac{3 \pm \sqrt{17}}{4}$

   D. $-\dfrac{1}{2}, 1$

4.   Which graph best represents the equation $y = x^2 - 4x + 5$?

A.

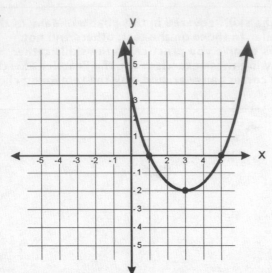

B.

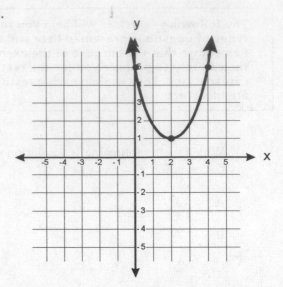

C.

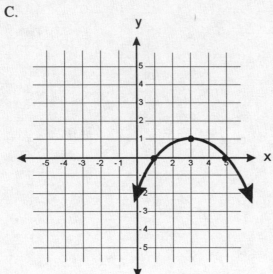

D.

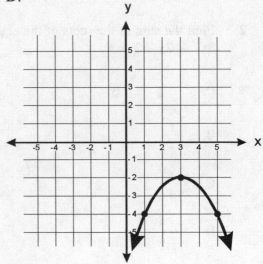

5.   Which equation represents the graph below?

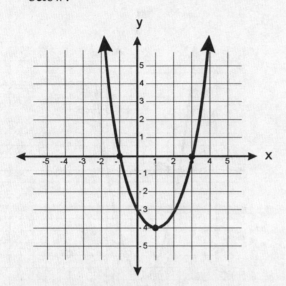

A. $y = x^2 + 2x - 3$

B. $y = 2x^2 - 4x - 6$

C. $y = -x^2 - 2x + 3$

D. $y = x^2 - 2x - 3$

6. Which of the following graphs best represents the solution set for $y \leq x^2 - 4x - 5$?

A.

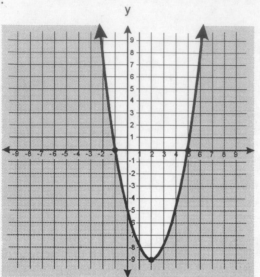

B.

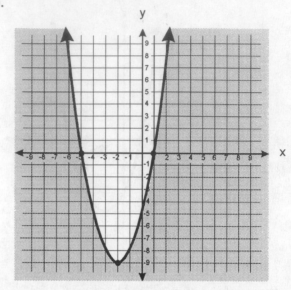

C.

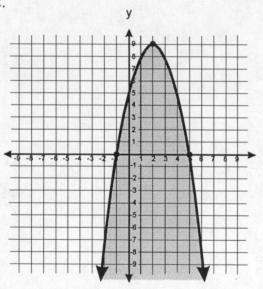

D.

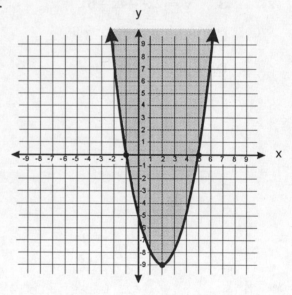

7.   Which of the following graphs best represents the solution set for $y \geq {}^{-}3x^2 + 3$?

A.

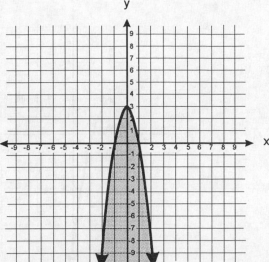

B.

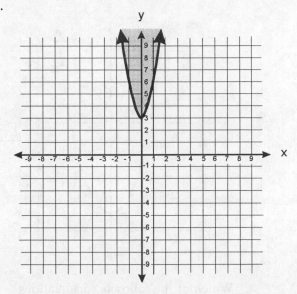

C.

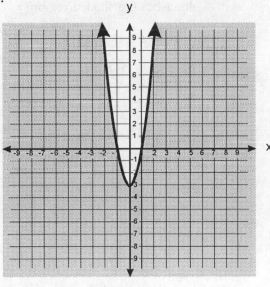

D.

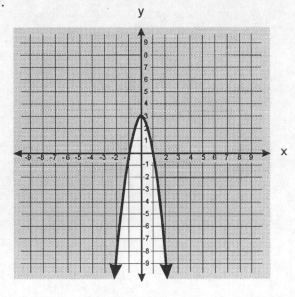

8. Use the graph below to answer the question that follows.

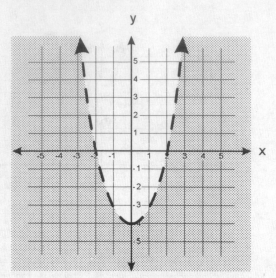

Which of the following inequalities describes the shaded region?

A. $y \geq x^2 - 4$

B. $y < {}^-x^2 - 4$

C. $y > x^2 - 4$

D. $y < x^2 - 4$

9. Use the graph below to answer the question that follows.

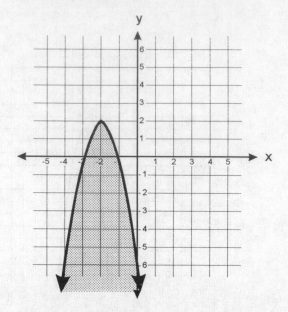

Which of the following inequalities describes the shaded region?

A. $y \geq 2x^2 + 8x - 6$

B. $y \leq {}^-2x^2 - 8x - 6$

C. $y \geq {}^-2x^2 - 8x - 6$

D. $y \leq 2x^2 + 8x + 6$

10. Maria is 4 years younger than Nancy. If the product of their ages is 60, what is the sum of their ages?

   A.   4

   B.   6

   C.   10

   D.   16

11. Jack left a diner at 8:00 a.m. and headed due east at 30 mph. Amy left the same diner at 9:00 a.m. and headed due north at 40 mph. If t represents the time Amy traveled, then which equation below represents the time when Amy and Jack will be 50 miles apart?

   A. $30(t + 1) + 40t = 50$

   B. $[30(t + 1)]^2 + (40t)^2 = 50^2$

   C. $30t + 40t = 50$

   D. $[30(t - 1)]^2 + (40t)^2 = 50^2$

12. One side of a square is decreased by 2 feet while the other dimension of the square is doubled to produce a rectangle having an area of 76 square feet. If s represents a side of the original square, which of the following equations expresses this relationship?

   A. $2s(s - 2) = 76$

   B. $(s + 2)(s - 2) = 76$

   C. $2s(s + 2) = 76$

   D. $s(s - 2) = 76$

13. A number, a, is 5 times the square of another number, b. Which of the following equations expresses this relationship?

   A. $a = \sqrt{5}\, b$

   B. $a = 5b^2$

   C. $a = 5\sqrt{b}$

   D. $a = (5b)^2$

14. The width of a square is decreased by 5 feet and its length is tripled to produce a rectangle. How long was the side of the original square if the area of the rectangle is 50 square feet more than the area of the original square?

   A.   2.5 feet

   B.   6.25 feet

   C.   10 feet

   D.   15 feet

Practice Exercise Explanations

1. **Correct Response: C.** This problem can be solved by factoring.

    $x^2 - 5x - 14 = 0$

    $(x - 7)(x + 2) = 0$

    $x - 7 = 0$ or $x + 2 = 0$ *Apply property of zero factors.*

      $x = 7$ $x = {}^-2$

    Check:

    $7^2 - 5(7) - 14 = 49 - 35 - 14 = 0$

    $({}^-2)^2 - 5({}^-2) - 14 = 4 + 10 - 14 = 0$

    Incorrect choices A and B are the result of not factoring correctly. Choice D uses the constant term as a solution. Another correct answer would be 7.

2. **Correct Response: A.** The factoring method may be used to solve this problem.

    $8x^2 + 2x - 3 = 0$

    $(2x - 1)(4x + 3) = 0$

    $2x - 1 = 0$ or $4x + 3 = 0$

      $2x = 1$ $4x = {}^-3$

       $x = \frac{1}{2}$ $x = -\frac{3}{4}$

    The solutions are $\frac{1}{2}$ and $-\frac{3}{4}$, which both check. The sum of the roots is

    $\frac{1}{2} + \left(-\frac{3}{4}\right) = -\frac{1}{4}$. Choice C is the result of an incorrect placement of the signs in the

    factoring step of the solution. Choices B and D give the individual roots instead of the sum.

3. **Correct Response: C.** Since the expression $2x^2 - 3x - 1$ has a discriminant of 17, it does not factor, and the quadratic formula should be used with $a = 2$, $b = {}^-3$, and $c = {}^-1$.

    $$x = \frac{{}^-b \pm \sqrt{b^2 - 4ac}}{2a}$$

    $$x = \frac{{}^-({}^-3) \pm \sqrt{({}^-3)^2 - 4(2)({}^-1)}}{2(2)}$$

    $$x = \frac{3 \pm \sqrt{17}}{4}$$

    Choices A and D are the result of incorrect factorizations, while choice B uses only a or 2 as a denominator for the quadratic formula.

4. **Correct Response: B.** The equation has the form $y = ax^2 + bx + c$, $a \neq 0$, and its graph is a parabola. Since $1 > 0$ ($a = 1$) and $c = 5$, the parabola opens upward and has a y-intercept of 5. Since $a = 1$ and $b = {}^-4$, the x-coordinate of the turning point, or vertex, is $-\frac{b}{2a} = \frac{-(-4)}{2(1)} = 2$. Substituting this x value into the equation gives the y-coordinate of the vertex: $y = 2^2 - 4(2) + 5 = 1$. Therefore, the turning point is at (2,1). The only graph that meets these criteria is choice B. Choice A results from incorrectly factoring $x^2 - 4x + 5$ and getting the zeros 1 and 5. Choice C is the result of factoring incorrectly and having the parabola open in the wrong direction. Choice D has the parabola opening in the wrong direction and finds the vertex using the zeros 1 and 5.

5.   **Correct Response: D.** You need to find an equation of the form $y = ax^2 + bx + c$, $a \neq 0$, because the given graph is a parabola. Further, since the parabola opens upward, a must be greater than 0, the zeros must be $^-1$ and 3, and the vertex $(1,^-4)$. Only choice D meets these criteria. Choice A is a parabola that opens upward but has vertex $(^-1,^-4)$ and zeros 1 and $^-3$. Choice B is a parabola that opens upward and has zeros $^-1$ and 3, but the vertex is $(1,^-8)$. Choice C is a parabola that opens downward and therefore could not be correct.

6.   **Correct Response: A.** First we must transform the inequality into an equation: $y = x^2 - 4x - 5$. We can tell from the equation that the parabola will open upward (since $a = 1$) and that the y-intercept is $^-5$. To calculate the x-coordinate of the turning point, we use the formula:

$$x = -\frac{b}{2a}$$
$$x = \frac{-(-4)}{2(1)}$$
$$x = 2$$

By substituting $x = 2$ into the equation, we find the y-coordinate of the turning point:

$$y = (2)^2 - 4(2) - 5$$
$$y = 4 - 8 - 5$$
$$y = ^-9$$

The turning point is therefore (2,-9).

Next we can test whether the point (0,0), which is in the interior of the curve, makes the original inequality true or false.

$$0 \leq 0^2 - 4(0) - 5$$
$$0 \leq ^-5$$
False.

Since a point in the interior of the curve made the inequality false, the exterior of the curve must be shaded.

Response B has the wrong turning point. Response C has the parabola opening downward and also has the wrong turning point. Response D has the wrong region shaded.

7.   **Correct Response: D.** Transforming the inequality into an equation produces $y = ^-3x^2 + 3$ (the x term has a coefficient of zero). We know that the curve will open downward ($a = ^-3$) and that the y-intercept is 3. Now we should find the turning point.

$$x = -\frac{b}{2a}$$
$$x = \frac{-0}{2(-3)}$$
$$x = 0$$

If the x-coordinate of the turning point is 0, the y-coordinate is:

$$y = ^-3(0^2) + 3$$
$$y = 3$$

The turning point is therefore (0, 3). So far graphs A and D satisfy all of this information.

Using (0, 0) as a test point in the interior of the parabola, we check to see if the original inequality is true or false for this point:

$y \geq {}^-3x^2 + 3$

$0 \geq 3$
False.

If a point on the interior of the curve produces a false statement, the exterior of the curve must be shaded.

Response A has the wrong region shaded. Responses B and C have the parabola opening upward.

8.   **Correct Response: D.** Response A would require a solid curve and would include the interior of the parabola. Response B would be a parabola opening downward. Response C would include the interior of the parabola. This can be determined by using the origin (0, 0) as a test point.

9.   **Correct Response: B.** Responses A and D are parabolas opening upward. Response C would have the exterior of the parabola shaded and a turning point of (2, 2).

10. **Correct Response: D.** To find the sum of the ages, you must first find each age. Let n = Nancy's age and n – 4 = Maria's age (4 years younger). The equation to solve is n (n – 4) = 60.

$n^2 - 4n = 60$ *The product of the ages is 60.*
$n^2 - 4n - 60 = 0$
$(n - 10)(n + 6) = 0$
$n - 10 = 0$ or $n + 6 = 0$
$n = 10$ $n = {}^-6$

Since neither age can be negative, the solution ⁻6 must be rejected. Nancy is 10 years old, and Maria is 6 years old. The sum of the ages is 10 + 6 = 16. Choice C represents Nancy's age, and choice B is Maria's age. Choice A is the difference of their ages.

11. **Correct Response: B.** This problem deals with distance and asks for an equation. Both a diagram and a table may be helpful.

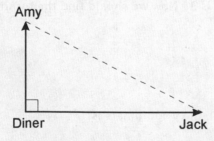

Table

	Rate	Time	Distance
Amy	40	t	
Jack	30		

Let t = time (in hours) Amy drove. Since Jack left one hour earlier than Amy, he traveled one hour more than Amy. Hence t + 1 = time Jack drove. Now, using the distance formula, distance = rate × time, and the fact that they are to be 50 miles apart, the diagram and the table may be updated.

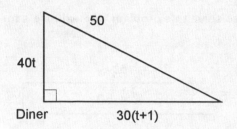

Table			
	Rate	Time	Distance
Amy	40	t	40t
Jack	30	t + 1	30(t + 1)

Finally, to get the relationship needed, apply the Pythagorean theorem.

$a^2 + b^2 = c^2$

$[30(t + 1)]^2 + (40t)^2 = 50^2$

Choice A has Jack and Amy going in opposite directions. Choice C has both persons traveling the same amount of time and in opposite directions. Choice D has Jack traveling 1 hour less than Amy instead of 1 hour more.

12. **Correct Response: A.** This problem involves areas and a change of shape and asks for an equation. A diagram would be helpful in planning the solution.

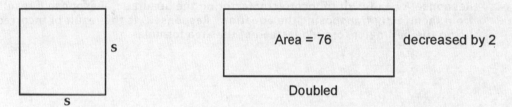

Let s = side of the square. If one side of the rectangle is the side of the square decreased by 2 and the other side is the side of the square doubled, the dimensions of the rectangle may be represented by s – 2 and 2s respectively. The diagram may then be updated.

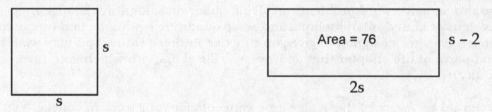

Using the formula to find the area of a rectangle, you get the following equation.

$A = \ell \times w$

$76 = 2s(s - 2)$

Choice B increases the length by 2 instead of doubling it. Choice C increases the width by 2 instead of decreasing it by 2. Choice D fails to double the length of the side.

13. **Correct Response: B.** The problem says that a number must equal 5 multiplied by another number, b, which must be squared. The equation that describes this is $5 \times (b)^2$, or $5b^2$. Choice A takes the square root of 5 instead of squaring b. Choice C takes the square root of b instead of squaring it. Choice D squares both 5 and b.

14. **Correct Response: C.** A diagram helps to solve this problem. We will use s for the side of the square and s^2 for its area.

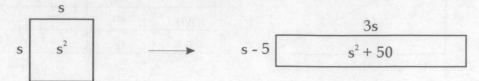

Using the formula for the area of a rectangle, we can see that

$$3s(s - 5) = s^2 + 50$$
$$3s^2 - 15s = s^2 + 50$$
$$2s^2 - 15s - 50 = 0$$
$$(2s + 5)(s - 10) = 0$$
$$s = -\frac{5}{2} \text{ or } 10$$

For the length of a side, a negative number makes no sense, so we conclude that the side of the original square was 10 feet long.

Response A is a result of incorrectly factoring the quadratic. Response B results from incorrectly transposing the equation. Response D is the result of incorrectly using the perimeter formula instead of the area formula.

Study Ideas

A careful study of the above exercises and the explanations of the answers will help you review important skills relating to solving problems involving quadratic equations. In these exercises you were asked to graph quadratic equations and inequalities, solve word problems involving quadratics, identify the algebraic equivalent of stated relationships, and solve quadratic equations and inequalities. The exercises are designed to give you practice in these skills. You may wish to reread parts of the chapter that address specific skills with which you have difficulty.

You should be aware of these algebraic concepts for your work in college. You may choose to consult an algebra textbook for more detailed explanations of these topics.

Chapter 18

SOLVE PROBLEMS INVOLVING GEOMETRIC FIGURES

This skill includes solving problems involving two- and three-dimensional geometric figures and using the Pythagorean theorem to solve problems involving right triangles.

Introduction

Geometry involves the study of certain shapes and their measurements. The formulas and techniques used in this branch of mathematics are very important in such diverse fields as architecture, art, science, construction, engineering, surveying, planning, and business. To use geometry effectively, you must understand how geometric shapes, also called geometric figures, are formed and how they can be used to solve problems. It is also helpful to be familiar with a number of special formulas that are used to make calculations in geometry. This chapter will review the definitions of the basic geometric figures, the appropriate units of measurement to use in calculations involving these figures, and the fundamental formulas of length, area, and volume.

Measurements

It is necessary to use measurement in geometry problems. Often, you will have to determine the length, width, height, volume, or area of a geometric figure to solve a problem. You will need to know how to read and use the various units of measurement to deal with geometry problems. This section discusses some of the most common units of measurement, as well as the types of measurement used most often in geometry problems.

Length

Length is actually a measure of distance. You may have to measure the length of a sports playing field, the width of a table, or the height of a box. All these measurements actually involve determining how far it is from one place to another (i.e., how long something is). Many different units are commonly used in measuring length. Several of those units are taken from a system of measurement called the English system, which is generally used in the United States. In this system of measurement, length is measured using units such as inches, feet, yards, and miles. The basic units of length from a second system, the metric system, are also used regularly. The centimeter, meter, and kilometer are commonly used units of measurement in the metric system.

Any distance must use one of these basic units of length, or some multiple or part of one of them. For example, to measure the dimensions of a room, you would normally use feet or meters, but you might have to subdivide part of the distance into smaller units such as inches or centimeters. You should use the unit of length that is most convenient in a particular situation.

Area

Area is a measurement of how much space is inside a two-dimensional object. For example, you might need to calculate how much space is inside a rectangle drawn on a piece of paper, or how much land is inside a square fence. The fundamental unit of area is a square that measures one length unit on each side. You may choose any unit of length and convert it to a unit of area. For example, if you choose the foot as the unit of length, the fundamental unit of area would be the square foot. A square foot is a measure of the amount of space inside a square that is one foot long on each side. The measurement one square foot is abbreviated 1 sq. ft. or 1 ft.^{2}. Area can also be measured in units such as square miles, square yards, square meters, and square kilometers. The area measurement of a rectangle that is 3 feet wide by 5 feet long is shown below.

Notice that the inside of the 3-foot-by-5-foot rectangle is made up of 15 squares that are one foot long on each side. Therefore, the area of this rectangle is 15 square feet (15 ft.^{2}).

Volume

Volume is a measure of the amount of space inside a three-dimensional object. For example, the amount of space inside a cardboard box is equal to the volume of the box. The fundamental unit of volume is a cube that measures one unit in length on each side. If you choose the foot as the length, the volume of the cube is one cubic foot. This volume is written 1 cubic foot or 1 ft.^{3}.

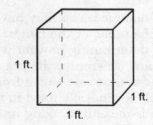

As in the case of area, you could use a different unit of length as the basis for measuring volume. Volume can be measured in cubic inches (in.^{3}), cubic yards (yd.^{3}), cubic meters (m^3), or cubic kilometers (km^3).

Powers of Units

Sometimes, the basic units of measurement are numbers raised to a power. You should notice that the basic units of length are not raised to a power. The basic units of area, however, consist of terms that are squared (i.e., raised to the second power). The basic units of volume consist of terms that are cubed (i.e., raised to the third power). Keeping this information in mind may help you choose the appropriate units to use for a problem.

Formulas

There are many important formulas that are used to solve geometry problems. Using these formulas may make it easier for you to answer geometry questions. The following chart shows some of the most common formulas for determining distance, area, and volume. These formulas will be discussed in more detail in the later sections of the chapter, but this chart may be a convenient reference for you.

P = perimeter (distance around a figure)   V = volume
C = circumference (perimeter of a circle)   A = area (surface area)

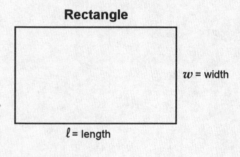

Rectangle

w = width

ℓ = length

$P = 2\ell + 2w$

$A = \ell w$

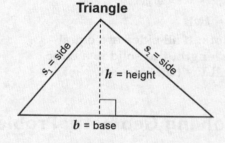

Triangle

s_1 = side s_2 = side

h = height

b = base

$P = b + s_1 + s_2$

$A = \frac{1}{2}bh$

Circle

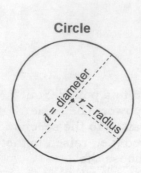

$C = 2\pi r = \pi d$
$A = \pi r^2$

Cylinder

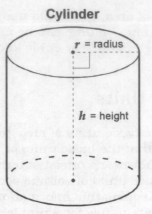

$V = \pi r^2 h$
$A \text{ (total)} = 2\pi r^2 + 2\pi rh$

Rectangular Solid

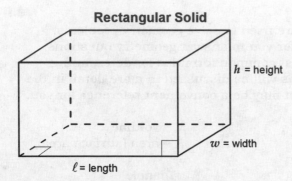

$V = \ell wh$
(Note: If all sides are equal
in length, the solid is a cube
and $V = (s)(s)(s) = s^3$)

Sphere

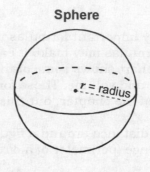

$V = \frac{4}{3}\pi r^3$

Solving Geometry Problems

It is easiest to solve geometry problems if you approach them in an orderly way.
You may find it helpful to use the following steps to solve geometry problems.

1. Draw a picture of the geometric figure described in the problem.

2. Label the measurements of the geometric figure you drew in Step 1 by
    using numbers given in the problem.

3. Determine what value the problem wants you to find.

4. Identify a formula that will allow you to determine that value.

5. In the formula, use the numbers from your drawing (i.e., from the problem)
    and solve for the appropriate value.

6. Check your answer to be sure it is reasonable and that it has the correct
    units.

Finding the Perimeter of Geometric Figures

A *perimeter* is the measurement around the outside of an object. For example, a sidewalk may form the perimeter of a city block, or a fence may form the perimeter of a piece of land. This section discusses problems that involve calculating the perimeter of two-dimensional geometric figures, such as triangles, rectangles, circles, and squares.

Rectangles and squares. The perimeter of a rectangle or square is the distance around the outside of the figure. You can find the perimeter of these geometric figures simply by adding the lengths of the four sides. Suppose, for example, that you need to find the perimeter of a rectangular desk, and you know that the long sides of the desk are 5 feet long and the short sides are 3 feet long. You could find the perimeter simply by adding the lengths of the two long sides to the lengths of the two short sides (5 + 5 + 3 + 3) to determine that the perimeter of the desk is 16 feet.

If the numbers in the problem were larger, it might be more difficult to add the numbers in this way. When this is the case, it is easier to use the following formula to find the perimeter of rectangles and squares.

Perimeter = 2l + 2w

In this formula, l is the length, and w is the width of the rectangle.

Notice that using this formula is similar to adding the length of all four sides, except that the formula takes advantage of the fact that the pairs of sides of the rectangle are the same length.

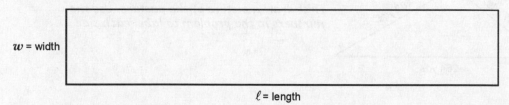

w = width

l = length

The following example shows how to use this formula to find the perimeter of a rectangle.

> Murray walked around a rectangular city block that is 250 feet wide and 350 feet long. How far did Murray walk?

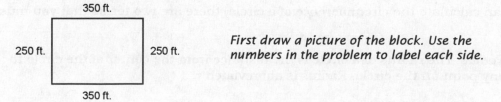

350 ft.

250 ft.   250 ft.

350 ft.

First draw a picture of the block. Use the numbers in the problem to label each side.

$2l + 2w = ?$
$2(350) + 2(250) = ?$
$700 + 500 = 1200$ ft.

You must find the perimeter of the rectangle. Use the formula $2l + 2w = perimeter$. Use the numbers from the problem to solve the formula.

Check your answer to be sure that you have used the correct units.

A square is a special kind of rectangle. You can add the lengths of the sides or use the formula given above to find the perimeter of a square. You can also use a special formula that takes advantage of all four sides of a square being the same length.

Perimeter = 4s, where s is the length of one side of the square.

Triangles. You can find the perimeter of a triangle by adding the lengths of the three sides.

$$Perimeter = s_1 + s_2 + s_3$$

In this formula, s_1, s_2, and s_3 represent the lengths of the sides of the triangle.

The following example shows how to use this formula to find the perimeter of a triangle.

A farmer wants to put a single-wire electric fence around a triangular pasture. One side of the pasture is 182 yards long, a second side is 147 yards long, and the third side is 264 yards long. How many yards of wire does the farmer need to put up the fence around the land?

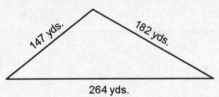

147 yds.   182 yds.

264 yds.

First draw a picture of the pasture. Use the numbers in the problem to label each side.

$s_1 + s_2 + s_3 = ?$
$182 + 147 + 264 = 593$ yd.

You must find the perimeter of the triangle. Use the formula $P = s_1 + s_2 + s_3$. Use the numbers from the problem to solve the formula.

Circles. The perimeter of a circle is called the circumference of the circle. Before you can calculate the circumference of a circle, there are two terms that you must know.

Radius: The radius of a circle is the distance from the center of the circle to any point on the circle. Radius is abbreviated r.

Diameter: The diameter of a circle is the distance from one point on the circle through the center to a point on the opposite side of the circle. Diameter is abbreviated d.

It is important to note that the diameter of a circle is twice as long as the radius of the same circle. You can use this fact to calculate one value if you are given the other (e.g., 2r = d or r = $\frac{1}{2}$d).

When you must solve problems involving circles, it is also important to know about a special value that mathematicians call pi. Pi is a fixed number that is approximately equal to 3.14. The exact value of pi can never be calculated because it contains an infinite number of places to the right of the decimal point. For most math problems, you should use 3.14 as the value of pi. In most problems, a special symbol, π, is used to represent the value of pi. Remember that π = 3.14.

You can find the circumference (perimeter) of a circle by multiplying the diameter (or twice the radius, 2r) times pi (π). The formula for finding the circumference of a circle is written as follows.

> Circumference = (π)(diameter) = (2)(π)(radius)
> C = πd = 2πr

The following example shows how to use this formula to find the circumference of a circle.

A circular hat box has a diameter of 12 inches. What is the circumference of the top of the box?

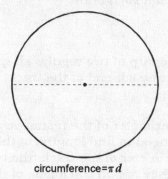

circumference=πd

First draw a picture of the top of the box.

Circumference = πd   *You must find the circumference*
                              of the circle. Use the formula
π(12) = ?   *πd = C. Solve the problem.*
3.14 × 12 = 37.68 in.

Geometry problems use the formulas for perimeter and circumference to find a variety of values. For example, a problem may tell you the perimeter and the length of one side of a rectangle, and then ask you to find the lengths of the three remaining sides. In a problem involving circles, you may be given the circumference of a circular window and asked to calculate the diameter of the window. Remember that you can use basic math operations to rearrange geometric formulas to solve for any value that is included in the formula.

Irregular shapes. You may be asked to find the perimeter of an object that is not a single, regular shape (i.e., square, rectangle, circle, triangle). If the irregular object has straight sides, you can find the perimeter by adding together the lengths of all the sides. Some irregularly shaped objects do not have straight sides, however.

Often, those objects are actually made up of two or more objects that do have a regular geometric shape. The key to finding the perimeter of an irregularly shaped object is to identify the types of regularly shaped objects within it. For example, a window may have a rectangular base with a semicircle above it.

Remember to use the following two rules when you must find the perimeter of an object that has an irregular shape.

1. If the shape has straight sides, simply add the lengths of all the sides. Perimeter = $s_1 + s_2 + s_3 + \ldots$.

2. If the object does not have straight sides, try to divide it into a number of regular shapes (e.g., rectangles, triangles, circles) that are easier to work with. Use the lengths of the sides of the individual shapes to find the perimeter of the irregular object.

The example below shows you how to find the perimeter of an irregular object.

A high school has an athletic track that is in the shape of a rectangle with semicircles at each end. If the rectangle is 100 yards long and 30 yards wide, what is the distance around the outside of the track?

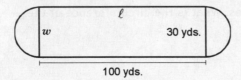

First, draw a picture of the track. Use the numbers in the problem to label the important parts of the diagram.

Notice that the track has an irregular shape that is made up of two regular shapes, a rectangle and a circle (there are two semicircles, one at each end of the track, that make up one whole circle).

To solve this problem, you must find a portion of the perimeter of the rectangle and the entire perimeter of the circle. Notice that you only need to find lengths of the two sides of the rectangle in your calculation of the perimeter of the track (the two widths do not make up part of the perimeter because they are on the inside of the shape). You should also notice that the widths of the rectangle also form the diameter of the circle (i.e., if you combine the two semicircles to make one whole circle, the newly formed whole circle has a diameter that is equal to the width of the rectangle).

100 yd. + 100 yd. = 200 yd.

Calculate the sum of the lengths of the sides of the rectangle. Remember to add in only the sides that are actually part of the perimeter of the track.

πd = circumference
π (30) = ?
3.14(30) = 94.2 yd.

The two semicircles can be combined to form a single circle. This new circle has a diameter of 30 yd. (the width of the rectangle). Use the formula πd = C and the numbers from the problem to find the circumference of the circle.

Length + circumference = perimeter of the track
200 + 94.2 = 294.2 yd.

You can find the total distance of the outside of the track by adding together the lengths of the sides of the rectangle and the circumference of the circle.

Finding the Area of Geometric Figures

Remember that area is a measure of the space inside a two-dimensional figure (for example, the amount of space on the floor of a rectangular volleyball court).

Rectangles and squares. You can calculate the area of a rectangle or a square by multiplying the length of one side by the width of one side, according to the formula A = l × w. In this formula, l is the length, and w is the width of the rectangle.

You can use the same formula to find the area of squares and rectangles. Because the sides of a square are all the same length, you can also use a special formula to find the area of a square. The formula A = s^2 simply squares the length of one side of the square.

The following example shows how to use the formula above to find the area of a rectangle.

> Maxine wants to put wall-to-wall carpet on the floor of her living room. If the room is 22 feet long and 16 feet wide, how much carpet does she need to buy?

To find out how much carpet Maxine must buy, you need to calculate the area of the room (i.e., the amount of floor space that will be covered by the rug). The problem tells you that the room is 22 feet long and 16 feet wide, which means that the room is rectangular.

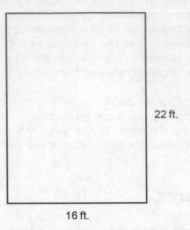

Draw a picture of the floor of the room. Use the numbers from the problem to label your drawing.

22 ft.

16 ft.

A = l × w   *Write the formula for the area*
A = 22 × 16   *of a rectangle. Put in the numbers*
A = 352 ft.^{2} *from the problem and solve.*

Be sure to check that you have used the correct units in your answer.

Sometimes, a problem like the one above asks for an additional step. For example, the problem above might have told you that the carpet Maxine wants to buy costs $1.75 per square foot. It might then have asked you how much it would cost her to buy enough carpet for the room (instead of asking you how much carpet she needs). You could calculate the cost of the carpet by finding the area of the room and then multiplying the number of square feet of carpet by $1.75.

Triangles. Finding the area of a triangle is very similar to finding the area of a rectangle. In fact, you can think of a triangle as half of a rectangle. Remember that the formula for the area of a rectangle is A = l × w.

Area of triangle = $\frac{1}{2}$(length × width)
A = $\frac{1}{2}lw$

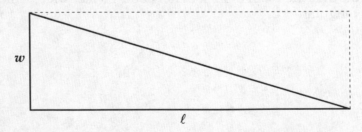

w

ℓ

The length of a triangle is equal to the length of the base of the triangle. As a result, the area formula for a triangle often uses the word *base* to replace the word *length*. The width of a triangle is often called its height. The height (width) is the distance between the base of the triangle and the angle directly above it (see the diagram above). The formula for the area of a triangle is written
A = $\frac{1}{2}$(base)(height) = $\frac{1}{2}$bh.

In some problems involving triangles, base and height are given. In other cases, you may have to calculate one of those values by using other pieces of information given in the problem.

A piece of land is in the shape of a triangle that has a base of 300 feet and a height of 400 feet. What is its area?

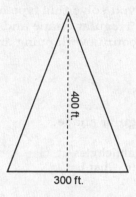

Draw a picture of the piece of land. Use the numbers from the problem to label your drawing.

$A = \frac{1}{2}bh$
$A = \frac{1}{2}(300)(400)$
$A = 60,000$ ft.^{2}

Write the formula for the area of a triangle. Put in the numbers from the problem and solve.

Circles. To find the area of a circle, you must use another special formula that involves the value π (pi). The area of a circle is given by the following formula.

Area = πr^2, where r is the radius of the circle and $\pi = 3.14$.

If a problem gives you the diameter of a circle, simply divide that value in half to find the radius ($\frac{d}{2} = r$).

The example below shows you how to find the area of a circle.

A fence surrounds a circular field that has a radius of 60 feet. What is the area of the field inside the fence?

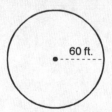

Draw a picture of the field. Use the numbers from the problem to label your drawing.

$A = \pi r^2$
$A = \pi(60)^2$
$A = 3.14(3600)$
$A = 11,304$ ft.^{2}

Write the formula for the area of a circle. Put in the numbers from the problem and solve.

Irregular shapes. Finding the area of an irregular shape is similar to finding the perimeter of an irregular shape. The first thing you must do is find the regular shapes within the irregular shape. Then find the area of each regular shape. Add those areas together to find the area of the irregular shape.

Calculating the area of an irregular shape provides an excellent example of why a diagram is necessary in working geometry problems. When you solve this type of problem, be sure to find the area of all the space inside the irregular shape and include all the space only once (make sure that you do not count overlapping areas twice).

A diagram makes it easier to solve most geometric problems.

The following examples show how to find the area of an irregular shape.

A high school track field is in the shape of a rectangle with semicircles at each end. If the rectangle is 100 yards long and 30 yards wide, what is the area of the field?

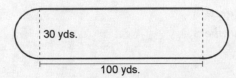

Draw a picture of the field. Use the numbers from the problem to label your drawing.

30 yds.

100 yds.

To solve this problem, you must find the area of the rectangle and the circle (two semicircles equal one full circle) that make up the field.

$A = \ell w$ *Write the formula for the area*
$A = (100)(30)$ *of a rectangle. Use the numbers*
$A = 3000$ yd.^{2} *from the problem to solve the formula.*

$A = \pi r^2$ *Write the formula for the area of a circle.*
$A = \pi(15)^2$ *Remember that the radius = $\frac{1}{2}$ diameter.*
$A = 3.14(225)$ *Use the numbers from the problem to*
$A = 706.5$ yd.^{2} *solve the formula.*

Total area = area of   *Add together the areas of the*
rectangle + area of circle *rectangle and the circle to get*
$A = 3000 + 706.5$ *the total area of the field.*
$A = 3706.5$ yd.^{2}

The total area of the field is 3706.5 square yards.

A rectangular piece of paper is 8 inches wide and 11 inches long. A student cuts out of one corner of the paper a triangular piece that is 3 inches long and 4 inches wide. What is the area of the piece of paper after the triangle-shaped piece is removed? Use the diagram that follows to help you answer the question.

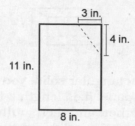

Notice that this problem already includes a diagram. You can therefore skip over the step of drawing and labeling the diagram.

You are asked to find the area of the piece of paper after the triangle-shaped piece is cut off. One way to do this is to find the total area of the rectangle and subtract the area of the triangle from it.

$A = \ell w$ $A = (8)(11)$ $A = 88$ in.^{2}	*Use the appropriate formula to find the area of the rectangle. Use the numbers from the problem to solve the formula.*
$A = \frac{1}{2}\ell w$ $A = \frac{1}{2}(3)(4)$ $A = 6$ in.^{2}	*Use the appropriate formula to find the area of the triangle. Use the numbers from the problem to solve the formula.*
Area remaining = area of rectangle – area of triangle $A = 88 - 6$ $A = 82$ in.^{2}	*Subtract the area of the triangle from the area of the rectangle.*

Surface area. *Surface area* is a special kind of area. It is the area on the surface of a three-dimensional object. For example, a shoe box has six surfaces: the four sides, the top, and the bottom. You can calculate the surface area of the box by determining the area of each of these individual surfaces, and then adding those separate areas together. Geometry problems often involve finding the surface area of two main types of objects, rectangular solids (e.g., cubes, boxes) and cylinders (e.g., cans, pieces of pipe).

Rectangular solids. A rectangular solid is a three-dimensional figure whose faces are rectangles. In a rectangular solid, the surfaces, or sides, that face each other always have the same area. The sides of a rectangular solid can be divided into three groups: top and bottom, front and back, and left and right. Both of the sides in a group have the same area (i.e., the top has the same area as the bottom, the front has the same area as the back, the left side has the same area as the right side). The diagram that follows shows a rectangular solid.

To find the surface area of a rectangular solid, you can calculate the area of the top (i.e., length × width), one side panel (i.e., length × height), and the end panel (i.e., height × width); add them together; and then multiply by 2. The formula for determining the area of a rectangular solid is given below.

Area = 2(area of top + area of front + area of side)

A = 2(ℓw + ℓh + hw)

Also note that in a cube all six surfaces have the same area (because all the sides of a cube have the same dimensions). As a result, you find the surface area of such a cube by finding the area of one side and multiplying that value by 6, or A = 6s^2.

The following example shows how to find the surface area of a rectangular solid.

Find the surface area of a rectangular solid with sides that are 8 inches long, 4 inches wide, and 6 inches high. Use the diagram below to solve this problem.

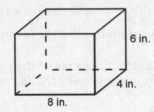

You can use the length, height, and width measurements given in the problem to find the area of the individual sides.

Area of top = ℓw
Area of top = (8)(4) = 32 in.^{2}

Area of front = ℓh
Area of front = (8)(6) = 48 in.^{2}

Area of side = hw
Area of side = (6)(4) = 24 in.^{2}

Total area = 2(area of top + area of front + area of side)
Total area = 2(32 + 48 + 24)
Total area = 2(104) = 208 in.^{2}

Cylinders. A cylinder is a three-dimensional figure that has a circular bottom (base), sides that rise up from the perimeter of the circular base, and a round top. The top and bottom circles are the same size. A can of soup is a common example of a cylinder. A piece of pipe that has a closed top and bottom is another example.

To find the surface area of a cylinder, you must calculate the surface area of the top and the bottom circles, as well as the surface area of the side.

You can think of the side of a cylinder as a rectangle that has been wrapped around the circular top and bottom, as a label is wrapped around a can. The width of the rectangle is the height, h, of the cylinder. The length of the rectangle is the distance around the circumference of the circle. Since a circle has a radius r, you can calculate the length of the rectangle by using the circumference formula, $2\pi r$. It is now possible to use the formula for the area of a rectangle, $A = \ell w$, to find the area of the side of the cylinder. In this case, w = height of the cylinder and $\ell = 2\pi r$, giving the formula $A = 2\pi rh$. You can use the formula for the area of a circle, πr^2, to find the area of the top and bottom of the cylinder. Remember that you must multiply this formula by 2 to find the area of both circles in the cylinder.

The entire formula for finding the surface area of a cylinder is as follows.

$$Area = (2\pi r^2) + (2\pi rh)$$

In this formula, r is the radius of the circular base, and h is the height of the cylinder. Note that the area of the base is multiplied by 2 because you must calculate the area of both the top and the bottom of the cylinder.

The following example shows you how to find the surface area of a cylinder.

Cylinder-shaped metal barrels will be used to store fertilizer on a farm. The farmer wants to paint the barrels with a rust-proofing paint to protect them. If one barrel is 36 inches tall, and its top has a radius of 12 inches, how much surface area will the farmer paint on each barrel (assume that both the top and the bottom are to be painted)?

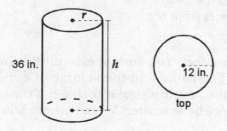

Draw a picture of the barrel. Use the numbers from the problem to label your drawing.

$A = (2\pi r^2) + (2\pi rh)$
$A = 2\pi(12)^2 + 2\pi(12)(36)$
$A = 904.32 + 2712.96$
$A = 3617.28$ in.^{2}

Use the appropriate formula to find the surface area of the cylinder. Use the numbers from the problem to solve the formula.

The farmer will paint a total surface area of 3617.28 square inches on each barrel.

Finding the Volume of Geometric Figures

At the beginning of this chapter, we said that volume is a measure of the space inside a three-dimensional object. Volume can be thought of as the amount of space something can hold. For example, an aluminum can is able to hold a certain amount of juice, or a box is able to hold a certain amount of paper. This section discusses formulas and procedures you can use to find the volume of common geometric figures, such as cubes, rectangular solids, and cylinders.

Rectangular solids. You can find the volume of rectangular solids (boxes, cubes, etc.) by using the following formula.

$$\text{Volume} = \ell \times w \times h$$

In this formula, ℓ is the length, w is the width, and h is the height of the solid.

The following example shows how to use this formula to find the volume of a rectangular solid.

Calculate the volume of a cube that is 2 feet on each side.

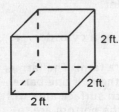

Draw a picture of the cube. Use the numbers from the problem to label your drawing.

2 ft.
2 ft.
2 ft.

$V = \ell wh$ *Use the formula for determining the volume of a*
$V = (2)(2)(2)$ *rectangular solid. Use the numbers from the*
$V = 8 \text{ ft.}^3$ *problem in the formula.*

Note that the answer is in units of volume, cubic feet. You should also notice that height, width, and length are equal in a cube. You could find the volume of a cube by taking the length of any side and cubing it (i.e., multiplying it by itself 3 times). The special formula for finding the volume of a cube is written $V = s^3$, where s is one side of the cube.

Cylinders. You can find the volume of a cylinder by using the following formula.

$$\text{Volume} = \pi r^2 h$$

In this formula, r is the radius of the top of the cylinder, and h is the height of the cylinder.

The following example shows how to find the volume of a cylinder.

A farmer uses cylinder-shaped metal barrels to hold fertilizer. The barrels are 3 feet tall, and the radius of the top of each barrel is 12 inches. What is the capacity of each barrel?

Capacity is a key word in this problem. It indicates that you must find the volume of each barrel.

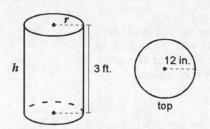

Draw a picture of the barrel. Label your drawing using the numbers from the problem.

Convert 12 in. to 1 ft.

$V = \pi r^2 h$
$V = \pi (1)^2 (3)$
$V = \pi (1)(3)$
$V = 9.42 \text{ ft.}^3$

Use the formula for the volume of a cylinder. Use the numbers from the drawing in the formula. Remember that one of the numbers in the problem is given in feet, and another is given in inches. You must either convert inches to feet or convert feet to inches before you solve the problem.

The volume of each barrel is 9.42 cubic feet.

Deciding Which Formula to Use

It is very important to choose the appropriate formula to solve a geometry problem. To choose the correct formula, you must read the problem carefully and decide what value you are to find. Choosing a formula may be easier if you use the following procedure.

1. Draw a picture of the geometric figure described in the problem.

2. Label all dimensions of the figure by using numbers or variables (i.e., letters) given in the problem.

3. Determine what value the problem wants you to find.

4. Identify a formula that will allow you to determine that value.

The following examples show you how to use this procedure to solve problems.

Murray walked once around a rectangular city block. What formula should be used to determine how far Murray walked?

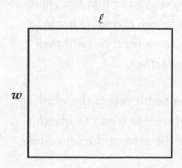

Draw a picture of the block, a rectangle. Decide what value you must find. In this case, you want to find the distance around the outside of a city block, or the perimeter of the block.

$P = 2\ell + 2w$

Choose the formula that allows you to find the value you need. Refer back to the chart of formulas at the beginning of the chapter to help you remember the appropriate formulas.

A phonograph record has a 12-inch diameter. What formula should be used to find the area of the phonograph record?

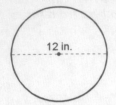

Draw a picture of the record and label it. Decide what value you must find. In this case, you are looking for the area of the record, which is circular.

$A = \pi r^2$ *Choose the formula that allows you to find the value you need.*

A rectangular box will be used to package fruit. What formula can be used to find the volume of the box?

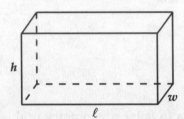

Draw a picture of the box. Decide what value you must find. In this case, you are looking for the volume of a box, which is a rectangular solid.

$V = \ell wh$ *Choose the formula that allows you to find the value you need.*

A window is in the shape of a rectangle with a semicircle above it. What formula should be used to find the number of square feet of glass needed in the window?

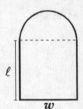

Draw a picture of the window. Decide what value you must find. In this case, you are looking for the number of square feet in the window. This tells you that you must find the area of the window. (Remember that square feet is a unit of area.)

Since the window is an irregular shape, you must find the areas of the two or more regular shapes that make up the window.

Area of rectangle = ℓw *Choose the formula that allows you to find the value*
Area of semicircle = $\frac{1}{2}\pi r^2$ *you need. You will need to use two formulas because the window is made up of two shapes. You will then need to add the two areas together.*

Your drawing will help you see that the diameter of the semicircle is the width of the rectangle (w). The radius of the semicircle is therefore $\frac{1}{2}$w. You can use this value to substitute for r in the formula in order to find the area of the semicircle.

Area of semicircle =

$$\frac{1}{2}\pi\left(\frac{w}{2}\right)^2 =$$

$$\frac{1}{8}\pi w^2$$

Area of rectangle = ℓw

Total area of window = rectangle + semicircle   *Add the two area formulas to find the total area of the window.*

Area of window = $\ell w + \frac{1}{8}\pi(w)^2$

Problems Involving Right Triangles

A triangle that contains one 90° angle is called a right triangle. In a right triangle, the 90° angle is called the right angle, and the side that is opposite the right angle is called the hypotenuse. (NOTE: It is important to remember that the hypotenuse of a right triangle is always longer than the other two sides.) Right triangles are very special geometric figures that have a number of unique properties. These properties make right triangles very useful for solving geometry problems.

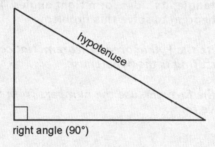

right angle (90°)

Some of the properties of right triangles are described by a mathematical expression called the Pythagorean theorem. This expression describes the relationships among the sides of a right triangle.

In the Pythagorean theorem, each side of a right triangle is given a letter name. The hypotenuse is always labeled *c*. The other two sides of the triangle are labeled *a* and *b*. The Pythagorean theorem states that if you square the values of a and b and add them together, their sum will be equal to the square of the value of c. This statement can be written in the form of an equation as follows.

$$a^2 + b^2 = c^2$$

This statement relates the lengths of the sides of a right triangle. If you know the length of any two sides of a triangle, you can use this statement to find the length of the remaining side. For example, suppose a problem tells you the length of the hypotenuse (c) and the length of one other side (a). You can find the length of the remaining side by using the numbers from the problem and solving for b as follows.

$a^2 + b^2 = c^2$

$b^2 = c^2 - a^2$

You can only use the Pythagorean theorem with right triangles; it does not work with any other type of triangle.

The following examples show how you can use the Pythagorean theorem to solve geometry problems.

To put a cover on a child's rectangular swimming pool, Maria needs to put a rope diagonally across the pool. She knows that the pool is 3 yards wide and 4 yards long. How long is the diagonal across the pool?

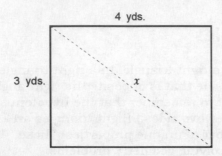

Draw a picture of the swimming pool, and use the numbers from the problem to label the sides. Label the diagonal x.

Since the pool is a rectangle, its sides form right angles. This means that you can use the Pythagorean theorem to solve this problem.

$a^2 + b^2 = c^2$ *Write the Pythagorean theorem. Notice that the side you must find is the hypotenuse.*

$3^2 + 4^2 = x^2$ *In the formula, use the numbers from the problem and*
$9 + 16 = x^2$ *solve for x.*
$25 = x^2$

$\sqrt{25} = \sqrt{x^2}$ *Find the value of x by taking the square root of both sides of the equation.*

$5 = x$

You should check your answer to see if you need to find a square root when you are using the Pythagorean theorem. Often, your answer will not be a perfect square (a number with a whole number for a square root). When that occurs, your answer may include a square root sign.

A 12-foot ladder is placed against a building. The base of the ladder is 4 feet from the base of the building. How high up the building does the ladder reach?

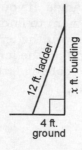

Draw a diagram of the building, ladder, and ground. Use the numbers from the problem to label the diagram. Label the building side of the triangle x.

Since the building is assumed to be perpendicular to the ground, the figure is a right triangle. You can use the Pythagorean theorem to solve for x.

$a^2 + b^2 = c^2$ *Write the Pythagorean theorem. Notice that you must find a leg of the right triangle.*

$4^2 + x^2 = 12^2$ *In the formula, use the numbers from the problem. Solve for x.*

$16 + x^2 = 144$
$x^2 = 144 - 16$
$x^2 = 128$

$\sqrt{x^2} = \sqrt{128}$ *Find the value of x by taking the square root of both sides.*

$x = \sqrt{128}$

$x = \sqrt{(64)(2)}$ *Factor the radicand.*

$x = 8\sqrt{2}$ *Simplify your answer.*

It is also possible to find a decimal approximation for x.

$x \approx 11.3$ feet

Find the height of an equilateral triangle with sides 8 cm.

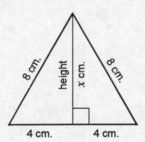

Draw the triangle. Label the height x.

Notice that the height of an equilateral triangle will bisect the base (i.e., divide it into two equal parts).

Use the Pythagorean theorem to find the height.

$a^2 + b^2 = c^2$

$4^2 + x^2 = 8^2$

$16 + x^2 = 64$

$x^2 = 64 - 16$

$x^2 = 48$

$$\sqrt{x^2} = \sqrt{48}$$

$$x = \sqrt{(16)(3)}$$

$$x = 4\sqrt{3}$$

A decimal approximation for x is 6.9 cm.

Practice Exercises

The following exercises will help you review the skills covered in this chapter. Many of the types of questions presented here will be similar to those on the test; others will not. Remember that the purpose of the exercises is to give you practice on the skills rather than merely to prepare you for the test. Following these exercises are the Practice Exercise Explanations. They explain each question, the correct answer, and why the remaining choices are incorrect.

1. Use the diagram below to answer the question that follows.

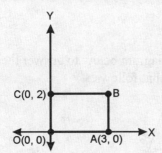

What is the perimeter of rectangle OABC?

A. 10

B. 5

C. 6

D. 6π

2. Use the diagram below to answer the question that follows.

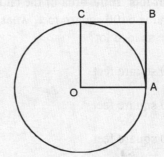

OABC is a square with a perimeter of 12 inches. What is the circumference of the circle with center O?

A. 3π

B. 6π

C. 8π

D. 9π

3. Use the diagram below to answer the
    question that follows.

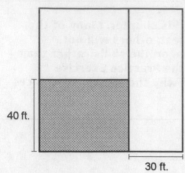

40 ft.

30 ft.

A square plot of land is partitioned into 3
rectangular lots. If the area of the entire
plot of land is 6400 square feet, what is the
area of the shaded lot?

A.   80 square feet

B.   180 square feet

C.   1200 square feet

D.   2000 square feet

4. Use the diagram below to answer the
    question that follows.

If the perimeter of this quartercircle is
$4 + \pi$, what is the area of the quartercircle?

A. π

B. 4π

C. 8π

D. 16π

5. Jill walked diagonally across a rectangular
    field that measured 100 feet by 240 feet.
    Which of the following expressions should
    be used to determine how far she walked?

A. $\dfrac{100 \times 240}{2}$

B. $\sqrt{100^2 + 240^2}$

C. $2(100 + 240)$

D. $\sqrt{100} + \sqrt{240}$

6. Use the diagram below to answer the
    question that follows.

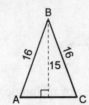

Which of the following expressions
describes the area of triangle ABC?

A. $(2)(15)\sqrt{16^2 - 15^2}$

B. $(2)(15)(16)$

C. $(15)\sqrt{16^2 - 15^2}$

D. $\dfrac{15 \times 16}{2}$

7. Use the diagram below to answer the question that follows.

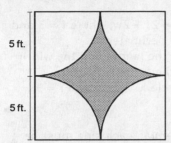

What is the area in square feet of the shaded region in the square?

A. $100 - 25\pi$

B. 75π

C. $100 - 10\pi$

D. 90π

8. Use the diagram below to answer the question that follows.

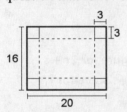

A 3-inch square is cut from each corner of a 20-inch-by-16-inch sheet of metal. The metal is folded along dotted lines as indicated in the diagram. What is the volume of the pan formed by the metal?

A. 420 in.³

B. 546 in.³

C. 663 in.³

D. 960 in.³

9. Use the diagram below to answer the question that follows.

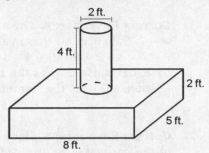

A pedestal for a statue is to have a height of 4 feet and a diameter of 2 feet. The pedestal's base is to be a rectangular solid that is 8 feet long, 5 feet wide, and 2 feet thick. What volume of cement is needed to construct the pedestal and its base?

A. $(80 + 16\pi)$ ft.³

B. $(80 - 4\pi)$ ft.³

C. $(80 + 8\pi)$ ft.³

D. $(80 + 4\pi)$ ft.³

10. Find the approximate length of the longest straight line that can be drawn on a 9-inch by 11-inch sheet of paper.

A. 6.3 inches

B. 11 inches

C. 14.2 inches

D. 18 inches

Practice Exercise Explanations

1. **Correct Response: A.** The appropriate formula to use is p = 2l + 2w, where l = 3 and w = 2. Substituting these values into the formula gives the perimeter, P = 2 × 3 + 2 × 2 = 6 + 4 = 10. Response B fails to multiply the length and the width by 2. Response C finds the area of the rectangle by using the formula A = lw. Response D uses the formula for the circumference of a circle, C = 2πr, with r = 3.

2. **Correct Response: B.** Since the four sides of a square are equal, each side must be $\frac{1}{4}$ of the perimeter, or 3 in. Side OA of the square is also the radius of the circle. Use the formula C = 2πr, where r = 3, to find the circumference. C = (2)(π)(3) = 6π. Response A does not double the radius. Response C divides 12 by 4, gets the incorrect value 4, and then uses it correctly. Response D finds the area of the circle.

3. **Correct Response: D.** First, use the formula for the area of a square, A = s², to find that each side of the plot of land is 80 ft. long.

   s² = 6400

   $\sqrt{s^2}$ = $\sqrt{6400}$

   s = 80

   The dimensions of the shaded lot can now be found to be 40 ft. and (80 – 30) ft. Using the formula A = lw, the area of the lot is 40 × (80 – 30) = 40 × 50 = 2000 sq. ft. Response A uses the length of one side instead of calculating area. Response B gives the perimeter of the shaded lot. Response C uses the length 30 without subtracting it from 80 to determine one side.

4. **Correct Response: A.** The perimeter is the distance around the figure, or 2r + s. Therefore, s must be $\frac{1}{4}$ the circumference of the circle, or $\frac{2\pi r}{4} = \frac{\pi r}{2}$. Solve for r, using the equation, P = 4 + π = 2r + $\frac{\pi r}{2}$.

   4 + π = 2r + $\frac{\pi r}{2}$

   7.14 = 2r + $\frac{(3.14)(r)}{2}$

   7.14 = (3.57)(r)

   r = $\frac{7.14}{3.57}$ = 2

   The area of the region is $\frac{1}{4}$ of the total area of a circle. A = πr², so the area is given by $\frac{1}{4}\pi r^2 = \frac{1}{4}\pi(2)^2 = \pi$. Response B finds the circumference of the whole circle. Response C uses the radius of 4 and finds the area of a semicircle. Response D uses the radius of 4 and finds the area of the complete circle.

5. **Correct Response: B.** The first step in solving this problem is to draw a diagram.

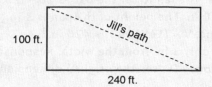

100 ft.

Jill's path

240 ft.

Since Jill's path across the rectangular field divides the field into two right triangles, this problem can be solved by applying the Pythagorean theorem: $a^2 + b^2 = c^2$. If her path across the field is p, the equation is as follows.

$$p^2 = 100^2 + 240^2$$

$$p = \sqrt{100^2 + 240^2}$$

Response A finds the area of each triangle formed by her path. Response C finds the perimeter of the whole field. Response D involves a misinterpretation of the Pythagorean theorem.

6. **Correct Response: C.** The area of a triangle is given by $\frac{1}{2}bh$, where b is the base and h is the height. In this triangle, h = 15, but you must calculate b. Using the Pythagorean theorem, you can calculate half of b as follows.

$$\left(\frac{b}{2}\right)^2 = c^2 - b^2 = 16^2 - 15^2$$

$$\frac{b}{2} = \sqrt{16^2 - 15^2}$$

$$b = (2)\sqrt{16^2 - 15^2}$$

The area, then, is as follows.

$$\frac{1}{2} \times (2)\sqrt{16^2 - 15^2} \times 15$$

$$= \sqrt{16^2 - 15^2} \times 15$$

Response A uses b × h as the formula for area. Response B uses one side as equivalent to b, multiplies this side by the height, and doubles the product. Response D uses 15 and 16 as h and b.

7. **Correct Response: A.** The shaded area equals the area of the square minus the area of each quartercircle. Each side of the square is 10, and the radius of each quartercircle is 5. Since there are four quartercircles, their combined area is the area of a circle with a radius of 5. Begin by using the formula for the area of a square.

$$A = s^2 = 10^2 = 100$$

Next, find the area of a circle with a radius of 5.

$$A = \pi r^2 = \pi 5^2 = 25\pi$$

The area of the shaded region is $100 - 25\pi$.

Response B incorrectly subtracts 25π from 100. Response C uses the formula for the circumference of the circle instead of for the area of the circle. Response D incorrectly subtracts 10π from 100.

8. **Correct Response: A.** To determine the volume of the pan, you must first determine the length, the width, and the height of the pan. The length of the pan is 20 – (2 × 3) = 14 in. The width of the pan is 16 – (2 × 3) = 10 in. The height of the pan is 3 in. Next, use the formula V = ℓwh to find the volume, V = (14)(10)(3) = 420 in.^{3}. Response B subtracts 6 in. from the length but only 3 in. from the width. Response C subtracts only 3 in. from each dimension. Response D uses the original dimensions along with a height of 3 in.

9. **Correct Response: D.** The volume is the sum of the volume of the base plus the volume of the cylinder. Since the base is a rectangular solid, its volume can be found by using the formula V = ℓ × w × h. The volume of the base is 8 ft. × 5 ft. × 2 ft. = 80 ft.^{3}. The volume of the cylinder can be found using the formula V = πr^2h. Before using the equation, notice that the radius of the cylinder is 1 ft., not 2 ft. The diameter of the cylinder is 2 ft. The volume of the cylinder is $(\pi)(1$ ft.$)^2(4$ ft.$) = 4\pi$ ft.^{3}. The volume of the base and the cylinder together is $(80 + 4\pi)$ ft.^{3}. Response A uses the diameter rather than the radius in calculating the area of the cylinder. Response B subtracts the volume of the cylinder from the volume of the base rather than adding the two volumes. Response C uses the formula V = $2\pi rh$ for the volume of the cylinder.

10. **Correct Response: C.** The first step is to draw a diagram.

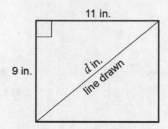

Since the longest straight line that can be drawn is a diagonal, and that line divides the paper into two right triangles, you can apply the Pythagorean theorem: $a^2 + b^2 = c^2$. Let the diagonal be d.

$d^2 = 11^2 + 9^2$

$d = \sqrt{11^2+9^2} = \sqrt{121+81} = \sqrt{202} \approx 14.2$ inches

Response A involves using the Pythagorean theorem to solve for a leg of the triangle instead of the hypotenuse. Response B is the result of drawing the line along the longer edge of the paper rather than diagonally. Response D results from adding 11 and 9.

Study Ideas

A careful study of the above exercises and the explanations of the answers will help you review important skills relating to solving problems involving geometric figures. In these exercises you were asked to identify the appropriate formula for solving geometric problems, to solve problems involving two- and three-dimensional geometric figures, and to solve problems involving right triangles using the Pythagorean theorem. The exercises are designed to give you practice in these skills. You may wish to reread parts of the chapter that address specific skills with which you have difficulty.

You should be aware of the basic geometric concepts discussed in this chapter and apply them to your work in college, at home, and on the job. The formulas and techniques of geometry are important in many fields.

Chapter 19

SOLVE PROBLEMS
INVOLVING GEOMETRIC CONCEPTS

This skill includes drawing conclusions using the principles of similarity, congruence, parallelism, and perpendicularity.

Introduction

Geometry is a branch of mathematics that is based on statements and definitions describing shapes and figures. In geometry problems, you must use these statements and definitions to prove whether other statements are true or false. You must also use reasoning skills to identify relationships between two statements or definitions or to identify patterns between geometric figures or numbers. Often, you will need to be able to recognize a connection between a statement and a geometric figure.

To identify these relationships, you must know the basic statements and definitions that are commonly used in geometry problems. In this chapter you will review some of the properties of segments and angles, parallel and perpendicular lines, and congruence and similarity.

Basic Definitions Used in Geometry

Geometry uses a number of basic terms. This section lists many of those terms and gives definitions for them. You will need to know these definitions to solve geometry problems. You may find it useful to refer back to this section as you work through other sections of this chapter.

Point. In geometry, a point indicates a position. Technically, a point has no size or dimensions, but it may be represented on paper as a dot. Points are often used to identify a position on a line, plane, or geometric figure. A point is usually named by writing a capital letter next to the dot representing it.

● P

Point P

Line. A line is a one-dimensional figure that extends infinitely far in two opposite directions (e.g., right and left, up and down). In geometry, all lines are assumed to be straight. A line is usually named for two points that are located on it.

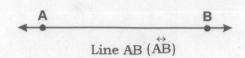

Line AB ($\overleftrightarrow{AB}$)

Plane. A plane is a flat surface that extends infinitely far in all directions. A plane is usually represented by a four-sided figure.

Line segment. A line segment is a part of a line. A line segment is made up of two distinct endpoints and all the points between them. A line segment is usually named for its endpoints.

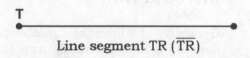

Line segment TR ($\overline{TR}$)

Ray. A ray is a portion of a line that has only one endpoint. The ray extends infinitely far from that endpoint. A ray usually takes the letter name of its endpoint (or its endpoint and another point on the line).

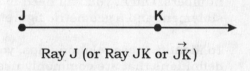

Ray J (or Ray JK or $\overrightarrow{JK}$)

Angle. An angle is the figure formed by two distinct rays that have a common endpoint. The common endpoint is called the vertex of the angle, and the rays are called the sides of the angle. An angle may be named by identifying the letter name of its vertex, or by naming a point on one ray, the vertex, and a point on the second ray.

Angles are measured in degrees. The measure of an angle is the number of degrees in the interior of the angle.

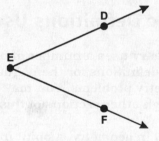

Angle E ($\angle E$) or
angle DEF ($\angle DEF$)

Right angle. A right angle is an angle that contains 90°.

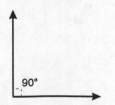

90°

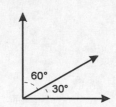

Complementary angles.
Complementary angles are two angles whose sum is 90°.

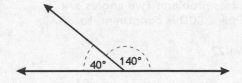

Supplementary angles.
Supplementary angles are two angles whose sum is 180°.

Adjacent angles. Adjacent angles are two angles on a plane that have the same vertex and a common side (but no interior points in common). ∠QSR and ∠RST are adjacent angles.

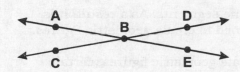

Vertical angles. Vertical angles are two nonadjacent angles that are formed by two intersecting lines. ∠ABC and ∠DBE are vertical angles.

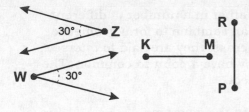

Congruent. Two geometric figures are congruent if they have the same shape and measure. For example, two congruent angles have the same number of degrees. Congruent line segments are the same length. The symbol for congruent is ≅. ∠Z ≅ ∠W, and $\overline{KM} \cong \overline{RP}$.

You should use the definitions above to solve the problems in the following examples.

Which angle in the diagram is congruent to ∠GAB?

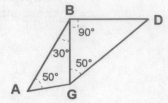

Use the definition of the word *congruent* to solve this problem. Two angles are congruent if they have the same measure. Therefore, ∠BGD is congruent to ∠GAB.

Which angles in the diagram are adjacent to ∠MKZ?

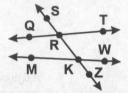

Use the definition of the word *adjacent* to solve this problem. Two angles are adjacent if they have the same vertex and a common side (i.e., if they are next to each other on the same side of a line). Therefore, ∠MKR and ∠ZKW are adjacent to ∠MKZ.

Solving Problems with Parallel and Perpendicular Lines

Many geometric figures are made up of lines or line segments. As a result, it is important to understand how lines can be combined to create geometric figures.

When lines or line segments are combined to create geometric figures, certain relationships are established. The way two lines come together affects the types of angles and figures that are formed. Often, it is possible to draw conclusions and make assumptions about angles and geometric figures just by knowing how lines were joined to make them.

Lines and line segments may be related to each other in a number of different ways. One of the most obvious ways that lines can combine to form geometric figures or angles is by crossing. When two lines cross, they are said to *intersect*. In geometry, two lines are said to intersect if they have a point in common. The diagram that follows shows two lines that intersect.

Notice that point P is found on both of the lines in the diagram.

Two lines that form right angles (90° angles) when they intersect are called *perpendicular lines* (⊥). $\overleftrightarrow{MN} \perp \overleftrightarrow{QR}$.

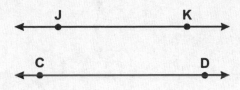

Two lines in a plane that never intersect are called *parallel lines* (∥). Two parallel lines are always exactly the same distance apart; they never get any closer or farther apart. $\overleftrightarrow{JK} \parallel \overleftrightarrow{CD}$.

Many geometric figures contain either parallel or perpendicular lines. For example, a rectangle is made up of two sets of parallel lines, one vertical pair and one horizontal pair. The vertical lines are also perpendicular to the horizontal lines. $\overline{AB} \parallel \overline{CD}$ and $\overline{AD} \parallel \overline{BC}$.

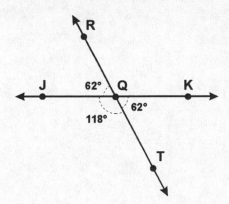

When two lines intersect, four angles are formed. The intersecting lines form four pairs of *adjacent angles* and two pairs of *opposite angles*. The two adjacent angles in each pair are *supplementary angles* (i.e., the sum of the measures of the two angles equals 180°). The angles that are opposite one another are equal in size. It is important to remember the relationships among the angles that are formed when two lines intersect.

Sometimes one line intersects two other lines. A line that intersects two other lines is called a *transversal*. Transversals also create special relationships among lines and angles. *Alternate interior angles, alternate exterior angles,* and *corresponding angles* are formed by transversals. It is important to know the definitions of these special types of angles. $\overleftrightarrow{AB}$ is a transversal.

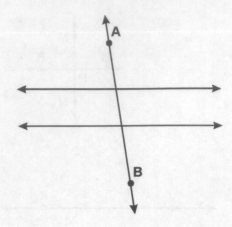

Alternate interior angles. When a transversal intersects two lines, two pairs of alternate interior angles are formed. The alternate interior angles are between the two lines that are intersected by the transversal, and they are on opposite sides of the transversal. ∠3 and ∠6 are alternate interior angles. ∠4 and ∠5 are also alternate interior angles.

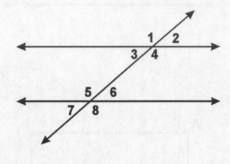

Alternate exterior angles. When a transversal intersects two lines, two pairs of alternate exterior angles are formed. The alternate exterior angles are outside the two lines that are intersected by the transversal, and they are on alternate sides of the transversal. ∠1 and ∠8 are alternate exterior angles. ∠2 and ∠7 are also alternate exterior angles.

Corresponding angles. When a transversal intersects two lines, several pairs of corresponding angles are formed. One of the angles of each pair must be between the two lines that are intersected by the transversal, and the other angle of each pair must be outside the two lines that are intersected by the transversal. The two angles in a pair of corresponding angles must be on the same side of the transversal. ∠8 and ∠4, ∠6 and ∠2, ∠7 and ∠3, and ∠5 and ∠1 are pairs of corresponding angles.

Use the definitions above to solve the problems in the following examples.

Based on the information in the diagram, which of the following must be true?

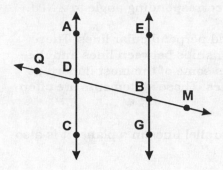

A. $\overleftrightarrow{QM}$ is a transversal.

B.   ∠ADQ ≅ ∠QDC

C. $\overleftrightarrow{AC} \perp \overleftrightarrow{QM}$

D.   ∠ADB and ∠MBG are opposite angles.

Use the definitions given above to solve this problem. A transversal is a line that intersects two other lines. Therefore, response A is a true statement. Two angles are congruent if they both have the same measure. ∠ADQ and ∠QDC could have the same measure only if they are both right angles. Since there is no indication that they are right angles, they are not congruent; therefore, response B is a false statement. Two line segments are perpendicular if they intersect to form right angles. Because ∠ADQ and ∠QDC are not right angles, $\overleftrightarrow{AC}$ and $\overleftrightarrow{QM}$ are not perpendicular; therefore, response C is a false statement. Opposite angles are two nonadjacent angles formed by two intersecting lines. Opposite angles share a common vertex but no common sides. ∠ADB and ∠MBG do not meet these criteria; therefore, response D is a false statement. The correct response to this question is response A.

Which angle is a corresponding angle to ∠NPJ?

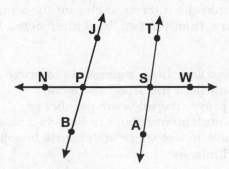

Pairs of corresponding angles are formed when a transversal intersects two lines. To be corresponding angles, one angle of the pair must be between the two lines that are intersected by the transversal, and the other must be outside the two lines that are intersected. Both angles in the pair must be on the same side of the transversal. Based on this definition, $\angle$TSP is a corresponding angle to $\angle$NPJ.

Many statements can be made about parallel and perpendicular lines. These statements can help you understand the relationships between lines and the angles that they form. The following list includes some of the most important statements about parallel and perpendicular lines. These statements are often useful for solving geometry problems.

1. If a line is perpendicular to one of two parallel lines in a plane, it is also perpendicular to the other line.

2. If two lines intersect to form congruent adjacent angles (i.e., adjacent angles that have the same measure), the lines are perpendicular.

3. If two parallel lines are intersected by a transversal, each pair of alternate interior angles is congruent (i.e., the angles have the same measure). Also, if a transversal intersects a pair of lines in such a way that the alternate interior angles are congruent, then the two lines intersected by the transversal are parallel.

4. If two parallel lines are intersected by a transversal, each pair of alternate exterior angles is congruent. Also, if a transversal intersects a pair of lines in such a way that the alternate exterior angles are congruent, then the two lines intersected by the transversal are parallel.

5. If two parallel lines are intersected by a transversal, each pair of corresponding angles is congruent. Also, if a transversal intersects a pair of lines in such a way that the corresponding angles are congruent, then the two lines intersected by the transversal are parallel.

6. If two parallel lines are intersected by a transversal, the exterior angles on the same side of the transversal are supplementary. Also, if a transversal intersects a pair of lines in such a way that the exterior angles on the same side of the transversal are supplementary, then the two lines intersected by the transversal are parallel.

7. If two parallel lines are intersected by a transversal, the interior angles on the same side of the transversal are supplementary. Also, if a transversal intersects a pair of lines in such a way that the interior angles on the same side of the transversal are supplementary, then the two lines intersected by the transversal are parallel.

In some geometry problems, you may be asked to use these statements to prove that certain angles in a geometric figure are congruent (i.e., have the same measure). In other problems, you may have to prove that lines are parallel or perpendicular to one another. You can use the statements above to help you solve such problems. The following examples show how to use these statements to solve problems involving parallel and perpendicular lines.

Use the statements above to solve the problems in the following examples.

Line CG and line FE lie in the same plane and are intersected by line AH. ∠GBD is congruent to ∠FDB. What does this indicate about the relationship between line CG and line FE?

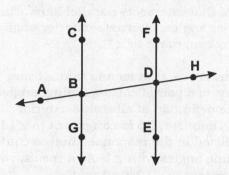

To solve this problem, you must consider three lines and two angles. Use the definitions given in the previous sections of this chapter to identify the relationships among these lines and angles. You may find it helpful to set up a table of statements about the problem and reasons why each statement is true.

Statement	Reason
1. $\overleftrightarrow{AH}$ is a transversal.	Definition of a transversal.
2. ∠GBD and ∠FDB are alternate interior angles.	Definition of alternate interior angles.
3. ∠GBD ≅ ∠FDB.	Given in the problem.
4. Line CG is parallel to line FE.	Alternate interior angles are congruent when two parallel lines are intersected by a transversal.

You should answer this problem by stating that line CG is parallel to line FE.

In the diagram below, $\overleftrightarrow{AB} \parallel \overleftrightarrow{CD}$. Which angle in the diagram is congruent to ∠1?

A. 2

B. 3

C. 5

D. 7

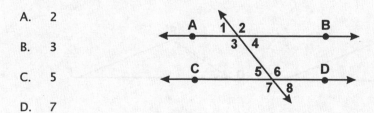

To solve this problem, you must identify the relationships among several angles. The easiest way to solve this problem may be to determine what type of angle ∠1 is and then to use the statements above to find an angle that must be congruent to it.

Notice that this diagram contains a transversal that intersects parallel lines. This is a clue that you should look for alternate interior angles, alternate exterior angles, or corresponding angles to find an angle that is congruent to ∠1.

∠1 is an exterior angle. By the definitions given above, that means that ∠1 may be part of a pair of alternate exterior angles or part of a pair of corresponding angles. The alternate exterior angle to ∠1 is ∠8 (by the definition of alternate exterior angles). The corresponding angle to ∠1 is ∠5. Therefore, ∠5 is congruent to ∠1 (by statement 5 above). None of the other angles listed in the response choices could form a pair of alternate exterior or corresponding angles with ∠1. As a result, you cannot prove that any of those angles are congruent to ∠1 based on the information stated in the problem.

Similarity and Congruence

Similarity and congruence are two of the most important concepts in geometry. These concepts help to identify lines, angles, and geometric figures that have something in common.

Earlier in this chapter, the definition of the word *congruent* was given as two figures having the same shape and measure. Line segments, angles, or geometric figures may be congruent. For example, if two triangles are congruent, their angles have the same measure, and their sides have the same length. The diagram below shows two congruent triangles.

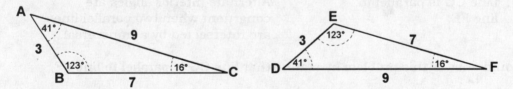

Figures that are similar have the same shape but are not necessarily the same size. For two figures to be similar, their corresponding angles must have the same measures, and their corresponding sides must be proportional. The diagram below shows two similar triangles. ∠B ≅ ∠E, ∠A ≅ ∠D, and ∠C ≅ ∠F; also, $\frac{AB}{DE} = \frac{BC}{EF} = \frac{AC}{DF}$.

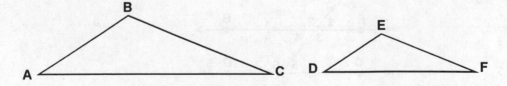

There are many types of geometric figures. A simple, closed, two-dimensional geometric figure with sides that are line segments and one interior region is called a polygon. Polygons are classified according to the number of sides they have. The following table identifies some of the most common polygons.

Number of Sides	Name	Diagram
3	Triangle	
4	Quadrilateral	
5	Pentagon	
6	Hexagon	
8	Octagon	
10	Decagon	

In many geometry problems, you must prove that two polygons are similar or congruent. These problems may give you information about angles or line segments that make up the polygon and then ask you to draw conclusions about the entire figure. Some problems may begin by telling you that two polygons are similar and then ask you to use that information to draw conclusions about line segments, angles, or polygons.

To prove that two figures are congruent, you must show that they have the same size and shape. You can only do that by finding a way to prove that all the corresponding measures in the two figures are equal.

To prove that two figures are similar, you must show that their corresponding angles have the same measure and that their corresponding sides are proportional.

Congruent triangles. In some cases, you may not need to show that all the measures in two figures are equal in order to prove that they are similar or congruent. For example, there are ways to prove that two triangles are congruent simply by proving that the three sides are congruent, that two sides and the angle between them are congruent, or that two angles and the side that connects them are congruent. The following statements explain these three ways to prove that two triangles are congruent.

Side/Side/Side (SSS). If the three sides of one triangle are congruent to the three sides of another triangle, then the two triangles are congruent. If side A is congruent to side a, and side B is congruent to side b, and side C is congruent to side c, the two triangles are congruent.

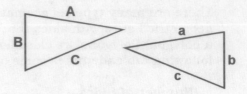

Side/Angle/Side (SAS). If two sides of one triangle and the angle between the sides are congruent to the corresponding sides and the angle of another triangle, then the two triangles are congruent. If side G is congruent to side N, side I is congruent to side M and $\angle a \cong \angle r$, the two triangles are congruent.

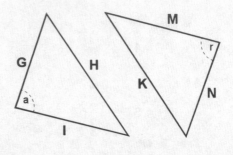

Angle/Side/Angle (ASA). If two angles and the side that connects them on one triangle are congruent to the corresponding angles and side on another triangle, then the two triangles are congruent. If $\angle d \cong \angle m$, $\angle e \cong \angle k$, and side R is congruent to side U, the two triangles are congruent.

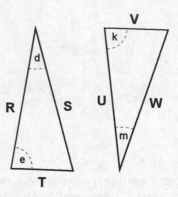

Similar triangles. To prove that two triangles are similar (i.e., have the same shape) it is not necessary to use the definition and prove that all the corresponding angles are congruent and all the corresponding sides are proportional. Just as with congruence of triangles, there are simpler methods to prove that triangles are similar. These include proving that corresponding angles are congruent, proving that two sets of sides are proportional and the included angles are congruent, and proving that the three sets of corresponding sides are proportional. The following statements explain these three ways to prove that two triangles are similar.

Angle/Angle/Angle. (AAA). If three angles of one triangle are congruent to three corresponding angles of a second triangle, then the two triangles are similar. If angle A is congruent to angle D, angle B is congruent to angle E, and angle C is congruent to angle F, then the two triangles are similar.

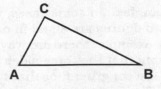
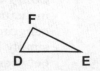

Side/Angle/Side (SAS). If two sides of one triangle are proportional to two sides of a second triangle and the included angles are congruent, then the two triangles are similar. If the ratio of side GH to side MK is equal to the ratio of side HJ to side KL (GH/MK = HJ/KL), and angle H is congruent to angle K, then the two triangles are similar.

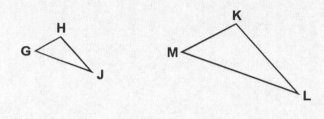

Side/Side/Side (SSS). If the three sets of corresponding sides of two triangles are proportional, then the two triangles are similar. If the ratio of RS to UV is equal to the ratio of TS to WV is equal to the ratio of RT to UW (RS/UV = TS/WV = RT/UW), then the triangles are similar.

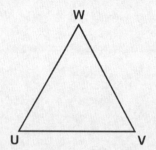

You may need to use these statements, or other statements listed in this chapter, to demonstrate that two angles, line segments, or polygons are congruent or similar. There are many other statements that can be used to show that figures are congruent or similar. You should consult a geometry book if you would like to find other statements that can be used to prove that figures are similar or congruent.

You may find it easier to prove that two polygons are similar or congruent if you use the following steps.

1. Study any diagrams that appear with the problem, or draw a diagram based on information in the problem.

2. Use numbers from the problem to label the known values in the diagram.

3. Determine what values you must find to prove that the figures are similar or congruent.

4. Use geometry statements and definitions to prove that the figures are similar or congruent.

Practice Exercises

The following exercises will help you review the skills covered in this chapter. Many of the types of questions presented here will be similar to those on the test; others will not. Remember that the purpose of the exercises is to give you practice on the skills rather than merely to prepare you for the test. Following these exercises are the Practice Exercise Explanations. They explain each question, the correct answer, and why the remaining choices are incorrect.

1. Use the diagram below to answer the question that follows.

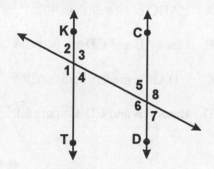

If line KT is parallel to line CD, and $\angle 7$ has a measure of 68°, what is the measure of $\angle 1$?

A.   22°

B.   68°

C.   90°

D.   112°

2. Use the diagram below to answer the question that follows.

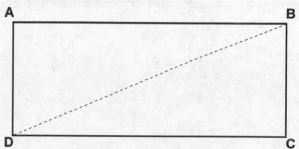

In rectangle ABCD, $\overline{AB} \parallel \overline{CD}$ and $\overline{AD} \parallel \overline{BC}$. Diagonal BD divides the rectangle into two triangles, $\triangle ABD$ and $\triangle CDB$. Which of the following is a valid conclusion about this figure?

A. $\triangle ABD$ contains three right angles.

B. $\overline{BD} \perp \overline{DC}$

C. $\angle ABD \cong \angle BDC$

D. $\angle ADB$ and $\angle CDB$ are supplementary.

3. Use the diagram below to answer the question that follows.

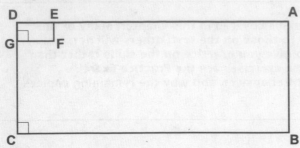

If rectangle DEFG is similar to rectangle DABC, and DE = 4, DA = 24, and AB = 12, what is the length of $\overline{EF}$?

A.   2

B.   4

C.   8

D.   16

4. Use the diagram below to answer the question that follows.

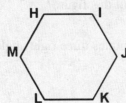

If polygon HIJKLM is similar to polygon ABCDEF, and HI = 40, AB = 20, and ∠K = 120°, what is the measure of ∠D?

A.   60°

B.   100°

C.   120°

D.   240°

5. Use the diagram below to answer the question that follows.

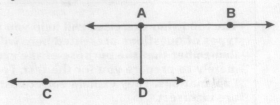

Lines AB and CD lie in the same plane and are connected by $\overline{AD}$. If $\overline{AD}$ is perpendicular to both $\overleftrightarrow{AB}$ and $\overleftrightarrow{CD}$, which of the following is a valid conclusion?

A. ∠ADC is greater than 90°.

B. Lines AB and CD are perpendicular.

C. ∠DAB is greater than ∠ADC.

D. Lines AB and CD are parallel.

6. In polygon RSTU, only sides RS and TU are parallel. What is the largest number of right angles that can be formed by the intersecting sides of this polygon?

A. 0

B. 1

C. 2

D. 4

7. Use the diagram below to answer the question that follows.

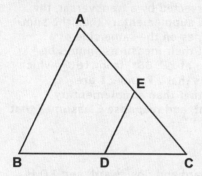

In triangle ABC, line DE is parallel to side AB. If triangle ABC is isosceles, with AC = CB, and the measure of angle C is 50 degrees, what is the measure of angle EDB?

A. 50 degrees

B. 65 degrees

C. 115 degrees

D. 125 degrees

8. Use the diagram below to answer the question that follows.

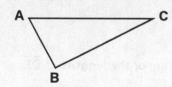

Triangle ABC is similar to triangle DEF. If AB = 12, DE = 4, and DF = 6, what is the length of AC?

A. 2

B. 8

C. 10

D. 18

Practice Exercise Explanations

1. **Correct Response: D.** When two parallel lines are intersected by a transversal, the exterior angles on the same side of the transversal are supplementary (i.e., the sum of their measures is 180°). $\angle 1$ and $\angle 7$ are exterior angles on the same side of a transversal that intersects parallel lines, so the sum of their measures should be 180°. To find the measure of $\angle 1$, subtract the measure of $\angle 7$, 68°, from 180°, which gives 112°. Therefore, $\angle 1 = 112°$. Response A assumes that $\angle 7$ and $\angle 1$ are complementary (i.e., their measures add up to 90°) rather than supplementary. Response B assumes that the two angles are congruent, and response C assumes that $\angle 1$ is a right angle.

2. **Correct Response: C.** If $\overline{AD}$ and $\overline{BC}$ are extended upward and downward, and $\overline{BD}$ is extended diagonally, it can be seen that $\overline{BD}$ is a transversal intersecting parallel lines. Alternate interior angles formed when a transversal intersects parallel lines are congruent. Since $\angle ABD$ and $\angle BDC$ are alternate interior angles, $\angle ABD \cong \angle BDC$. Response A is not valid because it is not possible for a triangle to contain three right angles. For $\overline{BD}$ and $\overline{DC}$ to be perpendicular, $\angle BDC$ would have to be a right angle. Since quadrilateral ABCD is a rectangle, $\angle ADC$ must be a right angle. The measure of $\angle BDC$ is less than the measure of $\angle ADC$. Therefore, $\angle BDC$ is not a right angle and $\overline{BD}$ is not perpendicular to $\overline{DC}$, making response B a false statement. Two angles are supplementary if the sum of their angles is 180°. Since $\angle ADB$ and $\angle CDB$ combine to form a right angle, they are complementary, not supplementary, and response D is not valid.

3. **Correct Response: A.** Because the rectangles are similar, their sides must be proportional in length. Therefore, you can set up a proportion to determine the length of corresponding sides.

    $$\frac{DE}{DA} = \frac{EF}{AB}; \frac{4}{24} = \frac{EF}{12}; 12 \times \frac{4}{24} = EF; 2 = EF$$

    Response B incorrectly assumes that DE $\cong$ EF. Response C is based on an incorrect ratio.

    $$\frac{DE}{AB} = \frac{EF}{DA} \text{ and } \frac{4}{12} = \frac{EF}{24}$$

    Response D is based on the incorrect assumption that the sum of the lengths of $\overline{DE}$ and $\overline{DA}$ is equal to the sum of the lengths of $\overline{AB}$ and $\overline{EF}$.

4. **Correct Response: C.** In similar polygons, corresponding angles are equal. $\angle K$ and $\angle D$ are corresponding angles, so $\angle K = \angle D = 120°$. Response A uses an invalid proportion to determine the measure of $\angle D$.

    $$\frac{HI}{AB} = \frac{\angle K}{\angle D}; \frac{40}{20} = \frac{120}{\angle D}; \angle D = 60°$$

    Response B assumes that the difference between the lengths of sides HI and AB is equal to the difference between angles K and D: HI − AB = 40 − 20 = 20; $\angle K - \angle D = 120 - \angle D = 20$; $\angle D = 100$. Response D is also based on an invalid proportion.

    $$\frac{20}{40} = \frac{120}{\angle D} \text{ and } \angle D = 240°$$

5. **Correct Response: D.** $\overline{AD}$ can only be perpendicular to both $\overline{AB}$ and $\overline{CD}$ if $\overline{AB}$ and $\overline{CD}$ are parallel to each other. Since $\overline{AD} \perp \overline{CD}$, $\angle ADC$ is a right angle; as a result, the measure of $\angle ADC$ is equal to, not greater than, 90°. Therefore, response A is not valid. Since $\overline{AD} \perp \overline{AB}$, $\angle DAB$ (like $\angle ADC$) is a right angle. Since $\angle ADC$ and $\angle DAB$, which are alternate interior angles, have equal measures, lines AB and CD are parallel. Two lines cannot be both perpendicular and parallel; therefore, response B is invalid. Response C is also invalid, since $\angle DAB$ and $\angle ADC$ have been shown to be congruent.

6. **Correct Response: C.** Sides RS and TU are parallel, so a perpendicular transversal ($\overline{RU}$) would form two right angles as follows.

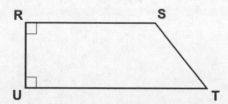

    Response A is incorrect because, although the polygon does not necessarily contain any right angles, the diagram shows that two right angles are possible. Response B is incorrect because if sides RS and TU are parallel, and $\angle SRU$ is a right angle, then $\angle RUT$ must also be a right angle. Response D is incorrect because in order for a four-sided figure to form four right angles, both pairs of opposite sides must be parallel, which is not the case for polygon RSTU.

7. **Correct Response: C.** Since the sum of the angles of a triangle is 180, and the two base angles of an isosceles triangle are equal in measure, we can calculate the measure of angle B by subtracting angle C's measure from 180 and dividing by 2: $\frac{(180-50)}{2} = 65$. If ED∥AB, angles EDB and ABD are interior angles on the same side of the transversal, which makes them supplementary (i.e., angle EDB + angle ABD = 180). Since angle ABD = 65, angle EDB = 115. Response A incorrectly assumes that angle EDB is congruent to angle C. Response B incorrectly assumes that interior angles on the same side of the transversal are congruent. Response D results from incorrectly subtracting 65 from 180.

8. **Correct Response: D.** In similar triangles corresponding sides are proportional. Thus $\frac{AB}{DE} = \frac{BC}{EF} = \frac{AC}{DF}$. Using the known lengths in this equation gives: $\frac{12}{4} = \frac{AC}{6}$.

    Solving gives $4 \, AC = 12 \cdot 6$
                              $4 \, AC = 72$
                              $AC = 18$

    Response A incorrectly uses the formula $\frac{AB}{DF} = \frac{DE}{AC}$. Response B incorrectly uses $\frac{AB}{DF} = \frac{AC}{DE}$. Response C uses AB + DE = AC + DF.

Study Ideas

A careful study of the above exercises and the explanations of the answers will
help you review important skills relating to geometric concepts. In these exercises
you were asked to draw conclusions using the principles of similarity, congruence,
parallelism, and perpendicularity. The exercises are designed to give you practice
in these skills. You may wish to reread parts of the chapter that address specific
skills with which you have difficulty.

Chapter 20

APPLY REASONING SKILLS

This skill includes drawing conclusions using inductive and deductive reasoning.

Introduction

Often, you will have to use reasoning and logic skills to solve problems. You may need to use reasoning skills to solve problems that involve geometric shapes, sequences of numbers or letters, the distribution of money, or time.

There are two basic types of reasoning that are commonly used to solve math problems, inductive reasoning and deductive reasoning. Some problems involve using only one type or the other, while some problems require that you use both. The next two sections of this chapter discuss inductive and deductive reasoning in more detail and provide some examples of how these reasoning patterns can be used to answer various types of questions.

Inductive Reasoning

Inductive reasoning is the process of drawing conclusions that are based on observations. In inductive reasoning, you must look at a few of the items in a group and then come to a conclusion about all the items in the group (i.e., you look at a few specific examples to come up with a generalization). In this type of reasoning, conclusions are based on observation and a fairly small amount of information. For example, suppose you go to the store and buy five pens that are all the same brand and type. When you get home, you take out one of the pens, and you notice that it has a small crack in one side. That pen will not write. So you take out a second pen. You see that the second pen also has a crack in it, and that pen will not write either. You take a third pen out of the bag. Before you try to write with it, you see that it is also cracked, and so you assume that it will not write. In this situation, you have used inductive reasoning. You have looked at a few pens, you observed something that is the same about them, and you have drawn a conclusion.

In the example given above, it was possible to identify a pattern that was common to all the pens. To use inductive reasoning effectively, you must be able to identify patterns. Math problems may ask you to recognize patterns in a sequence of numbers or shapes.

There are three basic patterns that show up regularly in math problems; increasing/decreasing, alternating, and circular. In an increasing/decreasing pattern, the elements of the pattern continually increase or decrease by a certain amount. For example, the number sequence 1, 2, 3, 4 is an increasing pattern in which the value 1 is added to each number in the sequence to find the next number. Another example of this type of pattern is the number sequence 10, 8, 6, 4, 2, in which the pattern involves subtracting 2 from each number in the sequence to find the next number. (NOTE: This is a decreasing pattern.)

In an alternating pattern, some feature varies in a regular way with every other element in a sequence. For example, the number sequence 1, 3, 2, 4, 3, 5, 4 has an alternating pattern. In this sequence, you add 2 to the first number to get the second number. Then you subtract 1 from the second number to get the third number. To continue the sequence, you must alternately add 2 to one number and then subtract 1 from the next number.

In a circular pattern, the elements in a sequence move through a particular set of changes and then return to their original positions. The number sequence 2, 4, 7, 2, 4, 7, 2 contains a circular pattern. To create this pattern, you must add 2 to the first number to get the second and then add 3 to the second to get the third. Next, you subtract 5 from the third number to get the fourth. The pattern then repeats itself.

The following examples show sequences of numbers, letters, and geometric figures that are typical of math problems involving inductive reasoning.

What is the next number in the sequence below?

1 7 3 9 5

To solve this problem, you should try to find a pattern in the sequence of numbers. Notice that the numbers go from small to large, then small to large again, and so on. This indicates that this is an alternating pattern. First, 6 is added to 1 to give 7, then 4 is subtracted from 7 to give 3. Next, 6 is added to 3 to give 9, and finally 4 is subtracted from 9 to give 5. The pattern here is add 6, then subtract 4. To find the next number, you must continue the pattern. The next step would be to add 6 to the last number given, 5, to give 11. The next number in this sequence is 11.

What is the next number in the sequence below?

2 3 5 8 12

In this sequence, the numbers continually increase in value. This is an example of an increasing pattern. First, 1 is added to 2 to give 3, then 2 is added to 3 to give 5, then 3 is added to 5 to give 8, then 4 is added to 8 to give 12. To find the next number in the sequence, 5 must be added to 12, which makes the next term 17.

What is the next letter in the sequence below?

B I P

This is a sequence of letters, not numbers. You can convert this sequence to a number sequence by assigning numerical values to each letter of the alphabet. Letting A = 1, B = 2, C = 3, D = 4, E = 5, and so on, you find that B = 2, I = 9, and P = 16. In its new numerical form, the sequence is 2, 9, 16. It is easy to determine that each term in the sequence is found by adding 7 to the preceding term:

This means that the next letter corresponds to the number 23 (16 + 7). That letter is W.

What is the next geometric shape in the sequence below?

This pattern includes a single geometric shape that changes position in a regular way. The triangle in the pattern rotates $\frac{1}{4}$ turn counterclockwise to create the next item in the sequence. Notice that the final item in the sequence is the same as the first item in the sequence. This indicates that this sequence of shapes follows a circular pattern. The next shape in the sequence should be the same as the second shape in the sequence. Thus, the next shape in the sequence should be as follows.

Deductive Reasoning

The second type of reasoning that is commonly used in math problems is called deductive reasoning. In this type of reasoning, you draw a conclusion by using accepted facts. You must use several general statements to arrive at a specific conclusion.

Deductive reasoning problems always begin with a fact or set of facts that are stated in the problem. These facts may be arranged as a word problem, or you may be given a numbered list of true statements to use in answering the question. To solve a deductive reasoning problem, you must use a step-by-step process, developing new statements that are based on the facts that you have been given in the problem. It is important for you to keep in mind that you must be able to prove each new statement you make by using the facts you have been given. Each new statement must lead toward one final statement, which is your conclusion. Each statement must also be supported by the statements that come before it.

People use deductive reasoning to solve many ordinary problems. Suppose, for example, that you go into a building looking for a particular office. You stop someone in the lobby to ask directions. The person tells you that the office you want is on the third floor and that it is either in room 310, 314, or 320. These are the facts you can use to solve your problem. To find the office, you go to the third floor, locate room 310, and find that it is not the office you want. Next, you go to room 320 and find that it is not the office you want. Therefore, you conclude that the office you want must be in room 314.

When you use deductive reasoning to solve problems, you must make sure that each new statement you create is true. You must be able to prove that these statements are true by using the facts given in the problem or by using accepted mathematical definitions and statements (such as the ones given earlier in this chapter). It is important to remember that you should not make assumptions that cannot be proven.

The following examples show how to use deductive reasoning to solve problems.

Four animals are kept in a barn at night. Each animal is kept in a separate stall. The animals must be put into the barn according to the following rules.

1. **If the horse is in the first stall, the cow cannot be in the second stall.**

2. **The cow must be in a stall next to the sheep.**

3. **The goat must always be put in the fourth stall.**

On one particular evening, the horse is in the first stall. Based on this information, which of the following conclusions is valid?

A. **The goat is in the stall next to the horse.**

B. **The horse is in the stall next to the cow.**

C. **The sheep is in the second stall.**

D. **The cow is in the fourth stall.**

The first step in solving this type of problem should be to identify the facts that are given in the problem. You may find it helpful to draw a diagram or to make a list of the things (in this case, animals) that are described in the problem.

Draw a diagram of the stalls in the barn and make a list of all the animals that are kept in the barn.

horse
cow
sheep
goat

Stall #1	Stall #2	Stall #3	Stall #4

You must make new statements and draw a conclusion based on this information. It may be useful to make a table of your new statements and the reasons why they are true.

Statement	Reason
1. The horse is in the first stall.	Given in the problem.
2. The cow is not in the second stall.	The first rule listed in the problem.
3. The goat is in the fourth stall.	The third rule listed in the problem.
4. The cow is in the third stall.	If the horse is in the first stall, the goat is in the fourth stall, and the cow is not in the second stall, then the cow must be in the third stall.
5. The sheep is in the second stall.	All the other stalls are filled. The sheep must be in the remaining empty stall.

Stall #1	Stall #2	Stall #3	Stall #4
Horse	Sheep	Cow	Goat

In your diagram, write in the appropriate stalls the names of the animals.

Look at the response options given in the problem and see which one is valid. In this problem, response C, *the sheep is in the second stall,* is a true statement that you found in reasoning through the problem. From your diagram, you can tell that the goat is not in the stall next to the horse (response A) and that the horse is not in the stall next to the cow (response B). Those two statements are false and are therefore not valid. The statement, *the cow is in the fourth stall,* (response D) is also false.

There are 25 students in a woodworking class. During the class, 13 of the students built a bookshelf, and 11 students built a birdhouse. Five students built both a bookshelf and a birdhouse. How many students in the class did not make either a bookshelf or a birdhouse?

This problem involves using facts given in the problem as well as basic arithmetic operations. Again, it may be easier to solve this problem if you make a table of new statements and reasons why those statements are true.

Statement	Reason
1. There are 25 students in the class.	Given in the problem.
2. Five students in the class built both a birdhouse and a bookshelf.	Given in the problem.
3. Twenty students did not build both a birdhouse and a bookshelf.	25 – 5 (total students minus the students who did build both)
4. Thirteen students built bookshelves.	Given in the problem.
5. Eight students built only a bookshelf.	13 – 5 (total students who made bookshelves minus students who made both a bookshelf and a birdhouse)
6. Eleven students built birdhouses.	Given in the problem.
7. Six students built only birdhouses.	11 – 5 (total students who made birdhouses minus students who made both a bookshelf and a birdhouse)
8. Fourteen students built either a birdhouse or a bookshelf.	8 + 6 (students who built only a bookshelf plus students who built only a birdhouse)
9. Six students made neither a bookshelf nor a birdhouse.	20 – 14 (students who did not make both a birdhouse and a bookshelf minus students who built one or the other)

Practice Exercises

The following exercises will help you review the skills covered in this chapter. Many of the types of questions presented here will be similar to those on the test; others will not. Remember that the purpose of the exercises is to give you practice on the skills rather than merely to prepare you for the test. Following these exercises are the Practice Exercise Explanations. They explain each question, the correct answer, and why the remaining choices are incorrect.

1. Use the diagram below to answer the question that follows.

Which figure should come next in this sequence?

A.

B.

C.

D.

2. What is the missing figure in this sequence?

A.

B.

C.

D.

3. Use the table below to answer the question that follows.

?	People who only ride the bus
?	People who only walk
19	People who ride the bus and walk
?	People who neither ride the bus nor walk

In a city, a poll was taken on the type of transportation people use each day. A total of 75 people said that they ride the bus, and a total of 23 people said that they walk. Of the 102 people polled, 19 both ride the bus and walk. How many people said that they neither ride the bus nor walk?

A.   4

B.   23

C.   79

D.   83

4. What are the next two letters in this sequence?

U F V E W D X

A.   C Y

B.   C B

C.   Y C

D.   C Z

5. Use the diagram below to answer the question that follows.

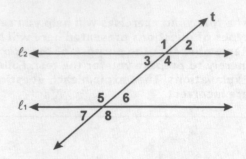

If angle 1 $\cong$ angle 5, what can be concluded about ℓ_1 and ℓ_2?

A. $\ell_1 \parallel \ell_2$

B. $\ell_1 \perp \ell_2$

C. $\ell_1 \perp t$

D. $\ell_2 \perp t$

6. A camp counselor must schedule three active sports activities (soccer, softball, and swimming) and three other activities (storytelling, a nature walk, and individual activities) on a day that runs from 8:00 A.M. to 5:00 P.M. In addition, each day must include a half-hour meeting and a lunch hour.

The following facts must also be considered in scheduling.

1. The swimming pool is available only in the morning.

2. None of the active sports should be scheduled right after lunch.

3. Lunch must be served at 12:00 noon.

4. Active sports should not be scheduled back to back.

Which of the following schedules is appropriate based on the information given?

A.	Meeting	8:00–8:30		B.	Swimming	8:00–9:30
	Nature walk	8:30–9:30			Individual activities	9:30–10:30
	Soccer	9:30–11:00			Nature walk	10:30–11:30
	Swimming	11:00–12:00			Meeting	11:30–12:00
	Lunch	12:00–1:00			Lunch	12:00–1:00
	Storytelling	1:00–2:00			Softball	1:00–2:30
	Softball	2:00–3:30			Storytelling	2:30–3:30
	Individual activities	3:30–5:00			Soccer	3:30–5:00
C.	Softball	8:00–9:30		D.	Soccer	8:00–9:30
	Nature walk	9:30–10:30			Nature walk	9:30–10:30
	Soccer	10:30–12:00			Swimming	10:30–12:00
	Lunch	12:00–1:00			Lunch	12:00–1:00
	Storytelling	1:00–2:00			Individual activities	1:00–2:00
	Swimming	2:00–3:30			Softball	2:00–3:30
	Individual activities	3:30–4:30			Storytelling	3:30–4:30
	Meeting	4:30–5:00			Meeting	4:30–5:00

Practice Exercise Explanations

1. **Correct Response: B.** There are two patterns in this sequence of figures. First, the figures alternate between squares and circles. Each shape is divided into four regions that contain dots; the dots create the second pattern. Each shape contains an open region, a region with one dot, a region with two dots, and a region with three dots. The dots are placed sequentially in adjacent regions, and the pattern of the dots rotates clockwise as the pattern moves from figure to figure. To match the shape pattern, the next figure in the sequence should be a square. To match the dot pattern, the next figure in the sequence should have a single dot in the top region, two dots in the right-hand region, three dots in the bottom region, and no dots in the left-hand region. Responses A and C are circles that do not contain the proper sequence of dots. Response D is a square, but the dots inside it are not arranged sequentially, and the open region is in the wrong location.

2. **Correct Response: C.** There are two patterns to identify in this sequence. First, each row and each column contains exactly one triangle, one square, and one circle. Second, the circles inside each shape alternate between shaded and open, alternating both across each row and down each column. The missing figure must be a triangle, and it must contain a closed inner circle. Responses B and D are the wrong shapes and would give too many circles or squares in the final row or column. In response A, the inner circle is open rather than shaded.

3. **Correct Response: B.** You can calculate the number that neither ride the bus nor walk based on the numbers given for those who ride the bus, walk, or do both. First, add the number of bus riders and walkers together. Then, subtract the number of people who do both, because this group is counted twice—once in the bus rider group and once in the walker group. Finally, subtract this difference from the total number of people polled to find the number of people who neither ride the bus nor walk.

   $75 + 23 - 19 = 79$

   $102 - 79 = 23$

   Response A adds 75 and 23, but forgets to subtract 19 before subtracting 98 from 102. Response C forgets to subtract from 102 and gives the number that either ride, walk, or do both. Response D subtracts 19 from 102.

4. **Correct Response: A.** Converting this letter sequence to a number sequence by assigning numerical values to the letters of the alphabet ($A = 1$, $B = 2$, $C = 3$, $D = 4$, etc.) gives this number sequence: 21, 6, 22, 5, 23, 4, 24. Use a diagram to find the relationship between the numbers.

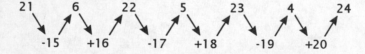

   This leads you to conclude that the two numbers can be found by subtracting 21 and then adding 22. Doing this gives 3 ($24 - 21$) and 25 ($3 + 22$). The numbers 3 and 25 convert to the letters C and Y. Response B results from subtracting 21 and then subtracting 1. Response C results from adding 1 and then subtracting 22. Response D results from subtracting 21 and adding 23.

5. **Correct Response: A.** Since ℓ_1 and ℓ_2 are cut by transversal t, angles 1 and 5 are corresponding angles. From the information given in the question, these two angles are congruent. If a transversal crosses two lines such that their corresponding angles are congruent, the two lines must be parallel.

   Since no numerical measures are given for any of the angles in the diagram, it cannot be determined that the transversal is perpendicular to the lines or that any of the angles are right angles. This eliminates responses B, C, and D.

6. **Correct Response: D.** Only Response D meets all of the conditions stated in the question. Response A has two active sports (soccer and swimming) back to back. Response B has an active sport (softball) right after lunch. Response C has swimming scheduled in the afternoon when the pool is not available.

Study Ideas

A careful study of the above exercises and the explanations of the answers will help you review important skills relating to applying reasoning skills. In these exercises you were asked to use inductive and deductive reasoning to solve problems. The exercises are designed to give you practice in these skills. You may wish to reread parts of the chapter that address specific skills with which you have difficulty.

Chapter 21

SOLVE PROBLEMS INVOLVING A COMBINATION OF MATHEMATICAL SKILLS

This skill includes applying combinations of mathematical skills to solve a problem or a series of related problems.

Introduction

In previous chapters of this guide, you learned how to apply mathematical skills to solve problems. In most cases, the problems involved the use of one particular type of mathematical skill, such as the interpretation of a graph or the solving of a quadratic equation. These individual mathematical skills are very valuable and your ability to apply them will be useful in college. However, in many problem situations you will be expected to apply more than one mathematical skill to reach a solution. In such situations, your first task will be to analyze the problem carefully to identify the particular skills and mathematical procedures that must be used in combination to reach a solution.

This chapter will present examples of problems that call for the use of several mathematical skills and processes. Each mathematical skill was discussed individually in a previous chapter of this guide. If you have difficulty with any of the procedures in this chapter, you may want to reread sections of previous chapters in which those procedures were discussed.

Using Mathematical Skills in Combination

Very often when you are solving real-world problems, you will have to use many math skills in combination. To reach an overall solution it will be important for you to separate the problem into manageable parts to be solved one at a time. As you think about the problem and begin to break it up, be sure to keep in mind the question that is being asked and be sure to give your answer in appropriate units.

The following examples are designed to show you how to integrate several math concepts when solving problems.

> A circular swimming pool is 25 feet in diameter and 5 feet 6 inches high. How many gallons of water will it take to fill the pool to a 5-foot level if there are 7.5 gallons of water in 1 cubic foot of water?

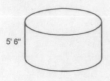

Draw a diagram. Use the numbers from the problem to label your drawing.

To solve this problem, first you must find the volume of the pool to the 5' level. This will give you an answer in cubic feet, which you will then have to use to reach a final answer.

$V = \pi r^2 h$ *Use the formula for determining the volume of a cylinder.*

$V = 3.14(12.5)^2 5$ *Use the numbers from the problem to find the volume. Remember that radius = $\frac{1}{2}$ diameter.*

$V = 3.14(156.25)5$
$V = 2453.125$ cubic feet

Now you need to find out how many gallons of water constitute a volume of 2453.125 cubic feet.

1 cubic foot of water = 7.5 gallons   *Use the information given in the problem.*

2453.125 cubic feet = (2453.125)(7.5) gallons   *Since there are 7.5 gallons in each cubic foot, you must multiply the total volume by 7.5.*

Total gallons = 18398.4375

So it will take approximately 18,398.4 gallons of water to fill the pool to a five-foot level.

Notice that, in solving this problem, you had to work in two separate steps. First you had to calculate a volume (in cubic feet) and then you had to convert that volume to another measure, gallons. In this case, as in many real-world problems, it is possible to imagine a number of other mathematical skills that *could* be asked for to obtain information of interest relating to this problem.

For example, it is reasonable to want to know the *cost* of filling the pool to the 5-foot level. In this case a cost per gallon (or per 100 gallons, or per cubic foot or cubic yard) could be given and you could be asked to calculate the cost from that information. Or, to take the example further, a rate of evaporation of the water could be given (e.g., 3 inches per week) and you could be asked to calculate the cost of not only filling the pool once, but keeping it full over the 13 weeks of summer. Or you could be given a ratio of chlorine to water and a cost per gallon of chlorine, and then asked to calculate the total cost of keeping the pool full of a water and chlorine mixture. And so on.

The point is that each mathematical operation should now be within your grasp. Often the most seemingly complex problem can be broken up into smaller problems, each of which you can manage with what you now know.

Let's look at another example.

Rectangle ABCD is similar to rectangle PQRS. What is the perimeter of rectangle PQRS?

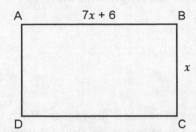

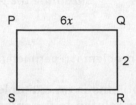

To solve this problem, you must use the properties of similar geometric figures and algebra (specifically, the quadratic formula) to obtain a value for x, and then use the geometric concept of perimeter to find a final answer. First is similarity.

$\dfrac{AB}{PQ} = \dfrac{BC}{QR}$ *Because the rectangles are similar, their sides must be proportional in length.*

$\dfrac{7x + 6}{6x} = \dfrac{x}{2}$ *Substitute the algebraic expressions for the appropriate sides.*

$6x\left(\dfrac{7x + 6}{6x}\right) = 6x\left(\dfrac{x}{2}\right)$ *Multiply the entire equation by 6x, the lowest common denominator, to clear the fractions.*

$\cancel{6x}\dfrac{7x + 6}{\cancel{6x}} = \dfrac{x}{\cancel{2}}\overset{3}{\cancel{6}}x$

$7x + 6 = 3x^2$

Now you have a quadratic equation to solve in order to find a value for x. Recall that there are 3 ways to solve a quadratic equation: factoring, completing the square, and using the quadratic formula, as will be done below.

$7x + 6 = 3x^2$

$3x^2 - 7x - 6 = 0$ *Transpose the equation so that it is in the form $ax^2 + bx + c = 0$.*

$a = 3$
$b = {}^-7$
$c = {}^-6$

$x = \dfrac{{}^-b \pm \sqrt{b^2 - 4ac}}{2a}$ *Write down the quadratic formula. Substitute the values of a, b, and c into the formula and solve for x.*

$x = \dfrac{{}^-(^-7) \pm \sqrt{(^-7)^2 - 4(3)(^-6)}}{2(3)}$

$x = \dfrac{7 \pm \sqrt{49 + 72}}{6}$

$x = \dfrac{7 \pm \sqrt{121}}{6}$

$x = \dfrac{7 \pm 11}{6}$

$x = \dfrac{7 + 11}{6}$ or $x = \dfrac{7 - 11}{6}$

$x = \dfrac{18}{3} = 3$ or $x = {}^-\dfrac{4}{6} = {}^-\dfrac{2}{3}$

Since the length of a side cannot be negative, x must be equal to 3.

Finally, you must find the perimeter of rectangle PQRS, knowing now that x = 3.

$P = 2l + 2w$	*Write the formula for perimeter of a rectangle.*
$P = 2(6x) + 2(2)$	*Substitute the expressions for the length and width of PQRS.*
$P = 2(6 \cdot 3) + 2(2)$	*Substitute the value of x.*
$P = 36 + 4$	
$P = 40$	

The solution for this problem is: perimeter = 40.

The following set of problems is an example of a series of related problems. Both parts of the problem are related to the information in the paragraph that follows.

Part 1

For a school project, Jackie needs to build a volcano. She plans to make a cone out of poster board and cover it with clay. The cone is to be a right circular cone with base radius 6 inches and height 8 inches. Poster board comes in sheets that are 1 foot, $1\frac{1}{2}$ feet, 2 feet, 3 feet, and 4 feet square. What are the dimensions of the smallest sheet of poster board Jackie can buy?

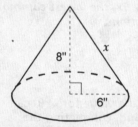

Draw a diagram. Use the numbers from the problem to label your diagram.

To find the dimensions of the poster board needed to make the cone, you have to open the cone up. Mentally cut the cone along the line marked x and lay it flat.

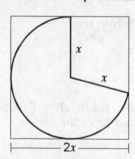

As you can see, you now have part of a circle with radius x inches. This circle can be inscribed in a square with side twice the radius of the circle. The square is the smallest piece of poster board from which the cone can be cut.

To find the length x, you must look back to the first diagram. The unknown quantity is the hypotenuse of a right triangle with legs 6" and 8". Use the Pythagorean theorem to find x.

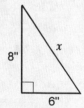

$c^2 = a^2 + b^2$	*Write the Pythagorean theorem.*
$x^2 = 8^2 + 6^2$	*Substitute the numbers from the problem.*
$x^2 = 64 + 36$	
$x^2 = 100$	
$x = \sqrt{100} = 10$	

Since the larger circle, from which the cone will be cut, has a diameter of 20 inches (2 times 10 inches), the smallest sheet of poster board Jackie can buy will be the 2-foot-square size. (Note that the problem states the sizes in which poster board is sold and there is no 20-inch-square size.)

Part 2

One package of clay will cover approximately 80 square inches. How many packages of clay will Jackie have to buy to make her volcano?

To solve this part of the problem you need to know the lateral surface area of the cone.

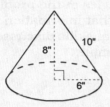   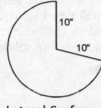

Again you must imagine the cone opened up. Draw a diagram. Use the radius you found in the preceding part of the problem to label your drawing. Now you have a portion of a circle.

Lateral Surface
of the Cone

To find the area of the portion of the circle, you need to find out what fraction of the whole circle you have. You can do that by dividing the edge of the portion of the circle by the circumference of the whole circle. Notice that the edge of the portion of the circle is the circumference of the base of the cone.

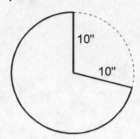

$c = \pi \cdot d$

Write the formula for circumference. Use it to find the circumference of both circles: the base of the cone and the large circle.

Base of cone

$c = \pi \cdot d$
$c = 3.14 \cdot 12$
$c = 37.68$ inches

Large circle

$c = \pi \cdot d$
$c = 3.14 \cdot 20$
$c = 62.8$ inches

$\dfrac{37.68}{62.8} = 0.6$

Divide to find what fraction of the large circle the portion of the circle is.

$A = \pi r^2$

Write the formula for finding the area of the large circle.

$A = 3.14 \cdot 10^2$
$A = 3.14 \cdot 100$
$A = 314$ sq. inches

The area of the portion of the circle is 0.6 times the area of the large circle.

Lateral surface area of the cone = 0.6(314)
                                                  = 188.4 sq. inches

Since one package of clay covers 80 sq. inches, you must divide to find the number of packages needed.

Number of clay packages = 188.4 ÷ 80
            188.4 ÷ 80 = 2.355

Since Jackie must buy whole packages of clay, she needs 3 packages.

Conclusion

These examples are typical of the kinds of combined problems you will encounter.
Study them carefully and think of other information you could be asked in any of
these problem situations (e.g., the cost of the volcano project in the last set of
problems; the length of a diagonal in either of the similar rectangles in the problem
before). Then try to think what you would need to know to find that information
and how you would go about it. Remember that the mathematical skills discussed
in the previous chapters are a good resource for solving even complex
mathematical problems.

Practice Exercises

The following exercises will help you review the skills covered in this chapter. Many of the types of questions presented here will be similar to those on the test; others will not. Remember that the purpose of the exercises is to give you practice on the skills rather than merely to prepare you for the test. Following these exercises are the Practice Exercise Explanations. They explain each question, the correct answer, and why the remaining choices are incorrect.

1. Use the diagram below to answer the following question.

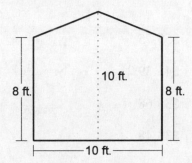

Max plans to paint his garage. The garage has a pentagonal front and back and rectangular sides. The diagram shows the front of the garage. The sides are 8-foot by 15-foot rectangles. One gallon of paint costs $18.50 and covers 350 square feet. Assuming he will need two coats of paint, how much will Max have to spend on paint?

A. $18.50

B. $37.00

C. $55.50

D. $74.00

2. Use the diagram below to answer the following question.

A rectangular park is 7 km long and 4 km wide. A hiker can walk on a path that runs around the outside of the park from point A to point B at an average rate of 5 km per hour. A hiker walking diagonally through the park can average 3 km per hour. Approximately how much faster is one route than the other?

A.   6 minutes

B.   28 minutes

C.   31 minutes

D.   88 minutes

3. A student in a class play needs to make five vests for costumes. Each vest requires $1\frac{1}{4}$ yards of wool fabric and $\frac{5}{8}$ yards of lining material. The wool costs $10.50 per yard and the lining material costs $2.79 per yard. How much will the student have to spend on fabric to make all the vests?

A. $74.35

B. $65.63

C. $63.85

D. $24.92

4. Find the area of the polygon enclosed by the three lines whose equations are $y = x + 2$, $y = {}^-4$, and $x = 6$.

A.   8 sq. units

B.   32 sq. units

C.   72 sq. units

D.   144 sq. units

5. Josh and Carlos plan to drive from Dallas, Texas, to Salt Lake City, Utah, together. Since they plan to take turns driving, they will make the trip taking no stops. They know that if they average 50 miles per hour it will take them 25 hours to reach Salt Lake City. The car they are taking averages 28 miles per gallon of gasoline at that speed. Gasoline prices will average $1.25 per gallon. What is the total estimated cost of the gasoline they can expect to use on the trip?

A. $55.75

B. $43.39

C. $35.68

D. $33.48

Use the diagram below to answer the three questions that follow.

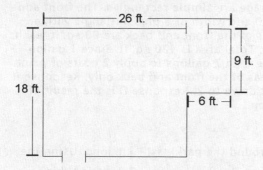

6.   The diagram is a drawing of Marsha's kitchen floor. Marsha plans to tile her kitchen floor with 6-inch by 6-inch square ceramic tiles. Each tile costs $4.50. How much will Marsha have to spend on the tiles?

A. $1863

B. $3726

C. $7452

D. $8424

7.   One can of ceramic tile glue is enough to tile 6 square yards. Each can costs $8.25. How much will Marsha have to spend on glue?

A. $ 62.70

B. $ 66.00

C. $189.75

D. $569.25

8.   Baseboard will have to be placed around the perimeter of the room except at the two door openings. Each door is 32 inches wide. The baseboard price is 45¢ per foot. How much will Marsha have to spend on baseboard?

A. $23.70

B. $36.90

C. $37.20

D. $40.80

Practice Exercise Explanations

1. **Correct Response: C.** The sides of the garage are simple rectangles. The front and back are each a rectangle with length of 10 and width of 8 plus a triangle with a base of 10 and height of 2. Thus, the areas of the front and back are 90 sq. ft. each. The areas of the sides are 120 sq. ft. each. Total area is 420 sq. ft. Since 1 gallon covers 350 sq. ft., it will take slightly more than 2 gallons to apply 2 coats of paint. Response A is the result of finding the areas of the front and back only. Response B results from rounding the gallons of paint down to 2. Response D is the result of incorrectly finding the area of the pentagon.

2. **Correct Response: B.** Route A (the path around the park) is 11 km long. Using the rate $\times$ time = distance formula, we get $5 \cdot t = 11$, or $\frac{11}{5}$ hours. Converting this to minutes, we get $t = \frac{11}{5} \cdot 60 = 132$ minutes. Route B (the diagonal route) is, by the Pythagorean theorem, $\sqrt{7^2 + 4^2}$, or $\sqrt{65}$. We can estimate this as approximately 8 km. Using $rt = d$ again, we get $3 \cdot t = 8$ for route B. Solving for t and converting to minutes gives $t = \frac{8}{3} \cdot 60 = 160$ minutes. Subtracting $(160 - 132)$ gives an answer of 28; route A is about 28 minutes shorter than route B.

    Response A results from incorrectly dividing rate by distance to get time. Response C is the result of multiplying rate by distance in both equations. Response D results from applying the Pythagorean theorem incorrectly to get $\sqrt{(7 + 4)^2}$ as the time for Route B.

3. **Correct Response: A.** Find the total yardage necessary for each fabric. Then multiply yardage by price per yard. Add the two amounts to get the total cost.

    $(5)\left(1\frac{1}{4}\right) = 6\frac{1}{4}$ yards of wool

    $\left(6\frac{1}{4}\right)(\$10.50) = \$65.625$ or $\$65.63$

    $(5)\left(\frac{5}{8}\right) = 3\frac{1}{8}$ yards of lining

    $\left(3\frac{1}{8}\right)(\$2.79) = \$8.71875$ or $\$8.72$

    $\$65.63 + \$8.72 = \$74.35$ total cost

    Response B is the result of forgetting to include the lining material. Response C results from an error in multiplying 5 and $1\frac{1}{4}$. Response D results from adding the yardage, adding the 2 prices, and multiplying the results.

4.   **Correct Response: C.** Draw the three lines on a graph. The polygon enclosed is a triangle with base 12 and height 12. Area is $\frac{1}{2}b \cdot h$ so A = 72 sq. units. Response A results from graphing y = 4 instead of y = ⁻4. Response B is the result of graphing x = 6 as a horizontal line and y = ⁻4 as a vertical line. Response D results from using the wrong formula for the area of a triangle.

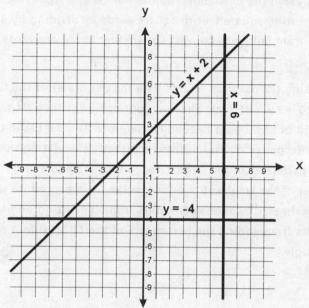

5.   **Correct Response: A.** Find the distance for the entire trip and divide by the miles per gallon. Multiply that result by the gasoline price per gallon.

     50 · 25 = 1250 miles
     1250 ÷ 28 = 44.6 gallons
     (44.6)($1.25) = $55.75

     Response B results from subtracting 1.25 rather than multiplying by it. Response C results from dividing by 1.25 rather than multiplying. Response D is the result of a multiplication error.

6.   **Correct Response: C.** The floor can be divided into two rectangles (one 18 × 20 feet, the other 9 × 6 feet), whose areas must be added together to produce a total area. Thus, A = (18 × 20) + (9 × 6) = 414 sq. ft. Since each tile is 0.25 square feet, 4 tiles will be needed for each square foot: (414)(4) = 1656 tiles. At a cost of $4.50 per tile, 1656 tiles will cost $7452.

     Response A results from assuming that 1 tile is needed to cover each square foot. Response B results from using 2 tiles per square foot. Response D is the result of treating the floor area as one large rectangle of 18 × 26 feet.

7. **Correct Response: B.** First the area of the floor must be converted from square feet to square yards: $414 \div 9 = 46$ sq. yd. Since each can of glue can tile 6 sq. yd., $\frac{46}{6} = 7.7$ cans are needed, which must be rounded up to 8 because only whole cans are sold. Eight cans at $8.25 will cost $66.00.

    Response A results from using the unrounded number of cans. Response C is the result of incorrectly converting square feet to square yards by dividing by 3 instead of 9. Response D results from failing to convert square feet to square yards.

8. **Correct Response: C.** Using the diagram to calculate the perimeter of the floor yields $26 + 9 + 6 + 9 + 20 + 18 = 88$ feet. The two door openings total 64 inches = $5\frac{1}{3}$ feet. The total amount of baseboard needed is therefore $82\frac{2}{3}$ feet, and the cost is $\left(82\frac{2}{3}\right)(0.45) = \$37.20$. Response A results from incorrectly calculating the perimeter by taking the perimeter of the large 18×26-foot rectangle and subtracting the perimeter of the smaller 9×6-foot rectangle, a procedure which works for area but not perimeter. Response B results from converting 64 inches to 6 feet. Response D results from adding the perimeters of the 18×20-foot rectangle and the 9×6-foot rectangle.

Study Ideas

A careful study of the above exercises and the explanations of the answers will help you review important skills relating to integrating math skills and concepts to solve problems. In these exercises you were asked to solve multistep problems that involve varied math skills. Each individual skill relates to information provided in previous chapters of this guide. The exercises are designed to give you practice in applying and combining these skills. You may wish to reread parts of this and other chapters that address specific skills with which you have difficulty.

Study References: Mathematics

These references for further study were suggested by members of the TASP Content Advisory Committee in Mathematics, the TASP Bias Review Panel, and the Remediation Subcommittee of the Texas Academic Skills Council.

Particular references are included because they relate to the TASP skills and are appropriate for college students. The titles listed here may also be available in learning centers and through developmental education programs on your campus.

Akst, G. R. *Improving Mathematics Skills.* San Francisco: Jossey-Bass, 1981.

Alwin, R. H., & Hackworth, R. D. *Algebra Programmed, Part I and Part II.* Englewood Cliffs, NJ: Prentice Hall, 1987.

Aufmann, R. N., & Barker, V. *Intermediate Algebra, An Applied Approach.* Boston: Houghton Mifflin, 1987.

Barker, J., et al. *Arithmetic.* New York: Saunders Publishing, 1987.

Barnett, R. *Review of Elementary Mathematics.* New York: McGraw-Hill Inc., 1977.

Barnett, R. *Schaum's Outline Series—Elementary Algebra.* New York: McGraw-Hill Inc., 1960.

Brand, N., & Nunley, B. *Passing Math: Fundamentals of College Algebra.* Dubuque, IA: Kendall/Hunt Publishing Co., 1986.

Commander, E.S., & Hawkins, C. *Geometry Basics/Data Analysis.* Dubuque, IA: Kendall/Hunt Publishing Co., 1991.

Hackworth, R. D. *Math Anxiety Reduction.* Clearwater, FL: H&H Publishing, 1985.

Hackworth, R. D., & Howland, J. W. *Programmed Arithmetic.* Clearwater, FL: H&H Publishing, 1983.

Keedy, M. L., & Bittinger, M. L. *Developmental Mathematics.* Reading, MA: Addison-Wesley, 1988.

Keedy, M. L., & Bittinger, M. L. *Developmental Mathematics—Arithmetic and Algebra.* Menlo Park, CA: Addison-Wesley, 1984.

Keedy, M. L., & Bittinger, M. L. *Essential Mathematics.* Menlo Park, CA: Addison-Wesley, 1987.

Keller, M. W. *Intermediate Algebra: A Text Workbook.* Boston: Houghton Mifflin, 1987.

Keller, M. W., & Zant, J. H. *Basic Mathematics and Algebra with Applications.* Boston: Houghton Mifflin, 1984.

Kruglak, H., & Moore, J. T. *Schaum's Outline Series—Basic Mathematics with Applications.* New York: McGraw-Hill Inc., 1973.

Lial, M. L., & Miller, C. D. *Beginning Algebra.* Glenview, IL: Scott, Foresman & Co., 1987.

Marchisotto, E. *Developmental Mathematics: Arithmetic, Algebra, and Measurement Geometry.* New York: John Wiley & Sons, 1987.

Miller, C., & Lial, M. *Introductory Algebra: A Text-Workbook.* Dallas: Scott, Foresman & Co., 1987.

Speigel, M. R. *Schaum's Outline Series—College Algebra.* New York: McGraw-Hill Inc., 1956.

Trivieri, L. A. *Basic Mathematics with Applications.* New York: Random House, 1988.

SECTION IV

Writing Skills Review

Introduction

Your ability to express yourself in writing will be one of the most important elements of your college career. Not only will your performance in college be judged in part on the basis of what and how you write, but the benefits you derive from college may also depend on your writing ability. Learning to write involves learning how to marshal and organize your thoughts and present them effectively.

In college, you will be expected to communicate often in writing. You will have to write homework assignments, outlines, notes, critiques, reports, papers, and essay questions on tests. Your writing assignments will benefit from your mastery of a few of the basic academic skills in writing. The Texas Academic Skills Program focuses on five particular skills that relate to writing ability. Each skill will be tested through multiple-choice questions on the TASP Test.

In addition to the five skills measured by multiple-choice items, the TASP Test will include a writing assignment: an essay written to a given audience for a purpose to be specified in an assignment on the test. The writing sample portion of the TASP Test will give you a chance to demonstrate your ability to put all of your skills together in the composition of an organized essay.

Organization of This Section

The first five chapters of this section describe and provide instruction on the five skills that will be tested with multiple-choice questions. The final two chapters of this section pertain to the writing sample portion of the TASP Test. The content of each of these seven chapters is briefly summarized below.

Chapter 22 relates to the skill of recognizing a writer's purpose, audience, and occasion for writing. The chapter describes the meaning of these terms and explains their importance in good writing. A writer must have a good grasp of purpose, audience, and occasion to help determine a style and level of expression that will prove effective.

Chapter 23 addresses three particularly important elements of good writing: unity, focus, and development. Writers must decide on a main point, express and maintain that point without distraction, and develop that point through detail and elaboration. This chapter describes those elements and gives examples of problems writers may have with them.

Chapter 24 describes how writers organize their writing. The chapter presents techniques of paragraph organization and explains the ways in which writers communicate to their readers the structure they are using in order to make comprehension easier.

Chapter 25 describes the construction of effective sentences and also describes factors that make sentences ineffective. The chapter deals with major sentence defects, such as the use of incomplete sentences. The chapter also covers agreement between subjects and verbs, the use of modifiers and negatives, the use of parallel structure in sentences to make reading easier, and the choice of words that precisely convey meaning.

Chapter 26 pertains to usage, that is, the ways in which words are formed (e.g., plurals of nouns, past tenses of verbs), used (e.g., the avoidance of double comparatives), and put together (e.g., punctuation) to form effective sentences.

Chapter 27 relates to the writing sample portion of the TASP Test. It describes a structured method for planning and writing an essay such as the one you will be asked to write on the test. The chapter presents several steps that help writers compose essays, including generating ideas, organizing ideas into paragraphs, writing a first draft, and editing and proofreading the draft.

The writing section of the study guide concludes with Chapter 28, which presents further information about the writing sample portion of the TASP Test, including a brief description of the way in which the writing samples will be scored. The chapter also includes a sample of the directions you will be given on the TASP Test, a writing assignment, and four sample essays that were written in response to that writing assignment. The four essays are used to illustrate the scoring procedure that will be used for the TASP Test. The chapter also presents an analysis of the sample essays based on their characteristics and the quality of the writing.

Please note that the purpose of the materials in this section of the study guide is to familiarize you with the skills eligible for inclusion on the TASP Test. In some cases, the chapters include material that may not appear on the test. Also, the practice exercises and examples are not necessarily in the format or at the level of difficulty you will find on the TASP Test.

Chapter 22

RECOGNIZE PURPOSE AND AUDIENCE

This skill includes recognizing the appropriate purpose, audience, or occasion for a piece of writing; and recognizing writing that is appropriate for various purposes, audiences, or occasions.

Introduction

Most of the writing required of you in college will be assigned by others, notably your course instructors, and will be used for two main reasons: to help you learn specific material by writing about it and to assess your understanding of the subjects you are studying.

However, whatever the writing situation—whether preparing a lab report, interpreting the symbolism in a novel, or writing a take-home exam on the causes of World War I—you must still make choices about the ideas, facts, logic, and language you use. Having a clear understanding of both your purpose for writing and the audience for whom you are writing will help you make these choices wisely.

Writing with Purpose

If you are uncertain about how to handle some college writing assignments, you may fall into the trap of trying to get through the task of writing an essay without truly understanding or thinking through its purpose. It is easy, for example, to focus on the subject of your essay and to forget that you must communicate that subject clearly to a reader. Writing with purpose means that you have made yourself consider both what you want your essay to accomplish and how you plan to achieve that goal. It means that you have distinguished between the topic of your writing and the purpose for your writing.

Here is an example of the difference between topic and purpose. If you simply decide to write a letter to your parents about your first semester in college, you have a form (the letter) and a topic (your first semester in college), but you have not yet discovered or decided why you are writing the letter. Is it to defend your decision to transfer to another school at the end of the year? To explain why you have decided to major in French? To assure your parents that the money they are investing in your education is well spent? To give them an idea of what your life is like at school, just as a part of keeping in touch? Your reasons for writing the letter will help determine both what you say and how you say it. For instance, a letter whose purpose is to explain your decision to go to another school might emphasize the negative elements of your present situation, while a letter describing campus life to your parents to keep them up to date on your daily activities would probably involve a more balanced presentation of positive and negative elements. The tone of the former would probably be fairly serious; the tone of the latter would be more likely to be informal or humorous.

Communicating with an Audience

From the example above, you can see that the nature of your audience—the people who will actually read your essay—is closely connected with your purpose. Your knowledge of your audience's expectations, level of interest, and level of understanding will guide you as you reach out to your reader. The letter whose purpose is to explain your decision to transfer to another school will require different handling, depending not only upon whether it is intended for your parents or for the dean of your college but also upon whether its audience is likely to be receptive to your decision or hostile to it. A letter explaining your decision to major in French will be one thing addressed to your parents and quite another addressed to a committee who will be awarding trips to Paris to eligible French majors.

A related consideration as you begin your writing task is the occasion for writing. Occasion is best thought of as the situation that the reader will be in when he or she reads what you have written. Occasion should guide you in your choice of topic, style, tone, ideas, and order as much as awareness of your audience. A speech for a political convention, an editorial in a community newspaper, and an essay written as an English assignment should each reflect the specific occasion for which it was written. As you think of your audience, you should also think of the likely situation (including place, time, mood, emotions, surroundings, fellow readers, and similar aspects of the environment) in which the reader will be receiving your message.

Purpose, Audience, and the Writing Process

A clear and sustained sense of purpose is central to the process of writing for an audience. Purpose establishes the relationship between writer and reader; it acts as a tool for selecting information and arguments and for structuring a presentation. Audience is equally important. The nature of your intended audience should affect your decisions about such elements as language, argument, and tone. To reach your audience successfully, you need to consider what knowledge and expectations your readers will have of your work, what they will want or need to know in order to make sense of your ideas, and what kind of presentation will accomplish your purpose with those readers.

The writing process is a series of related tasks that are all dependent on each other. These tasks include analyzing what you wish to write about, collecting your ideas, organizing your presentation, writing a first draft, and editing and polishing your work before producing a final version. All these tasks should be guided by your sense of purpose and your awareness of your reader's expectations and capabilities. Your clarity of purpose and your insight into your audience will be the standards against which you will measure your choices of content, organization, and style. Nothing should be retained that does not serve your purpose and help the reader connect with your thinking.

A Case Study

Let us say that you have been assigned a five-page paper for an economics class. You have been asked to describe the effect of two consecutive years of drought on the economy of a particular farming community and to analyze what the drought means for the economy of the state in which the community is located. You may begin by considering the reason for the assignment. Perhaps the professor assigned this paper to help you understand how certain principles of economics operate in the real world. He or she may also want to use the paper to assess your grasp of those principles, to gauge your ability to do appropriate research, and to judge your skill in making logical and convincing arguments. You should plan your writing to reflect these considerations.

Next, ask yourself what your reader (whether it is the grader of your paper or an imagined audience described by your professor for the purposes of the paper) will need to be told in order to understand and accept your ideas and findings. Also ask if there are any special aspects of the occasion for your writing that should influence what you choose to say and how you say it. For example, if the paper is to be read at a meeting of local farmers, your account of the economic effect will likely take a very different direction than if it is to be read by your professor, even though the basic concepts and facts would remain the same.

Your consideration of purpose, audience, and occasion will help you decide how much and what kind of research to do, what kinds of evidence you will have to use to support the assertions you make, and in what order you can best present your material. In the case of our hypothetical economics paper, an audience of local farmers will probably be more interested in practical than in theoretical issues. You would likely decide to spend less time describing the drought's effects—which the farmers already know all too well—and more time addressing possible ways to speed economic recovery. In a paper written solely for your college professor, on the other hand, you would probably want to provide a description of the economies of both the community and the state, and how they are related; to discuss relevant economic principles (such as the operation of supply and demand); and to present a carefully reasoned and unemotional account of the effects the drought would have on these factors.

Whatever approach you decide to take, however, the success with which you accomplish your purpose with a reader will also depend heavily on another factor: how well you *maintain* your purpose.

Maintaining Your Purpose

You are likely to find yourself writing for a wide variety of purposes in connection with your coursework. Here is a sampling of some possibilities.

To describe someone or something (a lecturer you have heard giving a talk; the anatomical features of a lab specimen)

To explain how to do something or why something behaves a certain way (how to change the dressing on a surgical wound; why human health depends on amino acids)

To inform someone about something (provide information about a student organization to someone who is considering joining it; tell a fellow student what to expect from a course you have taken)

To define a term or concept (distinguish between *manslaughter* and *negligent homicide;* compare the twentieth-century definition of God with that of the twelfth century)

To argue a point or position (defend a ban on genetic engineering; demonstrate why parents should read to their children from very early childhood)

To persuade someone of something (convince your college to install bicycle paths on campus; support or argue against a political position)

Actually, almost all writing of any complexity is a blend of purposes. In a single paper, for example, you might present facts for the purpose of informing your reader; use comparison and contrast in order to strengthen an argument; and provide descriptive detail in an effort to be persuasive. Such blending can be very effective as long as you maintain your primary direction and as long as everything you include in your writing furthers your central goal.

Blendings of purpose that introduce inconsistencies or irrelevancies, however, will confuse your reader and weaken your writing. There are several forms of inconsistency that are fairly common. One is a *shift in purpose:* You may begin an anthropology exercise by describing an island culture objectively, but become so involved that you start to advocate or criticize the values of that culture. Another is a *change of tone:* Although your debate presentation is aimed at persuading the judges that all medical research on animals should be outlawed, you give portions of your supporting evidence in a very objective, clinical tone, using technical language that does not persuade the judges because it is difficult to understand and lacks emotional power. A third is a *conflict of purposes:* Your engineering work group's assignment is to write up a winning contract proposal to remodel the campus pond. You have done a good job of researching, planning, and scheduling, but rather than using the standard format, you restructure the presentation to highlight particular figures and approaches, and you adopt a humorous tone. This not only makes the proposal more difficult to read and compare with other bids, but it calls your seriousness into question. Your goal (to win the contract) and the means by which you try to achieve it (an unusual proposal more attractive to you than to your client) are incompatible.

These kinds of flaws in your writing may cause a reader to question the reasoning behind your presentation. If an illogical shift in purpose makes your reader feel that the evidence you employ does not genuinely support the assertions you make, he or she will find your writing unconvincing. Read the following short paragraph and see if you can spot inconsistencies that make the writer's arguments less convincing.

[1]Since the election three years ago, 65 percent of our downtown retail stores and other businesses have moved to the fringes of the city or to suburban malls where the traffic flow is denser and the potential market greater. [2]How anybody could prefer shopping in a boring mall to the excitement of city shopping is another question. [3]Only about half the available apartments in the center of town are occupied now. [4]Several building sites stand half finished, among them some restorations of historic buildings and a public housing project. [5]The branch library is open only three days a week now, and both the Senior Citizens Center and the Free Health Clinic are closed. [6]The post office, however, is still open six days a week. [7]An estimated 22 percent of residents in this 30-square-block area are unemployed, up 13 percent from three years ago. [8]If our duly elected public officers have neither the greatness of heart nor the strength of will to stand firm in the defense of our faltering township, then it is up to us, her devoted citizens, to fill the breach.

You may have noticed three sentences that are inconsistent with the purpose of the paragraph as a whole. In Sentence 2, the writer has injected an irrelevant personal comment that not only does not support the purpose of the paragraph, but whose judgmental tone could well alienate a number of readers. Another sentence that does not fit is Sentence 6. The fact that the post office remains open seems irrelevant, if not contradictory, to the point the writer is attempting to make about the loss of services downtown. Finally, Sentence 8 has no place in this paragraph: the tone of its flowery and pretentious language would be much more appropriate for an emotional political speech than for the reasoned argument being presented here.

Inconsistencies of tone and purpose will make your writing less effective; be sure, when reviewing your own work, that you have maintained a consistent purpose and an awareness of audience and occasion throughout.

Practice Exercises

The following exercises will help you review the skills covered in this chapter. Many of the types of questions presented here will be similar to those on the test; others will not. Remember that the purpose of the exercises is to give you practice on the skills rather than merely to prepare you for the test. Following these exercises are the Practice Exercise Explanations. They explain each question, the correct answer, and why the remaining choices are incorrect.

Note the raised numbers that appear at the beginning of each "part" of the passages. In most cases, these numbered parts are sentences; in some cases, however, the parts are incomplete sentences (or sentence fragments) that are used for testing purposes. For this reason, the word *part* is used instead of the word *sentence* in questions that refer to the passages.

Read the passage below, written in the style of an education journal. Then answer the questions that follow.

^{1}In the last 20 years, film has become a standard tool in the classroom. ^{2}Teachers know that film can expand, illustrate, and reorganize information to provide new perspectives and stimulate new ideas; it can arouse curiosity, evoke emotion, and provide visual images that clarify concepts. ^{3}In addition, film clearly has the potential to shape behavior. ^{4}Remember that Florida kid who jumped off the top of a building after seeing the movie *Superman*? ^{5}We have long been familiar with film as a way of presenting current events and investigating contemporary issues and problems. ^{6}More recently, these educational roles have been filled by a similar medium even more accessible and more affordable: commercial television. ^{7}It is obvious that the influence of such media over the lives of our children will only continue to grow.

1. The writer's main purpose in this passage is to:

    A. prove that film may be dangerous in the classroom if used unwisely.

    B. demonstrate how teaching methods have changed in the last 20 years.

    C. examine the trend in education toward an even greater reliance on film and television.

    D. describe specific techniques for the effective use of film in the classroom.

2. Which of the following parts of the paragraph is NOT appropriate for the writer's purpose and intended audience?

    A. Part 1

    B. Part 2

    C. Part 4

    D. Part 6

Read the passage below, written in the style of a college agriculture textbook. Then answer the questions that follow.

[1]One of the most influential factors in the success of the American beef industry has been the introduction of cultivated crops to replace pasturage as the primary source of food for beef cattle. [2]Before this happened, land was becoming more expensive and less abundant, presenting ranchers with the problem of limited food resources for their herds. [3]When feed crops of corn and grain became available, ranchers were able to raise more cattle on their existing ranges. [4]In addition, each acre planted in feed crops would yield more usable food than an equal amount of pasturage, so each acre of ground became worth more both to the owner and to the national economy. [5]The nutritional value of crop feed is superior as well, since a pound of the consumed feed produces more weight in beef than a pound of forage. [6]Grazing also expends energy that, with the use of feed crops, can be put toward the beef weight of the cattle.

3. What is the writer's main purpose in this passage?

   A. to urge ranchers to feed cultivated feed crops to their beef cattle

   B. to demonstrate that the American beef industry is growing

   C. to inform the reader about how beef cattle should be fed

   D. to explain how feed crops have contributed to the American beef industry

4. Which of the following sentences, if added after Part 6 in the paragraph, would be most consistent with the writer's purpose and intended audience?

   A. We Americans should apply what we've learned in the beef industry to other industries that are experiencing economic troubles.

   B. Overall, feed crops are a more plentiful, more economical, and more cost-effective way of feeding beef cattle.

   C. Cultivated feed crops probably even taste better to cattle than grass does.

   D. Moreover, consistent utilization of feed crops such as corn and grain sorghum has been shown to have a moderating impact on susceptibility to drought and to insect infestation among the bovine population.

Read the passage below, written in the style of a college student handbook. Then answer the questions that follow.

[1]Campus dormitories offer three kinds of accommodations: the double room, the single room, and the suite. [2]Most students will occupy double rooms, with roommates matched by computer on the basis of the questionnaire each student completes during orientation or preregistration. [3]Single rooms and suites are generally reserved for those students who have completed at least 60 hours of coursework or who have special needs as described in Appendix A of this handbook. [4]Fees are slightly higher for single rooms, since each comes with its own bathroom. [5]Because the demand for these rooms usually exceeds the supply, students interested in a single may have to wait a semester or more for one to become available. [6]Suites accommodating four students are usually occupied by groups of people who apply for them together. [7]As members leave, the college may assign other students to the unit if the remaining residents cannot provide acceptable replacements. [8]Each suite consists of two double rooms equipped for sleep and study, joined by a study room.

5. This passage was primarily written for which audience?

   A. students who are planning to spend their junior year abroad

   B. professors who have just been appointed to the teaching staff

   C. students who will be attending the college for the first time

   D. administrators who have been employed at the college for several years

6. What is the writer's main purpose in this paragraph?

   A. to criticize the process by which dormitory room assignments are made

   B. to discourage incoming students from applying for single rooms or suites

   C. to instruct incoming students in how to select a dormitory room

   D. to acquaint incoming students with the kinds of dormitory housing available

7. Which sentence, if added to the passage, would NOT be consistent with the writer's purpose and intended audience?

   A. It is incumbent upon the students to procure suitemates who will complement the existing configuration of personalities in their entirety.

   B. Each dormitory contains all three types of living quarters.

   C. About 75 percent of dormitory housing consists of double-occupancy rooms.

   D. All dormitory housing is assigned on a first-come, first-served basis.

Read the passage below, written in the style of a student essay. Then answer the questions that follow.

[1]As a physics and astronomy major here at the university, I very frequently hear the question, "Why would you want to major in physics and astronomy?" [2]This question is usually accompanied by a pained and confused expression on the questioner's face. [3]While the question often makes me quite angry, I have to step back and be open-minded about the situation. [4]For lack of time, my answer is usually, "Because it's what I like!" [5]Sometimes, however, I am able to give a more energetic and detailed response. [6]I will attempt in this essay to explain my personal, although sometimes impractical, reasons for seeking a physics and astronomy major.

[7]My interest in astronomy began at an early age. [8]I have always found the stars and planets extremely interesting. [9]When I was ten, I received a powerful telescope from my grandparents, which I immediately put to use. [10]Then, in 1972, *National Geographic* magazine featured a beautiful pictorial on the solar system. [11]I read the magazine many times over because it introduced me to concepts that fascinated me. [12]The sizes, characteristics, orbits, and remoteness of the planets captured my interest. [13]One article in the magazine also pointed out that astronomy and physics are closely related; in fact, a person cannot know much about one subject without also studying the other. [14]That magazine was a source of insight and inspiration for me, and it helped me decide on the course of study I wanted to pursue in college.

8. The writer's main purpose in this passage is to:

   A. show why physics and astronomy is not a practical major.

   B. discuss the factors that led the writer to study physics and astronomy.

   C. encourage others to major in physics and astronomy.

   D. illustrate how physics and astronomy are related.

9. Which of the following sentences, if added where indicated in the second paragraph, would be most consistent with the writer's purpose and intended audience?

   A. Before Part 7: It's really nobody else's business why I like astronomy so much.

   B. After Part 9: That telescope made me feel closer to the stars and planets and started my more technical interest in astronomy.

   C. Before Part 12: In fact, I decided then and there that I would become a *National Geographic* subscriber for life.

   D. After Part 13: A thorough understanding of various branches of mathematics is essential in a number of the sciences today.

Practice Exercise Explanations

1. **Correct Response: C.** In this paragraph, the writer begins by describing some characteristics of film that make it educationally useful, points out that televison shares these and is even more readily available, and then asserts that these media will be increasingly influential on children's lives. Response A is incorrect because the paragraph stresses the advantages of film (and television) rather than the potential dangers. Responses B and D are incorrect because the paragraph does not compare teaching methods over the last 20 years or address specific techniques for using film in the classroom.

2. **Correct Response: C.** Part 4 introduces a casual tone that is inconsistent with the rest of the paragraph. The other choices listed are all consistent with the tone of the paragraph and support the writer's purpose. Part 1 (choice A) helps establish the value of film as an educational tool. Part 2 (choice B) suggests some of the useful possibilities of film. Part 6 (choice D) makes a connection between film and television that helps support the main point of the paragraph.

3. **Correct Response: D.** The paragraph illustrates by comparison that crop feed is preferable to grazing and has enabled ranchers to raise more pounds of beef. Response A is incorrect because the audience for this piece is clearly not ranchers, who have already become aware of the advantages of crop feed. Response B is incorrect because, although the paragraph asserts that the industry is growing, it does not discuss how or to what degree it is growing. Response C is incorrect because the paragraph gives readers no information about how beef cattle should be fed.

4. **Correct Response: B.** The paragraph is concluded appropriately by this summary of the virtues of feed crops. Response A is incorrect because its shift of purpose (from informing to persuading) and its change in tone (from objective to subjective) are inconsistent with the way the rest of the passage has addressed its purpose and audience. Response C is incorrect because its informal, humorous tone is inconsistent with the rest of the passage. Response D is incorrect because its language and style are inappropriately formal and stiff in the context of this paragraph.

5. **Correct Response: C.** The information presented in this paragraph would be most useful to incoming students attending the college for the first time. Students planning to spend their junior year abroad (choice A) would not need information about on-campus accommodations. New professors (choice B) and experienced administrators (choice D) would also be less likely than new students to need to know the information presented in this paragraph.

6. **Correct Response: D.** The paragraph describes the three types of dorm rooms available on campus. Response A is incorrect because the passage does not criticize the room-assignment process. Response B is incorrect because the passage does not attempt to persuade students to choose one kind of room or another; it simply states that most incoming students will not be eligible for single rooms or suites. Response C is incorrect because the passage does not describe the actual process of selection.

7. **Correct Response: A.** This sentence is not consistent with the writer's purpose and intended audience because it is redundant—it repeats information already given in Part 7—and because its tone is inappropriate—the language is too stilted and formal to be compatible with the rest of the passage. The other sentences all represent useful additions that are consistent with the purpose and audience of the passage. Response B answers a question that incoming students may well be expected to ask: Will I have to limit myself to certain dormitories to get a particular kind of room? Response C offers a statistic that gives a good idea of just how scarce the singles and suites are by showing what a large proportion of students typically live in double rooms. Response D, like response B, makes a general statement about room assignments that will help students manage the process of selecting housing.

8. **Correct Response: B.** This is a personal essay, written as a response to a question frequently asked of the writer. Choice A is incorrect because, while the writer admits that his or her own reasons for choosing this major may have been impractical, the passage does not demonstrate that physics and astronomy is an impractical major. The passage shows no evidence of being aimed at converting other students to this major, so choice C is not the correct response. Response D is incorrect because, although the writer mentions the relationship between astronomy and physics, the point is not further pursued in the passage.

9. **Correct Response: B.** The writer's stated purpose is to explain his or her personal reasons for studying physics and astronomy. Of the responses listed, only choice B contributes directly to this purpose. Choice A, in addition to being a digression inconsistent with the writer's purpose, is likely to be offensive to readers who are sincerely interested in what the writer has to say. Choices C and D are also digressions, irrelevant to the subject at hand.

Study Ideas

The exercises above are designed to give you practice in identifying a writer's main purpose and audience. Some questions ask you to identify sentences in a paragraph that are inconsistent with the writer's purpose and audience. Others call for you to choose a sentence that could be appropriately included in a given paragraph.

Review each exercise and its explanation carefully to make sure you understand *what* the writer's purpose is, *who* the writer's audience is, and *why* a particular sentence is or is not consistent with the writer's purpose and audience.

Take time to observe these elements in your personal reading. You will notice that purpose and audience vary considerably depending on just what it is you are reading: a novel, a newspaper editorial, a feature article in a magazine, a review of a performance, a scientific research paper, etc. After you read a paragraph, see if you can clearly identify the writer's purpose and audience. Did the writer maintain purpose throughout? Were there any distracting shifts in tone?

In your own writing, be sure to define your purpose and audience to yourself clearly, and write with these in mind. Remember that it is easy to shift your purpose unconsciously as you write. Be sure, as you review your draft, to ask yourself these questions: What is my purpose? Who is my audience? What is the occasion for which I am writing?

Chapter 23

RECOGNIZE UNITY, FOCUS, AND DEVELOPMENT IN WRITING

This skill includes recognizing unnecessary shifts in point of view or distracting details that impair the development of the main idea in a piece of writing, and recognizing revisions that improve the unity and focus of a piece of writing.

Introduction

With few exceptions, effective writing concentrates on one point at a time. In a unified piece of writing, all the separate parts are clearly related to each other and work together to make a single, coherent whole. Readers lose interest when a subject drifts or when the discussion of a topic does not lead to a specific point. A writer's ability to maintain unity and focus, therefore, is central to keeping his or her audience interested. To achieve unity, writers frequently make use of strategies that will be discussed in this chapter: focusing on and developing a single main idea, making sure that all details support the main idea, and writing from a single point of view.

Starting with Paragraphs

Most people think of the sentence as the basic unit of communication, and in a sense it is. But for the purpose of explaining an idea (which is the basic aim of most writing you will do in college), writers use paragraphs as their basic units.

The purpose of a paragraph is to develop just one idea, and it is important to limit each paragraph to a single point. But there is more to it than that. Good writing is marked by the clear and comprehensible development of that single idea. To be clear, a good paragraph provides sufficient explanation and examples but does not overwhelm the reader with detail. It presents a single idea that is both unified and focused.

There are of course many different ways to develop an idea. Some of these will be covered later in this chapter. No matter what kind of paragraph you write, however, it should be composed of sentences that "fit together." That is, the sentences of your paragraph should work together like a team to accomplish a goal: the development of a single main point.

Unity: The Key to Strong Paragraphs

To be effective, a paragraph must make just one central point. The main point is usually stated in a topic sentence. All the other sentences in the paragraph should support that point. If a paragraph includes more than one main point, it should be reworked so that each additional point becomes the focus of its own paragraph. If a sentence in the paragraph does not support the main point, it should be revised to do so or else deleted.

Paragraph unity requires one central idea or concept—not two or three, but one. Each paragraph should be held together by a unifying idea—the cement for the words and sentences. The unifying idea is especially important in academic writing, the kind you will be doing for your courses.

The following paragraph contains a sentence that destroys unity by introducing a point unrelated to the main point. See if you can identify that sentence.

> [1]Canada geese have remarkable instincts for travel. [2]After hatching in the spring and growing to adulthood during the summer months, they fly south in the early fall. [3]Migration may take these birds thousands of miles away from the nests where they were hatched, and autumn storms can blow them hundreds of miles off course. [4]Their preferred food is corn. [5]Yet in the spring of the year, they unerringly wing their way back to the marshes where they were born.

The main idea of this paragraph, established in the first sentence, is that Canada geese have powerful migratory instincts. Because Sentence 4 has nothing to do with this idea, it should be removed.

Now consider the following student paper written for a course in U.S. history.

> In the United States, the relationship between power and land ownership is undeniable, and the relationship extends back to the beginnings of our country. Consider who had power in the early years of the United States. It certainly was not Native Americans, Black Americans, or women; they were not even permitted to vote. Neither, for that matter, were White men—unless they owned land. And the more land a man held, the more power he had. The first seven presidents offer a good example of the relationship of land ownership to power. Five (Washington, Jefferson, Madison, Monroe, and Jackson) were plantation owners from Virginia and Tennessee; their land holdings were extensive.

The entire paragraph is devoted to establishing the relationship between land ownership and power in the early years of the United States. That is the unifying idea. It is important to note that the writer combines a series of details and even different topics—Native Americans, Blacks, women, the first seven presidents—to make the central point that land ownership determined power.

Focus as a Way to Achieve Unity

When you focus a camera on the image you wish to capture, the image sharpens. If you fail to adjust the focus, your picture will be fuzzy, and people will be unable to see the image clearly. Writing is like photography in this respect: if your writing is unfocused, your reader will be unable to see your meaning clearly.

For example, the subject matter of the following paragraph is careers; but what point is the writer trying to make?

> Business is always an appealing field. Graduates today have a choice of many different careers. Teaching salaries are low, according to many surveys, even though the profession requires a college education. The number of résumé services and job placement agencies has increased. Engineering is not as popular as it once was.

A writer might wish to revise the paragraph as follows.

> Graduates today have a choice of many different careers, although the choice is not always easy. Salaries in business careers tend to be high, but many people shy away from the pressures of the business environment. Education can be a fulfilling career, but teaching salaries are often low, even though the profession requires a college education. Engineering once held many opportunities; however, in the late 1980s those opportunities diminished considerably. It is instructive to note that the number of résumé services and job placement agencies has recently increased—a clear indication that many people are undecided about their future work and profession.

The writer has given the paragraph a focus. He or she has established a main point (that graduates have many choices but they are not easy ones), using the first sentence as a topic sentence. The other sentences have been revised to support the main idea by including both positive and negative aspects of each career.

Now consider another version of the paragraph. The general subject matter remains the same, but the writer, wishing to make a different point, has shifted the focus.

> Although graduates today have a choice of many different careers, the business field clearly offers more advantages than most. Teachers, for example, are notoriously underpaid and overworked. Job opportunities in technical fields such as engineering have diminished considerably in the last ten years. Jobs dependent on government funding, such as social work, are often highly politicized and may end abruptly if funds are cut off. There are always jobs available in business, however, and these jobs not only pay well initially, but also offer considerable opportunity for advancement. When people visit résumé services and job placement agencies these days, they are increasingly seeking employment in private businesses.

Note that the topic sentence has been changed and that the sentences have been revised to support the new main idea.

As you can see, a writer's focus determines what ideas will stand out clearly and what details or topics will remain in the background. A clear focus thus reinforces the purpose of a paragraph: it provides a strong sense of direction that helps the reader follow the writer's ideas.

Developing Ideas Fully

If there is one skill vital to your becoming a successful writer in college, it is learning to develop your ideas fully. Whether you study nursing, psychology, or English, the success of your writing will depend on the degree to which you can support your point of view. Attempting to present your ideas as convincingly as possible to a reader will also force you to think them through carefully; this process will more often than not deepen your own understanding of your subject matter and help make your arguments even more convincing.

Almost all paragraphs in a piece of expository writing include one sentence that states the main idea; this sentence is known as the *topic sentence*. The main idea stated in your topic sentence must be supported by the other sentences in the paragraph. This may be done in a number of ways; some of the more common approaches are shown in the following paragraph excerpts.

Reasons. The writer develops a paragraph by explaining the reasons for a particular point of view.

> The evidence is clear that the protective layer of ozone surrounding the earth is being destroyed. The average temperature in the United States has risen steadily over the past few summers. In addition, the incidence of skin cancers reported in the last decade has dramatically increased.

Concrete details. The writer supports a general main point by providing concrete or specific details.

> After a spring thunderstorm, the desert is magically transformed. An expanse of dry sand becomes a carpet of blue flowers. Faded green cacti are suddenly adorned with brilliant red blossoms.

Specific examples. The writer gives one or more examples of the main point.

> Authors often spend many years writing just one book. Joseph Heller, for instance, spent ten years working on his second novel, *Something Happened.*

Facts or statistics. The writer presents facts or statistics that support the main idea.

> Residents of the United States are reaping the benefits of improved health care. People who were born in 1950 could expect to live 68.2 years on average. Just 30 years later, life expectancy had jumped five and a half years, so that persons born in 1980 could expect to live to the age of 73.7.

Incidents or anecdotes. The writer uses a brief story or incident as an illustration of the main point.

> Professor Amis is famous for her lectures. I dropped in on her cultural anthropology class once last semester and couldn't find room to sit even in the aisle.

These are a few of the more common ways writers develop their paragraphs and essays. Remember that a variety of methods may be used in the same essay. One paragraph might develop its main idea (and contribute to the overall development of the entire essay) through the use of statistics, while another paragraph uses elaborative detail, another uses factual argument, and yet another presents an illustrative anecdote. Used carefully, these patterns can bolster each other and contribute diverse kinds of support to the main idea of the essay.

You should apply the principles of writing good paragraphs to your development of entire essays, as well. The main idea of each paragraph should combine logically with all the others to contribute to the unity and focus of your essay as a whole. If a paragraph does not support the essay's central idea, it should be revised to do so or deleted. Chapter 27 contains more information about how to achieve unity and focus throughout an entire essay.

The Importance of a Consistent Point of View

Good writing not only develops ideas fully, it also uses a consistent point of view to communicate them. Point of view can be first person (I or we); second person (you); or third person (he, she, it, or they). In most of your college writing you will probably want to maintain a single point of view, although there may be times that it would be appropriate to switch from one to another. An inappropriate or unnecessary switch, however, will distract your reader.

Consider the following example from a newspaper column.

> Superintendent of Schools John Lennox resigned today amid rumors that he had misappropriated school funds. Informed sources reported that Lennox had spent nearly $50,000 on a vacation home. I think he should have resigned earlier. Lennox was unavailable for comment.

In this example, the reporting on the superintendent's resignation begins in the third person (". . . he had misappropriated . . .") but is interrupted by the writer's injection of personal opinion in the first person ("I think . . ."). The result is jarring.

Certain points of view are appropriate for certain purposes, audiences, and occasions. Letter writing to a friend, for example, usually uses first and second person. Academic writing, by contrast, is generally more formal and relies most often on the third person.

Consider this example from the field of psychology. The author is attempting to stress the significance of an individual's early life in the formation of personality.

> Very little of a person's behavior is accidental. Psychologists believe there is a connection between an individual's early life and later personality. Initial experiences and feelings shape a person's view of the world. Most psychologists agree that an infant who feels loved will grow into an adult who sees the world positively. An infant who is ignored, by contrast, will not have his or her needs met. That individual will grow into an adult who sees the world negatively.

Note the point of view in this paragraph. It is written entirely in the third person. Had the writer added a personal opinion ("My own feeling about raising children is that . . .") or directly addressed the reader ("Can you imagine how an infant must feel . . ."), he or she would probably have distracted your attention from the main point.

It may on occasion be appropriate, or even necessary, to shift your point of view. For example, imagine that the above paragraph is the opening of a student paper about child care. The next paragraph could very easily be written as follows.

> In this paper, I will analyze the importance of early care for infants. I will show that parental care (or lack of care) can have a tremendous effect on a child's behavior. I will use works of Freud, Adler, and Benjamin as my main sources.

Because we expect the writer to explain the topic of an essay in such an introduction, the injection of the first person is not disruptive in this case.

In summary, there are few rigid rules about choosing a point of view. However, be on the alert whenever you find yourself shifting from one point of view to another. Then use your judgment—and avoid giving your reader unpleasant surprises.

Practice Exercises

The following exercises will help you review the skills covered in this chapter. Many of the types of questions presented here will be similar to those on the test; others will not. Remember that the purpose of the exercises is to give you practice on the skills rather than merely to prepare you for the test. Following these exercises are the Practice Exercise Explanations. They explain each question, the correct answer, and why the remaining choices are incorrect.

Note the raised numbers that appear at the beginning of each "part" of the passages. In most cases, these numbered parts are sentences; in some cases, however, the parts are incomplete sentences (or sentence fragments) that are used for testing purposes. For this reason, the word *part* is used instead of the word *sentence* in questions that refer to the passages.

1. Read the passage below, written in the style of a leisure studies textbook. Then answer the question that follows.

   [1]Fishing is one of the most popular recreational sports in the United States. [2]More people become involved in it every year. [3]Moreover, it is an activity that attracts participants from every geographic region of the country. [4]Unfortunately, acid rain poses a serious threat to our northeastern lakes and streams. [5]In short, people from all walks of life—from school teachers to computer programmers—are catching more fish every year.

   Which of the following numbered parts draws attention away from the main idea of the paragraph?

   A. Part 2

   B. Part 3

   C. Part 4

   D. Part 5

2. Read the passage below, written in the style of a student essay. Then answer the question that follows.

   [1]Since I was in third grade, the study of history has fascinated me. [2]Throughout grade school, biographies of famous people were my favorite books. [3]In high school, I found classes in science and math anything but interesting. [4]When I reached college, I took as many history courses as my advisor would permit.

   Which of the following sentences, if added after Part 3 in the paragraph, would best support the main idea of the paragraph?

   A. Not many other students were especially interested in history.

   B. Students in college often immerse themselves in the study of a specific discipline such as history.

   C. I really did try to be careful, at the time, not to go overboard with my enthusiasm.

   D. It was only classes that involved the story of past cultures that held my interest.

Read the passage below, written in the style of a college safety textbook. Then answer the questions that follow.

[1]Lightning kills more people than any other natural phenomenon. [2]However, there is little agreement even in the scientific community regarding the safety precautions that should be taken during a storm. [3]Everyone knows that it is wise to avoid standing near a tall tree, but that is where the agreement ends. [4]Clearly, education and other efforts to prevent needless deaths from lightning must begin with agreement on such a basic issue. [5]Sometimes it seems as though so-called "experts" can never agree on anything.

3. Which of the following sentences, if added where indicated, would best help to focus attention on the main idea of the paragraph?

    A. Before Part 1: Lightning will continue to result in many deaths in the years to come, since people simply ignore safety practices.

    B. Before Part 2: Insect bites, particularly bee stings, cause many more deaths than most people realize, but lightning causes the most fatalities of all.

    C. After Part 3: Even such basic points as the best posture to take during a storm—lying, standing, crouching—are marked by confusion.

    D. After Part 4: The safest place during a storm, most experts believe, is in a house with a lightning rod.

4. Which of the following numbered parts of the paragraph is LEAST relevant to the main idea of the paragraph?

    A. Part 1

    B. Part 2

    C. Part 4

    D. Part 5

5. Read the passage below, written in the style of a public health textbook. Then answer the question that follows.

    ¹Medical care is growing increasingly expensive, even as the quality of services continues to be questioned. ²Of the many strategies for reducing medical costs and at the same time increasing the quality of care, one in particular seems to hold promise. ³Reducing the length of stay in hospitals for those recovering from minor surgery would reduce costs significantly, since hospital rooms are one of the costliest aspects of modern health care. ⁴I was in the hospital once, and my room was very expensive. ⁵Many patients are finding that in addition to reducing costs, such an effort also hastens recovery; recuperation in the familiar surroundings of one's home, doctors speculate, may be less stressful.

    Which of the following changes would help focus attention on the main idea of the paragraph?

    A. Delete Part 1.

    B. Revise Part 3 to read, "Since hospital rooms are one of the costliest aspects of modern health care, reducing the length of stay in hospitals for those recovering from minor surgery would reduce costs significantly."

    C. Revise Part 4 to read, "For example, my room was very expensive when I was in the hospital."

    D. Delete Part 4.

6. Read the passage below, written in the style of a student essay. Then answer the question that follows.

    ¹To hear contemporary American politicians speak about immigration to the United States, one would conclude that our shores were the object of intense, and largely fulfilled, longing. ²According to the popular American view, immigrants simply couldn't wait to get here, renounce their native countries, learn English, and become Americanized. ³Careful study of patterns of immigration reveals a different story. ⁴I'm sure you're not surprised by this. ⁵Records show, for instance, that for every 100 individuals who came to American shores, 48 returned to their native lands. ⁶Thus, nearly half of all immigrants ultimately changed their minds about the American experience.

    Which of the numbered parts of the paragraph unnecessarily shifts the point of view taken by the writer?

    A. Part 1

    B. Part 2

    C. Part 3

    D. Part 4

7. Read the passage below, written in the style of an environmental studies textbook. Then answer the question that follows.

[1]The deadly poison DDT was routinely used by farmers in the 1950s to kill the insects that preyed on their crops. [2]Unfortunately, however, the chemical's effects could not be confined to the pests for whom it was intended. [3]Washed off the plants by rain, DDT found its way into rivers, contaminating fish. [4] _____ _____ .

[5] One such consumer, the bald eagle, was brought to the edge of extinction before DDT was banned. [6]It was only after DDT use was outlawed that the bald eagle population—as well as that of many other species of wildlife—began to increase once again.

Which of the following sentences would be the best replacement for the blank line labeled Part 4 in the paragraph?

A. Consumers of the fish were poisoned in turn.

B. This at least reduced the amount of DDT on the crops meant for human consumption.

C. You are probably wondering why somebody did not think of that.

D. We all feel sorry for the affected eagles, but what about the fish that died?

8. Read the passage below, written in the style of a student essay. Then answer the question that follows.

[1]Ever since television started covering politics, scholars have been interested in comparing the political reporting of the major networks. [2]One question of interest has been which stories each network picked to lead off its daily broadcasts. [3]One study compared the major television networks for one week of a presidential campaign. [4] _____ _____ .

[5]With just one exception, the next two stories were the same as well. [6]It seems, in at least this one respect, that there is little difference among the networks.

Which of the following sentences, if used in place of the blank line labeled Part 4, would best develop the main idea of the paragraph?

A. I am not really sure who was running in that particular election.

B. The results showed that the networks all had the same lead story every night.

C. Cable networks were not included in the study.

D. One has to wonder how many people were actually watching the news on those nights.

Practice Exercise Explanations

1. **Correct Response: C.** The main point of this paragraph is the growth of fishing. The sentence about acid rain distracts the reader from that main point. The other sentences all relate directly to the main point that fishing is a major sport in the United States.

2. **Correct Response: D.** The main idea of the paragraph is that the writer has been interested in history from an early age; the supporting sentences illustrate this interest throughout the writer's school years, as does choice D. Choices A and B are generalizations that do not keep the focus on the central point. Choice C is also a digression that leads the reader away from the main topic of the paragraph.

3. **Correct Response: C.** The main point of the paragraph is that there is little agreement on safety precautions during a lightning storm, and choice C develops the idea of disagreement over this issue. Responses A and B do not directly address the main point, so adding these sentences would impair paragraph unity. Choice D provides evidence of agreement by authorities, which is contradictory to the main point.

4. **Correct Response: D.** The comment in Part 5—that "so-called experts" frequently disagree—is irrelevant to the paragraph's main point that there is little agreement on safe behavior during electrical storms. Parts 1 and 2 (choices A and B) together establish this main point. Part 4 (choice C) is a relevant detail that addresses both lightning and safety precautions.

5. **Correct Response: D.** Deleting Part 4 eliminates an inappropriate shift in point of view from third person to first person. Since Part 1 (choice A) is the topic sentence of this paragraph, deleting it would eliminate the main point. The revision suggested to Part 3 (choice B) simply results in a rewording that has no effect on the main point. Rewording Part 4 (choice C) as indicated does not make it more relevant to the main point; the sentence still does not belong in the paragraph.

6. **Correct Response: D.** This sentence shifts the writing from the third person to a mixture of first person (I) and second person (you). Such a shift is not only unnecessary but inappropriate for this passage, which is fairly formal.

7. **Correct Response: A.** The sentence given in choice A is the only one that maintains the paragraph's focus on the effects of DDT on the environment. Response B does not maintain the writer's focus on the significance of all the chemical's adverse effects. Responses C and D shift the point of view from third person to second person (you) and first person (we), respectively, and do not contribute to the development of the main idea.

8. **Correct Response: B.** The main idea is stated in the first sentence of the paragraph; the sentences that follow describe an example that illustrates the main idea. The sentence in choice B is consistent with the purpose of describing the example. Choices A and D both shift the point of view. Choice C introduces a detail unrelated to the main idea.

Study Ideas

The exercises above address the related issues of unity, focus, and development in a piece of writing. They provide opportunities for you to identify flaws in the unity and focus of a passage and to revise paragraphs to improve these elements. Review the paragraphs, questions, and explanations carefully, making sure you understand both how the right answers contribute to unity and focus and why the wrong answers are incorrect.

In your personal reading, notice how writers have developed their main ideas and whether their development has provided a focus that helps unify their writing. Is the main idea clear? Do all the details support that idea? Is a single point of view maintained, and if not, is the unity of the piece damaged?

Consider these issues when you begin a writing assignment. As discussed in the previous chapter, define your overall purpose and audience. Then, as you begin developing your ideas in more detail, decide on your main points. Be sure that each main point is developed fully in its own paragraph(s). As you review your work, be on the alert for sentences that do not support the main idea; such sentences should be either revised, moved to a more appropriate location, or discarded.

Chapter 24

RECOGNIZE EFFECTIVE ORGANIZATION IN WRITING

This skill includes recognizing methods of paragraph organization and the appropriate use of transitional words or phrases to convey text structure, and reorganizing sentences to improve cohesion and the effective sequence of ideas.

Introduction

To communicate effectively, a writer must organize ideas so that a reader can follow his or her pattern of thought. Whether writing a paragraph or a longer composition, the writer must arrange ideas in a logical manner, so that the reader understands the relationship of supporting ideas to the main point as well as to one another. The writer must also give signals—for example, transitional words or phrases such as *first* or *in conclusion*—that will help the reader to grasp the pattern of organization.

Effective Organization in Writing

As you write, you should pay attention to how you are organizing your thoughts. Organization may be thought of in two ways. In the larger sense, it applies to the overall *structure* of your essay: What plan or strategy will you choose for presenting information to the reader? In another sense, it relates to the *methods* you will adopt to present your ideas clearly and to move from idea to idea within your presentation. The first of these definitions is sometimes referred to as the *sequence of ideas*. The second has to do with making sure the *transitions* between those ideas are accomplished clearly and smoothly.

Sequencing Ideas

The first major organizational decision you will have to make is how you wish to sequence your ideas. You have learned that there are some commonly used ways of *developing* ideas. There are also some common ways of *sequencing* or *ordering* your ideas. The type of paragraph you are writing will often suggest an effective sequence to use. A lab report for a chemistry class would lend itself to chronological (time) order—the first step in the experiment would be described first, the second step second, and so on. Similarly, a writer might choose chronological order to describe the events that led to a significant historical occurrence. A description of a room, on the other hand, might be organized according to spatial order (e.g., describing the room's features as a videocamera might film it).

Let us suppose, however, that you are to write an essay on whether American schools should include drug education programs as part of their curricula. As an important step in your brainstorming or prewriting process, you might think of several reasons why drug education in the schools is a good idea.

Idea A: Not every child has good role models in the home.

Idea B: Almost every child has been exposed to drug abuse in some way.

Idea C: Children who are educated about drugs make better choices and become more productive adults.

Idea D: Drug education should be offered by qualified professionals.

Your task now is to *sequence* these four ideas (sometimes called *subtopics*) so that your essay will achieve its maximum effect on the reader. One common way in which they might be organized is by **logical sequence**. If you recognize that one or more of your subtopics has caused the others to occur, you may wish to present the causes first and the effects later. Rearranged according to logical sequence, your list of subtopics might look like this:

1.   Almost every child has been exposed to drug abuse in some way. (Idea B)

2.   Not every child has good role models in the home. (Idea A)

3.   Drug education should be offered by qualified professionals. (Idea D)

4.   Children who are educated about drugs make better choices and become more productive adults. (Idea C)

The logical sequence presented here begins with a statement of a condition that presently exists (Sentence 1), moves to a possible solution that doesn't always work (Sentence 2), then presents a better solution (Sentence 3), and concludes with a statement of end result (Sentence 4). Once you have established an effective sequence of ideas, you are ready to begin developing each of these subtopics within its own paragraph (see "Developing Ideas Fully" in the preceding chapter).

Other common methods of sequencing ideas are discussed below.

Order of importance. The writer arranges supporting ideas in order of least important to most important or most important to least important. The former (least to most important) is usually preferred because the idea stated last is frequently the one that makes the strongest impression on a reader. Following this organizational principle, the ideas about drug education in the schools might be ordered as follows:

> Drug education in the schools is a good idea. Not every child has good role models in the home (Idea A). Besides, drug education is probably best offered by qualified professionals (Idea D). This education is essential because in our society few children will completely escape exposure to drug abuse (Idea B). With drug education in the schools, children can make better choices and become more productive adults (Idea C).

In this instance, the writer has determined that the ideas related to poor role models versus qualified professionals are perhaps less important to his or her overall argument than the ideas about how widespread drug abuse is and the hope that education offers for the future.

Deductive order. This is one of the most common ways of ordering ideas. Deductive order is used when a writer applies a generalization to specific instances. The writer begins with a general statement and follows it with specifics. The paragraph under "Sequencing Ideas: Order of Importance" above uses deductive order, in that the first sentence is a generalization, while the sentences that follow present more specific information in support of that generalization.

Inductive order. This arrangement of ideas moves from specific examples to the generalization that they illustrate. The paragraph under "Sequencing Ideas: Order of Importance" above could easily be rewritten using inductive order:

> It is time to face facts. Few children these days escape exposure to drug abuse (Idea B), and not all children have good role models in the home (Idea A). They need education about drug abuse, and that education is probably best offered by qualified professionals (Idea D). With proper education about drugs, children can make better choices and become more productive adults (Idea C). For all these reasons, the time has come to offer drug education in the schools.

In this method of sequencing ideas, the topic sentence of the paragraph is actually the final sentence. The writer is using the four more specific subtopics to build up to and support a generalization.

Chronological (time) order. Ideas are presented in their time sequence, the order of their occurrence. If the ideas above were rewritten to reflect a chronological consideration of the issue, the sequencing might look something like this:

> Drug abuse has been an especially challenging social issue since it first entered the mainstream of American life during the 1960s, with few children completely escaping exposure to drug abuse (Idea B). In addition, throughout the 1970s, drug abuse, along with other social problems, frequently meant that children had fewer good role models in the home (Idea A). Fortunately, in the 1980s, one response to this problem was the emergence of aggressive drug education programs offered by qualified professionals (Idea D). The next logical step for the 1990s would be to implement drug education in our schools, in order to ensure that children can make better choices and become more productive adults (Idea C).

Using Supporting Details Logically

Once you have decided what method you will use to sequence your ideas or subtopics logically, you are ready to begin marshaling support for your ideas. There are many ways in which ideas can be developed: you may elect to present **reasons**, **concrete details**, **specific examples**, **facts**, **statistics**, **incidents**, or **anecdotes** that support the truth or plausibility of your ideas (see "Developing Ideas Fully" in the preceding chapter). It is important, however, that whatever supporting details you choose be logically connected to the idea they are intended to support, as well as to each other. Carelessly mixing patterns of development or losing sight of what the point is you are trying to support may make your writing confusing. For example, look at the following paragraph. The writer has made an assertion of fact and followed it with supporting incidents. One sentence, however, is inconsistent with this general pattern.

[1]As a young child, the Polish girl who later became known to the world as Madame Curie gave evidence of her unique intellectual gifts. [2]She learned the alphabet from her older sister at the age of four and quickly taught herself to read, preferring reading to playing with blocks or other toys. [3]Her interest in science was foreshadowed by her attraction to the workroom of her father, himself a scientist. [4]Perhaps the reason she was so bright was that both of her parents were very intelligent. [5]She was fascinated by a barometer on the wall of this room and by a glass case containing scientific instruments and specimens of minerals.

Sentence 4 disrupts the pattern of logical development by giving, not another *incident* demonstrating Marie Curie's intelligent behavior, but a possible *reason* for her great intelligence. The reader is moved to wonder what that particular sentence is doing there—a sign of a weakness in the paragraph.

Other Organizational Patterns

In many of the examples above—in the paragraphs on drug education in the schools, for example—the writer is preparing a *persuasive* or *argumentative* essay. Your writing tasks in college may involve other purposes and goals. You will note, however, that whatever the rhetorical purpose involved, each of the paragraphs below follows a careful organizational pattern.

Comparison-contrast. The writer discusses similarities and/or differences between two subjects.

Students entering college soon discover that they spend fewer hours in the classroom than they did in high school. They also find that they have more long-range assignments than they have been accustomed to. And college teachers seem to be much less visible than their high school counterparts. These differences might give students the illusion of freedom, but they merely reflect the shift of responsibility to the student.

Definition. The writer explains the meaning of a word, phrase, or concept.

The term *workaholic* describes a person who is addicted to work, unable to break what can be a dangerous habit. Not content with eight hours at the office without a lunch break, the workaholic might dine with a client, bring home a briefcase full of paperwork at night, and return to the office on weekends.

Subdivision and classification. The writer divides something into parts, or places related items into separate categories.

Example of subdivision: The Middle Ages in the West can be divided into three periods. The Early Middle Ages, approximately A.D. 500 to 1000, was a time of cultural decline in Western civilization and was characterized by an agricultural economy. The High Middle Ages, about A.D. 1000 to 1300, saw the growth of cities, the rise of the middle class, and the establishment of strong monarchies. The Late Middle Ages, about A.D. 1300 to 1500, is known primarily for outstanding cultural achievements.

Example of classification: Historians take a variety of approaches to their discipline. Some believe that history is shaped by great men and women and focus on biography. Others emphasize the physical environment in their belief that geographical factors ultimately determine the course of events. A third group looks for an explanation of history in economic forces.

Transitions

The effective use of *transitions* is also very important to the clarity of your writing. If you look again at the paragraphs on drug education above, you will see that the writer has introduced key words and phrases into the text specifically to help the reader follow the argument. Words and phrases like "besides," "in addition," "in contrast," and "for example" help link the writer's ideas; they are examples of transitions. Transitional words or phrases are signals that help the reader follow a writer's thinking process. Even after creating a consistent pattern of development and a logical order of ideas, a writer will often use transitional words to make the connections between his or her ideas even more evident. Listed below are some examples of transitional words and phrases and some of the relationships they may be used to suggest.

Time: before, after, later

Space: above, to the left, behind

Addition: in addition, moreover, furthermore

Examples: for instance, for example, to illustrate

Contrast: on the contrary, in contrast, on the other hand

Comparison: likewise, similarly, also

Summary: therefore, in summary, in conclusion

Writers may use other transitional devices as well, such as the repetition of key words from one sentence to another, the use of words of similar meaning in two sentences, and the use of pronouns referring back to key concepts in a preceding sentence.

Organizing the ideas in your writing according to a reasonable and evident plan will help your reader understand your thinking. Making conscious decisions about your pattern and order of development and using appropriate transitional words will help you to accomplish this.

Practice Exercises

The following exercises will help you review the skills covered in this chapter. Many of the types of questions presented here will be similar to those on the test; others will not. Remember that the purpose of the exercises is to give you practice on the skills rather than merely to prepare you for the test. Following these exercises are the Practice Exercise Explanations. They explain each question, the correct answer, and why the remaining choices are incorrect.

Note the raised numbers that appear at the beginning of each "part" of the passages. In most cases, these numbered parts are sentences; in some cases, however, the parts are incomplete sentences (or sentence fragments) that are used for testing purposes. For this reason, the word *part* is used instead of the word *sentence* in questions that refer to the passages.

1. Read the passage below, written in the style of a college business textbook. Then answer the question that follows.

    [1]Those involved in international business should be aware of how customs and principles may vary from one culture to another. [2]Americans waiting for appointments in some countries might find that their hosts place a very different value on punctuality than they do. [3]Similarly, the degree of physical closeness acceptable for a normal conversation varies considerably among cultures. [4]The use of the first name too early or too late in a relationship is likewise a cause for misunderstanding. [5]_____ .
    [6]How important it is, then, for the businesspeople of our rapidly shrinking planet to learn about cultural differences.

Which of the following sentences, used in place of the blank line labeled Part 5, would best fit the writer's pattern of development in the paragraph?

A. Perhaps we will never understand the sources of these cultural differences.

B. Cultures may even differ about the correct method of bathing a baby.

C. Even the tone of voice in which a person says something may be misinterpreted by someone from another culture.

D. Those in business must also understand the economics of the country in which they conduct business.

2. Read the passage below, written in the style of an introductory logic textbook. Then answer the question that follows.

    (Note: an error in paragraph organization has been purposely included in this paragraph.)

    [1]Most of us have difficulty comprehending complex concepts about our universe. [2]Thus the tool of analogy can make a seemingly inaccessible idea reasonably clear to the layperson. [3]Our understanding of these concepts can often be aided by the use of analogy. [4]Many students remember a teacher using an orange and a grapefruit to demonstrate the concept of the earth's rotation on its axis and its simultaneous revolution around the sun. [5]Similarly, a simple balloon can help us understand the concept of an expanding universe.

    Which of the following changes would make the sequence of ideas in the paragraph clearer?

    A. Reverse the order of Parts 1 and 2.

    B. Place Part 2 after Part 5.

    C. Reverse the order of Parts 3 and 4.

    D. Delete Part 5.

3. Read the passage below, written in the style of a college geography textbook. Then answer the question that follows.

    The development of any culture is shaped to some extent by the resources and limitations of its geographical setting. This principle can clearly be seen in the study of early cultures. _____ , cultures without access to a major sea or an ocean, like early Russia, depended on rivers for trade and travel. _____ , ancient Greece, with its access to the Aegean Sea and the Mediterranean Sea, relied considerably on the sea for food and trade. But access to a sea or an ocean is not the only geographical feature that influences a culture. Climate, soil conditions, fresh water, and natural resources _____ affect the growth of a culture.

    Which words or phrases, if inserted in order into the blanks in the paragraph above, would help the reader understand the sequence of the writer's ideas?

    A. To illustrate; In contrast; also

    B. However; In conclusion; therefore

    C. On the other hand; Similarly; however

    D. Still; In addition; nevertheless

4. Read the passage below, written in the style of an introductory psychology textbook. Then answer the question that follows.

    [1]The social psychologist studies problems in our society in light of the principles of psychology. [2]One such problem is the phenomenon known as "urban stress," caused by overpopulation, dirt, and noise. [3]Another is the impact of media violence on our society. [4]Children exposed to violence on television have been known to behave violently toward their classmates. [5]The causes and effects of prejudice in our society are a third area of interest to the social psychologist. [6]Just as psychology can help us understand ourselves better as individuals, it can also lead us to a deeper understanding of problems, such as those mentioned here, that affect our society.

    Which numbered part of the paragraph interrupts the writer's pattern of development?

    A. Part 2

    B. Part 3

    C. Part 4

    D. Part 5

5. Read the passage below, written in the style of a college dance textbook. Then answer the question that follows.

    (Note: an error in paragraph organization has been purposely included in this paragraph.)

    [1]The term *modern dance* is generally used to refer to the serious and disciplined mode of dance that has evolved in this century. [2]Expressiveness is characteristic of this style of dance, distinguishing it from other forms of dance, such as folk and ballet. [3]However, the apparent spontaneity and freedom of movement of the style are not formless; they require the same intense study and practice as classical ballet. [4]Like other modern art forms, then, modern dance has its roots in scientific principle. [5]To achieve this effect of freedom, the dancer must become familiar with the natural laws that govern movement and must use those laws to express feeling.

    Which of the following changes would make the sequence of ideas in the paragraph clearer?

    A. Delete Part 1.

    B. Place Part 3 before Part 1.

    C. Delete Part 3.

    D. Reverse the order of Parts 4 and 5.

6. Read the passage below, written in the style of a college health textbook. Then answer the question that follows.

In studying the effects of air pollution on humans, two approaches are used: epidemiology and laboratory research. Epidemiology is the study of an observed effect on a large population in an attempt to associate that effect with a cause. Laboratory research begins with a cause and uses experiments to determine effects. Each approach has advantages and disadvantages. Epidemiology costs more, may yield incomplete data, and is difficult to control. _____ , research in laboratories is less expensive and can be carefully controlled. Laboratory experiments can also be repeated for verification. _____ , epidemiology can deal directly with human beings, whereas many laboratory experiments cannot be performed on people. Clearly a careful coordination of the two kinds of study would be most fruitful.

Which words or phrases, if inserted *in order* into the blanks in the paragraph, would help the reader understand the sequence of the writer's ideas?

A. On the other hand; However

B. Next; In addition

C. Likewise; Nevertheless

D. Consequently; In conclusion

7. Read the passage below, written in the style of an education textbook. Then answer the question that follows.

[1]The traditional, as opposed to the progressive, approach to education can best be defined by its basic assumptions. [2]The primary assumption of the traditionalist is that the main function of education is the transmission of culture. [3]Another assumption is that learning is best achieved in a formal context. [4] _____ . [5]Finally, the value of education is defended in deferred, rather than immediate, terms as "preparation for life." [6]A notable feature of all these assumptions is the lack of focus on the student who is to be educated.

Which of the following sentences, used in place of the blank line labeled Part 4, would best fit the writer's pattern of development in the paragraph?

A. The roots of traditional education can be found in the writings of ancient Greece.

B. The progressive educators do not agree with this assumption.

C. Most students educated under the traditional approach do not enjoy their schooling.

D. Next, the teacher is viewed as an authority, and certain subjects are valued as having central worth to education.

8. Read the passage below, written in the style of a college health textbook. Then answer the question that follows.

> Most people are aware that air pollution affects human health, but we must also study its effects on other aspects of the world we live in. Corrosion of materials, tarnishing of metals, and deterioration of textiles occur because of air pollution. Air pollution affects the tissues of plants and may eventually cause a decrease in the productivity of our crops. Probably most serious, and perhaps least understood, are the long-term effects of air pollution on our planet's ecology, the complex and delicate balance of living things. Thus, it is extremely important that we support scientists in their study of air pollution and ways to control it.

In what order are the details in this paragraph presented?

A. chronological

B. order of importance—most important to least important

C. order of importance—least important to most important

D. spatial

Practice Exercise Explanations

1. **Correct Response: C.** This paragraph is developed by specific examples, and choice C offers an additional example of a cultural difference that may affect a businessperson. Choice A is incorrect because the sentence is not an example, nor does it connect logically with the concluding sentence. Choice B is relevant to cultural differences but not to business; therefore, it would be inappropriate in this context. Choice D disrupts the pattern of organization because, although it relates to business, it does not follow the writer's pattern of giving examples of cultural differences relating to manners.

2. **Correct Response: B.** Part 2 draws a conclusion (signaled by the transitional word "thus") that does not follow logically from the first sentence. Used as the paragraph's final sentence, however, Part 2 provides both a logical conclusion based on the examples given and a good restatement of the main idea. Therefore, placing it after Part 5 would make the sequence of ideas clearer. Reversing the order of Parts 1 and 2 (choice A) would start the paragraph with the word "Thus"—a puzzling beginning. Because Part 3 leads logically to the listing of specific examples, reversing the order of Parts 3 and 4 (choice C) would make the paragraph less clear. Deleting Part 5 (choice D) would eliminate a relevant example that supports the main idea; this choice would not serve to make the sequence of ideas clearer.

   Note: One effective approach to a question such as this one is to try out each of the alternatives suggested as answer choices. For example, choice A suggests reversing the order of Parts 1 and 2. You should do this mentally by rereading the paragraph, reading Part 2 first and Part 1 second to see if this revision would make sense. Then do the same with the other choices.

3. **Correct Response: A.** In this paragraph, the opening sentence makes a general point about culture and geography. The second sentence narrows the topic to early cultures and leads logically to an example of an early culture in the third sentence. Thus, "to illustrate" (choice A) is appropriate as the first transition; the transition words listed first in choices B, C, and D do not fit sensibly in this context. The second transition introduces an example that contrasts with the first example. Therefore, "in contrast" is the most appropriate choice given; the transitional phrases listed second in the other choices do not suggest that a contrasting example will follow. The final sentence suggests that additional geographical factors other than seas and oceans affect cultures. "Also" is therefore an appropriate transition word to use in this space, whereas the final transitional words in each of the other responses are not appropriate.

4. **Correct Response: C.** Although Part 4 is related to the problem of violence, it breaks the pattern of the paragraph, which is based on examples of problems that the social psychologist studies. The writer begins with a statement about the concerns of social psychologists, and each sentence presents an example of a concern. Part 4 could be appropriate in a paragraph that developed the topic of violence, but it is not consistent with the pattern of this paragraph.

5. **Correct Response: D.** Part 4 is a concluding sentence that should be placed at the end of the paragraph; Part 5 should come immediately after Part 3, because of both its repetition of the word "freedom" and its elaboration of the argument presented in Part 3. Deleting Part 1 (choice A) would eliminate the topic sentence. Placing Part 3 before Part 1 (choice B) would start the paragraph confusingly. The word "however" implies the existence of a preceding paragraph, which is not given. Part 3 (choice C) strongly supports the main idea and leads into the sentence that should follow it (Part 5); therefore, deleting it would not clarify the sequence of ideas in this paragraph.

6. **Correct Response: A.** The paragraph is developed by comparison and contrast. Each statement about epidemiology is balanced by a contrasting statement about laboratory research. Both transitions indicated by the blanks introduce contrasts. Only choice A offers two words or phrases of contrast: "on the other hand" and "however." The transitional words and phrases listed in the other choices, if placed in order in the blanks, would not provide the reader with signals that clarify the writer's ideas.

7. **Correct Response: D.** The pattern of development in this paragraph is to define traditional education by looking at its basic assumptions. Choice D, introduced by the transitional clue "next," is the best choice. It alone continues the writer's pattern of development by offering another assumption of the traditionalists. Choice A introduces an irrelevant point about the history of traditional education. Choice B would be appropriate if this paragraph were developed by comparison and contrast rather than by definition. Choice C breaks the pattern of development by presenting an opinion about students' attitudes.

8. **Correct Response: C.** The paragraph begins with a general statement about the effects of pollution. The writer then provides explanatory details, beginning with the effects of pollution on materials, then on plant life, and finally (and "most serious") on ecology. The writer's details are carefully ordered, not merely listed at random. The point of the paragraph is more forceful because of this order.

Study Ideas

A careful study of the above exercises and the explanations of the answers will help you review important skills relating to organization in writing. In these exercises you were asked to identify methods of organizing ideas in a paragraph, to recognize effective order, and to identify the effective use of transitional words and phrases. Study the passages to determine how each sentence contributes to the effect of the passage as a whole, and note why the incorrect responses would interfere with effective communication by distracting the reader.

In your personal reading as well as your course reading, your understanding of paragraph structure can help you follow the writer's pattern of thought as well as comprehend his or her ideas.

When writing, be aware of the skills involved in effective organization. Review your writing carefully to determine if you have used patterns of development consistently, have sequenced your supporting ideas logically, and have used effective transitions that clearly communicate your train of thought to the reader.

Chapter 25

RECOGNIZE EFFECTIVE SENTENCES

This skill includes recognizing ineffective repetition and inefficiency in sentence construction; identifying sentence fragments and run-on sentences; identifying standard subject-verb agreement; identifying standard placement of modifiers, parallel structure, and use of negatives in sentence formation; and recognizing imprecise and inappropriate word choice.

Introduction

To communicate your ideas clearly, you must construct sentences that say what you intend them to say. Your sentences must be free of grammatical flaws and of errors in meaning and sense. If your writing is ungrammatical or vague, it will not convey the ideas you intend.

After you have decided what ideas you want to include in a piece of writing and have planned the structure of your work, you must begin putting your ideas into sentences that communicate those ideas effectively to your reader. You should write in complete and efficient sentences, using standard subject-verb agreement. Placing modifiers correctly, using parallel structure effectively, and employing negatives properly all help you present your ideas to the reader. Finally, you must choose words that convey precisely the message you want your reader to receive.

Edited American English

In this study guide, when we refer to "grammatical" writing or "standard" English, we are writing about a form of English that conforms to certain conventions of style, usage, and syntax. The formal name for this kind of English is "edited American English." This is the form of English that is used by writers in the United States to communicate in textbooks, government documents, magazines, newspapers, and the like. Many other forms of written and spoken English are acceptable in certain situations, but edited American English is the form that is generally considered acceptable in formal written communication.

Clauses and Phrases

You probably know that a standard sentence must have a subject and a verb. The following example is a standard sentence. Even though it is very short, it has both a subject and a verb, and it expresses a complete thought.

Fido slept.

A single word states the subject (*Fido*) and a single word states the verb (*slept*); together they express a complete thought. Sentences are not usually as simple as this one, however; they are more likely to consist of groups of words.

Old *Fido*, sighing contentedly, *slept* peacefully in the shade of the porch.

If you look carefully at this sentence, you can see that some words may be logically grouped together because they form units of meaning; examples of such groupings include "Fido . . . slept," "sighing contentedly," and "in the shade." Such units are divided into two basic groups: *clauses* and *phrases*. We will begin our discussion of effective sentence structure by looking at these two types of word groupings.

Clauses. A *clause* is a group of grammatically related words that contains a subject and its verb. There are two kinds of clauses: *independent* and *dependent* (or *subordinate*). Their names suggest the difference between them. An *independent clause* can stand alone as a sentence; a *dependent clause* cannot. Compare the two examples below.

1. Katie attends summer school

2. because Ellen wants to get to school early

Each of these clauses contains a subject and its verb ("Katie attends" in Example 1 and "Ellen wants" in Example 2). There is an important difference between them, however. The first example expresses a complete thought and can stand alone as a sentence. The second example does not express a complete thought; the reader expects some kind of conclusion to follow that makes its meaning clear. Example 1 is an *independent clause;* Example 2 is a *dependent (subordinate) clause*.

Phrases. A *phrase* is a group of words that expresses a meaning and acts as a single part of speech (e.g., as a noun or an adjective) but does *not* contain a subject and its verb. The following are examples of phrases.

1. the miniature train (noun phrase)

2. have been called (verb phrase)

3. on the ground (prepositional phrase)

4. eating and sleeping outdoors (verbal phrase)

Sentence Types

A sentence must contain at least one independent clause. However, sentences generally consist of combinations of phrases and clauses. The types of clauses a sentence contains determine the sentence's structural type: *simple, compound, complex,* or *compound-complex.*

A *simple sentence* contains a single independent clause, as in the examples below.

1. Katie attends summer school.

2. On Thursday mornings, Katie enthusiastically attends her favorite of all her summer school courses: chemistry.

Notice that, although the second sentence contains two prepositional phrases and is longer than the first, the subject and the verb "Katie attends" are the core of each sentence; both examples are *simple* sentences containing only a single independent clause.

A *compound sentence* contains two or more independent clauses joined together. Each of the following examples is a compound sentence. As you read each one, notice the method used for joining the clauses.

1. Katie attends summer school, but she still works 30 hours a week.

2. Katie attends summer school; however, she still works 30 hours a week.

3. Katie attends summer school; she also works 30 hours a week.

In Example 1, the two independent clauses are joined by a comma and a coordinating conjunction. (The *coordinating conjunctions* are *and, but, or, yet, for, nor,* and *so.*)

In Example 2, the independent clauses are joined by a semicolon and the conjunctive adverb *however* followed by a comma. (Some other *conjunctive adverbs* are *thus, consequently, then,* and *therefore.*)

In Example 3, a semicolon is used to separate the independent clauses; there is no linking word added.

A *complex sentence* contains *one* independent clause and one or more dependent clauses, as in the example below.

Katie attends summer school because she wants to finish her degree in three years.

Notice that the link between the independent and the dependent clauses is the word *because*. *Because* is a *subordinating conjunction*. The use of this type of conjunction is what makes the second clause dependent. (If the conjunction *because* were replaced with a semicolon, the sentence would become a *compound* sentence containing two independent clauses.) Some common subordinating conjunctions are *after, before, since, than, unless, when,* and *while.* A grammar book will provide you with a comprehensive list of these conjunctions.

A *compound-complex* sentence contains at least two independent clauses and at least one dependent clause. See the example below.

> Katie attends summer school because she wants to finish her degree in three years, but she continues to work 30 hours a week.

"Katie attends summer school" is an independent clause; "because she wants to finish her degree in three years" is a dependent clause; "but she continues to work 30 hours a week" is an independent clause.

You may wish to refer to the definitions presented above as we move on to a discussion of common problems in sentence construction.

Issues in Sentence Construction

Sentence Fragments

A sentence fragment is what its name suggests: only a part or fragment of a sentence, punctuated as if it were a complete sentence. Writers must be careful to avoid using sentence fragments when they really want to use sentences. A fragment is usually a phrase or dependent clause. The examples below are sentence fragments.

1. To go to the dentist on Saturday.

2. My brother, always planning to change his study habits.

3. The table in the middle of the room.

4. Because I hadn't met him before.

The following sentences show possible ways of changing these fragments to complete sentences. (The words that have been added to make each a complete sentence have been underlined.)

1. <u>Mary is scheduled</u> to go to the dentist on Saturday.

2. My brother, always planning to change his study habits, <u>has another new scheme</u>.

3. The table <u>stood</u> in the middle of the room.

4. <u>I felt nervous</u> because I hadn't met him before.

Sometimes writers use sentence fragments purposely for a specific effect. Fragments may appear, for example, in dialogue or as answers to questions, but such instances are rare in formal composition. Some examples follow.

> "He is a very difficult teacher," Mary said. "A fair one, though."

> Can anyone predict with assurance the course of our economy in the next five years? Not even the most astute economist!

In both examples the second "sentence" is actually a sentence fragment, but both are acceptable because they are used intentionally and effectively.

Always review your writing carefully to make certain that you have written complete sentences and that any sentence fragments are intentional and effective.

Run-ons (Comma Splices and Fused Sentences)

There are two types of *run-on* sentences. A *comma splice* results when two sentences (independent clauses) are joined by only a comma. A *fused sentence* results when punctuation between two sentences is omitted.

Comma splice: A storm was approaching rapidly, clouds quickly darkened the sky.

Fused sentence: A storm was approaching rapidly clouds quickly darkened the sky.

Possible ways of revising these sentences are shown below.

1. A storm was approaching rapidly. Clouds quickly darkened the sky.

2. A storm was approaching rapidly; clouds quickly darkened the sky.

3. A storm was approaching rapidly, and clouds quickly darkened the sky.

4. Because a storm was approaching, clouds quickly darkened the sky.

Subject-Verb Agreement

Standard English requires that you follow particular conventions of verb usage in your writing. One of these conventions is that the subject and the verb of a sentence must agree in number. That is, a singular subject must be accompanied by a singular verb, and a plural subject by a plural verb. This rule is demonstrated by the sentences below.

1. The girl sleeps.

2. The girls sleep.

In the first example, the singular subject *girl* is accompanied by the singular verb *sleeps;* in the second example, the plural *girls* is accompanied by the plural *sleep*. In these sentences, it is easy to decide what verb form to use, because the subjects are obvious. In other sentences, however, it may be more difficult to decide.

For example, a subject and a verb might be *separated* by several words, as in the following sentences. (The subject of each sentence has been underlined once and the verb twice.)

1. The harmonious <u>sound</u> of the violins <u>fills</u> the concert hall.

2. The sound <u>capabilities</u> of the keyboard <u>are</u> almost unlimited.

Although the subject and the verb are separated by prepositional phrases in both of these sentences, the number of the verb does not change. In the first sentence, the singular subject *sound* takes the singular verb *fills*. Notice that the plural noun *violins* is not the subject: the sentence is saying that *sound,* not *violins,* fills the room. In Sentence 2, the plural subject *capabilities* takes the plural verb *are;* the number of the verb is not changed by *keyboard,* which is the object of the preposition *of.*

Compound subjects may also cause confusion. If two subjects are joined by *and,* they form a compound subject; the verb that accompanies them must be plural. See the example below.

An audio <u>tape</u> and a <u>videotape</u> of that novel <u>are</u> available.

Since *tape* and *videotape* are both the subjects of this sentence, the verb must be the plural *are.*

Occasionally, however, a seemingly compound subject (or *false compound*) actually refers only to one person or to a single concept. In such a case, the verb is singular, as in the following example.

<u>Spaghetti and meatballs</u> <u>is</u> a traditional Italian dish.

Some *prepositional phrases* may cause confusion about whether the verb should be singular or plural. Examples of these are such phrasal prepositions as *along with, as well as, in addition to,* and *together with.* As with all prepositional phrases, however, these do not change the number of the subject or the verb in a sentence.

1. <u>Napoleon</u>, as well as Josephine, <u>was</u> frequently seen at the opera.

2. The <u>players</u>, along with their mascot, <u>were</u> already on the field.

Or words may also cause confusion. If two subjects are joined by *or, either, either . . . or,* or *neither . . . nor,* the verb must agree with the subject nearer to it. Look at the sentences below.

1. Neither his <u>poetry</u> nor his <u>novels</u> <u>are</u> among my favorites.

2. Either <u>cookies</u> or <u>ice cream</u> <u>is</u> available for dessert.

In Sentence 1, the verb *are* agrees with *novels,* which is nearer to the verb. In Sentence 2, the singular *is* agrees in number with the singular *ice cream,* to which it is nearer.

Inverted word order, another source of possible confusion, does not affect the number of the verb in a sentence. Ordinarily in English the subject precedes the verb, but this order can be inverted. The subject and the verb must still agree.

Among those most devastated by the crop failure <u>were</u> the small <u>farmers</u>.

Farmers is the subject of the verb *were* even though it follows the verb, just as it would be if the sentence were turned around:

The small <u>farmers</u> <u>were</u> most devastated by the crop failure.

When sentences begin with *there* (as in *there is* and *there are*), the writer must be careful to make the subject and the verb agree.

1. There <u>are</u> many <u>questions</u> to be answered.

2. There <u>is</u> an antique <u>flute</u> in the glass case.

In the first example, *questions* (rather than *there*) is the true subject of the sentence. In the second example, *flute* is a single subject requiring the single verb *is.*

Relative pronouns are pronouns such as *which, that, who, whom,* and *whose.* A relative pronoun refers to a noun (the pronoun's *antecedent*) coming just before it in a sentence. (Pronouns are discussed further in the following chapter.) In the sentence below, the relative pronoun is underlined twice, and its antecedent is underlined once.

Yesterday I met the <u>boy</u> <u>who</u> moved in next door.

In this sentence, *who* is used as a relative pronoun referring to the noun *boy.* When a relative pronoun is used to introduce a clause in a sentence, the number of the verb, the pronoun, and the antecedent noun must all be in agreement, as in the examples below.

1. The scientist who is concerned with the environment will dispose of laboratory waste in a responsible manner.

2. Wordsworth is one of the poets who are considered Romantic poets.

In Sentence 1, the relative pronoun *who* is singular because it refers to *scientist;* the verb, *is,* is therefore singular. In Sentence 2, the relative pronoun *who* is plural because its antecedent is the plural noun *poets;* the verb, *are,* is therefore plural.

If two or more singular subjects are joined by *and* but preceded by *every* or *each,* the verb is singular; see the following example.

> Each man and woman has a social security number.

When *indefinite pronouns* are used as subjects in a sentence, they frequently cause writers problems for this reason: some of them always take singular verbs, some always take plural verbs, and some may take either a singular or a plural verb, depending on the sentence. The indefinite pronouns *each, either, neither, one, anybody, everybody,* and *everyone* are among those that always take singular verbs. *Both, several, few,* and *many,* on the other hand, are always plural. Other indefinite pronouns, such as *all, any, most, none,* and *some,* may be plural or singular. Look at the examples below.

> Neither is ready to study calculus. (*Neither* is always singular.)

> Everybody in my class has a textbook. (*Everybody* is always singular.)

> Both of the politicians are coming to our school. (*Both* is always plural.)

> Some of the gravy was spilled. (Here *some* takes a singular verb, because it refers to the singular noun *gravy.*)

> Some of the children were too excited to sleep. (In this sentence, *some* refers to the plural noun *children,* so the verb is plural.)

> All the classrooms are filled. (In this case, *all* refers to a number of individual classrooms and is therefore plural.)

> All the money is spent. (In this case, *all* refers to a single amount of money and is therefore singular.)

Collective nouns are nouns that are singular in form but that refer to a group (e.g., *herd, flock, audience*). Words such as these, and words that refer to a fixed quantity (*one half, three quarters*), require a singular verb when they refer to the group as a unit and a plural verb when they refer to individuals or to parts of the group.

> Three fourths of the questions are multiple choice. (The context makes it clear that *three fourths* refers to individual questions; therefore, a plural verb is used.)

> Three fourths of the blueberry pie was eaten at lunch. (In this sentence, *three fourths* refers to a single amount; therefore, a singular verb is needed.)

Notice that in the following two examples, either a singular or a plural verb may be used, depending on the writer's meaning.

> The crew *wants* to turn back. (The crew is being treated as a single unit, so a singular verb is used.)

> The crew *want* to turn back. (Here the crew is being thought of as its individual members, so the plural verb *want* is used.)

Some nouns are plural in form but singular in meaning and usually require singular verbs. Examples of such words are *economics, measles,* and *physics.*

> Economics is a very complex subject.

Some nouns ending in *-ics,* such as *athletics* and *politics,* are singular or plural depending on context.

> Politics is a factor we cannot ignore.

> The politics of the candidates, not their consciences, are determining their positions on that issue.

When a sentence contains a *linking verb,* the verb must agree with the subject of the sentence, not with the noun that follows. (A linking verb is a verb followed by a word that renames or describes the subject.) See the examples below.

> Heavy rains are the difficulty. (In this sentence, *rains* is the subject of the plural verb *are.*)

> The difficulty is heavy rains. (In this sentence, the subject is *difficulty,* so the verb is singular.)

The title of a work, or a word referred to as a word, is always singular.

> 1. *Romeo and Juliet* is one of my favorite Shakespearean plays.

> 2. *Cats!* is one of the longest-running Broadway musicals.

> 3. *Umbrellas* is a plural noun.

In Examples 1 and 2, the singular verb is correctly used because the subjects are titles of created works. In Example 3, since the subject of the sentence is the word *umbrellas,* the singular verb is correct.

Misplaced Modifiers

Word order is very important in written English, for it tells readers the relationships among words or ideas in a sentence. Therefore, you should be very careful about where you place particular elements within a sentence. Some specific placement issues are addressed below.

When writing formal English, place adverbs and negatives (such as *almost, only, just, even, hardly, nearly,* and *not*) directly before the words they modify. Failing to do this may result in confusing, ambiguous, or ridiculous sentences.

Consider the sentence, "I got a B on the French test." The word *only* may be introduced into this sentence in several places, with very different meanings.

I got a *B* on the French test.

Only I got a *B* on the French test. (That is, nobody else got a *B*.)

I got only a *B* on the French test. (That is, I was expecting a higher grade.)

I got a *B* only on the French test. (That is, I got a different grade on every other test I took.)

I got a *B* on the only French test. (That is, no other French test was given.)

Consider also the placement of the word *not* in the following sentences.

1. All Americans are not Democrats, you know.

2. Not all Americans are Democrats, you know.

In Sentence 1, the wording is unclear. Most likely, the writer did not mean that there are no Americans who are Democrats, although that is the literal meaning of the sentence. The writer's probable meaning (that there are *some* Americans who are *not* Democrats) can be made clearer by moving the word *not* directly in front of the word it is meant to modify, as in Sentence 2.

Thus, even seemingly small and insignificant words can make a difference in meaning in a sentence, and careful writers are especially wary of such words.

Prepositional phrases, adjective clauses, and adverb clauses should also be placed near the element of the sentence they modify. Read the following examples, noticing how the placement of modifiers affects the meaning of the sentences.

1. The shape of that car is certainly adapted for driving on the highway, with its low body and smooth lines.

2. He wore socks rolled down to his ankles that were yellow.

In the first sentence, the prepositional phrase "with its low body and smooth lines" should follow *car*, which it modifies, rather than *highway*. In the second sentence, "that were yellow" is an adjective clause that should be placed after *socks*, which it modifies, rather than after *ankles*. Revising these two sentences as follows makes them clearer (as well as less unintentionally comical).

1. The shape of that car, with its low body and smooth lines, is certainly adapted for driving on the highway.

2. He wore socks that were yellow rolled down to his ankles.

Dangling Modifiers

A *dangling modifier* is a modifier that does not sensibly modify any element in a sentence. Because it does not modify an element in the sentence in which it appears, it is said to "dangle." The following sentence contains a dangling modifier.

> Discouraged by the lack of sales, his books were taken off the market.

Who was "discouraged by the lack of sales"? It could not have been "his books," although that is what the placement of the phrase suggests. The revision below corrects the problem.

> Discouraged by the lack of sales, he took his books off the market.

Now we are clearly told who was discouraged: the subject of the sentence, *he*.

The following two sentences also contain dangling modifiers.

> 1. Instead of assigning a novel, several short stories were given to the students to read.
>
> 2. To complete my assignment on time, the computer had to be repaired.

In Sentence 1, the phrase, "Instead of assigning a novel," does not modify anything in the sentence. In Sentence 2, the phrase, "To complete my assignment on time," seems to modify the subject, *the computer;* this, however, makes no sense. Look at the following revisions to these sentences.

> 1. Instead of assigning a novel, the teacher gave the students several short stories to read.
>
> 2. To complete my assignment on time, I had to have my computer repaired.

Double Negatives

A double negative is considered nonstandard in formal English writing. It involves the use of two negatives when a single negative is intended. The following sentence contains a double negative.

> I didn't get no presents for my graduation.

This sentence contains two negatives: *didn't* (which is a contraction for *did not*) and *no*. Logically, if someone did *not* get *no* presents, then he or she *did* get *some* presents—apparently contradicting what the writer means to say. Either of the following revisions would express correctly the writer's meaning.

> I didn't get any presents for my graduation.

> I got no presents for my graduation.

Using a negative with *hardly, barely,* and *scarcely* is also considered nonstandard, as in the following sentence.

I can't hardly wait until I finish my term paper.

Two alternative versions of this sentence are:

I can hardly wait until I finish my term paper.

I can't wait until I finish my term paper.

Wordiness and Needless Repetition

In effective sentences, every word contributes to the meaning of the sentence, and repetition is used only sparingly for emphasis. Consider the following wordy and repetitious example.

By the latter part of the season of autumn, it becomes apparent who the probable winner of the football conference championship will most likely be.

There are several ways to make this sentence more efficient. For example, the phrase *the latter part of* could be replaced by the single word *late*. The phrase *the season of autumn* is redundant (because autumn is a season): the single word *autumn* means the same thing. In addition, since the word *probable* and *most likely* suggest the same meaning in this sentence, one of them could be omitted. The sentence below is a more efficient version of the example.

By late autumn, it becomes apparent which football team will probably win the conference championship.

In general, you should economize on your use of words. Which of the following sentences do you think a reader would find clearer?

1. Subsequent to that point in time, the politician made contact with the lobbyists in person on account of the fact that he wanted them to give him their support.

2. Later on, the politician visited the lobbyists to get their support.

Parallel Structure

Parallel structure in writing refers to balancing the elements in a sentence grammatically. For example, if two elements in a sentence are paired, they should be written in the same form: both should be adjectives, phrases, participles, infinitives, etc. Parallel structure might be used in a series, in a compound element, in comparisons, or in contrasts. Effective parallelism can make your writing clearer and easier to read. Look at the examples below.

The homeless feel unwanted and as if they are not important.

The following revision makes this a more balanced, or parallel, sentence.

> The homeless feel unwanted and unimportant.

Study the following examples.

> (Unbalanced)   Effective writing demands breaking our bad habits and that we reinforce our good ones.
>
> (Balanced)   Effective writing demands that we break our bad habits and reinforce our good ones.
>
> (Unbalanced)   Many of the students protested the change, but it was welcomed by others.
>
> (Balanced)   Many students protested the change, but many welcomed it.

In general, parallel structure should be used for elements joined by coordinating conjunctions (*and, but, or,* etc.) and by correlative conjunctions (*either . . . or, neither . . . nor, both . . . and, not . . . but, not only . . . but also*).

You should be aware that parallel structure can sometimes be combined with effective repetition (as opposed to the needless repetition discussed earlier), as in the following example.

> The Republican appealed to some moderates as well as to conservatives; the Democrat appealed to some moderates as well as to liberals. (Here the repetition of specific words as well as the pattern serves to emphasize the point.)

Imprecise or Inappropriate Word Choice

Even when a sentence is grammatically correct and stylistically effective, the choice of a vague or an inappropriate word can distract the reader from your message.

Colloquial words. These are informal, conversational words. Using a good college dictionary or thesaurus can help you identify colloquial words. Generally, in formal writing, words your dictionary labels *informal* or *colloquial* are not appropriate except in dialogue.

> In Esther Forbes' book *Johnny Tremain,* Johnny goofs up by working on Sunday. (The phrase *goofs up* is too informal here.)

The following is a better version.

> In Esther Forbes' book *Johnny Tremain,* Johnny breaks the law by working on Sunday.

Contractions. Similarly, contractions are not generally used in formal writing.

> Many listeners felt the concerto wasn't fairly reviewed by critics after it was premiered by the Chicago Symphony last year. (The contraction *wasn't* should be replaced by the two words *was not*.)

Slang. As with colloquial language, slang should be used only when it is appropriate to your audience and purpose. It should generally be avoided in formal writing.

> Some people are grossed out by the portrayal of violence in William Golding's *Lord of the Flies*. (The slang expression *grossed out* is unacceptable in formal writing.)

A more formal version of this sentence is as follows.

> Some people are offended by the portrayal of violence in William Golding's *Lord of the Flies*.

Word choice. The mere fact that a word is long or impressive-sounding does not mean it is the most effective or appropriate choice. Often the best word to use is the short, common English word. Which of the following sentences seems clearer and more direct?

1. It was obvious from the manner in which they comported themselves that the adolescent females had larcenous intentions.

2. It was clear from their behavior that the teenage girls planned to steal something.

In addition, the more specific and concrete a word is (as opposed to general and abstract), the more effective it tends to be. Compare the following two sentences, noticing specific word choices in both.

1. The coach was amazed to see how much food the player could consume.

2. The coach was amazed to see how many hamburgers, french fries, and cupcakes the linebacker could eat.

We will close our discussion with a few word pairs that are commonly confused. You should take care to use the correct words in your writing. A dictionary will help you make the right choice, and most grammar books have a list of commonly confused words and/or a glossary of usage. Here are some examples with a few of their meanings.

affect/effect   *Affect* is commonly used as a verb meaning to *influence*.
                 He did not seem *affected* by the news.

                 Effect is frequently used as a verb meaning *to accomplish* or
                 as a noun meaning *a result*.
                 We have *effected* a change in policy.
                 The change should have several major *effects*.

allusion/illusion   *Allusion* is a noun meaning *a reference to something else*.
                     She made an *allusion* to our earlier disagreement.

                     Illusion means a *mistaken belief*.
                     He was under the *illusion* that the deadline had been
                     extended one week.

whose/who's   *Whose* is a possessive pronoun meaning *belonging to whom*.
               Whose radio do I hear?

               Who's is a contraction for *who is* or *who has*.
               Who's washing the dishes tonight?

climatic/climactic   *Climatic* is an adjective referring to *climate*.
                      A warming of the upper atmosphere will cause global
                      climatic changes.

                      Climactic is an adjective referring to a *climax*.
                      The *climactic* episode occurs in the sixth chapter of the
                      book.

principle/principal   The meanings of *principle* are *a rule of behavior* and *a law*.
                      His actions are always based on his *principles*.
                      The results of the experiment seemed to defy physical
                      principles.

                      Two meanings of *principal* are *head of a school* and *most
                      important*.
                      The *principal* spoke to all the students.
                      Your safety is my *principal* concern.

Practice Exercises

The following exercises will help you review the skills covered in this chapter. Many of the types of questions presented here will be similar to those on the test; others will not. Remember that the purpose of the exercises is to give you practice on the skills rather than merely to prepare you for the test. Following these exercises are the Practice Exercise Explanations. They explain each question, the correct answer, and why the remaining choices are incorrect.

Note the raised numbers that appear at the beginning of each "part" of the passages. In most cases, these numbered parts are sentences; in some cases, however, the parts are incomplete sentences (or sentence fragments) that are used for testing purposes. For this reason, the word *part* is used instead of the word *sentence* in questions that refer to the passages.

Read the passage below, written in the style of a college history textbook. Then answer the questions that follow.

[1]The Franco-Prussian War had far-reaching <u>affects</u> on France and her people. [2]The French had to pay the German Empire a sum of approximately one billion dollars, an amount that had a significant impact on the French economy. [3]In addition, the French lost all of Alsace and part of Lorraine, areas that have changed hands often in the history of these two powers. [4]A victory march through Paris caused <u>further</u> suffering for the French people. [5]The terms of settlement were extremely harsh, the only reason they were <u>accepted</u> was that the French were weary of war and eager for peace.

1. Which of the underlined words in the passage above should be replaced by a more precise or appropriate word?

    A. affects

    B. further

    C. accepted

    D. None of the words is used incorrectly.

2. Which of the following parts of the paragraph is not a standard sentence?

    A. Part 2

    B. Part 3

    C. Part 4

    D. Part 5

Read the passage below, written in the style of a student essay. Then answer the questions that follow.

[1]Advances in science are being recognized more and more as a mixed blessing. [2]They have made the world both a more comfortable and a more dangerous place in which to live. [3]On the one hand, the quality of our lives have been improved. [4]On the other hand a critical pollution problem has developed. [5]The very fact that science has lengthened our lifespan has contributed to a growth in population. [6]In turn, this growth has translated into an increase in waste materials and automobile emissions that pollute the environment. [7]In fact, statistics indicate that pollution is growing at an even faster rate than the population. [8]And these same advances have contributed to social problems many of which grow and develop in overcrowded and overpopulated cities that contain too many people.

3. Which of the following parts of the paragraph, if any, displays nonstandard subject-verb agreement?

   A. Part 2

   B. Part 3

   C. Part 4

   D. None of these parts displays nonstandard subject-verb agreement.

4. Which of the following parts should be revised to reduce repetition and improve the effectiveness of this paragraph?

   A. Part 1

   B. Part 5

   C. Part 7

   D. Part 8

Read the passage below, written in the style of a college science textbook. Then answer the questions that follow.

[1]Despite their name, killer whales are rather friendly animals—at least to humans. [2]Although they are ferocious hunters and will attack another species of whale larger than themselves, they are gentle in captivity. [3]Like their behavior, communication between these animals is an interesting subject to study. [4]Patterns of whistles, squeaks, and clicking sounds are uttered by the whales in a pod (the name for a group or herd of whales) and apparently was used to enable the pod to maintain its unity, even at considerable distances. [5]These patterns of sound are also helpful in finding food and in navigating. [6]Bouncing off an object and echoing, the whales hear the sound waves. [7]Like wolves, apes, and other animals, these whales remind us of the complexities of animal life that humans do not yet hardly understand.

5. Which of the following should be used in place of the underlined words in Part 4 of the passage?

    A. were used

    B. will be used

    C. is used

    D. are used

6. Which of the following should be used in place of the underlined words in Part 7 of the paragraph?

    A. do not yet understand

    B. don't hardly understand yet

    C. do not yet scarcely understand

    D. No change is needed.

7. Which of the following parts of the passage, if any, displays ineffective sentence construction?

    A. Part 2

    B. Part 3

    C. Part 6

    D. None of these parts displays ineffective sentence construction.

Read the passage below, written in the style of a college history textbook. Then answer the questions that follow.

[1]The ideas of the philosopher Confucius have influenced Chinese civilization for <u>many years</u>. [2]Born in the sixth century B.C., Confucius was concerned primarily with human beings and their relationships. [3]Such relationships, he believed, should be based on compassion, an unselfish feeling for others. [4]This compassion was to be carefully cultivated through the practice of unselfish behavior toward one's fellow humans. [5]A study of Confucius' ideas, then, reveals not only a profound concern for human beings and their interactions.

8. Which of the following phrases would be more precise than the underlined phrase in Part 1 of the passage?

    A. as long as one can recall

    B. some time

    C. more than two thousand years

    D. quite a while

9. Which of the following parts of the passage should be revised as indicated?

    A. Part 1: Change "Chinese civilization" to "the civilization of the Chinese people."

    B. Part 2: Insert the word "more" before "concerned."

    C. Part 3: Change the phrase "such relationships" to "relationships such as these."

    D. Part 5: Delete the conjunction "not only."

Practice Exercise Explanations

1. **Correct Response: A.** This question assesses the ability to recognize inappropriate word choice. Choice A is the best response because the word *affects* has been incorrectly used in the sentence to mean *outcomes* or *consequences*. This is not a meaning of the word *affects,* which is most commonly used as a verb meaning *to influence*. The correct word to use in this context is *effects*. Although *further* (choice B) is commonly confused with *farther* and *accept* (choice C) is often confused with *except,* both words are used correctly in this passage.

2. **Correct Response: D.** This question assesses the ability to recognize nonstandard sentences. Choice D is the best response because Part 5 is a *run-on* sentence: it consists of two independent clauses ("the terms of the settlement were extremely harsh" and "the only reason they were accepted was that the French were weary of war and eager for peace") that have been joined using only a comma. This is a type of run-on sentence known as a *comma splice.* A comma splice may be corrected by placing the word *and* after the comma, replacing the comma with a semicolon, or punctuating the clauses as two separate sentences. Of the other responses provided, choices A, B, and C are all standard sentences that need not be changed.

3. **Correct Response: B.** This question assesses the ability to identify nonstandard subject-verb agreement. Choice B is the best response because, to agree with the subject *quality,* the verb form used in Part 3 should be singular in number. Standard agreement requires that *have been improved* be changed to *has been improved*. Of the other responses provided, Parts 2 and 4 (choices A and C) display standard subject-verb agreement.

4. **Correct Response: D.** This question assesses the ability to recognize inefficient sentence construction. Choice D is the best response because the words *grow* and *develop* are too similar in meaning for both to be necessary, as are the words *overcrowded* and *overpopulated*. Nor is it necessary to add that the cities "contain too many people" after stating that they are "overpopulated." The sentences in Parts 1, 5, and 7 (choices A, B, and C, respectively) are all effectively crafted and should not be changed.

5. **Correct Response: D.** This question assesses the ability to recognize standard subject-verb agreement. The subject of the sentence is the noun *patterns*. Choice D is the best response because the verb form *are used* agrees in number with the subject and in tense with the present-tense verb *are uttered* in the first clause of the sentence. Of the other choices provided, *were used* (choice A) and *will be used* (choice B) are in the wrong tense, and *is used* (choice C) is singular, rather than plural, in number.

6. **Correct Response: A.** This question requires an understanding of the standard use of negatives in sentence formation. As written, the underlined section of Part 7 is a double negative meaning the opposite of what the writer intends. The easiest way to make the usage standard is to delete the modifier *hardly,* as has been done in choice A. Choices B and C are also double negatives and would therefore not improve the sentence.

7. **Correct Response: C.** This question assesses the ability to identify nonstandard placement of modifiers. Choice C is the best response because, as written, the phrase "Bouncing off an object and echoing" appears to modify *whales* rather than *waves*, the word that the writer intended the phrase to modify. In the other responses provided, all modifiers used in Parts 2 and 3 (choices A and B) are correctly placed and should not be moved.

8. **Correct Response: C.** This question assesses the ability to recognize precise word choice in a reading passage. Choice C is the best response because "more than two thousand years" gives readers a more definite idea of how long Confucian ideas have influenced Chinese society than does the phrase "many years," which could refer to a period of time ranging from twenty years to two hundred or two thousand years. Of the other choices provided, "as long as one can recall" (choice A), "some time" (choice B), and "quite a while" (choice D) are no more precise than the phrase used in the sentence.

9. **Correct Response: D.** This question requires an understanding of effective sentence structure. Choice D is the best response because *not only* is a correlative conjunction that is customarily used together with the conjunction *but also* in sentences; the presence of *not only* suggests that an additional clause will follow. Therefore, either *not only* should be dropped or a clause introduced by *but also* should be used to complete the sentence. Of the other choices provided, making the changes suggested in choices A and C would make Parts 1 and 3 wordier without improving them in any way. Inserting the word *more* before *concerned* in Part 2 (choice B) would suggest that a comparison is being made, which is not the case.

Study Ideas

Studying the above exercises and the accompanying explanations will help you review the skills involved in writing effective sentences. In some exercises you have been asked to identify sentences or parts of sentences that are not standard or not effectively expressed. In other exercises you have been asked to select a substitute for a nonstandard sentence or part of a sentence. Study these sample questions carefully to make sure you understand why some sentences are more effective than others. Note carefully that the correct choices communicate the writer's ideas efficiently and effectively. Notice also that the incorrect choices would confuse or distract the reader from the intended meaning.

In your reading, be aware of the sentence structure that writers use. Study the ways in which professional writers use English to express their ideas to their readers.

Most important, use these skills in your own writing. When revising, watch carefully for the flaws that weaken sentence structure, and substitute correct, standard, and effective writing. Paying attention to your sentence structure and working to write clear, economical sentences will improve your communication of ideas to your readers. Do not expect your first draft to contain only polished sentences. In fact, you may wish to write the first draft without much concern for sentence structure at all. But one step in your revision process should certainly be a careful scrutiny of your sentences to make certain that they do not violate the principles discussed in this chapter.

The chapter of this study guide that describes the writing sample will also discuss sentence structure in some detail.

Chapter 26

RECOGNIZE EDITED AMERICAN ENGLISH USAGE

This skill includes recognizing the standard use of verb forms and pronouns; recognizing the standard formation and use of adverbs, adjectives, comparatives, superlatives, and plural and possessive forms of nouns; and recognizing standard punctuation.

Introduction

Speakers and writers of English are faced with using a language that is in truth many languages. English is used differently by people from different regional or cultural backgrounds. The distinct language of a region or a group is usually called a *dialect*. Not only is the sound of the language different (because of different speakers' "accents"), but both the actual words and the patterns of words, phrases, and sentences are also different. Moreover, people instinctively use different types of English to suit different situations.

Edited American English. In this chapter, we address a particular type of adjustment that should be made by a writer who wishes to communicate effectively in fairly formal situations, such as those you will generally be faced with in college. The official term for the written standard English that is used by writers in the United States to communicate formally in textbooks, official government documents, magazines, newspapers, and the like is "edited American English." In this chapter we will generally refer to this type of English as "standard English" (as we have done throughout this study guide).

Writers should try to become comfortable switching between standard English and other dialects. At college, for an English class, you might write a short story with dialogue in the informal dialect of a specific group. In a scientific lab report, your writing will have to be less personal in its language and more precisely standard in its grammar, spelling, and punctuation. This holds true for all lab reports, book reports, term papers, exams, theses, and dissertations, just as it will also hold true later on in the workplace for job applications, résumés, memos, and business letters. Your audience will expect you to use standard word forms, spelling, punctuation, and grammar. Using nonstandard forms or ignoring the standard rules of grammar will detract from the effectiveness of your writing because readers will expect standard usage.

This chapter will help you become a critical evaluator of your own writing. Remember that whenever you write something for readers, you should make several drafts and several revisions. Read your own writing several times, and, if possible, ask others to read your drafts. The following are the points for which you should be examining your writing.

1. Make certain that your draft means what you intend (purpose), is specifically aimed at those who will be reading it (audience), and reflects the situation in which they are likely to read it (occasion). (See Chapter 22.)

2. Be sure you have chosen one subject to write about (unity) and that you continue to write about one main idea (focus) as you elaborate your points (development). (See Chapter 23.)

3. Look for a conscious and consistent organization that will be evident to your audience. (See Chapter 24.)

4. Make sure you follow patterns of standard English in both sentence construction (see Chapter 25) and usage—grammar, punctuation, and spelling (covered in this chapter—Chapter 26).

Perhaps the easiest way to get an idea of what is meant by the term *standard English* is to look at a passage containing some examples of *nonstandard English*. Read the paragraph below, and see if you can find instances of nonstandard English usage.

> [1]One of the first of the mainstream rock-and-rollers were Jerry Lee Lewis, a lanky blond whose curly hair would came undone after five minutes of a performance. [2]The minute Lewis stepped onstage, he will go wild. [3]He was even more wilder than Elvis Presley. [4]Lewis would kick back the piano stool stomp time bang the high keys with his foot and play a thundering bebop. [5]His unusually music was totally new to a first-time audiences ears.

You might have noticed the following examples of nonstandard usage in this paragraph.

Sentence 1 contains two. The first is the use of the plural verb *were* in combination with the singular subject *one*. Since the subject is singular, the verb should also be singular; *were* should be changed to *was*. The second is the nonstandard verb form *would came;* the standard form of this verb is *would come*.

Sentence 2 demonstrates nonstandard usage by mixing the *past tense* verb form *stepped* with the *future tense* verb form *will go,* making the meaning unclear. (Has the action already happened or is it going to happen?)

Sentence 3 uses the nonstandard comparative *more wilder*.

In Sentence 4, standard usage requires the placement of a comma after each element in a series—in this case after the words *stool, time,* and (optionally) *foot.*

Finally, in Sentence 5, there are two departures from standard usage. One is the use of an adverb to modify a noun; the adverb *unusually* should be replaced by the adjective *unusual*. The other is the omission of an apostrophe to show that the word *audience's* is possessive.

The paragraph has been revised below.

> [1]One of the first of the mainstream rock-and-rollers was Jerry Lee Lewis, a lanky blond whose curly hair would come undone after five minutes of a performance. [2]The minute Lewis stepped onstage, he went wild. [3]He was even wilder than Elvis Presley. [4]Lewis would kick back the piano stool, stomp time, bang the high keys with his foot, and play a thundering bebop. [5]His unusual music was totally new to a first-time audience's ears.

In this chapter, we will address the issue of standard and nonstandard usage in terms of some of the writing elements described above. Be aware, however, that the discussion below is meant only as a brief and partial review of the rules of standard English grammar and usage that you have studied throughout your school years. You should refer to textbooks on grammar and composition for a more detailed and comprehensive treatment of the subject.

A Writing Scenario

For the TASP Test, you will have to write an essay. Earlier sections of this study guide have suggested ways for you to think about your topic, audience, occasion, and purpose. Now watch a magazine writer at work, beginning an article on the thirtieth birthday of rock and roll music for a general audience of readers, aged 18 to 35 (say, readers of *Rolling Stone* magazine).

Look closely at how the writer correctly uses ordinary language to take readers back 30 years to the first dramatic moments of rock and roll. We will analyze how the grammar of standard English helps the writer do his or her job.

Here are the title and opening paragraphs of the story:

Rock and Roll: The First 30 Years

> To understand how Elvis Presley came to stir the musical soul of almost every teenager in the United States in the mid-1950s, you have to remember that he wasn't always the "King of Rock and Roll." In fact, there wasn't always a rock and roll to be king of. You have to go back before rock music even existed, back to the 1940s in the South, when it was mostly Black performers who sang the blues in bars and clubs, and mostly Black performers who used a loud, fast, pounding beat to communicate the message of the blues. These performers made a musical merger that they called rhythm and blues. This was the musical heritage that made possible the phenomenon of "the King."

When he walked into Sam Phillips' Sun Records studio, Elvis Presley was just an overgrown, show-off kid of 19 with greasy hair, pants pegged tight at the ankles, and big dreams of conquering not only Memphis and Tennessee, but the whole, wide musical world. Sam was not all that impressed the first few times Elvis played for him. He heard only passable guitar and a kid's voice that went from sweet (for schmaltzy music) to a slur (for the blues). It took Elvis two months to show Sam the frenzy, power, and suggestive growl that exploded on genuine "R&B" records. At one difficult recording session, Elvis and his boys began kidding around. Elvis broke loose into song, "Weeeeeeeelllllllll, that's all right, mama . . . ," and Sam knew right away that he had found what he wanted.

Verb Forms

Subject-verb agreement. In Chapter 25, we discussed subject-verb agreement in terms of effective sentence construction. Subject-verb agreement is also considered a usage issue. Look at the following sentence.

There weren't always a rock and roll to be king of.

The subject of this sentence—*rock and roll*—is singular, but the verb—*were(n't)*—is plural. Because the subject and the verb do not agree in number, the sentence demonstrates nonstandard *agreement*. It could equally well be said to demonstrate nonstandard *usage*, because the verb form *were* is not used in a conventional way. For a review of subject-verb agreement, refer to the previous chapter.

Verb tense. Another of the conventions regarding the use of verb forms has to do with *tense*. The tense of a verb indicates the time of an action. Look at the sentence, "Sam was not all that impressed the first few times Elvis played for him." Notice the form of the verb *play*. The *-ed* ending puts the verb in the *past tense*, telling us *when* Elvis made music—in the past.

The chart below shows the different forms used in each tense for the verb *play*. Each tense has both a *complete* form and a *progressive* form (that indicates the action is ongoing).

Tense	Sentence	Meaning
Present (complete)	He plays.	always, usually
Present (progressive)	He is playing.	ongoing
Past (complete)	He played.	finished in the past
Past (progressive)	He was playing.	ongoing in the past
Future (complete)	He will play.	at some future time
Future (progressive)	He will be playing.	ongoing in the future
Present perfect (complete)	He has played.	looking back from now
Present perfect (progressive)	He has been playing.	ongoing in the past
Past perfect (complete)	He had played.	done before a past act
Past perfect (progressive)	He had been playing.	ongoing before a past act
Future perfect (complete)	He will have played.	complete before future act
Future perfect (progressive)	He will have been playing.	ongoing before future act

Notice that different tenses use different forms of a verb. Present tense, for example, takes the form "He *plays*," not "He *playing*." The forms a verb may take are specified by its four principal parts: *infinitive, present participle, past,* and *past participle.* For the verb *play,* the principal parts are as follows.

Infinitive	Present Participle	Past	Past Participle
(to) play	playing	played	played

The verb *play* keeps the same stem (*play-*) in all of its forms; however, as you can see from the examples on the chart below, some verbs change their stems. For these *irregular* verbs, you must memorize the forms. A grammar book will provide you with this information.

Infinitive	Present Participle	Past	Past Participle
walk	walking	walked	walked
eat	eating	ate	eaten
be	being	was/were	been
begin	beginning	began	begun
go	going	went	gone

To understand the importance of verb tenses, let us look beyond a single sentence. Read the following paragraph about Elvis Presley's second appearance on television. Notice that while the specific verb tells *what* happens, the verb's tense tells *when* it happens. Tenses also help distinguish between what happens to Elvis and what the writer is saying directly to the reader.

> Every American over 35 knows how middle-class parents got their first look at "Elvis the Pelvis." Half the families in the country had turned on their television sets that Sunday night in 1956 for Ed Sullivan's "Talk of the Town." As one big national family, Americans had been tuning in every Sunday night for this hodgepodge variety show of magicians, mimics, jugglers, dancing dogs, and crooners in shiny suits. Everyone over 35 will remember that parents weren't at all ready for this rock and roll crooner in the pegged pants. Their kids were ready; the word was out. Ed Sullivan was ready, too. His cameramen had received strict instructions before Elvis took the stage: no shots below the waist of this sexy-sounding, hip-wiggling madman with the guitar.

Storytelling with Verb Tenses

Let us analyze the writer's use of specific verb tenses in this paragraph to order events in a dramatic way.

1. "Every American over 35 knows. . . ." Verb tenses do the main job here, allowing the writer to link us readers with the protagonist of the story, Elvis Presley, through our own experience or that of someone we know over 35—parents, an uncle, an older friend, perhaps. The writer swiftly takes us back 35 years: the first verb, *knows,* is in the present tense; the second, *got,* is past. Instantly, we are back in the 1950s.

2. "Half the families . . . had turned. . . ." Here the past perfect ("had turned") makes a fine point. The sets had been turned on before Presley appeared on the show. In other words, the audience was waiting—parents because they watched the show every week and kids because word had gotten around about Presley.

    The past perfect is different from the simple past. "Got" in the first sentence is in the simple past tense (something happened once). The past perfect "had turned," however, indicates that one action in the past (parents turned their TV sets on) happened before another action in the past (they saw Elvis).

    Notice the same relationship in the last sentence. Sullivan's camera crew "had received" orders about how to shoot Elvis in action *before* he "took" the stage. Both actions happened in the past, one before the other.

    Compare these verb forms with the verb form in the second sentence, "Americans *had been tuning in,*" which is the *progressive* form of the past perfect. Use of this tense indicates that, even before Elvis appeared, Americans watched the show every week.

3. "Everyone over 35 will remember" uses the future tense to draw us back to the present (i.e., when we are reading this passage), making us think again about ourselves or someone we know personally who might have seen that show. The writer is consciously drawing the reader back into the story, trying to avoid the feel of a history book about events far removed from us, almost saying, "Look around you; find someone over 35; ask him or her about the Elvis phenomenon." Notice how the verb tenses do the job here.

Think about how the writer has used verb tenses to convey meaning in the paragraph below.

> [1]What happened to Elvis and his music when he went from Sun Records in Memphis, Tennessee, to RCA Victor in New York City? [2]In that journey north, even in its earliest days, rock and roll lost some of its soul. [3]We hear the early strength in a Sun song, *Mystery Train,* when Elvis takes a line from an old country song about the loss and resignation of a man in chains, "Train I ride, 16 coaches long," and sings it with the shout of a man who knows that one day he will overcome, he will break those chains. [4]By the time he arrived in New York, however, Elvis had lost some of that shout.

Pronouns

Pronouns are words used to take the place of nouns. Consider the writer's use of pronouns as you read the following paragraph.

[1]At the end of the 1950s, Elvis went to Germany as a soldier with the U.S. Army, and Buddy Holly, Ritchie Valens, and J. P. Richardson (the Big Bopper) were killed in a plane crash. [2]It was the time Don McLean would later sing about in "American Pie" as "the day the music died." [3]Elvis was gone, rock musicians were dying, and rock and roll was going soft in the center. [4]The top song of 1960 was not a rock song. [5]Its sound came not from a guitar but from syrupy violins. [6]Its name came not from Memphis or New York but from Hollywood; it was a movie title, *A Summer Place*. [7]We think of the 1960s as unbroken rock and roll, but they also echoed with folk music and many other forms of popular music.

In this paragraph, the writer has used pronouns to avoid sounding repetitious. For example, look at Sentences 4, 5, and 6. In Sentence 4, the writer mentions "the top song of 1960"; the next two sentences also talk about "the top song," which they refer to as *it*. If you reread these sentences and mentally replace the pronoun *it* with "the top song of 1960" (or even, simply, "the song"), you will see why the writer has chosen to use the pronoun.

There are different kinds of pronouns. A *personal* pronoun (such as *I, you,* or *it*) takes one of three *persons* (first, second, or third) and is either singular or plural in *number*. A personal pronoun also takes one of three *cases:* nominative, objective, or possessive. A pronoun used as the subject or predicate nominative in a sentence takes the nominative case; a pronoun used as a direct or indirect object, or as the object of a preposition, takes the objective case; a pronoun that shows possession takes the possessive case. The following sentences show standard use of cases.

Nominative case	*He* is leaving.
	That person was *I*.
Objective case	We can't stop *them*.
	Hilary gave *him* a hug.
	Larry said goodbye to *him*.
Possessive case	*Our* trip will be a long one.
	That luggage is *theirs*.

The charts below show the personal pronouns.

NOMINATIVE CASE

	Singular	Plural
First person	I	we
Second person	you	you
Third person	he, she, it	they

OBJECTIVE CASE

	Singular	Plural
First person	me	us
Second person	you	you
Third person	him, her, it	them

POSSESSIVE CASE

	Singular	**Plural**
First person	my, mine	our, ours
Second person	your, yours	your, yours
Third person	his, her, hers, its	their, theirs

The other types of pronouns, and examples of each, are listed below. Note that a particular pronoun may be classed as one kind or another depending on how it is used in a sentence.

Relative pronouns	A *relative* pronoun is used to *relate* a clause to its antecedent, the noun to which the clause refers. The relative pronouns are *who, whom, whose, which,* and *that.* In the sentence, "The boy who ran home is my brother," *who* is a relative pronoun.
Interrogative pronouns	Interrogative pronouns are used in questions. *Who, whom, whose, which,* and *what* are the interrogative pronouns. *Who* is used as an interrogative pronoun in the question, "Who bought the tickets?"
Demonstrative pronouns	*This, that, these,* and *those* are the demonstrative pronouns. They are used to indicate a particular person or thing. *That* is used as a demonstrative pronoun in the sentence, "That is just what I have been looking for!"
Indefinite pronouns	Indefinite pronouns do not refer to a definite person or thing. *All, any, both, each, every, few, many, neither, nobody, none,* and *one* are some of the indefinite pronouns. "Nobody saw Mina's uncle" is a sentence containing an indefinite pronoun.
Reflexive pronouns	*Myself, yourself, himself, herself, itself, ourselves, yourselves,* and *themselves* are the reflexive pronouns. They are used for emphasis, as in the sentence, "You should do it yourself." (The pronoun *yourself* could be left out of this sentence, but it has been included to emphasize who should take action.) The nonstandard forms *hisself* and *theirselves* should not be used in formal writing.

A pronoun in a sentence must clearly refer to a specific noun; the noun to which a pronoun refers is called the pronoun's *antecedent*. A pronoun must agree with, or match, its antecedent in both *gender* and *number*. Earlier we discussed the issue of agreement between a verb and its subject. Subject-pronoun agreement follows similar rules. For example, if a pronoun's antecedent is singular, the pronoun must be singular; if the antecedent is plural, the pronoun must be plural. Look at the following sentences, in which the pronouns and their antecedents have been highlighted.

My *aunt* takes good care of *her* horses.

My *cousins* take good care of *their* horses.

Notice that each sentence shows agreement among all three elements: subject, verb, and pronoun.

Sometimes a pronoun's antecedent will be another pronoun, as in the examples below.

All of the children want *their* pictures taken.

Each of the boys wants *his* picture taken.

In general, your decisions about pronoun-antecedent agreement should follow the rules for subject-verb agreement. If the subject takes a singular verb, it takes a singular pronoun as well. If it takes a plural verb, it takes a plural pronoun.

Look for examples of nonstandard pronoun usage in the paragraph below.

[1]Rock and roll combined the simplicity of folk songs, the lament of blues, and the rhythms of country music. [2]They revolutionized the music world. [3]Rock and roll was a total departure from the blandness of pop music in the 1950s. [4]It had become utterly boring. [5]As for rock, however, us fans couldn't get it's rhythms out of our heads. [6]The difficulty no longer was to find music that we really wanted to hear. [7]The question was, "Who's music should we listen to next?"

In Sentence 2, the plural pronoun *they* is used to refer to the singular noun *rock and roll;* since the pronoun and its antecedent do not agree in *number,* this is nonstandard usage.

In Sentence 4, the pronoun *it* does not point clearly to its antecedent. Since the subject of Sentence 3 is "rock and roll," the reader assumes that the pronoun *it* in Sentence 4 refers to "rock and roll." After reading the sentence, however, the reader realizes that the writer must mean *it* to refer to "pop music in the 1950s." Sentence 4 should be revised to make this meaning clear.

In Sentence 5, there are two examples of nonstandard usage. One is the use of the objective case pronoun *us* instead of the nominative case pronoun *we* as the subject of the sentence. The other is the use of the contraction *it's* (meaning *it is*) instead of the possessive pronoun *its*.

Similarly, in Sentence 7, a contraction (*who's,* meaning *who is*) is used instead of a personal pronoun (*whose,* meaning *belonging to whom*).

The paragraph has been revised below.

> [1]Rock and roll combined the simplicity of folk songs, the lament of blues, and the rhythms of country music. [2]It revolutionized the music world. [3]Rock and roll was a total departure from the blandness of pop music in the 1950s. [4]Popular songs had become utterly boring. [5]As for rock, however, we fans couldn't get its rhythms out of our heads. [6]The difficulty no longer was to find music that we really wanted to hear. [7]The question was, "Whose music should we listen to next?"

Modifiers

Modifiers fall into two main categories: adjectives and adverbs. In Chapter 25 we discussed modifiers in terms of their placement within a sentence. Now we will look at them primarily in terms of the rules governing the forms they may take.

Adjectives. An adjective is a word used to modify, or tell something about, a noun. Look for examples of adjectives in the following paragraph.

> Watch the rock and rollers of the 1980s trying to recapture some of that early toughness. Punks and rockers wear black leather; their shaved heads are shiny with garish color and polished a pinky white. These modern rock and rollers emphasize the toughness of their musical roots by playing their music at ear-splitting sound levels. They are trying to shock their parents—who still consider themselves the true heirs to rock and roll—into voicing the same tired objections that their parents heard from their own parents.

The first two sentences contain the adjectives *the, that, black,* and *garish.* Two of the adjectives (*the* and *that*) work as *pointers* (that is, they *point* to the nouns they modify rather than *describing* them); *black* and *garish,* on the other hand, describe their nouns, helping the reader see them more vividly.

Adjectives generally give writers little trouble, with the exception of the demonstrative adjectives *this, that, these,* and *those.* You may recognize them as the demonstrative *pronouns* discussed earlier in this chapter. In fact, they are the same words. When used alone (as in the sentence, "*That's* what I meant!"), they are pronouns; when used together with a noun (as in, "*That idea* was mine!"), they are adjectives that point to the noun they precede.

Be sure you use demonstrative adjectives rather than pronouns to modify nouns, and be sure that the number of the adjective matches the number of the noun. See the following examples.

> Nonstandard: I have some of *them* Elvis Presley records.
>   (*Them* is a pronoun, not an adjective.)
>
> Standard: I have some of *those* Elvis Presley records.
>   (*Those* is a demonstrative adjective indicating which records.)

Nonstandard:	Do you like *these kind* of records? (*These* is plural, but *kind* is singular.)
Standard:	Do you like *this kind* (or *these kinds*) of records? (The singular *this* matches the singular *kind;* the plural *these* matches the plural *kinds.*)

Adverbs. Adverbs modify verbs, adjectives, and adverbs. Look for the adverbs in the paragraph below.

[1]In the record business, rock and roll first made itself felt on the sale of record singles, which were sold cheaply and were played again and again on juke boxes. [2]Soon, however, teenagers were spending money more freely. [3]They quickly became album buyers, arguing into the night over which of two albums was better, or what singer had released the best album. [4]Most important for the economy, recording companies were witnessing the birth of the nation's youngest and fastest-growing consumer market.

In this paragraph, as is usual, most of the adverbs modify verbs. In the first sentence, for example, *first* modifies the verb *made, cheaply* modifies the verb *were sold,* and *again and again* modifies the verb *were played.* But in Sentence 2, *more* modifies the adverb *freely,* and in Sentence 4, the adverb *most* modifies the adjective *important.*

Comparatives and superlatives. In addition to their basic forms, adjectives and adverbs have comparative and superlative forms. The comparative form is used to compare two items; the superlative form is used to compare more than two. For example, in Sentence 3 of the above paragraph, *better* (the comparative form of the adverb *well*) is used when two albums are compared; *best* (the superlative form) is used for a comparison of all the current singers.

Some comparatives and superlatives have special forms (e.g., good, better, best; bad, worse, worst). Others are formed by adding -er and -est to the basic form (e.g., fast, faster, fastest; happy, happier, happiest). Still others use the words *more* and *most* to express the comparative and the superlative (e.g., careful, more careful, most careful; dangerously, more dangerously, most dangerously).

Probably the most common problem with comparatives and superlatives occurs when a writer combines two of the forms (e.g., saying *most fastest* or *more shorter* instead of simply *fastest* or *shorter*); this is redundant and is considered nonstandard English.

Prepositional phrases. We also use *prepositional phrases* as adjectives or adverbs modifying nouns or verbs. A prepositional phrase consists of a preposition (such as *in, of, for, to, toward,* or *on*) and its object. For example, in the sentence "I went to the store," *to the store* is an adverbial prepositional phrase (modifying the verb *went*) that begins with the preposition *to* and is completed by the object of the preposition *store.* When you use a prepositional phrase to modify a word, you must be sure that you place the phrase appropriately in the sentence. You probably have seen examples, such as the ones below, of so-called "misplaced" modifiers.

I left his math book on the train in my backpack.
(What is in the backpack—the book or the train?)

We saw Ellen with Jim in a bright red dress.
(Who was wearing the red dress?)

He gave his paper to his teacher on television.
(What was "on television"—his paper or his teacher?)

Chapter 25 provides a more detailed discussion of standard placement of modifiers.

Conjunctions

To join words, phrases, and entire clauses, we use words such as *and, but, or, since, because,* and *although.* These words are called conjunctions. (See Chapter 25 for more on conjunctions.) Conjunctions can be used to signal the kinds of relationships between the writer's ideas.

For example, some conjunctions signal *time* relationships between two ideas in a sentence or in two sentences; examples of these include *before, after, while,* and *meanwhile.* Conjunctions may also signal *causal* relationships; *because, since,* and *for* are examples. Conjunctions such as *but, however, nevertheless,* and *still* express *contrasts* between ideas and/or opinions. Here are some examples of conjunctions being used to indicate time, cause, and contrast.

Time: *After* Elvis died, millions of fans visited his home.

Cause: I feel comfortable *for* I've been here before.

Cause: *Since* we're all friends, let's skip the formalities.

Contrast: I know you're ready; *still,* I'd like to wait a minute.

Contrast: Ted likes most music *but* not rock and roll.

Punctuation, capitalization, and spelling are known as the *mechanics* of writing. Punctuation is a writer's way of indicating pauses and voice changes that people who are *speaking* use without thinking. Skillful use of punctuation enables the writer to enliven his or her writing, to make it as expressive as spoken language. We will now look at five important marks of punctuation: commas, semicolons, colons, quotation marks, and apostrophes.

Standard Usage and Word Choice

One of the most important aspects of writing effective sentences is choosing the right words to express exactly what you mean to say. For maximum effect, words should be chosen with care and precision, and careful attention should be given to ensure that they follow the conventions of standard American usage. Some of the most common usage issues involve the following:

- **Double negatives.** A double negative occurs when a writer combines two (or more) negatives in a statement where a single negative meaning is intended.

  We can't do nothing about the weather. (The writer means, "We can't do anything about the weather.")

  The boy couldn't hardly read. (The writer means, "The boy could hardly read.")

- **Wordiness and needless repetition.** Be careful that every word in the sentence is necessary and that no words or phrases are needlessly redundant.

  I saw her at 9:45 P.M. at night wearing a dress that was short in length and yellow in color. (The phrases "at night," "in length," and "in color" are redundant and may be deleted from the sentence with no loss of meaning: "I saw her at 9:45 P.M. wearing a short, yellow dress.")

- **Imprecise or inappropriate word choice.** Effective writers are extremely careful in their word choice. Even if a sentence is grammatically correct, the choice of a vague or inappropriate word can be distracting to the reader. In formal writing, you may wish to avoid the use of **colloquialisms** and **slang**, **contractions**, and **excessively jargony, flowery, or impressive-sounding language**.

  Mr. Mains emerged from the conference with an extremely ticked-off look on his face. ("Ticked-off" is a colloquialism. To maintain the more formal tone of the sentence, you might substitute "irritated" or "angry.")

  Under the circumstances, taking an incomplete in the course wasn't an option. (In formal writing, the contraction "wasn't" should be replaced by "was not.")

  In order to strategize management options, present theoretical constructs should be seen to dictate more coherent operational contingencies. (This sentence contains too much jargony, overblown language. It could be rewritten as: "If management wants to keep its options open, it should make sure that practice keeps up with theory.")

Chapter 25 contains further discussion of these usage issues within the construction of effective sentences.

Punctuation

Read the sentences below aloud, pausing at the punctuation marks to hear how they help you understand meaning.

To understand how Elvis Presley stirred the souls of teenagers in the United States, we'd have to go back to the South in the mid-1950s.

Elvis Presley was just an overgrown, show-off kid with greasy hair, pegged pants, and wild, impossible dreams of conquering the world.

It took Elvis two months to show Sam what he wanted: the frenzy, power, and suggestive growl that exploded on genuine R&B records.

Elvis sang the words, "Train I ride, 16 coaches long" as if he were on that train himself.

The song's name didn't come from Memphis or New York but from Hollywood; it was a movie title, *A Summer Place*.

Commas. Commas indicate a slight pause in speaking or reading. Writers use commas in the following ways.

- To mark a series of three or more equals. ("I'm studying English, math, and computer science." Note that the comma before the word *and* is sometimes omitted in standard English; either usage is considered acceptable.)

- To separate adjectives of equal force that jointly modify the same noun. ("He had wild, impossible dreams.")

- To mark off a long introductory phrase or clause. ("To understand how Elvis came to stir the musical soul of almost every teenager in the United States, you have to remember. . . .")

- To mark off introductory words, especially those moved from their normal position in the sentence ("Furiously, he pounded the piano with two hands and his right heel") or those needing a pause. ("Finally, in the 1980s, we hear modern rock and rollers. . . .")

- To mark off one independent clause from another. ("Elvis played his first four songs, but nothing happened until the boys started joking around.")

- To mark off a subordinate clause coming before its controlling clause. ("Because most pop music was bland and sentimental, early rock singers had to write their own material.")

- To mark off a direct quotation. ("He started to sing, 'Train I ride. . . .' ")

- To mark off appositive phrases, descriptive material following a noun or pronoun. ("We know him today as Elvis, the King of Rock and Roll.")

- To mark a relative phrase or clause that is not essential to the basic meaning of the sentence. Compare these two sentences.

  1. I have all the Elvis Presley singles, which are not syrupy or sentimental.

  2. I have all the Elvis Presley singles that are not syrupy or sentimental.

In Sentence 1, the relative clause "which are not syrupy or sentimental" is set off by a comma because it is essentially a parenthetical remark. The basic meaning of the sentence—that the writer has all the Elvis Presley singles—is not lost if the clause is removed. In Sentence 2, however, the relative clause "that are not syrupy or sentimental" conveys an essential part of the meaning of the sentence—that the writer has only singles that are *not* syrupy or sentimental. In the first case, standard usage requires a comma; in the second case, it requires that the comma be omitted. (The different relative pronouns used—*which* and *that*—also indicate whether the clause is essential or nonessential.)

- To mark off other nonessential information in a sentence. ("He could, however, play a mean bass guitar.")

- To mark off items in dates and addresses. ("Elvis appeared on television on March 16, 1954, in a little studio on West 57th Street, New York City, New York.")

Semicolons. Semicolons are used to join closely related independent clauses. In most cases, the two clauses joined by the semicolon could reasonably be punctuated as two separate sentences; joining them, however, emphasizes the relationship between the two clauses. Semicolons are used in two ways.

- In place of a coordinating conjunction such as *and* or *but*. ("Elvis played and danced; Sam Phillips listened and watched." Here the semicolon replaces a comma and the word *and*.)

- Before adverbial conjunctions such as *in fact* or *however*. ("Rock was a growing movement; in fact, disc jockeys everywhere were demanding more rock singles." "Readers understand many styles of writing; however, you should always use a relatively formal style for your college essays.")

Colons. Writers use colons to serve two major functions.

- The first function is to introduce a list or (sometimes) a quotation. Used this way, the colon is roughly equivalent to the phrase "as follows" and makes such a phrase unnecessary; to use that phrase or a similar one (e.g., "for example," "namely") in addition to the colon would be redundant and nonstandard.

  A writer must always remember three things when planning and writing an essay: audience, purpose, and occasion.

  I am taking four courses this semester: Spanish, math, African literature, and home economics.

  You should buy the following items: a ruler, a calculator, two notebooks, at least three pens, and a good dictionary.

  Remember the words of Eleanor Roosevelt: "No one can make you feel inferior without your consent."

  Martin Luther King, Jr., put it most forcefully when he spoke these words: "We will not be satisfied until justice rolls down like waters and righteousness like a mighty stream."

- The second major function of the colon is to introduce a clause that explains or clarifies the clause that precedes the colon. Used this way, the colon is roughly equivalent to the phrase "let me explain"; again, the colon is used instead of such a phrase, not in addition to it.

  He was a sloppy writer who always took the easy way out: instead of laboring over his work and editing it carefully, he would rush out a first draft and hand it in unrevised.

  Ms. Diaz is a conscientious teacher: She always prepares her lessons carefully, she takes the time to make sure her students understand her points, and she invites open discussion of ideas.

Quotation marks. Quotation marks are used to indicate words quoted directly; names of poems, songs, magazine articles, etc.; and words used in an unusual way.

  He was angry. "What do you think you're doing?" he yelled.

  She said, "He's a real poet," but she added, "Sometimes I can't understand his lyrics. He confuses me."

Her favorite song is the ballad "Suzanne."

Her music is unusual, a kind of "religious" rock.

It is worth noting that it is a convention among American writers to indicate quotations within quotations by using single quotation marks within the usual double quotation marks. Often these single quotation marks look like apostrophes, but they serve a different function.

Charlie Reed told me, "My favorite short story is 'The Lottery' by Shirley Jackson."

Ms. Fleet asked, "When Martin Luther King, Jr., said, 'I have a dream,' what do you think he meant?"

Apostrophes. Apostrophes are used in two important ways. The first use is to indicate possession. The examples below demonstrate this use.

Is this John's book or Sondra's?

How much of these works are Socrates' ideas and how much Plato's?

It is important to know which are the parents' responsibilities and which are the children's.

Massachusetts' Bill of Rights is older than the United States'.

Everyone's rights are protected by the Constitution: men's, women's, boys', and girls'.

Odysseus' route home was no shortcut.

You will have noticed that sometimes the possessive is indicated by an apostrophe followed by an *s;* other times the apostrophe is used alone. In general, you should follow the rules below.

- An apostrophe and an *s* are used to indicate possession by a singular person or object, and by plural persons or objects whose plural forms do not end in an *s* sound.

- An apostrophe alone is used to indicate possession by plural persons or things whose plural forms end in an *s* sound, and sometimes possession by singular persons or things whose singular forms end in an *s* sound.

More simply stated: If the possessive word ends in *s,* add an apostrophe; if the possessive word ends in any sound other than *s,* add an apostrophe and an *s.* Note that this is a rule of thumb and is often violated; in general, use your sense of sound to tell you how to make a word possessive.

The second common use of the apostrophe is as a signal that one or more letters have been omitted from a word. This use of the apostrophe is most frequent in contractions, which are common phrases that have been shortened because they are used so often (e.g., *can't* for *cannot, won't* for *will not*). The use of such contractions is generally considered too colloquial, or casual, for formal writing and should be avoided.

Practice Exercises

The following exercises will help you review the skills covered in this chapter. Many of the types of questions presented here will be similar to those on the test; others will not. Remember that the purpose of the exercises is to give you practice on the skills rather than merely to prepare you for the test. Following these exercises are the Practice Exercise Explanations. They explain each question, the correct answer, and why the remaining choices are incorrect.

Note the raised numbers that appear at the beginning of each "part" of the passages. In most cases, these numbered parts are sentences; in some cases, however, the parts are incomplete sentences (or sentence fragments) that are used for testing purposes. For this reason, the word *part* is used instead of the word *sentence* in questions that refer to the passages.

Read the passage below, written in the style of a popular magazine article. Then answer the questions that follow.

[1]Rock music, like all manifestations of human culture, has both influenced and been influenced by the broader social context in which it evolved. [2]It is both a product of U.S. culture in the last half of the twentieth century and a musical and social force that has shape that culture. [3]Elvis Presley and his bold singing helped shape the manners and morals of the New South. [4]Yet Elvis's popularity was made possible only because of new recording technology, cheap records, and a vast new audience of teenagers. [5]Similarly, did rock music's blend of Black roots and White performers help make the civil rights movement of the 1960s a passionate cause among young people? [6]Or did the movement teach White youths the real pain that gave birth to the blues? [7]Or are both of them statements true?

1. Which one, if any, of the following changes is needed in the above passage?

   A. Part 2: Change "has shape" to "has shaped."

   B. Part 5: Change "did" to "does."

   C. Part 6: Change "teach" to "taught."

   D. None of these changes is needed.

2. Which of the following parts of the passage displays nonstandard usage?

   A. Part 1

   B. Part 3

   C. Part 4

   D. Part 7

Read the passage below, written in the style of a college anthropology textbook. Then answer the questions that follow.

[1]In addition to being one of the world's most vital food crops; rice is used to meet a broad range of needs. [2]The Japanese make an alcoholic beverage called *sake* from it, and brewers sometimes use it to make beer. [3]Equally important are the plant's by-products. [4]In some regions, farmers use rice bran, the brown skin surrounding a kernel, as a livestock feed. [5]Other people extract oil from the bran to make soap and margarine. [6]Rice grains also have rough outer shells, its hulls, that serve as an inexpensive fuel in many places. [7]Even dried rice stalks have their uses. [8]Many Asians use them to make hats and sandals, and to thatch the roofs of their homes.

3. Which one, if any, of the following changes is needed in the above passage?

    A. Part 1: Change the semicolon after "crops" to a comma.

    B. Part 4: Delete the comma after "bran."

    C. Part 8: Change the comma after "sandals" to a colon.

    D. None of these changes is needed.

4. Which of the following parts of the passage displays nonstandard usage?

    A. Part 2

    B. Part 3

    C. Part 6

    D. Part 7

Read the passage below, written in the style of a student essay. Then answer the questions that follow.

[1]San Antonio is one of the oldest cities in the United States. [2]At one time or another during its long history, it has been under the rule of Spain, Mexico, and the independent Republic of Texas. [3]Present-day San Antonio covers about 263 square miles and is the tenth most large city in the nation. [4]It is also an important cultural center. [5]Its theaters, museums, and symphony drawed visitors from all parts of the country last year. [6]Perhaps the city's greatest attraction is the Alamo, which was the site of a famous battle in the movement for Texas independence. [7]Although all the Alamo's defenders were killed, their heroism inspired others to continue the struggle to its successful conclusion. [8]Their sacrifice is remembered every April, when Fiesta San Antonio celebrates the formation of the Texas Republic.

5. Which one, if any, of the following changes is needed in the above passage?

    A. Part 5: Change "drawed" to "drew."

    B. Part 7: Change "were killed" to "was killed."

    C. Part 8: Change "celebrates" to "is celebrating."

    D. None of these changes is needed.

6. Which of the following parts of the passage displays nonstandard usage?

    A. Part 1

    B. Part 2

    C. Part 3

    D. Part 4

Read the passage below, written in the style of a biography. Then answer the questions that follow.

¹On March 4, 1933, Franklin D. Roosevelt took the oath as president of the United States. ²Although few realized it at the time, the country would never be the same again. ³Assuming office during the worst of the Great Depression, Roosevelt was soon forced to take actions that he hisself would have considered extreme only a few years earlier. ⁴There were programs to supply relief funds to local communities, to regulate industrial and agricultural production to provide old-age assistance to retired persons, and to protect labor's right to organize. ⁵In the process of enacting these measures, the new president made many enemies. ⁶Some thought that his policies endangered the free-enterprise system. ⁷Yet Roosevelt was also deeply loved by millions of Americans. ⁸"He was a beautiful man," one woman later recalled. ⁹"He was good to the poor and good to working people."

7. Which of the following parts of the passage displays nonstandard usage?

   A. Part 2

   B. Part 3

   C. Part 5

   D. Part 6

8. Which one, if any, of the following changes is needed in the above passage?

   A. Part 1: Delete the comma after "1933."

   B. Part 4: Insert a comma after "agricultural production."

   C. Part 8: Delete the comma after "man."

   D. None of these changes is needed.

Practice Exercise Explanations

1. **Correct Response: A.** This question requires an understanding of the correct usage of verb forms. Choice A is the best response because the standard form of the present perfect tense of *shape* is *has shaped,* not *has shape.* Of the other responses provided, the changes suggested in choices B and C would introduce nonstandard usage into Parts 5 and 6.

2. **Correct Response: D.** This question requires an understanding of the standard way to form and use adjectives. Choice D is the best response because *them* is a pronoun, a word that replaces rather than modifies a noun. Therefore, the pronoun *them* should be replaced with the demonstrative adjective *these.* Of the other responses provided, none of the sentences represented by choices A, B, and C contains examples of nonstandard English usage.

3. **Correct Response: A.** This question assesses the ability to recognize nonstandard punctuation. Choice A is the best response because a semicolon should not be used to connect a subordinate clause, which cannot stand alone as a sentence, to an independent clause. In Part 1, "In addition to being one of the world's most vital food crops" is a subordinate clause. Of the other choices provided, the comma after *bran* in Part 4 is used correctly together with the comma after *kernel* to set off an appositive phrase (choice B). In Part 8, the comma after *sandals* is used correctly to emphasize that the infinitive phrase "to make hats and sandals" is separate from the phrase that follows it.

4. **Correct Response: C.** This question assesses the ability to recognize nonstandard uses of pronouns. Choice C is the best response because the singular pronoun *its* does not agree with its noun antecedent *grains,* which is plural in number. *Its* should therefore be changed to *their.* Of the other responses provided, none of the sentences represented by choices A, B, and D contains examples of nonstandard English usage.

5. **Correct Response: A.** This question assesses the ability to recognize nonstandard verb formations. Choice A is the best response because only regular verbs form their past tense by adding *-ed* or *-d* to the infinitive form, and *draw* is an irregular verb. In Part 5, *drawed* should therefore be changed to *drew,* which is the standard way to form the past tense of *draw.* Of the other responses provided, the verbs listed in choices B and C are both correctly formed and in the appropriate tense.

6. **Correct Response: C.** This question requires an understanding of the standard way to form the superlative degree of comparison. Choice C is the best response because modifiers of one syllable, such as *large,* form their superlative degree by adding the suffix *-est.* In Part 3, *most large* should therefore be changed to *largest.* Of the other responses provided, none of the sentences represented by choices A, B, and D contains examples of nonstandard English usage.

7. **Correct Response: B.** This question assesses the ability to recognize nonstandard pronoun usage. Choice B is the best response because *hisself* is a nonstandard reflexive pronoun formation. To correct the error, *hisself* should be changed to *himself.* Of the other responses provided, none of the sentences represented by choices A, C, and D contains examples of nonstandard English usage.

8. **Correct Response: B.** This question assesses the ability to recognize nonstandard punctuation. Choice B is the best response because commas should be placed after each phrase (except the last) in a series. In Part 4, a comma should therefore be inserted after "agricultural production," the final words of the second phrase in a series of four phrases. As for the other choices provided, commas are placed after the year of a date when it is used with both the day and the month (choice A). Commas are also used to set off direct quotations (choice C).

Study Ideas

A careful study of the above exercises and the explanations of the answers will help you review important skills relating to the conventions of edited American English. In these exercises, you were asked to identify standard forms of different parts of speech, including nouns, verbs, and pronouns; standard forms of modifiers, including comparative and superlative adverbs and adjectives; and standard punctuation. You may wish to reread parts of the chapter that discuss particular points of usage; you may also wish to consult books on grammar and composition for additional information in general or for answers to specific questions.

In your personal reading as well as your course reading, take time to notice how standard (or nonstandard) English usage affects your understanding of a written passage.

When writing in college, be aware that most of your readers will expect you to use standard English. Readers generally find nonstandard usage confusing or distracting, or both. Always review your writing carefully to verify that your use of verb forms, pronouns, modifiers, plural and possessive nouns, and punctuation conforms to the conventions of edited American English.

Chapter 27

THE WRITING SAMPLE

Introduction

The ability to write well is one of the most useful skills a person can acquire. Writing is a powerful means of communicating; it enables one to inform, influence, and affect both individuals and organizations. It also has significant value as a tool for learning. Writing about something can be a way of clarifying meaning and making full sense of a topic. Finally, the ability to write well is important because good writing can bolster the credibility and persuasiveness of the writer.

The process of writing is a complex activity that involves generating ideas, organizing them, determining the best way to express them, and producing a final product that follows the principles of proper expression for a particular audience. Learning to write well requires a commitment of energy on your part as well as a familiarity with the basics of effective communication. But most of all, writing demands practice. The more often you write, the more situations for which you write, and the more topics about which you write, the more comfortable the act of writing will become for you.

Much of the writing you do in school, at work, and in your personal life is done under circumstances that permit time for careful planning, writing, and rewriting. There is time for research and experimenting and time to make choices about what to say and how to say it. A term paper for a college course or a letter you write to a manufacturer about a product are examples of this sort of writing. In both cases, you will usually have time to decide how to proceed, do some research, try out a few possible approaches, and have someone else read what you have written before you consider it finished.

Other times, however, you must write with little advance preparation and with predetermined limits on how much time you can spend getting it just right. Examples of this kind of work are your responses to essay questions on exams, certain on-the-job writing tasks, and the writing samples that are part of the TASP Test and many standardized tests. *Impromptu* writing, as this is often called, does not allow the kind of deliberation that goes on in other writing you do. Therefore, you need a practical strategy to make your impromptu writing as good as it can possibly be. This chapter will describe strategies that may be applied to all writing but are especially useful when you must write in situations such as the TASP Test or an exam for a college course.

The TASP Test Writing Sample

For the TASP Test writing sample, you will be given a writing assignment, or prompt. Your task is to write an essay that responds effectively to the prompt. Each prompt will describe an assignment, an audience, and a purpose for the writing. Your essay, or writing sample, will be scored on the basis of how well you respond to each of these dimensions. Chapter 28 provides a more in-depth discussion of the writing prompts and the scoring methodology.

Strategies for Impromptu Writing

Composing an essay or a writing sample for a test may concern some test-takers. Some people respond by grabbing a pen and scribbling furiously to make every second count. Others leave themselves two minutes at the end for reading what they have written, only to discover that there is no time left to make needed changes. Some test-takers receive the writing assignment, sit waiting for inspiration, and finally, when there is too little time left to complete the task, begin to write. None of these approaches will lead to success because the writers have failed to take control of the task.

The alternative to being frustrated by an impromptu writing assignment, whether the writing sample on the TASP Test, a surprise classroom exercise, or an unanticipated letter that must be in the mail by 2:00, is to develop a strategy for meeting the assignment. Having a strategy will help you approach the task with confidence. It will help you organize your thoughts as well as your time, and it will help you decide how to begin. It will also help you remember the main points you wish to make as well as decide what points to omit. The following pages present and explain one effective strategy by tracing the development of an impromptu essay in response to a sample prompt similar to those that appear on the TASP Test **(please note: Additional sample prompts appear at the end of Chapter 28 and within the Practice Test in Section V)**. This strategy is divided into four steps: evaluating the assignment, planning a response, writing a draft, and revising and editing. Learning to use these steps will help prepare you to do a good job when you write, whatever the writing assignment.

The writing assignments for the TASP Test may be provided in one of several formats. The formats do not have a substantial effect on the nature of the writing assignment itself. Rather, as you will see here, the difference is in the amount and manner in which information about the prompt is presented to you.

For the sample prompt we will work with in this chapter (dealing with taxes versus user fees as a way of paying for certain public services), we will present the prompt in a number of different formats.

The first format begins with a short introductory statement and the writing assignment.

> Are user fees or increased taxes the more appropriate way to pay for community recreational services? Proponents of user fees argue that such fees place the costs where they should be, on those individuals who are actually using the services. Proponents of taxes point out that all residents benefit from enhanced public services.
>
> Your purpose is to write an essay, to be read by a classroom instructor, in which you take a position on whether increased taxes or user fees are the best way to pay for community recreational services in a town. Be sure to defend your position with logical arguments and appropriate examples.

The second format provides arguments on both sides of an issue.

User Fees: Let Those Who Use Services Pay for Them

Paying the cost of recreational services provided by a town should fall on the shoulders of those who use those services, not on the shoulders of the residents as a whole. Unlike police and fire services, from which everyone benefits, recreational services, such as town swimming pools, are used by only some people and are discretionary rather than necessary. It is fair, therefore, that only the people who choose to use these services pay for them from fees collected for that purpose.

Taxes: Equity and Access to Facilities are the Issues

The cost of town services should be borne by all residents since everyone benefits from an enhanced quality of life. The argument that not all residents use a town's recreational services could be applied to other services as well. People without cars nonetheless pay taxes to repave streets; everyone contributes to the public schools whether they have children enrolled or not. Yet we do not think of charging user fees in these cases. Moreover, user fees concentrates the entire cost of the service on only some citizens, often too great a burden on low income residents. Is it fair that some children not be able to use a town swimming pool because their parents cannot afford inflated user fees?

> Your purpose is to write an essay, to be read by a classroom instructor, in which you take a position on whether increased taxes or user fees are the best way to pay for community recreational services in a town. Be sure to defend your position with logical arguments and appropriate examples.

The third format provides a somewhat longer introductory statement about the topic and concludes with the actual assignment.

> Paying for town services during tight budget times raises questions about who should pay for certain services. Recreational services are frequently discussed in this way. Many people argue that recreational services are optional discretionary services for a town. Not all residents use them. In fact, it is often easy to determine who does use such services. Rather than burden all tax payers with the cost of recreational services, some argue that user fees should be collected to cover these services from the people who are actually using them (e.g., admission fee for swimming pools, fees for recreational leagues). The more one uses the facilities, the more one would pay. This perspective is contested by those who argue on several grounds. First, almost all town services are used unequally by residents. Not everyone owns a car, and yet everyone pays for road repairs. Everyone pays taxes to support the public schools even through not everyone has children enrolled. We would never think of operating these services on the basis of user fees. Second, charging user fees may make some services prohibitively expensive for some citizens. We all benefit from an enhanced quality of life. Is it fair that children be denied the use of a swimming pool because their parents cannot afford the fees? Charging fees will make some services the exclusive domain of the well-to-do and deny access to the people who need them the most.

> Your purpose is to write an essay, to be read by a classroom instructor, in which you take a position on whether increased taxes or user fees are the best way to pay for community recreational services in a town. Be sure to defend your position with logical arguments and appropriate examples.

STEP ONE: Evaluating the Assignment

Let us imagine that you received the writing prompt or assignment above. How should you begin? The first thing is to figure out exactly what the assignment is asking of you. To do that, you will need to ask three questions.

1. What is my *purpose* for writing?_____

   _____

2. Who is my *audience?* _____

   _____

3. What is the *occasion* for writing or the situation in which my writing will

   be read? _____

   _____

Jot down your answers to these questions before reading further.

Your answer to the first question should resemble the following: "My purpose for writing is to take and defend a position on the user fee issue." The phrase *take and defend a position* is important because it suggests what you do and do not have to include in your writing. The tax question may have an interesting history, for example, but it is not your job to educate people about its history. Educating, or informing, is a different purpose for writing; your job is to *persuade*, or *convince*, your reader. A TASP Test writing prompt will always state your purpose for writing. As you plan and write your essay, always keep in mind your purpose for writing.

The answer to the second question might read, "The audience I am writing for is a classroom instructor." Identifying your reader or readers will help you determine the best way to reach them. It will help you decide which arguments will be most successful in persuading them to adopt your position. For example, it would not be a smart idea to tell your audience that raising taxes will not matter; your instructor is not likely to accept an illogical argument of this sort. Your audience will always be identified in the TASP Test writing prompt.

Your answer to the third question should resemble the following: "This will be an essay written for class." The answer to this question tells you something about how you should express yourself and the type of language you should use. You would not want to write, "Everybody should vote for a tax increase because kids don't want to pay for a place to shoot hoop and take a dip." This example uses too much slang and is too casual for the occasion. You will want to find a more formal tone that sounds mature and intelligent without being stuffy.

Successful writing begins with a clear understanding of what the assignment requires. Purpose? Audience? Occasion? Ask and answer those questions to evaluate any writing assignment you receive.

STEP TWO: Planning Your Response

The next step is to plan what you will write for the assignment. In the case of the sample question presented here, the first job will be to decide which side you will take on the tax increase versus user fees issue. In a hypothetical, or imagined, assignment such as this one, there are two ways you may proceed. One way is *personal preference*. If, in real life, you yourself frequently use free public recreation facilities, you may be opposed to the idea of paying for them. On the other hand, you may believe that people are generally taxed too much and should not be expected to pay more to support recreation. It is likely that your own sympathies will give you things to say. The other approach is *strength of ideas*. Even if you have no strong allegiance to either side of the issue, you may quickly think of some good arguments for one position. It may be wise for you to choose that side. The side you choose will not affect your score on the TASP Test. There is no right or wrong answer. Your writing sample will be scored based on the quality of your writing.

Once you have selected the position you wish to support, you will have the main idea for your writing. Then you will have to decide *how* to support it. You will now have to do some *inventing* (or *brainstorming*) and *evaluating*.

Invention means thinking of a set of ideas you *might* use in your writing. The goal here is not necessarily to develop a perfect set of arguments. The goal is to think of as many ideas as you can and to set them down quickly on scratch paper. There are a few techniques that you may find useful. One is to start writing as freely as you can about the topic. Begin with a sentence that reads, "What I want to say about this topic is . . ." and keep going for five minutes, writing as much as you can without stopping. Remember that this is *not* the final essay. Do *not* worry about grammar or spelling or whether your sentences are complete; just write. You may be surprised at how many ideas you can generate. A related technique is *listing*—jotting down words and phrases rather than sentences. At this stage, you should not judge the value of each entry on your list: simply get it down! An example of an invention list is presented below in the left column. The right column provides a place for you to make your own list, taking the opposite side in the essay.

Position: User fees should pay
for recreation improvements.

Position: Taxes should be raised
to pay for recreation improvements.

1. Not everyone uses park facilities   _____

2. Taxes should pay only for
    essentials   _____

3. Other things are more important   _____

4. If you want to swim or engage in
    other sports, pay for them   _____

5. Taxes are high enough already   _____

6. The recreation facilities are okay
    as they are   _____

7. Only a few people would benefit   _____

8. Don't raise taxes to pay for
    luxuries   _____

9. Pay for what you use!   _____

10. Improvements aren't worth
    the money   _____

11. Taxes for schools and police, etc.   _____

12. People would want to raise taxes
    for everything they value   _____

13. A choice of paying, with fees   _____

Evaluation, the next step, involves examining your list to see what is there, which entries you can use, and how you can use them. If you keep in mind the point you want to make in writing, it should be fairly easy to tell what is useful and what is not. For example, the list supplied here is a good one, but two items, Number 6 and Number 10, probably do not belong. Number 6 states that the facilities are "okay as they are" and Number 10 says "the improvements aren't worth the money." Both statements may be true, but they should be discarded because they are not directly related to the question. The question is whether taxes or user fees should pay for improvements to the facilities. Be sure your essay responds directly to the prompt.

Evaluate your own list and eliminate any ideas you would not use.

Once you have eliminated what you cannot use, you will want to decide how to use what is left. The best way to do that is to group items that seem to fit together. Some people find it helpful to draw lines to connect the items on the list; others like to group the numbers of the items together, as shown below.

Group A

2. Taxes should pay only for essentials.
3. Other things are more important.
5. Taxes are high enough already.
11. Taxes are for good schools and police protection.

Group B

4. If people want to swim or engage in other sports, they should be the ones to pay.
9. It's better to pay for what you use.
13. With user fees there is a choice of paying.

Group C

8. Taxes should not finance luxuries.
12. People would want to raise taxes to pay for everything they value personally.

Try connecting or grouping the ideas on your own list. The number of groups may vary. If your ideas seem to fit into two or three main groups, make what seems to you to be the best choice for placement of each item. Once you have the ideas grouped, it is useful to identify the main idea of each group to see what major point each group is making. Sometimes one item on the list will serve as the main point; other times you will need to generalize a main point. Look at the main points drawn from the three groups in the example.

A. Taxes should pay only for essential things.

B. User fees are fairer to everyone.

C. Taxes should not finance luxuries.

Try identifying or generalizing a main point for each of *your* groups.

Now you have a purpose for writing, some main points to make, some ideas to use, and a sense of how those ideas fit together. You can move on to the third step, writing the first version.

STEP THREE: Writing Your Draft

At this point, it is appropriate to discuss what your writing sample will look like. This assignment asks for a persuasive *essay*. An essay may be defined as "a group of connected paragraphs intended to prove or illuminate a central idea. . . ." The length of your essay will be controlled by the scope of the central idea and the amount of detail you will need to cover it (although the TASP Test asks you to write an essay of about 300 to 600 words). The number of paragraphs you use will be affected by both the depth in which you treat your idea and the manner in which you develop your idea. To phrase that in another way, if you have a narrow central idea and few parts to your explanation of it, then your essay will require fewer paragraphs than if your essay has a broad focus and many categories of explanatory material.

Most good essays, however, share the following three characteristics.

1. They have a beginning paragraph in which the writer introduces the subject and presents the central idea.

2. They have an unspecified number of middle paragraphs in which the support for the central idea is developed.

3. They have a final or concluding paragraph in which the writer summarizes the thoughts that have been expressed.

Essays may be as short as three paragraphs, but they are usually longer than that. They frequently contain a series of middle paragraphs, each presenting a different kind of support for or elaboration of the central idea. **Although the model that follows here uses a five-paragraph structure, it is by no means the only possible model. A four- or six-paragraph structure, for example, is equally valid.** Your most important consideration should be whether or not you have developed your ideas in a logical, thorough, and efficient manner rather than how many paragraphs you have used.

As you write, use the ideas you generated while you were planning your essay. Be sure that each paragraph has a strong topic sentence that states the main idea. Then write sentences that support this main idea as clearly as possible and with as much specific detail as you can. Be aware of the rules of sentence structure, grammar, and spelling, but do not at this stage try to make every line perfect. You can make final improvements when you reread and edit your essay.

Now try drafting your essay about the use of tax money to support and improve recreational facilities, using the ideas on your list.

Here is a sample draft essay on the subject, written for the purpose of persuading the reader that recreational facilities should be supported by user fees rather than by increased taxes. You may notice some problems that this essay has in terms of organization, nonstandard usage, etc. Step 4 of this chapter will discuss these issues, and Step 5 will present the essay in its final form. (Numbers have been added so that we may refer to each sentence.)

Introductory Paragraph	[1]Everyone should oppose proposed tax increases for improvements in recreation. [2]The people who use the facilities should pay user fees to finance those improvements.
First Support Paragraph	[3]The major reason for opposing this increase is that taxes are intended to pay for necessary things. [4]Such things as schools that are good and adequate police protection are funded through our taxes. [5]The money that we spend on taxes educates all our children and keeps our neighborhoods safe. [6]Many of us resent the high cost of taxes already. [7]Although we pay them. [8]However, we know that most tax money goes for basic services so we pay our bills. [9]But when tax bills go up to finance nonessential expenses such as tennis courts their is something wrong. [10]Tax dollars was never intended for luxuries.

Second Support Paragraph	[11]User fees are a wise alternitive to a tax increase. [12]Even if some basketball and tennis players will complain. [13]User fees guarantee that the cost of improvements in recreation will be carried by those who most enjoy the improvements. [14]Those citizens who never entered the parks and playgrounds will pay nothing. [15]Those of us who visit the courts and pool occasionally will pay a small fee. [16]Frequent users will assume the largest share; we should start doing that at the town dump, also. [17]Financing through user fees is the most fairest plan for everyone.
Third Support Paragraph	[18]Everyone will not want to use a fancy new swimming pool or choose to enjoy the results of a newly landscaped park. [19]Another reason we oppose the tax increase is only that a small percentage of the population will benefit from it. [20]Yet, funding improvements with taxes will mean that everyone will bare the cost. [21]As a result of this, the citizens of the town will be subsidizing the amusement and recreation of a few. [22]That is as unfair as it would be for the town to raise taxes to provide free chimney cleaning for peoples homes. [23]Those people whose homes do not have chimneys would be paying for those who do, town money should be spent for things that serve the majority.
Conclusion	[24]When you think about this topic, you should be against the recreation tax increase.

This draft is not the finished essay, but it is a good beginning. It supplies a clear picture of how the final essay will work, and the writer's arguments are clearly explained and supported. Also, although there are some errors, the writer has been fairly attentive to the rules of standard written English.

Once you have your own draft on paper, you will be able to begin making the changes that create polished writing. With your draft in hand, you may begin the fourth step: revision.

STEP FOUR: Revising and Editing

No matter how good a first draft may seem, it will always benefit from some refinement. Revising and editing are methods of changing a piece of writing in order to improve it. They require you to look at your work as objectively as possible and to evaluate it according to the following principles of good writing: appropriateness, unity and focus, development, organization, sentence structure, usage, and mechanical conventions. These principles are described below, with examples of some revisions that ought to be made to our sample essay. (The sentence numbers refer to the sample essay.) Pay careful attention to each of these principles. They are the characteristics upon which your TASP Test writing sample will be scored and are typical of scoring criteria for many other writing tests.

Appropriateness. For a writing sample to be appropriate, it must attend to the specific requirements of the assignment and to the general requirements of the essay format. Evaluating for appropriateness means asking whether the language and writing style reflect an awareness of purpose, audience, and occasion. This essay satisfies those concerns because it develops a group of arguments to persuade an audience and because its language and form are suitable for an essay for an instructor.

Tests for Appropriateness

Is the response in the form of an essay (not a poem, short story, outline, etc.)?

Does the essay consist of multiple paragraphs?

Does the entire essay address the topic or subject presented in the prompt?

Was the essay written with a specific audience and occasion in mind?

Is the language consistent with the essay's purpose, audience, and occasion?

See Chapter 22 for more information on making your writing appropriate for its purpose, audience, and occasion.

Unity and focus. Concern for unity and focus means looking at your draft in terms of how well it presents one central idea and how well it avoids wandering into issues that are not really part of that idea. The draft of the sample essay is generally successful in that respect. The introductory paragraph (Sentences 1 and 2) does an acceptable job of stating the central idea, but it would be improved by a more arresting and general statement of the subject before beginning the argument. In Sentence 16 of the second support paragraph, however, the writer introduces the idea of instituting dump fees. This has little to do with the rest of the essay and should be dropped to maintain focus.

As you edit and revise, remember that your entire essay must be unified and that the individual paragraphs must maintain focus. Avoid the temptation to expand your essay by bringing in topics that are not relevant.

Tests for Unity and Focus

Does the essay have one central idea?

Is the central idea clearly stated?

Is focus on the central idea maintained throughout the essay?

Is the writer's position about the main idea consistent throughout the essay?

Does each paragraph present a subtopic that is related to the essay's main idea?

Is each paragraph's subtopic stated clearly in a topic sentence?

Have digressions been avoided?

See Chapter 23 for more information about maintaining unity and focus in writing.

Development. A good essay offers relevant and convincing support for its central idea. It provides sufficient detail in the form of examples, reasons, and explanations, and it avoids the mistake of circling back on itself by simply repeating the same ideas in different words. The editing test for adequate development is this: have I given my audience enough information to understand fully what I mean? In the sample essay, the development of ideas is quite good because the writer has offered a series of supporting points and explained them clearly.

Tests for Development

Is the central idea supported in every paragraph?

Does support go beyond mere assertion to provide specific examples, explanations, and reasons?

Is the supporting detail relevant?

See Chapter 23 for more information about development in writing.

Organization. Deciding what is the best and most effective order for presenting ideas can be one of the most difficult decisions a writer has to make. Having the ideas on the page is not enough; they must be presented in an order that makes good sense. Concern for organization extends to the **logical sequence** of the sentences within your paragraphs and to the logical sequence of the paragraphs in your essay.

Organization also refers to the **clarity** of your writing. Ideas that are not sequenced logically can cause confusion. In addition, lack of control in one or more of the other six performance characteristics, such as an inappropriate text structure (see Appropriateness), the lack of a clearly stated main idea (see Unity and Focus), irrelevant support (see Development), poorly constructed sentences (see Sentence Structure), inappropriately chosen words (see Usage), and lack of control of spelling, punctuation, and/or capitalization (see Mechanical Conventions) can also contribute to lack of clarity and poor communication of meaning to the intended audience.

In the sample essay, there is a problem with paragraph order. The writer discusses fair and reasonable taxes in the first support paragraph, suggests an alternative source of funding in the second support paragraph, and then returns to a discussion of fair taxes in the third support paragraph. Better logic would be achieved by reversing the order of the second and third support paragraphs. Then the argument would move from the idea of fair taxes for essential services, to unfair taxes for luxuries, and finally, to an alternative to taxes.

Another organization problem in the essay appears within the third support paragraph. Sentence 18 presents an example that serves to support the idea expressed in Sentence 19. The paragraph would thus be better organized if the order of these sentences were reversed. The order of presentation would then be from *general* to *specific.* Writers frequently follow this order to organize paragraphs: putting the sentence that best expresses the message of the paragraph at the beginning and using the sentences that follow to support it. Also, the concluding paragraph (Sentence 24) ends the essay too abruptly and without summarizing the ideas presented in the preceding paragraphs. A better conclusion would attempt to tie everything together.

In other situations, the order of events in *time* (chronology) will control organization. (Example: First she opened the door, then she turned on the light, and then she took off her shoes.) Or, order may be ruled by *cause.* (Example: Because the bag was wet, the bottom ripped, and the groceries fell to the floor.) Another common organizational pattern is *emphasis.* (Example: I don't mind history, and I do pretty well in English, but chemistry is my favorite course.) When you are checking for effective organization, look for a clear order in which all the parts fit together to make your point.

Tests for Organization

Are the ideas arranged in an effective and logical sequence?

Do the ideas fit together within paragraphs?

Are there logical connections between and among paragraphs?

Do transitional words and phrases help reinforce the order of ideas?

Does your message come through (i.e., is the writing clear)?

See Chapter 24 for further discussion of organization in writing.

Sentence structure. As you edit your first draft, you should look very carefully for nonstandard sentence structure. It is especially important that you find and revise sentence fragments (constructions that are missing either a subject or a verb) and run-on sentences (constructions of two or more sentences with no punctuation between them). Fragments need to be expanded into complete sentences or joined with other sentences. Run-ons must be divided or restructured. In the sample essay, there are two sentence fragments (Sentences 7 and 12) and one run-on sentence (Sentence 23). These three sentences should be revised.

It is equally important to notice any other structural problems with your sentences. These include nonstandard subject-verb agreement (*dollars was* instead of *dollars were* in Sentence 10 of the sample); nonstandard placement of modifiers (*only that* in Sentence 19 should be changed to *that only* to make it clear that *only* modifies the phrase *a small percentage*); the use of nonparallel structure (*schools that are good and adequate police protection* in Sentence 4 should be revised to read *good schools and adequate police protection*); and faulty pronoun reference (the pronoun *it* in Sentence 22 does not refer to anything concrete).

Tests for Sentence Structure

Are there any sentence fragments or run-on sentences?

Is the sentence structure parallel?

Do subjects and verbs agree in the sentences?

Are modifiers and pronouns used correctly?

See Chapter 25 for a more detailed discussion of effective sentence construction.

Usage. Editing for usage means checking that the words you write are precise and correct and that the language you use conforms to the rules of standard English (officially known as "edited American English"). Be sure that your essay uses the standard forms of verbs, nouns, pronouns, adverbs, adjectives, and other words. (For example, in Sentence 17 of the sample essay, the double-superlative adjective *most fairest* is nonstandard and should be changed to *fairest*.) In addition, you should be sure that you have used words correctly. (In the sample essay, the word *their* in Sentence 9 should be changed to *there;* the word *bare* in Sentence 20 should be changed to *bear*.) Also, be certain that words are used precisely. (The vague word *things* in Sentence 4 should be replaced with a more precise word.)

Another usage issue is the improper choice of verb tense. Shifting *without reason* from a past tense verb to a present tense verb in the same sentence is an example of nonstandard usage. In Sentence 14 of the sample, the past tense *entered* should be replaced with the present tense *enter*.

The nonstandard use of negatives is another usage issue (*Everyone will not want* in Sentence 18 should be changed to *Not everyone will want*).

Ineffective repetition of words, phrases, or ideas is a usage problem, as is the inconsistent use of number, person, or point of view. Finally, the omission of words is considered an error in usage.

Tests for Usage

Are all verbs, nouns, pronouns, adjectives, and adverbs in standard form and/or tense?

Have the correct and most appropriate words been used?

Are there any inappropriate shifts in verb tense?

Are negatives used correctly?

Is needless repetition avoided?

Have any words been left out?

Are number, person, and point of view consistent?

See Chapter 26 for more about proper usage in writing.

Mechanical conventions. *Mechanical conventions* in writing include capitalization, punctuation, and spelling of common words. As you revise, be sure to use appropriate end punctuation (i.e., punctuation that ends sentences: periods, question marks, and exclamation points) and interior punctuation (e.g., commas, quotation marks, apostrophes, semicolons). In our sample, the word *peoples* in Sentence 22 is possessive and thus requires an apostrophe: *people's*. Edit carefully for misspellings. (For example, *alternitive* in Sentence 11 of the sample should be spelled *alternative*.) You may not be able to spell perfectly without a dictionary, but you should avoid as many errors as you can. Also, be certain that words are capitalized appropriately (proper nouns, the first word of any sentence) and consistently. If you write in block letters, be certain that a reader can distinguish between capitalized and uncapitalized words. By taking time to reread and edit your writing response, you will be able to find and correct mistakes.

Tests for Mechanics

Are there any errors in spelling or capitalization?

Are all words and sentences punctuated according to standard usage?

See Chapter 26 for more about the mechanics of writing.

A final note about the editing step: Do not be intimidated by all the guidelines you need to remember as you edit. Most likely, you are already familiar with the rules for standard usage. A careful rereading of your essay will help you find any places where you have departed from these rules. When rereading, try to read slowly, phrase by phrase; you might wish to point with your pencil to each word as you look for errors.

Now edit and revise the draft of your own practice essay.

STEP FIVE: Final Version

Below is the final version of our sample essay, edited and revised to conform to the guidelines we have discussed.

> Residents of many communities face the task of deciding how to pay for improvements in or maintenance of the town's recreational facilities. Some people advocate raising taxes to pay for these services. I oppose that plan, and I urge my fellow citizens to join me in voting for user fees to finance those improvements.
>
> The proper role of taxes is to pay for necessary services. Such essential services as good schools and adequate police protection are properly funded through taxes. The money spent on these services educates all of our children and keeps our neighborhoods safe. Although many citizens may feel some pain at the high cost of taxes, we pay them because we get our money back in basic, essential services. But when tax bills are increased to finance nonessentials such as tennis courts, there is something terribly wrong. Tax dollars were never intended to supply luxuries.
>
> Another reason for rejecting the tax increase is that only a small percentage of the population will benefit from it. Not everyone will want to use a fancy new swimming pool or a newly landscaped park. Yet funding such improvements with taxes will mean that everyone must bear the cost. In effect, all the citizens will be subsidizing the amusement and recreation of only a few. That is as unfair as it would be for the town to raise taxes to provide free chimney cleaning for people's homes. Those without chimneys would be paying to help out those who have them. Town tax money should be spent to serve the needs of everyone.
>
> Instead of raising taxes, communities should institute a system of user fees. User fees are a far wiser alternative than a tax increase because they guarantee that the cost of improved recreation will be carried by those who most enjoy the improvements. Those citizens who never enter the parks and playgrounds will pay nothing, while those who visit the courts and pool occasionally will pay a small fee. The frequent users will assume the largest share. Financing through user fees is the fairest option.
>
> I urge citizens to unite to defeat the recreation taxes. Taxes are for basic services, not luxuries, and those who want the benefits of better facilities should be the ones who pay for them.

Purpose, Audience, and Occasion

Purpose. Keep in mind that our sample assignment asked you to write a *persuasive* essay about the tax increase or user fee question. You adopted one side of the issue and made the best case you could to influence the voters' decisions. You attempted to make arguments that would convince readers of the logic or validity of a particular point of view. But what if the assignment had asked you to *inform* people of the positions held by both sides on the recreation tax question? That word *inform* would profoundly affect your responsibility as a writer. Instead of persuading the readers of your point of view, your job would be to present the issue and the beliefs of voters on both sides, without any attempt to sway opinions. Your purpose would be to add to people's understanding of the subject. You can see, then, that it is essential to identify your purpose for writing if you are to understand how you should proceed.

Audience. You will also need to make adjustments as you write for different audiences. If, for example, you were writing an explanation of the phases of the moon for your astronomy teacher, your explanation would be quite different from what you would write for a group of elementary school students. Good writers are aware of an audience's level of knowledge and sophistication, and they know how to match their writing to the audience's needs and expectations.

Occasion. Occasion refers to the particular circumstances and forms for writing. A letter to a friend is one kind of circumstance and a formal letter of application for employment is another. A short memorandum is not the same as a full-fledged technical report. Good writers are conscious of the different forms of written expression appropriate to various occasions.

Taking the Writing Sample Portion of the TASP Test

As mentioned earlier in this chapter, taking control of the situation will help you feel confident when faced with a timed writing sample. Both developing a strategy for writing your essay, as outlined in this chapter, and practicing your writing will help you perform well on this section of the test. Another useful approach is to work out a schedule for allocating your time during the writing period. The following is a suggested schedule for time management of a one-hour writing sample, together with some final reminders of points you will need to remember. The suggested time for generating your TASP Test writing sample is one hour.

Step One: Evaluating the Assignment   (5 minutes)

Remember that good writing begins with a clear sense of what the writing task demands. Define for yourself your *purpose* (what and why you are writing), your *audience* (those for whom you are writing), and the *occasion* (the situation in which your writing will be read).

Step Two: Planning Your Response   (5 minutes)

Invention and *evaluation* are the two stages to go through when planning your response. First create a set of ideas you might use in writing, and then evaluate them, discarding those that do not seem to belong and organizing those that do.

Step Three: Writing Your Draft   (30 minutes)

Write a response based on the ideas you developed in Step Two. Be sure the central idea of your essay is stated in an introductory paragraph. Be sure that each of your supporting paragraphs actually supports the central idea; be sure also that each paragraph has its own main idea and that that idea is clearly stated. Be careful to use specific details to support and explain your main idea. Write as well as you can, but do not at this point worry about making every sentence perfect. Do not surrender in the middle by telling yourself that you need to start over. Get through the draft!

Step Four: Revising and Editing   (20 minutes)

Reread what you have written. Make sure that your response to the assignment is clear, logical, and well organized. Make any necessary changes by adding, deleting, and replacing. Watch for ineffective sentences and sentences that are fragments or run-ons. Be sure you have observed subject-verb agreement in all sentences. Use words that are as clear and precise as possible. Be careful about grammar, punctuation, and spelling.

If you have more time to work on the writing sample, you may adjust the schedule, but it is a good idea to maintain approximately the same proportion of time spent on each of the strategies.

Chapter 28

ABOUT THE TASP TEST WRITING SAMPLE

The TASP Writing Prompt

The writing assignment, or prompt, that you will be given for the TASP Test is designed to elicit a response that will provide a direct measure of your ability to communicate effectively in writing. The prompt will require you to produce an original writing sample on a specific topic. The topic will be one that allows you to draw upon personal experience or general knowledge, regardless of your educational or cultural background. You will not be expected to demonstrate any significant familiarity with any subject area, such as history, art, or science.

As noted in the previous chapter, the prompt will require you to analyze an issue or topic and take and defend a position on that topic. The prompt will also present some ways of thinking about the topic and a certain amount of background information relevant to it. If you wish, you may make use of this information in formulating your essay; however, you certainly should utilize other relevant ideas, arguments, and information that may occur to you.

Each prompt is designed to elicit a response of approximately 300 to 600 words. The audience for which the sample will be written will typically be one that requires formal, rather than informal, writing, such as a classroom instructor.

At the end of this chapter are some samples of TASP Test writing topics. An additional TASP prompt, with four sample responses, is also included at the end of the Practice Test in Section V.

How the Writing Sample Is Scored

Writing samples prepared by examinees for the writing section of the TASP Test are scored through a process called *focused holistic scoring*. In this process, all papers are scored according to standardized procedures. Scoring sessions are held soon after each test administration.

The principle underlying the holistic scoring process is that a writing sample should be evaluated on the basis of how effectively it communicates a whole message to a specified audience for a given purpose. That is, scorers judge the overall effectiveness of the writing sample rather than score individual aspects of writing considered in isolation. Scorer judgments are based on the *quality* of the writing, not on length or neatness. Of course, essays must be long enough to cover the topic adequately; for the TASP Test, the suggested length for the writing sample is 300 to 600 words. (One page of average-sized handwriting consists of about 225 words.)

In general, a satisfactory essay is one that possesses the qualities described in the writing section of the TASP Test Skills List and covered in the writing section of this study guide. Scorers will score your essay based upon how well it adheres to the principles of appropriateness to the given audience, purpose, and occasion; focus and unity; development; organization; sentence structure; usage; and mechanical conventions. These skills are covered in detail in Chapters 22 through 27 of this guide. Your response should demonstrate adequacy across all seven TASP writing skills. A high level of performance in only one or two areas (e.g., usage and mechanical conventions) will not likely result in an adequate essay or a high score. Your essay will be scored based on how well it demonstrates mastery of the seven TASP writing skills working together to communicate a whole message effectively.

Each writing sample is scored independently by two readers. The scorers assign a rating of 1, 2, 3, or 4 to the essay. The following page contains a description of each of the four score points used in scoring the TASP Test writing sample. (Essays that are completely off topic, illegible, written in a language other than English, or otherwise unscorable receive a score of U.) The two ratings are added together for a writing sample score from 2 to 8. If the ratings from the two scores differ by more than one point, the essay undergoes additional scoring to resolve the discrepancy.

The passing standards for each section of the TASP Test are set by the Texas Higher Education Coordinating Board and the State Board of Education. The two boards, as well as committees of experts from Texas colleges and universities who advised the boards during the development of the test, felt strongly that the writing sample portion of the test should carry more weight than the multiple-choice portion. Consequently, an examinee's performance on the writing multiple-choice items affects the pass/fail status on the writing section *only* if the score on the writing sample is a 5; that is, if one scorer rates the essay a 3 (passing) and the other scorer rates the essay a 2 (failing), performance on the multiple-choice items provides additional information by which the pass/fail status is determined.

The passing standard currently adopted for the writing section is as follows.

- A writing sample score of *6 or above* is passing, regardless of performance on the multiple-choice items.

- A writing sample score of *4 or below* is failing, regardless of performance on the multiple-choice items.

- If the writing sample score is *5,* then approximately 70 percent of the writing multiple-choice items must be answered correctly for an examinee to pass the writing section.

Please be aware that passing standards are reviewed frequently and are subject to change.

Description of Score Points Used in Evaluating the TASP Test Writing Sample

Score Point	Description of Writing Sample
4 —	**a well-formed writing sample that effectively communicates a whole message to a specified audience** The writer maintains unity of a developed topic throughout the writing sample and establishes a focus by clearly stating a purpose. The writer exhibits control in the development of ideas and clearly specifies supporting detail. Sentence structure is effective and free of errors. Choice of words is precise, and usage is careful. The writer shows mastery of mechanical conventions, such as spelling and punctuation.
3 —	**an adequately formed writing sample that attempts to communicate a message to a specified audience** The focus and the purpose of the writing sample may be clear; however, the writer's attempts to develop supporting details may not be fully realized. The writer's organization of ideas may be ambiguous, incomplete, or partially ineffective. Sentence structure within paragraphs is adequate, but minor errors in sentence structure, usage, and word choice are evident. There may also be errors in the use of mechanical conventions, such as spelling and punctuation.
2 —	**a partially developed writing sample in which the characteristics of effective written communication are only partially formed** The statement of purpose is not clear, and, although a main idea or topic may be announced, focus on the main idea is not sustained. Ideas may be developed by the use of specific supporting detail, and the writer may make an effort to organize and sequence ideas, but development and organization are largely incomplete or unclear. Paragraphs contain poorly structured sentences with noticeable and distracting errors. The writer exhibits imprecision in usage and word choice and a lack of control of mechanical conventions, such as spelling and punctuation.
1 —	**an inadequately formed writing sample that fails to communicate a complete message** The writer attempts to address the topic, but language and style may be inappropriate for the given audience, purpose, and/or occasion. There is often no clear statement of a main idea and the writer's efforts to present supporting detail are confused. Any organization that is present fails to present an effective sequence of ideas. Sentence structure is ineffective and few sentences are free of errors. Usage and word choice are imprecise. The writer makes many errors in the use of mechanical conventions, such as spelling and punctuation.

Note: A score of U is given if the writing sample is off topic, illegible, primarily in a language other than English, or not of a sufficient length to score. A score of B is used if the writing sample is completely blank (i.e., the examinee made no response to the writing assignment).

Sample Directions and Writing Assignment

The writing sample (essay) portion of the TASP Test consists of a set of writing sample directions, a writing assignment, and three lined pages on which to write your final essay. Several blank pages, on which to write and edit the draft of your essay, are also provided. Note that you must write your final version of the essay in your answer document, not in the test booklet. Only essays in the answer document will be scored.

The writing sample directions explain this portion of the test and the characteristics on which your essay will be evaluated. The writing assignment describes the specific topic that should be the subject of your essay, the purpose for writing, and the audience for which the essay is to be written. Be sure to read the writing assignment carefully.

On the following pages are the writing sample directions and the TASP Test writing assignment from the previous chapter (about taxes and user fees).

Included as well are four examples of essays written in response to this writing assignment. One example is provided for each of the four score points used in the scoring process. Each example has been annotated to show characteristics of writing and types of errors that are taken into consideration during scoring.

When reviewing these examples and preparing for the test, please note the following points.

- The scores earned by these examples demonstrate the nature of holistic scoring. The essays identified as "4" and "3" papers do contain some mechanical errors and other flaws; however, overall those essays do demonstrate the characteristics of effective and correct writing.

- Although many writers use a five-paragraph structure in developing a short essay, other organizational structures (such as those utilizing four or six paragraphs, for example) are equally correct. The number of paragraphs a writer uses should be determined according to the manner in which the content is organized and conveyed.

- The annotations do not identify all errors or flaws that may be present in the examples. For reference purposes, consult Chapters 22 through 27 of this study guide for information on the principles of effective and correct writing.

As part of your preparation to take the test, you should read the writing assignment directions and use the sample assignment to write a practice essay. You can then compare your practice essay with the examples provided, using the annotations to help you identify specific problems or weaknesses in your practice essay. If possible, get a teacher to help you in evaluating your practice essay.

Writing Sample Directions

This portion of the writing section of the TASP Test consists of one writing assignment. You are asked to prepare a MULTIPLE-PARAGRAPH writing sample of about 300–600 words on an assigned topic. The assignment can be found in your test booklet. You should use the time available to plan, write, review, and edit what you have written.

Read the assignment carefully before you begin to write. Think about how you will organize what you plan to write. You may use any blank space provided in this test booklet to make notes or to prepare your writing sample. Additional paper is not permitted. Your score will be based solely on the version of your writing sample written in the space provided on pages 4, 5, and 6 of your answer document.

Your writing sample will be scored on the basis of how effectively it communicates a whole message to the specified audience for the stated purpose. You will be assessed on your ability to express, organize, and support opinions and ideas rather than the position you express. Pay particular attention to the seven characteristics listed below when preparing your writing sample. These seven characteristics will be used in scoring your writing sample.

- APPROPRIATENESS—the extent to which you address the topic and use language and style appropriate to the given audience, purpose, and occasion.

- UNITY AND FOCUS—the clarity with which you state and maintain your main idea or point of view.

- DEVELOPMENT—the amount, depth, and specificity of your supporting details.

- ORGANIZATION—the clarity of your writing and the logical sequence of your ideas.

- SENTENCE STRUCTURE—the effectiveness of your sentence structure and the extent to which your writing is free of errors in sentence structure.

- USAGE—the extent to which your writing is free of errors in usage and shows care and precision in word choice.

- MECHANICAL CONVENTIONS—your ability to spell common words and to use the conventions of capitalization and punctuation.

Be sure to write about the assigned topic and use MULTIPLE PARAGRAPHS. Please write legibly. You may not use any reference materials during the test. Remember to save some time to review what you have written and make any changes you think will improve your writing sample.

The final version of your essay should conform to the conventions of edited American English. Your written response should be your original work, written in your own words, and not copied or paraphrased from some other work.

Sample TASP Writing Assignment

Are user fees or increased taxes the more appropriate way to pay for community recreational services? Proponents of user fees argue that such fees place the costs where they should be, on those individuals who are actually using the services. Proponents of taxes point out that all residents benefit from enhanced public services.

Your purpose is to write an essay, to be read by a classroom instructor, in which you take a position on whether increased taxes or user fees are the best way to pay for community recreational services. Be sure to defend your position with logical arguments and appropriate examples.

SAMPLE "1" ESSAY

Are user fees or increased taxes the more appropriate way to pay for community recreational services? Proponents of user fees argue that such fees place the costs where they should be, on those individuals who are actually using the services. Proponents of taxes point out that all residents benefit from enhanced public services.

Your purpose is to write an essay, to be read by a classroom instructor, in which you take a position on whether increased taxes or user fees are the best way to pay for community recreational services. Be sure to defend your position with logical arguments and appropriate examples.

1   *In my opionon it is not right to change a users fee for such recreations; such as a park,*
2   *swimming pools, baseball fields, and playgrounds. If we allowed to start charging for these*
3   *facilities it may hurt the children. If a child plays in the summer and need $1.00 entrance fee*
4   *they are forced in the street instead ware they may get mixed up with drugs and possible*
5   *even with gangs.*
6   *Anthor problem is that a child may go swimming in a pool and if there is a sign that say*
7   *$1.50 entrance that child may turn around and were will he go after that.*
8   *We can say if circumstance were diffrent that a child would walk to the pool and as she*
9   *get up close see the sign which state entrance $1.50 and reach into her pocket and hand it to*
10   *the attendent standing at the gate and the attendent stamp her hand with red ink and she be*
11   *allowed to swim with friends. So as the summer wears on each time the girl go she see more*
12   *and more of her friends outside of the gate that surrounds the pool looking in. So one day*
13   *as she leave the swimming area she stop and ask her friend way she does not want to go*
14   *swimming any more and the boy sadly look up at her and say to her the boys parents can not*
15   *afford paying $1.50.*
16   *So I belive that the best way to solve this problem would be not to change for facilities. A*
17   *much better way to solve problem would be to collect money and have a fund riaser.*

FEATURES OF THE SAMPLE "1" ESSAY

APPROPRIATENESS

- Much of the style and language is inappropriate for the occasion. The majority of the discussion is a narrative (e.g., beginning in the third paragraph, the writer offers scenarios rather than a well-constructed and well-thought-out argument against user fees).

UNITY AND FOCUS

- The writer does not state and maintain one point of view; therefore, the focus is unclear and never established.
- There is little unity in the essay. The writer begins by stating that there are problems a child may face if required to pay a fee at a recreational facility. However, the discussion shifts from one about "problems" to one about other circumstances that a child may confront if the child were to meet another child who is unable to pay the user fee.

DEVELOPMENT

- The writer's use of details and examples to support the case being made is often minimal. For example, the meaning of the one sentence in the second paragraph is unclear because no supporting details or additional explanations are given.
- In other cases, too much unrelated detail is given (e.g., the child handing the $1.50 fee to an attendant who stamps the child's hand with red ink, and so on. The point the writer is trying to make is lost in the overabundance of irrelevant detail offered).

ORGANIZATION

- There is little evidence of a plan for writing. Because this essay relies so heavily on the narrative form, i.e., storytelling, the writer's points of discussion do not follow a prearranged plan. The writer seems to discuss ideas just as they have come into his or her head.
- The essay suffers from a lack of clarity at the sentence level. Problems with sentence construction and nonstandard usage block the clear presentation of ideas (e.g., lines 3–5, "If a child plays in the summer and need $1.00 entrance fee they are forced in the street instead ware they may get mixed up with drugs and possible even with gangs").

SENTENCE STRUCTURE

- Many of the sentences are poorly structured. There are many examples of nonstandard and run-on sentences that distract the reader (e.g., the first sentence of paragraph three).
- There are many problems with nonstandard subject-verb agreement (e.g., "each time the girl go" in line 11; "So one day as she leave" in lines 12–13).

USAGE

- There are many noticeable and distracting usage errors (e.g., "that child may turn around and *were* will he go" in line 7, or "ask her friend *way* she does not want to go swimming any more and the boy sadly look up at her and *say*" in lines 13–14).

MECHANICAL CONVENTIONS

- The writer's frequent and noticeable misuse of grammatical conventions distracts the reader. There are many examples of incorrect spelling (e.g., *"opionon"* in line 1, *"Anthor"* in line 6, and *"diffrent"* in line 8) and nonstandard punctuation (e.g., the incorrect use of a semicolon in line 1).

SAMPLE "2" ESSAY

Are user fees or increased taxes the more appropriate way to pay for community recreational services? Proponents of user fees argue that such fees place the costs where they should be, on those individuals who are actually using the services. Proponents of taxes point out that all residents benefit from enhanced public services.

Your purpose is to write an essay, to be read by a classroom instructor, in which you take a position on whether increased taxes or user fees are the best way to pay for community recreational services. Be sure to defend your position with logical arguments and appropriate examples.

1　　*Recreational Services in towns and city are a key component for keeping them productive*
2　*and well kept. I think increased taxes are a good idea to keep this opportunities open.*
3　　*Recreational Services are available to Children, Adults, Senior Citizens, families and all*
4　*types of groups. The most important group of people in which this opportunities would help*
5　*are teenagers. Most of the the problems in towns & in cities as far as conduct go are usually*
6　*blamed on teenagers. Teens who turn to drug or alcohol to entertain themselve because there*
7　*is no place to go and nothing to do. With all diferent types of recreational activies to choose*
8　*from Starting at a young age children will learn better ways of useing their time. Children will*
9　*also have a great sence of comunity. They themselves could in return help the community*
10　*rather then destroying it. There for not only thoes who participate in these activities will*
11　*benefet but also thoes who just live in the community.*
12　　*I think its about time to start preventing problems before they start, and I believe this is*
13　*one good way. Money is always the big issue. Taxes = less money in the eyes of most people.*
14　*How much money do we put into our towns due to vandalism and other problems due to*
15　*damage. What if the community came together more to deal with problems together.*
16　　*In todays society people have become very self oriented. People spend more time infront*
17　*of a T.V. or computer or machines then with other people. instead of going to a washing*
18　*machine in a basement people used to go to a laudry mat with other people. Instead of*
19　*interacting with people one will sit inside of an office alone typing into a computer. Every*
20　*thing that once meant walking in to town or talking to some one has been made into a*
21　*condenced version for the home. Due to this people become lonely, perhaps depressed. People*
22　*can't replace people for a computer, and with out the need for people life begins to loose its*
23　*interest, in life in general. Nothing can replace a shoulder to cry on, a hug, a kiss or a pat on*
24　*the back.*
25　　*I think the comunity should start to move backwards in technoloy instead of forwards.*
26　*People should start spending more time with people and if that means a few extra dollars*
27　*from every ones pocket then I think its worth it.*

FEATURES OF THE SAMPLE "2" ESSAY

APPROPRIATENESS

- The main topic is clearly announced.
- For the most part the language and style of the essay are appropriate for the occasion.

UNITY AND FOCUS

- There is some general focus to the essay, although the focus on the main idea (i.e., "increased taxes are a good idea to keep this opportunities open") is not always sustained.
- The essay is somewhat unified, although the writer introduces ideas unrelated to the essay's main idea (e.g., "Nothing can replace a shoulder to cry on, a hug, a kiss or a pat on the back" in lines 23–24).

DEVELOPMENT

- The writer does attempt to develop the essay through paragraph formation. However, many of the topics of the paragraphs move away from the announced major topics of the discussion. For instance, in lines 4–5, the writer says that teenagers are the most important group helped by recreational services. Yet the issue of teenagers or programs directed at teenagers is not addressed in subsequent paragraphs.
- The writer provides some supporting details, although many details in the essay are incomplete or unclear (e.g., in paragraph three, the idea of "preventing problems before they start" in line 12 is left undeveloped).

ORGANIZATION

- The writer's attempts to organize and sequence ideas do not follow a clearly stated plan.
- There are few transitional terms that assist the reader in following the writer's logic or order of discussion.
- There is an attempt at a concluding statement, although the points made do not add clarity to the ideas presented earlier.

SENTENCE STRUCTURE

- There are many examples of nonstandard and incomplete sentence structure that distract the reader (e.g., "Teens who turn to drug or alcohol to entertain themselve because there is no place to go and nothing to do" in lines 6–7 is a sentence fragment. "Every thing that once meant walking in to town or talking to some one has been made into a condenced version for the home" in lines 19–21 conveys little meaning).

USAGE

- There are noticeable and distracting errors in word usage (e.g., "I think the comunity should start to move backwards in technoloy instead of forwards" in line 25).
- There are errors of agreement in number between demonstrative adjectives and the modified nouns (e.g., **"this opportunities"** in line 2).
- The writer commits errors in standard word formation (e.g., **"with out the need"** in line 22).
- The writer commits errors in word choice (e.g., **"to loose"** in line 22).

MECHANICAL CONVENTIONS

- The writer demonstrates a weakness in applying standard rules of grammar.
- There are numerous examples of incorrect spelling (e.g., **"themselve"** in line 6, **"diferent"** in line 7, **"comunity"** in line 9).
- There are several examples of nonstandard punctuation (e.g., a period used instead of a question mark at the end of line 15; the unnecessary comma after **"interest"** in line 23).
- The writer does not follow the rules governing capitalization of first word in a sentence (e.g., **"instead"** in line 17).

SAMPLE "3" ESSAY

Are user fees or increased taxes the more appropriate way to pay for community recreational services? Proponents of user fees argue that such fees place the costs where they should be, on those individuals who are actually using the services. Proponents of taxes point out that all residents benefit from enhanced public services.

Your purpose is to write an essay, to be read by a classroom instructor, in which you take a position on whether increased taxes or user fees are the best way to pay for community recreational services. Be sure to defend your position with logical arguments and appropriate examples.

1   *To determine where the burden of payment for community recreational services should*
2   *fall, we first need to decide who benefits from the services. It is my belief that, after analyzing*
3   *what would happen to a community with recreational services, it would be determined that*
4   *the entire community benefits and thus should pay for them in taxes.*
5   *Recreational services consist of many things; sports teams, excercise classes, self defense*
6   *classes, and matenance of parks, fields and swimming pools. All these programs provide*
7   *outlets for members of the community to relax, learn things and meet new people.*
8   *It is a scientifically proven fact that kids who are involved in sports do better in school*
9   *and are off the streets. These are key benefits from recreational programs. A kid involved in a*
10 *school sport's team learns many things. He learns commitment and responsibility. He learns*
11 *team work and social skills in dealing with other children; but most importantly he learns self*
12 *esteem and self respect from seeing his improvment and his team's success. A child who is*
13 *involved in learning all these skills is not just a better person for himself but he will become a*
14 *productive member of society. A child involved in recreational programs is not on the streets,*
15 *involved in gangs or drugs, but he is learning many of life's lessons.*
16   *Shouldn't everyone who benefits from a program help pay for it? Doesn't a society which*
17 *only allows the rich to participate create an markedly noticable class system? I submit that*
18 *the whole community benefits from the availability of parks pools and sport programs and*
19 *that by instituting a users fee you will effectively be eliminating the availability of these*
20 *resources to a great many people. Their are many families who couldn't afford a $25 or $30*
21 *users fee for a sports team or a $1.50 or $3 charge to use the beach or pool. In addition, their*
22 *are many disabled and elderly members of the community of fixed incomes who although*
23 *they could benefit from these programs would not be able to participate for financial reasons.*
24   *The people of the United States believe as the ancient Greeks did on a sound body creating*
25 *a sound mind. As demonstrated in their vehement support of Olympic and professional teams.*
26 *Based on this, the benefit of such programs to the community and that having users fees*
27 *would limit availability and create an elitist society it is my position that the whole*
28 *community should pay through taxes for recreational sevices.*

FEATURES OF THE SAMPLE "3" ESSAY

APPROPRIATENESS

- The writer's topic is clearly stated, and the writer uses style and language that are appropriate for the purpose, audience, and occasion.

UNITY AND FOCUS

- The main idea (i.e., community recreational services should be paid for by taxes, in line 4) is clear and generally maintained throughout the essay. In the third paragraph, however, the writer's focus is interrupted by references to school sports which are not clearly connected to the issue of community recreational services.

DEVELOPMENT

- Development is adequate. The writer presents a number of examples and makes remarks that support the position on taxes.
- The essay contains a conclusion in which the writer attempts to tie the ideas together and to stress the benefits of the proposed use of tax revenues.

ORGANIZATION

- The essay is appropriately organized with ideas presented in a logical order.
- The writer uses the standard conventions of rhetorical questions and transitional terms to move from one developed argument to another.

SENTENCE STRUCTURE

- Sentence structure within paragraphs is adequate, although errors are present (e.g., line 25, "As demonstrated in their vehement support of Olympic and professional teams" in the concluding paragraph is a sentence fragment).

USAGE

- In general, word choice is appropriate and effective. There are several cases of needless changes in point of view (e.g., the third-person discussion in reference to the "community" is changed to second person in line 19), as well as some incorrect word choice ("*their*" in lines 20 and 21).

MECHANICAL CONVENTIONS

- There are several examples of incorrect spelling (e.g., "*excercise*" in line 5, "*matenance*" in line 6).
- There are several examples of nonstandard punctuation (e.g., an incorrectly used semicolon in lines 5 and 11; the absence of a comma after "*society*" in line 27).

SAMPLE "4" ESSAY

Are user fees or increased taxes the more appropriate way to pay for community recreational services? Proponents of user fees argue that such fees place the costs where they should be, on those individuals who are actually using the services. Proponents of taxes point out that all residents benefit from enhanced public services.

Your purpose is to write an essay, to be read by a classroom instructor, in which you take a position on whether increased taxes or user fees are the best way to pay for community recreational services. Be sure to defend your position with logical arguments and appropriate examples.

1   *While increasing taxes to benefit recreational services distributes the cost among a*
2   *greater number of people than users fees (and thereby lessening the amount the individual is*
3   *forced to pay), it is not a fair method of paying for community services. User fees target only*
4   *those who use the facilities whereas tax increases require that all citizens assist in paying.*
5   *Home owners who live out of town or senior citizens would end up paying for the children's*
6   *wading pool at the local park or a playground and, while these are beneficial for the*
7   *community as a whole, it seems ironic that such people would be forced to financially endorse*
8   *these projects. Also, people do not get to select where their money will go when they are*
9   *taxed. It is more appropriate to have a senior citizen willingly choose to give money for a*
10 *senior's center that he or she will frequent, rather than for a jungle gym to be built at a park*
11 *on the other side of town.*
12   *User fees would not target individuals to pay for something they will not use nor will*
13 *user fees require that people pay for a facility when they are having financial trouble. With*
14 *donations on a per use basis, the individuals are allowed to select how much money they will*
15 *give. The avid tennis player will spend more money on the community courts than the person*
16 *who hates tennis or the person who already has access to a place he or she can play. User*
17 *fees eliminate much of the argument over what will be provided by a town in this way, too. A*
18 *family who already has a swimming pool will give very little opposition to a community pool,*
19 *provided that they are not expected to pay for it.*
20   *The idea of a park that everyone can go to as much as he or she likes is fantastic,*
21 *unfortunately it is unrealistic. Taxation can cause unnecessary financial woes by requiring*
22 *money from all citizens. For specialized services (recreational centers, for example, rather*
23 *than necessary services such as city employed road or sewer workers) it is best that the*
24 *people who use them pay for them. This would follow the example of toll roads which are*
25 *paid for by drivers who choose to use them over alternate free routes.*
26   *In conclusion, user fees are a fair way of paying for community recreational services.*
27 *User fees target only those who use the facilities. User fees do not require people to pay for*
28 *services they do not use. In contrast to taxation, user fees are paid by the individuals who*
29 *make use of specialized services that do not directly benefit the entire community. I believe*
30 *that all towns and cities across the state will do a service to their citizens by considering and*
31 *instituting user fee programs for public services.*

FEATURES OF THE SAMPLE "4" ESSAY

APPROPRIATENESS

- The topic is clearly stated.
- The style and language are appropriate for the purpose, audience, and occasion.

UNITY AND FOCUS

- The central idea (i.e., user fees are a fair method of paying for community recreational services) is stated in the first paragraph and maintained throughout the essay. The examples are relevant to the central idea.
- There are no major digressions that detract from the unity and focus.

DEVELOPMENT

- The essay is well developed with several examples supporting each main point within a paragraph.
- The conclusion is strong and effective, with the writer restating the main points of the discussion in favor of "user fees."

ORGANIZATION

- The writer introduces the main issues (user fees and taxes) of the essay in the first paragraph.
- The writer then uses an expository "contrast" essay form to present arguments in favor of user fees.
- The plan of the essay is clear, and the sequencing of ideas is logical.

SENTENCE STRUCTURE

- The sentences are well constructed and vary in form.
- There are no major examples of nonstandard sentence formation.

USAGE

- The essay is free of any significant problems in usage, although there is some awkwardness in the last sentence of the third paragraph.
- The words are well chosen and appropriate for an explanatory essay.

MECHANICAL CONVENTIONS

- There are few, if any, instances of incorrect spelling.
- Overall the writer demonstrates a strong understanding of the conventions of grammar.

Scoring Features and the Study Guide

Now that you have seen how one sample writing assignment might be addressed and how four different attempts to address it might be scored, you should have a clearer idea about how to plan, develop, write, and review your essay for the TASP Test. If you had any trouble understanding the features of the various sample essays, refer to the chapters of this study guide that relate to those features:

Appropriateness	Chapter 22
Unity and focus	Chapter 23
Development	Chapter 23
Organization	Chapter 24
Sentence structure	Chapter 25
Usage	Chapter 26
Mechanical conventions	Chapter 26

Furthermore, Chapter 27 deals with putting the elements of composition together and writing an essay.

Improving Your Performance on the TASP Test Writing Sample

The surest way to improve your performance on the TASP Test writing sample is to improve your writing skills. Chapters 22 through 27 of this study guide provide detailed explanations of the skills that go into good writing. Read these chapters carefully and practice writing to develop those skills. Have a teacher or friend critique your writing; then practice revising and editing your work. Use the sample writing assignments, or prompts, provided in this chapter to simulate actual testing conditions: plan, draft, and revise an essay within one hour. Repeat this process until you are comfortable with the impromptu writing situation.

There are no shortcuts or easy ways to pass the writing sample portion of the TASP Test. There are, however, some basic do's and don'ts that will help your performance.

- *Do* read the directions and prompt carefully. Be sure you respond to the prompt and follow any cues or directions within the prompt. For example, if you are asked to state your position on an issue, be sure you do so. Pay attention to the audience for which you are required to write.

- *Do* plan and organize your essay before you begin to write. This will help you respond to the prompt and stay on topic.

- *Do* stay on topic. Avoid digressions into subjects or details that are not related to the topic. Support your main idea with examples and details.

- *Do* use a multiple paragraph structure. A single long paragraph fails to meet the organizational requirements of the essay.

- *Do* use the extra space in your test booklet for notes, outlines, a first draft, etc. Remember that only the final essay written on your answer document will be considered in scoring.

- *Do* write legibly. While neatness is not an issue in scoring, illegible handwriting may cloud your message. An edited final essay is fine, as long as your editing is clear and understandable. In other words, your final sample can have words crossed out or added as long as your intended meaning is clear.

There are also several things to consider on the *don't* side.

- *Don't* simply read the prompt and begin writing whatever comes to mind, assuming you can overcome deficiencies in focus, organization, and development with length.

- *Don't* come to the test with an essay prepared in your mind and try to fit it to whatever prompt you are given. Even a well-written essay may receive a low score if it does not represent an appropriate response to the prompt.

- *Don't* worry about counting the exact number of words you have written. While the suggested target is 300 to 600 words (approximately one and one-half to three pages), you will not be penalized if your essay is slightly longer or shorter. Be sure, however, that your response is of sufficient length to cover the topic effectively.

- *Don't* forget your purpose for writing. If you are writing a persuasive essay, for example, don't slip into descriptive or explanatory writing. This is a common problem and something you should look for specifically as you revise your draft.

Remember that the evaluation of your writing is based on how well you present and support your ideas, not on the content of the ideas. For instance, in the example in Chapter 27 about user fees versus higher taxes, the side you choose to defend is irrelevant.

Additional Sample Writing Assignments

Additional writing topics similar to the one you will receive on the TASP Test are provided below. Remember that the assignment may be accompanied by introductory information in one of a number of possible formats (see the previous chapter). We are presenting these samples in one format only.

We recommend that you take the time to read these assignments carefully and prepare a sample essay for each one. On your own or with a teacher, review your essays on the basis of the scoring features listed with the examples of essays presented earlier.

Sample Writing Prompts

1. Should health care be partially funded by an increased tax on alcohol and tobacco products? Proponents argue that these products contribute significantly to the overall health care costs of the country and that those who use them should pay for the medical expenditures they necessitate. Opponents would argue that such taxes are an attempt to legislate morality and an unfair reaction to habits that some people do not like.

    Your purpose is to write an essay to be read by a classroom instructor in which you take a position on whether taxes should be raised on alcohol and tobacco products to pay for health care in the United States. Be sure to defend your position with logical arguments and appropriate examples.

2. Should the federal tax on gasoline be raised significantly to help pay for public transportation and road improvements? Opponents argue that significantly higher gas taxes will hurt business by raising costs and will decease the freedom of mobility of the general public. Proponents say that we need the additional revenues to finance public works projects and that U.S. citizens pay less for gasoline than do citizens in other industrialized nations.

    Your purpose is to write an essay to be read by a classroom instructor in which you take a position on whether gasoline taxes should be raised. Be sure to defend your position with logical arguments and appropriate examples.

3. Should Texas pass a law requiring manufacturers to reduce the amount of packaging materials on products sold in the state? Proponents argue that much packaging is wasteful; it uses up resources and contributes to our waste disposal problems. Others say that a law like this would raise costs to Texas consumers if it does not apply nationwide and that consumers are used to packaging as it is.

    Your purpose is to write an essay to be read by a classroom instructor in which you take a position on requiring reduced packaging on products sold in Texas. Be sure to defend your position with logical arguments and appropriate examples.

Conclusion

In this chapter, we have provided you with essential information that should help you prepare for the writing sample portion of the TASP Test. Armed with this information, you should feel more confident about this portion of the test.

Study References: Writing

These references for further study were suggested by members of the TASP Content Advisory Committee in Writing, the TASP Bias Review Panel, and the Remediation Subcommittee of the Texas Academic Skills Council.

Particular references are included because they relate to the TASP skills and are appropriate for college students. The titles listed here may also be available in learning centers and through developmental education programs on your campus.

Adams, P. D. *CONNECTIONS: A Guide to the Basics of Writing.* Boston: Little, Brown, 1987.

Adelstein, M. E., & Pival, J. G. *The Writing Commitment.* New York: Harcourt Brace Jovanovich, 1984.

Arnaudet, M. L., & Barret, M. E. *Approaches to Academic Reading and Writing.* Englewood Cliffs, NJ: Prentice Hall, 1984.

Avery, L. A., et al. *Write On! Preparing to Write.* Dubuque, IA: Kendall/Hunt Publishing Co., 1988.

Axelrod, R. B., & Cooper, C. *The St. Martin's Guide to Writing.* New York: St. Martin's Press, 1988.

Blumenthal, J. C. *English 3200: A Programmed Course in Grammar and Usage.* New York: Harcourt Brace Jovanovich, 1981.

Bromberg, M., & Gordon, M. *Words You Need to Know.* Hauppauge, NY: Barron's Educational Series, 1987.

Carter, B., & Skates, C. *The Rinehart Handbook for Writers.* New York: Holt, Rinehart & Winston, 1987.

Clifford, J., & Waterhouse, R. F. *Sentence Combining: Shaping Ideas for Better Style.* Indianapolis, IN: Bobbs-Merrill Educational Publishing, 1983.

Corbett, E. P. J. *The Little English Handbook: Choices and Conventions.* Glenview, IL: Scott, Foresman & Co., 1987.

DeVillez, R. *Step-by-Step: College Writing* (3rd ed.). Dubuque, IA: Kendall/Hunt Publishing Co., 1987.

Donald, R. B., et al. *Writing Clear Paragraphs.* Englewood Cliffs, NJ: Prentice-Hall, 1987.

Elbow, P. *Writing Without Teachers.* New York: Oxford University Press, 1973.

Emery, D., Kierzek, J., & Lindblom, P. *English Fundamentals.* New York: Macmillan, 1985.

Flower, L. *Problem-Solving Strategies for Writing* (3rd ed.). New York: Harcourt Brace Jovanovich, 1985.

Fowler, H. R. *The Little, Brown Handbook.* Edited by Little, Brown. Boston: Little, Brown, 1986.

Griffith, K. J. *Writing Essays About Literature: A Guide and Style Sheet.* New York: Harcourt Brace Jovanovich, 1982.

Hairston, M. C. *A Contemporary Composition.* Boston: Houghton Mifflin, 1985.

Hart, A., & Reinking, J. *Writing for Career Education Students.* New York: St. Martin's Press, 1986.

Hawkins, M., et al. *The English Program.* Dubuque, IA: Kendall/Hunt Publishing Co., 1986.

Hawkins, M., et al. *Teacher's Manual: The English Program.* Dubuque, IA: Kendall/Hunt Publishing Co., 1986.

Hodges, J. C., & Whitten, M. E. *Harbrace College Handbook.* San Diego, CA: Harcourt Brace Jovanovich, 1986.

Hook, J. N., & Evans, W. H. *The Writer's Tutor: One Hundred Self-Correcting Lessons.* New York: Harcourt Brace Jovanovich, 1988.

Langan, J. *English Skills.* New York: McGraw-Hill Inc., 1985.

Langan, J. *Sentence Skills: A Workbook for Writing, Form C.* New York: McGraw-Hill Inc., 1988.

Lindemann, E. *A Rhetoric for Writing Teachers.* New York: Oxford University Press, 1987.

McMahan, E., & Day, S. *The Writer's Rhetoric and Handbook.* New York: McGraw-Hill Inc., 1988.

Neeld, E. C. *Writing: A Short Course.* Glenview, IL: Scott, Foresman & Co., 1987.

Neeld, E. C. *Writing Brief.* Glenview, IL: Scott, Foresman & Co., 1986.

Porter, T., & Barros, C. *The Literate Mind: Exposition, Argumentation, Self-Expression, Readers 1, 2, and 3.* Dubuque, IA: Kendall/Hunt Publishing Co., 1987.

Porter, T., Kneupper, C., & Reeder, H. *The Literate Mind: Reading, Writing, Critical Thinking.* Dubuque, IA: Kendall/Hunt Publishing Co., 1987.

Rackham, J. *From Sight to Insight: Steps in the Writing Process.* New York: Holt, Rinehart & Winston, 1984.

Seyler, D. *Read, Reason, Write.* New York: Random House, 1986.

Soteriou, P. E. *Integrating College Study Skills: Reasoning in Reading, Listening, and Writing.* Belmont, CA: Wadsworth, 1984.

Strunk, W., & White, E. B. *The Elements of Style.* New York: Macmillan, 1979.

Troyka, L., & Nudelman, J. *Steps in Composition* (4th ed.). Englewood Cliffs, NJ: Prentice Hall, 1986.

Walsh, J. M., & Walsh, A. K. *Plain English Handbook.* New York: Random House/McCormick, 1982.

Whimbey, A. *Mastering Reading Through Reasoning.* Stamford, CT: Innovative Sciences, Inc., 1985.

Wiener, H. *The Writing Room: A Resource Book for Teachers of English.* New York: Oxford Press, 1981.

Wiener, H. S., & Bazerman, C. *Basic Reading Skills Handbook.* Dallas: Houghton Mifflin, 1988.

Winkler, A., & McCuen, J. R. *Rhetoric Made Plain.* New York: Harcourt Brace Jovanovich, 1988.

SECTION V

Practice Test

Section V includes a full-length practice version of the TASP Test and some suggestions for getting the most benefit out of taking it. In addition to the test questions, you are provided with an:

- explanation for the correct answer for each test question (these explanations are meant to help you understand why the correct response is what it is and why the other answers are incorrect);

- answer sheet, which you may remove from the study guide to use; and

- answer key indicating the correct response for each question.

TASP Practice Test Directions

By now you probably know that you can use this study guide in many ways. For instance, you may choose to take the Practice Test as your last step in preparing for the TASP Test. Or, you might use the Practice Test as one of your first steps in assessing your skills in reading, mathematics, and writing.

Whatever your study plan, consider the Practice Test a valuable opportunity. It is not your only chance to practice your test-taking skills, though. Remember that another version of the test—the Pre-TASP Test—is available on some campuses. If you work through the study guide, and take the Practice Test and Pre-TASP Test, you will be able to gauge your skills, check your study progress, and judge your readiness for the actual TASP Test.

Set aside about four hours so that you can take the Practice Test without interruption. Work in a quiet place where you will not be disturbed. A reading room in the college library is an ideal location. You may take all three sections of the Practice Test at one time, or you may decide to split them up. Four-function (+, −, ×, ÷), nonprogrammable calculators [with square root (√) and percent (%) keys] are allowed. Reference materials are not permitted.

Remember, there is no penalty for guessing. Your score reflects only the number of questions answered correctly. Therefore, it will be to your advantage to analyze the answer choices, eliminate any that you are sure are wrong, and make an educated guess from the remaining choices. After the test you may choose to follow up on those specific skills about which you made a large number of guesses.

Use the answer sheet on the next page. Instead of flipping back and forth, you may decide to remove the answer sheet from the book. To make your Practice Test experience as similar as possible to the real test administration, follow the same rules that the real TASP Test will require. Fill in your answers carefully and completely. Be sure to mark just one response for each question. Make no stray marks.

Once you complete the test, check your answers against the Answer Key and the Skill Evaluation Chart.

_____

TASP Practice Test Answer Sheet

READING		MATHEMATICS		WRITING	
1 Ⓐ Ⓑ Ⓒ Ⓓ	22 Ⓐ Ⓑ Ⓒ Ⓓ	1 Ⓐ Ⓑ Ⓒ Ⓓ	25 Ⓐ Ⓑ Ⓒ Ⓓ	1 Ⓐ Ⓑ Ⓒ Ⓓ	21 Ⓐ Ⓑ Ⓒ Ⓓ
2 Ⓐ Ⓑ Ⓒ Ⓓ	23 Ⓐ Ⓑ Ⓒ Ⓓ	2 Ⓐ Ⓑ Ⓒ Ⓓ	26 Ⓐ Ⓑ Ⓒ Ⓓ	2 Ⓐ Ⓑ Ⓒ Ⓓ	22 Ⓐ Ⓑ Ⓒ Ⓓ
3 Ⓐ Ⓑ Ⓒ Ⓓ	24 Ⓐ Ⓑ Ⓒ Ⓓ	3 Ⓐ Ⓑ Ⓒ Ⓓ	27 Ⓐ Ⓑ Ⓒ Ⓓ	3 Ⓐ Ⓑ Ⓒ Ⓓ	23 Ⓐ Ⓑ Ⓒ Ⓓ
4 Ⓐ Ⓑ Ⓒ Ⓓ	25 Ⓐ Ⓑ Ⓒ Ⓓ	4 Ⓐ Ⓑ Ⓒ Ⓓ	28 Ⓐ Ⓑ Ⓒ Ⓓ	4 Ⓐ Ⓑ Ⓒ Ⓓ	24 Ⓐ Ⓑ Ⓒ Ⓓ
5 Ⓐ Ⓑ Ⓒ Ⓓ	26 Ⓐ Ⓑ Ⓒ Ⓓ	5 Ⓐ Ⓑ Ⓒ Ⓓ	29 Ⓐ Ⓑ Ⓒ Ⓓ	5 Ⓐ Ⓑ Ⓒ Ⓓ	25 Ⓐ Ⓑ Ⓒ Ⓓ
6 Ⓐ Ⓑ Ⓒ Ⓓ	27 Ⓐ Ⓑ Ⓒ Ⓓ	6 Ⓐ Ⓑ Ⓒ Ⓓ	30 Ⓐ Ⓑ Ⓒ Ⓓ	6 Ⓐ Ⓑ Ⓒ Ⓓ	26 Ⓐ Ⓑ Ⓒ Ⓓ
7 Ⓐ Ⓑ Ⓒ Ⓓ	28 Ⓐ Ⓑ Ⓒ Ⓓ	7 Ⓐ Ⓑ Ⓒ Ⓓ	31 Ⓐ Ⓑ Ⓒ Ⓓ	7 Ⓐ Ⓑ Ⓒ Ⓓ	27 Ⓐ Ⓑ Ⓒ Ⓓ
8 Ⓐ Ⓑ Ⓒ Ⓓ	29 Ⓐ Ⓑ Ⓒ Ⓓ	8 Ⓐ Ⓑ Ⓒ Ⓓ	32 Ⓐ Ⓑ Ⓒ Ⓓ	8 Ⓐ Ⓑ Ⓒ Ⓓ	28 Ⓐ Ⓑ Ⓒ Ⓓ
9 Ⓐ Ⓑ Ⓒ Ⓓ	30 Ⓐ Ⓑ Ⓒ Ⓓ	9 Ⓐ Ⓑ Ⓒ Ⓓ	33 Ⓐ Ⓑ Ⓒ Ⓓ	9 Ⓐ Ⓑ Ⓒ Ⓓ	29 Ⓐ Ⓑ Ⓒ Ⓓ
10 Ⓐ Ⓑ Ⓒ Ⓓ	31 Ⓐ Ⓑ Ⓒ Ⓓ	10 Ⓐ Ⓑ Ⓒ Ⓓ	34 Ⓐ Ⓑ Ⓒ Ⓓ	10 Ⓐ Ⓑ Ⓒ Ⓓ	30 Ⓐ Ⓑ Ⓒ Ⓓ
11 Ⓐ Ⓑ Ⓒ Ⓓ	32 Ⓐ Ⓑ Ⓒ Ⓓ	11 Ⓐ Ⓑ Ⓒ Ⓓ	35 Ⓐ Ⓑ Ⓒ Ⓓ	11 Ⓐ Ⓑ Ⓒ Ⓓ	31 Ⓐ Ⓑ Ⓒ Ⓓ
12 Ⓐ Ⓑ Ⓒ Ⓓ	33 Ⓐ Ⓑ Ⓒ Ⓓ	12 Ⓐ Ⓑ Ⓒ Ⓓ	36 Ⓐ Ⓑ Ⓒ Ⓓ	12 Ⓐ Ⓑ Ⓒ Ⓓ	32 Ⓐ Ⓑ Ⓒ Ⓓ
13 Ⓐ Ⓑ Ⓒ Ⓓ	34 Ⓐ Ⓑ Ⓒ Ⓓ	13 Ⓐ Ⓑ Ⓒ Ⓓ	37 Ⓐ Ⓑ Ⓒ Ⓓ	13 Ⓐ Ⓑ Ⓒ Ⓓ	33 Ⓐ Ⓑ Ⓒ Ⓓ
14 Ⓐ Ⓑ Ⓒ Ⓓ	35 Ⓐ Ⓑ Ⓒ Ⓓ	14 Ⓐ Ⓑ Ⓒ Ⓓ	38 Ⓐ Ⓑ Ⓒ Ⓓ	14 Ⓐ Ⓑ Ⓒ Ⓓ	34 Ⓐ Ⓑ Ⓒ Ⓓ
15 Ⓐ Ⓑ Ⓒ Ⓓ	36 Ⓐ Ⓑ Ⓒ Ⓓ	15 Ⓐ Ⓑ Ⓒ Ⓓ	39 Ⓐ Ⓑ Ⓒ Ⓓ	15 Ⓐ Ⓑ Ⓒ Ⓓ	35 Ⓐ Ⓑ Ⓒ Ⓓ
16 Ⓐ Ⓑ Ⓒ Ⓓ	37 Ⓐ Ⓑ Ⓒ Ⓓ	16 Ⓐ Ⓑ Ⓒ Ⓓ	40 Ⓐ Ⓑ Ⓒ Ⓓ	16 Ⓐ Ⓑ Ⓒ Ⓓ	36 Ⓐ Ⓑ Ⓒ Ⓓ
17 Ⓐ Ⓑ Ⓒ Ⓓ	38 Ⓐ Ⓑ Ⓒ Ⓓ	17 Ⓐ Ⓑ Ⓒ Ⓓ	41 Ⓐ Ⓑ Ⓒ Ⓓ	17 Ⓐ Ⓑ Ⓒ Ⓓ	37 Ⓐ Ⓑ Ⓒ Ⓓ
18 Ⓐ Ⓑ Ⓒ Ⓓ	39 Ⓐ Ⓑ Ⓒ Ⓓ	18 Ⓐ Ⓑ Ⓒ Ⓓ	42 Ⓐ Ⓑ Ⓒ Ⓓ	18 Ⓐ Ⓑ Ⓒ Ⓓ	38 Ⓐ Ⓑ Ⓒ Ⓓ
19 Ⓐ Ⓑ Ⓒ Ⓓ	40 Ⓐ Ⓑ Ⓒ Ⓓ	19 Ⓐ Ⓑ Ⓒ Ⓓ	43 Ⓐ Ⓑ Ⓒ Ⓓ	19 Ⓐ Ⓑ Ⓒ Ⓓ	39 Ⓐ Ⓑ Ⓒ Ⓓ
20 Ⓐ Ⓑ Ⓒ Ⓓ	41 Ⓐ Ⓑ Ⓒ Ⓓ	20 Ⓐ Ⓑ Ⓒ Ⓓ	44 Ⓐ Ⓑ Ⓒ Ⓓ	20 Ⓐ Ⓑ Ⓒ Ⓓ	40 Ⓐ Ⓑ Ⓒ Ⓓ
21 Ⓐ Ⓑ Ⓒ Ⓓ	42 Ⓐ Ⓑ Ⓒ Ⓓ	21 Ⓐ Ⓑ Ⓒ Ⓓ	45 Ⓐ Ⓑ Ⓒ Ⓓ		
		22 Ⓐ Ⓑ Ⓒ Ⓓ	46 Ⓐ Ⓑ Ⓒ Ⓓ		
		23 Ⓐ Ⓑ Ⓒ Ⓓ	47 Ⓐ Ⓑ Ⓒ Ⓓ		
		24 Ⓐ Ⓑ Ⓒ Ⓓ	48 Ⓐ Ⓑ Ⓒ Ⓓ		

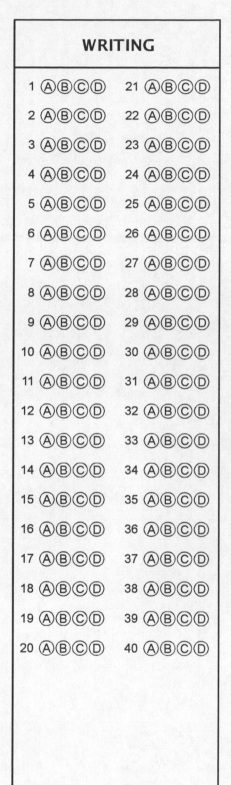

READING SECTION

The reading section of the test consists of 7 reading selections. After each reading selection, you will be asked to answer several questions related to the selection. Read each question carefully and choose the ONE best answer. You may refer back to the selection to answer the questions. There are a total of 42 multiple-choice questions in the reading section, numbered 1 to 42.

Record your answer on the answer sheet in the space that corresponds to the question number. Completely fill in the space having the same letter as the answer you have chosen.

In the reading section, the order of information requested by the questions does not necessarily correspond to the order of information in a given selection. Certain words and phrases within some selections have been highlighted for testing purposes, not for reasons of emphasis by the writers.

Read the passage below. Then answer the questions that follow.

Durkheim and the Development of Sociology

1   Sociology is defined as the study of human groups. In the broadest sense, sociology is concerned with understanding patterns of human relationships, their causes and their effects. Unlike psychology, sociology does not attempt to explain the behavior of a particular individual under certain circumstances. Rather, sociology focuses on social trends or other influences that affect whole groups or categories of people. Thus, while a psychologist might counsel an individual who feels worthless after retiring from a long and successful career, a sociologist would be more likely to examine societal attitudes that may contribute to the loss of self-esteem experienced by many retired persons in our society.

2   The emphasis that sociology places on human groups rather than individuals stems directly from the work of Emile Durkheim, a pioneering sociologist of the nineteenth century. Durkheim likened the nature of a social group to bronze, a unique metal that is formed when the metals tin, copper, and lead are melted and mixed together. Durkheim noted that bronze is much harder than any of its component metals. In the same way, he reasoned, the characteristics of a social group viewed as a whole cannot be determined simply by examining the characteristics of its individual members. Nor can individuals be understood strictly in terms of the individuals themselves; when people come together as members of a particular group, the group exerts considerable pressure on the individual to conform to what it considers acceptable ways of thinking, feeling, and behaving.

3   Besides developing a theoretical foundation for the study of social groups, Durkheim also conducted research designed to corroborate his theoretical work. Using landmark research methods, Durkheim collected and analyzed data from a number of countries that kept records on suicides. He wanted to show that social environment may have a profound effect even on those behaviors we consider most personal. The results of his study showed that suicide rates do indeed vary according to specific social characteristics. For example, Durkheim found that members of religions with strong prohibitions against suicide are less likely to commit suicide than are members of religious groups with weaker prohibitions. He also found a lower incidence of suicide among married persons than among persons who were single or divorced. Taken together, the findings of Durkheim's study provided convincing evidence that social groups do indeed exert pressures that control or regulate the behavior of individuals, including deeply personal behaviors.

4   Durkheim's rigorous research methods captured the attention of sociologists around the world, and were perhaps even more important to the future development of sociology than any specific research results could be. Within a short time, his specific approach to formulating and testing social theory became a <u>model</u> that guided the work of nearly all sociologists. This assured Emile Durkheim a lasting place as one of the key figures in the history of sociology.

◆ ◆ ◆ ◆ ◆ ◆ ◆ ◆

1. Which of the following best expresses the main idea of the selection?

    A. Both the social group theory and the scientific research methods developed by Durkheim have contributed much to the field of sociology.

    B. Durkheim believed that individual members of a group strongly influence the group's ways of thinking, feeling, and behaving.

    C. The research study conducted by Durkheim provided strong evidence that suicide rates vary among members of different social groups.

    D. Through his research, Durkheim made great strides in distinguishing sociology from psychology.

2. The writer's main purpose in writing this selection is to:

    A. outline the steps Durkheim followed in conducting his research study.

    B. describe the ways in which Durkheim's work has influenced sociology.

    C. persuade the reader that social groups control most of the behaviors of their individual members.

    D. explain the differences between sociology and psychology.

3. According to the selection, how do sociologists and psychologists differ?

    A. Sociologists are more concerned with explaining behavior than are psychologists.

    B. Psychologists focus more on individuals than do sociologists.

    C. Sociologists spend more time helping people solve their problems than do psychologists.

    D. Psychologists are more interested in understanding patterns of human relationships than are sociologists.

4. In comparing social groups to bronze, Durkheim wished to illustrate the idea that:

    A. a social group has characteristics that differ from those of its individual members.

    B. social groups are made up of three major component parts acting together.

    C. each social group is a unique entity that is unlike any other social group.

    D. social groups are extremely difficult to break apart once they have been formed.

5. Which of the following lists of topics best organizes the information in the selection?

   A. —Psychology vs. sociology
       —Sociology likened to bronze
       —Durkheim's suicide research
       —Durkheim's influence in distinguishing sociology from psychology

   B. —Sociology before Durkheim
       —Durkheim's early work
       —Durkheim's later work
       —Durkheim's influence on sociology

   C. —The focus of contemporary sociology
       —Durkheim's contributions to sociological theory
       —Durkheim's contributions to sociological research methods

   D. —Sociology as the study of human groups
       —Sociology in Durkheim's time
       —Sociology since Durkheim

6. Which of the following best defines the word model as it is used in the last paragraph of the selection?

   A. one of two or more alternative styles

   B. an artist's subject

   C. a small copy of an object

   D. a plan to be imitated

Read the selection adapted from *The Joy Luck Club* by Amy Tan.
Then answer the six questions that follow.

The Joy Luck Club

1   My mother started the San Francisco version of the Joy Luck Club in 1949, two years before I was born. This was the year my mother and father left China with one stiff leather trunk filled only with fancy silk dresses. There was no time to pack anything else, my mother had explained to my father after they boarded the boat. Still his hands swam frantically between the slippery silks, looking for his cotton shirts and wool pants.

2   When they arrived in San Francisco, my father made her hide those shiny clothes. She wore the same brown-checked Chinese dress until the Refugee Welcome Society gave her two hand-me-down dresses, all too large in sizes for American women. The society was composed of a group of white-haired American missionary ladies from the First Chinese Baptist Church. And because of their gifts, my parents could not refuse their invitation to join the church. Nor could they ignore the old ladies' practical advice to improve their English through Bible study class on Wednesday nights and, later, through choir practice on Saturday mornings. This was how my parents met the Hsus, the Jongs, and the St. Clairs. My mother could sense that the women of these families also had unspeakable tragedies they had left behind in China and hopes they couldn't begin to express in their fragile English. Or at least, my mother recognized the numbness in these women's faces. And she saw how quickly their eyes moved when she told them her idea for the Joy Luck Club.

3   Joy Luck was an idea my mother remembered from the days of her first marriage in Kweilin, before the Japanese came. That's why I think of Joy Luck as her Kweilin story.

It was the story she would always tell me when she was bored, when there was nothing to do, when every bowl had been washed and the Formica table had been wiped down twice, when my father sat reading the newspaper and smoking one Pall Mall cigarette after another, a warning not to disturb him. This is when my mother would take out a box of old ski sweaters sent to us by unseen relatives from Vancouver. She would snip the bottom of a sweater and pull out a kinky thread of yarn, anchoring it to a piece of cardboard. And as she began to roll with one sweeping rhythm, she would start her story. Over the years, she told me the same story, except for the ending, which grew darker, casting long shadows into her life, and eventually into mine. . . .

4   "I thought up Joy Luck on a summer night that was so hot even the moths fainted to the ground, their wings were so heavy with the damp heat. Every place was so crowded there was no room for fresh air. Unbearable smells from the sewers rose up to my second-story window and the stink had nowhere else to go but into my nose. At all hours of the night and day, I heard screaming sounds. I didn't know if it was a peasant slitting the throat of a runaway pig or an officer beating a half-dead peasant for lying in his way on the sidewalk. I didn't go to the window to find out. What use would it have been? And that's when I thought I needed something to do to help me move.

5   "My idea was to have a gathering of four women, one for each corner of my mah jong table. I knew which women I wanted to ask. They were all young like me, with wishful faces. . . .

6   "Each week one of us would host a party to raise money and to raise our spirits. The hostess had to serve special *dyansyin* foods to bring good fortune of all kinds—dumplings shaped like silver money ingots, long rice noodles for long life, boiled peanuts for conceiving sons, and of course, many good-luck oranges for a plentiful, sweet life. . . .

7   "We decided to hold parties and pretend each week had become the new year. Each week we could forget past wrongs done to us. We weren't allowed to think a bad thought. We feasted, we laughed, we played games, lost and won, we told the best stories. And each week, we could hope to be lucky. That hope was our only joy. And that's how we came to call our little parties Joy Luck."

◆ ◆ ◆ ◆ ◆ ◆ ◆

7. Which of the following statements best expresses the main idea of *paragraph 7* of the selection?

A. Joy Luck Club members were generally incapable of facing reality.

B. The weekly Joy Luck Club parties included an abundance of food and participation in games and storytelling.

C. The women went to the Joy Luck Club parties in the hopes of winning prizes that would make their lives easier.

D. Joy Luck parties were designed as happy events to help the women temporarily forget past sorrows and losses.

8. In paragraph 2, the author most likely uses phrases such as "unspeakable tragedies" and "hopes they couldn't begin to express in their fragile English" for what purpose?

A. to show how much these women needed to improve their English

B. to suggest the depth of the women's sorrow and desperation

C. to underscore the women's good fortune in having emigrated from China

D. to imply that the narrator's mother felt superior to these women

9. Which of the following is a valid conclusion based on the information in paragraph 4 of the selection?

   A. Frustration over her oppressive surroundings led the narrator's mother to conceive of the Joy Luck Club.

   B. The narrator's mother didn't go to the window to see what was going on outside because she was ill and unable to move.

   C. The heat and the unbearable smells from the sewers caused the narrator's mother to imagine terrible sounds and sights.

   D. Joy Luck was conceived by the narrator's mother simply as a means of generating income to escape her unpleasant living conditions.

10. Which of the following statements from the selection is presented as an opinion rather than a fact?

   A. She saw how quickly their eyes moved when she told them her idea for the Joy Luck Club.

   B. It was the story she would always tell me when she was bored, when there was nothing to do.

   C. Unbearable smells from the sewers rose up to my second-story window and the stink had nowhere else to go but into my nose.

   D. Each week we would forget past wrongs done to us.

11. Which of the following best summarizes the main points of the selection?

   A. The narrator's mother was living in a small town in China where she was quite unhappy. The weather was too hot and the streets were noisy and unsafe. To make herself feel better, she asked some friends to join a club that she invented so that she could have company.

   B. The narrator's parents arrived in San Francisco from China in 1949. They brought very few belongings, but were helped by the kind women at the First Chinese Baptist Church. Eventually, the wife made friends with some of the other women in the church. The women later decided to form a social club.

   C. The narrator's mother had had a very unhappy life. She and her husband did not always get along, and she had often been lonely. Sometimes, when she had nothing else to do, she would tell stories to her daughter about places she had lived and people she had known.

   D. The narrator's parents arrived in the United States with only a few of their most precious belongings. The narrator's mother met some friends and formed a club similar to one she had started in China. This club was designed to help the women forget the sorrows of their past and present and to have hope for the future.

12. In paragraph 3 of this selection, the author writes, "Over the years, she told me the same story, except for the ending, which grew darker, casting long shadows into her life." In this context, what does the author mean by casting long shadows into her life?

A. making her feel as if she was unaware of the past

B. affecting her life with painful memories from many years ago

C. confusing her with vague memories of her youth

D. hiding her memories of unpleasant events

Read the passage below. Then answer the questions that follow.

The Production of a Television Commercial

1   Everything in today's world is going faster and faster, and television commercials are no exception. At the start of the television age the standard commercial lasted 60 seconds, but most of today's commercials are only half that length and many are even shorter. The 15-second commercial, introduced a few years ago as a way to cut skyrocketing advertising costs, may soon be the most common in the United States. (Our television-watching counterparts in Japan and Europe are already being treated to 7½-second mini-commercials!)

2   What stands behind the message that blips onto and off of our television screens before we have time to get to the kitchen and back? Months of planning; hundreds of interviews with potential users of the product; hours of writing; dozens of actors, directors, and technicians; days of filming; and hundreds of thousands of dollars in payments to the television networks that will run the ad.

3   Take for example a recent commercial for a certain brand of cough drops. The manufacturer of the cough drops spent four months trying to think of a way to boost sales. After several surveys of cough drop users, the company decided to market a strawberry-flavored lozenge. Further surveys identified the typical users of the strawberry-flavored cough drop as persons between the ages of 15 and 30. This information was important in planning the content and style of the commercial (fast-paced and upbeat, with colorful graphics and lively music) and in determining when to air it (during situation comedies, prime-time dramas, and music specials).

4   The creative team at the advertising agency that handled the cough drop company's account then took over. After hours of discussion and writing, they came up with six scripts, from which the client chose two. One involved a young woman pulling a strawberry out of a box of cough drops. The outline, or <u>storyboard</u>, for the commercial looked deceptively simple: four sketches and a few lines of 'voice-over.' Yet these few words and images (just enough to fill 15 seconds) had been carefully selected to convey crucial information about the product: its effectiveness in suppressing coughs and soothing sore throats, the absence of sugar, and its strawberry flavor.

5   Turning this carefully calculated script into an effective commercial involved finding just the right actor: a young woman who would be attractive to the target audience and who could make her positive response to the cough drops look convincing. Forty-two actors were auditioned; one was chosen.

6   The actor wasn't the only element of the commercial that had to go through an audition. More than a hundred outfits were inspected before one was chosen for her to wear, and hundreds of strawberries had to be sorted through.

7   The filming began at 9:30 one morning. "All" the actor had to do was to open a box of cough drops, pull out a strawberry and munch on it. Yet her movements and facial expressions had to be just right, and achieving that perfection took three hours and 72 shootings, or 'takes.'

8   Even then—shooting completed—the job was far from done. Thousands of feet of film had to be reduced to a compact 45 feet of finished commercial. Using million-dollar, computerized equipment, the producer, writer, and art director selected the best two takes and mixed images and sound to produce a polished final product. The result? A simple, effortless-looking little film that shows none of the tremendous effort that went into producing it, but which should justify all of that time, creativity, and expense by boosting cough drop sales.

13. Which of the following best expresses the main idea of the selection?

A. Although most television commercials look simple and straightforward, they typically take a great deal of time, effort, and money to produce.

B. Because the development of television commercials involves so many steps, commercials are among the most difficult and complex types of film to produce.

C. The major factors in developing a successful television commercial are good planning of style and content and careful selection of actors.

D. A reduction in the average length of television commercials has made their development more complex and costly than it used to be.

14. At the end of the first paragraph, the writer includes a parenthetical remark about the 7½-second mini-commercials currently seen in Japan and Europe. The writer most likely includes this information to help readers understand that:

A. the United States has fallen behind its Japanese and European competitors in some important areas of development.

B. television commercials seen in the United States may well become even shorter than they are at present.

C. television commercials in other parts of the world use even more advanced technology than that used in the United States.

D. the quality of a television commercial is not necessarily related to its length.

15. According to information included in the selection, which of the following occurs first in the development of a television commercial?

A. developing alternative scripts

B. determining the general style of the commercial

C. selecting an actor or actors

D. identifying the commercial's target audience

16. Which of the following is the best assessment of the writer's credibility?

A. The approving tone of the selection and the author's thinly disguised enthusiasm for television commercials raise serious questions about his or her credibility.

B. Although readers are unable to assess the representativeness of the case study discussed in the selection, the considerable amount of factual detail presented inspires faith in the writer's credibility.

C. The writer's credibility is questionable because the selection devotes more attention to actors than to the technical personnel involved in making a commercial.

D. Although the selection provides useful information about the procedures involved in producing a television commercial, the writer's credibility is weakened by a failure to say more about the costs.

17. Which of the following sets of topics would best organize the information in the selection?

A. I. Television commercials around the world
II. Cough drop commercials as an example of television commercials in the United States

B. I. Recent trends in television commercials
II. Steps in making a television commercial

C. I. The role of networks and manufacturers in the production of television commercials
II. Professional personnel required for developing television commercials

D. I. Characteristics of television commercials
II. Goals of television commercials

18. Which of the following best defines the word storyboard as it is used in paragraph 4 of the selection?

A. a written description of a film's setting and characters

B. an enlarged script placed so that actors can read the words as they perform

C. a sequence of pictures and text illustrating the major segments of a film

D. the scenery used as a backdrop for the main action in a film

---

Read the selection adapted from *Child Development* by Neil J. Salkind and
Sueann Robinson Ambron. Then answer the six questions that follow.

Children's Fears

1   Children's fears come and go, but most children experience similar types of fears at approximately the same age. For toddlers, the worst fears are often associated with separation and change. Toddlers want their own mommy, daddy, spoon, chair, and bed. They are profoundly conservative little people. The most daring toddlers feel content if they can hold onto what they already know. Yet, children's fears are a useful index of their development. Fear of strangers appears to be a consequence of their first specific attachment, and its ending is a sign that they have acquired a more inclusive schema of faces and people in general. A child who is afraid of cats but not of rabbits evidently can differentiate one small animal from another. Fear of a particular person implies recognition of that person.

2   Just as children learn to fear things, they can learn what not to fear. As long as fears do not become too intense, a child's natural impulse to explore and discover things will be of help. Parents can be of assistance, both in overcoming fears and in preventing their development. They can prepare a child through play, stories, and happy prognostications for dealing with new situations that might be overwhelming; give prompt and unstinted comfort after a frightening experience or a bad dream; provide a night-light if the child is afraid of the dark; and devise ways in which a child can be gently and gradually—not abruptly—encouraged to take another look at feared objects and situations. Avoidance of the feared object reinforces the fear, and the fear becomes increasingly intense. Children's fears should be taken seriously, never ridiculed or

dismissed as silly or babyish. Often, if the caregiver can get the child to explain exactly what it is that is so frightening, the child can be reassured. The one thing not to do is force children into confronting a feared situation before they are ready to do so.

3   Almost all children are afraid of something and, as with adults, these fears are often well-grounded. If we are in an open field during a thunderstorm, we probably have good reason to be afraid of lightning.

4   But occasionally fear of something gets out of control and becomes a phobia. A phobia is an irrational fear of something. A child may be afraid of the dark and hesitate to go up the stairs alone at night. But when the child refuses to remain in a place where there is no light, such as the movies or his or her bedroom, the fear is taking too great a toll on the child's development.

5   There are many different ways that phobias are treated in children. One of these techniques, commonly referred to as contact desensitization, is a behavioral technique designed to eliminate unnatural fears. The basic premise of the technique is that any fear is learned, and that anything that is learned can be unlearned. If a child is overly sensitive to something like water, for example, the gradual introduction of the feared object coupled with a pleasant experience can help reduce the strength of the fear, making it more manageable.

6   This exact technique was used in one study with fifty snake-avoidant children ranging in age from three to nine years. To see which technique was most effective, the fifty children were divided into five groups:

A. Members of the "contact desensitization group" were told about snakes and how to approach them, were encouraged by an adult to approach a snake, were given praise when they tried, and watched one adult hold the snake.

B. The "contact desensitization without touch group" received all that group A did, but no one touched the snake.

C. The "verbal input plus modeling group" received verbal input and modeling (when the adult touched the snake).

D. The "verbal input only" received only verbal assurances from the adult.

E. Finally, one group of children received no treatment and, hence, was called the "no treatment group."

7   The researchers used something called the Behavior Avoidance Test to see if there was a reduction in avoidance of the snake. Here, an adult reads a series of instructions to each child, asking him or her to do things such as approach the snake, pet it, pick it up, and hold it. The instructions go from little contact with the snake to increasing contact. This way the researchers can see which group of children has the most contact.

8   The results showed that 82 percent of the children in the contact desensitization group reduced their fear of snakes. Children in the other groups also reduced their fear, but not as dramatically.

9   Fears are something we all have to live with. When they get out of hand, a technique like the one we described here can be very useful in assisting a child through a difficult experience.

◆ ◆ ◆ ◆ ◆ ◆ ◆

19. Which of the following details best supports the authors' point that children can be helped to overcome fears?

A. Fear of strangers usually ends when a child develops a more inclusive schema of faces and people.

B. Children should never be forced to confront a feared situation before they are ready to do so.

C. A child can sometimes be reassured after a caregiver has encouraged the child to explain the fear.

D. Many of children's fears are well-grounded and reasonable.

20. In paragraph 1, the sentence "The most daring toddlers feel content if they can hold onto what they already know" can best be described as having which of the following effects on the reader?

A. It focuses the reader's attention on the wide variety of children's fears.

B. It informs the reader of a specific type of fear.

C. It helps the reader understand children's fears from an adult perspective.

D. It allows the reader to decide how best to handle children's fears.

21. Based on the information presented in this selection, a child can best be helped to overcome a fear of riding an escalator by:

    A. talking with an adult about why riding an escalator is frightening.

    B. watching an adult ride an escalator, being encouraged to try it, and being praised if he or she does.

    C. being allowed to avoid escalators until the fear has diminished naturally.

    D. watching an adult ride an escalator and receiving verbal assurances from the adult that it is safe.

22. Which of the following details from the passage is *least* relevant to the authors' main topic?

    A. Parents can help prevent the development of fears in their child.

    B. Just as children learn to fear things, they can learn what not to fear.

    C. A child's fears should be taken seriously; they should not be ridiculed.

    D. In one study of children's fears, fifty children were divided into five groups.

23. Which three main topics would best help outline the information in this selection?

    A. I.   Universality of children's fears
        II. Helping children overcome fears
        III. Children's phobias and their treatment

    B. I.   Types of fears in children
        II. Treatment of fears in children
        III. Comparison of fears in children and adults

    C. I.   Normal fears experienced by toddlers
        II. Normal fears experienced by older children
        III. Phobias experienced by children

    D. I.   Children's fears of people
        II. Children's fears of situations
        III. Contact desensitization as a treatment for phobias

24. What is the meaning of the word <u>index</u> as it is used in paragraph 1 of this selection?

    A. an indicator or measurement of something

    B. a list or catalog of information

    C. an object used to point or indicate

    D. a relation or ratio of one quantity to another

> Read the selection adapted from "The Language We Know" (1987)
> by Simon J. Ortiz. Then answer the six questions that follow.

Writing as a Native American

1   My writing in my late teens and early adulthood was fashioned after the U.S. short stories and poetry taught in the high schools of the 1940s and 1950s, but by the 1960s, after I had gone to college and dropped out and served in the military, I began to develop topics and themes from my Native American background. The experience in my village of Deetziyamah and Acoma Pueblo was readily accessible. I had grown up within the oral tradition of speech, social and religious ritual, elders' counsel and advice, countless and endless stories, everyday events, and the visual art that was symbolically representative of life all around. My mother was a potter of the well-known Acoma clayware, a traditional art form that had been passed to her from her mother and the generations of mothers before. My father carved figures from wood and did beadwork. This was not unusual, as Native American people know; there was always some kind of artistic endeavor that people set themselves to, although they did not necessarily articulate it as "Art" in the sense of Western civilization. One lived and expressed an artful life, whether it was in ceremonial singing and dancing, architecture, painting, speaking, or in the way one's social-cultural life was structured. When I turned my attention to my own heritage, I did so because this was my identity, the substance of who I was, and I wanted to write about what that meant. My desire was to write about the integrity and dignity of a Native American identity, and at the same time I wanted to look at what this was within the context of an America that had too often denied its Native American heritage.

2   To a great extent my writing has a natural political-cultural bent simply because I was nurtured intellectually and emotionally within an atmosphere of Native American resistance. . . . The Acoma Pueblo, despite losing much of their land and surrounded by a foreign civilization, have not lost sight of their native heritage. This is the factual case with most other Native American peoples, and the clear explanation for this has been the fight-back we have found it necessary to wage. At times, in the past, it was outright armed struggle . . . ; currently, it is often in the legal arena, and it is in the field of literature. In 1981, when I was invited to the White House for an event celebrating American poets and poetry, I did not immediately accept the invitation. I questioned myself about the possibility that I was merely being exploited as an Indian, and I hedged against accepting. But then I recalled the elders going among our people in the poor days of the 1950s, asking for donations—a dollar here and there, a sheep, perhaps a piece of pottery—in order to finance a trip to the nation's capital. They were to make another countless appeal on behalf of our people, to demand justice, to reclaim lost land even though there was only spare hope they would be successful. I went to the White House realizing that I was to do no less than they and those who had fought in the Pueblo Revolt of 1680, and I read my poems and sang songs that were later described as "guttural" by a Washington, D.C., newspaper. I suppose it is more or less understandable why such a view of Native American literature is held by many, and it is also clear why there should be a political stand taken in my writing and those of my sister and brother Native American writers.

3   The 1960s and afterward have been an invigorating and liberating period for Native American people. It has been only a little more than twenty years since Native American writers began to write and publish extensively, but we are writing and publishing more and more; we can only go forward. We come from an ageless, continuing oral tradition that informs us of our values, concepts, and notions as native people, and it is amazing how much of this tradition is ingrained so deeply in our

contemporary writing, considering the brutal efforts of cultural repression that was not long ago outright U.S. policy. We were not to speak our languages, practice our spiritual beliefs, or accept the values of our past generations; and we were discouraged from pressing for our natural rights as Native American human beings. In spite of the fact that there is to some extent the same repression today, we persist and insist in living, believing, hoping, loving, speaking, and writing as Native Americans.

◆ ◆ ◆ ◆ ◆ ◆ ◆

25. Which of the following statements best expresses the main idea of paragraph 1 of this selection?

A. The artful nature of Native American life compels the author to explore and write about that heritage.

B. Art is an important part of Native American life and should be a part of everyone's existence.

C. The author remembers his childhood, especially his parents and the elders in his community, in a very positive way.

D. A desire to return to traditional Native American values led the author to write about Native American issues.

26. The effect of the quoted word "guttural" as the author uses it in the second paragraph of the selection is to:

A. convey the sound of the Acoma Pueblo language to readers who are unfamiliar with it.

B. emphasize the dramatic effect on the White House audience of the author's reading of his poems and performance of traditional Pueblo songs.

C. describe most accurately how the author felt about his White House reading of his poems.

D. communicate the newspaper's lack of understanding and respect for the author's presentation.

27. Which of the following caused the author to change his mind about declining his invitation to the White House?

   A. He realized that he had not been invited to the event as a representative of Native Americans.

   B. He remembered the sacrifices that his ancestors had made for the privilege of going there, even if only to be ignored.

   C. He was eager to read his poetry to an audience of other poets and literary critics.

   D. He wanted his writing and the writing of other Native American men and women to take on a more political tone.

28. Which of the following assumptions most influenced the author's main argument in this selection?

   A. Literature can be a powerful tool for asserting the cultural values and political rights of ethnic groups.

   B. The artistic traditions of Native American peoples are similar to those of European cultures.

   C. All writings produced by Native Americans express, either directly or indirectly, a political position.

   D. The major responsibility of Native American writers is to celebrate and preserve the cultural traditions of their people.

29. Which of the following topic lists best summarizes the main points of the selection?

   A. —Arts of Native American family
      —Invitation to White House
      —Brotherhood of Native American writers

   B. —Native American background as topic for writing
      —Importance of attending White House poetry event
      —Vitality of contemporary Native American writing

   C. —Native American writing
      —Achievements of ancestors
      —Future of Native Americans

   D. —Writing in 1940s, 1950s, and 1960s
      —Involvement of Native Americans in many forms of art
      —Writing about Native American heritage

30. What is the meaning of the word spare as it is used in paragraph 2 of the selection?

   A. frugal

   B. extra

   C. meager

   D. free

Read the passage below. Then answer the questions that follow.

Bacteria Farming

1   Most people consider bacteria dangerous. After all, these microorganisms cause a host of serious human diseases, including tuberculosis, typhoid fever, pneumonia, and food poisoning. In fact, however, only a small percentage of bacteria cause diseases, while many bacteria are actually beneficial to humans. For example, doctors use bacteria to produce vaccines and other medicines. Bacteria are also critical to many industrial processes, from fermenting wine to recycling wastes, and scientists use bacteria to study many of the biological processes common to all living things.

2   With such a wide variety of economic and scientific applications, it is no surprise that several laboratories around the United States grow and sell bacteria as a crop. These laboratories use specialized farming techniques to produce one of the nation's most valuable biological commodities.

3   Like plants, bacteria have specific growth requirements. In particular, they need a place to grow and they need a supply of nutrients. Bacteria may be cultivated in containers ranging from small test tubes to giant steel tanks. The organisms are placed in a container along with a nutritionally balanced liquid or jelly, called a culture medium, which provides vitamins, minerals, and fluids to the growing bacteria. The growth container and culture medium must be kept at a constant temperature that is appropriate for the type of bacteria being cultivated. Most bacteria used in medicine and industry grow best between 20° and 45°C.

4   In a closed container, bacteria exhibit a definite growth pattern. The figure shows a typical bacterial growth curve. All bacteria follow this pattern, a fact that is very important to anyone who wants to cultivate them in large numbers.

FIGURE 1

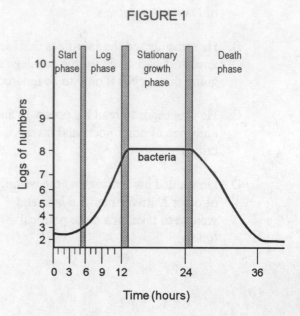

5   When bacteria are first placed in a growth container, they must adapt to their new environment, and growth is slow while they are making this adjustment. This period is called the "start phase" of the bacterial growth cycle. At the end of this phase, as the bacteria become accustomed to their new living conditions, they begin to grow and reproduce rapidly. During the second phase, called the "log phase," a population explosion occurs. In a large tank, millions of new bacteria may be produced every hour during this phase. Eventually, however, the bacterial population reaches the maximum size possible, given the limitations of the growth container. At this point, the bacteria enter the "stationary growth phase," during which they continue to reproduce, but at a slower rate. After a time, the bacteria use up their supply of nutrients and their wastes accumulate in the growth container. The final period in the growth cycle, called the "death phase," occurs when the bacteria begin to die faster than they reproduce.

6   People who grow bacteria for science and industry take advantage of this unique growth cycle. Bacteria are harvested during the "stationary growth phase," yielding a good crop of usable organisms. By carefully monitoring the growth pattern, bacteria farmers can also decide when to add more nutrients to the culture medium or to transfer the bacteria to new growth containers. In this way, they can prevent large losses during the "death phase." By applying a knowledge of the growth requirements and patterns of bacteria, these modern day agriculturalists are able to help everyone derive the maximum benefit from these versatile organisms.

◆ ◆ ◆ ◆ ◆ ◆ ◆ ◆

31. Which of the following statements from the selection best expresses the main idea of the first paragraph?

   A. Most people consider bacteria dangerous.

   B. Only a small percentage of bacteria cause diseases, while many bacteria are actually beneficial to humans.

   C. These microorganisms cause a host of serious human diseases.

   D. Bacteria are critical to many industrial processes, from fermenting wine to recycling wastes, and scientists use bacteria to study many of the biological processes common to all living things.

32. The writer's main purpose in this selection is to:

   A. explain how bacteria are cultivated.

   B. identify harmful and beneficial forms of bacteria.

   C. compare methods of growing bacteria.

   D. demonstrate the beneficial uses of bacteria.

33. According to information presented in the selection, which of the following would most likely hasten the "death phase" of the bacterial growth cycle?

   A. transferring the bacterial population to a smaller growth container

   B. neglecting to monitor growth during the "start phase" of growth cycle

   C. increasing the amount of liquids in the culture medium

   D. failing to make adjustments in the temperature of the culture medium

34. Ideas presented in the selection are most influenced by which of the following assumptions?

   A. Bacteria farming is more useful and profitable than most other types of farming.

   B. All organisms exhibit similar growth rates.

   C. The greatest strides in medicine and industry have come about through the use of bacteria.

   D. Scientific knowledge often has important commercial applications.

35. According to the graph, a bacterial
    population begins to decrease in size after
    approximately how many hours of
    incubation?

    A. 6

    B. 12

    C. 24

    D. 36

36. Which of the following best defines the
    word <u>yielding</u> as it is used in the last
    paragraph?

    A. surrendering

    B. producing

    C. giving up

    D. granting

Read the passage below. Then answer the questions that follow.

The Road to Civil Rights

1   The period immediately following the Civil War was a time of great hope for Black Americans. It was also a time of momentous constitutional change, as the nation sought to extend those liberties enshrined in the Bill of Rights to all Americans, Black and White. The Thirteenth Amendment abolished slavery, the Fourteenth Amendment guaranteed all citizens equal protection of the laws, and the Fifteenth Amendment declared that no one could be denied the right to vote "on account of race, color, or previous condition of servitude." In subsequent decades, however, it became all too apparent, at least to Blacks and an unfortunately small number of concerned White Americans, that the promises contained in these amendments were not being honored. By century's end, racial segregation was still an inescapable fact of American social life, in the North as well as the South. At the same time, most southern states had adopted devices such as the poll tax, literacy test, and White primary to strip Blacks of their right to vote.

2   The struggle to close the gap between constitutional promise and social reality would pass through two important stages. In the first stage, organizations such as the NAACP worked through the courts to restore the meaning of the Reconstruction-era amendments. These efforts <u>culminated</u> in the 1954 Supreme Court decision in *Brown v. Board of Education of Topeka,* which outlawed segregation in public schools. The decision also stated that separate facilities were inherently unequal, thus providing a legal basis for subsequent suits to desegregate other kinds of public accommodations.

3   As it turned out, the principles enunciated in the *Brown* decision were more easily stated than enforced. Court orders to desegregate public schools often encountered massive resistance. Seeing this, Blacks and their supporters began to adopt new tactics. As they did, the struggle for Black rights entered its second stage, a stage that would be characterized by direct action rather than legal challenges, and would be played out in the streets rather than the courts. In turning to civil disobedience, leaders such as Martin Luther King, Jr. made it possible for all victims of racial injustice to take action in a way that was direct and forceful, but also peaceable. And through the power of their moral example, they soon won widespread support for their cause. In response to these developments, Congress took steps to restore the full meaning of the Fourteenth and Fifteenth Amendments by passing the Civil Rights Act of 1964 and the Voting Rights Act of 1965.

4   The enactment of these measures by no means marked the end of the civil rights movement. There was still much to be done. Yet the passage of these acts nevertheless had far-reaching significance. The acts not only helped correct social inequities that had persisted far too long, they also showed that the Constitution means something, however long it may sometimes take to give substance to that meaning. This is no small matter in a nation of laws.

◆ ◆ ◆ ◆ ◆ ◆ ◆ ◆

37. Which of the following statements from the selection best expresses the main idea of the first paragraph?

A. The period immediately following the Civil War was a time of great hope for Black Americans.

B. The Thirteenth Amendment abolished slavery, the Fourteenth Amendment guaranteed all citizens equal protection of the laws, and the Fifteenth Amendment declared that no one could be denied the right to vote "on account of race, color, or previous condition of servitude."

C. In subsequent decades, it became all too apparent that the promises contained in the Thirteenth, Fourteenth, and Fifteenth Amendments were not being honored.

D. Most southern states had adopted devices such as the poll tax, literacy test, and White primary to strip Blacks of their right to vote.

38. The content of paragraph 3 indicates the writer's belief that:

A. the first stage of the civil rights movement was a failure.

B. Supreme Court decisions have less influence on United States society than Congressional actions.

C. social movements are able to influence the political process.

D. the costs of civil disobedience sometimes outweigh its benefits.

39. According to the selection, many communities refused to enforce the *Brown* decision. Blacks and their supporters tried to overcome this problem by:

A. demanding that Congress pass additional civil rights legislation.

B. engaging in nonviolent direct action.

C. selecting new leaders for the civil rights movement.

D. requesting the assistance of the Supreme Court.

40. Which of the following assumptions most influenced the views expressed by the writer in this selection?

A. Nations that profess a belief in the rule of law should ensure that all laws are observed.

B. Social injustice can be eliminated most effectively through amendments to the Constitution.

C. As a rule, people must be forcibly compelled to respect the rights of others.

D. Without forceful leaders, social movements are unlikely to gain broad support.

41. Which of the following statements best summarizes the information presented in the selection?

   A. After the Civil War, the Thirteenth, Fourteenth, and Fifteenth Amendments were adopted to protect and extend the rights of Black Americans. By century's end, however, racial segregation was still an inescapable fact of American social life. It would remain so until the 1954 Supreme Court decision in *Brown v. Board of Education of Topeka,* which called for the full desegregation of all kinds of public accommodations.

   B. During the past century, there have been significant changes in the leadership of the civil rights movement. Organizations such as the NAACP spearheaded the initial phase of the struggle for Black rights. As legal action gave way to direct action, however, leadership came primarily from individuals like Martin Luther King, Jr.

   C. Adopted immediately after the Civil War, the Thirteenth Amendment abolished slavery, the Fourteenth Amendment guaranteed Blacks equal protection of the laws, and the Fifteenth Amendment gave Blacks the right to vote. Blacks and their supporters have long struggled to give meaning to these amendments.

   D. Efforts by Black Americans and their supporters to close the gap between the constitutional promises of the Reconstruction-era amendments and the realities of American social life passed through two important stages. The first stage, which focused on legal action, culminated in the *Brown* decision of 1954. This stage was followed by a direct action phase that resulted in the passage of the civil rights acts of the sixties.

42. Which of the following best defines the word culminated as it is used in paragraph 2 of the selection?

   A. initiated a lengthy process

   B. completed the initial phase of a project

   C. began a period of decline

   D. reached the highest point of achievement

MATHEMATICS SECTION

The mathematics section of the test consists of 48 multiple-choice questions. Read each question carefully and choose the ONE best answer. Record your answer on the answer sheet in the space that corresponds to the question number. Completely fill in the space having the same letter as the answer you have chosen.

Appropriate definitions and formulas are provided below and on the following three pages to help you perform the calculations on the test.

Definitions and Formulas

Definitions

$=$	is equal to		$\perp$	is perpendicular to
$\neq$	is not equal to		$\parallel$	is parallel to
$\approx$	is approximately equal to		$\sim$	is similar to
$>$	is greater than		$\cong$	is congruent to
$<$	is less than		$\ncong$	is not congruent to
$\geq$	is greater than or equal to		$\pm$	plus or minus
$\leq$	is less than or equal to		$\overline{AB}$	line segment joining points A and B
π	≈ 3.14		$\overleftrightarrow{AB}$	line containing points A and B
$\angle$	angle		$m(\overline{AB})$	length of $\overline{AB}$
$m\angle$	measure of angle		AB	length of $\overline{AB}$
$\lrcorner$	right angle		$\lvert\overline{AB}\rvert$	length of $\overline{AB}$
$\triangle$	triangle		$\frac{a}{b}$ or a:b	ratio of a to b

Abbreviations for Units of Measurement

U.S. Standard   Metric

		U.S. Standard			Metric
Distance	in.	inch		m	meter
	ft.	foot		km	kilometer
	mi.	mile		cm	centimeter
				mm	millimeter
Volume	gal.	gallon		L	liter
	qt.	quart		mL	milliliter
	oz.	ounce		cc	cubic centimeter
Weight/Mass	lb.	pound		g	gram
	oz.	ounce		kg	kilogram
				mg	milligram
Temperature	°F	degree Fahrenheit		°C	degree Celsius
Time	sec.	second			
	min.	minute			
	hr.	hour			
Speed	mph	miles per hour			

Conversions for Units of Measurement

U.S. Standard

Length	12 inches = 1 foot
	3 feet = 1 yard
	5280 feet = 1 mile
Volume (liquid)	8 ounces = 1 cup
	2 cups = 1 pint
	2 pints = 1 quart
	4 quarts = 1 gallon
Weight	16 ounces = 1 pound
	2000 pounds = 1 ton

Metric

Length	10 millimeters = 1 centimeter
	100 centimeters = 1 meter
	1000 meters = 1 kilometer
Volume	1000 milliliters = 1 liter
	1000 liters = 1 kiloliter
Weight	1000 milligrams = 1 gram
	1000 grams = 1 kilogram

Time   60 seconds = 1 minute
60 minutes = 1 hour
24 hours = 1 day

Formulas

Quadratic formula: If $ax^2 + bx + c = 0$, and $a \neq 0$,

$$x = \frac{-b \pm \sqrt{b^2 - 4ac}}{2a}$$

Line

$$\text{Slope} = m = \frac{y_2 - y_1}{x_2 - x_1}$$

Slope-intercept form for the equation of a line
$$y = mx + b$$

Point-slope form for the equation of a line
$$y - y_1 = m(x - x_1)$$

$$\text{Distance} = \sqrt{(x_2 - x_1)^2 + (y_2 - y_1)^2}$$

$$\text{Midpoint} = \left(\frac{x_1 + x_2}{2}, \frac{y_1 + y_2}{2}\right)$$

Distance
$$d = rt$$

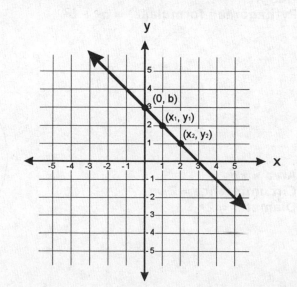

Geometric Figures

Square
Area = s^2
Perimeter = $4s$

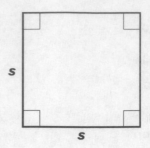

Rectangle

Area = ℓw

Perimeter = $2\ell + 2w$

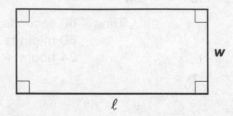

Triangle
Area = $\frac{1}{2} bh$

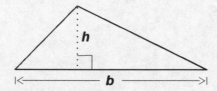

Right triangle
Pythagorean formula: $c^2 = a^2 + b^2$

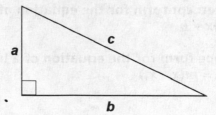

Circle
Area = πr^2
Circumference = $2\pi r$
Diameter = $2r$

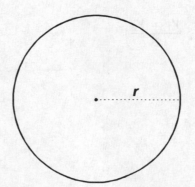

Sphere

Surface area $= 4\pi r^2$

Volume $= \dfrac{4}{3}\pi r^3$

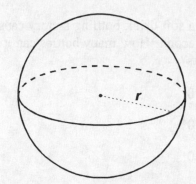

Cube

Surface area $= 6s^2$

Volume $= s^3$

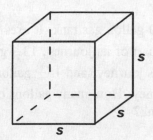

Rectangular solid

Surface area $= 2\ell w + 2\ell h + 2wh$

Volume $= \ell wh$

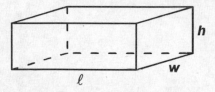

Right circular cylinder

Surface area $= 2\pi rh + 2\pi r^2$

Volume $= \pi r^2 h$

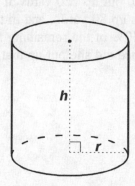

1. A machine in a soft drink bottling factory caps
    3 bottles per second. How many bottles can it
    cap in 15 hours?

    A. 2.7×10^3

    B. 1.6×10^4

    C. 1.8×10^4

    D. 1.6×10^5

2. A truck has a full 50-gallon gas tank. It uses $7\frac{1}{4}$
    gallons on the first part of its journey, $13\frac{1}{2}$ gallons on
    the second part of its journey, and $15\frac{1}{4}$ gallons on the
    third part of its journey. How many gallons of gas
    remain in the gas tank?

    A. 14

    B. $14\frac{1}{4}$

    C. 15

    D. 36

3. A rancher is planning to put up 220 yards of fencing.
    In the morning she puts up 80 yards, and in the
    afternoon she puts up 40% of the remaining fence.
    What percent of the fence did she put up that day?

    A. 36%

    B. 51%

    C. 62%

    D. 76%

4. During a bike-a-thon a local company pledges to
    donate $1.25 for every $4.00 pledged by the public. If
    the public pledges a total of $156.00 dollars per mile,
    how much will the company donate per mile?

    A. $2.75

    B. $48.75

    C. $195.00

    D. $499.20

5. Use the pie charts below to answer the question that
    follows.

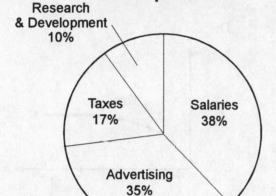

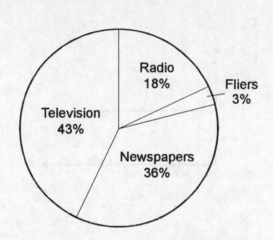

    The first pie chart represents a company's
    expenditures, and the second pie chart shows a
    breakdown of the company's advertising expenditures.
    What percent of the company's expenditures is spent
    on radio advertising?

    A.   6.3%

    B.   11.7%

    C.   18.0%

    D.   35.0%

6. Scientists have stocked Wilson's pond with a species of fish. The scientists note that the population has steadily decreased over a period of time until the population is approximately half the number of fish originally stocked. If the number of fish are plotted on the y-axis and the amount of time on the x-axis, which of the following could result?

A.

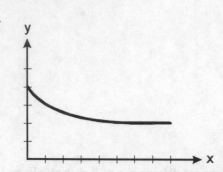

B.

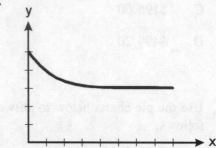

C.

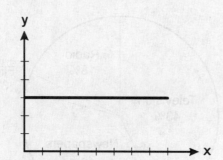

D.

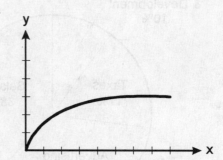

7.   A student has received scores of 88, 82, and 84 on
     three quizzes. If tests count twice as much as quizzes,
     what is the lowest score the student can get on the next
     test to achieve an average score of at least 70?

     A.   13

     B.   48

     C.   70

     D.   96

8.   Use the distribution curves below to answer the
     question that follows.

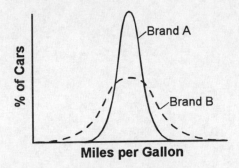

     The distribution curves above show data on the gas
     mileage for two different brands of car. Which of the
     following correctly analyzes the information presented
     in these distributions?

     A.   the mean gas mileage of brand A is greater than
           the mean gas mileage of brand B

     B.   data was collected for more cars of brand A than
           of brand B

     C.   brand A cars have smaller variability in gas
           mileage than brand B cars

     D.   brand A cars get poorer gas mileage than brand
           B cars

9. Use the graph below to answer the question that follows.

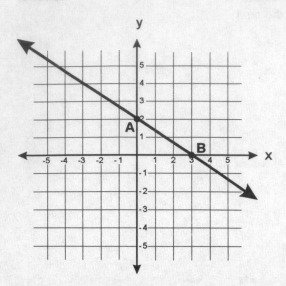

Which of the following equations represents line *AB*?

A. $y = -\frac{2}{3}x + 2$

B. $y = \frac{3}{2}x + 3$

C. $y = -2x + 3$

D. $y = 3x + 2$

10. What is the slope of the line passing through $(0,-1)$ and $(3,-2)$?

A. $\frac{1}{3}$

B. $-\frac{1}{3}$

C. 3

D. -3

11. Which of the following is an equation of the line passing through (–2,4) and (6,0)?

A. $y = \frac{1}{2}x + 3$

B. $y = -\frac{1}{2}x + 3$

C. $y = -2x + 3$

D. $y = -\frac{1}{2}x + 6$

12. Use the graph below to answer the question that follows.

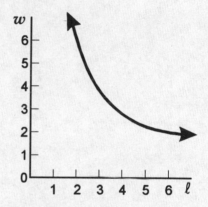

The graph shows how the width (*w*) depends on the length (*l*) for a rectangle of constant area. What is the value of w for $l = 8$?

A. 1

B. $\frac{3}{2}$

C. 4

D. 96

13. If $-\frac{1}{3}x + 7 = 16$, what is the value of $2x + 1$?

A. $^-5$

B. $^-27$

C. $^-53$

D. $^-137$

14. If $5r = 9t + 7$, what is the value of t?

A. $t = \frac{5r-7}{9}$

B. $t = \frac{5r+7}{9}$

C. $t = \frac{5r}{9} - 7$

D. $t = \frac{5r}{9} + 7$

15. What is the solution to the system of equations
$x^2 - x + 6 = y$ and $2x + 2y = 36$?

A. $(0,6), (9,9)$

B. $(2\sqrt{3}, 18 - 2\sqrt{3}), (-2\sqrt{3}, 18 + 2\sqrt{3})$

C. an infinite number of solutions

D. no solution

16.   Which of the following graphs shows the solution of
        $y + 2x + 2 = 0$ and $y = x^2 - 9$?

A.

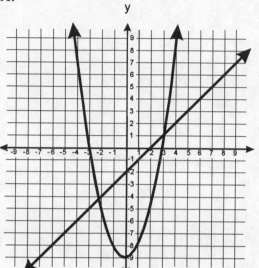

B.

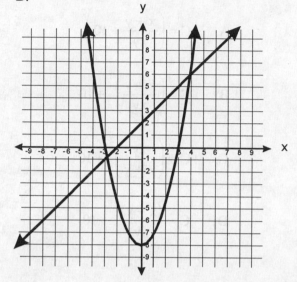

C.

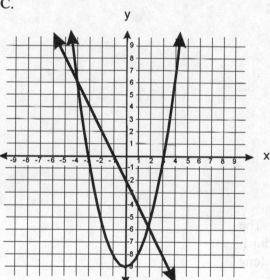

D.

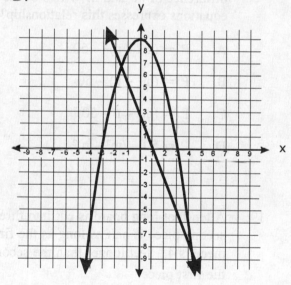

17. C is 10 more than the square of the quotient of the sum of x and y and the product of x and y. Which equation expresses this relationship?

A. $C = \left(\dfrac{x+y}{xy} + 10\right)^2$

B. $C = \left(\dfrac{x+y}{xy}\right)^2 + 10$

C. $C = \left(\dfrac{xy}{x+y}\right)^2 + 10$

D. $C = \dfrac{(x+y)^2}{xy} + 10$

18. The number P is 50 less than the square of the difference of m^2 and n. Which of the following equations expresses this relationship?

A. $P = (m^2 - n)^2 - 50$

B. $P = (m^2 - n) - 50$

C. $P = (m^2 - n - 50)^2$

D. $P = 50 - (m^2 - n)^2$

19. A ten-foot-long board is cut into three pieces. The second piece is half as long as the first. The third piece is $4\frac{1}{2}$ feet longer than the second. How long is the first piece?

A. $1\frac{1}{10}$ feet

B. $2\frac{1}{5}$ feet

C. $2\frac{3}{4}$ feet

D. $3\frac{1}{3}$ feet

20. Angel has $1.80 in nickels, dimes, and quarters in his pocket. He has twice as many quarters as nickels. The number of dimes in his pocket is one more than the number of nickels and quarters put together. Which set of three equations could be used to determine how many nickels, dimes, and quarters Angel has?

A. $5N + 10D + 25Q = 180$
    $Q = 2N$
    $D = N + Q + 1$

B. $5N + 10D + 25Q = 180$
    $N = 2Q$
    $D = N + Q + 1$

C. $5N + 10D + 25Q = 1.80$
    $Q = 2N$
    $D + 1 = N + Q$

D. $0.05N + 0.10D + 0.75Q = 180$
    $Q = 2N$
    $D + 1 = N + Q$

21. Robin Chang collected $175 in the second week of her school charity drive. This was $35 more than she collected in the first week. How much did she collect in the two weeks?

A. $210

B. $315

C. $385

D. $420

22. One factor of $x^2 - 2x - 24$ is:

A. $(x - 24)$

B. $(x - 4)$

C. $(x - 6)$

D. $(x + 6)$

23. $\dfrac{x^2 - x}{x^2 + 3x + 2} \div \dfrac{x^2 + 2x}{x^2 - 1} =$

   A. $\dfrac{x^2}{x^2 + 2x + 1}$

   B.   1

   C. $\dfrac{x^2 - 1}{x^2 - 4}$

   D. $\dfrac{x^2 - 2x + 1}{x^2 + 4x + 4}$

24. $\dfrac{9c}{24cx - 18c^2} =$

   A. $\dfrac{3}{8x - 6c}$

   B. $\dfrac{1}{15x - 9c}$

   C. $\dfrac{8x - 6c}{3}$

   D. $\dfrac{3}{6x - 8c}$

25. $\dfrac{a^{3/2}b^3c^5}{a^2b^{1/3}} \div a^2b^{5/3}d^{1/2} =$

   A. $a^{3/2}b^{13/3}c^5d^{1/2}$

   B. $\dfrac{a^6b^6c^5}{d^{1/2}}$

   C. $\dfrac{a^{3/8}b^{3/2}c^5}{d^{1/2}}$

   D. $\dfrac{bc^5}{a^{5/2}d^{1/2}}$

26. If $f(x) = 2x^2 + \frac{1}{2}x - 4$, what is $f(-\frac{1}{2})$?

    A. $-\frac{13}{4}$

    B.   5

    C. $-\frac{15}{4}$

    D.   3

27. Use the graph below to answer the question that follows.

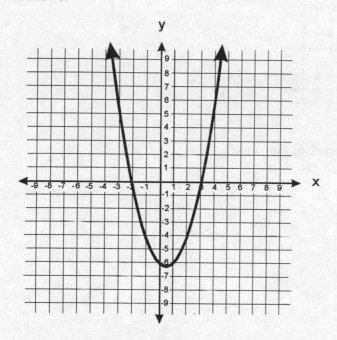

Which equation is represented by this graph?

    A. $y = {}^-x^2 + x + 6$

    B. $y = x^2 - x - 6$

    C. $y = {}^-x^2 - x - 6$

    D. $y = x^2 - x + 6$

28.   Use the graph below to answer the question that
      follows.

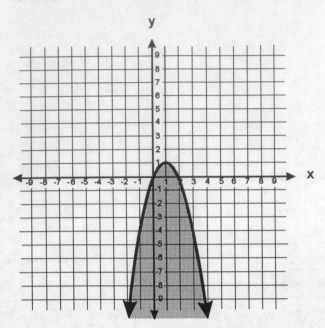

Which of the following inequalities describes the
shaded region?

A. $y \leq -x^2 - 2x$

B. $y > -x^2 + 2x$

C. $y \leq -x^2 + 2x$

D. $y \leq -x^2 + 2x + 2$

29.   Which of the following expressions should be placed in
      each set of parentheses below in order to solve the
      equation by completing the square?

$x^2 + 6x + (?) = 15 + (?)$

A. $\dfrac{3}{2}$

B.   3

C.   6

D.   9

30. Which of the following expressions appear as a step in solving $3x^2 = x - 5$ using the quadratic formula?

A. $\dfrac{-1 \pm \sqrt{61}}{6}$

B. $\dfrac{1 \pm \sqrt{-59}}{6}$

C. $\dfrac{1 \pm \sqrt{61}}{6}$

D. $\dfrac{1 \pm \sqrt{59}}{6}$

31. The height of a rocket in feet is given by the equation $h = 128t - 32t^2$ where t is the time in seconds after it is fired and h is the height in feet. At what time is the rocket at a height of 128 feet?

A. 1 second

B. 2 seconds

C. 3 seconds

D. 4 seconds

32. Use the diagram below to answer the question that follows.

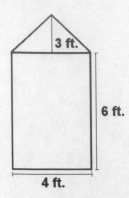

A window is rectangular with a triangular top section. What is the total area of glass needed for the window?

A.   24 square feet

B.   30 square feet

C.   36 square feet

D.   48 square feet

33. Use the diagram below to answer the question that follows.

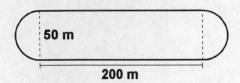

The drawing above represents a race track. The ends are semicircular. What is the approximate distance in meters a runner runs in 8 laps around the track?

A.   560 m

B.   4000 m

C.   4460 m

D.   5710 m

34. An observatory dome is hemispherical in shape with a radius of 18 meters and is built using 12 equal sections. Which of the following formulas describes the surface area of <u>each</u> section?

A. $\frac{1}{12} \cdot \frac{1}{2} \cdot \frac{4}{3} \pi (18)^3$

B. $\frac{1}{12} \cdot 4\pi (18)^2$

C. $\frac{1}{12} \cdot \frac{1}{2} \cdot 4\pi (36)^2$

D. $\frac{1}{12} \cdot \frac{1}{2} \cdot 4\pi (18)^2$

35. Use the diagram below to answer the question that follows.

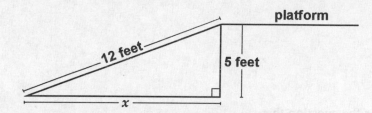

A ramp 12 feet long is leaning against a raised platform which is 5 feet above the ground. What is the distance from the ramp's contact point with the ground and the base of the platform?

A. 7 feet

B. 8.5 feet

C. $\sqrt{119}$ feet

D. 13 feet

36. Figure ABCDE is similar to figure FGHIJ. If AE = 5,
FJ = 20, and BC = 40, what is GH?

A. 10

B. 25

C. 45

D. 160

37. If pentagon ABCDE is similar to pentagon GHIDF,
and DI = 20, CD = 50, and DE = 45, what is DF?

A. 112.5

B. 25

C. 18

D. 15

38. Use the diagram below to answer the question that
follows.

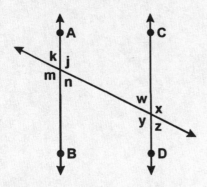

Line AB is parallel to line CD. What is the sum of the
measure of angle k and the measure of angle y?

A. 90°

B. 100°

C. 180°

D. 360°

39.   Use the diagram below to answer the question that
       follows.

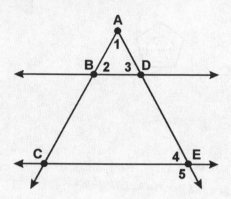

       If △ABD is an equilateral triangle, and line BD is
       parallel to line CE, what is the measure of angle 5?

       A.   60°

       B.   90°

       C.   120°

       D.   180°

40.   Use the statements below to answer the question that
       follows.

       1. All people wearing hats have brown hair.
       2. Some of the people have red hair.
       3. All people who have brown hair like pizza.
       4. People who have red hair like hamburgers.
       5. Carl has brown hair.

       Which of the following statements must be true?

       A.   Carl likes pizza.

       B.   Carl has red hair.

       C.   Carl is wearing a hat.

       D.   Carl likes hamburgers

41. Use the pattern sequence below to answer the question that follows.

    ?

What is the missing design in the sequence?

A.

B.

C.

D.

42. Bess, Tara, Gerard, and Clifton all work for the same company. One is a writer, one a researcher, one an artist, and one an engineer. Use the statements below to answer the question that follows.

   I.   Bess and Gerard eat lunch with the engineer.
  II.   Clifton and Tara carpool with the researcher.
 III.   Gerard works in the same building as the writer and researcher.

Who is the researcher?

A. Tara

B. Bess

C. Clifton

D. Gerard

43.   Use the pattern below to answer the question that
       follows.

What is the missing figure?

A.

B.

C.

D.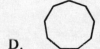

44. Use the diagram below to answer the question that follows.

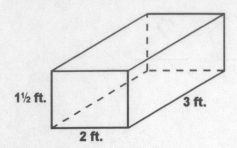

1½ ft.   3 ft.

2 ft.

A rectangular box has dimensions $1\frac{1}{2}$ feet $\times$ 2 feet $\times$ 3 feet. What is the length of the longest object that can be put in the box, if the object can be placed in any position?

A. 3.6 feet

B. 3.9 feet

C. 6.5 feet

D. 15.25 feet

45. Sarah is planning to rent an apartment. She makes the table below in order to compare the monthly cost of renting two different apartments.

Apartment	Rent ($)	Average Monthly Electricity Use (kWh)	Commuting Cost ($/day)
A	575	250	1.50
B	600	225	.75

If electricity costs 5¢ per kilowatt-hour (kWh), which of the following statements is true?

A. Apartment A will be cheaper.

B. Apartment B will be cheaper.

C. Apartments A and B will cost the same per month.

D. She cannot determine which apartment will be cheaper.

Use the information below to answer the three questions that follow.

A water treatment plant is built with three cylindrical tanks to contain the water for a town. Each tank has a radius of 15 feet and a depth of 25 feet.

46. If there are about 7.5 gallons in a cubic foot of water, approximately how many gallons of water can be treated at the plant at any one time?

    A. 7.1×10^3

    B. 1.3×10^5

    C. 4.1×10^5

    D. 4.1×10^6

47. Engineers know that the amount of water lost due to evaporation is directly proportional to the surface area of the holding tanks and that the local climate causes water to evaporate at the rate of about $\frac{1}{10}$ gallon of water per hour for each square foot of water exposed to the air. About how many total gallons of waste water may enter the three tanks each day to maintain full capacity?

    A. 2.1×10^2

    B. 1.7×10^3

    C. 5.0×10^3

    D. 5.0×10^4

48. The three tanks are occasionally cleaned by draining them. The following table gives the depth of water as the tanks are being drained:

Time (hours)	Depth (feet)
0	25
1	17
2	9
3	1

Which of the following equations will give the depth (D) at any time (t)?

A. $D = {}^-8t - 25$

B. $D = -\frac{1}{8}t + 25$

C. $D = 8t + 25$

D. $D = {}^-8t + 25$

WRITING SECTION

The writing section of the test consists of two subsections: a multiple-choice subsection and a writing sample subsection.

MULTIPLE-CHOICE
SUBSECTION

The multiple-choice subsection of the writing test consists of 16 passages. All parts (e.g., sentences, sentence fragments) of the passages are identified by number. The questions refer to the numbered parts of the passages.

After each passage, there are several questions to answer related to the passage. Read each question carefully and choose the ONE best answer. There are a total of 40 questions.

Record your answer on the answer sheet in the space that corresponds to the question number. Completely fill in the space having the same letter as the answer you have chosen.

In the writing section the term "nonstandard" refers to language use that does not conform to the conventions of edited American English.

Read the passage below, written in the style of a student letter to a college newspaper.
Then answer the questions that follow.

¹The parking situation on this campus is truly outrageous. ²Sure, for full-time students who live on campus, convenient parking isn't a big deal. ³But by now everyone—except, evidently, those responsible for campus parking—must know that there are a lot of us commuter students who struggle to balance a job, a family, and academics. ⁴We are not the ones you see strolling leisurely from dormitory to class to dining hall to student hangout. ⁵Nothing in our lives is leisurely: we race from job to classroom to the library to the daycare center to the grocery store and finally, exhaustedly, back home.

⁶We commuter students don't have time to park our cars in lots that require us to walk a mile to get to the nearest classroom building or the library. ⁷Sure, it's nice to look at all those neat lawns and walk along those pretty paths and not see any ugly cars anywhere. ⁸But wake up! ⁹We're here to get an education, not to fritter away our time in some kind of ecological never-never land. ¹⁰I say forget the lawns and build a couple of convenient parking lots for we harried commuters!

◆ ◆ ◆ ◆ ◆ ◆ ◆

1. Which of the following sentences, if added between Parts 3 and 4 of the first paragraph, would be most consistent with the writer's purpose and intended audience?

   A. We commuter students don't drive to campus just because it's nice to have a car around in case we want to go shopping or to the movies.

   B. Even a cursory survey of the situation should be sufficient to reveal the significant burdens that such a demanding life style must place on the average commuter student.

   C. One must accept the statistically verifiable fact that, as a group, commuter students take more difficult courses than students who live on campus.

   D. I am aware that commuter students cannot and should not request special treatment from campus officials.

2. Which one of the following changes is needed in the second paragraph?

   A. Part 6: Change "nearest" to "nearer."

   B. Part 7: Change "it's" to "its."

   C. Part 9: Change "our" to "their."

   D. Part 10: Change "we" to "us."

Read the passage below, written in the style of a student essay. Then answer the questions that follow.

Note: An error in paragraph organization has been purposely included in the second paragraph.

[1]Measuring public opinion has unfortunately become a growth industry in the United States. [2]As each major election approaches, newspaper readers and television viewers are swamped with trivial data from the latest polls. [3]Indeed, public opinion polls have proven a valuable addition to the political process in the twentieth-century United States. [4]With a minimum of research, the average citizen can find out what percentage of Americans on any given day <u>think</u> candidate X is trustworthy, loyal, and kind to animals. [5]Is it all really necessary? [6]Do we need to know such things in order to vote intelligently? [7]Plainly, we do not.

[8]If not conducting public opinion polls, what should the media be doing? [9]To be sure, this may not be the best way to make friends. [10]Rather than counting heads, newspaper and television networks ought to spend more time analyzing a candidate's positions on the issues. [11]And when these positions are so lacking in substance as to make such analysis impossible, the media should inform their audiences of the fact. [12]It would, however, be a real service to the voting public.

♦ ♦ ♦ ♦ ♦ ♦ ♦ ♦

3. Which of the following changes would help focus attention on the main idea of the first paragraph?

   A. Delete Part 3.

   B. Delete the phrase "with a minimum of research" from Part 4.

   C. Change Part 6 from an interrogative to a declarative sentence by dropping the word "Do."

   D. Change Part 7 from the plural to the singular, as in "Plainly, I do not."

4. Which of the following should be used in place of the underlined word in Part 4 of the first paragraph?

   A. thinking

   B. will think

   C. thinks

   D. should think

5. Which of the following changes would make the sequence of ideas in the second paragraph clearer?

   A. Reverse the order of Parts 8 and 9.

   B. Place Part 9 after Part 11.

   C. Reverse the order of Parts 10 and 11.

   D. Delete Part 12.

Read the passage below, written in the style of an education textbook. Then answer the questions that follow.

¹Current methods of foreign language teaching often aim for more than mastery of vocabulary and grammar. ²A new topic called "pragmatics" has been added to the curriculum. ³Researchers have observed that every language community has different rules not only about how to construct meaningful sentences, but about when, where, and how to say them—and when to remain silent. 4 _____

⁵And as a result, more students than ever before are learning to look for cues to appropriate behavior when speaking a foreign tongue.

⁶For example, how do individuals know when it is their turn to speak in a conversation? ⁷Every language community has specific signals involving body

gestures, shifts in tone of voice, and other subtle cues that indicate when a speaker is ready to let someone else have a turn talking. ⁸What is the proper way to greet people? ⁹Every culture has it's rules about who should greet whom first and which verbal and physical form of greeting is appropriate for different circumstances. ¹⁰The proper greeting usually depends on such factors as the speakers' gender, status, type of relationship between the speakers, and relative age of the speakers.

¹¹Such questions were largely ignored in traditional foreign language teaching. ¹²This may explain why until recently students could study a language for years and yet have great difficulty using it for real-life communication.

♦ ♦ ♦ ♦ ♦ ♦ ♦

6. Which of the following sentences, used in place of the blank line labeled Part 4, would **best** fit the writer's pattern of development in the first paragraph?

A. Simply remaining silent is, in fact, often the best way to understand what another person is really trying to say.

B. Consequently, many teachers now instruct their students in the pragmatics, or practical applications, of correct vocabulary and grammar.

C. Another topic of great interest to researchers today is the difference between adults' and young children's approaches to language learning.

D. Of course, pragmatics is of less concern to students whose primary aim is to learn to read, rather than to speak, another language.

7. Which of the numbered parts should be revised to reduce its unnecessary repetition?

A. Part 6

B. Part 7

C. Part 8

D. Part 10

8. Which of the following changes is needed in the second paragraph?

A. Part 6: Change "their" to "they're."

B. Part 7: Change "specific" to "specifically."

C. Part 8: Change "proper" to "properly."

D. Part 9: Change "it's" to "its."

Read the passage below, written in the style of a student essay. Then answer the questions that follow.

[1]A good book is like a good friend. [2]It may not be affection at first sight, but after about page thirty, or the third time you get together with your new acquaintance, you know whether or not to pursue the relationship. [3]When you've finished the book. [4]You can feel that your life is suddenly richer. [5]As you go about your business, you find yourself pondering and reliving certain of its parts, just as your daily life keeps triggering thoughts about something peculiarly wise or amusing your new friend has said.

[6]One of the greatest pleasures derived from a good book—as from a good friend—is the way in which it grows with you through the years. [7]You happen to pick it up and read it again, after barely surviving yet another mid-life crisis, and you are delighted and comforted that there are still some things in life you can count on. [8]You are delighted—and downright amazed—that this same old book has somehow magically been transformed. [9]How can it be that it suddenly speaks to you of new things, things you didn't see there before, things that happen to be exactly relevant to what's on your mind and in your heart right now, just like a best friend?

◆ ◆ ◆ ◆ ◆ ◆ ◆

9. Which of the following parts of the first paragraph is a nonstandard sentence?

   A. Part 1

   B. Part 3

   C. Part 4

   D. Part 5

10. Which of the following sentences, if added between Parts 7 and 8 of the second paragraph, would be most consistent with the writer's purpose and intended audience?

   A. I rarely read the same book more than once, though; I think that is a waste of time.

   B. Within that realm of fictional escapism, you extract solace and intellectual gratification.

   C. That, of course, is not true of the books that you are forced to read for most college literature courses.

   D. You are comforted by the fact that your friend still has all of the same wonderful qualities that captured your affection when you first met.

Read the passage below, written in the style of a college history textbook. Then answer the questions that follow.

[1]For more than two hundred years, the proper role of government in American society has been a topic of intense political discussion. [2]Long, long ago, the main outlines of the debate were shaped by the conflicting views of Alexander Hamilton and Thomas Jefferson. [3]As a spokesman for the northeastern banking and commercial interests, Hamilton believed the federal government should make every effort to promote economic growth. [4]Accordingly, he proposed the enactment of high tariffs on imports to protect new industries, the creation of a national bank to provide large loans for government and business enterprises, and the construction of roadways and lighthouses to stimulate trade. [5]The passage of these and related measures, Hamilton believed would enable the United States to realize its destiny as a great industrial nation.

[6]But not all Americans shared Hamilton's vision. [7]People from the plantations and farms of the South and West hoped to preserve a quiet agricultural world of independent landowners. [8]They believed that the creation of an urban, industrial society would diminish their political influence. [9]They also believed that a federal government with Hamiltonian powers would threaten their individual liberties. [10]It was for these people that Jefferson spoke. [11]In doing so, he initiated a debate that in some respects still continues today.

♦ ♦ ♦ ♦ ♦ ♦ ♦ ♦

11. Which of the following sentences, if added between Parts 6 and 7 of the second paragraph, would be most consistent with the writer's purpose and intended audience?

A. Some folks knew better than to jump on Hamilton's bandwagon, which was sure to face a bumpy road once the country really got going.

B. On the contrary, many people living in the United States, including Thomas Jefferson, did not want their new nation to become heavily industrialized.

C. How anybody could fail to see the fact that Hamilton clearly had the best plan for the future of this country is totally beyond me.

D. Rather, there were those who viewed the Federalist geopolitical and economic strategy as a movement toward tyrannical despotism and away from democratic ideology.

12. Which of the underlined words in the first paragraph should be replaced by more precise or appropriate words?

A. proper role

B. Long, long ago

C. economic growth

D. high tariffs

13. Which of the following changes is needed in the first paragraph?

A. Part 2: Place a colon after the word "by."

B. Part 3: Change "As" to "Like."

C. Part 4: Move "Accordingly" after the word "enactment."

D. Part 5: Place a comma after the phrase "Hamilton believed."

> Read the passage below, written in the style of a sociology textbook. Then answer the questions that follow.

Note: An error in paragraph organization has been purposely included in the first paragraph.

[1]Historians and lawyers have much in common. [2]One shared characteristic is the kinds of tasks they are required to perform. [3]For example, a major task of both lawyers and historians is collecting evidence to construct and support an argument. [4]For instance, sources such as tax records, interviews, and photographs are as much tools of the historian's craft as they are of the lawyer's. [5]In addition, lawyers and historians sometimes even use similar kinds of sources in their work. [6]And, like lawyers, historians too have their adversaries. [7]Academics who object to the views of one of their peers can argue just as forcefully as rival counsel in a legal proceeding.

[8]This, however, brings us to a major difference between lawyers and historians. [9]Where lawyers are most often called upon to defend a person or institution, historians must defend a point of view, an interpretation of the past that is seldom shaped by the facts alone. [10]Historians have debated for years whether Dwight D. Eisenhower's presidency was one of relative unawareness or great subtlety. [11]This explains why historical controversies are less easily resolved than legal disputes. [12]In a legal dispute, establishing the facts generally led to a final decision; in history, a "final interpretation" is a rarity.

◆ ◆ ◆ ◆ ◆ ◆ ◆

14. Which of the following changes would make the sequence of ideas in the first paragraph clearer?

A. Delete Part 1.

B. Reverse the order of Parts 1 and 2.

C. Delete Part 3.

D. Reverse the order of Parts 4 and 5.

15. Which of the following editorial changes would help focus attention on the main idea of the second paragraph?

A. Delete Part 8.

B. Reverse the order of Parts 8 and 9.

C. Delete Part 10.

D. Add a sentence after Part 11 describing the major steps involved in deciding a legal dispute.

16. Which one of the following changes is needed in the second paragraph?

A. Part 8: Change "between" to "among."

B. Part 9: Change "where" to "when."

C. Part 11: Change "less" to "least."

D. Part 12: Change "led" to "leads."

Read the passage below, written in the style of a college history textbook. Then answer the questions that follow.

[1]Recent scientific evidence has shed new light on the disappearance of the Minoan civilization, which flourished on Crete and other islands of the eastern Mediterranean for nearly a thousand years before it was abruptly and utterly destroyed around 1450 B.C. [2]The Minoans were among the first peoples to build ships that could sail across the Mediterranean Sea, and they traded with islands as far away as Sicily. [3]The largest island in the Mediterranean, Sicily has been a trade center for thousands of years. [4]Excavations in Crete have revealed well-built roads, terraced gardens, and palaces many stories high equipped with running water and adorned by elegant frescoes depicting the playful and carefree life the Minoans enjoyed. [5]These frescoes show women exercising independence and equality with men, something entirely unheard of in the rest of the ancient world.

[6]The disappearance of the Minoans and their culture was long considered an unsolvable mystery, but recent geological evidence indicates that it was caused by a volcanic eruption on the Minoan island of Thera (now called Santorini) about 70 miles from Crete. [7]_____

_____

[8]In addition, the explosion sent tidal waves 150 feet high sweeping across the other Minoan islands at speeds of up to 300 miles per hour. [9]If there were any survivors left in the ruins of the great Minoan palaces, they had to leave their island homes because the volcano covered the islands with thick layers of ash that probably made them uninhabitable.

◆ ◆ ◆ ◆ ◆ ◆ ◆ ◆

17. Which of the following numbered parts is LEAST relevant to the main idea of the first paragraph?

   A. Part 1

   B. Part 2

   C. Part 3

   D. Part 4

18. Which of the following sentences, if used in place of the blank line labeled Part 7, would **best** develop the main idea of the second paragraph?

   A. Geologists estimate that the massive eruption obliterated 50 square miles of land on Thera.

   B. Another intriguing Minoan mystery is the practice of bull vaulting, known to us only from ancient wall paintings.

   C. Accurately predicting volcanic eruptions must have been as difficult then as it is today.

   D. The science of geology is becoming an increasingly reliable source of historical information.

Read the passage below, written in the style of a college economics textbook. Then answer the questions that follow.

[1]As federal budget deficits have grown in recent years, there have been increasing calls for a constitutional amendment that would require Congress to balance the budget each year. [2]Congress has added only 26 amendments to the Constitution since it was ratified in 1788. [3]Supporters of the amendment contend that federal spending is now out of control. [4]They further insist that there is little likelihood that the budget will be balanced at any point in the foreseeable future. [5]These people argue that legislators invariably find it easier to spend money than raise taxes; they say that Congress will continue to spend unchecked unless it is pressured to do otherwise. [6]If something is not done soon, they warn, such uncontrolled spending will do serious long-term damage to the economy.

[7]Although no one defends huge budget deficits, many economists believe that a balanced budget amendment would create more problems than it would solve. [8]For example, such an amendment would prevent Congress from creating jobs or reducing taxes in response to an economic slowdown. [9]The result might be a depression comparable to the Great Depression of the 1930s. [10]These are seriously concerns, and they should be given careful consideration by anyone who believes that a balanced budget amendment is a cure-all for the nation's current economic woes.

◆ ◆ ◆ ◆ ◆ ◆ ◆ ◆

19. Which of the sentences, if added between Parts 9 and 10 of the second paragraph, would be most consistent with the writer's purpose and intended audience?

A. Does that sound like a very smart idea?

B. Some question the fiscal wisdom of instituting a macroeconomic policy that reduces the national debt but negates federal social responsibility.

C. Personally, I think a balanced budget amendment would really help this country by forcing Congress to get its act together.

D. Other economists worry that a balanced budget amendment would prompt Congress to shift responsibility for public service programs to state and local governments that lack the money to pay for them.

20. Which of the following numbered parts draws attention away from the main idea of the first paragraph?

A. Part 1

B. Part 2

C. Part 3

D. Part 4

21. Which of the following changes is needed in the above passage?

A. Part 5: Change "than" to "then."

B. Part 6: Change "soon" to "sooner."

C. Part 7: Change "Although" to "Because."

D. Part 10: Change "seriously" to "serious."

Read the passage below, written in the style of a sociology textbook. Then answer the questions that follow.

[1]Population growth trends in developed countries have passed through several phases. [2]Before about 1850, birth rates and death rates were both high. [3]The large number of births and deaths that occurred each year tended more or less to cancel each other out, so that populations remained fairly constant or exhibited relatively low growth rates.

[4]This began to change after 1850, when industrialization led to a substantial rise in living standards for the general population and advances in medical science markedly reduced the number of deaths caused by infectious diseases. [5]The rapid decline in death rates that resulted was accompanied by a much slower decline in birth rates. [6]Thus, far exceeding the number of people who died each year, developed countries grew increasingly populous.

[7]By 1950, _____ , population growth rates in the developed countries again dropped off substantially. [8]The main reason was the continuing decline in birth rates, which occurred gradually as the role of children in the family changed and parents began deciding to have fewer offspring. [9]_____ , in the decades since 1950, birth rates and death rates have both been low. [10]This has resulted once again in populations that are growing only slowly or not at all.

◆ ◆ ◆ ◆ ◆ ◆ ◆ ◆

22. Which words or phrases would, if inserted *in order* into the blanks in the third paragraph, help the reader understand the logical sequence of the writer's ideas?

A. as a result; Furthermore

B. for example; On the other hand

C. however; Consequently

D. in conclusion; Yet

23. Which of the following parts of the passage displays nonstandard placement of a modifier?

A. Part 1

B. Part 2

C. Part 5

D. Part 6

Read the passage below, written in the style of a college writing textbook for first-year students. Then answer the questions that follow.

¹Beginning writers often have a hard time setting an appropriate length for their paragraphs. ²And they generally have an even harder time locating a reference source that offers reasonable advice about how to deal with this problem. ³Composition textbooks are often distressingly vague when they discuss this topic. ⁴One might learn, for example, that paragraphs should not be too short because one- or two-sentence paragraphs make a composition disjointed and difficult to follow. ⁵At the same time, they should not be too long: lengthy paragraphs can be dense and confusing to the reader.

⁶The truth is that there are no hard-and-fast rules for determining how long paragraphs should be. ⁷Actually, this is just as well because rules usually restrict creative impulses, not only in writing, but also in other artistic areas. ⁸There are, however, two general principles that writers should keep in mind. ⁹The first is that the main purpose of a paragraph is to develop an idea. ¹⁰The second is that writing is broke into units such as paragraphs to help readers understand the writer's message. ¹¹All decisions about paragraph length should reflect both of these concerns.

◆ ◆ ◆ ◆ ◆ ◆ ◆ ◆

24. Which of the following sentences, if added between Parts 3 and 4 of the first paragraph, would be most consistent with the writer's purpose and intended audience?

A. If you ask me, those books aren't even worth the trouble it takes to read them.

B. These books can be very useful, however, when a writer is looking for information on subjects other than paragraph length.

C. In these texts, sections on paragraph structure tend to concentrate on what to avoid rather than what to do.

D. These tomes are rife with rambling, ambiguous theoretical discourse that fails to provide any constructive counsel.

25. Which of the following editorial changes would help focus attention on the main idea of the second paragraph?

A. Delete Part 7.

B. Combine Parts 8 and 9 by changing the period after "mind" to a comma.

C. Add a clause to Part 9 giving some examples of ideas that might be presented in a paragraph.

D. Delete Part 11.

26. Which of the following parts of the passage displays nonstandard use of a verb form?

A. Part 1

B. Part 4

C. Part 6

D. Part 10

Read the passage below, written in the style of a college communication textbook. Then answer the questions that follow.

[1]"Are we going to support this development project, or are we going to let this town become a howling wilderness?" [2]Of course, this is a rhetorical question—no answer is really expected. [3]It is also a fallacious question, based on a false assumption. [4]Clearly, the speaker is attempting to persuade people not by logic, but by deceit. [5]This and similar rhetorical tricks are known as "informal fallacies."

[6]The informal fallacies that public speakers sometimes employ to sway an audience include such techniques as making appeals to emotions (arousing feelings of anger, for example), special pleading (presenting only one side of a question), and making faulty analogies (treating two things as essentially similar even though they have significant differences). [7]Although most informal fallacies are designed to cloud the issue being discussed, some can also be used to place an opponent on the defensive. [8]_____

[9]The use of fallacious arguments may sometimes be effective, but it is never honest. [10]Informal fallacies have no place in reasoned discussion.

◆ ◆ ◆ ◆ ◆ ◆ ◆

27. Which of the following sentences, if added between Parts 3 and 4 of the first paragraph, would be most consistent with the writer's purpose and intended audience?

A. Despite the speaker's implication, a town would not be reduced to "a howling wilderness" by its failure to support a development project.

B. I bet a lot of readers think that most towns would be better off if they had more "howling wilderness" and less development anyway.

C. How could a speaker think anybody would fall for such a crazy argument?

D. It's pretty obvious that the creator of that "howling wilderness" sentence was just trying to pull a fast one on us.

28. Which of the following sentences, if used in place of the blank line labeled Part 8, would best support the main idea of the second paragraph?

A. Newspaper editorials make use of many different rhetorical and persuasive devices, including informal fallacies.

B. It is no easy task, for example, to respond convincingly to the question, "Why do you think you're the only important person in this room?"

C. The increased use of informal fallacies in writing and speaking reflects the fact that most people no longer believe that "honesty is the best policy."

D. But public speakers do not always intend to persuade; speakers may also address an audience to inform, explain, demonstrate, or entertain.

Read the passage below, written in the style of a popular magazine. Then answer the questions that follow.

[1]The two halves of the human body generally work together so well that it may be surprising to learn that they are controlled by two separate centers of consciousness, the right and left sides of the brain. [2]Just like the outside of the body, the brain is symmetrical, comprising two identical halves, each half, or hemisphere, controls the movement, sensation, hearing, and vision of the opposite side of the body. [3]Thus the left hemisphere of the brain controls the right side of the body; the right hemisphere controls the left side.

[4]The two sides of the brain have different specialties. [5]The left side controls speech and other communication involving words and numbers, as well as the process of reasoning. [6] _____

[7]The hemispheres are connected by a special nerve bridge that allows information to pass rapidly between the two sides of the brain. [8]This is what enables the two hemispheres to coordinate their activities and function as a single unit.

◆ ◆ ◆ ◆ ◆ ◆ ◆

29. Which of the following sentences, used in place of the blank lines labeled Part 6, would **best** fit the writer's pattern of development in the second paragraph?

   A. The right side controls the perception of patterns, the ability to recognize people and places, and the process of imagination or visualization.

   B. This is by far the more interesting side of the brain, which may explain why it has been more extensively studied than the right side.

   C. The right-left division within the brain was not widely recognized before the twentieth century.

   D. Some scientists believe that this fact may cause left-handed people to be better in artistic areas, while right-handers have stronger verbal skills.

30. Which of the following parts of the passage is a nonstandard sentence?

   A. Part 1

   B. Part 2

   C. Part 4

   D. Part 8

Read the passage below, written in the style of a popular magazine. Then answer the questions that follow.

[1]Too many people are afraid to take on woodworking projects because they think they are not qualified to do their own carpentry. [2]But the fact is that anybody can successfully complete projects such as hanging doors or building bookshelves. [3]Woodworking is difficult only if you do it by the "trial and error" method. [4]If you take time to organize your work, you can do your own woodworking and achieve professional results.

[5]The best woodworkers know that each project must be planned carefully. [6]Before you buy a nail or cut a board, you must analyze your project and define the work that needs to be done. [7]Then you should develop a written plan for the job. [8]_____

[9]There are many fine do-it-yourself handbooks available that can guide you as you design your project. [10]You should also talk to the salespeople at your lumber and hardware stores; they can often provide advice that will save you both time and money.

[11]Once you have finished your plans and your planning is complete, you can use your completed plan to begin the final construction phase. [12]Follow your plan exactly; don't try to improvise as you go along. [13]If you have planned well, you will quickly discover how easy and rewarding it can be to do your own carpentry.

◆ ◆ ◆ ◆ ◆ ◆ ◆

31. Which of the following sentences, if added between Parts 2 and 3 of the first paragraph, would be most consistent with the writer's purpose and intended audience?

   A. Let's face it: if I can be a woodworker, so can you.

   B. Keep in mind, however, that you shouldn't force somebody to try woodworking if they really don't want to do it.

   C. No one should panic at the thought of nailing down a few loose boards or building a new magazine rack.

   D. For a novice suddenly cast into the world of joists, sills, and sashes, confidence is a primary asset.

32. Which of the following sentences, used in place of the blank line labeled Part 8, would **best** support the main idea of the second paragraph?

   A. Unlike metalworking, woodworking can be done with fairly few expensive tools and relatively little specialized training.

   B. Professional carpenters and architects usually have extensive drafting training and regularly use technical drawing techniques in their work.

   C. Some personal computers have highly sophisticated graphics capabilities that enable you to inspect a design from all possible angles.

   D. Draw detailed sketches showing all necessary measurements and make a list of the materials you will need (including their costs).

33. Which of the numbered parts should be revised to reduce its unnecessary repetition?

   A. Part 1

   B. Part 6

   C. Part 7

   D. Part 11

> Read the passage below, written in the style of a natural history article. Then answer the questions that follow.

[1]Along with alligators and crocodiles, turtles are among the world's most oldest reptiles—the last survivors of the age of the dinosaurs, when giant reptiles of all kinds dominated the earth. [2]Yet today, after 200 million years of existence, some species of turtle are in danger of extinction.

[3]In particular danger is the green turtle, a sea turtle found in temperate oceans throughout the world. [4]Although they are not commonly eaten in North America, green turtles are prized as a delicacy elsewhere, and they are hunted extensively. [5]These turtles are at a distinct disadvantage in the hunt because of one unfortunate trait: they must come ashore to lay their eggs. [6]Once on land, the female turtle is easy prey. [7]Her buried clutch of eggs <u>are</u> also vulnerable—to find the eggs, a hunter need only follow the mother's unmistakable tracks up the beach.

[8]Fortunately, countries around the world have taken steps to protect green turtles by restricting turtle hunting or banning it altogether. [9]_____, conservationists have begun efforts to restore turtles to areas where they have been nearly wiped out. [10]_____, eggs are collected and transported to beaches where they were once found in abundance. [11]_____, they are placed in a nest that is fenced in and carefully guarded until the newly-hatched babies are able to scramble to the relative safety of the ocean.

34. Which words or phrases would, if inserted *in order* into the blanks in the third paragraph, help the reader understand the sequence of the writer's ideas?

    A. Nevertheless; Moreover; In other words

    B. In addition; First; Next

    C. Eventually; Furthermore; As a result

    D. By contrast; However; Still

35. Which of the following should be used in place of the underlined word in Part 7 of the second paragraph?

    A. were

    B. will be

    C. is

    D. was

36. Which of the following changes is needed in the above passage?

    A. Part 1: Delete the word "most."

    B. Part 2: Change the phrase "Yet today" to "Although today."

    C. Part 4: Change "commonly" to "common."

    D. Part 5: Put quotation marks around the phrase, "they must come ashore to lay their eggs."

Read the passage below, written in the style of a college fine arts article. Then answer the questions that follow.

Note: An error in paragraph organization has been purposely included in the second paragraph.

[1]Martha Graham's innovative dancing and choreography have had a profound influence on the development of modern dance in America. [2]Her concept of dance as an expression of the inner self led to the creation of a highly athletic disciplined, and passionate dance technique.

[3]Graham was born in 1893. [4]Her professional dancing career began when, as a teenager, she trained and performed with the Denishawn dance company, where she remained for seven years. [5]Her use of violent movement and discordant music in those original works was disturbing to many people, and her creations were not well received at first. [6]The company's traditional emphasis on grace and lyricism, however, was ultimately too confining for her, and in the mid-1920s she began to choreograph, or design, her own dances. [7]She pursued her own course, however, and during the 1940s created some of her most acclaimed works, including *Letter to the World,* based on the life of poet Emily Dickinson, and the joyous *Appalachian Spring,* for which Aaron Copland composed the score.

[8]Although Graham spent years struggling against the disapproval of audiences who disliked and ridiculed her work, the power and substance of her unique vision proved in the end to be undeniable. [9]Martha Graham's technique has long since been recognized as a truly monumental contribution to the art of modern dance.

◆ ◆ ◆ ◆ ◆ ◆ ◆

37. Which of the following changes would make the sequence of ideas in the second paragraph clearer?

   A. Reverse the order of Parts 3 and 4.

   B. Place Part 7 before Part 3.

   C. Reverse the order of Parts 5 and 6.

   D. Delete Part 7.

38. Which of the following changes is needed in the above passage?

   A. Part 1: Add a comma after "choreography."

   B. Part 2: Add a comma after "athletic."

   C. Part 8: Replace the comma after "work" with a semicolon.

   D. Part 9: Change "recognized" to "recognizing."

Read the passage below, written in the style of a student essay. Then answer the questions that follow.

---

[1]Why do we remember some things, but forget others? [2]That question has puzzled scientists for years. [3]Recently, however, psychologists have discovered some of the answers about how the human memory functions.

[4]Psychologists believe that the human memory has three distinct parts. [5]The first part, called the sensory memory, stores information for one second or less. [6]One function of the sensory memory is to hold the image of your surroundings so that you don't forget where you are each time you blink. [7]The second part of the memory, short-term memory, holds information for up to one minute. [8]The third and most permanent part of the memory is the long-term memory. [9]Once information enters long-term memory, it may be retained for the rest of a person's life.

[10]Recent research indicates that how often we use a piece of information determines which type of memory will be used to store it. [11]Some computer memories also have sorting systems that arrange information according to how frequently it is used. [12]Data that we need for a brief time, such as a telephone number we call only once, will probably be stored in short-term memory and then discarded. [13]But information we use repeatedly, such as the name of a close friend, is more likely to be held in long-term memory.

◆ ◆ ◆ ◆ ◆ ◆ ◆

39. Which of the following sentences, if added between Parts 7 and 8 of the second paragraph, would be most consistent with the writer's purpose and intended audience?

A. The intrinsic differences between the sensory and the short-term memories are apparent at both the biological and psychological levels.

B. I guess that's why a lot of people have a hard time keeping track of little things that they only need to remember for a minute.

C. Information such as new telephone numbers or addresses may be stored in this part of the memory.

D. Don't you think it's kind of neat how the brain keeps everything organized that way?

40. Which of the following editorial changes would help focus attention on the main idea of the passage?

A. Add a clause to Part 3 naming some psychologists who have done research on the human memory.

B. Rephrase Part 5 so that it reads, "The sensory memory, which stores information for one second or less, is the first part."

C. Reverse the order of Parts 4 and 5.

D. Delete Part 11.

WRITING SAMPLE SUBSECTION

DIRECTIONS FOR WRITING SAMPLE

This portion of the writing section of the TASP® Test consists of one writing assignment. You are asked to prepare a MULTIPLE-PARAGRAPH writing sample of about 300–600 words on an assigned topic. The assignment can be found in your test booklet. You should use the time available to plan, write, review, and edit what you have written.

Find the assignment and read it carefully before you begin to write. Think about how you will organize what you plan to write. At the test, space for your writing sample is limited to the pages provided for that purpose in your test booklet and your answer document. Additional paper is not permitted. Your score will be based <u>solely</u> on the version of your writing sample written in the space provided in the answer document.

Your writing sample will be scored on the basis of how effectively it communicates a whole message to the specified audience for the stated purpose. You will be assessed on your ability to express, organize, and support opinions and ideas rather than the position you express. Pay particular attention to the seven characteristics listed below when preparing your writing sample. These seven characteristics will be used in scoring your writing sample.

- APPROPRIATENESS—the extent to which you address the topic and use language and style appropriate to the given audience, purpose, and occasion.

- UNITY AND FOCUS—the clarity with which you state and maintain your main idea or point of view.

- DEVELOPMENT—the amount, depth, and specificity of your supporting details.

- ORGANIZATION—the clarity of your writing and the logical sequence of your ideas.

- SENTENCE STRUCTURE—the effectiveness of your sentence structure and the extent to which your writing is free of errors in sentence structure.

- USAGE—the extent to which your writing is free of errors in usage and shows care and precision in word choice.

- MECHANICAL CONVENTIONS—your ability to spell common words and to use the conventions of capitalization and punctuation.

Be sure to write about the assigned topic and to use MULTIPLE PARAGRAPHS. Please write legibly. You may not use any reference materials during the test. Remember to save some time to review what you have written and make any changes you think will improve your writing sample.

The final version of the essay should conform to the conventions of edited American English.

Writing Sample Assignment

Do the benefits of technology outweigh the risks? Technological advances have lengthened human life, allowed people to travel in space, and enabled us to communicate with one another from any place on earth. But technology can also consume enormous amounts of natural resources, pollute the environment, or be used to create powerful weapons of war.

Your purpose is to write an essay, to be read by a classroom instructor, in which you analyze the impact of a particular technological advance on modern society.

- Select *one* of the following technological innovations: the telephone, the computer, the automobile; the television, the tractor; the skyscraper; or the nuclear power plant.

- Discuss the advantages and/or disadvantages of that technology for individuals and society.

Be sure to support your analysis with logical arguments and appropriate examples.

_____

_____

_____

_____

_____

_____

_____

_____

_____

_____

_____

_____

_____

_____

_____

_____

Practice Test Answer Key

Reading	Mathematics	Writing
1. A	1. D	1. A
2. B	2. A	2. D
3. B	3. C	3. A
4. B	4. B	4. C
5. C	5. A	5. B
6. D	6. A	6. B
7. D	7. B	7. D
8. B	8. C	8. D
9. A	9. A	9. B
10. C	10. B	10. D
11. D	11. B	11. B
12. B	12. B	12. B
13. A	13. C	13. D
14. B	14. A	14. D
15. D	15. B	15. C
16. B	16. C	16. D
17. B	17. B	17. C
18. C	18. A	18. A
19. C	19. C	19. D
20. C	20. A	20. B
21. B	21. B	21. D
22. D	22. C	22. C
23. A	23. D	23. D
24. A	24. A	24. C
25. A	25. D	25. A
26. D	26. C	26. D
27. B	27. B	27. A
28. A	28. C	28. B
29. B	29. D	29. A
30. C	30. B	30. B
31. B	31. B	31. C
32. A	32. B	32. D
33. A	33. C	33. D
34. D	34. D	34. B
35. C	35. C	35. C
36. B	36. D	36. A
37. C	37. C	37. C
38. C	38. C	38. B
39. B	39. C	39. C
40. A	40. A	40. D
41. D	41. A	
42. D	42. B	
	43. C	
	44. B	
	45. A	
	46. C	
	47. C	
	48. D	

Practice Test Skill Evaluation Chart

Below you will find the answers to the Practice Test. Alongside the correct response is a space. There you should indicate with a check mark if your answer is correct. Leave any incorrect answers blank.

The questions are in numerical order and arranged horizontally by skill. For example, for Reading question 7, the correct answer is "D." Question 7 deals with the reading skill "understand main ideas and supporting details." Questions 1, 13, 19, 25, 31, and 37 also deal with main idea and supporting details.

Once all your correct answers are checked, simply add up your check marks for each skill (that is, horizontally across the page) and write the number of correct answers in the space provided on the far right. Having this information, you can decide which skills may require extra work. Each skill is covered in an instructional chapter in this book.

Skill/Questions/Correct Answers   Your Score

Reading

Meanings of Words and Phrases

6 D___	12 B___	18 C___	24 A___	30 C___	36 B___	42 D___	___/7

Main Idea and Details

1 A___	7 D___	13 A___	19 C___	25 A___	31 B___	37 C___	___/7

Writer's Purpose and Meaning

2 B___	8 B___	14 B___	20 C___	26 D___	32 A___	38 C___	___/7

Relationship among Ideas

3 B___	9 A___	15 D___	21 B___	27 B___	33 A___	39 B___	___/7

Critical Reasoning Skills

4 A___	10 C___	16 B___	22 D___	28 A___	34 D___	40 A___	___/7

Study Skills in Reading

5 C___	11 D___	17 B___	23 A___	29 B___	35 C___	41 D___	___/7

Mathematics

Word Problems with Integers, Fractions, Decimals, and Units of Measurement				
1 D___ 2 A___ 3 C___ 4 B___				___/4

Problems Involving Data Interpretation and Analysis				
5 A___ 6 A___ 7 B___ 8 C___				___/4

Graphs of Number Relationships				
9 A___ 10 B___ 11 B___ 12 B___				___/4

One- and Two-Variable Equations				
13 C___ 14 A___ 15 B___ 16 C___				___/4

Word Problems with Variables				
17 B___ 18 A___ 19 C___ 20 A___ 21 B___				___/5

Algebraic Expressions and Functional Notation				
22 C___ 23 D___ 24 A___ 25 D___ 26 C___				___/5

Quadratic Equations				
27 B___ 28 C___ 29 D___ 30 B___ 31 B___				___/5

Problems with Geometric Figures				
32 B___ 33 C___ 34 D___ 35 C___				___/4

Problems with Geometric Concepts				
36 D___ 37 C___ 38 C___ 39 C___				___/4

Reasoning Skills				
40 A___ 41 A___ 42 B___ 43 C___				___/4

Solve Applied Problems				
44 B___ 45 A___ 46 C___ 47 C___ 48 D___				___/5

Writing

Purpose and Audience								
1 A	10 D	11 B	19 D	24 C	27 A	31 C	39 C	/8

Unity, Focus, and Development								
3 A	15 C	17 C	20 B	25 A	28 B	32 D	40 D	/8

Effective Organization								
5 B	6 B	14 D	18 A	22 C	29 A	34 B	37 C	/8

Effective Sentences								
4 C	7 D	9 B	12 B	23 D	30 B	33 D	35 C	/8

Edited American English								
2 D	8 D	13 D	16 D	21 D	26 D	36 A	38 B	/8

Interpreting Your Score

Do not try to use the Practice Test as a predictor for how you might score on an official TASP Test. As mentioned in the beginning of this study guide, there may be differences between the two tests in both format and level of difficulty. Also, no "mastery" or "passing" scores have been determined or suggested for the Practice Test.

On the other hand, the Practice Test can provide valuable information as to your degree of preparedness on the skills that are eligible for testing in the Texas Academic Skills Program. If you answered all the questions associated with a given skill correctly, you may need only to refresh your memory of that skill as you prepare for the TASP Test. If you missed all or most of the items associated with a skill, you should plan to spend more time working in that area. You may also want to talk with someone on your campus about getting additional help with the content of skills on which you performed poorly. In addition to working with the content of this study guide, there may be special programs or courses that would benefit your preparation.

Practice Test Explanations: Reading

1. **Correct Response: A.** This selection focuses on the profound impact of Emile Durkheim on the development of sociology. Choice A, which indicates Durkheim's primary contributions to the discipline, thus best expresses the main idea of the selection. Of the other responses listed, choice B is a misinterpretation of Durkheim's social group theory, choice C is too narrow in scope to constitute the main idea of the selection, and choice D reflects a misunderstanding of information presented in the selection.

2. **Correct Response: B.** This question assesses the ability to recognize a writer's purpose for writing a given selection. Choice B is the best response because the writer's primary intention is to inform readers of Emile Durkheim's influence on the development of sociology. Although choices A and D relate to ideas and issues that the writer addresses in developing the main theme of the selection, they do not reflect an accurate understanding of the primary purpose of the work. Choice C reflects a misinterpretation of the writer's basic intent, which is to inform and describe rather than to persuade.

3. **Correct Response: B.** In the first paragraph, the writer states that sociology does not attempt to explain the behavior of a particular individual. Choice B is therefore the best response to the question because, unlike psychologists, sociologists tend to be concerned with people as members of groups rather than as individuals. Of the other choices listed, both sociologists and psychologists are concerned with explaining behavior (choice A), while psychologists are likely to spend more time than sociologists helping people solve their problems (choice C). Concerning choice D, the text explicitly states that sociologists are interested in understanding patterns of human relationships.

4. **Correct Response: A.** This question requires an understanding of the analogy that Durkheim used to illustrate the nature of social groups. Choice A is the best response because, according to the selection, Durkheim observed that just as the hardness of bronze cannot be predicted by knowing about the hardness of its component metals, the characteristics of a social group as a collective unit cannot be determined by analyzing the traits of the group's individual members. Choices B, C, and D all reflect misinterpretations of Durkheim's reason for comparing social groups to bronze.

5. **Correct Response: C.** This question assesses the ability to organize information for study purposes. Of the alternative choices provided, choice C is the best response because it represents the most complete and accurate listing of the main themes presented in the selection. By comparison, the other choices provided not only omit one or more major themes, but also state main ideas in ways that are either inaccurate or misleading. For example, social groups rather than sociology are compared to bronze in the second paragraph (choice A), and the author does not attempt at any point in the selection to examine sociology before or after Durkheim (choices B and D).

6. **Correct Response: D.** This question assesses the ability to use context clues to determine the intended meaning of a word with multiple meanings. Within the context of the fourth paragraph of the selection, the best definition of the word *model* is a plan to be imitated (choice D). The reader knows this because the writer goes on to state that Durkheim's approach "guided the work of nearly all sociologists." Although choices A (one of two or more alternative styles), B (an artist's subject), and C (a small copy of an object) are all possible meanings of the word *model,* they inaccurately convey the word's meaning as it is used in this context and distort what the writer is trying to say in the paragraph.

7. **Correct Response: D.** In the seventh paragraph, the writer discusses what the Joy Luck parties meant to the women who attended them. That choice A is the best response is evidenced not only by information contained in the paragraph, but also by the extensive discussion of the mother's past losses in preceding parts of the selection. Of the other responses provided, the women realized that the parties were at best a brief respite from the often hard reality of their lives (choice A), and they did not expect to win prizes of any significant value at these gatherings (choice C). Concerning choice B, feasting on various delicacies was an important feature of the parties, but it was not the main reason that the women organized them.

8. **Correct Response: B.** This question assesses the ability to recognize the likely effect on an audience of a writer's choice of certain phrases. That choice B is the best response is confirmed by the following sentence in which the writer observes that her mother "recognized the numbness in these women's faces." Of the other responses provided, the women were trying to improve their English, but not because they had any particular desire to give fuller expression to past tragedies (choice A). The passage does not tell us how these women felt about having emigrated from China (choice C), nor is there any suggestion that the narrator's mother felt superior to the women (choice D).

9. **Correct Response: A.** This question assesses the ability to draw conclusions from a passage. Choice A is the best response because information contained in the fourth paragraph indicates that the narrator's mother conceived of the Joy Luck Club in an effort to come to grips with the harshness of her current circumstances. She had no illusions, however, that Joy Luck would generate the money needed to escape those conditions (choice D). Of the other responses provided, the paragraph tells us nothing about the mother's state of health on the night in question (choice B), and it was the actual screaming sounds from the street that led her to imagine terrible sights that evening (choice C).

10. **Correct Response: C.** This question assesses the ability to distinguish between fact and opinion in a reading selection. Choice C is the best response because it is based on a on intentional exaggeration on the part of the writer's mother: that the smells had nowhere else to go but to her nose. By comparison, the observations contained in choices A, B, and D all represent efforts to convey accurate descriptions and recollections of various matters.

11. **Correct Response: D.** This question assesses the ability to summarize a reading passage for study purposes. Choice D is the best response because it provides the most accurate and complete statement of the main points discussed in the passage. By comparison, the other responses provided all omit important elements of the story; choices A and C also misinterpret parts of the selection.

12. **Correct Response: B.** Within the context of the selection, choice B is the best definition of *casting long shadows into her life* because the following paragraph provides a vivid description of the hard life the writer's mother had experienced in earlier years—a life that she could never forget (choice A). Of the other choices provided, the mother appears to have had a remarkably clear recollection of the past (choice C), and made little or no effort to erase those memories, however unpleasant they may have been (choice D).

13. **Correct Response: A.** This selection focuses on the complex procedures involved in the development of television commercials. Choice A, which notes that commercials require a great deal of time, effort, and money to produce, thus best expresses the main idea of the selection. Of the other choices listed, the selection provides no evidence that commercials are more difficult to produce than other types of film (choice B), nor does it indicate that shorter commercials are more costly and complex to develop than longer commercials (choice D). Choice C is too narrow in scope to constitute the main idea of the selection. It may also be inaccurate, as it does not take into consideration all the important information presented in the selection.

14. **Correct Response: B.** This question assesses the ability to infer a writer's purpose for including particular content in a reading selection. Choice B is the best response because it is most in accord with the main purpose of the first paragraph, which is to inform readers that television commercials have become increasingly shorter in recent decades. Of the other choices listed, the writer makes no effort at any point in the paragraph to compare U.S. development or technology with that of other nations (choices A and C) or to assess the quality of television commercials (choice D).

15. **Correct Response: D.** This question assesses the ability to identify the proper sequence of steps presented in a reading selection. Choice D is the best response because the writer implies in the third paragraph that businesses typically conduct several market surveys before making any decisions related to the style or content of a television commercial. These surveys are designed to identify the typical users of the product to be advertised. Without such information, the producers of television commercials would have no guidelines for developing scripts (choice A), determining general style (choice B), or selecting actors for commercials (choice C).

16. **Correct Response: B.** Choice B provides the best assessment of the writer's credibility. Even though readers are unable to judge the representativeness of the example presented, the amount of detail contained in the selection indicates that the passage is based on extensive research. That the passage evidences considerable enthusiasm for television commericals does not detract from the writer's credibility because the selection is not intended to promote or defend the interests of the advertising industry (choice A). Of the other choices provided, the comparative amount of space devoted to actors and technical personnel has little bearing on the writer's credibility (choice C), and there was no compelling reason for the writer to present additional information about costs (choice D).

17. **Correct Response: B.** This question assesses the ability to organize information for study purposes. Choice B is the best response because it most accurately targets the main themes presented in the selection. Each of the alternative answers contains at least one element that represents a minor detail from the selection rather than a major point. For example, the writer devotes no more than passing attention to television commercials around the world (choice A), the role of networks and manufacturers in the production of television commercials (choice C), and the goals of television commercials (choice D).

18. **Correct Response: C.** Within the context of the fourth paragraph of the selection, the best definition of the word *storyboard* is a sequence of pictures and text illustrating the major segments of a film (choice C). The reader knows this because the writer indicates that a *storyboard* is an outline for a commercial that is composed of both images (i.e., "sketches") and words (i.e., "lines of 'voice-over' "). The definitions provided in choices A, B, and D each misinterpret the information provided by the writer about the purpose and components of a *storyboard*.

19. **Correct Reponse: C.** This question assesses the ability to recognize ideas that support the main idea of a paragraph or a passage. Choice C is the best response because encouraging children to explain why they are afraid, and then offering reassurance, is one means by which caregivers can help children to deal with their fears. Of the other responses provided, Choice A describes a way in which children overcome their fears without assistance, and Choice B indicates what caregivers should not do rather than what they can do to aid children. Choice D mentions something that caregivers should bear in mind when helping children to conquer their fears, but it says nothing about how they might offer such aid.

20. **Correct Response: C.** This question assesses the ability to recognize the likely effect on an audience of a writer's choice of certain words. Choice C is the best response because adults can readily understand the sense of security one feels when dealing with the familiar. The sentence says nothing about the actual fears of children (choices A and B), nor does it provide advice on how to help children overcome their fears (choice D).

21. **Correct Response: B.** This question assesses the ability to identify a solution to a problem presented in a passage. Choice B is the best response because contact desensitization studies show that fear reduction is most likely to occur when children are told how to approach the object of fear, encouraged by an adult to do so, praised when they try, and allowed to watch an adult do so as well. The techniques described in choices A and D may also reduce a child's fears, but contact desensitization studies show that they are not as effective as the approach outlined in choice B. Although children should not be forced to confront a feared situation before they are ready to do so, allowing them to avoid the object of fear (choice C) does nothing to eliminate the fear.

22. **Correct Response: D.** Understanding and dealing with children's fears are the main topics discussed in the passage. Choice D is therefore the best response because it says nothing about the nature of children's fears or the ways in which adults can help children to overcome them. By comparison, choice A states a major theme of the passage, choice B provides information about the learning process of fear reduction, and choice C offers advice about how to respond to children's fears.

23. **Correct Response: A.** This question assesses the ability to organize information for study purposes. Choice A is the best reponse because it provides the most accurate and inclusive statement of the main themes of the selection. Of the other responses provided, choices B and C misinterpret information presented in the selection. For example, the passage does not compare the fears of children and adults (choice B) or distinguish between the fears experienced by toddlers and older children (choice C); the latter also fails to list a major theme of the selection—how caregivers can help children to overcome their fears. Although the information provided in choice D is accurate, it does not reflect the flow and balance of major ideas discussed in the selection as well as choice A.

24. **Correct Response: A.** Within the context of the selection, choice A is the best definition of the word *index* because it most accurately describes the situation to which the word refers: allowing an observer to measure or gauge a child's level of development. Although choices B, C, and D are all acceptable definitions of the word *index*, they do not convey the correct meaning of the word as it is used in the passage. Their adoption in this context would be contrary to the writer's intentions.

25. **Correct Response: A.** In the first paragraph, the author explains why he chose to make topics and themes from his Native American background the focus of his writings. Choice A, which notes the connection between the writer's heritage and literary work, thus best states the main idea of the paragraph. Of the other responses provided, the writer certainly appreciates the artistic endeavors of Native American people; but it is unclear whether he believes art should be a part of everyone's existence (choice B); nor does he appear to have ever abandoned traditional Native American values (choice D). Concerning choice C, the author does have positive memories his parents and childhood, but these recollections do not constitute the main idea of the paragraph.

26. **Correct Response: D.** This question assesses the ability to recognize the likely effect on an audience of a writer's choice of a certain word. Choice D is the best response because the word "guttural" is often used to describe strange or disagreeable utterances, and the following sentence suggests that the newspaper disapproved of the author's poems. Of the other responses provided, "guttural" may be used to describe the sound of language, but that does not appear to have been the newspaper's intention in using the word (choice A); nor was the newspaper attempting to describe how the author felt about his poems (choice C). Concerning choice B, "guttural" is not a word that one would customarily use to characterize an audience's reaction to a perfomance.

27. **Correct Response: B.** This question assesses the ability to identify cause-effect relationships. Choice B is the best response because information in the passage indicates that memories of the sacrifices made to send tribal elders to Washington most influenced his decision to accept the White House invitation. Of the other responses provided, the author went to Washington despite a feeling that he was possibly being exploited as a Native American (choice A). There is no indication that he was especially eager to read his work before an audience of other poets and literary critics (choice C); and while he may have wished that the writings of other Native Americans assume a more political tone, that was not the reason why he changed his mind about the White House invitation (choice D).

28. **Correct Response: A.** Choice A is the best response to the question because the selection focuses on the ways his literary work and that of other Native American writers have been influenced by their cultural heritage, a heritage that has been marked by cultural repression on the part of U.S. policymakers. It thus follows that the author would view literature as a powerful means of asserting both the cultural values and political rights of Native Americans. Of the other responses provided, the author makes no effort to compare European and Native American artistic traditions (choice B), nor does he suggest that all Native American writings express a political position (choice C). Concerning choice D, much of the author's own work is intended to preserve Native American cultural traditions, but he does not insist that other Native American writers follow his example.

29. **Correct Response: B.** This question assesses the ability to identify a summary of a reading passage for study purposes. Of the responses provided, choice B is the best response because it provides the most informative and complete listing of the main points discussed in the selection. By comparison, many of the topics listed in the other choices are so vaguely phrased as to be of little help for study purposes; nor do any these responses note the importance of the author's Native American background to his literary work, which is a central theme of the passage.

30. **Correct Response: C.** Within the context of the second paragraph of the selection, the best definition of the word *spare* is meager because the author implies that U.S. policymakers largely ignored the many appeals of tribal elders. Of the other responses provided, adoption of choices A or D would distort the meaning of this part of the selection, and choice C is not an accepted meaning of the word *spare*.

31. **Correct Response: B.** The first paragraph of the selection is intended to distinguish between the negative and positive attributes of bacteria. Choice B, which notes that bacteria can be beneficial as well as harmful to humans, thus best expresses the main idea of the paragraph. By contrast, choices A, C, and D state that bacteria are either dangerous or useful, but do not indicate that they possess both of these characteristics.

32. **Correct Response: A.** The writer's primary intention in this selection is to examine important factors and procedures involved in bacteria farming. Therefore, choice A is the best response to the question. Although choices B and D relate to background issues and ideas that the writer addresses in developing the main theme of the selection, neither constitutes the primary purpose of the work. Concerning choice C, no effort is made in the selection to compare different methods of growing bacteria.

33. **Correct Response: A.** This question assesses the ability to identify cause-effect relationships in a reading selection. Choice A is the best response because the accumulation of wastes in the growth container is a major factor in bringing about the "death phase" of the bacterial growth cycle. Of the other responses provided, there is no compelling reason to monitor growth during the "start phase" of the growth cycle (choice B), increasing the amount of liquids in the culture medium is more likely to postpone than hasten the "death phase" of the growth cycle (choice C), and the culture medium should be kept at a constant temperature (choice D).

34. **Correct Response: D.** This question assesses the ability to recognize an assumption on which the validity of an argument depends. Choice D is the best response because an important theme of the selection is that, to be commercially successful, bacteria farmers must understand and take advantage of the organism's unique growth cycle. The selection provides no indication that the assumptions listed in choices A, B, and C had any influence on the writer. At no point in the selection does the writer attempt to compare the benefits of bacteria cultivation with other types of farming (choice A), to examine the growth rates of other kinds of organisms (choice B), or to assess the comparative influence of different factors on progress in medicine and industry (choice C).

35. **Correct Response: C.** This question assesses the ability to interpret information presented in a graph. The selection states that a bacterial population begins to decrease in size as it passes from the "stationary growth phase" to "death phase" of the bacterial growth cycle. According to the bacterial growth curve presented in the graph, this point is reached after approximately 24 hours of incubation (choice C). Of the other choices provided, the graph shows that a bacterial population is still increasing in size at the 6 and 12 hour marks (choices A and B), and is at the end of its "death phase" after 36 hours of incubation (choice D).

36. **Correct Response: B.** This question assesses the ability to use context clues to determine the intended meaning of a word with multiple meanings. Within the context of the last paragraph of the selection, producing (choice B) is the best definition of the word *yielding*. The reader knows this because the writer is discussing the good crop of usable organisms that bacteria farmers are able to produce and harvest during the "stationary growth phase." Although choices A, C, and D are all possible meanings of *yielding*, they do not convey the meaning intended by the writer in the context of the last paragraph.

37. **Correct Response: C.** In the first paragraph, the writer attempts to set the stage for the remainder of the selection by describing the gulf that developed between the promises contained in the Civil War era amendments and the realities of American social and political life. Choice C, which notes that the important provisions of the amendments were not honored in later decades, thus best expresses the main idea of the paragraph. Of the other responses provided, choice A is too narrow in scope to constitute the main idea of the paragraph, while the primary function of choices B and D is to furnish details that support the main idea.

38. **Correct Response: C.** This question assesses the ability to use the content of a reading passage to determine a writer's opinions. Choice C is the best response because a main purpose of the writer in the third paragraph is to show that political authorities in a democratic society are responsive to popular demands for change. The other choices provided all represent misinterpretations of the writer's intentions in the paragraph. The paragraph contains no criticism of the first phase of the civil rights movement (choice A), nor is any effort made to evaluate the comparative influence of Supreme Court decisions and Congressional actions (choice B). Concerning choice D, the paragraph indicates only that civil disobedience is sometimes an effective means of securing political change.

39. **Correct Response: B.** This question assesses the ability to identify a solution to a problem presented in a reading selection. Choice B is the best response because the writer states that when court orders to desegregate public schools encountered massive resistance, Blacks and their supporters adopted new tactics that emphasized nonviolent direct action. Although this campaign of civil disobedience eventually prompted Congressional action, there is no evidence in the selection that initial efforts to secure enforcement of the *Brown* decision focused on the enactment of civil rights legislation (choice A). Of the other responses provided, choices C and D are both unsupported by information presented in the selection.

40. **Correct Response: A.** Choice A is the best response to the question because the selection focuses on the century-long struggle of Blacks and their supporters to give meaning to the Civil War era amendments. Therefore, implicit throughout the selection is an assumption that nations should ensure that all their laws are observed, to whomever they may apply. The other choices provided all reflect a misunderstanding of the writer's argument in the selection. Amendments to the Constitution are not singled out for their effectiveness in eliminating social injustice (choice B), and at no point in the selection does the writer contend that people must in general be forcibly compelled to respect the rights of others (choice C). Concerning choice D, the selection suggests that the success of a social movement depends more on the justice of its cause than the forcefulness of its leaders.

41. **Correct Response: D.** This question assesses the ability to summarize information for study purposes. Choice D is the best response because it provides the most accurate and complete statement of the main themes of the selection. Of the other responses provided, choices A and B not only omit one or more of the selection's main ideas, but also misinterpret information presented in the passage. For example, the selection does not argue that the *Brown* decision ended segregation in American social life (choice A), nor does it contend that individuals were more important than organizations during the second stage of the civil rights movement (choice B). Although the information provided in choice C is accurate, it does not well reflect the flow and balance of the ideas presented in the selection and is too narrow in scope to constitute an adequate summary of the selection.

42. **Correct Response: D.** Within the context of the selection, choice D is the best definition of the word *culminated* because the next paragraph makes it clear that the *Brown* decision marked the highest point of achievement of the first phase of the civil rights movement. According to the third paragraph, subsequent progress would depend more on nonviolent direct action than the legal challenges that characterized the first stage of the movement. Choices A, B, and C are not accepted meanings of the word *culminated*. Their adoption in this context would also distort the broader meaning of the selection.

Practice Test Explanations: Mathematics

1. **Correct Response: D.** To solve this problem, you must multiply the number of bottles capped per second times the total number of seconds in 15 hours:

   (3 bottles/sec) (60 sec/min) (60 min/hr) (15 hr)

   1.6×10^5 bottles

   Notice that all the units cancel except the number of bottles. Choice A results from omitting one of the factors of 60. Choice B results from miscounting the number of decimal places in the answer. Choice C results from interpreting the problem as saying "3 seconds per bottle" instead of "3 bottles per second."

2. **Correct Response: A.** To solve the this problem, first add the total number of gallons of gas used, then subtract that number from the initial number of gallons:

   $7\frac{1}{4} + 13\frac{1}{2} + 15\frac{1}{4}$

   $\frac{29}{4} + \frac{27}{2} + \frac{61}{4}$ *Change to simple fractions.*

   $\frac{29}{4} + \frac{54}{4} + \frac{61}{4}$ *Find common denominator.*

   $\frac{144}{4} = 36$ *Add and reduce.*

   $50 - 36 = 14$ *Subtract.*

   Choice B results from adding incorrectly. Choice C results from adding only the integer parts of each number. Choice D is the total number of gallons of gas used.

3. **Correct Response: C.** This is a multistep problem involving subtraction, percents, and addition. First find how much fencing is left after the morning, then find 40% of this remaining fencing, then add those two numbers:

   $220 - 80 = 140$ *Subtract.*
   $(40\%)(140) = (0.40)(140) = 56$ *Multiply.*
   $80 + 56 = 136$ *Add.*
   $\frac{136}{220} \times 100\% = 62\%$ *Find percentage.*

   Choice A is the percent of fencing that was put up in the morning. Choice B is the result of adding the amount of fencing put up in the morning plus 40% of the amount of fencing put up in the morning. Choice D is the result of adding the amount of fencing put up in the morning plus 40% of the original amount of fencing to be put up.

4. **Correct Response: B.** This problem is solved by using proportions.

   $\frac{\$1.25}{\$4.00} = \frac{x}{\$156.00}$

   $x = \frac{(\$1.25)}{\$4.00} (\$156.00) = \$48.75$

   Choice A results from subtracting $1.25 from $4.00. Choice C results from multiplying $1.25 times $156.00. Choice D results from setting up the proportion incorrectly.

5. **Correct Response: A.** This problem involves taking a percentage of a percent. Eighteen percent of the advertising expenditures (which is 35% of the total budget) is spent on radio advertising.

$$(0.35)(0.18) = 0.063 = 6.3\%$$

Choice B results from calculating 18% of the non-advertising expenditures. Choice C is the percentage of advertising expenditures spent on radio advertising. Choice D is the percentage of total expenditures spent on advertising.

6. **Correct Response: A.** Solving this problem involves correctly interpreting the information on the graph. At time t = 0, the pond is stocked with a certain number of fish. This eliminates choice D, since on that graph there are no fish in the pond initially. The number of fish steadily decreases. This eliminates choice C, since that graph shows the number of fish remaining constant through time. (This also eliminates choice D, since that graph shows the number of fish as increasing through time.) Eventually, there are approximately half the number of fish originally stocked. This eliminates choice B, since on that graph, the number of fish is never half the number of fish initially stocked.

7. **Correct Response: B.** To solve this problem, let x equal the test score needed. Then, since the test counts twice as much as the quizzes, x must appear twice in the expression for the average:

$$\frac{88+82+84+x+x}{5} = 70$$

$$\frac{254+2x}{5} = 70 \qquad\qquad \textit{Simplify.}$$

$$254 + 2x = 350 \qquad\qquad \textit{Multiply by 5.}$$

$$2x = 96 \qquad\qquad\qquad\; \textit{Subtract 254.}$$

$$x = 48 \qquad\qquad\qquad\;\; \textit{Divide by 2.}$$

Choice A results from including x twice, but dividing by 4 instead of 5. (There are 5 grades to be counted: 3 quizzes, and the test grade, twice.) Choice C is the average the student needs, not the test score. Choice D results from only counting x once, but dividing by 5.

8. **Correct Response: C.** Solving this problem involves correctly interpreting a distribution graph. The mean of a (symmetric) distribution curve is where it attains its maximum value. Both curves in the graph have approximately the same mean, which eliminates choices A and D. The distribution curves give the percentage of cars that have a given gas mileage, which eliminates choice B. The variability of the data is reflected in the width of the distribution curve. Since curve A is narrower than curve B, brand A cars have smaller variability in gas mileage than brand B cars.

9. **Correct Response: A.** Solving this problem involves correctly interpreting information from the graph of a line. The slope-intercept form of a line is y = mx + b, where m is the slope of the line and b is the y-intercept. The y-intercept of the given line is 2, which eliminates choices B and C. The slope of the line is:

$$m = \frac{\Delta y}{\Delta x} = \frac{y_2 - y_1}{x_2 - x_1} = \frac{0-2}{3-0} = -\frac{2}{3}$$

Choice D has slope m = 3. Only choice A fits both criteria.

10. **Correct Response: B.** The slope of the line through two points is:

$$m = \frac{y_2 - y_1}{x_2 - x_1}$$

$$m = \frac{-2 - (-1)}{3 - 0} = \frac{-2 + 1}{3 - 0} = -\frac{1}{3}$$

Choice A results from calculating $\frac{y_2 - y_1}{x_1 - x_2}$.

Choice C results from calculating $\frac{x_1 - x_2}{y_2 - y_1}$.

Choice D results from calculating $\frac{x_2 - x_1}{y_2 - y_1}$.

11. **Correct Response: B.** This problem involves finding the slope of the line, and then substituting the coordinates of a point on the line to eliminate the incorrect answers.

$$m = \frac{y_2 - y_1}{x_2 - x_1} = \frac{0 - 4}{6 - (-2)} = \frac{-4}{8} = \frac{-1}{2}$$

This eliminates choice A, which has $m = \frac{1}{2}$, and choice C, which has $m = -2$. Of the remaining two choices, only choice B passes through both given points:

$4 = -\frac{1}{2}(-2) + 3$ *Substitute -2 for x and 4 for y.*

$4 = 4$

$0 = -\frac{1}{2}(6) + 3$ *Substitute 6 for x and 0 for y.*

$0 = 0$

12. **Correct Response: B.** To solve this problem, you must recognize that the graph represents an inverse variation relation. If a rectangle has constant area, then length × width = constant, or ℓw = constant. The graph passes through the point (3,4) so that, at that point, $\ell = 3$ and $w = 4$. Therefore, the constant for this rectangle is $3 \cdot 4 = 12$. Now, if $\ell = 8$, then $8w = 12$ or $w = \frac{12}{8} = \frac{3}{2}$. Choice A results from incorrectly estimating the w-value of the graph at $\ell = 8$. Choice C results from subtracting 12 − 8 instead of dividing 12/8. Choice D results from multiplying (12)(8) instead of dividing 12/8.

13. **Correct Response: C.** This problem requires determining the value of an unknown in an equation and using that value to solve a second problem. The first step is to solve the first equation for x.

$-\frac{1}{3}x + 7 = 16$

$-\frac{1}{3}x = 9$ *Subtract 7 from each side.*

$x = -27$ *Multiply each side by -3.*

Now, use $x = -27$ in the second problem.

$2x + 1 = ?$

$2(-27) + 1 = ?$

$-54 + 1 = -53$

Choice C, ⁻53, is correct. Choice A, ⁻5, results from multiplying the right side by $-\frac{1}{3}$ instead of ⁻3. Choice B, ⁻27, results from solving only the first equation. Choice D, ⁻137, results from adding rather than subtracting 7 in the first problem-solving step.

14. **Correct Response: A.** This problem involves finding the value of an unknown in an equation and expressing it in terms of another unknown. To find the value of t in terms of r, the first step is to isolate t on one side of the equation.

$9t + 7 = 5r$

$9t = 5r - 7$ *Subtract 7 from each side.*

$t = \frac{5r-7}{9}$ *Divide each side by 9.*

Choice B results from a sign error when subtracting 7 from both sides. Choice C results from dividing only one term, rather than both, by 9. Choice D results from both of the above errors.

15. **Correct Response: B.** This problem involves solving two equations simultaneously, one of which is quadratic, and the other of which is linear. We may solve this system of equations by substitution. Since $y = x^2 - x + 6$ (first equation), substitute $x^2 - x + 6$ for y in the second equation, and solve that equation for x:

$2x + 2(x^2 - x + 6) = 36$ *Substitute.*

$2x + 2x^2 - 2x + 12 = 36$ *Distribute.*

$2x^2 + 12 = 36$ *Simplify.*

$2x^2 = 24$ *Subtract 12.*

$x^2 = 12$ *Divide by 2.*

$x = \pm\sqrt{12} = \pm2\sqrt{3}$ *Take the square root.*

Now solve for y:

$y = x^2 - x + 6$

$= \left(\pm2\sqrt{3}\right)^2 - \left(\pm2\sqrt{3}\right) + 6$ *Substitute for x.*

$= 12 \mp 2\sqrt{3} + 6$ *Simplify.*

$= 18 \mp 2\sqrt{3}$ *Simplify.*

Therefore, $y = 18 - 2\sqrt{3}$ when $x = +2\sqrt{3}$, and $y = 18 + 2\sqrt{3}$ when $x = -2\sqrt{3}$. The correct answer, then, is $\left(2\sqrt{3}, 18-2\sqrt{3}\right), \left(-2\sqrt{3}, 18+2\sqrt{3}\right)$. In choice A, (0,6) is a solution of the first equation, and (9,9) is a solution of the second equation, but they are not solutions of both equations simultaneously.

16. **Correct Response: C.** This problem involves solving two simultaneous equations in two variables by graphing. The first equation is a line with slope m = $^-2$ and y-intercept b = $^-2$:

$$y + 2x + 2 = 0$$

$$y = {}^-2x - 2 \qquad \textit{Solve for y.}$$

$$y = mx + b \qquad \textit{Slope-intercept form of a line.}$$

$$m = {}^-2, b = {}^-2 \qquad \textit{By inspection.}$$

Since the slope is negative, the graph of the line slopes down and to the right. This eliminates choices A and B, since both lines have positive slopes. The second equation is a parabola that opens up (since $y = ax^2 + bx + c$ with a>0 is a parabola that opens up). This eliminates choice D. Only choice C fits all of the properties of the two equations.

17. **Correct Response: B.** This problem involves writing algebraic relationships from verbal descriptions. The sum of x and y is x + y, and the product of x and y is xy. The quotient of these two expressions is $\frac{x+y}{xy}$, and the square of this quotient is $\left(\frac{x+y}{xy}\right)^2$

Ten more than this expression is $\left(\frac{x+y}{xy}\right)^2 + 10$, which is equal to C. Choice A is the square of 10 more than the quotient of the sum of x and y and the product of x and y. Choice C is 10 more than the square of the quotient of the product of x and y and the sum of x and y. Choice D is 10 more than the quotient of the square of the sum of x and y, and the product of x and y.

18. **Correct Response: A.** The difference of m^2 and n is $m^2 - n$, and the square of this expression is $(m^2 - n)^2$. Fifty less than this expression is $(m^2 - n)^2 - 50$, which equals P. Choice B is 50 less than the difference of m^2 and n. Choice C is the square of 50 less than the difference of m^2 and n. Choice D is the difference of 50 and the square of the difference of m^2 and n.

19. **Correct Response: C.** This problem involves writing an algebraic expression for the relationships between the lengths of the three pieces of the board. Let the lengths of the three pieces be a, b, and c. Then, the sum of the lengths of the three pieces is 10 feet: a + b + c = 10. But the second piece (b) is not as long as the first (a): b = $\frac{a}{2}$. And, the third piece (c) is $4\frac{1}{2}$ feet longer than the second (b or $\frac{a}{2}$):

$$c = b + 4\frac{1}{2}$$

$$= b + \frac{9}{2} \qquad \textit{Simplify: } 4\frac{1}{2} = \frac{9}{2}$$

$$= \frac{a}{2} + \frac{9}{2} \qquad \textit{Substitute for b.}$$

$$= \frac{a+9}{2} \qquad \textit{Combine fractions.}$$

Now substitute back into the first equation:

$a + b + c = 10$

$a + \frac{a}{2} + \frac{a+9}{2} = 10$ *Substitute for b and c.*

$\frac{2a}{2} + \frac{a}{2} + \frac{a+9}{2} = 10$ *Common denominator.*

$\frac{4a+9}{2} = 10$ *Combine fractions.*

$4a + 9 = 20$ *Multiply by 2.*

$4a = 11$ *Subtract 9.*

$a = \frac{11}{4} = 2\frac{3}{4}$ *Divide by 4.*

Choice A results from using the incorrect relation that the second piece is twice as long as the first. Choice B results from using the incorrect relation that the third piece is $4\frac{1}{2}$ feet longer than the first piece. Choice D results from dividing the 10-foot board into three equal pieces.

20. **Correct Response: A.** This problem involves writing relations between different quantities as a system of three linear equations in three variables. If we write all money quantities in cents, then Angel has 180 cents in his pocket. The total number of cents in nickels is 5N (5 cents for each nickel, times the number of nickels N), the total number of cents in dimes is 10D (10 cents for each dime, times the total number of dimes D), and the total number of cents in quarters is 25Q (25 cents for each quarter times the number of quarters Q). This gives the first equation: 5N + 10D + 25Q = 180. This excludes choices C and D. Since the coefficients on the left side and the number on the right side are written in different units (cents and dollars). The second sentence says that Angel has twice as many quarters as nickels, so that the number of quarters Q is two times the number of nickels N. Q = 2N. This excludes choice B, in which the relation is reversed. The third sentence says that the number of dimes D equals the number of nickels N plus the number of quarters Q plus 1: D = N + Q + 1. Only choice A has all three of these equations.

21. **Correct Response: B.** This problem involves writing an equation from the given verbal information, and solving it. If $175 was collected this week, and this was $35 more than was collected last week, then $175 – $35 = $140 collected last week. The total amount of money collected in the two weeks, then, was $140 + $175 = $315. Choice A assumes that $35 was collected in the first week. Choice C assumes that $35 less was collected in the second week than in the first week. Choice D assumes that $70 less was collected in the second week than in the first week.

22. **Correct Response: C.** To solve this problem, you must factor the quadratic expression. The factors of 24 are $1 \cdot 24$, $2 \cdot 12$, $3 \cdot 8$, and $4 \cdot 6$. One of each pair of factors must be positive and the other negative, since the constant term is negative (–24):

$(x + \quad)(x - \quad) = x^2 - 2x - 24$

The only pair of factors that sums to –2 (the coefficient of x) is +4, –6:

$(x + 4)(x - 6) = x^2 - 2x - 24.$

Choice A is the result of factoring incorrectly. Choices B and D are the results of choosing the wrong signs to the factors.

23.   **Correct Response: D.** This problem may be solved by inverting the second rational expression and factoring, then simplifying and multiplying.

$$\frac{x^2-x}{x^2+3x+2} \div \frac{x^2+2x}{x^2-1}$$

$$\frac{x^2-x}{x^2+3x+2} \cdot \frac{x^2-1}{x^2+2x}$$ *Invert the second expression and change division to multiplication.*

$$\frac{\cancel{x}(x-1)}{(x+2)\cancel{(x+1)}} \cdot \frac{\cancel{(x+1)}(x-1)}{\cancel{x}(x+2)}$$ *Factor and cancel.*

$$\frac{(x-1)^2}{(x+2)^2}$$ *Simplify.*

$$\frac{x^2-2x+1}{x^2+4x+4}$$ *Multiply out.*

Choice A results from multiplying the two rational expressions instead of dividing. Choice B results from canceling before inverting the second expression, then inverting and canceling again. Choice C results from incorrectly canceling and multiplying.

24.   **Correct Response: A.** This problem involves simplifying a rational expression.

$$\frac{9c}{24cx-18c^2}$$

$$=\frac{3\cdot 3\cancel{c}}{3\cancel{c}(8x-6c)}$$ *Factor 3c out of expressions in numerator and denominator.*

$$=\frac{3}{8x-6c}$$ *Cancel 3c.*

Choice B results from correctly canceling the c but subtracting coefficients instead of factoring and canceling. Choice C results from taking the reciprocal of the correct answer. Choice D results from correctly canceling the c but incorrectly canceling the coefficients.

25.   **Correct Response: D.** This problem involves dividing and simplifying two rational expressions, and using the laws of exponents.

$$\frac{a^{3/2}b^3c^5}{a^2b^{1/3}} \div a^2 \, b^{5/3} \, d^{1/2}$$

$$\frac{a^{3/2}b^3c^5}{a^2b^{1/3}} \cdot \frac{1}{a^2b^{5/3}d^{1/2}}$$ *Invert second expression and change division to multiplication.*

$$\frac{a^{3/2}b^3c^5}{a^4b^2d^{1/2}}$$ *Simplify denominator by adding exponents of common bases.*

$$\frac{bc^5}{a^{5/2}d^{1/2}}$$ *Simplify by subtracting exponents of common bases.*

Choice A results from multiplying the two expressions instead of dividing. Choice B results from correctly inverting the second expression and adding exponents of common bases in the denominator, but then multiplying exponents instead of subtracting in the last step. Choice C results from correctly inverting and adding exponents of common bases in the denominator, but then dividing exponents instead of subtracting in the last step.

26. **Correct Response: C.** This problem involves evaluating a function for a particular value of its variable.

$$f(x) = 2x^2 + \tfrac{1}{2}x - 4$$

$$f\left(-\tfrac{1}{2}\right) = 2\left(-\tfrac{1}{2}\right)^2 + \tfrac{1}{2}\left(-\tfrac{1}{2}\right) - 4 \qquad \textit{Substitute } -\tfrac{1}{2} \textit{ for } x.$$

$$= 2\left(\tfrac{1}{4}\right) + \tfrac{1}{2}\left(-\tfrac{1}{2}\right) - 4 \qquad \textit{Square } \left(-\tfrac{1}{2}\right).$$

$$= \tfrac{2}{4} - \tfrac{1}{4} - \tfrac{16}{4} \qquad \textit{Simplify and rewrite last term using common}$$
$$\textit{denominator of 4.}$$

$$= -\tfrac{15}{4} \qquad \textit{Simplify.}$$

Choice A is $f(\tfrac{1}{2})$. Choice B is $f(2)$. Choice D is $f(^-2)$.

27. **Correct Response: B.** This problem involves determining the equation of a function from its graph. The graph is a parabola that opens up so that it has the form $y = ax^2 + bx + c$ where a is positive. This eliminates Choices A and C. The graph passes through the points $(^-2,0)$, $(3,0)$ (the x-intercepts), and $(0,^-6)$ (the y-intercept). The only choice in which substituting these values for x and y makes the equation true is choice B.

28. **Correct Response: C.** This problem involves identifying an inequality from its graph. To solve this problem first identify the equality. The graph is a parabola opening down, that passes through the points $(0,0)$, $(1,1)$, and $(2,0)$. Only choices B or C, when written as equalities, satisfy all three of these points when the coordinates are substituted into the equations. To determine which choice is correct, pick a point inside the shaded region and substitute the coordinates into the expression, leaving a question mark for the inequality sign:

$$0 \; ? \; ^-(1)^2 + 2(1) \qquad \textit{Substitute } (1,0).$$

$$0 \; ? \; ^-1 + 2$$

$$0 < 1$$

Zero is less than one, so choice C is correct.

29. **Correct Response: D.** This problem requires carrying out a step in solving a quadratic equation by completing the square. To complete the square, make sure the coefficient of x^2 is 1, take half the coefficient of x, square it and place the result in each set of parentheses.

$$x^2 + 6x + (\;\;) = 15 + (\;\;)$$

$$\left(\tfrac{6}{2}\right)^2 = (3)^2 \qquad \textit{Half of coefficient of } x \textit{ is 3.}$$

$$x^2 + 6x + (9) = 15 + (9) \qquad \textit{Place 9 in each set of parentheses.}$$

$$x^2 + 6x + 9 = 24 \qquad \textit{First three terms are a perfect square.}$$

$$(x + 3)^2 = 24$$

Choice A results from taking one half of one half the coefficient of x. Choice B results from taking half the coefficient of x, but not squaring it. Choice C results from incorrectly squaring 3.

30. **Correct Response: B.** To solve this problem, you must first put the expression in standard form and then use the quadratic formula:

$3x^2 = x - 5$

$3x^2 - x + 5 = 0$ *Bring x - 5 to left side.*

$a = 3, b = {}^-1, c = 5$ *Coefficients.*

$x = \frac{{}^-b \pm \sqrt{b^2 - 4ac}}{2a}$ *Quadratic formula.*

$x = \frac{1 \pm \sqrt{({}^-1)^2 - 4(3)(5)}}{2(3)}$ *Substitute for a, b, and c.*

$= \frac{1 \pm \sqrt{1 - 60}}{6}$

$= \frac{1 \pm \sqrt{-59}}{6}$

Choice A results from incorrectly putting the expression in standard form, and uses $3x^2 + x - 5 = 0$. Choice C results form an incorrect use of the quadratic equation ($b^2 + 4ac$ instead of $b^2 - 4ac$). Choice D results from an incorrect use of the quadratic equation ($4ac - b^2$ instead of $b^2 - 4ac$).

31. **Correct Response: B.** This problem involves using the quadratic model to solve for a particular value of one of the variables. To solve this problem, substitute known height for h and solve for t:

$h = 128t - 32t^2$

$128 = 128t - 32t^2$ *Substitute 128 for h.*

$32t^2 - 128t + 128 = 0$ *Put in standard quadratic form.*

$32(t^2 - 4t + 4) = 0$ *Factor out 32.*

$t^2 - 4t + 4 = 0$ *Divide by 32.*

$(t - 2)(t - 2) = 0$ *Factor.*

$t - 2 = 0$ *Zero factor rule.*

$t = 2$ *Add 2 to both sides.*

Choice A results from an error made inputting the equation in standard quadratic form. Choice C results from incorrectly factoring. Choice D results from incorrectly solving the quadratic equation.

32. **Correct Response: B.** To solve this problem, the total area of the geometric figure must be calculated. This is best done piece by piece. The area of the lower rectangular part of the window is 6 ft. × 4 ft. = 24 square feet. The area of the upper triangular part of the window is:

$\frac{1}{2} bh = \frac{1}{2} (4 \text{ ft})(3 \text{ ft}) = 6$ square feet.

The total area is the sum of the two sections: 24 square feet + 6 square feet = 30 square feet.

Choice A is the area of just the rectangular lower section of the window. Choice C is the area the window would have if it were a rectangle 4 feet wide and 9 feet high. Choice D is twice the area of the rectangular lower section of the window.

33. **Correct Response: C.** To solve this problem, you must calculate the perimeter of the figure, including the two semicircular end caps, and then multiply by 8 for the 8 laps. There are two straight parts of the track, each 200 m long, for a total of 400 m. Each end cap is a semicircle, making a full circle of radius 25 m. The circumference of the circle is $c = 2\pi r = 2\pi (25m) \approx 157$ m. The total perimeter of the track, then, is approximately 400 m + 157 m = 557 m. The runner runs 8 times around, for a total of 8×557 m = 4456 m. Choice A is the approximate length of one lap. Choice B is the length of 8 laps around a rectangular track measuring 200 m × 50 m. Choice D counts each end cap as a full circle instead of a semicircle.

34. **Correct Response: D.** This problem involves knowing the formula for the surface of a sphere. The surface area of a sphere of radius r is $4\pi r^2$. Therefore, the surface area of a hemisphere is half that of a sphere: $\frac{1}{2} \bullet 4\pi r^2$. If a hemisphere is divided into 12 equal sections, each section has $\frac{1}{12}$ of the area of the hemisphere: $\frac{1}{12} \bullet \frac{1}{2} \bullet 4\pi r^2$. If the radius of the hemisphere is 18 m, the formula for one section of the hemisphere is $\frac{1}{12} \bullet \frac{1}{2} \bullet 4\pi (18)^2$. Choice A is the formula for $\frac{1}{12}$ the volume of a hemisphere of radius 18 m. Choice B is the formula for the entire surface area of a hemisphere of radius 18 m. Choice C is an incorrect formula, since it uses the square of the diameter of the hemisphere instead of the radius.

35. **Correct Response: C.** Solving this problem involves using the Pythagorean theorem. The ramp forms the hypotenuse of a right triangle whose base is the ground, and whose vertical side is the wall of the platform:

$12^2 = x^2 + 5^2$ *Pythagorean Theorem.*

$x^2 = 12^2 - 5^2 = 144 - 25 = 119$ *Solve for x^2.*

$x = \sqrt{119}$ *Square root.*

Choice A is the difference between the length of the ramp and the height of the platform. Choice B is the average of the length of the ramp and the height of the platform. Choice D is the hypotenuse of a triangle whose sides have lengths 5 and 12.

36. **Correct Response: D.** To solve this problem, you must use the properties of similarity to set up a proportion between two pairs of sides of the two figures. Corresponding sides of the two figures are proportional:

$\frac{AE}{FJ} = \frac{BC}{GH}$

$\frac{5}{20} = \frac{40}{GH}$

$GH = \frac{20 \bullet 40}{5} = 160$

Choice A results from incorrectly setting up the proportion. Choice B results from adding the lengths of the two sides of the first figure, and equating that number to the sum of the lengths of the two sides of the second figure. This is incorrect because in similar geometric figures, the lengths of corresponding sides are proportional, but the sides do not necessarily add up to the same lengths. Choice C is the sum of the lengths of the two given sides of the first figure.

37. **Correct Response: C.** To solve this problem, you must use the properties of similarity to set up a proportion between two pairs of sides of the two figures. Corresponding sides of the two figures are proportional:

$$\frac{DI}{CD} = \frac{DF}{DE}$$

$$\frac{20}{50} = \frac{DF}{45}$$

$$DF = \frac{45 \cdot 20}{50} = 18$$

Choice A results from setting up the proportion incorrectly. Choices B and D result from assuming that the lengths of the two pairs of sides sum to the same number. In similar geometric figures, the ratios of corresponding sides are equal, but the lengths of the sides of the two figures do not necessarily sum to the same number.

38. **Correct Response: C.** To solve this problem, you must use the properties of parallel lines. In the figure, angle k and angle w are corresponding angles, so that the measure of angle k equals the measure of angle w. Angle w and angle y are supplementary angles, since they lie on the straight line. Supplementary angles add to 180°. Therefore, the measure of angle k plus the measure of angle y is 180°.

Choice A results from incorrectly using angle w and angle y as complementary angles. Choice B results from incorrectly summing supplementary angles to be 100°. Choice D results from summing angles k, j, m, and n.

39. **Correct Response: C.** To solve this problem, you need to use the properties of triangles and of parallel lines. The angles of a triangle add up to 180°. An equilateral triangle has three equal angles, so that each angle is 60°. Therefore, the measure of angle 3 is 60°. Since line BC is parallel to line CE, angles 3 and 4 are corresponding angles. The measure of angle 4 is 60°, since corresponding angles are congruent. Angles 4 and 5 are supplementary angles, since they lie on a straight line. Supplementary angles add up to 180°. Therefore,

m ∠4 + m ∠5 = 180°

60° + m ∠5 = 180°

m ∠5 = 120°

Choice A is the measure of angle 4. Choice B is the measure of a right angle, and Choice D is the sum of angle 4 and angle 5.

40. **Correct Response: A.** This problem involves an application of inductive reasoning. Since Carl has brown hair (by statement 5), Carl must like pizza (by statement 3). Choice B (Carl has red hair) cannot be true since he has brown hair (by statement 5). We do not know whether Carl is wearing a hat (choice C). It is true that Carl has brown hair (statement 5), but there is no statement saying that all people who have brown hair are wearing hats. Statement 1 says that all people wearing hats have brown hair. We do not know whether Carl likes hamburgers (choice D). There is no statement that says that people who have brown hair like hamburgers, though there is one (statement 4) that says that people who have red hair like hamburgers.

41. **Correct Response: A.** This problem involves an application of inductive reasoning, in this case determining the missing design from a pattern sequence. This type of problem is solved by using the given information to determine how the pattern changes, and then predicting what the missing design should be. The pattern is discerned by trial and error. In this case, the pattern is that the external shape becomes the internal shape of the design to its right (or vice versa). Since the external shape of the design to the left of the blank is a diamond, that must be the internal shape of the correct response. Since the internal shape of the design to the right of the blank is a semicircle, that must be the external shape of the correct response. Adding together these two shapes gives choice A. Choices B, C, and D are designs that do not fit in the pattern sequence.

42. **Correct Response: B.** This question involves the application of deductive reasoning to solve a given problem. This problem is best solved by setting up a matrix using the persons as one dimension and the jobs as the other.

	Writer	Researcher	Artist	Engineer
Bess				
Tara				
Gerard				
Clifton				

Then, using the given statements, fill in the matrix. Since the information is in the form of who is not what (e.g., Bess and Gerard are not the engineer), put an X in the appropriate places to rule out the jobs each person *cannot* hold. For statement I, Bess and Gerard cannot be the engineer.

	Writer	Researcher	Artist	Engineer
Bess				X
Tara				
Gerard				X
Clifton				

Add statement II, which indicates that Clifton and Tara cannot be the researcher.

	Writer	Researcher	Artist	Engineer
Bess				X
Tara		X		
Gerard				X
Clifton		X		

Finally, add statement III, which indicates that Gerard cannot be the writer or the researcher.

	Writer	Researcher	Artist	Engineer
Bess				X
Tara		X		
Gerard	X	X		X
Clifton		X		

The only empty cell under researcher corresponds with Bess; therefore, choice B must be correct.

43. **Correct Response: C.** This problem involves an application of inductive reasoning, in this case determining the missing design from a pattern sequence. This type of problem is solved by using the given information to determine how the pattern changes, and then predicting what the missing pattern should be. In this case, the designs are polygons with different numbers of sides, so the first step is to write down the number of sides in each polygon:

    3 6 4 7 5 __

    This is two sequences mixed together. Every other term in the sequence increases by one:

    3 4 5
    6 7 __

    The missing number is 8, so the missing polygon is the one with 8 sides.

44. **Correct Response: B.** Solving this problem involves using the Pythagorean Theorem twice.

    The largest straight distance in the box is always a diagonal through the middle of the box. This diagonal forms the hypotenuse of a triangle whose side is the edge, and whose base is the diagonal of the bottom of the box.

    To find the diagonal of the bottom of the box, we find the diagonal of a 2-foot by 3-foot rectangle using the Pythagorean Theorem:

    Diagonal of bottom of box $\sqrt{2^2 + 3^2} = \sqrt{13}$ feet

    To find the length of the diagonal through the middle of the box we use the Pythagorean Theorem again:

    $$c = \sqrt{a^2 + b^2} = \sqrt{(1.5)^2 + (\sqrt{13})^2} = \sqrt{2.25 + 13} = 3.9 \text{ feet}$$

    Choice A is the length of the diagonal in the bottom of the box. Choice C results from adding the lengths of the three sides of the box. Choice D results from not taking the square root of $a^2 + b^2$.

45. **Correct Response: A.** This is a multi-step problem in which you must calculate each contribution to the monthly cost of each apartment. For apartment A, rent is $575 per month. This apartment uses 250 kilowatt-hours of electricity, at 5¢ per kilowatt-hour, for a total of (250 kWh) × ($0.05/kWh) = $12.50. The total cost of commuting from apartment A is ($1.50/day) × (30 days) = $45.00. Therefore, the total monthly cost of apartment A is $575.00 + $12.50 + $45.00 = $632.50. For apartment B, rent is $600 per month; electricity is (225 kilowatt-hours/month) × ($0.05/kilowatt-hour) = $11.25; and commuting cost is ($0.75/day) × (30 days) = $22.50. Apartment B's total monthly cost is therefore $600.00 + $11.25 + 22.50 = $633.75. Therefore, apartment A is cheaper.

46. **Correct Response: C.** To solve this problem, you must calculate the volume of each tank, multiply by 3 for the three tanks to get the total capacity of the plant in gallons, and then multiply by 7.5 to get the total number of gallons.

For tank 1, $V = \pi r^2 h$ *Volume of a cylinder.*

$$= \pi (15 \text{ ft})^2 (25 \text{ ft}) \quad \textit{Substitute.}$$

$$= 1.8 \times 10^4 \text{ ft}^3$$

For 3 tanks, $V = 3 (1.8 \times 10^4 \text{ ft}^3)$

$$= 5.4 \times 10^4 \text{ft}^3$$

Each cubic foot contains approximately 7.5 gallons, so we multiply to get the total number of gallons:

$$(5.4 \times 10^4 \text{ft}^3)(7.5 \text{ gal/ft}^3) = 4.1 \times 10^5 \text{gal}.$$

Choice A results from dividing by 7.5 instead of multiplying. Choice B is the number of gallons in one tank. Choice D results from incorrectly placing the decimal point.

47. **Correct Response: C.** To solve this problem, you must calculate the number of square feet of surface area exposed to the air in all three tanks and multiply by the amount of water that evaporates per square foot per day.

Surface Area

$$= (3 \text{ tanks}) (\pi r^2)$$
$$= 3\pi (15 \text{ ft})^2$$
$$= 2.1 \times 10^3 \text{ ft}^2$$

Number of gallons evaporating per day =

$$\left(\tfrac{1}{10} \tfrac{\text{gal}}{\text{hr·ft}^2}\right)\left(24 \tfrac{\text{hr}}{\text{day}}\right)\left(2.1 \times 10^3 \text{ft}^2\right)$$

$$= 5.0 \times 10^3 \text{ gal/day}$$

Choice A is the number of gallons evaporating per hour. Choice B is the number of gallons evaporating per day from one tank. Choice D results from incorrectly placing the decimal point.

48. **Correct Response: D.** This problem involves using the data in a table to write an equation that models the data. Since the depth is decreasing as time increases, the slope of this linear relation is negative. This eliminates choice C. When time equals zero, the depth is 25 feet. Substituting these values into the equations eliminates A, since the values do not make that equation true. At time equals 1 hour, the depth is 17 feet. When we substitute these values into the equations, only equation D is satisfied.

Practice Test Explanations: Writing

1. **Correct Response: A.** In this letter, the writer uses the personal voice and informal, emotional language to persuade a campus community that its parking facilities are inadequate. The sentence presented in choice A is consistent with the letter's style because of the personal voice used (*we*), the use of the informal *it's,* and the sarcasm implied in the suggestion that some students have cars for trivial reasons. Of the other choices listed, the sentence in choice B is incorrect because it involves an inappropriate shift to formal language and the impersonal voice. Choice C is incorrect not only because of its irrelevance to the focus of the letter, but also because its use of the pronoun *one* and its appeal to statistical evidence give the sentence an apparent objectivity that is inconsistent with the writer's highly subjective approach. In choice D, even though the personal voice is used, the sentence's formal tone makes it inappropriate in this context.

2. **Correct Response: D.** This question assesses the ability to recognize the standard use of pronouns and comparatives. Choice D is the correct response because, since the pronoun is used as the object of the preposition *for*, it should be in the objective case (*us*) rather than the nominative case (*we*). Choice A is incorrect because the change from *nearest,* which suggests many buildings, to *nearer,* which suggests only two buildings, would be illogical in this context. Nor should the change described in choice B be made, because the expression *it's* correctly conveys the intended abbreviation of *it is,* while the possessive adjective *its,* meaning *belonging to it,* would not make sense here. In Part 9, *our* should not be changed (choice C) because it agrees in person and number with the subject of the sentence (*we*).

3. **Correct Response: A.** The main idea of the first paragraph is that the spread of public opinion polls is an unfortunate and unnecessary development, since such polls generally address insignificant questions. Part 3, however, states precisely the opposite point of view and should be deleted; thus, choice A is the correct response. Choice B is incorrect because the phrase "with a minimum of research" is a supportive detail in a sentence that effectively points out the ease with which trivial information can be collected and spread. Choice C is incorrect because changing the rhetorical question "Do we need to know such things . . . ?" into an assertion that "We need to know such things . . ." contradicts the main idea of the paragraph. Revising Part 7 from the plural to the singular (choice D) is incorrect because the resulting sentence would be an inappropriate reply to the rhetorical question in Part 6, which uses the pronoun *we.*

4. **Correct Response: C.** This question requires the ability to identify the standard sentence structure, in this case, standard subject-verb agreement. The subject of Part 4 is *percentage,* which is a singular noun and therefore requires a singular verb, i.e., *thinks. Americans* does not affect the number of the verb. Therefore choice C is correct. Choice A is incorrect because *thinking,* the present participle of the verb *to think,* requires the helping verb *is,* which is missing here, to make sense. Choice B is incorrect because, although the substitution of the future tense *will think* would produce a grammatically correct sentence, it would be illogical here: the polls do not report what people *will think* but what they *do* think. Choice D is incorrect for similar reasons: the substitution of *should think* would be logically incorrect.

5. **Correct Response: B.** This question requires the ability to organize the sentences of a paragraph in such a way that the paragraph is cohesive and presents an effective sequence of ideas. Part 8 introduces the main idea of the second paragraph by asking, "what should the media be doing?" The sentence that follows Part 9 is not a logical next sentence for two reasons: it does not address the question in any way, and it contains a demonstrative pronoun (*this*) that does not have a clear antecedent. Choice B, placing Part 9 after Part 11, would solve both problems. Moving Part 10 to follow Part 8 would provide an answer to the question; and putting Part 9 after Parts 10 and 11 would provide *this* with a clear antecedent: the writer's suggestion for what the media should be doing. The other revisions suggested would impair, rather than clarify, the sequence of ideas in the paragraph.

6. **Correct Response: B.** This question assesses the ability to recognize effective organization in writing. The first paragraph of the selection is organized by cause and effect. It makes the point that, as a result of recent research findings regarding language use, current approaches to foreign language teaching often include a new topic, called *pragmatics,* in addition to vocabulary and grammar. The most appropriate addition to this paragraph is the sentence presented in choice B. The transitional adverb *consequently* is a signal that the next statement is a logical result of previous assertions. In fact, the sentence in choice B draws a clear causal connection between the findings of research and their application in the classroom. Choice A is incorrect because it digresses from the topic at hand: it elaborates on the usefulness of silence in human communication in general, without any specific connection to foreign language teaching. Choices C and D are incorrect because neither develops the main idea of the paragraph: choice C introduces a new topic, and choice D interrupts the flow of development by minimizing the importance of pragmatics before the concept has been fully explained.

7. **Correct Response: D.** This question assesses the ability to recognize ineffective repetition and inefficiency in sentence construction. Only Part 10 (choice D) requires revision to reduce needless repetition. This sentence, which gives examples of factors that may determine the proper greeting between speakers, is confusing because of wordy and repetitive references to "the speakers." This repetition is unnecessary since the grammatical and logical context makes it clear that the factors listed are related to the speakers. It would be clearer and therefore more effective if the factors were simply listed as "the speakers' gender, status, type of relationship, and relative age."

8. **Correct Response: D.** This question requires an understanding of the standard formation of pronouns and modifiers. Choice D is the correct response because *it's* is a contraction of *it is,* which does not make sense in this context. Instead, the phrase "every culture has . . ." requires the possessive pronoun *its,* indicating that the rules *belong* to the culture. Choice A is an incorrect response because Part 6 appropriately uses the possessive adjective *their* to refer to the relationship between *individuals* and *turn; they're* is the contraction of *they are,* words that do not fit this context. The revision suggested in choice B is also inappropriate; since *specifically* is an adverb, it should not be used to modify a noun. In Part 8, the adjective *proper* is used correctly to modify the noun *way* and should not be changed to its adverbial form (choice C).

9. **Correct Response: B.** This question requires the ability to recognize a sentence fragment. The correct response is choice B because Part 3 is a subordinate clause, introduced by the subordinating conjunction "when"; its meaning depends on a main, or independent, clause, which is missing. None of the parts identified in choices A, C, and D are nonstandard sentences. Parts 1 and 4 are both simple sentences, and Part 5 is a complex sentence.

10. **Correct Response: D.** This question requires the ability to recognize writing that is appropriate for a given purpose and audience. The sentence presented in choice D has several features that make it appropriate for insertion into the second paragraph. For example, its beginning phrase, *You are comforted,* echoes the phrasing of Part 7: *you are delighted and comforted.* In addition, the sentence as a whole elaborates on the main idea that a good book is like a good friend. Choice A would not fit into the paragraph because it states an idea that is precisely the opposite of the writer's opinion, and, in addition, introduces a sudden and inappropriate change in point of view. Choice B is incorrect because the formal, highly abstract language of this sentence is inconsistent with the relatively personal and intimate tone of the passage. Finally, choice C is incorrect because it would interject an inappropriate and irrelevant comment—the passage is about good books in general and does not make any judgment about where good books can or cannot be found.

11. **Correct Response: B.** This question requires the ability to recognize appropriate language for a given purpose and audience. The passage seeks to describe to its intended audience of college students some of the major differences between a Hamiltonian and a Jeffersonian political viewpoint. The sentence presented in choice B would be most consistent with the writer's purpose and audience because it provides information relevant to the topic and uses language that is objective and impersonal, yet is neither very formal nor particularly informal. The sentence in choice A would not fit well within the context of this passage because its "folksy" tone and vivid imagery differ from the more restrained tone of the passage. Choice C would be inappropriate because the purpose of the suggested sentence is to argue and persuade in a personalized voice, functions that would be inconsistent with the passage. Even though the sentence in choice D would support the writer's argument, its highly abstract and difficult language does not match the language used throughout the rest of the passage.

12. **Correct Response: B.** This question calls for the ability to recognize imprecise and inappropriate word choice. The expression *long, long ago* (choice B) should be replaced both because it is imprecise (why not identify the specific years during which Jefferson and Hamilton carried on this debate?) and because it conjures up associations with fairy tales rather than with a historical account. None of the words listed for the other answer choices need to be replaced; they are all precise and appropriate in their context. The *proper role* (choice A) of government is exactly the topic of ongoing discussion, and *high tariffs* (choice D) were, in fact, one of the means by which Hamilton sought to promote *economic growth* (choice C).

13. **Correct Response: D.** This question requires the ability to recognize edited American English usage. The first paragraph contains no examples of nonstandard usage except for the one described in choice D. A comma is needed after the clause "Hamilton believed," because nonessential, or nonrestrictive, clauses, of which this is an example, should be set off by commas. This clause is nonessential because the basic meaning of the sentence would not change if it were deleted. As for choice A, it would be inappropriate to insert a colon after the word *by* in Part 2 because *by* is not followed by an example, a series, an explanation, or any other material that should be grouped as a separate unit. The revisions suggested in choices B and C are unnecessary because they would not change the meaning or improve the clarity of Parts 3 and 4.

14. **Correct Response: D.** This question requires the ability to recognize effective organization in writing. The sequence of ideas in the first paragraph is clear and effective, except in Parts 4 and 5, which should be reversed (choice D). Part 1 states the main idea; Part 2 provides an example to elaborate on the main idea; and Part 3 presents specific illustrations to explain Part 2. If the order of Parts 4 and 5 is reversed, the two sentences then do just what Parts 2 and 3 do: provide an example of the main idea and then give illustrations of this example. Therefore, none of the revisions suggested in answer choices A, B, and C would improve the paragraph.

15. **Correct Response: C.** This question requires the ability to recognize unity and focus in writing. Both the first and the second paragraph of the passage draw comparisons and contrasts between lawyers and historians at a very general level. The introduction of a single specific example drawn from history breaks the flow of ideas; therefore, Part 10 should be deleted, choice C. On the other hand, Part 8 should be neither deleted (choice A) nor moved (choice B) because this sentence provides both an effective transition between the two paragraphs and an introduction to the second paragraph. The revision suggested in choice D would also be inappropriate because the addition of such detailed information would draw the focus away from the main idea.

16. **Correct Response: D.** This question requires the ability to recognize an example of nonstandard usage, in this case the use of inappropriate verb tense in a sentence. Choice D is the best response because the use of *led* in the first clause of Part 12 introduces an inappropriate change from the present tense to the past tense: *led* should be replaced by the present tense *leads. Between* (choice A) is used correctly in Part 8 because two distinct groups, lawyers and historians, are being compared. The substitution of *when* for *where* in Part 9 (choice B) would result in an illogical sentence, because the word *where* is used here to mean *whereas* rather than to designate a place or a time. The revision described in choice C would inappropriately replace the comparative form *less* with the superlative form *least,* resulting in nonstandard usage.

17. **Correct Response: C.** This question requires the ability to recognize distracting details that impair the development of the main idea in a paragraph. The first paragraph of the passage clearly develops the idea that Minoan civilization had reached admirable levels before its sudden disappearance. The flow of this development is disrupted by irrelevant details about Sicily, presented in Part 3; therefore, choice C is the correct response. Part 1 (choice A) is an effective topic sentence for the entire passage. Parts 2 and 4 (choices B and D) provide details that effectively support the main idea of the paragraph.

18. **Correct Response: A.** This question requires the ability to organize sentences to present an effective sequence of ideas. The second paragraph describes the volcanic eruption that obliterated Minoan civilization. Of the four sentences given, choice A would best fit the structure of this paragraph, because it furnishes additional, relevant facts about the historic eruption. Choice B would be inappropriate here because it introduces an entirely different topic from the one addressed in this paragraph. Choice C is too general a statement to fit well within this factual account of a specific volcanic eruption. While choice D is related to the overall topic of the passage, it is not relevant to the main idea of the second paragraph.

19. **Correct Response: D.** This passage is written for an audience of college students. Its purpose is to assess the merits of a balanced budget amendment. Choice D is the best response because it adds relevant detail to the writer's analysis and is written with the appropriate tone and level of formality. As for the other responses provided, the introduction of a rhetorical question addressed directly to the reader (choice A) and use of slang as well as the first person singular (choice C) represent inappropriate shifts in tone. Although choice B adds relevant detail to the passage, it contains overly technical language that is not in keeping with the level of vocabulary used elsewhere in the selection.

20. **Correct Response: B.** This question assesses the ability to recognize distracting details that impair the development of the main idea in a piece of writing. The main idea of the first paragraph is that increasing numbers of people believe a balanced budget amendment is needed to bring federal spending under control. Choice B draws attention away from the main idea because it deals with constitutional history rather than the economic concerns that are the primary focus of the paragraph. As for the other choices provided, Part 1 (choice A) expresses the main ideas of the paragraph, and Parts 3 (choice C) and 4 (choice D) contain information that the writer uses to develop the main idea.

21. **Correct Response: D.** This question requires an understanding of standard American English word usage. Choice D is the best response because *seriously* is an adverb, not an adjective. Adverbs are used to modify verbs, adjectives, and other adverbs rather than nouns. It is therefore correct to change the adverb *seriously* in Part 10 to the adjective *serious*, which can be employed to modify the noun *concerns*. Of the other choices provided, the conjunction *than* is used properly in Part 5 (choice A) and *soon* should not be changed to its comparative form in Part 6 (choice B). The change suggested in choice C is inappropriate because replacing *Although* (which means *in spite of*) with *Because* (which means *on account of*) would suggest a causal relationship between the first clause and the rest of the sentence that does not make sense.

22. **Correct Response: C.** This question assesses the ability to use transitional words to develop text structure. Choice C is the best response because the first blank calls for a word that emphasizes the discontinuity between the trend discussed in Part 7 and that examined in the preceding paragraph. Of the responses provided for the first blank, *however* is the only word that indicates such a change has occurred. By contrast, choices A (*as a result*) and D (*in conclusion*) suggest that no new information is presented in Part 7, and choice B (*for example*) indicates a degree of continuity that would be inappropriate in this context. Similarly, choice C presents the only appropriate transitional word to replace the second blank because *consequently* signals a logical conclusion based on previously presented evidence, and Part 9 presents such a conclusion. None of the transitional words listed second in the other choices suggests this connection between Part 9 and the ideas presented earlier.

23. **Correct Response: D.** This question assesses the ability to identify standard placement of modifiers. Choice D is the best response because the participial phrase "far exceeding the number of people who died each year" does not modify any noun or pronoun in Part 6. As a result, the sentence is difficult to understand. To restore meaning to Part 6, the phrase needs to be deleted. The placement of all modifiers used in choices A, B, and C complies with standard American English usage.

24. **Correct Response: C.** This passage is written for an audience of first-year college students. The writer's main purpose in the first paragraph is to expose the inadequate manner in which many composition textbooks deal with the topic of paragraph length. Choice C is the best response because its content supports the paragraph's main purpose, and it is written with the appropriate tone and level of formality. Of the other responses provided, choices A and D adopt a harsh, dismissive stance that is at variance with the writer's more restrained approach. Although the tone of choice B is similar to that used in the passage, it is incorrect because it contradicts the main purpose of the paragraph by commending rather than criticizing composition textbooks.

25. **Correct Response: A.** This question assesses the ability to recognize revisions that improve the focus of a piece of writing. The main idea of the second paragraph is that there are two general principles that writers should use as guidelines for determining the appropriate length of paragraphs. Part 7 (choice A) therefore contradicts the paragraph's main idea and makes it difficult to understand exactly what the writer is trying to say. As for the other responses provided, combining Parts 8 and 9 would not help concentrate attention on the main idea (choice B), and implementing choice C would weaken rather than strengthen the paragraph's focus. Given the paragraph's main idea, Part 11 is an appropriate concluding sentence and should not be deleted (choice D).

26. **Correct Response: D.** This question requires an understanding of the standard use of verb forms. Choice D is the best response because in Part 10 *is broke* is a nonstandard formation of the present tense: the present tense of the verb *to be* (*is*) should never be used in combination with the simple past tense of another verb. To correct the error, *is broke* should be replaced by the verb phrase *is broken*. Of the other responses provided, the verb forms used in choices A, B, and C all comply with standard American English usage.

27. **Correct Response: A.** This passage is written for an audience of college students. The writer's main purpose in the first paragraph is to describe a common type of informal fallacy. Choice A is the best response because it clearly relates to the writer's purpose and is written with the appropriate tone, person, and level of usage. Of the other responses provided, choices B and D depart from the paragraph's main purpose and are written in the first person rather than the third person. In addition to being stated in less formal diction than that used in the passage, choice C also diverts attention from the writer's main purpose, which is to provide readers with an understanding of informal fallacies rather than to criticize those who employ such rhetorical tricks.

28. **Correct Response: B.** This question assesses the ability to recognize examples of well-developed writing. The main idea of the second paragraph is that speakers should avoid the use of informal fallacies. Choice B is the best response because it supports the main idea by helping to demonstrate why it is unfair to use informal fallacies as a means of argumentation. Of the other responses provided, choices A and D represent statements that are unrelated to the paragraph's main idea, and choice C shifts the focus of the paragraph from an argument against the use of informal fallacies to an analysis of the social implications of their increased use.

29. **Correct Response: A.** This question requires an understanding of effective paragraph organization. The second paragraph of the passage is developed through specific details. Its main purpose is to describe the operation of the two sides of the brain. Choice A is the best response because it supports the main purpose of the paragraph by providing relevant details about the right side of the brain. The information presented in choices B, C, and D is unrelated to the writer's purpose. Using any of these statements in place of Part 6 would weaken the organization of the paragraph.

30. **Correct Response: B.** This question assesses the ability to recognize nonstandard sentence structure. Choice B is the best response because Part 2 is a run-on sentence: two sentences written as though they were one. To correct the error, the comma after *halves* should be changed to a period, and the first letter in *each* should be capitalized to show that it is the first word of a separate sentence. As for the other responses provided, Parts 1 (choice A), 4 (choice C), and 8 (choice D) are all complete, effective sentences.

31. **Correct Response: C.** This passage is written for an audience composed of individuals who are interested in woodworking but have no formal training in the craft. The writer's main purpose in the first paragraph is to persuade readers that woodworking is not as difficult as it appears. Choice C is the best response because it is written with the appropriate level of formality, and its reassuring tone clearly supports the main purpose of the paragraph. Choice A is overly informal and is written in the first person rather than the second or third person that is used elsewhere in the passage; choice B shifts attention from the main purpose of the first paragraph; and choice D introduces technical terms that are more likely to intimidate than reassure the intended audience.

32. **Correct Response: D.** This question assesses the ability to recognize examples of well-developed writing. The main idea of the second paragraph is that successful woodworking projects require careful planning. Choice D is the best response because it offers readers useful advice on how to begin making such plans. As for the other responses provided, choice A diverts attention from the paragraph's main idea by comparing woodworking with metalworking, as do choices B and C by presenting information unrelated to the needs of the novice woodworkers that the writer is trying to reach.

33. **Correct Response: D.** This question assesses the ability to recognize ineffective sentence construction. Choice D is the best response because Part 11 is needlessly repetitive. Part 11 should be made more concise; it could, for example, be revised to read: "Once your planning is complete, you can begin the final construction phase." As for the other responses provided, Parts 1 (choice A), 6 (choice B), and 7 (choice C) are all efficiently constructed and should not be revised.

34. **Correct Response: B.** This question assesses the ability to use transitional words to develop text structure. Choice B is the best response because the blanks in Parts 9, 10, and 11 call for transitional words that link the three sentences with Part 8 in a unified developmental sequence. Of the responses provided, *In addition, First,* and *Next* are the only links that convey an appropriate combination of unity and progression. By contrast, the first words in choices A (*Nevertheless*) and D (*By contrast*) indicate discontinuity between Parts 8 and 9. Choice C is incorrect because *Eventually* does not fit the context of Part 9. Similarly, the second and third transitional words listed in choices A, C, and D do not link the paragraph's ideas in a unified, logical manner.

35. **Correct Response: C.** This question assesses the ability to identify standard sentence structure, in this case, standard subject-verb agreement. Choice C (*is*) is the best response because the subject *clutch of eggs* is singular in number and agrees with the present tense used throughout the paragraph. As for the other responses provided, choice A (*were*) is a plural verb in the past tense, choice B (*will be*) is in the future tense, and choice D (*was*) is in the past tense.

36. **Correct Response: A.** This question requires an understanding of standard American English word usage. Choice A is the best response because the superlative adverb *most* should not be used before one-syllable modifiers, such as *old,* that form their superlative degree by adding the suffix *-est*. As for the other responses provided, changing *yet* to *although* would change an independent clause to a dependent clause, making Part 2 a sentence fragment (choice B). In Part 4, the adverb *commonly* is used correctly to modify the verb *eaten* (choice C). Putting quotation marks around the clause "they must come ashore to lay their eggs" in Part 5 (choice D) would convey the inaccurate impression that the clause is a direct quotation from another source.

37. **Correct Response: C.** This question assesses the ability to reorganize sentences to improve the sequence of ideas in a passage. Reversing the order of parts 5 and 6 (choice C) is the best response because Part 6, which tells readers why Graham left the Denishawn dance company, directly continues a topic that is introduced in Part 4. Also, the writer's observation in the first clause of Part 8 is a logical extension of information presented in Part 5. As for the other responses provided, implementing the changes suggested in choices A and B would make it difficult to follow the writer's line of reasoning, and deleting Part 7 (choice D) would remove information that is related to the main idea of the passage.

38. **Correct Response: B.** This question requires an understanding of standard punctuation. Choice B is the best response because, when there are three or more items in a series, commas should be used to separate the items. Therefore, a comma should be placed after *athletic*, the first in a series of three adjectives. Placing a comma after *choreography* in Part 1 (choice A) would make the sentence difficult to understand by needlessly separating its subject and predicate, and semicolons should not be used to connect a subordinate clause (*Although Graham . . .*) with another clause (choice C). In Part 9, replacing *recognized* with the participle *recognizing* (choice D) would distort the meaning of the sentence.

39. **Correct Response: C.** This passage is written for college students. Its main purpose is to describe some aspects of the human memory. Choice C is the best response because it provides specific examples of the use of short-term memory and is written with the appropriate tone and level of formality. None of the other responses provides supporting detail. In addition, the language of choice A is overly formal, choice B represents an inappropriate shift to the first person singular, and choice D contains slang (*kind of neat*) and a shift in point of view that do not fit the context of the passage.

40. **Correct Response: D.** This question assesses the ability to recognize revisions that improve the focus of a piece of writing. The main idea of the passage is that the way people use a piece of information determines which type of memory will be used to store it. Part 11, however, introduces an irrelevant fact about how computer memory is sometimes stored; choice D ("Delete Part 11") is therefore the best response. As for the other responses provided, adding the names of particular psychologists (choice A) would divert attention from the passage's main idea, the revision suggested in choice B does not change the meaning of Part 5, and reversing the positions of Parts 4 and 5 (choice C) would not make sense logically.

Practice Test Writing Samples

The following are examples of writing samples at each score point in the Practice Test concerning technology. The writing samples were generated by students in a tryout and retain the spelling, punctuation, and other mechanical conventions in the original versions. The chapters in *The Official TASP® Test Study Guide* that address the writing prompt contain a discussion of the characteristics of writing at each of the four score points. You may find it helpful to compare your response to the assignment in the Practice Test with those presented below.

Sample "1" Paper

Enviroment have been one of the major issue to look at over the technology improve in this century. For my understanding technology means new improve different ways to better our lives and especially the enviroment which we live. These technology have advantages and disadvantages concerning our enviroment.

Automobiles one of the major polluter of our enviroment. Automobiles help us for transportation. This one easy and major advantage of all technology.

There are many disadvantage in this technology.

One of the major disadvantage is fumes. Fumes may sound like it's not a major problem, but if you do imagine how many automobiles we has in this earth, you will see the problem. Fumes which are produced by our automobiles don't get to be recycle all of it goes to our enviroment because of fumes now we have a problem at Ozone.

I think the major focus we should be looking when we invite new technologies is to make sure we able to recycle the pollution which are produced by these new technologies not just to let them go and pollute our enviroment.

Sample "2" Paper

The automobile is one technological innovation that has had a big impact on modern society. The automobile has created many advantages for our society but at the same time it has created many disadvantages for our society.

The automobile has many advantages to it that has helped our society for many generations now. Before there were automobiles people had a heck of time getting around from place to place. They had to walk so if they wanted to visit someone who lived far away from them it took a least a couple of weeks before they got there. Another reason why this was a problem was because if they were going on a long trip they needed to pack many items and they would have problems carring everything. Then there were horses, this seemed to be a great improvement because not only did it shorten the amount of time it took for someone to travel but it was also easier for them to carry with them whatever they needed for the trip.

Although the automobile has many advantages to it there are also many disadvantages to it. The biggest disadvantage that there is is that automobiles give off carbon minoxide and this affects our ozone layer. If this continues who knows by the year 2000 we could all be killed off because our ozone layer might be diteireatated.

As you can see the automobile has helped us in many ways but it has also caused us many problems. But what the help so hasn't everything else in this world.

Sample "3" Paper

The automobile is arguably the most important technological breakthrough this century. It has virtually changed the face of the world we live in, enhancing communication and transportation to the point that it has made the world a smaller place.

The automobile has changed the way we live by making the transportation of goods easier and cheaper. It has also become a nessecity and part of the American Dream.

Ironically, one of the most beneficial technological advances, the automobile also has some serious drawbacks. Running on fossil fuel (gasoline), the huge demand for gasoline has serious risks. The War in the Gulf, proved we are willing to go to war over the limited supply of gasoline.

Cars also present an immense environmental problem. The carbon-monoxide emmitted from automobile exhausts gets trapped in the atmosphere, letting heat from the sun enter but not escape. This increases global temperatures, creating a "Greenhouse effect" that could cause devastating effects on earth.

An increase in global temperatures would melt the polar ice caps, increasing worldwide waterlevels (drowning all coastal cities), as well as kill plants and animals, who can't survive a heat wave.

Luckily, today, legislation is being made and technology is available for the development of low and zero-emission automobiles.

I believe technology should be used for the benefit of all and in moderation. If the technology for the car created a serious environmental problem, new technology can solve the problem.

Sample "4" Paper

The television is an invention that has both negative and positive consequences. Whether or not a person considers the invention of the television to be a positive event, it has certainly made a large impact on the way we spend our free time. The average American has five hours of leisure time each day and spends about one-third of that watching television, i.e., more than any other leisure activity. As a nation, we are television-crazed. No matter what our choices are for programs to watch, we always find something. The number of channels is multiplying rapidly as the demand grows. There is talk of as many as 400 channels within a decade. Television is one of the things that binds our country together. Although we, as a people, are very diverse, most of us (98%) have one thing in common: we own television sets.

Television has both pros and cons. One positive aspect of television is its ability to relax. After a hard day's work, there is nothing more soothing than plopping down in front of the television and letting the mind wander. Television can make us laugh, cry, and understand more about how different types of people live. We can spend a night as a member of the Cosby family, journey to Africa to see the wildlife, or cheer as the Texas Rangers win a game.

One of the most positive aspects of television is its ability to show us live action in others parts of the world. Newspapers cannot convey this information until the next day, in most cases. Those of us who are too lazy to skim through a newspaper can get a summary of the day's events by simply watching the television for a half-hour.

We learn through television. Movies and documentaries can teach us about important people, issues, geographical areas and animals. Because television has the ability to captivate audiences, it is sometimes a more effective teaching aid than people, computers or books.

On the other hand, it also has some disadvantages. With all the time we devote to television, we tend to neglect our other duties. Watching television is a useful method of procrastination. We spend so much time sitting that we have become a lazier country with heart troubles. Eating and television watching go so well together that we have also become a heavier and more obese people. Television has generally caused a decline in health.

Another negative aspect of television is all of the violence and sex that is shown. Children are being exposed to these things much earlier and this might relate somewhat to the increased violence among children.

Because we tend to trust what we see on television, we may be somewhat misinformed. News programs decide what and what not to show. They are, in a sense, deciding what is important to the country. Television has a large impact on our country as a whole. The L.A. Riots of 1992 probably would not have happened if the beating of Rodney King had not been shown repeatedly on television.

Overall, the benefits of television outweigh the detriments. Television is soothing and healthy in small doses. We have the choice of how much and what we watch. If we can make these decisions wisely, we can all continue to benefit from the invention and innovations of television.

Glossary

absolute value: the distance of a number from zero on the number line, expressed as a positive value. That is, both 3.5 and -3.5 are the same distance from zero on the number line, and both have the same absolute value, 3.5.

active voice: a verb form that expresses action performed by its subject

adjacent angles: two angles on one line with the same vertex and one common side

adjective: a word that modifies a noun or pronoun

adverb: a word that modifies a verb, adjective, or adverb

algorithm: a special method of solving a problem

analogy: a comparison between two things that have a partial resemblance

anecdote: usually a short account of a personal or biographical event

angle: a geometric figure formed by two distinct rays that have a common endpoint

antecedent: a word or phrase to which a pronoun refers

apostrophe: a punctuation mark that stands for missing letters or indicates possession

appositive: a word or phrase that explains or identifies another word or phrase coming just before it

area: the measure of space on a plane; space within a set of boundaries on a flat surface (measured in square units)

assumption: something that is taken for granted

audience: those for whom a writer is writing

average: the sum of two or more quantities divided by the number of quantities

axiom: a definition

axis: a horizontal or vertical line in a graph (plural—axes)

axis of symmetry: a line around which a parabola or other figure is symmetrically arranged

base: a number that may be raised to various powers

bias: prejudice; leaning to one side of an issue

binomial: a polynomial expression with two terms

Cartesian coordinate system: a system made up of two real number lines (axes), one that is horizontal and one that is vertical, that intersect and are perpendicular to each other

causal chain: a cause-and-effect description in which one event causes a second, which in turn causes a third, and so on

central tendency: the middle or center of a group of numbers; measures of central tendency include the mean, median, and mode

chronological order: arrangement in time sequence

circumference: the distance around the outside of a circle

clarity: clearness

clause: a group of words related grammatically and containing a subject and predicate

cliché: a word or expression that has lost its power from overuse

coefficient: see *numerical coefficient*

collective noun: a singular noun that refers to a group

colloquial language: conversational, or informal, language

colon: a punctuation mark used before an example, explanation, or series

comma: a punctuation mark used to separate sentence parts

comma splice: two independent sentences joined by a comma; a kind of run-on sentence

complementary angles: two angles whose sum is 90 degrees

completing the square: a method for solving quadratic equations

complex sentence: one independent clause together with one or more dependent clauses

compound sentence: a sentence containing two or more independent clauses

compound-complex sentence: a sentence containing two or more independent clauses and one or more dependent clauses

compound subject: in a sentence, two or more nouns used as the subject

conclusion: the end of a piece of writing where the main point is repeated or summarized

concrete language: language that is about substances, persons, or things rather than abstractions

congruence: (of two geometric figures) having angles and sides of equal measure

conjunction: a word that connects words or groups of words in a sentence

connotation: the meaning associated with a word

context, context clue: the words or ideas that surround an unfamiliar word and provide clues to its meaning; clues may be in the form of examples, definitions, restatements, or explanations

conversion: in mathematics, the process of changing a quantity expressed in one unit of measurement to an equivalent quantity in a different unit of measurement (e.g., one foot may be coverted to 12 inches)

coordinate: the label of a point on a number line or the Cartesian coordinate system

credibility: the condition of being believable

critical thinking: thought that involves a careful analysis of information

dangling modifier: a modifier that does not clearly modify any word in a sentence

decimal: a number containing a decimal point and representing a part of a whole

deductive order: a sequence of ideas that moves from the general to the specific

deductive reasoning: drawing a specific conclusion from a general premise

degree (of a polynomial):   the largest exponent in a mathematical expression

demonstrative pronoun: a pronoun used to indicate a particular person or thing

denominator: the term on the bottom or right side of a fraction

denotation: a word's literal meaning

dependent clause: (also called a subordinate clause) a clause that cannot stand alone as a sentence

dependent system: a system of equations with infinite solutions

diameter: the distance from one point through the center to the point opposite on a circle (twice the radius)

difference: the result of subtracting two numbers

direct variation: a mathematical relationship in which two values change in the same way

dividend: a quantity to be divided

divisor: the quantity by which a dividend is divided

edited American English: the form of English that is used by careful writers in the United States to communicate in textbooks, magazines, newspapers, and the like

endpoint: the point at which a line segment or ray begins or ends

equation: a statement of balance or equality

equivalent fractions: two or more fractions that are equal in value but are represented with different numerators and denominators

estimation: approximation, often by means of rounding off

explicit: clearly or directly stated

exponent: a number that describes the number of times a number (the base) is to be multiplied by itself

exponential notation: use of a fractional exponent to denote a radical expression. The index of the radical expression (e.g., 2 for a square root) becomes the denominator of a fraction that is used as an exponent. For example, $\sqrt{5}$ becomes $5^{\frac{1}{2}}$ in exponential notation, and $\sqrt[3]{79}$ becomes $79^{\frac{1}{3}}$.

expository writing: writing that explains or describes

expression: a quantity or operation in math

extrapolate: using values on a graph, table, or chart to estimate a value that lies beyond the given ones

extrapolation: drawing conclusions about facts beyond the range of available information

fact: something that is true and verifiable

factor: two or more numbers that can be multiplied to produce a specific product

factored expression: a mathematical expression rewritten as a product

factoring: expressing a mathematical expression in terms of its factors

fiction: writing that focuses on imaginary characters and events

figure of speech: also referred to as figurative language or figurative expressions; used to make descriptions more vivid and to bring fresh meaning to writing; includes metaphor, simile, hyperbole, and personification

first-degree polynomial: a polynomial that contains no exponents

flashback: an interruption in the regular sequence of events to return to an earlier event

focus (in writing):   the center or target of a writer's attention

FOIL: FOIL stands for first, outside, inside, last—a method for multiplying two binomials

formal outline: a concise way to organize and summarize information in terms of main ideas and subordinate details; uses a system of Roman numerals, letters, and numbers to identify topics and subtopics

fraction: a number used to represent a part of a whole or a part of a group

function: in mathematics, a rule, usually expressed as an equation, for transforming one value into another value. More formally, a function is a rule used to assign to each element of one set (called the *domain* of the function) exactly one element from another set (called the *range* of the function). In the function $y = 6x + 3$, each value of x is transformed into a new value by first multiplying the starting value by 6 and then adding 3. In **functional notation,** this equation could be written $P(x) = 6x + 3$.

fused sentence: two independent sentences joined without necessary punctuation; a kind of run-on sentence

geometry: a branch of mathematics involving the study of shapes, figures, and planes

graphs: pictorial representations of data including bar, line, pie, picto-

grouping symbols: parentheses, brackets, braces

hyperbola: the graph of an inverse variation equation

hyperbole: overstatement or exaggeration used to produce a serious or comic effect; not meant to be taken literally

hypotenuse: the side of a right triangle opposite the right angle

hypothesis: an unproved theory

identity: in mathematics, an equation involving a variable for which any assigned value produces a true statement; an equation with an infinite number of solutions

implicit: suggested or indirectly stated

imply: to suggest without directly stating

improper fraction: a fraction in which the numerator is larger than the denominator

inconsistent system: a system of equations with no solution

indefinite pronoun: a pronoun that does not refer to a specific person or thing

independent clause: (also called a main clause) a clause that can stand alone as a sentence and has a subject and predicate

index: see *radical expression*

inductive order: a sequence of ideas that moves from the specific to the general

inductive reasoning: drawing a general conclusion from a particular fact or group of facts

inequality: a statement relating two unequal quantities

infer: to draw a conclusion based on evidence

integers: the natural numbers, their negatives, and zero; whole numbers

interpolate: using values on a graph, table, or chart to estimate a value between two given values

intercept: the point where the graph of a line crosses either the x- or y-axis

interjection: an exclamation that is set off from the rest of a sentence; usually followed by an exclamation point

interpolation: drawing conclusions about facts within the range of available information

interrogative: a word used to form a sentence that asks a question

intersect: to cross

inverse variation: a mathematical relationship in which two values change in opposite ways

least common denominator: (LCD) the smallest number divisible by all denominators in a problem

length: distance

like terms: two or more terms that contain the same variable raised to the same power

line: a one-dimensional figure that extends infinitely far in two directions

line segment: part of a line, with two distinct endpoints

linear equation: a mathematical expression whose terms consist of numbers or first-degree polynomials

literal language: writing that uses the ordinary rather than figurative meanings of words

logic: a system of reasoning or argument

magnitude: the size of a number

main idea: in a piece of writing, the major point being made by the writer; may be either clearly stated or implied

mean: (a measure of central tendency) the arithmetic average of a group of values, produced by adding the values in the group and dividing the sum by the number of values in the group

median: (a measure of central tendency) the middle value in a group of numbers when the numbers are arranged in order of size. If the number of values in the group is odd, the median is simply the middle value; if the number of values is even, the median is the arithmetic average of the two middle values (i.e., the sum of the two middle values divided by two).

metaphor: a figure of speech that emphasizes the common qualities of two unlike things; differs from a simile in that the comparison is presented without the use of introductory words that signal a comparison

misplaced modifier: in a sentence, a modifier that has not been placed next to the word it modifies

mixed number: a number that consists of both a whole number and a fraction

mode: (a measure of central tendency) the most frequently occurring value in a group of values

modifiers: a word, phrase, or clause, used as an adjective or adverb, that describes or limits the meaning of another sentence element

monomial: a mathematical term that consists of a number, a variable, or a product of a number and one or more variables

narrative writing: writing that tells a story or gives an account of an event

natural numbers: the numbers used in counting

nonfiction: writing that is based on real characters, events, or things

notetaking: a method for organizing and summarizing information; may take the form of a list, outline, map, or diagram

noun: a word that names a person, place, thing, idea, or action

null set: a set containing no elements; the empty set

number line: a line used to represent numbers and numerical relationships

numerator: the term on the top or left side of a fraction

numerical coefficient: the numerical part of a monomial containing a number and a variable

objective writing: writing that is neutral; writing that does not favor either side of an issue

objectivity: the state of being without bias

occasion: the situation the reader will be in when reading a piece of writing

opinion: a judgment; a belief that is open to debate

order of ideas: the sequence in which ideas are presented

order of importance: the sequencing of ideas according to their significance

ordered pair: two numbers used to represent the position of a point on a coordinate plane

origin: the point labeled zero on a number line or the Cartesian coordinate system

parabola: the graph of a quadratic equation; a U-shaped curve that is symmetrical about a line called the *axis of symmetry*. The point at which the axis of symmetry intersects the parabola is called the vertex, or turning point, of the parabola.

parallel lines: lines on the same plane that never intersect

parallel structure: in a sentence, the use of elements that display similar or balanced grammatical structure

part of speech: the way a word is used (there are eight parts of speech: noun, pronoun, verb, adjective, adverb, preposition, conjunction, and interjection)

passive voice: a verb form that expresses action performed on its subject

pattern of organization: the scheme used by a writer to arrange the content of a piece of writing

percent: a number that represents hundredths

perimeter: the measure of a figure's outer boundary

perpendicular lines: lines on the same plane that intersect in a right (90 degree) angle

personification: a figure of speech that gives human qualities to nonhuman things, objects, or ideas

phrase: a sentence part that does not contain a subject and predicate

pi: the circumference of a circle divided by its diameter (approximately 3.14)

plane: a flat surface that extends infinitely far in all directions

point of view: used as a technical term *in writing* to refer to the person (i.e., first, second, third) in which a piece of writing is presented; *in reading,* it is the opinion, viewpoint, or stand taken by a writer

point-slope formula: an equation for a line in the form $y - y_1 = m(x - x_1)$. In this form, m is the slope.

polygon: a two-dimensional closed figure with sides that are line segments

polynomial: a mathematical expression involving the sum of a number of terms. Each term is either a real number or the product of a real number (called a *numerical coefficient)* and a variable with a nonnegative integer exponent. A polynomial with one term is called a *monomial;* a polynomial with two terms is a *binomial;* and a polynomial with three terms is a *trinomial.*

postulate: assumption

power: see *exponent*

predicate: a verb or verb phrase

prefix: a word element found at the beginning of some words; adding a prefix to a word either changes the word's meaning or creates an entirely new word

premise: a statement that may serve as the foundation of an argument

preposition: a word governing a noun or pronoun to form a phrase that modifies another sentence element

prepositional phrase: a preposition and its object

prime number: an integer that can only be divided by itself and 1

product: the result of multiplying numbers

pronoun: a word that takes the place of a noun

proportion: a mathematical statement that says that two ratios are equal

purpose (in writing): what a piece of writing is intended to accomplish

Pythagorean theorem: a formula relating the length of the sides of a right triangle ($a^2 + b^2 = c^2$)

quadrant: one of four distinct parts on the Cartesian coordinate system

quadratic: a second-degree polynomial; may have one, two, or no solutions

quadratic formula: the formula used in solving quadratic equations; $x = \frac{-b \pm \sqrt{b^2 - 4ac}}{2a}$

quadrilateral: a four-sided polygon

quotation marks: punctuation marks used most often to enclose directly quoted material

quotient: the result of dividing numbers

radical expression: an expression involving a radical sign ($\sqrt{}$). The number or variable inside the radical sign is called the *radicand.* The number (if any) on top of the hook to the left of the radical sign is called the *index;* if no index is expressed, the index is understood to be 2 and the radical expression is a square root.

radical sign: a sign that indicates a root

radicand: see *radical expression*

radius: the distance from the center to any point on the outer boundary of a circle (plural—radii)

range: the numerical distance between the highest and lowest values in a group of numbers; the difference between the highest number and the lowest number

ratio: a special value used to compare two numbers by division; usually written as a fraction

rational expression: a fraction

rational number: a real number that can be represented as a ratio of two integers

ray: a straight line that extends infinitely far in one direction from a point

real number system: (as distinct from the complex number system) the set of numbers commonly used in most mathematical operations, including integers, fractions (or rational numbers), and irrational numbers. Real numbers correspond to points on the number line; in the real number system, the expression $\sqrt{a}$ has no meaning if a < 0.

reciprocal: the multiplicative inverse of a fraction

reflexive pronoun: a personal pronoun in the *self* or *selves* form

relative pronoun: a pronoun that relates a clause to its antecedent

relevance: the state of being to the point

right triangle: a triangle that has one angle of 90 degrees (right angle)

rise: the amount of vertical change in a line

root: the word element that is the main part of any word; *in math,* a solution of a quadratic equation, or a number which, when multiplied by itself a given number of times, produces a given value (e.g., 2 is the fourth root of 16 because 2 must be multiplied by itself four times to produce 16)

run: the amount of horizontal change in a line

run-on sentence: nonstandard joining of independent clauses; two types of run-on sentences are the comma splice and the fused sentence

scientific notation: a method of writing numbers that uses the form $N(10^P)$, where N is a number between 1 and 10 and P is an exponent

semicolon: a punctuation mark used most often to join closely related independent clauses

sentence fragment: a dependent clause or a phrase punctuated as a complete sentence

sequential order: organization of facts, events, or ideas based on logical, chronological, or spatial order

signed numbers: numbers that are positive or negative

similarity: (of two geometric figures) having angles, but not necessarily sides, of equal measure; that is, in similar figures, all corresponding angles are congruent and all corresponding sides are proportional

simile: a figure of speech that shows how two unlike items are alike in some way; introduced by words such as *like, as,* and *similar to*

simple sentence: an independent clause that stands alone as a sentence without other clauses

slope: the amount of slant a line has; mathematically it is the ratio of the amount of vertical change to the amount of horizontal change between two points on a line

slope-intercept formula: an equation for a line in the form $y = mx + b$. In this form, m is the slope of the line and b is its y-intercept.

solution: an answer that makes an equation into a true statement

solution set: all numbers that yield a true statement when substituted in an equation

square root: a number that when squared will be a given number

standard English: see *edited American English*

standard form: written according to conventions of edited American English

structure: the method of development a writer uses

subordinate detail: a piece of information that is less important than another

suffix: a word element found at the end of some words; adding a suffix to a word either changes the word's meaning or creates an entirely new word

sum: the result of adding numbers

sum of the roots: the result of adding all the roots (solutions) of an equation

summary: a concise presentation of a larger body of information

supplementary angles: two angles whose sum is 180 degrees

supporting detail: information in a piece of writing that supports, illustrates, or elaborates the main idea

syllogism: the basic form of deductive reasoning where a conclusion is drawn from two statements or premises

system of equations: a set of equations in which the values of the variables must be consistent across the equations if the system is to have a solution

tables: charts or other diagrams that present data in tabular form

term: a number, variable, or product of numbers and variables

text mapping: a graphic method for organizing and summarizing written information into main ideas and subordinate details

thesis: a point set forth and defended in writing

tone: attitude as expressed in a writer's work

topic sentence: a sentence that introduces the main idea of a paragraph

transitions (in writing): words that serve to link ideas in an evident order

transposition: a method for isolating terms when solving linear equations

transversal: a line that intersects two lines

trinomial: a polynomial expression with three terms

turning point: the vertex of a parabola; the point at which the parabola and its axis of symmetry intersect

unit of measurement: the standard in which quantities that result from measurements or other calculations are expressed (e.g., inch, centimeter, hour, gram)

validity: the state of being sound; based on clear logic or facts

variability: the spread of the values in a group of values; the distance of the values from the mean of the values

variable: an unknown

verb: a word that expresses action, being, or state of being

vertex: the point at which two sides of an angle intersect; *also* the turning point of a parabola

vertical angles: two nonadjacent angles formed by two intersecting lines; vertical angles have a common vertex

volume: measure of capacity (measured in cubed units)

x-axis: in the Cartesian coordinate system, a horizontal line with zero as its central value, negative numbers to the left of zero, and positive numbers to the right of zero

x-coordinate: in the Cartesian coordinate system, the first number in an ordered pair, indicating the placement of a point in the Cartesian plane in relation to the numbers on the x-axis. That is, if 3 is the x-coordinate of a point, the point is directly above or below the number 3 on the x-axis.

x-intercept: the point at which a line crosses the x-axis in the Cartesian coordinate plane

y-axis: in the Cartesian coordinate system, a vertical line with zero as its central value, negative numbers below zero, and positive numbers above zero

y-coordinate: in the Cartesian coordinate system, the second number in an ordered pair, indicating the placement of a point in the Cartesian plane in relation to the numbers on the y-axis. That is, if 3 is the y-coordinate of a point, the point is directly right or left of the number 3 on the y-axis.

y-intercept: the point at which a line crosses the y-axis in the Cartesian coordinate plane

Feedback Form

The Official TASP® Test Study Guide

We are interested in your reaction to this study guide. Please take a moment to complete this form, then fold it and mail it back to National Evaluation Systems.

1. Did you take the Quick Pre-Test (Chapter 3) as a part of using this study guide? yes ___   no ___

2. Did you refer to the Glossary during your use of this guide? yes ___   no ___

3. Did you take the Practice Test? yes ___   no ___

4. Did you use any of the references? yes ___   no ___

5. Are there features you would like to see added to or expanded in the study guide?

   _____

   _____

   _____

6. Were there any parts of the study guide that you found confusing, unhelpful, or poorly organized? Try to be specific in your comments.

   _____

   _____

   _____

7. Were there any parts of the study guide that you found particularly helpful or good?

   _____

   _____

   _____

8. Please add any other comments you care to make.

   _____

   _____

   _____

Thank you!

National Evaluation Systems, P.O. Box 140406, Austin, TX 78714-0406

OFFICIAL TASP® TEST STUDY GUIDE REQUEST FORM

The Official TASP® Test Study Guide is sold in many bookstores at the list price of $12.00 each. It may also be ordered by mail for $16.00 each, which includes $4.00 each for shipping, handling, and tax. Fill out both the order form and mailing label and send them with the appropriate payment in an envelope addressed to:

The Official TASP® Test Study Guide
National Evaluation Systems, Inc.
P.O. Box 140347
Austin, TX 78714-0347

Please allow four weeks for delivery.

------------------------------ ✂ CUT HERE TO DETACH ------------------------------

ORDER FORM FOR THE OFFICIAL TASP® TEST STUDY GUIDE

Use this order form when ordering **more than one copy** or ordering without submitting a TASP Test Registration Form. Please send *The Official TASP® Test Study Guide* @ $16 (includes $4 for shipping, handling, and tax).

Number of Study Guides Ordered	Cost Per Copy	Amount Due
_____	$16 each	$ _____

All orders must be accompanied by payment in full. Do not send cash. Orders received without payment cannot be processed.

☐ Check/Money Order enclosed (Payable to NES)

This is your mailing label. Type or print clearly.

From: **TASP Test**
National Evaluation Systems, Inc.
P.O. Box 140347
Austin, TX 78714-0347

Date _____

Name _____

Street Address _____
(Do not use P.O. Box numbers.)

City _____

State _____ Zip _____

Daytime Phone: Area Code: (___) Number _____

------------------------------ ✂ CUT HERE TO DETACH ------------------------------

ORDER FORM FOR THE OFFICIAL TASP® TEST STUDY GUIDE

Use this order form when ordering **more than one copy** or ordering without submitting a TASP Test Registration Form. Please send *The Official TASP® Test Study Guide* @ $16 (includes $4 for shipping, handling, and tax).

Number of Study Guides Ordered	Cost Per Copy	Amount Due
_____	$16 each	$ _____

All orders must be accompanied by payment in full. Do not send cash. Orders received without payment cannot be processed.

☐ Check/Money Order enclosed (Payable to NES)

This is your mailing label. Type or print clearly.

From: **TASP Test**
National Evaluation Systems, Inc.
P.O. Box 140347
Austin, TX 78714-0347

Date _____

Name _____

Street Address _____
(Do not use P.O. Box numbers.)

City _____

State _____ Zip _____

Daytime Phone: Area Code: (___) Number _____

TEXAS ACADEMIC SKILLS PROGRAM™

OFFICIAL TASP® TEST STUDY GUIDE REQUEST FORM

The Official TASP® Test Study Guide is sold in many bookstores at the list price of $12.00 each. It may also be ordered by mail for $16.00 each, which includes $4.00 each for shipping, handling, and tax. Fill out both the order form and mailing label and send them with the appropriate payment in an envelope addressed to:

The Official TASP® Test Study Guide
National Evaluation Systems, Inc.
P.O. Box 140347
Austin, TX 78714-0347

Please allow four weeks for delivery.

------------------------------ ✄ CUT HERE TO DETACH ------------------------------

ORDER FORM FOR THE OFFICIAL TASP® TEST STUDY GUIDE

Use this order form when ordering **more than one copy** or ordering without submitting a TASP Test Registration Form. Please send *The Official TASP® Test Study Guide* @ $16 (includes $4 for shipping, handling, and tax).

Number of Study Guides Ordered	Cost Per Copy	Amount Due
_____	$16 each	$ _____

All orders must be accompanied by payment in full. Do not send cash. Orders received without payment cannot be processed.

☐ Check/Money Order enclosed (Payable to NES)

This is your mailing label. Type or print clearly.

From: TASP Test
National Evaluation Systems, Inc.
P.O. Box 140347
Austin, TX 78714-0347

Date _____
Name _____
Street Address _____
(Do not use P.O. Box numbers.)
City _____
State _____ Zip _____
Daytime Phone: Area Code: (___) Number _____

------------------------------ ✄ CUT HERE TO DETACH ------------------------------

ORDER FORM FOR THE OFFICIAL TASP® TEST STUDY GUIDE

Use this order form when ordering **more than one copy** or ordering without submitting a TASP Test Registration Form. Please send *The Official TASP® Test Study Guide* @ $16 (includes $4 for shipping, handling, and tax).

Number of Study Guides Ordered	Cost Per Copy	Amount Due
_____	$16 each	$ _____

All orders must be accompanied by payment in full. Do not send cash. Orders received without payment cannot be processed.

☐ Check/Money Order enclosed (Payable to NES)

This is your mailing label. Type or print clearly.

From: TASP Test
National Evaluation Systems, Inc.
P.O. Box 140347
Austin, TX 78714-0347

Date _____
Name _____
Street Address _____
(Do not use P.O. Box numbers.)
City _____
State _____ Zip _____
Daytime Phone: Area Code: (___) Number _____